Albert C

Albert Camus is among the most significant French writers of the twentieth century. His novels, *The Plague* and *The Outsider*, have a timeless power and appeal and are studied all over the world, and his philosophical work has had an enduring influence. His life was turbulent and he was involved with the major political and moral issues of his day but his private self – until now – has been less well known.

Olivier Todd has been authorised by Camus' family to write the first definitive life. Opening with his impoverished childhood in Algiers, Todd brings the historical context to life, shedding light on Camus' later agonising conflict between sympathy for the working class Algerians and for the French colonials – like his own family – with a stake in their adopted land. He follows Camus' break from the sun and sea that he loved, his involvement with the Resistance in France and his immersion in the life of the Parisian literati after the success of his first novel. This life too presented impossible choices and perpetual struggle: his intimacy with the Gallimard family, despite their collaborationist activities; his involvement in the conflict between Sartre and de Beauvoir; his own battles with debilitating bouts of tuberculosis and with the passionate, restless nature that would never let him settle. Because Todd understands his subject and his times so well, he brings to this rich, generous biography a rare immediacy and perception, evoking a great writer and his would with memorable force and engaging subtlety.

Albert Camus:

A Life

Olivier Todd

TRANSLATED BY
BENJAMIN IVRY

Chatto & Windus
LONDON

This edition first published by Chatto & Windus 1997

2 4 6 8 10 9 7 5 3 1

Published in French as *Albert Camus: une vie* in 1996
by Editions Gallimard

Copyright © Olivier Todd 1996
English translation copyright © Benjamin Ivry 1996

Olivier Todd and Benjamin Ivry have asserted their rights
under the Copyright, Designs and Patents Act 1988 to be identified as the
author and translator respectively of this work

First published in Great Britain in 1997 by
Chatto & Windus
Random House, 20 Vauxhall Bridge Road,
London SW1V 2SA

Random House Australia (Pty) Limited
20 Alfred Street, Milsons Point, Sydney,
New South Wales 2061, Australia

Random House New Zealand Limited
18 Poland Road, Glenfield,
Auckland 10, New Zealand

Random House South Africa (Pty) Limited
Endulini, 5A Jubilee Road, Parktown 2193, South Africa

Random House UK Limited Reg. No. 954009

A CIP catalogue record for this book
is available from the British Library

ISBN 0 701 1 6062 4

Papers used by Random House UK Limited are natural,
recyclable products made from wood grown in sustainable forests.
The manufacturing processes conform to the environmental
regulations of the country of origin.

Printed and bound in Great Britain by
Mackays of Chatham PLC, Chatham, Kent

Contents

Photographic inserts follow pages 000 and 000.

Translator's Note

The present book is an abridged and edited English version of Olivier Todd's biography of Albert Camus, which was published in France in 1996. While all relevant information about the life and work of Albert Camus has been retained, some material not of sufficient interest to the British and American general reader has been omitted to improve the narrative flow. Anyone seeking more background detail can, of course, consult the original French. The notes at the end of the French edition have also been deleted. While one of the virtues of Todd's book is his energetic research, in order to keep this edition an accessible length we decided to integrate necessary information into the text rather than including the extensive documentation of sources. Again, scholars can turn to the French edition for a full accounting.

I wish to thank Richard Howard for his shining dedication and inspiration at a number of literary tasks, translation among them. At Alfred A. Knopf, Judith Jones provided wise counsel, and she was ably assisted by Kenneth Schneider.

—Benjamin Ivry

Preface

The author of *L'Etranger*, never forgetting that he was the noted writer Camus, protected his family and private life. He kept an eye out for the devourer hidden behind every biographer. When critics like Jean-Claude Brisville, Germaine Brée, Roger Quilliot, and Carl Viggiani questioned him about his life, he told them very little.

In 1978, the pioneering biographer Herbert Lottman depicted Camus the man. I've also attempted to describe him as such, without forgetting that he was a writer. During research in France, Czechoslovakia, and Italy, in conversations with people from France, Algeria, America, and England, while exploring public and private archives, as well as colonial files in Aix and Komintern reports in Moscow, I've often had the feeling of trying to walk across the horizon. Camus used to say, "There is no true creation without secrecy."

This book is entitled *Albert Camus: A Life*, meaning the one that I've written. A hundred biographies are possible for every human being. I hope to have revealed the important moments and personalities of one life. I have also based the book partly on eyewitness accounts. Any literary personality has real enemies during his life and as many false friends afterwards. Historians, judges, and biographers run up against the fragility of eyewitness accounts. Thirty-five years after Camus's death, it was time to take stock. Certain of his intimate friends weren't known at all or were only slightly known until now. Before Francine Camus's death on December 24, 1979, decency also imposed a certain reserve.

Camus showed Quilliot a typed version of some of his diaries—"the backstage of a work," Quilliot remarked. I've used the *Carnets*, but sometimes I feel that Camus wrote them with posterity looking over his shoulder, not the way Gide wrote his succulent *Journals*, but rather with the discretion of Johnson explaining himself to Boswell.

Nevertheless, Camus did not write in code when he put down his observations, thoughts, and adventures, as did Pepys and Hugo. In his letters, the reader is drawn to center stage. I have had the luck of discovering unpublished letters, where an unexpected Camus appears. The authenticity of a letter isn't proof of whether it is sincere. But a letter without too much literary veneer does give the feelings, ideas, and information that a writer wants to convey to its recipient.

Camus once said, "The idea that every writer . . . portrays himself in his books is one of the puerilities bequeathed to us by Romanticism. A man's works often describe his longings or temptations, and almost never his own true story." Nevertheless, apart from his successes in artistic transposition, Camus's work is highly autobiographical. Roger Grenier, who knew him, spoke about the writer's "masks."

In 1959 Camus was asked which part of his work critics had neglected. He replied, "The obscure part, what is blind and instinctive in me. French critics are mainly interested in ideas." This rough generalization also describes Camus in the rich French literary, philosophical, and political turmoil from 1930 to 1960.

At age twenty, he wrote, "Just as after a writer's death we exaggerate the importance of his work, so an individual's death makes us overestimate his personal importance to us." France makes a habit of hagiographic elegies, but later, for years on end, the dear departed may be regularly assassinated.

In his first novel, published eleven years after his death, Camus described a character: "He wanted to hold his life in his hands, like a warm piece of bread that you squeeze and knead." A biography is only an *essay*. I have attempted to discern the gestures, hands, and heart of a working writer and to give his different voices back to Camus.

Albert Camus

A Life

Chapter One # Matriculation Number 17.032

On September 22, 1913, on the Saint-Paul Farm outside the city of Mondovi in Algeria, Lucien Auguste Camus wrote to his employer, "The grape harvest at Saint-Paul ended this morning at 10 a.m." Mondovi is 420 kilometers west of Algiers, and Lucien Camus worked there for the Ricôme wine company as a cellarman. He lived on the farm in a low-built house with a clay floor, two rooms and a kitchen next to the wine cellars.

In the production of wine, vineyard owners reigned at the top of the economic ladder. Then came the estate managers; the directors of grape growing, who supervised the vines; and the cellarmen, who worked with the grapes after harvest. White laborers were used for disbudding, pruning, and wine pressing. "Native" workers lived around the farms in tents that clung to hovels made of wooden planks. Day workers might be local tribesmen and prison laborers, who returned to jail after each day's work. Europeans and Arabs worked side by side, but they had little social contact, except at the bordello in nearby Bône, the hometown of Saint Augustine.

Once Lucien Camus recommended an Arab worker who wanted to change jobs: in his letter of reference for this laborer, named Rabad Oustani, who had refused to sabotage wine production despite orders from a French supervisor, Lucien wrote, "Although he is a native, he has much more know-how than the ignoble individual who urged him to sabotage the filtering of the wine during the night. Because he refused to do it, he had to quit his job."

Born in 1885 at Ouled-Fayet, outside Algiers, Lucien Camus was a de-scendant of the first generation of Frenchmen to settle in Algeria. He was not a rich colonist, but a simple salaried foreman. In his professional notes, the cellarman would sometimes include a literary touch, such as during the very hot summer of 1913, "The birds are silenced . . . by the heat, and the wine tastes like a heated pond."

The vineyard employee Lucien Auguste Camus, twenty-eight years old, had blue eyes, brown hair, and a mustache. He measured five feet six inches, which was then above average height. He had served with the Zouave regiment in Morocco as a second-class soldier in 1907 and 1908. His military papers described him as a "coach driver."

Orphaned at the age of one, he had been placed by his siblings in an orphanage. One of his grandfathers had come from the Bordeaux region, and a great-grandfather was from the Ardèche in France. The Camuses had a family legend that they were from Alsace, no doubt because in Algeria, a political refugee from Alsace had more prestige than a poor immigrant from Bordeaux.

On November 13, 1910, Lucien Auguste had married Catherine Hélène Sintès, who was three years older than he, and three months later their first son, Lucien Jean Etienne, was born. In autumn 1913, Catherine Hélène and her small son traveled for eighteen hours by train from Algiers en route to Bône. After the long train ride, on wooden seats, the pregnant woman and her son were packed into a wagon that carted trunks and furniture, to Saint-Paul.

Shortly after his family arrived, Lucien Camus wrote to a colleague at the Ricôme company, "Things aren't going well at home, the little boy and his mother have fevers, bad luck, but they're a little better the last two days." Malaria, a constant threat, was borne by the wind blown over from nearby putrid swamps and the stagnant Lake Fetzara. Only fifty years before, an epidemic of cholera and plague had killed half the colonists.

Lucien also had difficulties with his workers. He was "twice physically threatened by a native driver." And he was bothered by Europeans who lived in Bône, writing in a letter on June 24, 1914: "It's true that all these people from Bône seem as sweet as lambs, but deep down they're deceitful and treacherous as foxes." When business obliged him to drive his cart to Mondovi, small boys would hang on to the vehicle just for a lark, and rather than using his whip to get rid of them—other drivers would have—Lucien simply cried "Emchi!"—Go away!

On November 8, 1913, Lucien Camus appeared at the mayor's office in Mondovi to register the birth of his second son, born the day before. The baby was given only one Christian name, Albert. The two witnesses to the newly registered infant were Jean Piro, a merchant, and Salvatore Frendo, a delivery man for a local grocer.

Mondovi had been designed by military engineers, who organized the sharply rectangular city into twenty neighborhoods of twelve houses each. The city offered hunting clubs, which Lucien Camus would have enjoyed if he had had the time; he'd proved himself a good shot in military service.

Silent films were shown at Mondovi, but the Camuses did not use the farm car to go into town for amusements.

Lucien Camus earned ten to twenty francs a day, not much more than a common laborer. He complained to his supervisor at Ricôme wines, M. Classiault, that the manager of the Saint-Paul Farm "didn't hide his displeasure that Ricôme is only buying 131 barrels." When Classiault reacted by chewing out the disgruntled manager, Camus, aware that employees had guns and would use them if provoked, warned his boss, "I beg you not to make a big deal about it, and not to threaten him, because this fellow is capable of anything."

Around Algeria, there were debates over France's role in the country's future, and what rights the Arabs should have. A month after Albert's birth, the daily *L'Echo d'Alger* published a series of articles by a professor of law, Emile Chauvin. He declared that France's purpose in Algeria was "to substitute civilization and reason for barbarity and fanaticism, and to aim for the assimilation, the unification of the races," in order to make them as French as possible. Frenchmen like Chauvin believed that in the very distant future, natives *might* be transformed into citizens of the French Republic. For the time being, declared Chauvin, France "intends to energetically maintain the principle of French supremacy, by not allowing native, non-French advisers to participate in mayoral elections. . . . We cannot accept the idea of giving French citizenship and thereby political rights to men who persist in thinking and acting outside of all our legal and moral strictures."

Lucien Camus was much too occupied as cellarman to get involved in such debates. He noted to his employer in the winter of 1913, "I sent out 1,553 full barrels, but got back only 1,543 empty barrels. . . . Something suspicious may happen before the season's work is over. . . . I have to stand guard during the day and part of the night."

The new year began badly. On January 4, 1914, he noted, "I plan to move, when the weather is good . . . we've had torrential rains here for several days. . . . You can't even wash the barrels, there is so much mud all over."

That spring Lucien received a draft notice from the French army, but his employer tried to intervene to have his military service postponed until the quiet season in winemaking. Catherine and their two sons, three-year-old Lucien and eight-month-old Albert, were threatened by malaria. On July 14, the cellarman wrote to Classiault, "I plan to move my family to Algiers at the end of the month, for health reasons."

Finally called up to the First Zouave Regiment, Lucien was just in time for Germany's declaration of war on France on August 3. Wearing the Zouave uniform—a fez, billowing red pants, and a blue vest—the dashing Lucien had the matriculation number 17.032.

His regiment was sent overseas in a crowded ship, the *Lamarsa*. The soldiers lived on a diet of beans and beef, and after a few hours at sea the ship stank of vomit. They landed at the southern French city of Sète. From there, the troops traveled in boxcars to Narbonne, got off at Massy-Palaiseau, crossed Paris, and then looked for the German foe.

The Zouaves' red-and-blue uniforms made them an easy target for German Maxim machine guns, and Lucien Camus was among the first French soldiers wounded in the bloody Battle of the Marne. From the town of Montreuil-sous-Bois, Lucien sent his wife, who had returned to Algiers on August 30, a postcard that showed a municipal fountain in the city of Noisy-le-Sec. The message read, "A big kiss for you and the children and hello to my friends. Send me your news, my health and news are all fine, no worries."

A few days later he sent another card from Saint-Brieuc in Brittany, showing a school that had been transformed into a makeshift army hospital. One window was marked with an X, with the message, "My dear Hélène, I'm sending you a picture of the hospital where I'm being treated, just above the X. Kiss the children for me, Your husband."

Lucien did not write this card himself, and he died of his wounds on October 11, 1914. Of the 1,357,000 Frenchmen killed in the First World War, Algeria contributed 25,000 Frenchmen and 22,000 Arabs who had served in the French army. Of these, fifty casualties came from Mondovi, including twelve Arabs.

Lucien Camus's body was never sent home to Algeria. Instead, the French bureaucratic system sent his widow the dead soldier's military passbook, marked as having served in "the German campaign from August 28 to October 11, 1914."

Lucien had spent a tenth of his short life in the army. As the first man in the life of his son, he would be the one Albert knew least. He left behind a few documents and sepia photographs, his posthumous war medal, and some shrapnel from the shell that killed him. They were sent to his widow by the staff of the Saint-Brieuc hospital where he died.

Albert and his father, Lucien, had lived together for only eight months.

Chapter Two

"Mosquito, You've Been Accepted."

On May 7, 1921, Catherine Hélène Sintès-Camus was informed by the French Pension Ministry that as a war widow, she was entitled to eight hundred francs per year, plus three hundred francs for each of her children until they reached the age of eighteen. At the time, a cleaning woman earned one thousand francs a year.

As war orphans, Lucien and Albert were entitled to free medical treatment. During the war, their mother had worked in a factory, stacking cartridges in boxes. The workers earned up to five francs per day, but now the widow Camus worked as a cleaning woman in private homes and businesses, such as the butcher shop on the rue de Lyon in Algiers. She lived in her mother's apartment with her brothers, Etienne and Joseph, and her two sons.

The children, Lucien and Albert, felt that their grandmother talked too much, and their mother not enough. Camus's mother came from a family of Spanish origin, from Minorca. Dark, small, and partly deaf, she could neither read nor write. Although she was able to read lips, some people thought her mute, or mentally retarded. Others thought that she was suffering from badly treated meningitis. Albert believed that his mother began to have hearing and speech problems after a bout of typhoid fever or typhus. Still others thought she had had a cerebral attack upon hearing about her husband's death. She would slide over certain words, hissing instead of pronouncing sounds like s or z, and say "coucou" when she meant to say "couscous." She would use her hands to express herself, joining them to imply that a man and woman were having a love affair.

Present and yet distant, this terrified woman would not intervene with the children in the way Camus's grandmother did. Nor would she complain when an aunt snubbed her. Catherine Hélène, known in the family by her second name, would neither laugh nor cry in front of her family, maintaining a steady smile on her face. When Lucien and Albert quarreled, she would only say, "I doan like arguments, I doan like fights."

She had red, rheumatic hands and wore black or gray blouses all year long. She would lean on her elbow on the windowsill, watching the street through the potted geraniums. In spring and summer, she took a chair out to the sidewalk and listened to the neighbors' gossip.

Later, the family moved further down the rue de Lyon, from number 17 to number 93, in the heart of Belcourt, a working-class quarter in east Algiers, on the border of the Arab quarter, Marabout. On the ground floor of the house were a barber, a wine seller, and a milliner. Behind the building was an orange tree and a rickety shack where the barber lived, along with the Arab family of a street sweeper, whose son, Omar, played with Albert.

The Sintès-Camus home was a three-room apartment with a long corridor. The name of the grandmother, Madame Sintès, was on the lease. She occupied one room. The main room, whitewashed, had a table, a desk, a sideboard, and a mattress on the floor, hidden by a covering. Albert and Lucien's uncle Etienne, who was partially mute, slept there. Hélène and her two sons shared the third room, which was crowded with a mirrored wardrobe, two iron bedframes—a single for the mother, a double for the boys—and a night table between them. A net covering was draped over a fiber trunk. Etienne's brother, Joseph, also lived in the apartment until 1920, and at one point a woman cousin named Minette slept in the hallway for some months.

On the landings the Turkish toilets—a hole with a drain—stank. There was no electricity or running water, and jugs of water had to be fetched from street faucets. Everyone washed in the kitchen sink and once a week took a shower in a zinc tub. Above a table in the main room was an oil lamp.

Grandmother kept her coins in a cookie box, as no one in the family had a bank account. On New Year's Day 1921, Grandmother explained to Albert that now he was "grown up," and he would be getting practical gifts from now on. Grandmother and Mother would get up early to do the marketing, stopping to gossip with the delicatessen owner, as the trolley's early-morning runs along the rue de Lyon made the house shake.

Catherine Hélène prepared dishes like jugged hare, and snails with oil. She would wait patiently, while the snails disgorged, simmering her sauce of lard, onions, tomatoes, and pepper. One of the children took the prepared dishes over to the butcher's to get them cooked.

Grocery stores sold tomatoes, figs, melons ripened in the sun, and fat, juicy Algerian apricots, while fishmongers offered sea bream and mullet. On Thursdays and Sundays, Hélène would prepare desserts, flavoring pastries with lemon and orange blossom, while the boys hovered around the kitchen. Their grandmother would yell at them, but never sent them outside, because she didn't want them "hanging around."

The mother's life was one of silence and work. She never remarried, although in 1930 she did have one suitor, Antoine, a Maltese fishmonger, a handsome, mustached man who wore a bowler hat. She put on makeup and a bright smock, but Etienne made a scene—the typical North African European protecting his sister. When Hélène cut her hair, her mother called her a whore. She wasn't given a chance to remarry.

Etienne used to hang out at a café near the house, where he would drink anisette, a drink that according to a local saying "rolled off the tongue like the piss of Baby Jesus." As Etienne gossiped and played cards, his nephew Albert learned the rules of the French card game belote. In Belcourt, on the left bank, lived the humble French people of Algiers. They were joyous, generous, vain, quarrelsome, quickly excited and as quickly discouraged. The lower-level French laborers of Belcourt often despised their Arab neighbors, but they also felt inferior to the ruling class of French civil servants, who could afford to take vacations back in France.

In Belcourt, the lower-class French rubbed elbows with Arabs and believed they understood them, speaking in condescending generalities of "Ahmed" or "Fatma" instead of using their full Arab names. With Arabs they shared the spit-roasted lamb *méchoui* during picnics on the beach, but would never think of receiving Arabs in their homes. Both lower-class Arabs and whites had a hatred for the police, even during a *baroufa*, the typical street brawl. The poor also feared unemployment. Arabs, Jews, Neapolitans, Spanish, Corsicans, and people from Marseilles were all accused of stealing jobs. Xenophobia flourished, with a kind of solidarity between Arabs and the poor. On the rue de Lyon, French, Arab, Italian, and Spanish accents could be heard.

Afternoon was nap time, and Albert hated having to lie next to his grandmother, with her rancid old-lady smell. Over her bed, Grandmother had hung her own portrait. With her hair in a tight bun, a chain around her neck, and clear, piercing eyes, the old lady was starchy.

Her daughter and sons accepted Madame Sintès's authority, and when Grandmother whipped the boys, Catherine Hélène would just stand by, begging her not to hit them too hard. Lucien, the elder and thus the first to be held responsible for mischief, took more beatings than his brother. Grandmother was especially fond of Albert. With some talent for histrionics, she would hide in her room, complaining of stomach aches, or ask the boys in front of guests if they preferred Mother or Grandmother. And she complained that her daughter didn't take care of her, and that her son Joseph had gone far away.

Uncle Etienne would take Albert to the Sablettes beach, where they played with the family dog, Brilliant. Etienne had a quick temper, and he no longer spoke with Joseph, who called him "a rude beast." On Thursdays, Albert helped Uncle Etienne in his work as a barrel maker. A careful craftsman, Etienne was obliged to work a sixty-hour week. Once he deliberately cut the palm of his hand and got sick leave.

Uncle Joseph had a better job, working for the railroad, and was married to a piano teacher. As a railway employee, Joseph could travel around the countryside free, buying chickens and rabbits from farmers and reselling them, or giving some to his mother to raise in her courtyard. Madame Sintès decided that Albert had become a man on the day he helped her kill one of their chickens. Etienne agreed that the boy "had courage," compared with big brother Lucien, who had refused to kill the fowl. But Madame Sintès was usually strict: when Albert hurt a finger by getting it pinched in a seat at school and the blood was flowing freely, his grandmother gave him a whipping for disturbing the household.

The family's favorite entertainment was going to the Musset cinema, next door, or the Alcazar, nearby on the rue de l'Union. Albert was embarrassed to have to read aloud the silent film titles for his illiterate mother and grandmother. To cover up, his grandmother would say loudly, "I've left my eyeglasses at home, so you'll have to read them to me."

Although Lucien was a friendly and sociable boy, he was a less gifted student than Albert, but was more talented at soccer. Lucien would look after Albert, sharing boxes of coconut candy with him. At the age of fourteen, Lucien was hired as a messenger at the Ricôme wine company, with a starting salary of eighty francs per month.

In 1923, Albert went to the boys' primary school on the rue Aumerat, a ten-minute walk from the rue de Lyon apartment. Students wore charcoal-gray blouses, like the teachers, and had to ask permission to sit down. It was a typical French school of the Third Republic. In winter, fires were lit in cast-iron stoves. Each wooden desk had an inkwell containing a purple ink, into which the children dipped their Sergent-Major pen nibs. Like their students, the instructors wore charcoal-gray shirts. Blackboards, cluttered with white, pink, and blue pieces of chalk, were side by side on the wall with Vidal de La Blache's geographical maps, representing France and its Algerian colony in the same color. The standard world atlas, Schroeder and Galouedec's, colored the entire French empire a uniform light purple. On the classroom walls there were also photographs of the cathedrals of Strasbourg and Notre-Dame de Paris and the Mont-Blanc—parts of a country that to the Algerians of Belcourt seemed like a paradise with its châteaux, kings, and revolutionaries.

Classes in history, geography, and civics hammered into the students the idea of France as a maternal power. In 1923, the second-year courses were run by an established instructor, Louis Germain. Tall and stiff, with precise pronunciation, Germain played the clarinet as an amateur, but he followed the musical score so strictly that some listeners said, "All Germain knows is the metronome markings." The teacher used to slap unruly students and spank their bottoms with what he called his "barley sugar," a fat ruler made of red wood. Unyielding about spelling, punctuation, arithmetic, and composition, Germain would organize contests of mental arithmetic and give twice-monthly slide shows about geography and natural history to his rapt students. A relative free-thinker, he would tell his students that some people practiced no religion at all. As a social progressive, Louis Germain was aware of the Socialist leader Jules Ferry's famous "Letter to Teachers," in which he said that teachers "replace fathers of families." During the four years of World War I, Germain would read aloud in class a novel about trench warfare by Roland Dorgelès, *Les Croix de bois,* which described bayonet attacks, the wounded, and war's horror. He later told Albert, "I've always considered your poor father as a personal friend," although the men had never met.

At Belcourt, a few young Arabs were admitted into primary school, and in Germain's second-year class, out of thirty-three students, only three were Arabs. Germain wanted Albert to continue his studies into high school, seeing that his student was happy in class, but did not realize how poor he was. He would tell Albert later, "Your pleasure at being in class was always apparent, and your face was so optimistic that looking at it, I never guessed your family's real situation. I only had a clue when your mother came to see me about entering your name on the list of scholarship candidates."

Grandmother was against scholarships for Albert, feeling that he should work for his living the way Lucien did. But with Catherine Hélène's encouragement, Germain explained about the boy's skill in reading, writing, and the spoken word, and that the scholarship would pay for a high-school diploma, after which Albert could get a better job.

Albert was a good student, especially in French. Starting in January 1924, Germain, who had lots of free time because he had separated from his wife, gave two free hours of supplementary lessons every day for four students, including Albert, who had ranked first in his class the month before. Once he was a scholarship candidate, Albert was treated with more respect at the apartment on the rue de Lyon. Germain also spoke to Albert on his grandmother's behalf, saying that her bark was worse than her bite.

In school, the boy discovered the world of words, as there were no books at home. On Thursdays and Sundays, when there was no school, Albert would walk by his friend Pierre Fassina's house and the boys would go tree climbing in Essai Park. Young Camus had the reputation of being a brawler: when one schoolmate took him to be Alsatian and called him a *boche,* an insulting French term for a German, Albert insisted on having a fistfight with the boy and gave him a black eye. Pierre and Albert would roam through the streets, wearing espadrilles with holes in them, cotton pants, and sweaters. In the spring the friends, along with brother Lucien, would attend soccer matches, often preceded by a parade with a marching band.

The working people of Belcourt admired priests less than they did teachers. Albert had been baptized, and was confirmed at the Church of Saint Bonaventura in Algiers, but no one in his family was a churchgoer. There was never any talk of hell, paradise, or purgatory, and when somebody died, Grandmother would say, "Well, he's farted his last. . . ."

Religious observance was limited in Belcourt, but still, most burials were under the auspices of the church. The Algerian parish priests rattled off the catechism, inspiring guilt in their young students. The priests stressed the subject of impurity, that masturbation would cause deafness and sometimes blindness or insanity, too. From the Belcourt point of view, the Catholic Church seemed definitely on the side of the rich.

Madame Sintès did insist, however, that Albert have his first communion before entering high school. When Albert talked during catechism class, he was slapped by the priest, which he remembered far longer than the lesson of the day. After the communion ceremony, wearing a sailor suit and armband, Albert went back to school. Louis Germain later commented, "I remember your coming to class with your communion friends. You were so visibly happy and proud of the costume you were wearing and the special day you were observing that I was sincerely happy at your joy, feeling that if you made your communion, it was because you wanted to. . . ."

The anticlerical leftists in Algiers, who had gained power in 1924, plastered posters around showing Joan of Arc at the stake, being burned by cardinals and monks. The poor folk of Belcourt were not generally observant, and they were suspicious of priests. The Catholics of Spanish origin would celebrate Mardi Gras by burning a priest in effigy. When they passed a priest in the street, people would murmur "Tocaferro"—Touch iron. It was believed that church people brought bad luck. Camus was brought up on the outskirts of a superficial Catholicism. The priests in Algeria spoke of heaven, but on earth they tended to pit their parishioners against one another. To a Spanish congregation in Bab el-Oued, Spanish-language sermons denounced the French in Algeria, claiming that they did not attend mass, nor did they produce enough children. But the young people in Algeria were more concerned with the earth, the sand, the sun, and the sea.

And there was school: For the scholarship competition, Louis Germain came to pick up the candidates in Belcourt and took them to the big high school, buying them croissants to eat as encouragement. On their way out, he was waiting for them, and he studied the rough drafts of their answers. Two days later, the jury posted the results, and Albert Camus and Pierre Fassina were granted scholarships.

Louis Germain said to Camus, "Bravo, Mosquito, you've been accepted."

Chapter Three   ## Silence and Words

*I*n the bed they shared, Lucien Camus slept against the wall so that when Albert woke up at five-thirty a.m. to go to high school, he wouldn't have to climb over his brother. With his friend Pierre Fassina, Albert would take a trolley car crowded with laborers at the rue de Lyon stop; he used to spend the half-hour trip balanced on the trolley's lower step. One day he and Pierre were shocked when the passengers forced an Arab to get off the trolley because he had lice on his djellaba.

There were two high schools in Algiers, a small one in the chic Mustapha Heights neighborhood and a larger one to the south in the Bab el-Oued quarter. The snobbish students of the chic school called the larger one, which Albert attended, "the Jewish school." The disciplinary supervisor, nicknamed "the Rhinoceros," would wait for the children at the entrance to the school every morning.

Albert would arrive before seven a.m., because his scholarship for non-boarders entitled him to breakfast—coffee with milk (or sometimes hot chocolate), bread, butter, and jam—as well as lunch. Breakfast was at seven-fifteen, and classes started at eight or nine. If Albert didn't have any classes, he went to study hall. From many rooms in the school, students could see the ocean, which gave them something to dream about.

When Albert had to fill in forms about his parents' occupations, writing "domestic" to describe his mother made him know "shame, and the shame that comes from feeling ashamed." Whenever there were forms to be filled out by parents, Albert would bring them back blank, because his illiterate mother would not have known what to do with them.

Although he was Catholic, Albert did not want to study the catechism, but he did study Latin, which bored him. He did better in French literature, geography, natural sciences, and mathematics, thanks to the preparation of

13

Louis Germain's class. For the first time, Albert found himself with children from privileged families, and he noted later, "Before, everyone was like me, and poverty seemed to be utterly natural in this world, but in high school, I learned about comparisons."

Albert played a little of the Basque sport pelota, and lots of soccer, after breakfast, during recreation period at four p.m., and before evening study hall. He got the reputation of being a good goalkeeper and center forward. He remained on the amateur level, although he did play at the Montpensier Sports Club and on the junior team of the Algiers Racing University team, the RUA. He would go flying at opponents with his cleats, and was kneed in the groin for his trouble. Once he blocked a shot by taking it full force in the chest, and fainted under the goalposts. The October 28, 1930 bulletin of the RUA soccer club congratulates his junior team after a match they lost by a score of one to nothing, adding that "the best of all was Camus, who was only beaten because of a mishap, but who gave a splendid exhibition."

Camus was also occupied by his studies, with good results in literature but only a passing grade in math. For years he would refer to his teachers as "masters," but he could be insolent to them and would be given up to four hours of detention if he was rowdy. While serving detention, he would gaze at the banana trees in Marengo Park near the school, which was better than looking at the assistant dean, M. Clérian, whose mouth the students compared to a hen's behind.

The high school was considered on the level of a good school in provincial France, and there were some outstanding teachers, such as M. Lespes, a geographer who specialized in Algeria. He would yell at lazy students, "If you don't do a goddamn thing in my class, I'll throw you into a Jesuit factory, and make you into good little Jesuitties!"

Another teacher, a royalist and member of the far-right-wing Action Française movement, would stand on a chair and shriek his grief over the beheading of Louis XVI during the French Revolution: "And they killed the King!"

The students got a then-standard view of colonial history, with France as benefactor, civilizer, and enlightener of its colonies. Apart from schoolbooks, Camus also haunted the city library, where he would devour adventure stories by authors like Michel Zévaco, Jules Verne, and Alexandre Dumas, graduating from them to the more adult Honoré de Balzac. The more he would read in the large family living room, the further removed he seemed to be from the rest of his family's concerns.

When his mother and grandmother visited the school for Prize Day, they did not look like other boys' relatives. His mother wore a hat decorated with brown tulle, while his grandmother sported a black Spanish scarf, which Albert tried without success to keep her from wearing. His grandmother explained that the scarf kept her warm, and she could not afford to get sick, which shamed the boy even more.

Most of his friends did not come to the Camus family apartment on the rue de Lyon. Instead, he would visit their houses. At home, Albert was admired but little understood. Soon he was better informed than anyone else in the family, and could not easily share what he had learned at school, not even with Lucien. For all of them, a French poem had no meaning at all.

Albert had wanted to write ever since he was age seven, but still had no clear plan about how to become a writer. His family hoped he would be an elementary school teacher.

During school vacations, his grandmother could not understand why the boy was not working: "I've never had any vacations myself!" Answering a want ad, Albert got a job in a ironmonger's shop, for eight hours a day at 150 francs per month, which was more than Lucien's salary at Ricôme's office. Then he found a job with a maritime broker, where he filed mail and bills, translated lists of provisions from English into French, and visited customs officers. He liked the job at first, but then grew bored with it. After he turned over his first paycheck, his grandmother handed him back a twenty-franc coin.

Once again Albert felt *different*, as none of his school friends worked during vacation time, and some even took trips to France. Albert was humiliated, too, because he hadn't told his boss he would be leaving on September 15 to go back to school. He had to admit that he hadn't been looking for permanent employment and that he had to work during the summer because he was poor. At the office, Albert learned about administrative jobs, where one rarely saw the results of one's efforts—"this office work which comes from nowhere and ends up with nothing. Everything revolved around buying and selling, mediocre actions which were impossible to appreciate."* His uncle Etienne's barrel workshop required skilled hands, and a new barrel could be admired or rejected. Albert developed the idea of a worker as an artisan who made an object.

During the summer at the ironmonger's, a female employee had dropped a box of pins, and when Albert crouched down to pick them up for her, he looked up and saw her knees separate underneath her dress, which affected him more than the smell of Pierre's aunt's lipstick, or the women's hands that he brushed against in the crowded trolley car.

His palling around deepened into friendships, as Albert became more choosy. Some were French boys from Algeria, like Pierre Fassina, Claude de Fréminville, and André Belamich, while others came from France, like Georges Didier. Georges hated cursing and made Albert stop using God's

* From *LePremier Homme*

name in vain. In philosophy class, Georges decided to become a Jesuit, a vocation that fascinated Albert, the nonbeliever. He saw his young friend as "seized by the absolute . . . wholly involved in his loyal passions."

Young Camus's education soon became more complicated, because his earlier passion for philosophy was giving way to a love for literature.

Chapter Four

Metaphysics and Politics

C amus did not return to high school at the end of his first academic term in December 1930 because he was running a fever, having coughing fits, and spitting blood. Doctors diagnosed tuberculosis, which in the poor quarters of Belcourt and Bab el-Oued was often a death sentence. Camus summed up his state of health: "Fatigue from too much sports and too much sunbathing resulted in spitting blood." Some people in his family believed he had caught cold after swimming in the sea, while others thought it happened after a soccer match.

He had begun coughing and spitting blood in August, and a Dr. Lévi-Valensi treated him before the summer was over. He would spit blood after taking a bath, or a walk, or if the weather was too hot. Albert's mother never panicked, but remained at his side.

As a war orphan, he had the right to free treatment, and he entered the general ward of Mustapha Hospital in Algiers. The doctors diagnosed pulmonary tuberculosis in the right lung, without pleural complications. Albert sensed the threat of death and hated the hospital. He later noted down other patients' conversations overheard in the ward: " 'Whatever happen to Jean Pérès?' 'The one who worked for the gas company? He's dead, although he had only one lung infected, because he wanted to go home. . . . He was always on top of his wife, two or three times a day, and that will finally kill a sick man.' "

Before antibiotics were developed, the most common treatment for tuberculosis, which was practiced on Camus, was artificial pneumothorax, or collapse therapy: a doctor injected air between the chest wall and lung to force the lung to collapse, and while it rested, the tubercular lesions would heal. Every week or two there would be another injection, and then X rays to see how the patient was doing.

Suddenly aware of his own mortality, Camus spent his time in bed reading Epictetus, who had written, "Illness is an obstacle for the body, but not necessarily for the will." His philosophy teacher, Jean Grenier, was worried by Camus's unexplained absence from school and took a taxi to Belcourt with one of Camus's classmates to see how the boy was doing. By then, Albert was back at home but too embarrassed to speak to his teacher—"suffocated by timidity and gratitude," as he put it. Trying to find a positive side to his illness, Camus decided that it was "a remedy against death, because it prepares us for death, creating an apprenticeship whose first step is self-pity. Illness supports man in the great attempt to shirk the fact that he will surely die."

The pneumothorax treatments worked, and he began to breathe more easily. Stimulated by reading André Gide's novel *Amyntas*, which romanticized a tubercular patient's illness, Camus had feverish visions, which he described later in his book *La Mort heureuse*: "The images came, huge fantastic animals who nodded their heads above desert landscapes."

After he was released, his uncle and aunt Gustave and Antoinette Acault took Albert into their apartment on the rue de Languedoc, where he could have his own room and avoid the threat of infecting Lucien by continuing to share a bed with him at home. At the Acaults' house, he was stuffed with hamburgers at dinnertime, as the doctors said that overeating was a good remedy for tuberculosis.

His uncle Gustave soon became a father figure for Albert, more than his teacher Louis Germain had been. Uncle Gustave's walrus mustache, checked shirt, and the white apron and cap that he always wore in his butcher shop made him into a familiar local character. Gustave would tell his nephew that knowing how to live well was better than knowing endless information, and a smart guy was better than a pedant.

Gustave was a Mason, an avid reader of Voltaire, and more cultivated than most Europeans in Algeria. He read Anatole France and James Joyce, too. In his uncle's library Camus discovered the complete works of Honoré de Balzac, Victor Hugo, and Emile Zola, as well as Paul Valéry and Charles Maurras.

Uncle Gustave was an anarchist in politics, and he and Albert would have long discussions about books and politics, talking as equals. The childless Acaults treated Albert as their son, taking him to the seaside, and imagining for him a career as a high-school teacher. Gustave also secretly hoped that one day Albert might take over the butcher shop, earn a good living, and still have time to write.

In his uncle's house, Camus learned about domestic comfort. Later he would recall that in his mother's home "things had no names, and we spoke of deep-dishes or the pot on the chimney, etc. But at [Gustave's] house, there was glazed earthenware from the Vosges region, or dishes from Quimper, etc." Albert began to "wake up to the idea of there being a choice."

By October 1931, Camus's tuberculosis was in remission and he was able to return to high school, in a philosophy class taught by Jean Grenier. There Camus met a new friend, Robert Jaussaud, a boy who had just arrived from France, where the Front Populaire had made young people politically aware. He and Albert would go on long hikes, discussing matters such as the injustices done to local Moslems.

In class, Grenier spoke about metaphysical serenity and Indian religions. Although Camus was not the class valedictorian, he did receive the best grade for a philosophy composition in his third term, and his high-school diploma was conferred with the grade average of twelve out of twenty, which was considered "rather good" in French academic terminology.

His next challenge would be the preparatory class for university. Instead of the high-pressured studying that went on in Paris schools, the Algiers class was relaxed, with students having fun and playing soccer with students from other preparatory classes. Camus enjoyed himself with friends like Claude de Fréminville and André Belamich; but he did have two serious questions for Jean Grenier, namely: Should he continue his philosophy studies? And would he be able to write things worthy of publication?

Albert appreciated Grenier's attention, and in April 1933 he devoured his teacher's book *Les Iles*. Camus wrote on a stray piece of paper about Grenier the author: "He is completely in [the book] and the admiration and love that I feel for him is growing. . . . Will I ever know how much I owe him? . . . I must learn to train my sensitivity which is too prompt to gush out, and yet not hide it under coldness and irony." He added, "I place too much emphasis on my contradictions, and become obsessed by my personality's natural weakness. . . . Damned pride."

One classmate, Maurice Perrin, later recalled that Camus was "cold, sarcastic, and distant," behaving like a coxcomb. Even so, he was impressed by Albert's "maturity." Perrin recalled that Albert "always wore a gray flannel suit, a small, round felt hat, a wide, deep-blue scarf with white polka-dots, white socks, and polished shoes." This formal attire was different from that of his other classmates, who were disheveled, usually wearing depressing gray shirts and rope belts. Camus walked around with a briefcase full of art magazines and unheard-of books, quoted the Russian philosopher Leon Chestov as well as Proust, and made fun of other famous writers, like Stendhal, who he felt worked a sort of "terrorism" on French writers.

One of Camus's French compositions, "The Novel as Literary Genre," was honored by being read aloud in front of the class. He spoke of the great Russian novelists, lifting a number of ideas from André Gide's novel *Les Faux-Monnayeurs*, and argued for a "polyphony of the novel," made of interwoven themes, and characters confronted by a single problem. Camus saw printed texts as words to be spoken or declaimed. He took a literature class with another teacher, Paul Mathieu, where he did not always get the highest grade but was always original and peremptory.

In writing compositions, Camus would often borrow heavily from other writers, especially Nietzsche, for subjects like an essay on "Tragedy and Comedy," which received a grade of twelve out of twenty: "Greek tragedy was born from the need to escape a life that was too painful. The Greeks did not try to make life more agreeable, they annihilated it with tragedy and dreams. The only purpose of tragedy, like comedy, was to bring forget-fulness."

Camus's classmates would criticize him, but one student defended the boy, saying he liked Camus, who usually looked sad when he arrived at school in the morning. Maurice Perrin later recalled that he "never became close pals" with Albert, who he felt at the time "was involved in sterile aes-theticism, which for the moment [isolated him] from his generation."

Jean Grenier would lend Albert books when they met at his home or in cafés, such as a novel by a friend of his, André de Richaud, *La Douleur*. It dealt with subjects that Camus knew about, such as a mother, poverty, and lovely skies.

His closest friends were Claude de Fréminville and André Belamich. Claude had an insatiable appetite for reading, while André was obsessed with classical music. He wrote on the classroom blackboard once, "Intelli-gence is an old whore."

When academic prizes were distributed on July 5, 1933, Camus won first prize in French composition and second prize in philosophy, a subject in which he had earned a grade of fourteen out of twenty for his final exam. He also was given a prize in history studies. Yet Jean Grenier felt that Camus had not gotten the "hang of academic things."

Camus was contributing juvenile verse and stories to a literary maga-zine, *Sud*, which Grenier read with interest. In the December 1931 issue, Ca-mus published a poem that owed a great deal to Paul Verlaine's "L'Heure exquise," and an autobiographical story entitled "The Last Day of a Stillborn Man." The narrator declares, "I am eighteen years old, and I can hardly re-member my gentle, well-behaved, and sickly childhood. . . . I had well-established principles: God, the immortal soul, living for others, and despising carnal pleasures." He goes on to discuss sexual desire: "I knew she was easy, and we started a conversation, until my desire became infinitely greater than love. . . . When I felt her breasts against my chest . . . she be-came frightened and backed away and I returned to the mountains, running and laughing."

And his narrator was depressed: "I haven't got anything any more, I don't believe in anything, and it's impossible to live like this, having killed morality inside me. I have no more purpose, no more reason to live, and I will die."

Camus also wrote four critical essays in *Sud*, including a banal analysis of Verlaine, and another about the popular poet and lyricist of turn-of-the-century Parisian poverty, Jehan Rictus. Albert tried to find a critical method: "True and sincere works should not be analyzed, because literary dissection kills emotion. . . . What is most seductive . . . is the contrast between [Rictus's] low and filthy life and the naive limpidity of his soul."

He also contributed a little article, "Our Century's Philosophy," about Henri Bergson's book *Les Deux Sources de la morale et de la réligion*. He had read the 1929 edition of Bergson's *Matière et mémoire* and was violently disappointed with the new book: "I impatiently awaited this book, which should have crowned Bergson's life work. His philosophy was a question, a problem raised which lacked an answer, and this book was written, but it disappointed me as an answer." Although he found that Bergson was still making "an apology for intuition and criticizing intellience," he wondered why the philosopher did not "write a work like a master who is teaching about the truth." Camus sought a fixed system, and complained that Bergson's method, to "put intelligence aside as dangerous, basing an entire system on immediate knowledge and basic sensations," was to "set aside all of our century's philosophy."

In the June 1932 issue of *Sud*, Camus had a six-page essay on music. Grenier jotted down his own personal reactions on the magazine's margins: "Superfluous . . . uninteresting . . . nonsense," Camus declared that music meant harmony, and developed analyses of Schopenhauer and Nietzsche's ideas about music, coining a new word: "Nietzsche took Schopenhauer's ideas and extravaganted them."

At the end of 1933, Camus wrote a short story about a character named Beriha, which was criticized in detail by a bookish school friend, Max-Pol Fouchet, who would go on to a literary career in France. Fouchet found that Beriha was too logical, which Camus denied: "I put Dreams and Action ahead of logic, because I see logic as pure intelligence, empty and to be despised."

Camus made stray notes at this time which would reflect on his later work: "Should one accept life as it is? That would be stupid, but how to do otherwise? . . . Should one accept the human condition? On the contrary, I think revolt is part of human nature. . . . Whether one accepts or revolts, one is confronting life." His view could be solemn: "Let's not kid ourselves, pain always exists, and there's no shilly-shallying that it is probably the essential part of life. . . . When a young man is on the threshold of life, before doing anything, he is usually soiled by grim lassitude and deep disgust at meanness and vanity, even while he is trying to avoid them. . . . He knows that metaphysical lewdness is mere vanity."

He took many notes and reread his favorite authors, like André Gide: "I was enraged by the mediocrity of my thoughts, while considering the deep feeling I have for Gide." Camus felt that Gide's novel *Les Nourritures terrestres* was "an apology for sensation . . . a forbidden paradise. . . . My liking for Gide doubles when I read his *Journal*. Isn't he human, though? I continue to prefer him to every other writer, and by inverse reaction, I detest Cocteau."

When Jean Grenier presented him with a copy of Marcel Proust's novel *A la Recherche du temps perdu*, Camus said he admired Proust's "combining sweeping power with minute detail." For Camus, Proust represented the typical artist, and in Proust, "everything is said, and there's no need to go back to the same subjects again."

The aspiring young writer confessed, "I only know one thing, my mystical soul is burning to give itself with enthusiasm, faith, and fervor." To this end, he assembled texts under the title "Intuitions," which he showed to no one, in which "reveries born of great lassitude, reveal an over-mystical soul's need to find an object for his fervor and faith." One text described Camus in a dialogue with a madman, who said, "I am too much in love with my lies and hypocrisies not to confess them fervently."

He also tried to write poems, clumsy and overalliterative, which proved that his most poetic path would be as a prose writer.

Chapter Five   **White Socks**

N ear the Acaults' butcher shop was rue Michelet, Algiers's version of
Fifth Avenue. At the angle of rue Michelet and rue Tirman was the
Notre-Dame bookstore, which Albert haunted, run by two French-
women whom Uncle Gustave called "the Virgins."

High-school students hung out on the street, and Camus and his pal
Fréminville would sit on the terrace of the Café des Facultés watching pretty
girls pass by. In October 1932, Camus wrote to Fréminville, "What other city
offers as many riches all year long, the sea, sun, hot sand, geraniums,
and . . . olive and eucalyptus trees? We can be happy here. . . . I could never
live anywhere but Algiers, although I will travel because I want to know the
world, but I'm sure that anywhere else, I'd always feel in exile."

The young people met at the Café de la Bourse and would go back up
to the city through the side streets of the lower Casbah, where there were lots
of Arabs, a minority in Algiers. The city had 170,000 white residents and only
55,000 "natives."

Camus and his friends would take walks to the citadel's ramparts, returning by way of the El-Ketar cemetery, where they would sit by the tombs,
reading inscriptions in French, Spanish, Italian, and Maltese, which re-
counted colonial history. The sea was in sight, the blue-brown limestone
quarries at Bab el-Oued, and the Notre-Dame d'Afrique basilica, a frightful
piece of architectural pastry. They would return by the rue Kataroudji, with
its notary offices and whorehouses.

Camus loved the city's bustle, and the calm found just outside the center. Most people who met him in 1932 and 1933 thought he was content, but
in fact Camus felt tormented, as he confessed to friends like Robert Jaussaud
and Claude de Fréminville, whom Albert called "the best . . . the most
gifted," although Jean Grenier, who didn't like the boy, disagreed. Claude

wrote poems about Oran, with its yellow stone cathedral and graffiti on city walls of giant penises shooting huge jets of sperm.

Both Claude and Albert felt themselves to be Spanish as well as French and would say "buenas tardas" to one another. Claude and Robert Jaussaud were politically conscious and pushed Albert to be aware of the inequality of wages and social problems for Arabs. The young men would exchange books and read verses aloud such as Baudelaire's "L'Etranger," alternating lines.

As Fréminville was planning a trip to France, Camus wrote him exalted letters: "Be a flame of joy at the crossroads, don't think that you are evil, you are a good and sensitive child who wants to be immoral, but be what you are, don't change. . . . Be wicked and prideful, and put up with insulting joy. It won't matter because you will remain avid or tender beneath it all. . . . Tenderness does not exist. . . . I don't believe in anything anymore. . . ." Albert said farewell to his friend but asked him to "write if you can."

Camus was having considerable success with girls, charming them with his gray-green eyes. He was particularly fond of cynical young Simone Hié, who had a lovely freckled oval face, a straight nose, brown eyes with green highlights, long legs, and a sexy walk. Simone had many boyfriends, including Max-Pol Fouchet. Albert first saw Simone at Max-Pol's, where the young people would meet to listen to music, with the window curtains drawn, following André Gide's advice. The daughter of a woman ophthalmologist, Simone called herself Max-Pol's fiancée. Known as "S" to her circle, she was a year younger than Albert, and the gossip was that she slept with boys, which was uncommon for unmarried girls in her social class in Algiers.

Her eyelids painted mauve and blue, wearing fake eyelashes and a see-through dress, Simone was graceful and mysterious, with a touch of vulgarity. Wrapped in a black fur, she had a touch of Greta Garbo, Marlene Dietrich, or Nadja, the heroine of André Breton's surrealist novel. Clinging to a cigarette holder, she admitted she was a liar. Her stepfather would say, "Simone, you'll end up a whore."

Camus got back in touch with Fréminville, writing to him in France on June 16, 1933, that he had not liked Claude's chapbook of poems: "You understand, old boy, why I'm not afraid to tell you the truth, because the real Fréminville will love me more if I'm sincere. . . . I admit that Walt Whitman can be heard in your verses, and perhaps Paul Claudel, but I confess I can't hear Henry James. So be proud, and don't get upset. . . . I insist on . . . staying in contact with you, above all now, when I've decided not to see anyone anymore and to live alone."

At nineteen, Camus had left his uncle Gustave's apartment on the rue de Languedoc after Gustave would not allow Albert to bring girls to his room, especially Simone. Max-Pol Fouchet often traveled as a militant in the Socialist Youth movement, and his ties to "S" became weaker. Camus met

Max-Pol at Essai Park, and they walked down to the beach, where Camus told him that Simone "won't come to see you anymore, because she has made her choice." Max-Pol accepted this news without a murmur and Albert remarked, "I wondered if you were a genius, and now you've proved it." Fouchet may have felt relief at getting rid of "S," since she was a drug addict. A few years before, her mother had given her a morphine injection for menstrual cramps, and since then Simone had been stealing her mother's prescriptions to obtain drugs. When her mother discovered what was going on, "S" began to get prescriptions from other doctors. Seductive and disturbing, Simone would quote André Breton, give huge tips to cab drivers, sing obscene songs, and dissect Gabriel Audisio's poetic novel *Jeunesse de la Méditerranée*. When she was on drugs, she would become distant and introverted, obsessed by a single line from the Dadaist poet Tristan Tzara, which irritated Albert.

To try to break her habit, Albert managed to obtain boxes of progressively diluted ampules for her from his friend Louis Bénisti's brother, a pharmacist in Bab el-Oued. Simone would shoot up at the home of Professor Jacques Heurgon on the rue Michelet and at the university, where she took courses after failing her entrance exam. Her high-heeled shoes and gray-blue fox stole caused quite a stir. She would stride down the street and men's heads would turn, and that made Camus jealous. He wanted to beat up anyone who looked at her with sexual interest. Sometimes he felt, as he confessed to a friend on July 27, 1933, that "love means nothing. . . . I've been forced to separate from my parents [the Acaults], and my brother took me in."

The kindly Lucien Camus, who lived at 117 bis rue Michelet, did not understand his younger brother, but loved him anyway. Uncle Gustave had cut off Albert's allowance, and Camus reported, "I live almost alone, penniless, and uncertain." Lucien was working as a sales representative and accountant and would help Albert when he could. But he earned only 1,800 francs a month, and he planned to marry a young seamstress on that, and gave money to his mother as well. So Albert was forced to earn his living, as he told Claude de Fréminville: "I'm thinking about journalism as a way to continue my studies. . . . I feel a sort of happiness in believing that I have infinite possibilities."

He decided to give up "the too-easy path . . . of revolt and anathema." He told Claude that he was struck by Algiers's beauty: "There is an immense brightness in the bit of sky I can see from my window and although I don't know why, it makes me think of one of our walks under the clouds, when we romantically strolled beneath the lightning and rain. It was very beautiful. . . . I believe that lovely things and lovely souls are often sad and always tragic, even when they laugh and get carried away."

At twenty, Camus knew his sadnesses were transitory: "These lassitudes are not conclusive. . . . Suffering is nothing, what counts is knowing how to suffer." He criticized Fréminville's Oran, "Each time I go to your frightful city, I am appalled by its rich vulgarity, and I much prefer Algiers." Camus was reading little and writing less, but "one must accept these mental hibernations."

Camus mentioned money worries in all his letters between the end of 1933 and the beginning of 1934. He had no more scholarship money, and his hope of finding a job as a publishing house secretary had failed, while another job possibility, as a tax collector, "did not stimulate my appetite." He asked Fréminville to use connections to help him find a job writing for the newspaper *Oran Matin*, hoping to continue studying by correspondence at the same time. Camus did not consider himself a rank beginner, as he had already written for the journals *Sud* and *Alger Etudiant*, as well as doing a column about musical recordings for *La Presse libre*.

Uncle Gustave had urged him to take a teaching job, but Albert feared that would stifle his artistic development. In November 1933, he received a diploma in moral studies and sociology, but in his final exam his marks were uneven; he failed in classical literature, so he had to take it again the following November.

Informing Fréminville that he was reading Thomas Mann, Nicolas de Malebranche, and Paul Claudel, studying German, and enjoying science, Camus stated, "I've given myself four years to write the works I want, because my illness will not allow me more than that. . . . When we're twenty, we think we have rights, but I am more and more convinced that we only have duties."

He warned Fréminville about "the facility that spoils the finest works. . . . I am so weary and broken. . . . I feel myself getting old, at twenty. . . . I know very well that I am suffering, and living fully. I know that the sublime cannot do without the tragic, although the contrary is sometimes true, when tragedy squeezes us too tightly and prevents us from weeping." Camus was going through "days of bitterness and unbelief" and felt protective towards Claude, his "very pure and childlike friend."

He returned to the subject of journalism: "No magazine suits me, because I don't want to publish, as it is finer and surer to create for the sake of creation, and not hope for some pale immortality. . . . If I had to publish, I'd wait three or four years, because works must be carried inside you for at least that long. . . . I don't believe in precocious genius."

During the first half of 1934, Fréminville stayed in Paris, where Camus wrote him, asking again for help with employment and reminding his friend, "My health does not allow any night work, and I can't leave right now." That was because he and Simone had got back together again, after some arguments: "I am in a hurry to live a lot, with lots of experiences, and both of us ask you to help us."

Camus planned to visit Fréminville in Paris in June: "I won't come alone . . . but don't imagine anything romantic or too easy, it's much more serious than that."

Dressed like a dandy in white pants, felt hat, and bow tie, Camus attended courses with Simone at the University of Algiers, given by a philosopher of science, René Poirier. Albert excelled in written assignments but was not the best at oral exams in the small class, and Poirier felt that despite the excellent organization of Camus's essays, he seemed detached from subjects.

Poirier was assisted by another philosophy professor, Jean Grenier, who was more interested in literature than the science-obsessed Poirier. Another professor who impressed Camus was Jacques Heurgon, who taught Roman history and literature, and in 1934 gave a class on the Roman emperors, including Caligula. Heurgon liked Camus, and felt it was a shame that the young man had no Greek and was only average in Latin, noting on Albert's translation of a brief passage from Tacitus, "Just passable, intelligent but still too uneven and unsure."

Camus was already certain that he would write, and he idolized the thirty-two-year-old French novelist André Malraux, who came to visit Jean Grenier in Algiers. But Grenier did not invite any colleagues or students to meet him. Of the hundreds of books that Camus read at this time, the two that most impressed him were Grenier's *Les Iles* and Malraux's *La Condition humaine*.

Grenier, fifteen years older than Camus, established a good rapport with his student, often exchanging thoughts about *Les Iles*, a 150-page essay on the attraction he felt for desert spaces, for islands, and for his cat, Mouloud. Camus regarded this type of essay as something he could develop himself, and he saw Grenier as close to the French writers François-René de Chateaubriand and Maurice Barrès. Camus appreciated his teacher's hidden irony and the touch of madness in the way he would read aloud a dialogue by Plato, wailing like a Russian tragic actress.

Camus also liked Grenier's odd way of referring to his premonitions as "my 'monitions." Grenier advised his student to visit Greece and Italy and Southeast Asia, recommending that Camus ask for an all-expenses-paid job as a teacher in Saigon. Both Camus and Grenier adored cats and dogs; yet despite their affinities, they kept a respectful distance, using the formal "vous" to address one another.

The tight-fisted Grenier had an existential difficulty in paying for a round of drinks, but he did generously give Camus a number of concepts from *Les Iles*, such as grandeur, revolt, heroism, and plenitude. In his writing Grenier also evoked his passion for the Mediterranean, which seduced

Camus as well. When Grenier and Camus were discussing things at a café terrace, other students would interrupt at their own peril. Camus would reply to the question "I'm not bothering you, am I?" with "Yes, you are!" and refuse to shake hands with the interloper.

Camus snubbed some people for arbitrary reasons: Once he decided he didn't like a fellow student, a young man from Oran named Henri Sansom, and kept calling him "Monsieur" Sansom until he took the hint and went away. Some women students hated Camus because he either ignored them or chased after them or rejected their advances; and he ignored the only Arab student in the philosophy department. Camus flaunted his sense of superiority in a way that put many people off.

He kept up a rather precious correspondence with Simone Hié, and the two surprised everyone except her mother by deciding to get married. Camus was twenty years old and Simone, nineteen. Simone's mother, Dr. Sogler, felt that Albert could only help her daughter. Their friend Louis Bénisti feared they were making a mistake, and that by marrying Simone, Camus was playing at being an angel, or a St. Bernard dog, trying to rescue her from drugs. Bénisti had heard Camus furiously criticize marriage as an "unnatural" institution, and the "sad symbol" of a wedding ring as a way of imprisoning people.

Albert and Simone did not swear to be faithful to one another, since they believed that they shouldn't deprive themselves of possible happiness if they grew weary of one another's bodies. Camus said, "I want to get married, kill myself, or subscribe to *L'Illustration* magazine, do something desperate, you know what I mean?"

The ceremony took place on June 16, 1934, and although the young couple became legally independent of their families, they were still financially dependent. Dr. Sogler rented an apartment for the couple and the Acaults, who were reconciled with Albert, gave him a little money and lent him a Citroën.

When Camus's mother asked him what he wanted as a wedding gift, he replied, "A dozen pairs of white socks."

Chapter Six   **"Little Bits of Soul"**

I n 1934, Claude de Fréminville joined the French Communist Party and urged his friends to follow suit. Camus warned him, "Above all, don't tie yourself to a youthful 'credo.'. . . We tend to call it cowardice when we abandon former mistakes. . . . If I went towards communism, and it's possible I would, I'd put my vitality, power, and intelligence into it, I might put all my talent and soul, but not all my heart."

Camus explained further, "I have a deep-seated attitude against religion, and for me, communism is nothing if not a religion." When Fréminville insisted, Camus replied on April 30, 1934, that he refused to ask for a Communist Party membership card: "To belong would mean to force myself to hide my other beliefs. . . . I can't help it if everything pushes me towards silence and my own life, and away from whatever is social. If it's a question of action, I act every day. . . . Incidentally, I am paying for it, I am neither happy nor joyful."

Fréminville planned to publish a literary magazine in Algiers, and Camus decided to contribute an article on André Malraux, the first time he tried to write about a young living author. He tried to find parallels between Malraux's books and those of Jean Grenier. Camus soon got involved in the proposed magazine's editorial policies. He suggested that the editor be strict with articles, "mine included," asked for a serious design, and offered to donate 50 francs per month. He was earning 300 francs per month by tutoring, apart from the money he received from his uncle Gustave and his mother-in-law.

Camus refused to contribute to Fréminville's project of an issue in honor of the stodgy French novelist Romain Rolland, and when Claude sent an article about jazz by a certain Mouchot, Camus called it "very badly written, with no interesting ideas." When Camus found out that "Mouchot" was in fact the pen name of Fréminville, he wrote to his friend again, saying "I had to go and beat up on you. . . ."

On September 3, 1934, Fréminville wrote to their mutual friend André Belamich about Camus's political commitment, and how the proposed magazine "will save the three of us from an evil Trotskyite influence which frightens me. . . . Should we leave Camus all alone? . . . Try to understand how necessary it is to reach out to him."

Albert had his mind on literature, while Claude thought only about politics. Camus advised his Communist friend, "Don't turn your back so resolutely on everything that resembles the divine, and beware of calling love what is only a manifestation of that God. . . . Above all, don't think of their kind of a just God, imagine him as being capricious and unjust instead, as in the Bible's Book of Exodus. Otherwise, how can one expect our hopeless human condition to change one day?"

The Camuses lived in a small house in the Parc d'Hydra neighborhood. Jean de Maisonseul, a student of Le Corbusier, decorated their apartment. Simone's mother paid the rent of 450 francs a month. Camus kept up his correspondence with Fréminville, in one letter praising his beloved philosopher Blaise Pascal: "If you knew how ravishing Pascal is . . . clear, profound, and unforgettable about the human heart and in his despairing glory." In the same letter, he suddenly switched to a good recipe for coffee, telling Claude that he mustn't pour boiling water into the coffee pot bit by bit, "but first a fourth of lukewarm water, and then the rest of the boiling hot water in three pours."

Fréminville accused his friend of being basically an intellectual, and Camus protested, "You know how much I love people, how I am touched when old housekeepers feel distressed because they've been mistreated, or workers who drink with me in the cafés of Belcourt."

When Fréminville sent him his writings to be evaluated, Camus would praise isolated sentences like "Antonio heard the sky beat like a broken sail on a boat," commenting, "That's how I like sentences to be, like vases that contain a blend of mixed perfumes, inseparable and moving." Camus would also point out his friend's spelling mistakes and when his language became too crude: "Why should you begin your story, 'Shit, a kick in the balls!' and mention on the first page 'an old cunt,' a 'prick,' etc.? To me it seems a typical Fréminville provocation."

Albert told André Belamich that he often had doubts about himself, but never about Fréminville, who recommended that he read Faulkner's *Sanctuary*. Camus found Franz Kafka's *The Trial* to be his kind of novel, while Faulkner was more to Claude's taste. Camus felt that André Gide's novel *Les Faux-Monnayeurs* was "perhaps Gide's best book," and he admired Katherine Mansfield's *Journal* and *Letters* more than her short stories.

Fréminville compared Camus to Mansfield, which puzzled his friend: "I don't know why you compare me to her, unless it's because of a hesitation about creating?"

In early 1935 he announced to Claude that he was working on a novel, *Le Quartier pauvre*: "I've written about a third of it, the first part and almost all of the second part. I'll send you the first part soon, and you'll tell me what you think. One thing I must know is if it can be sensed that I worked on it with emotion and love. When it is all finished, in June [1935] maybe, I'll try to publish it."

Helped by his teachers' recommendations, Albert found a part-time job in the Algiers motor vehicle registration department, which he called "idiot work." His boss, M. Pommier, used to scold the unmotivated young employee for not knowing how to write, although it is possible that Pommier was referring to Camus's penmanship rather than to his compositional skills.

For two years, Camus had been rewriting his book, also called *L'Hôpital du quartier pauvre* or *Les Voix du quartier pauvre*. Influenced by Proust and Faulkner, it had ornate sentences like "The immense park screamed beneath the wind, and intense life reared up under the rain." *Le Quartier pauvre* remained in draft form, and Camus later blended it with another project.

Preoccupied by his work problems, Camus insisted to Fréminville, "I don't want to be a teacher, and I'm trying to find a way out . . . although I'm told there is none, which is depressing. In the phony high-school atmosphere, where colleagues frown at you, students lie about their real feelings. Right now I'm giving high-school courses at night school, preparing office, bank, and postal workers for a philosophy degree examination. It's a sympathetic group of ten, who work in offices until 6 p.m., then take courses until 11 p.m. some evenings, yet manage to pass their exams. I like them a lot." Camus preferred his adult students to the adolescents he taught, whom he called "dirty little pretentious brats."

He planned to join Fréminville in Paris: "If only it were possible, I'd be glad to get my diploma there. Paris! Grenier says it's the only city in the world. What a joy to work with you, and go to exhibits, concerts, the Louvre, and the old Paris streets I dream of, called the rue Brisemiche, Pot-de-Fer, etc."

From March to June 1935, Camus studied for two diplomas: "I know a third of each program . . . at least fifty books to read, and then I'll have more than ever the 'sadness of culture.' " He received an honorable mention in history of philosophy as well as in logic.

Camus decided to stay in Algiers because Simone was still taking drugs and needed to be watched. She sometimes lived at her mother's home and often stayed in clinics. Albert wanted to finish his book by 1935, but did not manage to do so, and the magazine project failed as well. He thought about writing a play with Fréminville, *Fait divers*, in a style influenced by Charles

Vildrac, a favorite writer of the French Communists and Socialists, and the Catholic poet Paul Claudel. Camus admitted that the combination "may seem idiotic, but I think theater must be arbitrary and yet obey conventions, with something monstrous in its style and spirit. A human interest story, or real life, crushes you, but is every day's richest emotional material." Camus explored the idea of dramatizing "the powerful conflict that a sick woman and a dead girl create in every sensitive conscience, the conflict created by the afterlife, pride or resignation (Claudel)." He was also toying with the idea of a play about Caligula.

At the same time Camus was giving a class for students who had failed the June 1935 philosophy high-school diploma exam, in order to prepare them for their next attempt in October. While the assembled group drank tea and smoked, twenty-one-year-old Camus criticized his students' work, then sent them follow-up letters, such as one that blamed a student, Solange Sarfati, for "too docile obedience" because her essay did not distinguish between the opinions of Blaise Pascal and Paul Valéry, an omission which Camus found stupid.

One day Simone interrupted the course by yelling, "Albert, you left your slippers in the kitchen," at which Camus smiled at his female students and said, "Never get married, ladies." That fall, when classes were held at a student's home near the Sainte-Marcienne church, wedding bells rang during one class and Camus said, "Poor people, they don't know what they're doing. Never marry, ladies, never marry."

Solange Sarfati recalls that Camus encouraged her in her desire to be a doctor, although her brothers pressured her to accept the less ambitious job of pharmacist. Albert declared, "Don't listen to them, Solange, you'll be a fine doctor."

He planned to rewrite the book he'd promised to Fréminville between June and November, and he began another work as well. Simone enjoyed children's stories by the seventeenth-century Frenchman Charles Perrault and by the Brothers Grimm; and to amuse his distressed wife, he wrote *Le Livre de Mélusine*, subtitled "A Tale for Children Who Are Too Sad." The Mélusine story was based on the premise that "it is time to create new worlds, to escape from the intense melancholy one expects." The author explained on page two that writing a moralized fable required "great inventive qualities" that he lacked. The fairy-tale form eluded him, and he included clumsy verses about mythical fairies like Mélusine, Morgane, Urgèle, and Viviane: "I'm thirsty for your humanity. . . . I love your parched roads, watered with hope."

Camus was not a fantasy writer, and he never showed *Mélusine* to Fréminville. He struck a truer note with enigmatic messages that he would leave beside the sleeping Simone before he left the apartment to go to classes, such as, "Because we want to, we shall, and I'll take my little girl by the hand and sit her down beside me."

Max-Pol Fouchet wrote a letter of reconciliation from a tuberculosis sanitorium, and Camus replied that with Fouchet ill and Fréminville far away, "We are all striving to mask with prepared language our desperate search for an unadorned and simple truth, that our condition is hopeless." In his letter to Max-Pol and in another to Fréminville, Camus spoke of "little bits of soul" that are in letters to friends, and he asked Fouchet to find articles and lessons for him to do.

But when Max-Pol returned to Algiers, he saw little of Camus, who had, after all, stolen his fiancée and pretended to be more leftist than Fouchet, a busy political activist. Camus kept his circles of friends separate and isolated his wife from them, as Simone's behavior could be disruptive. For instance, she would walk half-dressed around their apartment on the rue Michelet. Still addicted to morphine, Simone represented a defeat for Camus. Friends would see her looking dazed in the apartment; she then would head for her room and rejoin the company later, looking calmer. Some friends thought that Simone made Camus suffer, but that he hid his feelings behind ironic smiles or sarcastic silence.

Albert appreciated the solidity of art and architecture studies as opposed to the abstractions of literary courses. In a 1935 letter of introduction for a young Algiers architect to Fréminville, Albert noted, "You know, an architect is always superior to a simple student, because he is obliged to consider things as they are, otherwise the house will fall on his head."

Camus had another painter friend, one of Algiers's most gifted draftsmen and furniture designers, Sauveur Galliero. He also saw a lot of another friend, a high-school English teacher named Yves Bourgeois, a political activist with sympathies for unions, pacifism, and anarchy. Bourgeois would go on holidays with Albert and Simone, without understanding what the couple shared in common, as they seemed quite different from each other. During one vacation, Albert and Yves were having a drink while Simone paraded around wearing Yves's jacket. Albert explained with a smile, "She has a life of her own." "Maybe so," replied Yves, "but she's got my jacket!" Camus decided that Bourgeois was "the husband type."

Until the summer of 1935, when his other lung became infected with tuberculosis, Camus was an enthusiastic swimmer and camper, and he loved attending soccer and boxing matches. He was treated by a doctor, Stanislas Cviklinski, known as "Stacha," who also tried unsuccessfully to break Simone's addiction by putting her on a strict month-long diet of glycerine water. Cviklinski was a fan of literature, like most people in Algiers's cultural circles, who were either aesthetes or political activists. Or, like Camus, both at once.

Chapter Seven # The Temptation to Action

*I*n his *Carnets* Camus would put down his thoughts, more to help plan future works than as a vehicle for an intimate journal. He sketched out pages for works to come, spoke of himself and future characters, and looked for "measure" when he felt that he was leading a "disordered life." He tried to organize his disorder, noting in 1935, "What saves us during our worst suffering is the sense of being abandoned and alone. . . . Our abandonment braces and exalts us while we are endlessly sad. . . . Happiness is often no more than the sense of pity about our own misery."

Camus decided to visit the Balearic Islands off Spain with Simone in 1935, as Spain was a second homeland for him. He reflected in 1936, "The wages of a trip are fear. . . . Far from our country and our language, a French newspaper becomes invaluable, during those late hours in cafés when one wants to touch other men's elbows, a vague fear seizes us and an instinctive desire to get back to the shelter of our old habits, the surest thing traveling brings us."

During his trip, Camus was tempted to escape the world and live in a monastery: "On top of a hill I saw a monastery, all yellow and baked earth, as they are here. A monk told me he would rent me a room if I wished, provided I did my own cooking and didn't mind seeing no one for days. . . . At 800 meters up, I'd work on my book alone, and I'd finish it."

Camus suffered from what he called "flu" but was an attack of tubercular fever, and he linked travel with illness: "When we are feverish and receptive, and the least little shock shakes us at the heart of our being. . . . One never travels for pleasure, since there is no pleasure in traveling. . . . I see it more as a form of asceticism. . . . We travel to cultivate our most private instinct, which is that of eternity. Pleasure takes us away from ourselves. . . . Traveling, like a greater and more serious science, brings us back again."

34

Back from the Balearic Islands, Camus decided to take a boat trip with a friend, Paul Raffi, along the North African coast as far as Tunis, but the trip was interrupted at the port of Bougie (Bejaïa), Algeria, when his previously healthy lung became infected. He wrote to Jean Grenier on August 4, 1935: "On Friday I came down in a cargo ship but the moment I arrived in Bougie, a bout of black-water fever forced me to see a doctor. He advised me to get home quickly, fearing that because of my condition, this attack might be tubercular in origin."

Back in Algiers, without Simone, he visited the Villa Shéhérazade, belonging to new friends, the Raffi family. The father had made money in the arms industry and the sons, Paul and André, became close friends of Camus. At the Raffi home, Camus met two young women from Oran who lived together, Marguerite Dobrenn and Jeanne Sicard. Jeanne was a brunette, the same age as Camus, with a high forehead and gray-blue eyes. A student of literature, she was self-assured and capable of being haughty, hence Camus's nickname for her, "Bittersweet." Jeanne came from a family of rich tobacco manufacturers. Marguerite, a historian, was a year older than her friend, and smaller. There was an inquisitive look behind her eyeglasses, and she had a timid charm. Together the women formed an inseparable couple.

Camus felt great affection for this female couple, and as he had no need to play the seducer with *them*, he discovered the pleasure of certain "sweet and restrained forms of women's friendship." He would tell Marguerite and Jeanne, as well as another friend, Jeanne Terracini, about his projects, saying that he counted on his pen for his livelihood and glory.

Camus also had male friends, like Charles Poncet, the Belcourt leader of the Communist peace movement Amsterdam-Pleyel, which fought fascism. Poncet had met Camus when both arrived early at a meeting of the Amsterdam-Pleyel group in the basement of an Algiers bistro. Camus explained to Poncet that the leaders of Amsterdam-Pleyel had sent him to encourage the activities of the Belcourt group: "I know these Belcourt guys, they're champions at playing bowls, card games like belote, or drinking anisette. But as for politics . . ." He proposed to create a revolutionary political theater, and Poncet promised his support. For a long time Poncet did not know that Camus was married, as he did not wear a wedding ring, and he never spoke about Simone.

Another friend, Robert Namia, came from a family of Jewish colonists from near Blida, a city to the southwest of Algiers. Namia had a series of jobs in an architect's office; he was violently antiwar and was a faithful reader of *Commune*, the official publication of the Comintern in France.

When not busy with politics, the young people would take walks around Algiers, pausing in cafés, where the men ordered anisette drinks and the women, barley water. Plates of olives, chickpeas, and fritters were served free with each round of drinks. On their own, the men visited the Lower Depths, a bistro in the sailors' quarter favored by whores and pimps. The bar was decorated with a full-sized guillotine and a skeleton with a bouncing phallus hidden by an old sheet. The place was run by a dwarf named Coco, who blessed his clients by waving a dildo in the air like a bishop's mitre, to the amusement of Camus, who sat among dockworkers smoking hashish. The young men would talk about books and sing obscene words to popular melodies. Camus, who wrote his books in chaste language, was amused by raw conversation. In restaurants with his friends, Camus often refused to be treated to meals; although he lacked money, he preferred to be the host.

After dinner, the friends would go to cinemas like the Variétés or the Bijou Palace—they preferred American westerns and detective movies, or Soviet films if there was nothing else being shown. Camus felt that theater was superior to cinema as an art form.

Camus no longer played soccer, as he got out of breath too easily, but if he saw an empty can in the street, he would immediately start to kick it. Like his friend the painter Sauveur Galliero, he enjoyed observing the modest folk of the Bab el-Oued and Belcourt neighborhoods and watching the obsessed players of boules, with their extravagant and majestic gestures.

Camus would visit again the Essai Park he had known in his childhood, with its tropical vegetation and adolescent Arab boys walking around with jasmine flowers behind their ears, their little fingers intertwined in friendship. On the beaches, European and Arab kids mingled. The young people enjoyed the free pleasures of sun and water, which was often so hot that it was said to be "like horse piss." On Sundays, Camus would borrow his uncle's car and with friends would drive out to camp near the ruins of the city of Djemila, 150 kilometers away from Algiers. The ruins stimulated certain questions in Camus's mind: "I am astonished that while we have such refined ideas about other subjects, we are so deprived about the subject of death. . . . We do not know how to speak of death or of colors, either."

Sometimes Camus and his friends would drive to Cape Bengui to the east of Algiers, or Tipasa's Roman ruins to the west, which became a favorite place for strolls. Camus would read parts of a lyrical essay to his friends: "In springtime, gods dwell in Tipasa, speaking through the sun and wormwood perfume, the sea in its silver armor, the unbleached blue sky, flower-covered ruins and great bubbles of light in piles of rocks. . . . At certain hours, the countryside is blackened by the sun. . . . We enter into a yellow and blue world of Algeria's summer landscape, where we are greeted by a perfumed and bitter sigh."

The friends also went camping to the back country, at the gorges of Chiffa, between the cities of Blida and Médéa. There, a female monkey that Camus once caressed created a jealous scene when a woman friend happened by. A farmer's wife offered the travelers sardine sandwiches for lunch, and Camus dipped his in his coffee with gusto.

Since 1934, the leftist French Popular Front had been trying to defend democratic freedom against the threat of fascism. Camus had reservations about the Socialist leader Léon Blum and the leftist figurehead Romain Rolland, whom he disliked as a man and writer. Some farsighted political observers had already denounced Soviet communism, but most novices like Camus were ignorant of Stalin's acts and still confusedly admired Lenin. Camus attended many Communist Youth meetings, and by the spring of 1935, Claude de Fréminville had convinced Camus to join the Communist Party. Camus informed his friends like Max-Pol Fouchet, who were amused by the news. Others, such as Louis Bénisti, thought that Camus was joking, but Camus's girlfriends took his political dreams seriously.

On Sundays, Jean Grenier would invite students and friends to his home, where he spoke informally about communism, saying that at Camus's age, one must become committed and try the experience of politics, otherwise one simply retired from the world. "If you're doing philosophy, politics is necessary," said Grenier. He had pushed Camus to sign up with the Communist Party, which was looking for local leaders. Grenier, who had written "An Essay Against the Orthodox Mind," felt that as a Communist Camus would "play a great political role . . . assured of a career worthy of a new Julien Sorel," the ambitious working-class hero of Stendhal's *Le Rouge et le noir*.

Camus did not view politics in a careerist way, but saw it as a way to fight inequalities between Europeans and "natives" in Algeria. Since communism promised equality, Camus decided to be a Communist. He wrote to Grenier from Tipasa on August 21, 1935, "You are right to advise me to join the Communist Party."

He announced to Fréminville that even before leaving for the Balearic Islands, he had taken the plunge: "I've joined the Communist Party, where I will work loyally as a soldier, not in the leadership committee. My skills will be used in journalism for *La Lutte Sociale* [the Party's bimonthly journal] and in Marxist classes, etc. We must experience the hardships and triumphs of Communism, and in one year I'll take stock, or we can do so together. . . . I'm at an important turning point." He explained that he still had reservations: "I believe that communism's excesses are based on a certain number of misunderstandings that can be painlessly disavowed. . . . What had stopped me for a long time, and what I believe stops so many, is communism's lack of religious emphasis, and the Marxists' pretense of constructing a morality that depicts man as sufficient unto himself. . . . We might see communism as a springboard and ascetism that prepares the ground for more spiritual activities. In short, it's a way to shirk false idealism and mechanical optimism, and establish a situation where man can rediscover his sense of eternity."

Camus did not claim to have read Karl Marx's *Das Kapital*, as copies were rare in Algiers, nor did he pretend to be a Marxist. He was having a try at Communism, an idea sparked by world events, as part of a quest for the absolute.

Chapter Eight   **Heroism and "A Load of Crap"**

Camus knew about the hardships of workers in the Belcourt neighborhood of Algiers, and a little about Arab poverty. By joining the French Communist Party, he felt he was defending his mother, who was an illiterate cleaning woman, and his uncle Etienne, the barrel maker. For the writer, the Party was a kind of secular church.

Few in number and regularly persecuted, Algerian Communists fought against war in general, although inconsistently so. As a war orphan, Camus was swayed by this apparently pacifist stance. He hoped that the reactionary upper classes in Algeria and France would be defeated by the Arab and French revolutionary working class. Since the bourgeois class had compromised itself with the Nazis and Fascists, he felt that world socialism was needed more than ever.

Camus also saw joining the Communist Party as a way to fight for the rights of Algerian "natives." In a similar way, to be against fascism, imperialism, and colonialism was part of the same political package. He was impressed by an Algerian Communist, Amar Ouzegane, who felt that all Europeans, even the Communists, had paternalist views about Arabs.

Camus spent time in Algiers Circle of Progress meetings, talking with members of the Islamic Studies Association, led by the sheiks Ben Badis and El Okbi. He tried to see how the Algerian Communist Party could grow closer to native Algerians, but he did not really know working-class Arabs, only the educated, French-speaking elite.

He felt sympathy for militant activists, as he wrote to Claude de Fréminville on July 22, 1935: "I believe there is more truth in the human relations between Communists than in what they declare their beliefs to be." At a Communist film club, he saw a Soviet film, *Torn Socks*, and returned home "very exalted . . . I sometimes feel the resonance of the new communism, and how much I admire André Malraux."

Simone was hospitalized, and Camus complained, "I'm too alone here, and so I often go to Belcourt where I can find myself again." He recruited his friends Jeanne Sicard and Marguerite Dobrenn to join the Party, but did not participate in indoctrination sessions with Communist leaders. The Party headquarters was on the rue de Lyon in Belcourt, near the Camus family apartment. All told, there were only 150 members of the Algerian Communist Party, with only ten percent Arabs, who made up ninety percent of the country's population.

The Party leaders encouraged Camus to run local front organizations, such as the committee that planned lectures and similar events as part of the Amsterdam-Pleyel peace movement. On April 2, 1936, Camus gave a lecture at the Stella cinema, which attracted the attention of Algiers policemen, who filed two separate reports on the evening. The police stated, "Mr. Camus gave the history of the Popular Front movement, saying that in order to understand the Popular Front, one must understand Europe's current situation, with Fascist Germany's violence, Fascist Italy's colonial war [in Ethiopia], and Nationalist Japan's effort to make China into a colony."

Camus had told his audience, "The dangers of war and death are everywhere, and fascism is just an expression of capitalism's dire straits. Capitalism is bankrupt because under its power, a collectivity works for the profit of a privileged minority. . . . While forty million unemployed people across the world wonder what they will eat tomorrow, we are burning raw materials and throwing them into the sea. People are beginning to understand what their own interests are, and are revolting against the Fascist yoke." He went on to analyze fascism's success in Italy and Germany: "Fascism has many ways of keeping people in their place, such as the power of words like 'fatherland,' 'glory,' and 'honor,' which are synonyms for the Fascists' safety-deposit boxes. Then there is war. Finally and above all, there is the division of the people. . . . Artisans, small businessmen, workers, intellectuals, the middle class, and the lower middle class ought to unite to shake off the Fascist oppressor's yoke."

The policemen noted down that Camus said, "Capitalism even tends to pit the native-born part of our country against the Jews." They quoted his parallel between Algeria's tradition of anti-Semitism and Germany, "which is trying to isolate France through anti-Semitism."

Camus sought only "a little more justice, freedom for all, guaranteed work for all in the best conditions, with no fear of the future, and above all, in world peace." The meeting, which had begun at 6:45 p.m., ended by 8:00, to much audience applause.

The Communist Party was wary of intellectuals, but gave them special employment; and Camus was a roving intellectual agent without a specific job title, who gave speeches, worked at the Cultural Center, and ran a popular theater.

Albert's Communist friends got together every fifteen days, and although they were uninterested in Marxist theory, they tried to organize a circle of sociological studies, with Marguerite Dobrenn as secretary. This was in addition to the Théâtre du Travail and the Cultural Center, where Marguerite, Jeanne Sicard, and Camus were active members. They were all Communist dilettantes, and only Camus had any contact with Party leaders.

On January 1, 1936, Camus wrote to Fréminville, "Basically, at the very bottom of life, which seduces us all, there is only absurdity, and more absurdity.... And maybe that's what gives us our joy for living, because the only thing that can defeat absurdity is lucidity." He had confessed to Fréminville at the end of 1935, "Unlike you, I see [communism] as an adventure and a wager more than a sure form of communion.... If you weren't intelligent, you might fall into sentimentality, a big load of humanist crap, what assholes think of as fraternity and communion....

"My year looks likely to be busy—(1) The Party, Newspaper, Marxist School, and Speech. (2) The possible creation of a worker's theater, and I thought you might write a play. (3) Essays that I want to write—Europe facing North Africa, about André Malraux—the metaphysics of Marxism—something about the experience of Death, and its 'social value' in a culture and civilization. (4) To finish my diploma—on Neoplatonism and Christianity. (5) A work about poor neighborhoods, etc., etc.

"I'm a little frightened, but what the hell, if I don't do it all this year, it will be another year, and if not, at least I'll use all my strength. I want to use up all of my youth."

André Gide moved to a second rank of interest as André Malraux intrigued Camus more and more. In July 1935 Malraux, the heroic writer and herald of revolution, arrived in Algiers by hydroplane and gave a speech at Belcourt, and Camus wrote about the exciting event in *La Lutte Sociale*. He observed that in Malraux's books, such as *La Tentation de l'Occident* and *La Condition humaine*, the characters were admirable and moving in their struggles against a prideful European world.

Malraux was important for Camus and his generation because he defended Communists in China and Germany, at least according to legend, and although he was never actually a Party member, almost no one knew this fact. In *La Condition humaine*, Malraux hammered home a truth that Camus understood very well, that for impoverished, exploited classes, dignity meant "the opposite of humiliation."

Malraux, like the young Camus, thought as much about political action as about art: "I think there are few novelists in our time who have not seen journalism collected into books and realized the new novelistic form they represent, and quickly became discouraged." For Malraux, journalism "continues the strongest traditions of the French novel, from Balzac to Zola, with the entrance of a character into a world which he reveals to us, as he discovers it for himself."

In June 1936, Camus finished his graduate work and told Fréminville, "Every discipline is stupid, but every game has its rules, and if you want to express yourself, follow the rules of the game. It may be foolish, but expressing oneself with inarticulate shouts is no better than unadorned life, and I'm convinced that there is a division between Art and life. . . . What will last is perhaps a shout that is a little truer, a page one writes that will find its chosen reader. To produce that one page takes a life's work."

Camus had theatrical projects for Claude: "once everything is started and brought to life in performance, to shake up discouraged actors and joke with them, believing in everything that will be performed onstage, and of which nothing will remain the next day except the need to sweep up and add up box-office receipts. I don't know any more exalting experience than to be an actor and technician, a rigorous financial expert who is sensitive to style. If you were with me, it would be even more beautiful."

His uncle Gustave Acault refused to lend his car anymore, and Camus was looking to buy a used motorbike and spend the summer with Fréminville.

Chapter Nine   # Saint Augustine Without Marx

amus had decided to become a teacher. The University of Algiers
gave him a student loan of 4,500 francs, which allowed him to survive, although in considerable poverty. He planned to earn the rest of
the money he needed by tutoring pupils and with money from his mother-
in-law, Dr. Sogler. He would have preferred to teach in Algeria but also
toyed with the idea of going to France, or to Asia, as André Malraux had. At
age twenty-two, he saw himself as a civil servant, working without pleasure
but with a regular salary.

A candidate for the teacher's license had to write a thesis, a sort of doc-
toral dissertation, about one hundred pages long. Camus chose an ambitious
subject, "Christian Metaphysics and Neoplatonism: Plotinus and Saint Augustine." The chairman of the university's philosophy department, René
Poirier, accepted the title and subject of Camus's project, although Jean Grenier had suggested a work on the Hindu religion. One advantage of Plotinus
for Camus was that neither Poirier nor Grenier was a specialist on the ancient philosopher.

Camus's thesis was a stodgy, well-constructed essay with notes and critical apparatus. In it he tried to reconcile Greek thought and Christianity,
explaining how Plotinus contributed to this reconciliation. Camus had sympathy for Christianity—without God—which encouraged commitment in
the world, but he preferred the Greek philosophers' view of the world to
Christian thought. He reproached Christianity for focusing on individual sin
and collective guilt.

Although Camus was a militant Communist at the time he wrote his
thesis, he did not mention Marx or Engels, whom he had scarcely read, and
wrote his essay in the cloying French academic philosophy style. He chose
Greece as a subject even though he had never studied the language, and

Christianity when his knowledge of the religion was scanty. Both Augustine and Plotinus were Africans, and Camus saw himself as a Mediterranean man. He felt strangely like a Greek in a Christian universe and questioned how one could have a religious temperament without belief. He was attracted to communism as a religion without God, and Plotinus and Saint Augustine intrigued him as characters, closer to his heart, body, and intelligence than other philosophers. Plotinus represented Neoplatonism, which declared that the world of ideas was the real world, and Camus sought to reconcile reality and appearance. He was also seduced by the aesthetic side of Plotinus, and his search for ecstasy. Saint Augustine was the theologian of God's transcendence and impenetrability, who said, "God, make me chaste, but not yet," and Camus too sought the satisfaction of the senses, while finding God incomprehensible. He appreciated Augustine's passion and his search for righteousness. Through Plotinus and Augustine, Camus sought reasons for optimism while examining arguments in favor of universal pessimism. He found that a sense of tragedy and joy in life were complementary.

To prepare his thesis, Camus carefully read and scribbled in the margins of the two volumes of Augustine's *Confessions* in the Garnier Classics edition. The thesis was written in a heavy style, sometimes striving for literary effect: "We see Christian heresy's glittering motley as a metaphysical fairground." To please Grenier and pad out his thesis, Camus included much about apparently irrelevant Indian philosophers in his potpourri. He quoted and paraphrased numerous experts in philosophy, often forgetting to attribute his quotes. Camus also borrowed from past Augustine scholars in an unoriginal way. A later reader of the thesis, the Augustine expert Paul Archambault, called Camus's work "very muddled and confused." In his theological debate, Camus was in the tradition of neither Plotinus nor Augustine, but of Pelagius, a theologian for whom man builds his own spiritual and worldly destiny.

Behind the flood of quotations, Camus did make some personal observations: "Plotinus' philosophy showed an artist's point of view. If things can be explained, it means they are beautiful, and Plotinus transported an artist's extreme emotion about the physical world into the world of understanding. . . . Plotinus described intelligence in a sensual way."

Camus felt that the Gospels put death at the center of modern man's preoccupations, and he preferred the luminous and innocent Greeks, as he saw them. He was repelled by Augustine's sermons about asceticism and restraint, although he was fascinated by them, too. Rejecting the Christian notion of sin, Camus saw the soul as "the desire for God and nostalgia for a lost fatherland." He praised Augustine's role in religious history: "For many years he remained the only hope and shield against the Western world's misfortunes"—which marked an advance on Camus's youthful conviction that Christianity was merely a religion for old ladies.

While Camus was finishing his thesis, his cat, Moniou-Blanc, died. He wrote to Marguerite Dobrenn on April 16, 1936, "Moniou Blanc died last night, and I found him in the morning all rigid lying in a puddle of urine. They say he was poisoned, but they always say that when an animal dies."

He handed in his thesis on May 8, 1936, and waited for the reaction, disturbed by one of his periodical quarrels and breakups with Simone, who had left a clinic and gone to live with her mother. With his university work done, Camus took two weeks off to savor life, as he noted in his *Carnets*: "May 16. A long walk in the hills with the sea below and the delicate sun, wild roses growing on every bush, fat syrupy flowers with purple petals. Returning home to the sweetness of friendship with women, young women's sober and smiling faces. . . . No false notes."

On May 25, Camus was granted his graduate diploma, with a grade of twenty-eight out of forty for his thesis. This was good enough to suggest that he would have a promising career as a teacher, although René Poirier felt that his work on Augustine and Plotinus showed more of a literary talent than a grasp of philosophy.

By the end of springtime, 1936, Camus had his diploma, had begun work on his own writing, and toyed with the idea of getting an advanced teaching degree as Jean Grenier had done. He thought of staying in Algeria, or else following Grenier's advice to go to Paris, where reputations were made. If he left Algeria, it might not be with the unstable Simone.

Camus had freed himself from God, but not from the need to construct a code of behavior. It was easier to base a ready-made social morality on communism than to create a whole new, personal morality. To the question of how to live without God, who does not exist, Camus had three answers: live, act, and write.

Chapter Ten ## The Letter from Salzburg

amus's English-teacher friend Yves Bourgeois, a kayak enthusiast, had recently paddled from Innsbruck to Budapest, and he suggested a similar trip to the Camuses. Yves admired Albert's endurance in keeping up with all his activities, while remaining affable, courteous, and elegant, and was intrigued by Simone, whom he visited in the clinic in Ben Aknoun.

Simone spoke of studying classical dance, while Albert agreed to put aside his own work in order to take her on the trip, to get her away from morphine pushers. Bourgeois gave the couple some kayak lessons before they left Algiers for Marseilles. At the beginning of July 1936, the trio crossed the Mediterranean and arrived in Lyons by train.

On July 13, Camus wrote to his friends Jeanne Sicard and Marguerite Dobrenn, "Don't expect any news about my trip. I hate the 'impressions' style of writing. . . . This trip has an aura of fear for me, which may seem unclear when I say it like that, but if I become a writer, I'll try to explain it one day."

Camus found Lyons sinister and grandiose, "bourgeois in its comforts, food, morals, and even whores. . . . A city of hypocrites and suppressed people, whom I detest with all my heart, because they do everything possible to avoid life. They park themselves behind dishes of quenelles and filet of sole cooked in cream. They are typical Frenchmen, in their flat mediocrity. . . . Instead of calling people shits, I'll call them inhabitants of Lyons."

He enjoyed the working-class suburb of Lyons, Villeurbanne: "A Communist local government, with a skyscraper and other architecture designed by Le Corbusier. . . . There is a hammer and sickle on the town hall, and workers carry a mechanical piano through the streets on a wheeled cart to announce dance parties. Tomorrow I'll walk with them as they parade around."

46

When the trio was sitting at a café terrace on the place des Terraux in Lyons, one of Bourgeois's former students came over to chat. He was a member of the far-right-wing Patriotic Youth group, which irked Camus, who said, "You can't talk to these sort of people." Camus was further irritated when Bourgeois said provocatively, as they passed Saint-Irénée Church during a stroll, "Did you happen to know that I'm a Christian?"

Bourgeois rented a second kayak, and they bought third-class train tickets to Austria, via Switzerland. Camus was tired by the time they got to Innsbruck. He wrote to Marguerite and Jeanne on July 17: "What bores me the most about the Tyrol . . . is its Tyrolian aspect, and Innsbruck is a comic-opera town where men walk around in short pants and a feather in their hat."

Their plans were to get into their canoes at Innsbruck and to go camping along the way. Camus discovered he had accidentally brought along an Algerian lottery ticket, and requested of Jeanne and Marguerite, "There are no Algerian newspapers here, so look at the third section and see if the number 136918A will win us millions, a farm, and happiness."

At Innsbruck, they stayed at the same traveler's inn, the Golden Eagle, where Goethe had stayed over a century before. They followed international news, noting that in Spain, General Franco was trying to overthrow the Republican government, but Camus and Bourgeois were convinced that the Fascist would fail.

Bourgeois put the kayaks into the water on July 19 and led the way with the suitcases. But after the first step of the journey, Camus woke up in their campsite in severe pain. They reached a town called Kufstein, on the Austrian-German border, where he wrote to Marguerite and Jeanne, "I felt extremely tired and only then did I recall that doctors had forbidden me any extensive exercise of my shoulders. I decided to give up the canoe and travel alongside on foot or by bus. . . . Each time I realize that I'm an invalid, I realize how I am unlike what I'd prefer to be."

Camus said "One day I must write a 'Psychology of the Body,' to add to the countless number of my works in progress. . . . Here the women are blond, tall, and stupid. The men are honest, servile, and inoffensive. I learnt that Heinrich Heine said that the Tyrolians were infinitely stupid, which is saying a lot, but there is basic truth to it."

Simone and Yves continued to travel by kayak without him. Bourgeois sensed tension between Albert and Simone when they all shared a room in a hotel at the resort of Berchtesgaden, which scandalized the hotel owner. He felt that Camus did not sufficiently admire the natural beauty of Berchtesgaden. Indeed, the Austrian Alps terrified Camus and gave him a claustrophobic feeling of suffocating. They headed to Salzburg, site of the expensive summer music festival, where, although they could not afford concert tickets, they planned to stay a few days. They rented two rooms, and one morning Camus somberly told Bourgeois that he was separating from Simone. At the general delivery window of the local post office, Camus had found a letter addressed to Simone from an Algiers doctor, and opened it to discover that the man who furnished Simone with her drugs was also her lover. On July 26, he wrote to Marguerite and Jeanne that two hours after he arrived in Salzburg, he had received "one of the most painful blows" of his life, which "has been completely changed by it. I don't like confiding in people, but I simply want to inform you friends of the fact that as soon as I return to Algeria, I will live *completely* alone. . . . Never speak to me about it."

The trip continued, and Camus wrote to his friends again: "I'm writing this letter just after emerging from a mystery play written by Hugo von Hofmannsthal and directed by Max Reinhardt, *Jedermann, or the Play of the Rich Man's Death*. It was performed on the square in front of the cathedral at 5 p.m., and it taught me a lot of things, but, above all, it was strangely moving. Towards the end of the play, dusk fell and the rich man died repentant, as the character of Faith leaned over his grave, saying, 'He has been stripped of everything, even his life.' "

Again he wrote to Jeanne and Marguerite: "I'm going to continue the voyage in spite of everything, because of Bourgeois, who hasn't suspected or noticed anything." This was not strictly true, as he had already informed Bourgeois of his intention to leave Simone. Camus stopped at Linz for a lung collapse treatment, noting telegraphically in his *Carnets*: "Linz—Danube and workers' suburbs—Dr. Gutweiss—suburbs—little Gothic cloister—Solitude."

The three crossed the Czech border, with Camus following by train. Yves and Simone paddled along the Vltava River, and paused at Budejovice, a city whose name would later inspire one of Camus's plays. At one point, Simone asked Bourgeois for money to get an abortion, and returned two hours later, smiling; later he realized that she must have bought some drugs.

In August 1936, Camus spent four days alone in a cheap hotel room in Prague, "deadly" days full of "anguish."

On August 6, he wrote to Marguerite from Prague, "An immense city . . . where I feel completely out of my depth. Since yesterday I haven't been able to shake a stupid depression which prevents me from enjoying what is admirable here. . . . I have enough money for eight days but I'm still managing to worry about the subject. . . . The fact that I'm going to spend three days in nervous waiting [for Simone], which I know can only depress me in the state I'm in." He hated the food: "I mustn't spend more than ten crowns for each meal. . . . I point to a dish on the menu which I can't read . . . and get a mix of semolina flour and meat, made disgusting with an incredible amount of cumin seasoning."

Camus had wanted to visit Prague's Jewish cemetery, but did not manage to locate it, which shows how upset he was, since this famous tourist landmark is not hard to find. The next day he wrote to Marguerite, "I'm feeling better, and I've seen the cathedral and a vast quantity of baroque churches which don't inspire me." On the same day he wrote to Claude de Fréminville, "For more than a month, I've been living like a depressed near-madman, and in the past few days my mood is even worse." Later, on returning to Algeria, Camus would write a failed novel that he never published, *La Mort heureuse*, in which the protagonist, Mersault, went through many of the same moods in Prague that the writer had felt. He wrote to Fréminville, "It is hard to follow the events in Spain from here, and each time I pick up a French newspaper, it's with anguish, as the news is often contradictory, but at least our side has not been overwhelmed." He told Claude about Simone's lover, commenting bitterly, "She used to hang around doctors' waiting rooms."

Despite the strain, Simone continued to amuse Yves during the trip by asking waiters to translate the menus into German and English, finally ordering something that was not on the menu, such as enormous plates of mushrooms that she devoured. The trio saw a poor staging of a Maxim Gorky play, and Bourgeois and Camus swore to do better when they put on Gorky's *The Lower Depths* in Algiers. They went to Dresden, with Bourgeois rowing his kayak alone. Simone and Albert took the train, going to the Dresden Fine Arts Museum and dutifully admiring Raphael's *Sistine Madonna*, and finding the city to be "the Germanic version of Florence."

In another letter to Marguerite, on August 14, he wrote, "I remember that when I was eighteen years old, I thought that time spent sleeping was a waste, I had a mad and avid thirst for everything that awaited me, people I didn't yet know, words that I hadn't yet spoken, works, books, and men. I didn't feel that I could do without it, and I'm not sure that I've changed since then. . . ."

Bourgeois shipped his kayaks to France and the friends traveled on together, stopping at the cities of Botzen and Breslau on the way to Silesia. Camus found the Silesian plains "pitiless and barren, dunes with birds flying in the clayey sky above the sticky earth." They went back into Czechoslovakia, and Camus generalized about that country and Germany: "This terrain without appeal, dreary, filthy, foggy—something pitiless yet strangely compelling." They ran out of money and waited for a cable from Simone's mother, who sent the money along with a single word: "Enjoy."

Camus wrote to Claude de Fréminville on August 22 from Olmütz, "I've just come from Germany, where everything smells of hatred." They spent a morose week in Olmütz, with Simone seeming distracted and drugged, and finally got to Vienna. She spent lots of time in her hotel room, primping, while Camus and Bourgeois quietly went to see the Ring boulevard.

Camus decided to cut short the trip, canceling planned detours to Venice and Genoa. He later described Vienna in *La Mort heureuse*: "Vienna was a refreshing city insofar as there was nothing to see, the oversized Saint Stephen's Cathedral bored him, and he preferred the coffee-houses."

The trio bought their discount train tickets to Italy, which required that they stay a week in the country to get the low rate, despite their fatigue. Camus felt relieved to get away from German and Slavic people and be among Mediterraneans again. They took a train to Vicenza, and then to a little town, Monte Berico, where they stayed for a week. Camus particularly appreciated the airy view from their hotel on a hilltop: "In Prague, I was suffocated between walls, but here the world is open for me." During their stay in Monte Berico, Camus went sightseeing and played bocce ball with Bourgeois, while Simone remained in her room or vanished for a while. Simone and Albert behaved to each other like distant friends, and soon left for Milan, which they did not stop to visit, but took the train to Marseilles and then the boat for Algiers.

On September 9, when they arrived in Algiers, the couple broke up, Camus staying at his brother's apartment and Simone moving in with her mother.

Camus would later sum up his painful trip in *L'Envers et l'endroit*: "Any country where I wasn't bored was a country where I didn't learn anything." He added philosophically about his ruined relationship with Simone: "At least it was good to have had a great love, an unhappy passion in one's life." He soon began writing *La Mort heureuse*, in which the protagonist is betrayed by an unfaithful woman: "There was no doubt about it, that that man had slept with Marthe. . . ." In a letter to Marguerite, he focused on the six days spent in the Italian countryside at Monte Berico: "I benefited a lot from it, I didn't write a line and spoke very few words, and I wonder if that isn't what happiness means."

Camus said he was thinking about renting a small apartment with his mother, "who is getting old and who needs looking after. . . . I think with much affection about the faithfulness and simplicity with which you wrote me all summer, but let's draw a curtain over that—because of the sun, as Gabriele d'Annunzio wrote."

Chapter Eleven

Banned Playwright

B efore leaving for the European trip, Camus had sent confident letters to Marguerite Dobrenn and Jeanne Sicard to announce that the 1936–37 season of the Théâtre du Travail would include Maxim Gorky's *The Lower Depths*, Machiavelli's "La Mandragola," Honoré de Balzac's *Vautrin*, Francisco de Rojas's *La Celestina*, and a revival of the company's adaptation of Malraux's short novel *Le Temps du mépris*.

Theater had long been one of his life's great occupations. At primary school, Camus played the role of d'Artagnan in Alexandre Dumas's *The Three Musketeers*, and in high school he would read aloud plays by Molière and Marivaux. He loved working on a team, and Camus and his friends despised the popular theater with its unlikely plots and silly eroticism. Through the Communist boulevard and the theater, Camus discovered that he was a natural leader, and he thought about how to approach classic adaptations by André Gide, and Pushkin's plays.

Camus was inspired by the work of the French director Jacques Copeau, founder of the Théâtre du Vieux-Colombier, who put the text first, staging plays with minimal scenery and direction. Camus agreed that the text was the key element in the theater and that everything else must be subservient to it.

The Théâtre du Travail had opened on January 25, 1936, with the Malraux adaptation, *Le Temps du mépris*. The evening was a benefit for unemployed workers, who were let in free. Camus had sent the adaptation to Malraux for his opinion, and he received a one-word telegram in reply: "Act." Malraux's brief reply—"Joue" in the original French—also had the meaning of "play" or "enjoy," and was in the more intimate singular verb form, rather than the more formal "Jouez." The conservative newspaper *L'Echo d'Alger* ran a positive review by a friend of Camus's, Lucienne Jean-

Darrouy, who pointed out that the audience "belonged to every stratum of society."

Le Temps du mépris was the story of a Communist, Kassner, who escapes after being interrogated by the Nazis. Camus worked the tale into a two-act play, with short lyrical scenes in Kassner's prison cell and the interrogation chamber, his reunion with his wife, and a public meeting in which the real-life audience participated. He divided the play's scenes in a way that made his friend Charles Poncet think of a "tragic comic strip." In his staging of the play, Camus lifted ideas from such directors as the German Erwin Piscator and the Russians Vsevolod Meyerhold and Konstantin Stanislavsky.

Performances took place in the large auditorium of the popular Padovani Bathhouse in Bab el-Oued. The scenery was designed by Louis Miquel in minimalist style. Audiences of seven hundred people crowded into the hall for the performances, and a police report stated that on a given Saturday night, there were three hundred women in the audience, "including some prostitutes." After the performance was over, the actors would speak to the audience about the real-life model for the character Kassner, the German Communist leader Thaelmann, who had been imprisoned by the Nazis. The play was an occasion to present Communists as democrats and to hate Nazis as villains.

The audience was so galvanized by an orator's rousing speech, delivered by Robert Namia, that they spontaneously began singing the Communist hymn "The Internationale." The stately Professor Alazard from the University of Algiers, who had founded the city's art museum, raised his fist in the Communist salute. The play was filled with blatant propaganda, such as the moment when Marguerite Dobrenn, wearing a kerchief on her head, stood in a spotlit corner of the stage and declared that "Vladimir Ilyich [Lenin] deeply loved the people!" Some participants would later recall that the level of acting was barely acceptable, and that there was lots of onstage screaming in the histrionic acting style of the time. Pierre Salama, the brother of a school friend of Camus's, who saw all the performances, thought at the time, "Albert has a flat and hollow voice, and although he's happy to be acting, he is performing in the melodramatic style, which is not his strong point. . . ."

Camus's second theatrical effort, *Révolte dans les Asturies*, was more ambitious. In September 1934, the far-right-wing Spanish government had brutally suppressed a miners' strike, and Camus's group created a play on the subject. The actors were asked to improvise their own lines, in the commedia dell'arte tradition; but in the end, they would perform a text almost entirely written by Camus, with help from Jeanne Sicard, Yves Bourgeois, and Alfred Poignant. The play contained a certain violent irony, and discussed many themes important to Camus, like the Spanish labor movement. "If a strike leads to death, which is the case here, it can reach a certain form of grandeur that is specific to man, namely absurdity."

Révolte dans les Asturies was meant to be performed in the Salle Cervantès in Algiers, and the police prefect gave his approval, but the far-right-wing mayor of Algiers, Augustin Rozis, would not grant the troupe use of the hall. The leftist newspaper *L'Algérie Ouvrière* complained that the play would have been performed "as a benefit for poor European and native children, and thus we see M. Rozis's contribution to the first popular, lively, and intelligent show of the Algerian theater." The ban stimulated Camus, who wrote to Jeanne Sicard and Marguerite Dobrenn at Eastertime, 1936, that there was "charming work for yours truly, protest letters to newspapers in the polemical style. . . . Still to be organized, the printing of two thousand pamphlets, one hundred posters, a protest rally if possible, a sandwich-board man in town, and cars with protest banners, and I've only just begun."

Camus thought about staging Gorky's *Lower Depths* as a replacement for the banned play, or else announcing a third performance of *Le Temps du mépris* and reading the forbidden *Révolte dans les Asturies* instead. He stated, "I feel myself capable of every excess, becoming a Dominican priest, devoting myself to the reform of unwed mothers, writing an article for *L'Illustration* magazine, claiming that André Breton's poetry is dynamic, or finding a prostitute and taking her to my room, writhing at her feet while calling her 'my little dove' and speaking of God, putting the tea samovar on the table, and begging her to spit all over me so that, losing my pride in humility, I might become a repentant, absolved sinner."

Jokingly, Camus claimed that he was mulling over a longtime desire to write a detective novel with a group, in the way that the banned play was created. There was a project to read and partly stage a scene from *Révolte dans les Asturies* in the Rio cinema in Algiers, and Camus said that the sets should "surround and press down on the spectator, forcing him to enter the action, which a more classical approach would want him to view from outside. . . . Ideally, the person in seat number 156 will see things differently than the one in seat 157."

Révolte dans les Asturies survived thanks to a twenty-one-year-old publisher, Edmond Charlot, who printed it in a limited edition at Algiers.

From 1936 to 1939, Camus's circle devoted themselves to theater. Jeanne Sicard and Marguerite Dobrenn admired Camus, but they were critical of his habit of seducing young women, even though Marguerite admitted that they fell into his lap without any effort on his part.

Camus also had a rival in the group, André Thomas-Rouault, the nephew of the painter Georges Rouault, who owned a paint and wallpaper store, and would challenge Camus's opinions about theatrical matters. A British composer, Frank Turner, wrote music for the group, and a rich woman, Marie Viton, Countess of Estournel, took charge of costumes and assisted in stagings. Viton wore distinctive skirts in Prince of Wales checks and flew airplanes as a hobby. There were few working-class members in the troupe, apart from a Communist Polish Jew, Maks Widorschik, a furniture maker, who built the sets designed by Louis Miquel. There was also an Arab, who did technical jobs in the theater, and young Belkadi, who made his living as a house painter.

The group staged little plays in the suburbs of Algiers in December 1936 at events organized by the newspaper *La Lutte Sociale*, and also prepared a realistic play, Ramon Sender's *Le Secret*, about a worker interrogated by the police.

Camus planned to direct a play by Pushkin and wanted to act the role of Molière's Don Juan and to stage the Irish playwright John Millington Synge's *Playboy of the Western World*. He also acted in radio dramas for Radio Algiers, and in a farce by Georges Courteline, *Article 330*, which was a vulgar but funny play that criticized the judicial system, for the Belcourt branch of the Algiers Women's Union.

In his exuberance Camus would make holes in cane chairs by leaping on top of them. Rehearsals were held at actors' homes or at Communist Party headquarters, and although Camus had many friends, he enjoyed posing as a solitary boss, as he told a friend in September 1936: "I run this theater alone, by thunderous decree." Before staging Aeschylus' *Prometheus Bound*, he instructed Louis Bénisti, "I want to use popular elements, Greek masks smeared with burgundy color." Bénisti would make a sketch and Marie Viton would then create the costumes.

Each production, which was performed two or three times only, took several weeks' work. There were challenges, such as how to obtain period scenery for Ben Jonson's *Epicene, or the Silent Woman*; Bénisti finally gave up and put a nineteenth-century French sideboard in the Napoleon III style on stage for want of something more historically accurate.

The friends would gather at couscous restaurants and Camus and Robert Namia would debate about suicide, the difference between Japanese hara-kiri and the Ancient Roman version.

As the Spanish War heated up, the friends read Shakespeare's *Hamlet* aloud at the home of André Thomas-Rouault. One night Robert Namia said mysteriously that he would not be able to attend the next rehearsal and hemmed and hawed when asked why not. Camus exclaimed, "Shit, where will you be?" Namia replied that he would be going to Spain to fight on the Republican side against Franco's Fascists, as other Frenchmen, such as André Malraux, were already doing. Camus declared brusquely, "The rehearsal's over." Later that evening, when they were eating a North African stew of mutton and vegetables, called tajine, at a friend's house, Camus told

Namia, "You're a lucky man." With the condition of his lungs, Camus could not possibly join the International Brigade.

Many theatrical projects did not work out, and among the cancellations were productions of Shakespeare's *Hamlet*, *Othello*, and *Romeo and Juliet*; John Ford's *'Tis Pity She's a Whore*; Machiavelli's comedy *The Mandrake*; and *Vautrin*, based on the character created by Balzac.

As a director Camus would scold the actor Jean Negroni for being late to rehearsals, but forgave him when Negroni explained, "I couldn't come earlier because I was drunk." One young actress, a Mlle Garcin, was accompanied everywhere in rehearsals by her father, who was so worried about Camus's reputation as a lady-killer that he would not let his daughter out of his sight in the theater. When it finally reached the stage, *Prometheus Bound* did not please most of the audience.

On September 14, 1936, Camus wrote to Marguerite Dobrenn thinking about a farm, "which must be in Algeria, or at the least in the Provence region of France. The main thing is that it won't be in Germany, and that it has cypress trees." Camus explained that he was relishing "the evenings here, in an almost green light, when beautiful women walk up the rue Michelet, isn't that admirable enough to fill a life?" He noted to Jeanne Sicard, "All I expect are real friendships, like my two ideal daughters. . . . I'm doing my own work with discipline. . . . I'm watching the days go by without being able to think or decide, and in ten years I'll call that happiness." A few days later, he wrote to his "two little pigheaded people" to say that he would "no doubt have to settle for tutoring and a graduate fellowship I've been promised," but the fellowship did not come through. He joked, "Enough about my base side, now for the noble part: fifty years from now, I'll publish a 'History of My Ideas,' which will inform you all, and I've already found the title for the first chapter: 'How My Genius Was Born.' There's lots of [the philosopher] Alain and of Julien Benda in it."

The two young women were ending their vacation in Oran, and Camus told them he longed to order iced drinks "on the boulevard Ourdinot, next to the stand where a female dwarf plays a radio." Although surrounded by friends, he told Marguerite and Jeanne, "Yesterday, I noticed that I don't have any friends right now. . . . For me, who loves company so much, it's rather curious; I read endlessly and work for myself and cannot manage to be serious when someone speaks to me."

Camus gave up on Céline's novel *Mort à Crédit* (Death on the Installment Plan), reading "with the greatest attention up to page 23, and that's when I abandoned it, as it's only bragging about being disgusted, which wants to seem pessimistic, but is really hoping to sell 300,000 copies." He had been reading with admiration Jakob Wassermann's novel *The Maurizius Case*, but wished the author "had gone farther in this story of sexual jealousy." In October 1936 he wrote to Jeanne and Marguerite describing how he had read Wassermann's novel "in the train, facing an old Arab, who was an amiable old scum." The Arab explained that he was paralyzed and asked if Camus could fetch him a bottle of mineral water. Camus, trying to read, said, "I'm going to explain it to you: You get off the train, walk a little, turn right, and there's a sign that says 'Restaurant.' That's all you need to know." The Arab said, "You don't want to go yourself," and Camus replied, "You catch on fast," and the two men laughed. Camus added, "Then he wanted me to admire the boils on his thighs for a good half-hour."

Still thinking about theater, Camus decided to have Le Temps du mépris performed on a double bill with Prometheus Bound: "I am fascinated by the idea of performing [the Aeschylus] in the same evening as the Malraux, to compare two efforts at tragedy more than two thousands years apart." He was less enthusiastic about a new production of Gorky's realist play The Lower Depths. He declared theatrically to Marguerite and Jeanne: "Ah my friends, what shame doth cover mine face when I think of everything I haven't done yet and which I should have done so long ago. But I'm basically full of courage, no matter how foolish and disillusioned I may seem. . . . I'm sure that if I manage to keep my lucidity and freedom of action, I won't regret it this year." He commented about rehearsals for the Gorky play, "An unemployed young laborer named Prédhumeau, who is playing the role of a policeman, said, 'This play is only about the dregs of society.' . . . I've got only one hope left, that Mexico or India will colonize Algeria, but there's no hope that they will, because they're too intelligent."

Camus asked Jeanne for musical advice about the production, as he had "no musical knowledge, apart from what one can pick up by loving the music one takes to naturally."

Camus was rewriting Paul Nizan's translation, and complained, "As usual, whatever I write is always too overwrought." He wanted a brief trumpet call every time Jupiter was mentioned, "and then the themes intertwine until the end when Prometheus is set aflame, amid a din of trumpets, explosions, and thunder. Then a brief moment of calm, with a flute and guitar trying to make themselves heard, but Jupiter's trumpets break out with even more force from the four corners of the stage and drown out everything, only Prometheus is silent, and thus the whole tragedy is summed up at the end and symbolized in the musical architecture."

When Jeanne Sicard suggested writing polytonal music for the play, Camus did not grasp her technical arguments about music, but asked her again, "Don't you think it's possible for a Bach-like oboe and a guitar from Catalonian sardana dances to be heard amid the trumpet's blare, and have them drowned out afterwards? . . . Excuse me if I'm saying stupid things."

He dreamed of going camping with Robert and Madeleine Jaussaud, along with Marguerite and Jeanne: "In the evening at the camp, I'd speak to you [Jeanne] about the immortality of the soul, and Marguerite would say simply and quietly, 'What happened to the sausages?' That's what I call happiness, little girl, to speak about sausages when others are interested in the soul's destiny."

Also in October, he wrote his friends that he was being invited out to many social occasions, although he did not know why, and would utter a few paradoxes and be done with it, such as a maxim he had invented about women: "They inspire in us the desire to create masterpieces, and prevent us from finishing them."

He begged Jeanne Sicard not to forget him, amid all his worries to get *The Lower Depths* onstage "in any way, and however unprepared it may be, on November 29. . . . Delay is impossible."

Camus always knew how to get past obstacles.

Chapter Twelve   The "Political Agitator"

In June 1936, Camus had been looking for a room or apartment in which to write. He'd told Marguerite Dobrenn and Jeanne Sicard, "I'm fed up, kids. I've been on a sinister search for an apartment, and those I can afford are horribly ugly." His apartment search delayed his work for the Théâtre du Travail: "I have a ferocious need for an apartment, to find myself, and see things with lucidity and open eyes, because I hate people who are always 'in delirium.' Happiness, somewhere between lucidity and grandeur, would be fine, but how to achieve it without twenty square meters of one's own?"

Off to look at another apartment, Camus said that if it had a fireplace, Marguerite and Jeanne, who were in Oran preparing their roles in a stage version of *The Brothers Karamazov*, could come over "to drink mulled wine, made with orange, cinnamon, by the fireplace. Continue to practice undulating Russian gestures. . . . Everyone here seems foolish and graceless, except the charming Louis Bénisti, who looks like a biblical character and with whom I often speak about painting and sculpture, which I haven't done in years."

Camus was planning to spend the next year in Algiers, working on theater projects, but he wrote to Marguerite and Jeanne on October 29, 1936, "I'm not sure to be here when you get back [from Oran]: I'm negotiating with a sanitorium in the Haute-Savoie region of the Alps that needs a teacher for children patients, so I might get stuck there at 1,500 meters' altitude. . . . If the deal doesn't work out, which I secretly hope, I'll get an office job here so I can work eight hours like my little pals, which would not be hysterically amusing, but I'm scraping the bottom of the barrel. . . ."

He was already imagining taking tea with the two women when he got out of a hypothetical office job at six p.m., and told them he had given up the search for an apartment, realizing that he couldn't afford one, and would be obliged to live with his brother Lucien.

Christiane Galindo, a young woman from Oran, was helping Camus to forget about Simone. Marguerite and Jeanne had asked Camus to look after Christiane when she came to Algiers, and he helped her to find a secretarial job by examining the want ads, for himself as well, "in the secret hope that a Hindu prince will be looking for a male secretary with a Western education." If Christiane Galindo came to Algiers for two weeks, Camus suggested, she could "eat a naturist diet, which is excellent for the health and the pocketbook, and see things close-up. . . . Ordinarily I would take her as a lodger at my place, but I no longer have a place nor any money. . . ."

He jokingly referred to Jeannie and Marguerite as his children, and now he had found a third in Christiane: "For the third child, these successive acceptances of paternity are starting to do me in, but I am incapable of refusing such a sacred duty. I've found a firm offer for her, as a farm machine company has needed a secretary for three days." Camus had still found no work for himself: "For over a week, I haven't even had the ten cents to pay for a stamp, so I named my brother my secretary, and he mails off my letters."

When she arrived, Christiane Galindo turned out to be a lovely, tanned brunette. She found a job as a stenographer at a Peugeot dealership in Algiers, and became Camus's lover in a long and tender relationship which began in January 1937. Unlike Simone, Christiane had an open and healthy personality, and her beauty and generosity touched Camus's friends, who thought she spoiled him.

In his novel *La Mort heureuse*, Camus described the house that he shared with Christiane, Jeanne, and Marguerite—named the Fichu House after the family that owned it—located high atop Algiers on Laperlier Hill, surrounded by olive, pine, and cypress trees: "In the neighborhood they call it 'the three women students' house,' and it is reached by a steep path which begins and ends flanked by olive trees. . . . You arrive in a sweat and out of breath, push a little blue gate and avoid being scratched by the bougainvilleas, and there is still a stairway to climb, as steep as a ladder, but in a blue-tinged shade which already quenches your thirst. They and the fellow call it the House on Top of the World, looking out on the whole landscape like a balloon's basket hanging in the sky, brilliant above the world's colored dance." Once they were able to admire the view, no visitors "complained about the steep path or fatigue, and each day we had to suppress our joy." The Fichu House was decorated with props from the Théâtre du Travail and filled with Camus's pets, including a dog, Kirk, a red cat, Cali, and a black cat, Gula.

Camus was secretary general of the Algiers Cultural Center, an initiative of the French Socialist government, the Popular Front, and his friends joined him to promote cultural life in the city through the Théâtre du Travail, the visual arts, literature, and a French-Moslem Union, in which Claude de Fréminville participated.

In February 1937, at an evening lecture under the auspices of the Algiers Cultural Center, Camus spoke about whether a Mediterranean culture was possible. He rejected Italian dictator Benito Mussolini's idea that Mediterranean culture meant imperial Rome and its imitators, pointing out that Spain had contributed much to culture as well. Camus saw Spain as the link between Mediterranean Europe and Africa as a basis for understanding North African culture. He felt that Northerners were a different breed, explaining, "I spent two months in Central Europe, from Austria to Germany, wondering why I felt uneasy and so deeply concerned, and I've only recently understood that these (Northern) people were tightly buttoned up, with no idea of how to let themselves go."

Members of the Cultural Center, who heard guest lecturers from France, defended the Blum-Viollette plan for better conditions for Arabs in Algeria. As governor of Algeria, Maurice Viollette wanted to give French citizenship to the Moslem élite, and in a 1931 book, *L'Algérie vivra-t-elle?*, he predicted that if this did not happen, France would lose Algeria as a colony between 1945 and 1950. Léon Blum, who was briefly president of France under the Popular Front, drew up the Blum-Viollette plan to give political rights to two hundred thousand Moslem voters, but under pressure from French political classes, including the Radical Socialists, the plan was not adopted, despite the support of people like Camus and his friends.

The Cultural Center offered evenings of Arab culture, but hardly any Arabs came. On May 24, 1937, there was a benefit evening for the Spanish Republicans at war with Franco's Fascists, and Camus led the applause for the guests of honor, a group of Spanish Republican naval commanders. For young people in the mid-1930s, the choice between sympathizing with communism and with fascism seemed clear. Camus would say that he was a progressive, but did not talk much about his Communist Party membership.

Camus's leftist circle was greatly influenced by two writers, André Malraux and André Gide. The latter's book, *Retour de l'URSS*, published in November 1936, marked a definitive disillusionment with Soviet communism. Gide criticized the depersonalization of Russian collectivism and stated that there were far too many poor people in the USSR. Both Camus and Charles Poncet were troubled by Gide's book and wanted to program an evening debate about it. However, the Paris bureau of the Amsterdam-Pleyel organization sent a letter saying that such a debate might not be "opportune."

The debate was held anyway in 1937, although fewer than forty listeners attended, and no Communists among them, not even Camus. Poncet was sure that the Communists had organized a silent boycott of the evening, and Camus may have gone along with this edict, as he was usually present at Cultural Center evenings, even those of less immediate interest to him.

In June 1937, a Communist Youth Group speaker, Gabriel Préd-humeau, accused Camus of embezzling money from the Cultural Center—an odd idea, since the center had no money and Albert and his friends, particularly Jeanne Sicard, paid for events out of their own pockets. Préd-humeau persisted in making unsavory references to Camus's sexual success as boss of the Théâtre du Travail. Camus wanted to punch him in the nose, but finally just decided to ban Prédhumeau from theater activities.

Another militant Communist, Jean Deguerce, attacked Camus for staging, in addition to Communist-approved works like Gorky's *Lower Depths,* Jonson's comedy *Epicoene* at the Théâtre du Travail. Camus weathered these criticisms and became involved in the troubles of an Algerian Moslem political leader, Messali Hadj, who fought for national liberation, although not immediate independence. At the beginning of 1937, Messali Hadj founded the Algerian Popular Party (APP). Nationwide labor strikes and demonstrations followed, and in July, Messali Hadj was arrested and deported from Algeria as a dangerous agitator. It was said that because many members of his Popular Party were ex-Communists, the official Communist Party was active in trying to get rid of the troublemaker. Camus was sympathetic to the APP and felt close to some of the party's activists without knowing them intimately. He told Amar Ouzegane, the Algerian Communist Party's secretary, that he disagreed with the Communists' opposition to the Popular Party. Ouzegane tried without success to convince him of the contrary, as he was jealous of Messali Hadj's popularity with the masses.

Along with other Europeans in Algiers, Camus supported the hopes of a Moslem elite. Ouzegane warned Camus that his support of Messali separated him from the Communist party line, but Camus insisted that in this case the Communist Party had been wrong in its analyses of Messali, and ignoble in its actions.

The Algerian Communists had previously considered Camus a useful ally, noting that some conservative families had refused to let their children study in the classes Camus taught because he was said to be a Communist. He belonged to a Communist circle of intellectuals, including friends like Jeanne Sicard, Marguerite Dobrenn, and Claude de Fréminville. Along with three Arab manual laborers who were pals of Camus, they would meet at the Fichu House to talk informally about anything and everything, seriously addressing world problems.

The French Communists called Messali's Popular Party a group of pseudonationalists, agitators, and government agents; at meetings of the intellectual circle, Camus would insist on supporting Arab civil and social rights, which, he pointed out, used to be the Communist Party line too, before they began the battle with the APP and decided that the fight against fascism was more important than the struggle against injustices to native peoples. As a result, Camus was summoned along with a friend, Maurice Girard, to a special hearing of local Communist Party members and grilled about his beliefs, and at the end of the meeting Girard handed in his Party membership card. Camus, refusing the advice of friends that he too should resign from the Party, decided to force the Communists to throw him out, if they wanted to.

Amar Ouzegane, in his role as Party secretary, appreciated Camus for not being the typical European in Algeria and not suffering from "Western ethnocentrism." Ouzegane had taken up a collection for Camus when the young writer was ill and out of money, but now he saw Camus as an aesthete with only a rudimentary political understanding.

Although Camus had not been an unconditional supporter of the Popular Front, he did pin his hopes on the Blum-Viollette plan; and when the Radical Socialists in Algeria, who represented rich colonists, opposed the plan, Camus wrote a Manifesto of Algerian Intellectuals, published on May 2, 1937. The manifesto, in favor of the Blum-Viollette plan, appeared in the monthly bulletin of the Algerian Cultural Center, with an anticolonial message: "Culture cannot live where dignity is killed. . . . A civilization cannot prosper under laws which crush it." Camus said that culture could not be spoken of "in a country where 900,000 inhabitants are deprived of schooling and civilization."

A French Communist, Robert Deloche, advised the Party about the situation in Algeria in a report that was also sent to the Comintern in Moscow. Deloche stated that it was "necessary to purge certain Trotskyite agitators, such as Albert Camus . . . who have developed a systematic campaign of calumny against the directors of the French Communist Party and its political line." Amar Ouzegane was also criticized, for, among other things, being "always very well dressed," and the fact that Camus too was a snappy dresser may have offended some puritan Communists.

A few months later, Claude de Fréminville, accused by the Communists of printing propaganda for Messali, left the Party, rather than being noisily expelled. Jeanne Sicard and Marguerite Dobrenn also quit, tearing up their cards shortly afterward.

In less than two years, Camus had lost his wife and his political party. He was not traumatized by the break with the Communists (sometime between July 1937 and early 1938), because he felt he had betrayed no one, remaining faithful to the European and Arab working classes. One immediate result of the whole affair was that he would avoid doing political theater.

A few months before Camus was expelled from the Communist Party, his first book, *L'Envers et l'endroit,* was printed in an edition of 350 copies. Jean de Maisonseul wrote to say that he felt that Camus used the first person singular too often, and Camus replied on July 8, 1937: "I agree with you, Jean, one must remain on the sidelines." He went on to say that he had allowed himself "to say everything will all my passion . . . [and] a mania for nakedness" of emotion, with which he finally had become disillusioned. He planned a later book with a "more exterior" approach, explaining, "The work of art does not count for me today, even if certain pages are well written, because my heart and my flesh have written them well, and not my intelligence."

In the five essay-novellas of *L'Envers et l'endroit,* Camus wrote about his mother and his grandmother, who was "nothing but an actress." Camus meditated about youth: "Young people don't know that experience is a defeat, and that you have to lose everything in order to know a little bit. . . . Just as it took me a long time to understand my attachment to, and love for, the world of poverty where I spent my childhood, only now can I perceive the lessons of the sun and the land where I was born."

Camus tried many different prose rhythms and styles in this book, which was received with general indifference; the Paris press did not react at all. The first review, which appeared in the *Oran Républicain* newspaper, accused Camus of mimicking Jean Grenier's prose style. After a few more articles came out, Camus told Jean de Maisonseul, "The same words kept recurring, like 'bitterness' and 'pessimism,' etc. They don't understand and I sometimes tell myself that it's my fault that I wasn't understood."

Camus had replaced politics with literature, as he noted in his *Carnets* in December 1937: "Those who have grandeur inside them do not do politics." However, he remained interested in politics, and wrote an "Essay on the Forty-Hour Work Week," which he could not get published, although it was neatly typed by Christiane Galindo. In the essay Camus objected to the fact that the government had voted the forty-hour work week for laborers but then ignored it, claiming that the forty-eight hour week was better for production. He spoke of his family, without naming them: "There are entire families where the men, for example, are barrel makers and the women are cleaning women, and that's how they balance their budgets. As soon as children reach the age of apprenticeship, they are put to work as well, so that they'll 'produce' something. . . . The only historical inevitability is the one which we create. . . . In that dangerous freedom where man finds himself alone facing the destiny he alone creates, he can find his most secret fraternity, in fertile joy."

In breaking with the French Communist Party, Camus had refused to compromise his feeling for the Arabs, and his ideas about art, to Party pressures that would make political content paramount in art.

Chapter Thirteen

Intellectual Worker

amus wrote to his friend Jacques Heurgon on July 26, 1937, "I love to write because of the ardent, secret passion it demands." The same day, he wrote to Marguerite Dobrenn with his travel plans for the next weeks: to go from Algiers to Marseilles, Arles, Avignon, Orange, and Paris. He invited Marguerite and Jeanne Sicard to join him, warning that Claude de Fréminville, who was about to get divorced, would also come along. Camus found North Africa too hot in the summer, even if swimming in the sea made him "black and seductive." He told Marguerite that he was not going to get married, and felt in a romantically adventurous mood.

However, the travel plans soon broke down. When they reached Avignon, Camus began to feel ill with a nameless fear that often oppressed him when traveling. Next, he went to Lyons, and felt homesick for Algiers, where he could keep a balance between work and playing in the sun, although "a fragile one, no doubt." He thought of going next to Lago di Gardo, and urged Jeanne and Marguerite to come, even if they had no money, as they could share expenses. He wanted to be in Florence so much that he could taste it.

Meanwhile, he spent almost a week in Paris, a city that inspired in him an emotion he found hard to describe any way but "tenderness. . . . I know Paris intimately, by heart, as if I had been born there. . . . No doubt my impoverished past makes me feel that way. Belcourt resembles certain quarters of Paris (rue Mouffetard, la Cité, etc) so closely. . . . I now have the kind of attachment for this city that one has for women who cheat on you, which is to say I'd be extremely unhappy if I lived here, but at the same time so enriched, that I'd be obliged to write." He was more elliptical about Paris in his *Carnets*: "August 1937, the tenderness and emotion of Paris, cats and children, people drifting, gray colors, the sky and big parade of stone and water."

After visiting the 1937 Paris World's Fair, he traveled to a town in the Hautes-Alpes region, Embrun, at 870 meters' altitude. He announced to Marguerite Dobrenn on August 17, "I've decided to stay a month here, if only to prove to friends that it won't help me at all." Charles Poncet criticized Camus for not obeying doctors, who wanted him to check into a sanatorium. He found the Embrun resort "horribly boring."

The book project *La Mort heureuse* returned to his thoughts, as he told Marguerite: "A strange thing happened to me, I started to think about my novel. . . . I didn't used to think of myself as a novelist, but started to see my characters with such intensity that I left the real world for a time. . . . If I have any doubts left, they are only about whether I'll be able to realize the world that lives inside me." He said that his novel would be "something really bizarre and strange, but very much alive, don't worry about that," warning her to expect "boredom to the ninth degree." Were it not for work that occupied him, Camus would have "already spit in the face of my neighbor at the dining room, who takes pills all the time 'to make her regular.' " This woman informed her husband within earshot of Camus about "the least little incident in her intestinal functionings."

On August 21 he wrote again to Marguerite to say that his stay at Embrun had been useful, "something that allowed me to be alone with myself. In Algiers I was exhausted and my body got out of control, I acted like an idiot and didn't have time to think about myself. Here, I'm starting to get control over my body, and through sheer boredom starting to understand certain things. . . . I'm more encouraged about life here."

He noted in his *Carnets* some first ideas that would develop into the novel *L'Etranger*: "A man who had looked for life where it is normally found, in marriage and a job, etc., notices all at once, after reading a fashion catalogue, how he had been a stranger [*étranger*] to his own life, life as it is portrayed in fashion catalogues." Mersault, the hero of *La Mort heureuse*, would serve as a basis for Meursault, the main character of *L'Etranger*. Still working on *La Mort heureuse*, Camus drew up a three-part outline for the book, which he did not follow, while also sketching out a three-part outline for *L'Etranger*: "First part—his life until then. Second part—the Game. Third part—abandonment of compromises and truth being in nature." He wrote in his *Carnets*, "This month of August has been a turning point, taking a big breath before letting everything go in a delirious effort. . . . I must live and create, live until I weep from living."

He still hoped that Marguerite and Jeanne would visit him at Embrun, and despite his own money difficulties he offered to lend them a small sum if it would make their trip possible. Claude de Fréminville arrived first at Embrun, looking depressed because of his marital problems, and then Jeanne and Marguerite finally came. Albert took the train with his women friends, stopping first at Marseilles, where he was fascinated to find odd, greasy stains in his hotel room behind the radiator, which gave him "the sort of liberation that comes from dubious and shady things." The closer he got to Italy, the more relaxed he felt, as his *Carnets* for September 8 reveal: "Blue evenings on the Ligurian coast, my tiredness and need to cry, solitude and the necessity for love, and finally Pisa, vivid and austere, its green and yellow palazzos, domes, and gracefulness along the grim Arno River. . . . Something which had been bleeding inside me has now begun to heal." Camus studied the Arno River, noted street graffiti such as "Alberto fa l'amore con la mia sorella," and ogled pretty Italian girls, who stimulated "the hot beast of desire carried in the hollow of one's loins, moving with fierce sweetness."

From Florence, he wrote to Claude de Fréminville on September 10, 1937, about their meeting, which had not been a success: "Since I left Embrun, I realized how hard it was for you and me, and I walk around all day feeling as though I want to cry, which is my way of being happy. . . . Something has finally collapsed inside me that was like a cyst, getting harder every day. Oh, Claude, how much better we are when we're happy. . . . It's terrible when one gets out of the habit of really living."

In Italy, he admired Florentine and Sienese painters of the early Renaissance, noting, "Their stubbornness in painting buildings smaller than men was not because they did not know about perspective, but because they viewed the men and saints they depicted honorably. . . . [Images] to be used in a stage set."

While traveling, Camus labored over his writing and rewriting, as he despised writers who published their first drafts: "Those who don't want to rewrite just want to shine more quickly. Despicable. Start over again." When he arrived in Algiers, Marguerite showed him photos she had taken of him in Florence, and he asked her to destroy them: "I really look like a barber's assistant in them, and I prefer not to know the truth."

On his return, he asked the Algiers Board of Education for work as a substitute teacher and was granted a job as grammar instructor in Sidi-bel-Abbès, a colonial city sixty kilometers from Oran and twelve hours by train from Algiers. An ugly place, Sidi-bel-Abbès was a French Foreign Legion troop base. Camus arrived on Saturday to meet the school's principal and the next day was on the train back to Algiers, unable to abandon his friends and lovers and stay in the hideous provincial town. He noted with a shudder of horror, "If I would have got through the first few days, I certainly would have stayed on, and that was the danger." Writing to his friend Jacques Heurgon about his "stupid adventure" at Sidi-bel-Abbès, he declared, "It finally seems to me that I've made a wager that forces me to create something meaningful, otherwise my life will be totally absurd."

He wanted to write but did not think about making a career of it, "of gaining advantages from it," as he said to Grenier. "I haven't that many pure things in my life, and writing is one of them. . . . The only thing is to decide which is the most aesthetic form of suicide, marriage and a forty-hour-a-week job, or a revolver."

Chatting with Charles Poncet about the theater, Camus declared that propaganda plays were doomed to failure, since the possibilities of choice and expression were limited. For Camus, freedom was the essential power of the theater. He decided to found an independent theater company, the Théâtre de l'Equipe, taking its name from a film directed by Julien Duvivier, *La Belle Equipe.* Inspired by Jacques Copeau, Camus wanted to train his own team of actors. In October 1937, Camus drew up a manifesto for his new theater group: "The Théâtre de l'Equipe, without political or religious prejudices, hopes to make its spectators into friends." He assembled friends like Robert and Madeleine Jaussaud, Jeanne Sicard and Marguerite Dobrenn, and Charles Poncet. One of Poncet's friends who joined, Célestin Récagno, was a trained actor, but too hostile to politics to have been part of the activist Théâtre du Travail group. Récagno turned out to be a true character, insisting on real chicken and wine to wolf down during a scene in *The Brothers Karamazov,* and amusing Camus by exhaling garlicky breath in his direction at every occasion.

Camus planned to adapt André Malraux's novel *La Condition humaine* for the stage and to perform Aristophanes' *The Acharnians* in Paul Nizan's translation. But material worries were pressing, and Camus could not survive on what he earned from occasional tutoring. With help from friends, he was finally offered a job at the Algiers Geophysics Institute, as a temporary assistant in meteorology, at one thousand francs per month, about half the pay of a beginning teacher in France. Methodically, Camus put on a scientist's white lab coat to work on climatological statistics, classifying twenty years of barometric measurements taken from 350 weather stations. He filled out index cards with information and drew graphs of climate progressions for eleven months, until September 1938.

He now had been working on his novel for nearly two years. Thinking of it, he noted, "The 'real' experience of solitude is the least literary thing imaginable—a thousand miles away from the literary idea of solitude." *La Mort heureuse* was a shaky story, but it would nevertheless serve as a source for his later writings. In it he wrote about his father and mother, his uncle, and his illness, interwoven with a badly told story. A modest employee, Patrice Mersault, visits a rich invalid named Zagreus, with whom he shares a mistress named Marthe. Mersault kills Zagreus and takes his money, travels to Prague, returns to Algeria, gets married, and divorces. The moral of the story is that Mersault wants to live life fully, and does so, as opposed to the whining Zagreus. Camus used friends as models for characters in the novel, including Christiane Galindo, but without mentioning his affair with her. He laughed at the rumor going around town that he was living with three women lovers at the Fichu House.

Camus's best writing at the time went into his *Noces*, essays that he started in 1936 in a tone of lyric joy. He lost another opportunity to live in France when the writer Gabriel Audisio, who worked at the Algiers Tourist Office in Paris, was not able to find him a job there. But as *Noces* made clear, Camus did not miss Paris: "What is lovable about Algiers is what everyone experiences, the sight of the sea from every street-corner, a certain heaviness of sunlight. . . ."

He gathered sweethearts, disagreeing with André Gide's manner of hypocritically "asking us to suppress our desire in order to make it more acute, thus becoming "complicated" or "cerebral" types, as whores would describe such men. Christianity also seeks to annul desire, but that is more natural, since they see that as a mortification of the flesh." Camus preferred the behavior of his friend Vincent the barrel maker: "He drinks when he's thirsty, if he desires a woman he tries to sleep with her, and if he loves her, he marries her."

Camus appreciated the direct local humor, which mixed sex and death: "The favorite joke of Algiers' morticians when their hearses are empty is to pass pretty girls in the street and holler, 'You want a ride, sweetie?' There seems to be a symbol there, even if it's an unfortunate one." Camus also relished local slang, and entertained friends with stories in sing-song dialect with guttural Arabic accents, accompanied by obscene gestures, about his *catz*, the slang word for penis, or *angorade*, which meant a lover's unfaithfulness.

In the summer of 1937, he was feeling serene, taking in a small salary and getting on with his writing, when he met a young woman named Francine Faure. She was an excellent pianist, who specialized in Bach, and a mathematician, who studied at the university for her teaching license. She was aware of her own indecisiveness, and Camus courted her gently. With her dark eyes and high cheekbones that gave her a Tartar look, Francine was ravishingly beautiful. Her smile revealed pretty teeth, and her dancer's legs moved with suppleness and natural elegance. When Camus and his friends swore or told dirty stories, she would take offense. Francine loved being courted, but it was not easy to approach her. In his private life, Camus wanted his own freedom to be respected, and his other girlfriends—Christiane Galindo, Blanche Balain, and Lucette Meurer—accorded him this freedom, but it would not be as easy with Francine Faure.

Camus had convinced Edmond Charlot to publish the poems of Blanche Balain with an extravagantly laudatory preface by himself, predicting a great future for her. Blanche was a law student, to whom Marie Viton had introduced him at the Algiers-Maison-Blanche airport. Camus immediately suggested that she act in *La Célestine*, which his theater troupe was staging. Blanche's father, a military officer, complained to Edmond Charlot about Camus's wooing his daughter and sent the girl to Morocco, where she received letters from Camus written in a protective tone: "my child," "my little girl." He wrote to her, as a way of breaking up with her, about the charms of solitude, and how she should profit from her trip to Morocco.

In December 1937, Lucette Meurer, a pharmacology student, was introduced to Camus in front of the Algiers post office by Manette Chaperon, Francine Faure's cousin. Both young women lived at a girls' hostel on the boulevard Saint-Saëns in Algiers. Lucette also became his lover, and acted the role of the servant in his adaptation of Dostoyevsky's *Brothers Karamazov*. He would speak about poetry with Blanche, while with Lucette the subjects were more often novel-writing and politics. Camus later said he never fully understood how serious Lucette felt about him, as she was secretive, shy, and restrained; but he was not in love with her, feeling only "tenderness, desire, and lots of friendship-comradeship." To Lucette, as well as to Christiane Galindo and other girlfriends, he would talk endlessly about Francine Faure.

On February 10, 1938, he wrote to Francine about his daily activities:

> In ten days we will be performing again, and on the program will be *Return of the Prodigal Son* adapted from André Gide, and Charles Vildrac's *Le Paquebot Tenacity*. Tonight I hang up posters, and on Sundays I'll do scenery and every evening we rehearse and yell at one another. As you see, Art is a flower that can also bloom on the dungheap.
>
> I'll send you a program when they're ready and if you want, I'll have a seat reserved for you. . . . Have you read Montherlant's little book about Algiers? If not, I'll send it to you, you'll love it. . . . For a week now, "The Karamazovs" has been dead, a critical success but a financial disaster. But at least I can return to my own concerns now. I'm happy that you liked "The Karamazovs." I must say that I defended the play against all our friends, and I nearly imposed it on the theater, and today they are all converted. You guessed it, I played the role of Ivan, and I cannot tell you the profound joy I felt in doing it. Grenier told me, "I was sure you'd take that role, because Ivan is intelligence without God or love." That was severe, but true. . . .
>
> I've been writing nonstop—I can tell you, can't I?—a whole novel, which I finished recently [*La Mort heureuse*]. . . . Only it

was all written in exasperation, carried inside me for hours to be written down only in the evenings. Now, despite polite compliments from Grenier and Heurgon, what they say clearly shows it's a failure, too herky-jerky to be artistic.

For some days, that was a serious blow, as I had thought of it as my last chance, but I was wrong and now things are better. . . .

No doubt I'm not making myself understood, but I don't know how to say it any better, and what I'm doing has always been a mystery to me, which is no doubt the reason for its clear limits. All of this must seem very futile to you, but it's so very important to me.

Last year, I was afraid to take myself seriously but now, I'm no longer playing games and I want to be a writer. No doubt I have a lot of work to do. Grenier told me that what handicapped me most were my pretentiousness and pride. I can't tell you how right he was.

Each time I see him—too rarely—what he tells me revolts me for a few days, then I understand it and I realize how much I love that man. To finish about myself, I'll add that I've also written a little book of essays about Florence, Djemila, Tipasa, and Algiers. . . .

Every time that you tell me, "But we can't speak about Bach," I think of the magnificent model he is for all artists, with jubilation and generosity, overabundance in the simplest, most natural language. That's how one should write, but to do it, one must have a pure heart, which is the one thing in the world I'll never have.

Camus apologized for his outpouring of confidences: "I reread this letter and feel a bit ashamed to be talking to you with such freedom about things I usually keep to myself. But this year, I haven't 'communicated' with anyone—except twice with Grenier—and it's a great joy to do it with you, and although I wanted to be honest and clear, I still ended up saying foolish and pretentious things. I might say, as you will, that it's the fault of the letter, but I remember when you were here, I was equally clumsy and pretentious. Too bad."

Camus was thinking again of going abroad: "I'm waiting for an answer about Southeast Asia. I made my request as I do everything of this kind, violently and in a moment of disgust, and I'm still ready to leave. But right now, I only have a one percent chance of obtaining the medical certificate that would finally let me get my teaching degree. . . . If I got it, I'd start work again and stay a year in Algiers to get a degree in science—biology, no doubt—if I don't, what else can I do? I need money badly, and in Southeast Asia I would earn it. I was wrong to tell you that I've got nothing to win or lose. One writes these things because they come naturally to one's pen and feel good to say. I hope you took it as it deserved to be taken. . . ."

Chapter Fourteen

An Older Brother

When Jeanne Sicard left Algiers for Paris, Camus wrote to her on August 19, 1938, saying, "Your life here is no longer a learning experience, and sometimes a place can imprison us. We belong to a clique, which is not a good thing, even though the clique is friendly."

He was planning a new theatrical troupe, although "few actors are still participating. . . . I'll always miss this marvelous atmosphere. . . . I owe it some of my purest joys and a number of solid friendships." Jeanne had faith in *La Mort heureuse*, which he was rewriting, as well as *Noces*. The latter was written in stylized prose that he felt was "clumsy and too stiff."

Camus was planning to obtain a philosophy teacher's license, and he put together the documents for the necessary application, including a doctor's certificate. The educational services refused to accept applicants with tuberculosis, to avoid paying pensions to invalids. Dr. Lévi-Valensi, who had been treating Albert since August 1931, wrote a medical report, noting that the patient had a pneumothorax "for pulmonary tuberculosis . . . which had infiltrated into almost the entire left lung, with infection beginning at the top of the right lung." The patient had gained weight, and Lévi-Valensi had continued lung-collapse therapy until May 1938, but "with no incidents" and no interruption of high school or college studies for the young man. (The doctor was painting a rosy picture to help Camus, for he had in fact taken several months off from studies because of illness and been obliged to repeat one philosophy course.) The doctor concluded that the applicant could be a teacher "without any danger to himself or those around him."

In September, Camus went through another medical examination for the teacher's diploma, and Dr. Emile Pouget also gave him the go-ahead, finding that the applicant had "a good constitution," weighed 143 pounds, and measured five foot ten. He "shows no infirmity, with normal hearing and sight. . . . Nothing to report about the heart. . . . Nothing abnormal in the urine." The doctor agreed with his colleague's diagnosis, that Camus showed "no clinical signs of developing pulmonary tuberculosis . . . and must be considered cured, with no relapse to be feared." Both doctors recommended that he be allowed to take the exam to become a teacher.

But on October 8, the surgeon general of Algeria declared that Camus could not be declared "free of tuberculosis, according to current rules." No appeal of the decision was possible, so Camus would never be named a teacher, and was obliged to look for work elsewhere.

Camus was no longer a political activist, but followed with concern the rise of fascism and anti-Semitism in France, echoed in Algeria. He found fault with his uncle Etienne, who, more out of reflex than conviction, criticized the Jews. Camus maintained his respect for Soviet communism, even though he was suspicious of the French Communist Party, saying that in Russia "at least they shoot generals, instead of slaveys, as we do here."

In October 1938, a new liberal newspaper, *Alger Républicain*, was created to help to fight the new climate. The owner, Jean-Pierre Faure, hired Pascal Pia, who had worked in Paris as an editor of the Communist evening daily, *Ce Soir*, to run it. Although Pia was offered low pay, he would be given complete control of the publication. Faure had to name an editorial secretary, and on Pia's recommendation he contacted Camus before the summer of 1938. Camus reported to Marguerite Dobrenn on July 22, 1938, "I still haven't definitely accepted the editorial job, and I'm undecided about what to think of it. Right now I need calm and tranquility in order to write. If I knew where to go and to make a firm decision, everything would be simplified, but for several years I haven't had a long period of relaxation and abandonment. Everything I do necessarily reflects that." Then just a week later he wrote again to Marguerite: "The editorial job is waiting for me. I'll rewrite articles and contribute culture and arts columns from 5 p.m. to 1 a.m. I can sleep mornings and have part of the afternoons for myself. So much for the future."

He was thinking of another novel and a play, and wrote in his *Carnets* the beginning of a novel that became *L'Etranger*: "Today Maman died, or maybe yesterday, I don't know. I got a telegram from the home, 'Mother deceased, burial tomorrow, sincerely yours.' I can't tell, maybe it was yesterday. . . ."

In September 1938, Camus had a meeting with Pascal Pia, but did not speak with him right away about his adaptation of *Le Temps du mépris* or of his published work *L'Envers et l'endroit*. Camus wrote in his *Carnets*, "The pleasure one finds in relations with men, the subtle giving or asking for a light, a complicity between cigarette Freemasons."

Pascal Pia, whose real name was Pierre Durand, was ten years older than Camus, the age of a big brother. Tall and dark, Pia inspired confidence in others. He had used an infinite number of pen names, from "Marcel Lapompe" to "Louise Lalanne," when he was writing prefaces to illegally reprinted obscene eighteenth-century texts. Both Camus and Pia had lost their fathers in the First World War; and though Pia's mother was an accountant who worked for a railway company, to bring her into line with Camus's cleaning-lady mother Pia would joke that she was really a concierge. Pia had worked at numerous small jobs in Paris and counted among his friends pimps and thugs as well as writers like Antonin Artaud and André Malraux. Pia knew Algeria, having served there in the Third Zouave Regiment. He was a great admirer of Baudelaire, who had written that "absurdity is a deliverance for tired people."

Camus was exhausted when he met Pia, plagued by boils. Their personalities were different, Pia being a total pessimist while Camus believed that man could and should try to be happy. Skeptical but not cynical, Pia was the opposite of a careerist.

The first issue of *Alger Républicain* came out on October 6, 1938, eight pages priced at forty centimes, which was too much for Arab workers to be able to read it regularly. In the first issue was an article on illiteracy by Camus's reporter friend Lucienne Jean-Darrouy; and Camus soon got two more women friends, Lucette Meurer and Yvonne Ducailar, onto the paper's staff as writers for the women's pages.

Since readers were curious about the new editor in chief, Pia published a brief autobiographical article on October 14, 1938, half-invented as a practical joke, with credits such as having served in the Merchant Marine and having written a thesis on the seventeenth-century writer Tallemant des Réaux.

Pia and Camus both distinguished between the rich colonists and the poor white workers in Algeria, and both hated politicians as a class of professional liars, feeling that a journalist's job was to expose lies. Pia did not share Camus's admiration for André Gide and had never belonged to the Communist Party. But he saw Camus as intelligent, sensitive, and cultivated, without any illusions about the left wing, a man who did not accept the established order, especially in Algeria, and who had more life experience than most men of his age.

A week before the newspaper was launched, Hitler, Mussolini, Britain's Neville Chamberlain, and France's Edouard Daladier signed the Munich Pact, which was meant to avoid war for the future. The politics of *Alger Républicain* were that of the failed French political movement the Popular Front, led by the socialist León Blum. The paper declared that its enemies were "the traveling salesmen of fascism, and industrial, agrarian, and banking feudalism." They fought German anti-Semitism as well as "the social conservatism that tries to keep our native friends on an inferior level." To this end, the *Alger Républicain* printed news that other papers ignored, such as the fact that six thousand foreign Jews living in France had offered to join the French army. The paper insisted on "immediate social equality for all Frenchmen, whatever their origins, religion, and philosophy," and "the progress of Algerian natives towards political equality."

Despite Pia's serious approach to journalism, there were front-page photos of music-hall celebrities like Mistinguett and American film stars like Joan Crawford and Cesar Romero. Sports coverage expanded from one page to two.

Pia noticed that Camus, although a beginner in journalism, wrote better than the other staffers, as he haunted police stations, taking crime reporting seriously. At the end of his 1938 *Carnets*, Camus reported a typical scene:

> The lovely world where two old journalists are screaming at one another in the middle of the police station, surrounded by laughing cops. Their senile fury cannot be expressed in blows, so takes the form of astonishing rudeness: "You shit!" "You big cunt!" "Filthy cunt!" "Guzzler!" "Pimp!"
> "I'm clean."
> "There's a difference between the two of us."
> "Yeah, a big one. You're the cunt of all cunts."
> "Keep it up and I'll break your face and kick your ass in."
> "I've got more muscles than you on the end of my dick, and I'm clean, I am."

Camus did not propose to devote himself entirely to journalism, and wanted to save his energy for a novel, a play, and essays. His next book would be published by Edmond Charlot, who had already produced *Révolte dans les Asturies* and *L'Envers et l'endroit*. He was not starstruck by his newspaper job, writing to Jean Grenier at the end of 1938, "I'm doing journalism, articles about dogs run over in the street, reporting, and a few literary pieces. You know better than I how disappointing this business is, but at least I have an impression of freedom here, no constraints, and everything I do seems lively. There are also lowly satisfactions, but there's nothing to do about that."

If he had been able to take the philosophy teachers' exam, he would not have become a journalist: "That's why I accepted the job of writer at the *Alger Républicain*." The paper's basic problem, apart from finances, was separating news from opinion. The only professional journalist on the staff, Lucienne Jean-Darrouy, had previously worked for *L'Echo d'Alger*, a fact that she lorded over her colleagues, irritating Camus. Other contributors included Robert Namia, who had been wounded in the anti-Franco International Brigade in Spain, and François Mary, a defrocked priest who was a better bon vivant than writer. Contributors joined at random, such as a seventeen-year-old student, José Bacri, who proposed to Pia an article on a philosophy lecture he had attended. Pia thought it well written, but when it appeared in print, Bacri's piece had been rewritten and was signed "Albert Camus." When Bacri went to the newspaper office to complain, Camus apologized but then proceeded to give Bacri a journalism lesson; and the young man later contributed articles for the children's page.

Pia relied on Camus to replace him on occasion to read proof, and when the soccer results came in on Sunday nights, Camus was delighted when his team, the RUA, won. There were only two Moslem workers on the paper, and one of them was a police informer, according to Pia. Only rarely did Moslem writers contribute editorials, and then in line with Algeria remaining part of the French family of nations. The paper started out with a circulation of thirty thousand, which quickly dropped to less than twenty thousand. In the office, the laborers knew that Camus had left the Communist Party, but felt that he was still a leftist, which was the important thing.

To attract readers, the paper decided to serialize fiction, but had no money to pay novelists, so Pia ran works in the public domain, such as Stendhal's *Les Cenci* and works by Honoré de Balzac. Since not every newspaper buyer was attracted by Stendhal, they also printed in serial form the translated screenplay of the Hollywood film *The Adventures of Robin Hood* starring Errol Flynn. Fiercely critical of the French president, Edouard Daladier, the newspaper changed its focus with the worsening world situation, using its firepower against the Nazi and fascist threat.

Camus had still not finished *Noces* and was planning to "return to work on Plotinus" for his philosophical essay. He spoke a lot about the absurd with friends, and studied books by the scholar George Gurvitch, *Current Trends in German Philosophy* and *Essays in Sociology*. But journalism got in the way of his theatrical activity. In the previous season, 1937–38, Camus had worked on four plays, but during the 1938–39 season he staged only John Millington Synge's *Playboy of the Western World*, on March 31 and April 2, which was reviewed in the newspaper by Camus's friend Charles Poncet, writing under a pen name. The Théâtre de l'Equipe praised itself as "a theater without stars, where the actors don't go to high society parties, but are machine operators, painters, electricians, poster hangers, and costume makers, too." Camus was still interested in Aristophanes' *The Acharnians*, and in August 1938 he proposed to make a tour to Oran with the Théâtre de l'Equipe, and thought about asking for subsidies from that city's far-right-wing mayor, the Abbé Lambert. It proved impossible to do both theater and newspaper work, so Camus canceled his theater projects and instead sought purity in journalism.

Chapter Fifteen **Battles**

*I*n the summer of 1939, Camus felt confused, as he wrote to Francine
Faure, "I don't know if I'm going to take my vacation, and if I did, I'd
want a month doing my own work in a place I liked. But I can't think
about that today—I received the typed copy of *Caligula* [his new play] and
on rereading it, I see I'll have to rewrite it all. Everything seems difficult to
me, and I have to make an adaptation of *La Condition humaine* and get on
with my novel. All that requires more energy than I've got, and how can anyone work when there's an ignoble threat of war?"

He wrote to Francine again a few days later: "Unless there's a miracle,
everything will collapse. I'm thinking of one of T. E. Lawrence's last statements: 'The world is waiting for a great movement of generosity or a great
wave of death.' The wave is here, and for it to recede, each of us must do everything we can in his little circle to start the movement."

Although he was happily in love with Francine, Camus felt out of sorts
with himself. After a brief vacation during which he worked on his own projects, from October 6, 1938 to October 28, 1939 he had learned the journalist's trade, helping to produce nearly four hundred issues of the *Alger
Républicain*.

He was tempted by journalism because of the pressure of a daily deadline, the quickened pace of European history, and his penchant for being a
moralist. The newspaper's politics were sympathetic to the working classes
and Moslems and opposed Franco in Spain, Nazism, and fascism. Ever
since *Révolte dans les Asturies* had been banned, the paper had certain accounts to settle with Algerian right-wing politicians.

On October 12, 1938, Camus's first news article appeared in *Alger
Républicain*, about workers' buying power after the Popular Front and the
French leader Paul Reynaud's laws on overtime pay. Camus admitted that

the Popular Front had slightly improved the unskilled Arab laborers' condition, "but for a man who earned eleven francs per day, this small improvement is still only a last resort. . . . As for the European worker, inequalities in salary and the cost of living have cancelled advances which were so difficult to win." As a newcomer to economic subjects, Camus wrote about them with a heavy hand, such as a December 3, 1938 "Dialogue Between a President of the Council and a Worker Who Earns 1,200 Francs Per Month," which reads like a high-school homework assignment.

But two days earlier, on December 1, he wrote an impressive report about conditions in the hold of a prison ship, where captives were in detention before being deported to Cayenne: "In case of a prison riot, the ceiling of each cage has . . . a spigot ready to vomit hot steam on the prisoners. . . . I see three Arabs who are looking at Algiers, pushing each other around for a glimpse through the porthole." Camus, as a reporter of European origin, confessed, "I don't feel proud to be here. . . . On the way out, one of the men asked me in Arabic for a cigarette and I knew that the rules forbade it. What a derisory response to someone who was only asking for a sign of complicity and a human gesture . . . but I didn't reply." Camus said that outside the ship, he "would have preferred not to see elegant ladies on the embarcation dock, who had come out of curiosity. . . . It isn't a question of pity, but something else. There is no spectacle more abject than seeing man brought to below a human condition."

Camus also reported on trials, and in his novel-in-progress he revealed a sardonic knowledge of both the judicial system and the press: in his *L'Etranger*, a reporter tells Meursault, who is on trial, "You know, we've blown up your case a little, since summertime is the slow season for newspapers and only your story and a guy who killed his father were worth anything." Camus even introduced himself as a reporter into Meursault's trial, in an Alfred Hitchcock–style appearance in his own work, as one of the journalists: "much younger than the others, dressed in grey flannel with a blue tie, he put his pencil down and looked at me. In his slightly asymmetrical face, I only saw his light-colored eyes which examined me attentively, without expressing anything you could put your finger on, and I had the weird impression of being looked at by myself."

He published over 150 articles, about crime, senatorial elections, the city budget, and welfare aid to North African emigrants in France among other subjects. Camus won himself a name as a courtroom reporter, more of a militant than an objective witness: in six months he took sides in three major trials. In the first, he defended Michel Hodent, who worked under the supervision of the Wheat Office, responsible for buying wheat harvests to prevent speculation. In doing so, Hodent had offended rich European and Arab merchants, and he was arrested along with his warehouseman and charged with embezzlement. Hodent wrote appreciatively to Camus, who followed the trial and kept it in the public eye in *Alger Républicain*, listing the court's errors and demanding that the accused man be acquitted. Camus even published an open letter to Algeria's governor general in which he deftly tried to appeal to the governor's humanity rather than challenging him: "We observe you at parades, through edicts and official speeches, but where is the man behind all that? . . . In a world where poverty and absurdity make so many people lose their humanity, to save a single man means to save oneself, as well as a bit of humanity's future which we all hope for."

The Hodent trial took place in Tiaret, a town of sixteen thousand inhabitants to the southeast of Oran, and Camus lived there while writing his articles. He described in his *Carnets* what he did after court had recessed for the day and his article for that day was written:

> At Tiaret, a group of male schoolteachers told me that they were "bored as shit."
> "And what do you do when you're bored as shit?"
> "We get bombed."
> "And then?"
> "We go to the whorehouse."
> I accompanied them to the whorehouse, through the snow, which fell in fine but solid flakes. They were all drunk. A doorman made me pay two francs to get into a huge rectangular room strangely painted with diagonal black and yellow lines, where people danced to music from a record player. The whores were neither pretty nor ugly.
> One of them said, "You wanna ball?"
> The man refused unconvincingly.
> The whore said, "I'd really like you to put that thing inside me."

Camus developed an ironic style for covering the Hodent trial in the newspaper: "You will no doubt have noticed that the reasonings of the court do not get to the heart of the case, which may be because this case does not have a heart." The day before the verdict, he informed his readers, "Tomorrow the judges at Tiaret do not have to decide about an affair, but to choose between two causes, and will find on the one hand a man [Hodent] without medals or titles, money or ambition, and on the other, an elite in name only." Hodent was finally acquitted, partly because of Camus's articles.

He covered another difficult case when Sheik El Okbi, a modernist reformer, was accused of having taken out a contract to murder the Grand Mufti of Algiers, the city's main Moslem religious leader. The police arrested some prostitutes and underworld thugs, who confessed but then took back their confessions. El Okbi and another accused man, Abbas Turqui, were set free provisionally in February 1938. The Mufti's family appealed the court's decision, and the sheik and his fellow defendant went back to trial. The complex affair, botched by policemen and a series of judges, involved bribed, tampered, and perjured witnesses, vanishing police informers, kidnappings, and evidence such as blood samples and pieces of a typewriter that were mysteriously lost.

Nearly three years after the murder, the two men and three other "natives" were back in the accused box. The colonials saw El Okbi as a dangerous advocate of reform, who had been described by the late Grand Mufti as a "progressive agitator." El Okbi and Abbas Turqui again were acquitted, although their co-defendants were sentenced to long prison terms. Writing under the pen name Antar, Camus praised the "greatness" of the fight to save El Okbi, who was opposed to racism and Hitler, comparing the defendant to Socrates and Galileo.

A number of defense witnesses served on the governing board of the *Alger Républicain*, and Camus assumed that since the murdered Grand Mufti was a reactionary ally of the French administration and defender of the status quo, and Sheik El Okbi was a liberal, he had to be defended by anticolonialists. In fact, it seems that El Okbi was indeed guilty as charged of inciting others to murder the Grand Mufti, and Camus let himself be exploited because of his contempt for the colonial administration.

To Camus, who could not forget that *Révolte dans les Asturies* had been banned, the mayor of Algiers, Augustin Rozis, represented the worst side of colonialism. Rozis admired the French nationalist writer Charles Maurras and Fascists like Franco, and hated labor unions and the Blum-Viollette project to improve the lot of Algerian Arabs. Along with the mayors of Oran and Sidi-bel-Abbès, Rozis was one of the first Algerians invited by Franco for an official visit to Fascist Spain. Rozis sent a special telegram to French President Edouard Daladier to refuse to admit Spanish Republican refugees into his city.

Month after month, Camus and Pia steadfastly attacked Rozis. If crime increased, the paper wrote, "True, Mr. Rozis is the mayor, but that's no reason for gangsters to run the streets." If budget questions were raised, the *Alger Républicain* noted, "Mr. Rozis costs the city more than 60,000 francs per year, and think how many Spanish children could be helped for that sum." When Hitler's Germany was in the headlines, the paper jibed, "Do you know 'Herr von Rozis'? That's what the German radio calls the mayor of Algiers to congratulate him." When Rozis was in a battle with city employees, Camus wrote, "I would be understating my beliefs if I said he was grotesque, unlawful, and odious." When a city gas main exploded, Camus urged Rozis "not to use an odious tone when impoverished accident victims, many of them artisans, humble seamstresses, and ticket takers, ask you to take an interest in their problems."

Pia and Camus had different working hours. Pia stayed at the office until the newspaper was put to bed at 2 a.m., making corrections until the final moment. At first Camus worked from the beginning of the afternoon until midnight, but then he began to arrive earlier at the office. In March 1939, only eight months after Camus obtained his press card, he began a series of eleven articles which ran over four months, "Poverty in Kabylia."

Camus had the advantage of not being an official investigator, hemmed in by civil-servant guides. He took the bus and walked through mountain villages, staying at cheap hotels. He wrote to a friend, Irène Dayan, "I am not finding the peace I had expected on this voyage. I'm arriving at an age when one should not reasonably speak of peace." One drawback in his assignment was that Camus did not speak Arabic or the Berber language, needing interpreters along the way, and perhaps as a result seems never to have noticed that the Kabyles were a specific people. His first article, "Greece in Rags," began like a passage from *Noces*: "One thinks of Greece when one climbs slopes in Kabylia, seeing the little villages grouped around natural landmarks and men draped in white wool, roads bordered with olive, fig, and cactus trees, the simplicity of life and landscape and the harmony between man and the soil." Camus had never seen Greece.

But soon his article turned from travelogue to social protest: "In no other country I know is the human body more humiliated than Kabylia. . . . The country's poverty is horrible." Most Kabyle men went to France to earn a living, and those who stayed home lived on official charity. Camus stated that he had "a bad conscience" as a European when he saw the beggars, schoolchildren fainting from hunger, towns without doctors, and villages with no sewers. He noted what some Kabyles told him through an interpreter: " 'Long live the war, because then at least they'll give us something to eat.' It's as if they thought one absurdity could cure another." He noted dryly, "To explain the low pay and disparity with European workers who get paid twice as much, colonists say that natives profit from nature, because they eat five to six kilograms of grapes every day!"

Camus observed "colonists' general scorn for poor people in this area," but he did not blame Kabylia's poverty entirely on colonization. History too was at fault: "In truth, every day we brush by a people who are living three hundred years behind the times. . . . It is despicable to say that these people do not have the same needs that we have. . . . If colonial conquest can be justified, it will be insofar as it helps conquered people keep their personalities, and we owe it to this land to let a proud and humane population stay faithful to themselves and their destiny."

Camus was outraged by the workload imposed on Kabyles, which he called "slavery," blaming Kabyle landowners as well as colonists for obliging employees to labor for twelve hours per day for ten francs' pay. He wrote, "I don't think that charity is a useless emotion, but I think that sometimes its results are useless, and a constructive social policy is better."

Camus's series ended on June 15, 1939, having attracted much criticism from Algiers rightists, and he commented, "It seems that to point out poverty in a French territory makes one a bad Frenchman today."

Despite his progressive hopes, Camus had seen the Popular Front government civil servants refuse to implement the modest suggestions in the Blum-Viollette project. After his articles appeared, Algerian Governor General Le Beau went to Kabylia, perhaps in part impelled by the reporter's descriptions. Some ethnologists who read Camus's articles found they idealized the poor too much, and spoke from too haughty a position, yet no journalist in memory had written such a powerful series of articles.

World events would soon push Algerian problems to a lower level of world importance. On August 22, 1939, Charles Poncet invited a group of friends over to his home to eat couscous, including Robert and Madeleine Jaussaud and Jeanne Sicard, and all were astonished when the always punctual Camus arrived late. The journalist explained, "Sorry, but we had to redo the entire front page of the paper. My friends, that's it, war is almost certain. Stalin and Hitler have reached an agreement, and tomorrow Ribbentrop will be in Moscow to sign a friendship pact with the Soviet Union."

In his article about these events, using the pen name "Vincent Capable," Camus wrote, "Should we discuss things with Hitler? . . . I am mostly for discussions, on the condition that they never stop." Camus feared repression in France: "The exterior danger and interior danger seem to me to be equal." Over the following days, *Alger Républicain* refused to believe in the Hitler-Stalin nonaggression pact, calling it "much ado about nothing. . . . This treaty only confirms two accords which are several years old." Only when the Soviets attacked Poland did the editorial staff of *Alger Républicain* realize what the real situation was.

Camus also wrote an ardent defense of the Spanish Republicans and the International Brigade that fought on their behalf. When journalist Joseph Prudhomme in a rival newspaper, *La Dépêche Algérienne*, called the International Brigade mercenaries paid by French taxpayers, Camus replied with a disdainful article in *Alger Républicain*: "As usual, Joseph Prudhomme shows the morality of his pretentious and lying style. . . . It is terribly tiring to despise people."

Despising people came easily to Camus, justifiably or not.

Chapter Sixteen   **The Reading Room**

*I*n the fourth issue of *Alger Républicain*, a new feature appeared, "The Reading Room": "Like most of this newspaper's departments, this column has no ambition to be regular or systematic." Although Paris publishers were not eager to send review copies to a new Algerian paper they had never heard of, Camus wrote fifty articles over the following months about news, books, and the arts. He also wrote about the Théâtre du Travail's work and advised his friend Edmond Charlot about his publishing list. Camus slept little, smoked lots of Bastos cigarettes, ate meals only when he could, and took occasional weekend beach trips with his friends Robert and Madeleine Jaussaud.

In his reviews, Camus preferred to write about books he liked, revealing some ideas about novel writing in general. In a review of the German novelist Erich Maria Remarque's *Three Comrades*, he commented, "An important experience can often inspire a strong literary work, but will not for all that make someone into a writer." Writing about a book by René Janon, Camus observed, "Malraux says somewhere that reporting seems to him another form of novel writing." Sometimes Camus used a review for political propaganda, such as a collection of articles by the Stalinist heroine of the Spanish Republican forces, Dolores "La Pasionaria" Ibarruri: "This may not be a great book, but it's a cry that once heard is unforgettable." In macho fashion, Camus praised La Pasionaria's "manly shouts," which he likened to the style of the French novelist Henry de Montherlant. He panned Marie Mauron's *Le Quartier Mortisso* because he had "counted thirty alexandrines in the first three chapters in the novel, which is a serious fault. . . . One cannot be exalted all day long, because it gets tiring and inhuman." He also used the books column to make personal observations about women, such as, "It is certain that one does not always desire the woman one loves." He also expressed a rare opinion about the Moslem religion, while reviewing a book by Abd Errahman Ben El Haffaf, writing that Mohammed's teachings contained a generosity of mind that encouraged respect for mankind.

Camus was sometimes self-serving as a reviewer: he praised a book he partly translated and published himself, a selection of Andalusian popular ballads, which appeared from the ephemeral publisher Cafre Editions, "Ca" and "fre" being Camus and Fréminville, lauding the book and himself as "the anonymous translator whose artistic taste equals his modesty." When Camus's *Noces* was published by Edmond Charlot, the "Reading Room" column was entirely devoted to an ad for the new book. *Noces* sold very few copies, although the author did receive a letter of praise from Henry de Montherlant, who advised him to come to Paris.

In another review, Camus described the novelist Jean Giono: "He belongs to the line of moralist prose-writers who make up part of the French literary tradition." But he later criticized Giono in a brief observation signed with the pen name "Conscientious Objector": "Jean Giono, decorated with the Legion of Honor, answered his former friends' indignation by saying that the award was a private matter. So is a man's conscience." Reviewing the novel *Bread and Wine* by Italian ex-Communist Ignazio Silone, Camus observed, "Our epoch teaches us . . . that revolutionary art cannot do without artistic greatness, or else it falls into the lowest forms of thought. . . . There is no middle ground between low propaganda and exalting creativity, between what Malraux called 'the will to prove' and a work like *La Condition humaine.*"

In October 1938, he reviewed Jean-Paul Sartre's *La Nausée*, remarking, "A novel is only philosophy put into images, and in a good novel, all the philosophy goes into the images." Although he was dazzled by Sartre's novel, its philosophy irritated him, and he felt that its plot was unbelievable, with so much moralizing. He found in the hero of *La Nausée*, Roquentin, a "fundamental absurdity. . . . The error of a certain literature is to believe that life is tragic because it is miserable. . . . To observe that life is absurd is not an end, but a beginning." He acknowledged that Sartre had "moving gifts . . . at the same time generously shared with us and wasted. Taken separately, each chapter in this extravagant meditation attains a sort of perfection in its bitterness and truth," but he did not find the book as a whole to be "a work of art." Still, he praised Sartre's "limitless gifts . . . a mind from which anything can be expected . . . a singular and vigorous mind whose next works and lessons we await impatiently." He compared Sartre with Kafka, thinking that the observation was original, whereas an earlier reviewer in Paris, Sartre's friend Paul Nizan, had already called the author of *La Nausée* a "French Kafka."

Camus had mulled over this review for some time. Four months earlier, at the end of July 1938, he wrote to his friend Lucette Meurer, "I read Jean-Paul Sartre's *La Nausée* a few weeks ago, and I have a lot to say about this book. It's too close to a certain part of me for me not to like it, but that's exactly the part I want to react against. When one writes a novel, one puts a philosophy into images and the entire challenge is to put that philosophy entirely in the images. But in *La Nausée*, the philosophy and images are separate from one another, and juxtaposed. That bothers me because I agree with the philosophy, and it pains me to see it lose its power as one reads. I'm expressing myself badly, but by a curious coincidence, I've thought a lot about this book. . . . Since your friend the Tahitian woman knows Sartre, I'd be pleased to have some details about him as a man. . . ." (Camus called their friend Yvonne Ducailar "the Tahitian woman" because she had been photographed wearing an exotic pareo.)

Camus's most serious literary enthusiasms remained André Malraux and André Gide. He called Gide "one of the century's most endearing minds." As for Malraux, "It is fashionable . . . to denounce the romantic attitudes of a writer like Malraux. The question is not to know if Malraux prefers the epic aspects of revolution to economic constructions—although his novel *L'Espoir* answers that accusation—but to know that he risks his life every day to justify his way of seeing."

Reviewing *La Conspiration*, another novel by a member of the French Communist Party, Paul Nizan, Camus declared that "Nizan poses the great problem for intellectuals of our time, that of joining [the Communist Party]. . . . When all is said and done, it's as futile a problem as that of immortality, a matter which a man must settle for himself and which he must not be judged on. . . . One joins in the same way that one gets married." Camus felt that the artist must come before the militant: "Malraux, who joined, is a great writer, although one wishes one could say the same thing about Louis Aragon. On the other hand, Mr. Henry Bordeaux has never thought of joining, and that doesn't improve his talent, which is mediocre. Henry de Montherlant, who refuses to be regimented in any way, remains one of the most astonishing prose writers of the century. Paul Nizan, who is a provocative partisan, is a thoroughbred writer and proved it in his essay 'Chiens de garde' and book *La Conspiration.*"

In March 1939, the "Reading Room" column spoke about Sartre's collection of novellas *Le Mur*, which Camus liked more than *La Nausée*, and emphasized the "prodigious interest of M. Sartre's tales and at the same time their profound mastery." However, he did have doubts about Sartre's characters being "free, but their freedom was of no use to them, at least that's what M. Sartre shows us. This is surely the source of these pages' emotion, so often upsetting and pathetically cruel. In this universe, man is freed from the ties of prejudice and his own nature, and forced to look at himself, and be made aware of his deep indifference to anything which is not himself." Camus concluded about Sartre's man: "His condition is absurd. . . . [He] is alone, and imprisoned in that freedom. This freedom is limited by time, and death is a quick and vertiginous denial of it."

Camus stated that every great novel had its own philosophy: "A great writer always brings his own world and preaching with him, and M. Sartre's argues for Nothingness, but also for lucidity." He did not approve of Sartre's sometimes rude language: "Obscenity in literature may attain grandeur, and contains in itself elements of grandeur, if we think of Shakespeare's obscenity, but it must be justified by the work itself. In *Le Mur*, I would say that this is the case in the story 'Erostrate' . . . but not in 'Intimité,' where the sexual descriptions often seem gratuitous." Camus saluted the powerful literary originality of both *Le Mur* and *La Nausée*, but criticized their metaphysical and moral baseness.

In another review, Camus studied his Algerian roots while praising Edmond Brua's *Fables bônoises*, as a "masterpiece of absurdity and humor . . . (showing) the morality of our soulless people, who overflow with life. . . . The Algerians have a language, although not yet a literature." For Camus, the only writer to try to describe the psychology of Algerians was Henry de Montherlant in his book *Images d'Alger*.

Chapter Seventeen

Persistent Hopes for Peace

*I*nternational politics and the Second World War wrenched Camus away from his literary concerns. Exempted from the draft in 1931 32, he chose to return to the draft board on September 9, 1939, but "remained exempted," according to his military records. On November 11 he tried one last time to get into the army, but failed.

He explained to Grenier in the spring of 1940, "I became involved . . . but because I didn't want my illness to shield me in this business, and also because I felt solidarity with the poor fellows who were drafted without knowing why. The draft commission that examined me found me unfit for service and continued my exemption, and since then another commission called me up with other exempted men of my category, and exempted me again."

On September 3, 1939, Britain and France had declared war on Germany, and Nazi armored cars rolled into Warsaw. In his *Carnets*, Camus noted the reactions of local Algerians: "Some people are getting urgent operations by reputable Algiers surgeons, because they're afraid that otherwise they might be drafted. . . . On the railway platform, the mother of a reserve soldier, who is at least thirty, tells her son, 'Be careful, now.' War has been declared, but where's the war? Apart from the news which one must believe, and the posters one must read, where can a sign of the absurd events be found? Not in the blue sky over the blue sea, or in the cries of seagulls in the cypress trees which line the hillsides. Nor is it in the youthful glare of light in the Algiers streets."

Camus had many memories, especially about the death of his father: "No doubt later, the mud, blood, and immense discouragement will come." The *Alger Républicain* announced that it would produce a new paper, *Le Soir Républicain*, to be edited by Albert Camus. On September 15, 1939, the first issue came out, priced at forty centimes.

The *Alger Républicain* was an eight-page paper, while the new publication was printed on both sides of a single sheet, with mostly unsigned articles. It was an afternoon journal, hitting the streets at four p.m., and declared itself to be against propagandist and chauvinistic brainwashing. Camus had little staff and learned about the news from press services.

Le Soir Républicain reported in its first issue that the USSR might join Germany in crushing Poland, which happened, but also wrote that Hitler would abdicate as Führer to dedicate himself to literature and the fine arts, and be replaced by Hermann Goering, which did not happen. *Le Soir Républicain* presented itself as the best-informed newspaper, but in fact it had some problems with its sources. Camus tried to make up for this by sprinkling boxed quotations throughout the paper by philosophers like Spinoza and Voltaire and writers like Guy de Maupassant and André Maurois. Some of the quotes were anonymous, invented by Camus himself about the ongoing war: "The marvelous thing about this hellish enterprise is that each government leader has his flag blessed and solemnly mentions God before going out to exterminate his fellow man."

On October 6, 1939, the day when Germany and the USSR divided Poland, Camus wrote to Francine Faure, "After considerable reflection, I'm going to attack my novel. . . . I see the form and content around me in the poverty here, the simple people, and their resigned indifference. They give an image of a rather frightening world without tenderness. This time I feel that I'm going to work without any feeling of [unreadable word] inside me, and this readiness is marvelous. But it makes me sad and worried, as if I were struggling beneath a too-heavy load. If only I could complete it successfully, I would like to be done with the three projects I am planning right now, I'd like peace to come, and to leave for Italy with you, to laugh and live innocently."

The following day, he wrote again to Francine, "Yesterday, I really began my work. As I told you—and myself as well—I would start my novel, in fact I began my essay on the Absurd. It is far more ready inside me than the novel, and I was able to finish the first chapter—the first draft at least—about Don Juan. For some time I've been writing more freely and what I produce is clearer, and without flourishes. I am trying less for effect, and yesterday I was pleased by my chapter, although I have not yet reread it and don't know what it's worth. I hope to continue without stopping."

Albert and Francine were busy breaking up and getting back together again, although he kept his confidence in the young woman, to whom he reported, "The *Alger Républicain* is dead, and tomorrow's issue will be its last, with only *Le Soir Républicain* continuing. Three-quarters of the staff has been fired, almost forty people will be unemployed, and at *Soir* the only ones remaining are Pia, a writer, and myself. Who knows how long that will last. . . . Pia plans to leave in a month or two and let me run the newspaper. I'll be better paid and busier. I forgot to tell you that the business broke down because the Fournier [publicity] agency suddenly withdrew its offer, probably after external pressure. Things will get nastier when we publish a new column of 'Explanations of the War' in the paper. A captain in the censorship office told one of the writers about me that I'd better watch out, adding, 'What a shame that a boy with such talent should be a bad Frenchman—sic and double sic! This morning, as I was again asked to stop running the 'Explanations of the War,' I replied that to fight Hitler, we had to fight Frenchmen who wanted to introduce Hitler's methods in France. That's where things stand now."

Camus had a sudden urge to destroy part of his past, as he confessed to Francine the following day: "I just spent my afternoon emptying two trunks full of five years of correspondence, and burned all these letters in a sort of rage. I didn't save any, not those which were dearest to me, nor those which flattered or moved me. Letters from Grenier, Heurgon, Claude, Jeanne and Marguerite and Christiane, all these and the rest were burned. I have five years less weighing on my heart. I reread a few of them at random, from when I was a young man, and then a man, and I found that I haven't kept the same face for any two people. I have never made anyone happy who loved me, that's for sure, which is so little that I can't even regret anything. To really do it right, I'd need to burn your letters as well, since what good are these pieces of evidence? I was about to do it, and I don't know what prevented me. I still have lots of things to burn, old papers, ridiculous essays, some letters from writers like Max Jacob, Gabriel Audisio, André Malraux, Henry de Montherlant. That will be the second wheelbarrow, but today the fire gave me a temperature and I wanted to stop for a minute and think."

Camus felt the war was absurd because it could have been avoided. The day after Warsaw was invaded by the Nazis, Camus wrote in the newspaper, "Never have left-wing militants had so many reasons to despair. . . . Many of us have not really understood the man of 1914. . . . We know that at a certain limit of despair, indifference takes over and with it the sense and desire for inevitability." In his article, Camus sought "fragile and precious images from a past time when life had a meaning, the joy of bodies playing in sunlight and water, late springtimes bursting with flowers. . . . It is perhaps the outer limit of revolt to lose one's faith in humanity. Perhaps after this war, trees will flower again, since the world always finally wins out over history, but on that day, I don't know how many men will be there to see it."

On the left, before the war, the USSR had been considered humanity's hope; but now that the Soviets were on the Nazis' side, Camus wrote in *Le Soir Républicain* on December 13, 1939, "at present, everything leads us to believe that the Soviet Union is now an imperialist power." Camus predicted "more carnage" if peace was not made, which angered his friend Robert Jaussaud, who wanted to know how Hitler could be stopped if peace was the only priority. The two friends quarreled; Jaussaud was upset, too, because he felt that Albert had behaved badly with Christiane Galindo.

Albert's brother, Lucien, was mobilized in Constantine, Algeria, but Albert was not even asked to join the auxiliary forces. With Lucien absent, he visited his mother at the rue de Lyon apartment two or three times a week, and he noted her sparse conversation in his *Carnets*: "Mom said, 'The weather's starting to change. . . . Will the street lighting be reduced during the whole war? . . . It will be sad in wintertime.' "

Camus did not quarrel with his former Communist comrades, and *Le Soir Républicain* was the only Algiers daily to protest when Communist leaders were rounded up and imprisoned, whether or not they approved of the German-Soviet nonaggression pact. He wrote in his *Carnets*, "Everyone has betrayed us, those who pushed others to resistance and those who spoke of peace."

Camus was opposed to "revolutionary imperialism" and to Nazi or Fascist imperialism. Few other leftists dared to write as Camus did in 1939 that "today the USSR can be classed among the countries that prey on others." He saw both communism and Nazism as religions with their own mystiques, but he did not reject the German people as a whole.

Le Soir Républicain's editor in chief wrote almost the whole paper, and signed his work with pen names like "Vincent Capable," "Demos," "Irène," "Liber," "Nero," "Petronius," "Zaks," and "Cesare Borgia." Under the pen name "Marco," Camus wrote that the French and English people didn't want to see Germany crushed, divided, and in servitude, which was not strictly true about public opinion in the two countries. The positions the paper took shocked its readers, and its owner Jean-Pierre Faure, too. On November 6, 1939, two months after war was declared, Camus and Pia wrote an article together in which they examined the war's causes and legitimized Germany's annexing of the Sudetenland, where millions of Germans lived, from Czechoslovakia:

We still think:

1) That Hitler's claims included a rather curious mixture of legitimate claims [the Sudetenland] and unjustified pretensions.

2) That over the past few years, the international policy has been to grant his unjustified claims and refuse the legitimate ones, only to give in to what one had refused before, after being threatened.

3) In any case, one can't live forever on a treaty or de facto situation, and notions of winners and losers are subject to tragic changes.

Pia and Camus denounced the Treaty of Versailles, which ended the First World War, and Hitler's demands for more territory. As a political analyst, Camus did not believe in historical determinism, and was above all a moralist and man of goodwill: "We believe there is only one inevitability in history, the one we create. We believe that the war could have been avoided, and can still be ended to everyone's satisfaction." But by October 1939, it was impossible to find a compromise that would have satisfied Hitler's imperial ambitions. Camus quarreled with some friends who agreed with his opinions on literature but not on politics, like Blanche Balain, to whom he wrote on November 11, 1939: "You ask me about my position, but you don't need to, because you already know what you want and have already accepted the death of millions of people, consciously or not, in the name of an ideal or inevitability that you're still trying to define. It's painful, no doubt, but you think it is a matter of fate that there is war, and you accept its inevitability. . . . But war is not inevitable, it could have been avoided, and it still can at any time." He went on to tell her that he had tried to enlist, "wanting to risk my life, although not agreeing with the stakes being offered me." He was "disgusted by the hate which submerges us today" and felt that the "only values worth defending" were "love and the mind."

Camus admired England, where a pacifist candidate could run for office in the present warlike climate. He and Pia wrote a manifesto that remained unpublished, in which they explained that their newspaper could not "support the professionals of nationalism, whose lyricism is drawn from others' bloodshed, because we are deeply pacifist." "Pacifist" was a dangerous word, once war had been declared, and the French government was hunting down and imprisoning revolutionary pacifists from the Socialist workers' and farmers' party led by the activist Marceau Pivert.

The iconoclastic *Soir Républicain* had troubles with censorship, which was more severe in Algeria than in France. Camus and his newspaper accepted censorship about military matters, but "we do not accept mental censorship." Censors, led by a Lieutenant Colonel Florit, cut some articles, such as one, aptly enough about censorship, written by Léon Blum and reprinted from a Parisian newspaper, *Le Populaire*.

Because the news in *Le Soir Républicain* was not its strong point, instead of taking a strong editorial line about the war, Camus reprinted what the rest of the national and foreign press had written about events. This gave the censors the thorny problem of whether to ban parts of articles that had already appeared in France or England. Camus reprinted part of a London *Daily Mail* article from September 23, 1939, which explained that Stalin signed the nonaggression pact not because he loved Hitler or wanted to save democracy but in Russia's own interest, following a realistic policy. Camus offered many historical analyses of the Treaty of Versailles, to gain a perspective on current events.

As a creative editor, Camus invented the column "Explanations of the War," in which he evaded censorship by recommending books that meant nothing to the censors but were antiwar, such as the philosopher Alain's *Mars, or War Judged* and Jaroslav Hašek's farcical novel *The Good Soldier Schweik.* The column advised readers to read John Maynard Keynes's *The Economic Consequences of the Peace,* about the disastrous results of the Treaty of Versailles. When Camus printed parts of the Versailles Treaty itself, censors cut some parts of it, finding them objectionable. They also cut out sections of Voltaire's chapter on war from his *Philosophical Dictionary,* which Camus reprinted one day. In his column, Camus attacked war songs, under the pretext of studying soldier's music, finding "odious" one World War I tune that went, "Everybody advance to the firing line, it's the supreme battle. . . ." He also printed what he called a new French army song, which the censor somehow let by:

It's the bay, the yo, the net, the ba-yo-net, that brings us victory!
It's our lit, our tul, our balls, our little balls that bring us glory!

Camus was aware of the absurd side of current events, and he shared these with Francine: ". . . I don't think I'm the only person to find all this absurd. On the contrary, I think that it's a useful view for us all. . . . People say 'That's absurd,' but then they pay their taxes and put their daughter into a religious school, because they think that there's nothing else to do, after one has said that things are absurd, whereas in reality, that's only the beginning. I can't explain in a few words what would take a whole book to say. . . . Philosophical thought only begins when we challenge the logic of clichés with rigor and honesty."

Two days later, at the end of November 1939, Albert confessed to Francine that he was feeling sluggish: "Since yesterday I have been full of doubt. Last night I started to write my essay about the absurd. Until now I'd only written scattered fragments, whatever suited my mood of the moment, but the real work remains to be done. It must be written, from beginning to end, and everything must fit into one work, which is what I started to do yesterday, and after a half hour, everything fell apart. I wrote two pages which are puerile, compared to what I really think. I was not seeing clearly, and got lost in the details. I stopped short, and suddenly thought that maybe I'm not capable of writing this, since anyone can have ideas, but to make them fit into a work and to master them creatively is what makes a writer. . . . Until now, I've amused myself by writing, feeling, and living. Now for the first time, I'm starting a long sustained work, and as I planned it, it cannot be a partial success, it needs total transparency to fully succeed, which is different than just planning it."

Five days later, on December 3, 1939, things looked even worse, and Camus wrote to Francine: "I've abandoned my work. When I write now it's only by sheer will, instead of the hot flame I felt that I wanted to capture. But now it's only a more or less brilliant game that I'm following, without participating, which isn't the same as writing with all of oneself. I haven't put that vibration into it which gives it essential value. It needs momentum and a sense of self-release, but I'm tense and nervous about my need to do what I must at any cost. The truth is, I've forgotten how to write, and I even notice it when writing letters quickly. . . . I prefer to leave nothing behind, rather than a work that betrays everything I feel."

In his "Explanations of the War" column in December 1939, Camus quoted the German philosopher Johann Gottlieb Fichte: "In order to show courage, there is no need to take up arms. Often in our lives, we must show more courage to remain true to our convictions by rising above the world's opinions." In his paper, which had little advertising and a circulation of less than six thousand, Camus proclaimed that its readers must "refuse all available regimes in Europe, and not just Nazism, fascism, and Franco's rule. . . . In our eyes, socialism does not mean the devotion to one man, a sect, a catechism, or even to a class or government. . . . Socialism is a striving by thought and action to improve the material and moral conditions of members of a society by collectivizing the economy."

Camus liked to quote a sentence written by Paul Nizan in his *Chronique de septembre*, a study of the failed Munich peace accord, that a journalist is "an instantaneous historian." Despite the efforts of Pia and Camus, the future of *Le Soir Républicain* looked bleak. The newspaper's owners suspected that the paper advocated anarchist politics, which were hardly commercial. Unlike the other local newspapers, which cheered for victorious war, Camus's paper continued to think that war could be avoided, mainly because all-out war had not begun between France and England on one side and the German foe. He overestimated Hitler's desire for peace and discounted the Nazi war machine's buildup from a military point of view.

Censorship battles continued, and on January 10 a M. Bourrette, divisional commissioner of the Algiers Special Police, asked to see Albert Camus, editor in chief of *Le Soir Républicain*. The commissioner notified Camus that by a decree dated January 9, 1940, the Algerian governor general was suspending the newspaper's publication. The newspaper had already been "momentarily" shut down before, on October 28, 1939; and at the end of the work day on January 10, 1940, police arrived at the newspaper office and seized 110 copies of *Le Soir Républicain*, which were to be sent to subscribers, and confiscated 1,051 unsold copies at newsstands.

The end of *Le Soir Républicain* was partly suicide. On the night of January 10, Camus and Pia had long talks with ten of the paper's workmen, who wanted their pay immediately. Pia explained that they would be paid in installments and suggested that meanwhile they look for other jobs.

After the death of Le Soir Républicain, Pia had no choice but to return to Paris, where he was offered jobs at La Lumière, a paper with ties to the Freemasons, and Paris-Soir. Camus also had to look for a job, and until Pia could find him something in France, he tried to find tutoring jobs or another journalistic position. Camus found himself without a profession or savings, and, like Pia, he was considered a suspicious character by the government.

Camus had learned to be a courtroom reporter, editorial writer, and literary critic, and in less than two years he had developed a journalistic morality. With two daily newspapers, which both died rapidly, Camus experienced bitterness, joy, lucidity, and the absurd.

Chapter Eighteen　　**A Beach at Bouisseville**

Camus had worked eight hours a day, six days a week at the newspaper, and now that he was unemployed, he had time to write an essay on the absurd, a novel, and a new draft of his play.

On July 25, 1939, he wrote to Christiane Galindo, "My work . . . is pursuing me. I just this minute finished *Caligula*, and it's unbearable, because I feel that I can do better than that, and I must rewrite it. I'm moving on Saturday and I'll start my novel at my mother's home, and all that will take a lot of time." He also planned to spend some time on his private life, and told Christiane, "There's another reason I haven't mentioned: I'm afraid to see F. [Francine] again; I want to see her but I don't want to get back together in any way, because I've got better things to do. Maybe it's better just to let everything die. For my works, I need freedom of mind, and freedom, period."

In August 1939, Camus suggested visiting Greece on a trawler boat with Christiane and some members of the Théâtre de l'Equipe, like Louis Miquel and the architect P. A. Emery. Camus felt stressed about his writing projects: "I can't get my mind off *Caligula*, because it must be a success. With my novel and my essay on the absurd, it makes the first stage of what I'm no longer afraid to call my works. . . . A dangerous and difficult step to get past, which will decide all the rest. . . . I feel clumsy and tormented when I look at my work. Yet I believe in it, that it could be fine in its own way—I mean my thing about absurdity."

Camus had been taking notes for his essay for over two years, and had worked a lot at his mother's apartment, where he stayed for three months out of financial necessity, from September through November 1939. He had nearly lost the notes to his essay when he burned his letters. Thinking of Francine Faure, he speculated, "A long time ago, two or three years ago, I thought I might be allowed to take a chance on normal happiness, like anyone else. . . . But then I ruined everything. A little while ago, Francine, whose honest heart I love, called me and I agreed once again to try to be a man like any other. . . . I'd be lying, and Francine would know it, if I said I accepted that without any regrets. I am missing lots of pleasure and people, but I'm making an effort to accept it."

His being refused for army service still upset him: "I thought that finally I'd be alone and free to despise others, in a shelter or on the front, but I was refused this mean consolation. At least today, I would like to preserve what remains of truth, youth, and friendship amid all the ruins."

Among the people important to him was Yvonne Ducailar, whom he met in October 1939. A graduate student at Algiers University working as a substitute philosophy teacher at a girls' high school, she had been presented to Camus by Lucette Meurer on the outdoor terrace of a café. Yvonne would visit Charlot's bookstore and attend meetings of the Théâtre de l'Equipe, where Camus advised her to read the books of the Russian philosopher and critic Leon Chestov. Yvonne admired Camus's natural superiority, his kindness and friendliness, his irony which bordered on cynicism, his way of being serious lightly, and his eyes when he spoke, "as if his soul were blossoming in them."

At the time, he was living in a isolated little house near the church of Notre-Dame-d'Afrique. Yvonne knew, as did Blanche, Lucette, and Christiane, that Albert was engaged to be married to Francine Faure. In 1938 and 1939 in Oran, Francine told Christiane Galindo that she wondered if she should agree to sleep with Albert, and by autumn 1939 she had decided to do so, while Albert kept seeing his other girlfriends, including Lucette and Yvonne.

He spent the first three months of 1940 in Oran, divided among his love affairs. He theorized about his appetites in *Noces*, "It isn't always easy to be a man, and even less to be a pure man." His heart and body required the right to unlimited love. Working on his essay about the absurd, he dealt with revolt and freedom, but also matters of conscience, death, suicide, the actor he had been, and the seducer who stated that "the lover, the actor, and the adventurer are playing absurd roles . . . as are the chaste man, the civil servant, and our country's president."

He dealt with the relations between novels and philosophy, Franz Kafka and Sisyphus, and described the character Don Juan, writing, "If loving was enough, then things would be too simple, but the more one loves, the more the absurd is reinforced. . . . It is not from lack of love that Don Juan goes from woman to woman. . . . It's because he loves them equally and gives himself fully each time, that he needs to repeat this gift and this deeper exploration."

Francine tried to be understanding and patient. Camus wrote that "each woman hoped to give Don Juan what no one had ever given him before, and in this, each one is deeply wrong, and only makes him feel the need for repetition. . . . Why must one love few people in order to love a lot?" He generalized about sexual matters: "Books and legends are responsible for a collective way of seeing that makes us call love that which ties us to certain people. . . . All I know about love is a mix of desire, tenderness, and intelligence that links me to one such person, and this combination is not the same for everyone, so I cannot describe every experience with the same term, nor need I use the same gestures with every one."

Don Juan's insatiability was explained: "If he leaves a woman, it's not necessarily because he no longer desires her, because a lovely woman is always desirable, but that he desires a different woman, which is not the same thing." Camus imagined Don Juan ending his days in a Spanish monastery, and saw pleasure and asceticism as "the two faces of the same destitution." By choosing Francine, he was trying to destroy the past, as when he burnt all his letters.

Francine's older sister Christiane Faure kept a protective watch on her. Francine told her family that she thought she would marry Albert Camus, a tubercular young man with no money or job, who was getting divorced because he loved freedom and who did not really want to get remarried. When Francine showed her family a photo of Albert, Christiane commented, "He looks like a little monkey." Francine replied, "The monkey is the animal that resembles man the most."

Although they did not yet live together, Francine was already part of Albert's life, a gracious and serious companion. She had a weakness for sickly men, and previously had been involved with a tubercular law student and had a schoolgirl crush on her uncle Charley, a skirt chaser with a wooden leg. She was aware of her powers of seduction and her musical talent. Albert, one year older than Francine, was paternal with her.

The Faures were not one of the great families of Oran, but they were strongly united, the mother and her daughters, Christiane, Suzy, and Francine, the youngest. The Faure family rented apartments along the rue d'Arzew. Unlike the Camus family, they knew about their ancestors. A Jewish Berber grandmother, Clara Touboul, had suffered from depression after her husband died young of cancer and her son was badly wounded in the First World War. Fernande Faure's husband had been a lieutenant in a Zouave regiment and was killed in September 1914 during the Battle of the Marne, as was Albert's father. Francine was born two months after her father's death. During the war, Fernande vowed to become an observant Christian if her brother survived the butchery. Her three daughters were baptized, rather belatedly, and went through the motions of first communions. Of the three girls, Suzy was the most firmly agnostic, while Francine, although not a believer, would attend midnight mass to hear the music.

Fernande went back to school after her husband's death, and worked as a dressmaker and at a government-controlled building society to support her three daughters, selling porcelain on the side to make extra money. She finally landed a job at the post office, where she energetically worked her way up the ladder from switchboard operator to executive. She also took care of household chores, and in her spare moments she enjoyed reading the letters of Madame de Sevigné and stories by Colette and Chekhov, as well as traditional literary magazines like *Conferencia*. She was fearsomely authoritative with her girls, loving and possessive, and as the baby of the family Francine was especially adored. The other two girls, Christiane and Suzy, had been literature students at Paris's Lycée Fénélon and became teachers, Christiane at the girls' high school in Oran. Francine got her diploma as a math teacher in Algiers.

The women of the Faure family watched with concern as Francine first broke up, and then reunited with Albert. At the beginning of 1940, with no social position, money, or permanent home, Camus traveled between Algiers and Oran, but settled in the latter city, proposing marriage to Francine without swearing to be faithful to her. Camus's circle of friends was mostly feminine, as he explained to Lucette Maurer in a July 1938 letter: "People attract me insofar as they are impassioned about life and avid for happiness, which is perhaps why I have more women friends than men." He admitted to Lucette that friendship between men and women always contained "something equivocal, a double game, that falsifies feelings at their source, which I think is because few men manage to clearly understand their desires, to know where they begin and end."

Camus needed women as friends and lovers, and Christiane Galindo, Lucette Meurer, and Yvonne Ducailar had never said they wanted to marry him. They knew he was committed to Francine. On January 5, he wrote to Yvonne from Oran, "You haven't told me much about yourself, my little girl, but I'd like to know what you're doing. . . . Everything that's happened doesn't prevent me from feeling something new and young inside me whenever I think of you, and maybe if we can wait a little, we'll have more days to share together and to better experience. I wish that for myself, and desire it. When all this mud and clouds will pass, I think I'll see more clearly. I no longer recognize myself in what I was in Algiers. But I do recognize myself in a certain life which I shared with you. I'm floundering and expressing all this very badly, but it's simple enough to say that I'm happy when I feel your presence in my life, and add that I feel confident and relaxed with you. Write to me, Yvonne, a long letter if you can. I can never write often or much, but I want you to trust me, and I want to press you against me."

Although in Oran for the moment, Camus was hoping to find a journalism job in Algiers, and in the meantime gave French and philosophy lessons. Camus knew plenty of people in Oran, and also stayed in contact with friends in prison, as did Pia. One such incarcerated friend, an Arab Communist named Smaïli, wrote to Pia from Algiers prison in January 1940, praising Pia and Camus, "who had the remarkable courage to worry about the poverty of our Moslem brothers"; such people, the prisoner noted, "can be counted on the fingers of one hand."

Camus got to know Oran, which he in many respects found "magnificent. . . . It is fertile and brutal and I think I could live here for many months." He praised the beaches around Oran, "every summer morning looking like the creation of the world," but joked about the city itself: "Oran, an extravagant city where the shoe stores display horrible plaster models of deformed feet and shop windows place party jokes next to red, white, and blue wallets, and where one can still drink extraordinary coffee in chipped glasses at counters slippery with grease and the feet and wings of flies." He added, with some feeling, "Incomparable and loose city with its parade of imperfect and moving young women, wearing no makeup and incapable of showing emotion, who fake coquetry so badly that their ruses quickly become stale."

Camus hated Oran's Colonial House, a pretentious building erected to the glory of the Empire, but he did like the area outside the city, which was more rough and African-looking than the outskirts of Algiers. He felt that in the city itself, "one learns the very temporary virtues of a certain boredom."

He stewed about the lack of cultural life in Oran, where the cinemas would more likely program a Hollywood silent film such as *Ben-Hur* starring Ramon Novarro rather than the Russian director Sergei Eisenstein's classic *Battleship Potemkin*. By denouncing Oran's provincialism, Camus was also defending Algiers by comparison.

He would eat sardines and snails with hot sauce in little restaurants at Oran's old port, in the company of his best friend, Pierre Galindo, Christiane's brother. A stroll to Bouisseville, outside Oran, impressed Camus, giving him a strong and mysterious scene for the novel he was working on, *L'Etranger*. The beaches were far from the city and could only be reached by bicycle or car. One Sunday morning, between eleven and noon, a group of Galindo's friends were on the beach at Bouisseville, where the men were swimming and playing soccer with a inflatable rubber ball. One of Camus's friends, Raoul Bensoussan, excitedly ran up to his brother and explained that he had just had a run-in with two Arabs on the beach. Raoul had been jostled by the Arabs, and he felt that they had showed disrespect to his girlfriend in some fashion. Raoul returned with his brother to argue with the Arabs, and after a brawl he was injured by one of them, who had a knife. That afternoon, during lunch by the seaside, Raoul resolved to have his revenge, and armed with a small-caliber automatic pistol, he went looking for the two Arabs, who were arrested by local police, although the Bensoussans did not press charges. One of the Arabs had a police record, and they were charged with disturbing the peace rather than assault. Camus heard the details of this conflict many times over and incorporated many of them directly into *L'Etranger*.

Despite such inspiration to his work, Camus grew impatient with Oran. He still lacked money, and had asked friends to sell some of his books in Algiers to raise cash, and none of the job possibilities he had hoped for came through. He sent to the Théâtre de l'Equipe the manuscript of his adaptation of Pierre de Larivey's book *Esprits*, which he hoped to stage.

He returned to Algiers on January 30, and on February 13, when he was still living at his mother's home, he wrote to Pascal Pia in Paris that "until yesterday, I had no news about your departure," but had learned that Pia had received severance pay from the newspaper, "the royal sum of 3,500 francs." Camus suggested that he would appear at the labor court to defend his own case as well as Pia's, and ironized about their bosses at *Alger Républicain* and *Le Soir Républicain*: "Through inaction, we must absolutely not let these great men think that loutishness is a universally accepted virtue, and thus it will be a public health matter, because even if you use the money to buy a female elephant for your Sunday strolls, it would be better spent than to keep their venomous sheet going for a few more days. Personally, I'd be delighted to participate in this health project."

Camus was finally given his back pay for December and ten days in January. He wrote again to Pascal, "I don't have a dime left and cannot possibly join you in Paris. [The printer] Andréo paid me one thousand francs for my layout and my two days' work, which is what I'm living on, and it's running out terribly quickly. Andréo told me that I might run a government magazine, but I replied that I have no desire to be a whore, even a well-paid one." In his February 13 letter he admitted that he missed Pia: "Although I'm happy to know you're in Paris, I can't personally congratulate myself for that. There is a lack of men here, and I feel a bit alone. I think I've already expressed this to you clumsily, but it hurt me to part from you. Together we have defended things that are worth defending, and that would be enough to explain my regrets and my friendship, if I didn't have the esteem and gratitude for you which you know about."

Six days later, Camus reported to Pia that he had reconsidered his plans: "I've decided to leave Algiers for Paris, because I haven't found any work here. At the end of the week, I'm going to leave Algiers for Oran, where they've found me a few philosophy lessons, and there I'll wait for your telegram, which will be welcome. . . . I can always find enough money to pay for the trip to Paris, once I know I'll be earning a living there. As for Francine Faure, she and I are agreed that I must live where I want to live, and I think that she'll join me in Paris."

Camus lost his lawsuit at the labor court, as he reported from Oran to Pascal Pia: "The blow was rotten but aboveboard, as [*Alger Républicain*] pled necessity, that the firing was imposed by the government because of Mr. Camus's 'insane' articles, which were 'detrimental to the national interest.' The labor court judges turned pale."

He decided that he no longer liked Oran: "It isn't amusing here at all, I'm suffocating and waiting for the occasion to leave. I've asked for a job abroad and would be ready to leave at a moment's notice, even to Valparaiso." He did not want to dissipate his energies, in order to finish his books, and needed solitude, which he hoped to find far away from his girl-friends.

Pascal Pia did find him a job, and the news of Camus's departure set off a "fine family drama," with Fernande Faure tearfully reproaching him for not making Francine happy and being egoistic, which, Camus admitted in a March 1940 letter to Christane Galindo, was strictly true. Francine stayed in Oran, but promised to join Albert in Paris at the end of the academic year.

Before he left, Albert solemnly promised to marry Francine, which Fernande and Christiane had imposed as the necessary requirement for his intimacy with the girl. Camus left Algeria on March 14, 1940.

Three days later he wrote to Yvonne Ducailar to complain about the "exhausting" boat trip to Paris, during which he ate little, drank almost nothing, and didn't sleep at all. But physical deprivation fit his mood, and his belief in the asceticism necessary for creative work.

He had written in his *Carnets* for September 27, 1939:

Hence the absolute necessity of proving oneself . . . through rigorous chastity. Before any theoretical enterprise, which tries to glorify the here and now, one must strain for a month of asceticism in every sense.

Sexual chastity.

Chaste thoughts—forbidding desire to wander, and thoughts to disperse.

A single, constant subject for meditation, and to refuse anything else.

To work at fixed hours, continuously, without fail, etc., etc.—and moral asceticism, too.

For his novel in progress, Camus considered different titles, like *A Happy Man, Modesty, A Free Man, A Man Like Any Other,* and, finally, *The Stranger.*

Chapter Nineteen   Exile

On March 16, 1940, a depressing Saturday, Camus arrived in Paris. He ate a meal and drank martinis. Then, having "slept his fill," he saw things "from a more equitable angle." Pia had reserved a room for him at the Hôtel Poirier at 16 rue Ravignan in the eighteenth arrondissement, near the boulevard de Clichy and the Montmartre cemetery. Camus found the hotel "perfectly amusing. . . . I must admit that it's more or less sordid and squalid, inhabited by pimps and failed artists, but nothing is more middle-class than a houseful of pimps, and these gentlemen live there with their 'ladies,' who don't work in the hotel where they live. That would be immoral." He was amused by the signs posted all over the hotel, "Watch Out for the Light!" The managers were worried about being fined, and perhaps even about German bombs, if blackout rules were violated. Camus wrote: "The owner goes to bed at 5 a.m. and refuses to take care of clients until noon. The rooms are made up in the evenings, and everyone finds that normal. I do too, to be fair." He tried to borrow an alarm clock from an "unbelievable and nice princess who is like Jenny Diver in *The Threepenny Opera*, smoking while she paced endlessly around the room." She promised to lend him the clock and "she told me to go to bed and not to worry because she had the pass-key to my room. . . . I found her simplicity just brilliant, and I returned to my room, wondering dreamily about the destiny of the last few hundred-franc notes that I had left." Camus thought he would stay in Paris only for a year or two: "You can't live here, you can only work and vibrate here."

A *Paris-Soir* editor agreed to see Camus, telling him, "We don't do any politics here!" Camus responded very calmly, "Of course!" Camus was hired as an editorial secretary, like Pia, earning three thousand francs per month, which was considered good pay for five hours of work a day. Yet Camus took a risk, because he was hired for only a one-week trial period. *Paris-Soir*, which sold about one million copies, was a giant machine compared to the *Alger Républicain*.

His first day, Camus worked from 6:00 a.m. to 11:30 a.m., and "all was copacetic," as he reported to friends at home, writing about the cold wave in Europe and pieces of ice floating in the Seine. He reported that his technical job interested him and "left him intact." He worked in the page layout department. One of his bosses, Hervé Mille, felt that while this young man was more concerned with aesthetics than with news value, what he designed was very attractive. Pia had a more professional approach.

Camus insisted on his independence and his ideological integrity and did not feel that he was responsible for the contents of *Paris-Soir*. Leftist friends like Robert Poncet nicknamed the paper "Pourrisoir"—Rotten Evening—but Camus did not write a word of the newspaper. The largest seller in the French press, *Paris-Soir* was not quite as putrid as its detractors claimed. Under directions from its owners, the paper adhered to only one political side, the opinions of the government, whatever they might be.

Paris-Soir was four pages long and priced at fifty centimes, aimed at civil servants in the Ministry of Foreign Affairs as much as at auto workers in Boulogne-Billancourt. This daily was much beneath *Le Figaro* and *Le Temps* but was a step above certain British scandal sheets. Insipid editorials alternated with articles by François Mauriac, Léon Blum, Georges Duhamel, Alexander Kerensky, and H. G. Wells. To add some syrup to the formula, an academician whom Camus despised, Henry Bordeaux, wrote about his visits to the Pope.

Camus saved his energy for his novel and wasted nothing, asking Francine to send him literary material: "At least I hope you held on to the text of *La Mort heureuse*. If so, look attentively at chapter 2, where I believe you'll find (1) the passage at the beginning where Emmanuel and Mersault run after a truck on the docks, (2) everything which has to do with 'Sundays at the Window.' If these two passages are indeed in chapter 2, just send the whole chapter to me at rue Ravignan." He was disappointed and agitated to learn that Francine did not want to join him in Paris.

Camus chatted with editorial secretaries and typographers. As he had not been in the business for long, he had much to learn, and was a good listener. During one talk, an employee, Henri Coquelin, said that he certainly wouldn't want to work alongside a tubercular colleague. Daniel Lenief, another worker, kicked Coquelin under the table and took him aside for a moment. Coquelin apologized to Camus and they became friends, eating spaghetti dinners together, although Camus never told Coquelin that he was a writer. Camus spent little time with reporters, walking by the newspaper's stars, like Joseph Kessel, and lesser reporters, like Roger Vailland, who were well paid although they worked very little, without making any contact. He mostly felt comfortable with other technical workers. Janine Thomasset was a pretty twenty-year-old executive secretary who was taking up an office collection for a wedding party. Janine noticed Albert, a handsome young man in a tweed jacket who smoked corn-paper cigarettes, and when she asked him to contribute, he joked, "You never said good morning to me, and now you're asking for money!"

As war clouds gathered, Camus would smile at speeches by Paul Reynaud, the new president of the council, especially when Reynaud declared that all Frenchmen who would not work would be "crushed." Despite the charm of the Hôtel Poirier, Camus switched to the Left Bank's Hôtel Madison, facing the church of Saint-Germain-des-Près in the sixth arrondissement. There he concentrated on his work-in-progress, and noted in his *Carnets*: "March 1940. More and more, faced by the world of men, the only possible reaction is individualism." Camus was earning his living, and he wrote to Claude de Fréminville, who had been drafted, to say that his "conscience was at rest."

Fréminville was hoping to place his own poems in Paris's literary reviews, but Camus warned him that "the NRF [*Nouvelle Revue Française*], *Esprit*, etc. are beneath contempt and the power of stupidity seems to be contagious." By contrast, he admired a small Italian-American publication, *The World*, run by Guglielmo Ferrero, who had been exiled to the United States.

In Paris's sad, sticky springtime Camus noted the "mediocrity of souls and faces." Algerians often find French faces inexpressive by comparison to what they are accustomed to. Camus thought of Algeria as "a kind of paradise lost." He wrote to Fréminville that there were intellectual compensations: "I saw Malraux and had lunch with him. He has eyes like yours and a certain something else of you. A bit more now, because you've lost weight. I was at a private showing of his film on Spain and I was overwhelmed. What a joy to be able to admire something wholeheartedly."

He wrote a lot of letters and repeated to Yvonne Ducailar how moved he had been by Malraux: "Afterwards, I had an appointment with Malraux and Pia and I spent a fascinating hour with a person full of tics, feverish and disorganized, but an amazing intelligence." Camus had met one of his great men. He mentioned a magazine that Edmond Charlot planned to publish, but Malraux said, "Either a magazine will have no influence, or if it does, that magazine will be closed down."

Camus liked to admire things, whether films or books, but he had not noticed any works of lasting value in Paris's theaters. He worked "like a desperate man," often suffering from fever and frightful headaches, and needed strong willpower to keep going physically. "And I've got it," he affirmed. He spoke to Fréminville as an equal: "You know that after the 'exercise' of *Noces*, I felt that I could undertake what I wanted to, an art of the absurd. I have already told you about it: several parts with each section embodied with different techniques, and their results illustrate the consequences of an absurd grappling with life. I am explaining this badly, but it's really less systematic and less abstract. I've begun the first part. As you know, *Caligula* is finished. *L'Etranger* is three-quarters written—you've read the first chapter. My essay on the absurd is half-written. This summer I will finish all three things at the same time. (I'm going to revise *Caligula* a little.)" Camus planned far ahead: "I'll begin the next part. You see that all this is vast, but for the first time, I am aware of all I want to do and I am sure of bringing it to completion."

The man who praised happiness questioned himself: "Happy? Let's not talk about it. . . . But even if my life is complicated, I haven't stopped loving. At this time there is no distance between my life and my work. I'm doing both at the same time, and with the same passion." He was worried about his individualism and detachment from events: "Empires may fall and crush us in part, but life must go on. But if we had to die, that would be too bad."

Edmond Charlot proposed to Camus and Fréminville to buy the backlist of Cafre Editions, which they had created in Algeria some years before, and they agreed. Camus had grown accustomed to Paris, and now said he would stay for three years. He wrote to Irène Dijan that afterwards, he planned to take up again his "little career as Wandering Jew." As seen from Paris, Oran had a lot of charm. Camus mused: "All of Algeria must be full of flowers." In Paris, for every Malraux and some "really good fellows," there were many "phony artists, wheeler-dealers, and dreadful thinkers." Camus had almost finished his novel, and he wrote, " 'L'Etranger'—who can know what that word means?" He felt no need to write anything but his own works, and especially nothing for *Paris-Soir*: "Events are going at such speed that the only wise and courageous attitude to have is silence. This can be used as a sort of sustained meditation which will prepare us for the future."

Camus had no taste for forced conformity. Later he would speak out very loudly: "I have no real ambition, apart from a certain plan, but if I had to aspire to what is called a 'name,' it would be to use it at such times as these. For example, at the beginning of the war it would have been useful." In Paris, for the time being, he had to "wait and work." He would stroll in the Latin Quarter, admiring blond women students and thinking about his destiny: "So what? I'll be a journalist and die young. . . . What more could I ask and why should I regret the lives I haven't had?" But he did miss them, wanting several lives, one with Francine and another with Yvonne. At the hotel, Camus got on with his novel and wrote home, "I've just been informed that bombs are falling on Paris. Life is beautiful." He was waiting for Francine and would have liked Yvonne to be there as well: "Yesterday . . . I was in a Montmartre restaurant next to an old boy who spent a lot of time ordering the cheapest dishes on the menu. Facing me was a small and dirty Italian violinist who swallowed the croutons in his soup without chewing them. I would have got a stomachache, but it seemed to go down easily for him. On the other side there was a fairly ugly girl who stunned me by giving me the eye. Everyone was picking their teeth, sniffing, and counting their pennies, and I asked myself what I was doing there and why I consented to this sinister world."

Camus wanted to detach himself from the "stupidities" of this war, and at the same time he wanted to enlist and take part in uniform. He was obsessed by his bad health and his body, which "disgusted" him. He got even thinner and paler, losing the tanned look he had in Algiers. He noted some sinister events: "The day before yesterday, the woman who lives above me threw herself off the balcony into the courtyard. Everything is still splattered with blood. She died after saying, 'Finally!'" In April he wrote in his *Carnets*: "At *Paris-Soir* I feel the entire heart of Paris and its abject mind that of a silly shopgirl. Mimi's mansard roof [from *La Bohème*] has become a skyscraper, but her heart has remained the same, and it is rotten."

Albert thought endlessly of Yvonne and Francine, and wrote to the former: "I'm probably going to waste my life, if common sense is any judge. I mean I'm going to marry F., unless she refuses me (I haven't had any news for a long time)." In the same letter he informed Yvonne, "I'm not saying I love you." So, according to Camus, he did not love either Francine or Yvonne. This may have been a sign of sincerity, apology, showing off, or genuine perplexity, a desire not to hurt or the contrary. He said he repressed his desire to love in the unusual and perhaps derisory life he was leading, thus trying to explain the irrational nature of his passions: "And to legitimize what I want to create, I absolutely must deny it." He felt a passion for Yvonne, which he told her about, and he also felt affection for Francine, which he did not tell Yvonne about. He felt "stupidly hurt. . . . But that has no more importance than all the rest, the way I have arranged my life, the harm I can do to others, and the terrible vanity of all this agitation."

Albert did not dare admit that he loved two women, out of fear of seeming ridiculous or clumsy. He ended one letter to Yvonne by saying, "I want so much to kiss you, and also to turn away," and added a postscript the same evening: "What I was trying to tell you was I too am continuing to gamble on a losing streak." He promised never to write again in this manner. A few days later, he said that he would join Yvonne in "accepting chance and the worst." They led parallel lives. As a letter writer, Camus was like the moralist-philosopher in his writings: "For the rest, let the absurd little God have his way. You know he is elegant and proper, rather ironic and terribly quick when he strikes. His religion teaches us never to refuse to be hit and to know how to cash in." Albert stated that in certain ways, his novel "resembled" Yvonne, and he planned to have it published in October, along with his essay and play.

Like his hero Meursault, Camus had problems with the idea of marriage. He felt that in one sense, marriage had no importance. He wrote in his novel-in-progress: "In the evening, Marie came to look for me and asked me if I wanted to marry her. I said I didn't care, that we could do it if she wanted to. Then she wanted to know if I loved her. I answered in the way I already had once before, that it didn't mean anything, but that no doubt, I didn't love her. She asked, 'Why will you marry me, then?' I told her that it didn't matter and that if she wanted to, we could get married. Anyway, she was the one who asked, and I agreed. Then she said that marriage was a serious thing. I answered, 'No.' She was quiet for a moment and looked at me in silence. Then she spoke, simply wanting to know if I'd have accepted the same proposal from another woman to whom I was attached in the same way. I said, 'Naturally.' Then she asked herself if she loved me, and of course I couldn't know anything about that subject. After another moment of silence, she whispered that I was bizarre and no doubt she loved me because of that, but that one day perhaps I would disgust her for the same reason. As I remained silent, having nothing more to say, she took me in her arms and smilingly said that she wanted to marry me. I said we would do it as soon as she wanted. Then I spoke to her about the boss's proposition and Marie said she would like to know Paris. I informed her that I had lived there for a while and she asked me how it was. I told her, 'It's dirty. There are pigeons and black courtyards. People have white skin.'"

The character Meursault was inspired by Camus, Pascal Pia, Pierre Galindo, the Bensoussan brothers, Sauveur Galliero, and Yvonne herself. Marie was not Francine. Camus the writer mastered his novel in a way that Camus the man did not control his life. Meursault never asked himself any questions, whereas Camus was always examining his actions and motivations. Meursault was also far from Caligula, but both characters were close to Camus as masks of a writer who felt self-doubt and self-confidence at the same time. Caligula yelled, "What is love? Of little importance!" and "Unhappiness is like marriage. You think you are choosing and then you are chosen." Or: "To live is the opposite of to love. . . . To love someone is to accept to grow old with him. I'm not capable of this love."

On April 5, 1940, the newspaper *La Lumière* published an article by Camus reacting to a essay in which François Mauriac named the literary heirs of the writer Maurice Barrès as André Malraux, Henry de Montherlant, Louis Aragon, and Pierre Drieu La Rochelle. Camus disagreed, finding Montherlant and Malraux far from Barrès. The young writer felt that Barrès "only magnified on paper" his ethics, while Malraux and Montherlant had transformed them "into an exalting code for life" as they had actually lived it.

Camus no longer wished to write journalism, which he saw as incompatible with literature under the circumstances: "The people who create—I mean great artists, not literary journalists—are almost always men of action, contrary to popular belief, who have chosen this form of action to exercise their will." He added a topical parenthesis: "Hitler had ambitions as a painter, but he did not have enough intelligence to be anything but a dictator." Camus felt that his own work must go before anything else, but there was a price to pay for this attitude: "To create, you must necessarily have a slightly hard heart." He did not believe in genius: "But talent is another matter, it can be acquired by work."

Camus sent out his texts and articles, typed in Oran by Christiane Galindo, as well as some handwritten pages from his novel. He felt on solid ground when he was constructing his work, but always went from relative satisfaction to total doubt, sometimes from one moment to the next: "At times I think what I am accumulating represents something unique. Other times, it's discouragement about the universe I wanted to create and what it ends up looking like. Maybe I took on something here which is beyond me. And yet, at certain moments, what power and lucidity I feel in myself!" He constantly doubted his overall view of his work: "But now I am no longer a judge of anything, and I work like a deaf man. We'll see the results. What's funny here is that I see lots of people, mostly phony great men, and I bring to them the world which I have created. It's a strange feeling of power to give up nothing of the essential things which one possesses."

Camus's ambition was immense, and so was his humility. *Paris-Soir's* mediocrity offended him, but also nurtured him. *Paris-Soir* was obliged in spite of itself to become more interested in international politics and to spend less time on its brainless readership. After May 11, the Germans began bombing France heavily, following the invasions of Belgium, Holland, and Luxembourg. Camus was absorbed by *L'Etranger,* working as if he were walking on a "tightrope, in passionate and solitary tension." In a discouraged mood, he wrote to Francine, "I've just reread all that I've written of my novel. I was seized with disgust and it seemed to me a failure from the ground up, that *Caligula* was hardly better and that my initial plans had been stymied by the limits of what I had managed to do. I turned away from my papers sadly, but it's almost as if I were already resigned. All of this is not good."

But he got hold of himself: "I get lots of invitations and solicitations, and I accept only one out of five. But I'm not complaining about that either, because that's the condition for writing, so that I may write with great joy inside me. I've never worked as much. This room is miserable. I live alone and

I am weary, but I don't know if it's despite all this or because of it that I am writing all I wanted to write. Soon I will be able to judge what I'm worth and decide one way or another."

On May 1, 1940, ten days before the general offensive of the German army and sixteen days before the Allies' evacuation of Dunkirk, Albert wrote to Francine with tears of sadness and joy: "I'm writing to you at night. I have just finished my novel and I'm too overexcited to think of sleeping. No doubt my work isn't finished, I have things to go over, others to add and rewrite. But the fact is, I've finished and I wrote the last sentence. Why do I turn immediately towards you? I have the manuscript in front of me, and I think of all it cost me in effort and will—how much involvement it required—to sacrifice other thoughts, other desires to remain in its atmosphere. I don't know what it's worth. At certain moments these days, I am terribly proud of some of its sentences, whose tone and truth go through me like lightning, but at other times I see only ashes and clumsiness. I am too absorbed in this story. I am going to put these pages in my drawer and start work on my essay, and in two weeks I'll take it out again and rework the novel. Then I'll have it read by people. I don't want to dwell on it too much, because in fact I've been carrying it for two weeks and I saw quite well from the way I wrote it that it was already marked out inside me. That makes two months that I'm working on it every day and part of the night. Curiously, if I leave to go to the newspaper with a page half-written, when I get back I can finish the sentence effortlessly, with perfect lucidity. I have never written anything with this continuity and this facility. I sleep badly right now, and suffer from insomnia. Sometimes when I wake up, I see clearly a whole series of works that I will write like this one, as if under dictation, as if now everything was clear among my projects and in the universe I wanted to depict. Tonight, I'm exhausted. Lately, I've been asking myself if my work at *Paris-Soir* isn't tiring me out too much. But in fact the novel is also responsible, because it also demanded a continuous effort which seemed easy but which in fact exhausted me."

Camus expressed his own doubts about his work with irony: "The strangest thing is that I don't even know if I am satisfied. Yet it's the only thing which has allowed me to get away from myself, and I think I'd forgive Paris for everything, for having allowed me to live like this, completely concentrated upon what I was doing." He hoped to ward off the evil eye: "Even if it has no value, there is value in the joy of work itself that no one can destroy and which I'd be feeling myself tonight if I weren't so tired. . . . But I imagine that the reader of this manuscript will be at least as tired as I am, and the continual tension that can be felt in it might discourage many readers." Camus admitted, "I sought this tension and worked to put it in my book. I know it is there." Camus was also feeling a certain self-satisfaction: "I don't know if it is good. Grenier told me that Montherlant spoke to him about Nice and about me 'with lots of warmth.' M. did not know that Grenier knew me, and asked what I am doing. That gave me the idea to send Montherlant my two manuscripts when they are finished; and to explain to him what I want. I think that only he could help me publish them all together."

Yet Montherlant was far from Camus in spirit. Both sang the praises of sport and the human body, both were sensitive to poverty and the humiliation of the Arab and Kabyle peoples; but Montherlant had an aristocratic paternalism which Camus never had.

He was very upset that Francine was not coming to join him, and his book reminded him of his exile and of the kingdom on the other side of the Mediterranean: "I think of a sentence from my novel: 'Over there, over there too, evening is like a melancholy respite.' " He thought of evenings in Algiers and Oran: "How much I would like that respite by the seaside." Now he planned to spend 1940 and 1941 in Paris or elsewhere in France, before returning to "rediscover the green sky" of Algeria. Throughout May the Allied defeats continued, although there was no trace of the war in Camus's surviving *Carnets*, but his letters show that he was not indifferent to events. In his May 1 letter to Yvonne he wrote, "I am writing this to you at the newspaper office, amid the general hysteria created by events here. Men will die by the thousands so there is something to be excited about."

Camus renounced both Yvonne and a planned trip to Portugal. Yvonne and Albert had sworn to tell each other the truth, and there was a man in Yvonne's life in Algiers, whom Camus called "Al Capone." He pretended to accept this other man's existence: "I prefer to know about it than to imagine it." He refused to be jealous, or at least tried to suppress the emotion: "I'm thinking of you. For example, I think that I could never get married to you. Nor anyone else, of course. But even less to you. Only, I feel that I could always live with you, meet you, travel, desire you, drink, find you lovely, and all the rest." Camus's analysis of his love for Yvonne took on the air of a postmortem. Camus had achieved his dream of a monastic existence: "For three months I have been cloistered. I stopped everything in order to put into shape what I had to say now (I haven't touched a woman for all this time, and I think that it's the first time in my life)." He observed with a sort of sad smile, "I told you one day laughingly that things always end where they began and our beginning was in a cemetery."

Camus still thought he might have to serve: "This month I am going to take another draft examination. But I don't care if I am accepted. What I have to do and to live through, I can do as well in the middle of battle as in the middle of Paris. As for the risks of death, they are of no importance. There was an air-raid alert this morning. I was awakened by sirens, the hum of airplanes, and shooting from anti-aircraft guns. But I went back to the sleep of the just, although people were screaming and getting upset around me." Camus wanted to take part in the war: "If I could, I would ask to join the French troops on the eastern front and to be shipped out to Syria. Naturally, not out of conviction but because I'd prefer that to the mindlessness of a French barracks. Can you imagine me somewhere near Puy or in the Franche-Comte?" he asked Christiane Galindo.

He felt self-doubt akin to discouragement, as he confessed to Francine in a letter on May 13: "This morning when I didn't have to work, I put my novel in a drawer and I took out my essay, to organize my projects. I am terrified by the amount of effort and conscience that it will require. I was overwhelmed by these notes, plans, etc. I'm afraid of being overwhelmed by a too-ambitious project. In reality, it could be the conclusions from an entire life, but on the other hand, what I want to do has value because of its outsized aspect. If I'm incapable of doing it, then I need only get a job selling cars. As I don't really want to do so, I must therefore get past all the difficulties. However, it would feel very good not to get past anything at all, and just to let myself go."

Camus weighed his different projects: "I've also had some worries about the magazine I was planning with Charlier [a printer in Algeria]. He hounded me to do it in Paris, but my life here has allowed me to think about a lot of questions, and especially about politics, if I may say so. On the one hand, I do not approve of the idealistic and optimistic look that C. gives all this. And, above all, it seemed to me that before we undertake or suggest anything, we have to know exactly what we want. I'm certainly sure about some things—you know what they are. But I find that to start from zero in this domain requires more profound thought and more radical beliefs. It takes time, and silence seems to me the only valuable behavior today. First, because it expresses better than anything else the contempt one may feel, and secondly, because it allows you to think and to see clearly what it is you want. Only as soon as you are sure of the least useful truth, you must act immediately, and even if it means sacrificing everything. I thought that way, and I still think so, therefore I'm going to write to Charlier that I don't want to create a magazine or a movement. It's plain and perfectly clear."

He stated in a letter dated May 14: "You are right, Kafka always says the same thing, but the truth is always monotonous. He needs patient readers and finally, what grandeur! I answered almost all your questions and worries in yesterday's letter, which I'm sending with this one. The preference which you've always shown for my essay is a little odd. It's almost as if things of the intelligence attract you more than 'exterior' works. And yet, I know that's not absolutely true in every case. I'm a bit anxious about the work I still have to do. For the moment, everything that I've written about [*Le Mythe de*

Sisyphe] pleases me, because I feel a sort of constant flame in it, and an accent which cannot be indifferent, it seems, despite the dryness and tension of the subject. But I still must make it into a work, a single face that follows through its nuances and its emotions. For that, one must be continually far-sighted. Of course, it's only a question of will, but these thoughts do not calm my anxieties."

On May 15, Holland fell to the Germans. At the end of the month, part of the editorial and administrative staff of *Paris-Soir* were transferred to Nantes, but Camus stayed in Paris, "in the middle of an almost deserted newspaper; on double duty. Paris is dead and there is a latent threat. We go home and wait for the alarm or for anything at all. I'm regularly stopped in the streets for verification of identity: the atmosphere is charming."

Pia was drafted and was serving at Maisons-Laffitte under his real name, Pierre Durand. Camus often dined at the home of Enrico and Jeanne Terracini. Enrico, a Jewish salesman of wool and furs, was a cousin of Umberto Terracini, one of the founders of the Italian Communist Party, and Jeanne had published a book with Charlot Editions. Enrico had fled with his wife from Italy to Paris, where their apartment on the rue Condorcet in the ninth arrondissement became a center for political refugees. Jeanne did not believe that France could be defeated, but Camus urged the couple to leave Paris at once: "Go away. You're going to find the Gestapo downstairs soon."

On June 10, Italy declared war on France, and the Norwegian army surrendered to the Germans. On May 22, Camus was still able to write to Francine, "As the days go on and the dangers become clearer, Paris becomes more anguished. I gave myself until June 15 to finish my work. I really must tell you that later, I wanted to try to enlist again. But things are going too fast, and I feel that I cannot sacrifice any longer my deep motivations for an occupation that is secondary in my order of values. These days, volunteers are asked to drive ambulances on the front, but these volunteers have to take care of their own material needs. I wrote to offer my services, but asked to be considered as a second-class soldier without material responsibilities. I am waiting for an answer. I know that this decision will cause you pain, but you understood me in September, and the same reasons are still valid. This war has not stopped being absurd, but one cannot retire from a game when it becomes deadly. I gave myself a time limit in order to be freer to live without restraint later, but that was my way to feel more comfortable about my status. If I am accepted, I'll finish my work in the middle of the brawl, I'm sure, just as I would have done in the silence and solitude of Paris. As soon as things are decided, I'll ask you to help me and I'll send you detailed 'instructions' about my three manuscripts."

Chapter Twenty   # Exodus

A s a solitary Paris-dweller, Camus felt closer to the French people than
to the government. On June 9, the Minister of Information, Jean
Prouvost, also the owner of *Paris-Soir*, ordered Pierre Lazareff to evac-
uate all the remaining staff to Clermont-Ferrand. Camus and other techni-
cians were told to leave Paris for Clermont. The next day, journalists,
typesetters, proofreaders, and accountants started to leave in vans and autos,
completing their evacuation on June 12. Two days later, German troops
marched down the Champs-Elysées in Paris. That day Camus the Algerian,
the man from Algiers, felt "truly French." Between two and three million
people were on the roads: civilians and military Frenchmen as well as Dutch
and Belgian refugees. They took to the roads from fear of bombings, feeling
grief and shame at the defeat which had turned into a debacle. Telephone
lines were cut, and of necessity some *Paris-Soir* drivers were mobilized by the
armed forces. On the road as well, Camus drove a car with a woman proof-
reader at his side, traveling by night to avoid bombings. The car finally made
it to the place Jaude in Clermont-Ferrand, giving off smoke and short on gas,
oil, and water. Camus's friend Daniel Lenief, who was standing nearby, saw
that as soon as the writer had stopped the car, he ran to open the trunk,
which contained a valise with the manuscript of *L'Etranger*.

Camus found Clermont-Ferrand to be "precisely the stage set for *La
Nausée*," as gray as the town of Bouville in Sartre's narrative. Yet Clermont
also had its own kind of charm, as the 150 staffers Lazareff established in the
city discovered. Camus shared a hotel room with Daniel Lenief, while the
Paris-Soir staff set to work in offices located just behind a lunatic asylum,
where a madman screamed audibly all day. Among the secretaries at work
were the young Françoise Giroud and Janine Thomasset, both of whom
would work with Camus in other circumstances later.

After ten days in Clermont, the *Paris-Soir* staff was ordered to retreat once again. On the night of June 16–17, Philippe Pétain became prime minister. Camus missed the famous June 18 radio broadcast by the exiled General Charles de Gaulle, who called for resistance, because he was on the road to Bordeaux, spending three days "amidst a crowd of refugees and defeated soldiers." He also missed a boat at Bordeaux by only a few hours which would have allowed him to "go fight elsewhere."

The Germans occupied Bordeaux, and in the journalistic maelstrom Camus realized what was happening: "Life in France is hell for the mind now," he wrote three days after the French surrender, on June 22. He was wary of postal censorship: "I have no need to tell you what I think or what it does to me," he explained to Yvonne. He believed that the *Paris-Soir* staff would "return to Paris to put out the newspaper amidst the Occupation troops."

On June 26, Jean Prouvost was suddenly named high commissioner for propaganda by the collaborationist Vichy government, and *Paris-Soir* soon contained articles about how the eighty-five-year-old Marshall Pétain had "the arteries of a man of forty." *Paris-Soir* also printed anonymous anti-Semitic articles about "heterogeneous elements" or foreign émigrés: "Let us eliminate them." Pétain arrived in Vichy on the first of July and had himself proclaimed head of the French government on the tenth. Camus saw these events as a strange parenthesis "in all this madness." Sometimes he was sure he would be "out of work," with a total savings of two thousand francs and no train or other way back to North Africa: "If there was a boat, I'd go on foot to Marseilles in ten days and get on the boat. Life here is impossible," he told Yvonne.

More than the gray atmosphere, the political climate affected him: "It isn't just ignoble Clermont-Ferrand, but the cowardice that surrounds me and is found everywhere. . . . What we are going to experience now is unbearable to think of, and I am sure that for a free man, there is no other future, apart from exile and useless revolt. Now the only moral value is courage, which is useful here for judging the puppets and chatterboxes who pretend to speak in the name of the people." Pétain talked endlessly on the radio, and Camus wrote, "I am suffocating here."

Albert and his colleagues took walks, went out drinking, and watched the youth of Auvergne celebrate with songs the feast of Saint John in the mountains. Rationing was stringently applied, but army surplus cigarettes were available—fortunately, as Camus was a heavy smoker. For meals the *Paris-Soir* staff often took potluck in the tiny room where Lenief's brother lived with two friends.

In town, Camus ran into Pierre Salama, the brother of Myriam, a classmate of his at the University of Algiers, with other cadets from the infantry school at Fontenay-le-Comte. Camus admired Salama's uniform and invited him for a drink. Salama explained that uniformed soldiers were not allowed to enter cafés. So Camus took off his jacket and said, "Put this over it, then you'll be dressed as a civilian. I won't need this jacket for much longer, any day now I'll be arrested." Camus felt that as a former Communist and an employee of Lazareff, a Jew who ran an anti-Hitler newspaper, he was perhaps listed in the Vichy police files.

On July 8, Camus wrote to Francine, repeating his obsession about escaping, "There's no more transport to North Africa. If there is soon, I could get to Marseilles on foot (there are no more trains, cars, or gasoline) and get on board. While waiting, I am sharing a fairly pleasant apartment with colleagues (if anything can be agreeable in this ignoble region). We do our own cooking and laundry, and we wait. By the time you receive this, everything will be settled one way or another: even more so because I'm told that the only means of communication with Algeria is by telegraph. That's why these letters are ridiculous, and that's also why I am very close to stopping writing them."

Camus was not at all a Pétain supporter: "Cowardice and senility, that's all we are being offered. Pro-German policies, a constitution like those of totalitarian regimes, horrible fear of a revolution that will not happen, all this as an excuse for sweet-talking enemies who will crush us anyway, and to preserve privileges which are not threatened. Terrible days are in store: famine and general unemployment along with the hate they bring, which won't be prevented by an old geezer's speeches. Military dictatorship and the censor will not keep me from saying as much as I please. We must also be aware of anti-British propaganda, which hides the worst motivations. I don't know why I am saying this, I only know that I will maintain what I believe to be true in my own universe, and as an individual I will give in to nothing. I don't need to tell you that we have lost the battle, and that those who led us in spite of ourselves to this disastrous war have further strengthened their power after this unnamable defeat."

Defeats do not only produce lucid heroes: "With one or two exceptions, there are only cowards around me. In a few weeks I've seen too many frightful things and my heart is drowned by all that. I am suffocating and I want to leave. Now I only think of Algeria, as the country I love and where those I love are living, but also as the last French soil that is still free (without that ignoble thing called Occupation) and where one can be disengaged and live as an individual. I may be wrong, but this is how I feel—with this power as well (to reassure you) which never left me, and which you know as well as I do. I kiss you, my dear. The idea seems inconceivable to me that there can still be a universe of love, of human truth, of people like you. It is perhaps their greatest crime to have mutilated so many souls. In any case, write to me and be patient if you don't hear anything from me, I will get out of here in one piece. Don't expect anything and live as we must live. I love you very much for your courage and your fidelity."

As a small comfort, Camus adopted a dog and named him Blaise Blatin, the first name after an author he revered, Blaise Pascal, who was born in Clermont-Ferrand, and the second after the rue Blatin, where *Paris-Soir* had its offices. He socialized with Rirette Maîtrejean, the former girlfriend of the leftist-wing Victor Serge. Camus had a weakness for anarchists.

He worked on his essay about the absurd, and on August 5 he wrote to Francine, who was still in Algeria: "I have nothing to tell you, nothing to reply to your letters. I have no desire to speak about myself or about anything else. Only this: *Paris-Soir* asked me to work a little longer, until August 15. After then, I'll be available. . . . I'm going to be obliged to give up my profession. There is a 'statute' being prepared for journalists that I have the misfortune to consider dishonorable or nearly so. What's more, all the Jews are being thrown out of our office, even those who have returned from fighting the war. So I am going to choose another profession. . . . I want you to arrange a job for me as soon as possible (farm or commerce or no matter what). Above all I want you to ask Pierre [Galindo] if he'd like to share something with me. I think you can get land with easy payments for official concessions now. As he is on the spot, he can see about it. I'm not afraid of working a lot, if it is a free job, and I want to do it with Pierre more than anyone else. That's all. But time is wasting and I'd like you to think about it seriously. I'm well and I kiss you."

On September 6, Camus wrote to Claude de Fréminville: "Unemployment is widespread and *Paris-Soir* in particular has fired half its personnel. They still need me, but it may only be a question of time." When he went to Lyons, Camus looked for a job for Claude, who was hoping to come to France: "If you could be an editorial secretary, it's a profession which has remained clean and pays well." As Camus acquired political certainties, he put some order in his private life, choosing Francine and leaving Yvonne, at least by letter. With Yvonne he assumed a paternal tone as he often did when he was breaking up: "Farewell, my little girl. You seem to be very far away and I haven't felt as helpless in years, but all that is my own fault. I want, I really want to leave everything and to forget everything." He nearly pushed Yvonne to make the decision instead of him: "I don't want you to answer this." But he concluded by seeming to deny what he had just written: "Just try not to forget me."

When he arrived at Lyons, Camus's divorce from Simone Hié was finally pronounced. He had promised to marry Francine as soon as he got a divorce. He caught up with his friends and acquaintances. Some, like Max Beral, a Communist friend from Algiers, had been killed. Pascal Pia arrived at Clermont after crossing France on foot. Pia was part of a troop forgotten in a forest in the Paris region and had not been taken prisoner. When he got to Paris, Pia tried to claim Camus's suitcases at the Hôtel Madison, but observing policemen and German soldiers in the vicinity, he left.

Camus abandoned the idea of having his two works that were nearly finished, his play and his novel, published: "I understood . . . that what I wrote still needed a lot of time to become valid. Besides, I don't plan to publish anything in France for many years, apart from praise of the family." Camus was ridiculing the Pétain government's obsession with "family values." The writer felt hesitations and doubt: "I have no joy, not even that of writing. Maybe it would be better to abandon everything."

At the beginning of October, *before* there was any German pressure on the matter, the French government at Vichy announced new racial laws against the Jews, which among other things abolished the Crémieux decree, which accorded French nationality to Algerian Jews. On October 23, Camus wrote to Irène Dijan, who was Jewish: "All this is particularly unfair and particularly abject, but I want you to know that the thing is not looked upon with indifference by those not directly involved. In other words, this is the time to show solidarity with you, and I insist on participating in that solidarity. This is what I am saying; and what I will say each time it is necessary: Let the wind pass, it cannot last, it will not last if each one of us in his place just calmly affirms that this wind smells bad." He also wrote to Liliane Choucroun, another Jewish friend he had known at the University of Algiers, to assure her of his support. A teacher by profession, Choucroun no longer had the right to work after the new laws were passed.

Pierre Lazareff also lost his French citizenship, and left for the United States. Hervé Mille took over the direction of *Paris-Soir* in Lyons, where many Parisian journalists had settled. Among the *Paris-Soir* staffers, the former surrealist Roger Vailland was fascinated by the Vichy minister Pierre Laval, but Pia and Camus were very hostile to the Vichy ideology and could not stand Laval's tirades about morality or the soil. Pia had reclaimed his job as editorial secretary and worked in Lyons.

Camus showed *Caligula* to Pia, who was enthusiastic about the play. The two friends thought about publishing a magazine, to be called *Prométhée*, and got a number of literary personalities interested in the project, including the eminent Gallimard editor Jean Paulhan, the philosopher Bernard Groethuysen, the poet and novelist Raymond Queneau, and André Malraux too. The plan was that Malraux's half-brother Roland would collect the texts in Paris and get them taken to the free zone in the south for printing.

In Lyons, food was even scarcer than in Clermont-Ferrand, and the black market flourished. Camus worked at the newspaper and in a modest hotel room in a former brothel, where the décor amused him, especially a ground-floor salon decorated with images of naked women. His room was cold, and no one swept up the abundant snow in the street. Camus had never found Lyons very welcoming at the best of times, and *Paris-Soir* had become a vehicle of Pétainist propaganda, although not as ignoble as Paris newspapers like *L'Oeuvre*, run by Marcel Déat.

Because Camus had promised to marry Francine, she joined him in Lyons at the end of November. He was not at the train station to meet her, as he had mixed up the train schedule. They got married on December 3, exchanging copper wedding rings. Witnesses at the town hall were Pia, Lenief, and friends from the newspaper. There was no religious ceremony, nor was there a wedding meal, just a celebratory drink afterwards.

In Lyons, as in Paris and Algiers, Camus liked the printing plant, with its comradeship and its smell of damp paper, lead, and ink. The typographers were an elite group of workers, often cultivated, with anarchist sympathies. Camus participated joyfully at parties known as "allas," where people drank to their friends' health, singing trade or military songs. Camus worked the night shift, and returned to the hotel between 2 a.m. and 5 a.m.

The couple had no typewriter in their room, and when *Le Mythe de Sisyphe* was finished, Francine copied it over by hand. Camus planned to cut the text, which began with the line: "There is only one serious philosophical problem, which is suicide." The book ended by observing "this hideous and distressing world where even moles get involved in hoping."

The planned trilogy was finished: a play, a novel, and an essay. Edmond Charlot invited Camus to publish them with his press, and although the writer was tempted, he did not accept the offer, no doubt still hoping for publication in Paris. On December 12, he wrote to Claude de Fréminville, who was still in Algeria, advising him to write a book "to be published in two or three years. . . . Leave everything else aside and maybe you will observe again that Oran is a great city and a livable place. I have always believed that you have talent, and there is no reason why I should be mistaken. But at this time, one must have the strength to turn away and to accept it all as a means of isolating oneself."

He added, "I will soon have finished what I see as 'the first stone,' and I'll know soon enough if it's bad. In that case, I'll abandon everything, but without anger, I believe. You can't reach a man's age (which is ours now) without frightful heartbreaks, but that has so little interest for others, and basically it is of no importance. Thus one may lose what made one's strength, and no one would know." Having finished three major works in less than five years, Camus expected to be neither published nor recognized. He tried to cheer up Fréminville, explaining to him that it was wrong to live in isolation and advising him to see Camus's own friends in Oran, above all his women friends. And Fréminville should see Pierre Galindo, "one of the only men for whom I feel complete friendship, but you'll have to win him over." Camus had been married for nine days with Francine, and concluded: "I've done lots of foolish things for some time, and foolish things do not result in happiness either for others or for myself. But you know that I remain faithful to my friends and especially to you, which is the only luxury today."

Cramped in their hotel room, the Camuses looked for an apartment with Pia's help. They did not have time to move before Camus was a victim of a new staff reduction at *Paris-Soir*. One solution was to leave for Oran, where the couple would not need to pay any rent.

So in January 1941, the Camuses boarded the ship *President-Dal-Piaz* at Marseilles, heading home.

Chapter Twenty-one **Stopover at Oran**

In Oran, the Audóeud galleries ran along the rue d'Arzew, offering cafés, stores, and two cinemas. The Camuses moved into an apartment at number 67 of the rue d'Arzew, an apartment previously occupied by Christiane, who went to live with her mother at 65 rue d'Arzew. The apartment had balconies and over one hundred square meters of surface area, with a living room, two bedrooms, a bathroom, a kitchen, and on each side of a laundry area, two terraces made of dark tiles. On a mantelpiece Albert put a little gilded wood Buddha which he had kept since the breakup with Simone.

The Faures gave Albert a warm welcome, pleased that this man who had rebelled against marriage for so long had finally wed Francine. But at age twenty-seven, he did not have a job. Often somber, he rarely opened his mouth. He found his mother-in-law authoritarian, which in fact she was. Francine's family seemed very bourgeois compared with Camus's own humble background, but not when matched with other Oran dynasties.

Sometimes Camus was needlessly aggressive, such as the time Madame Faure asked him to give her "best regards to Madame Camus." Albert cut her off, saying curtly: "There is no *Madame* Camus." The Faure dining room had linen tablecloths, while the Camuses had always used oilcloth. Albert would put on working-class manners just to irritate "the colonel's wife," as he called her: during one meal, he made a point of conspicuously placing a wine bottle on the floor beside his chair. But he did get along with Christiane, who admired him, as she would have liked to be a writer.

Francine worked as a substitute teacher and her mother, Fernande, was still employed at the post office. The Faures were not considered Jews, because only one grandmother of the family, Clara Touboul, was Jewish, and the girls were baptized.

Edmond Charlot wrote from Algiers, insisting that Camus join him there, but he could not guarantee a decent salary. So Camus stayed on in Oran.

Basic food necessities were expensive and even rarer than in mainland France—there were shortages of everything, from oil and sugar to meat and milk. Camus saw a lot of Pierre Galindo, who was demobilized. In the evenings, they would go back to their favorite cafés, where they drank muscat. Saturdays they went to hear flamenco music, and they also shared a passion for soccer.

Camus had a faithful group of friends in Oran and in Algiers, where he often went. They had the same political opinions as he did, and they moved naturally from sheltering Spanish Republicans to rejecting Vichy ideology. Camus said he was ready to take any job, even as an antiques vendor or truck farmer. He dreamed of a farm which he might cultivate with Pierre Galindo and Julio Davila, a friend from Oran, who was now married to Christiane Galindo. Camus spoke about painting to Francine's cousin Robert Martin, the owner of a bookshop-gallery, and he became close to the Bénichous, a family of brilliant Jewish intellectuals. Starting from humble origins, Paul Bénichou had graduated from Paris's prestigious Ecole Normale Supérieure, while André Bénichou, who was closer to Camus and his senior by three years, loved Baudelaire and Rimbaud and had a particular passion for Proust. André had suffered from an episode of pleurisy, which led Camus to speak of "we consumptives." André's wife, Mado, was a friend of Francine's. Albert did not like to show his unpublished work, but he lent the manuscript of *L'Etranger* to André, who read it in a single night. To André, Camus was a great writer.

Vichy's politics rekindled anti-Semitism in Algeria. André Bénichou was fired from his job as lycée teacher. On his passport, the words "French citizen" were replaced by "native Jew." When the Crémieux decree was abolished, 111,021 Algerian Jews lost their French citizenship, and Admiral Abrial, the anti-Semitic governor general of Algeria, placed machine guns around the principal cities in case the Jews decided to demonstrate. Quotas were established for Jewish students in public schools; first it was fourteen percent of the total enrollment, then seven percent. Unlike French Jews, Algerian Jews were not deported to concentration camps or obliged to wear a yellow star, but they were persecuted nonetheless. André Bénichou, like other Jewish teachers suddenly unemployed, applied for authorization to give private courses, and despite his record as a Communist free-thinker, this permission was tentatively granted. The vast majority of Europeans in Algeria supported Marshal Pétain, and when Fernande Faure joined a Gaullist strike at the post office for a few minutes, she was suspended from her job for two months: Camus's mother-in-law had guts.

The Camus and Faure families took up a collection to help a penniless Jewish friend, Louis Bénisti, who no longer had the right to teach drawing, which was his profession. The Camuses put Bénisti up for a few days while Fernande gave shelter to Nicola Chiaramonte, a writer and remarkable thinker who was a friend of Malraux's and a former tailgunner of his air squadron in Spain.

Seeing well-informed travelers like Chiaramonte, Camus and his friends began to think that they might be able to "do something." Refugees were arriving from France, hoping to leave for Morocco, England, or America. Chiaramonte left for New York as residents of Oran and Algiers asked themselves how they might fight the Vichy government and the Germans. Camus knew that even if he escaped to England, he would not be accepted in the French Freedom Fighters based there—unlike Edgar Bensoussan, who was now an aviator—because of his lung condition. Still, Camus and his circle prepared for action. Algerian Communists had been publishing clandestinely the journal *La Lutte Sociale* since November 1940, but the Communist Party had little influence. A network of Resistance formed in Algeria, at first intellectual and then active. Many Jews were involved in the group, whose primary goal was to defend youngsters who were prevented from studying at the University of Algiers. Camus spoke with Louis Bénisti about organizing "something."

Among the cultured milieu of the opposition to Vichy, Camus had a rival in Jean-Paul de Dadelsen, a young teacher of German and a gifted poet. Dadelsen was a handsome man who wore yellow gloves and kissed ladies' hands. Laughingly he told Camus, "I'll be the twentieth century's greatest poet, and you, its greatest prose writer."

Camus circulated freely between Oran and Algiers. Sometimes Francine, who had less free time than her husband, would accompany him to meet with her friends from the Théâtre de l'Equipe. The former theater members thought of staging a production of Chekhov's *Ivanov*, whose plot, about a ruined landowner who becomes anti-Semitic and kills himself after learning the futility and absurdity of existence, seemed timely. Francine also studied roles like Elvire in Molière's *Don Juan* and Ophelia in *Hamlet*, but all the theatrical projects were stillborn.

The painter Sauveur Galliero came through Oran, and Robert Martin organized a show of Galliero's work at his bookshop-gallery. Camus lent Sauveur money and refused to be paid back, explaining, "I owe you a lot." Sauveur had not yet read *L'Etranger* and did not know that Meursault was partly based on him.

At school, the remaining teachers, including Francine, were obliged to be present eight hours each day. Camus would wander around their apartment through "long empty days." He had forgotten how to take a vacation and wanted to divide his time between Oran and Algiers, where he met Yvonne. He would also see his mother and Yvonne's sister at Trouville, near Oran, but everything seemed futile in Oran, as he wrote to Yvonne in January 1941: "I am suffocating here. I am unhappy and I've decided to leave. I don't love anything or anybody and I finally said so to Francine." As an actor, Camus overdramatized things from time to time: "So now, I am only left with dead things, which I don't care if I perpetuate or not. I'll do what is expected of me." On February 21, 1941, he noted in the *Carnets* with dry precision, "Finished *Sisyphe*. The three absurd works are done. Beginning of freedom."

He asked Yvonne to write him, to send a telegram or write care of general delivery. One day, with luck, they would buy tickets "for the end of the world." He claimed that he was trying in vain to work, when he was in fact putting the final touches on his corrected versions of the absurd works. He always confided more to his correspondents than to his *Carnets*, as another letter to Yvonne from February proves: "Until now, I have always known what I wanted to do with my life, and I always did what was needed. Now I have the impression that I am losing the match. I feel myself nibbled away, put under a glass cover, annexed bit by bit. It's as if I were dispossessed of my own life, simply by lassitude, as if I had given up in a boxing match." Camus and Pierre Galindo were boxing fans and would often go to the Gallia stadium to watch the European champion Marcel Cerdan fight. Camus continued, "Every day I am astonished not to see a reaction appear that I know well in myself. That's when I'm astonished to see that I am passively waiting to be helped by events." If Yvonne were at his side, he would no longer have the "withering impression" of being alone and opposed by those around him.

He did not understand the obscure, secret tie that attached Yvonne to himself. He met one of Yvonne's friends, Marica Toubiana, who was charming but "tremendously married." Marica claimed that Camus wasn't an intellectual at all. Albert looked up from his meal of sardines washed down with Cinzano and replied that he absolutely was an intellectual, and managed to be so quite cheerfully.

He used his *Carnets* to analyze his ties with Francine, Yvonne, and women in general: "What does a heart control itself by? By loving? Highly doubtful. We know what it is to suffer from love, but we don't know what love is. . . . Here [love] is privation, regret, and empty hands. I won't have its explosion, but its anguish stays with me. Hell, which everyone believes is Paradise, is hell nonetheless. What drains me, I call life and love. Departure, constraint, breaking up this dark heart scattered inside me, the salty taste of tears and love." He resolved "to renounce that servitude which is attraction to women." In his desire to change his path, Camus uttered nonsense: "If I had given in to my deep inclination, I would now be a civil servant working eight hours a day and I'd try to believe it was very good. Now maybe this isn't any better, but I always did try. Maybe also one day, I'll have had enough of making efforts. Turning away from everything must be a kind of disgusting peacefulness."

Camus was concerned about his health and his relationship with Yvonne, as he explained to her: "Nothing is more ignoble than illness. Here again the temptation to abandon oneself is too great. . . . Maybe in fact it isn't a passion that [you and I] share, but if I try to see things as they are, without sudden crazes and high fevers, I must admit that I'm not looking for anything more than this. Of course I cannot deny that at this moment I think of you as something which is not in my present life. . . . It's a perspective that rather lacks grandeur."

Camus spent much time with friends, especially Pierre Galindo. Uncouth, rough, but not brutal, Pierre was "the only person here whom I would be happy to live with," Camus said. He would take walks to enjoy the countryside around the city, which had no cultural life, according to him. His irritation at the Faure home was often transformed into hatred for the city, and he would take trips outside Oran, alone or with friends: "Yesterday, I spent the day at Trouville. It was very fine weather with a strong cold wind on the plateau. There was lots of clover and very fragile autumn crocuses. I spent a fine day doing nothing. I met a large dog, half Alsatian, half Kabyle, which moved like an injection into a culture medium, so I called him Proto (as in Protozoa). He stayed with me all day, and I was happy to have him. There are times when the only companions I feel good with are animals, especially dogs. I wanted to take him with me, but the buses won't carry him. He accompanied me and when the bus started, he looked at me with generous eyes. I hope I find him again."

Camus took in many dogs in his life, Kirk at the Fichu House in Algiers, where he lived in 1936, Blaise Blatin in Clermont-Ferrand, and Proto. In 1940, Camus would return to Trouville, but he lost Proto in Oran.

He became accustomed to the luminous regions around Oran: "It seemed years since I left this kind of country, and I found it again as if it were new." He liked to walk until he was quite exhausted, so that after a shower he felt half happy and half asleep. By the beginning of April, Camus was resigned to staying in the city, and therefore with Francine. He took the step backward of giving private lessons, as in the days when Madame Sogler paid his rent. He was almost twenty-eight years old, and the Faures were giving him free housing.

Francine earned a salary, but he was like a superannuated student. His royalties from Charlot Editions were meager, and Camus did not know if his three absurds would be published. Edmond Brua sent him his latest book, a parody of Corneille's *Le Cid* in Algerian dialect. Camus wanted to write about it, as he once had written about the humorous *Fables bônoises* in *Alger Républicain*; but times had changed, and no one in Algeria would print an article by Camus.

André Bénichou asked him to give French classes at his school, which was later called Le Cours Descartes. Camus was a big success with the girls and boys—he was a star, and his students knew it. The students admired his way of bending his head, and his tone of voice. Camus was able to survive on what Bénichou paid him, along with what he earned at another school, Les Etudes Françaises, where he taught French, history, geography, and philosophy as well as coached the soccer team.

Almost everyone at the two rue d'Arzew apartments taught: Francine; her sister Christiane, who worked at a girls' lycée and also gave private lessons to Jewish students preparing for the baccalaureate examination (they were no longer permitted to attend public schools); Francine's sister Suzy taught at yet another school for Jewish pupils.

When not working, Camus had his favorite spots in Oran which he would visit ritually, like the place d'Armes with its immense, rough fig trees, and the boulevard Séguin, filled with people strolling about, even early in the morning. He would visit the Spanish neighborhood, La Calère; the colorful Jewish quarter; and the swarming Moslem Village Nègre, with its cafés full of men drinking tea, wearing a mint leaf over their ears. There was the Promenade de l'Etang, with its lovely terraces over the port, at the foot of the Spanish fortifications. Here Camus found the light and warmth of Africa.

Camus had a soft spot for the beaches of the Oran region. Both real and mythic, his Algeria was sea, sun, and beaches. Oran's beaches were a trial of patience to get to, located far from the city center. Since gas was rationed and buses rare and overcrowded, Camus and his friends went there by bicycle. The Camuses preferred the beaches to the west of the city, in little seaside resorts.

After the narrow beach of Bouisseville, where Meursault met his fate in *L'Etranger*, and after Mers el-Kebir, they would arrive in Aïn-El-Türck. There they would refresh themselves with an iced lemonade called *agua limón*. Then the group would pedal out to the dunes, which were covered with reeds. Often the friends would set up camp and sometimes walk around naked, surprising an occasional fishermen. Albert would sunbathe with his eyes closed and arms in cruciform position, though his friends were concerned that with his fragile lungs, too much sun would be dangerous. Everyone would sing rounds, or old folksongs like the English "Greensleeves." When they were hungry, the campers would steal melons from a farmer's field. On one such trip, Camus told André Belamich about a crime he had read of in the newspaper: an exiled man returned home, but his mother and sister did not recognize him, and they slit his throat. Camus would refer to this story in later work.

At Oran, Camus was like two separate people: in public he seemed joyful and accustomed to the city; his private side was secretive and anxious, confessing to friends that he was depressed: "The return to Oran, considering the conditions of my life here, is not a step forward." He wrote to Lucette Meurer, Yvonne's friend, "I would like to see (in the simplest meaning of that word) Y. here, if she wants to." He went back to his work: "My life is based on the idea that I have something to say and that I will be freed from everything when I have said it."

When he finished the three absurd works, he had conquered freedom, but he had to conquer it all over again, because he was thinking of a new book. "I am exasperated with Oran and with everything. If I had enough money, I would go away for a few days to live alone on a mountain or a deserted beach." In June, he spent eight days camping on beaches behind Cap-Falcon: "Things are going as badly as possible for me." He asked Lucette to sell the few pieces of furniture and other objects he owned in Algiers because he needed money. He also tried to recover numerous books he had lent to friends, with uneven success.

The publisher Edmond Charlot wrote to Lucette that "the rumor is running around insistently" that Camus planned to return to Algiers. Albert replied to Lucette: "This diplomatic phrase is flattering, but untrue. Tell the rumors to stop running." He did not even have the thousand francs for the fare to Algiers during his two weeks of vacation at the beginning of July. Thanks to André Bénichou, Camus was able to earn some money by teaching philosophy classes all summer long.

Albert was haunted by Yvonne, and being caught between her and Francine was heartbreaking. He told Yvonne in the middle of summer: "Even if I'm wrong and you are suffering, what do you care about the rest of it? I see nothing vulgar in this situation, because neither you nor I has put anything vulgar into it. If someone had judged it as such, we would have known that it wasn't. We still know it now. We also know that nothing has been spoiled or compromised. It will never be absurd for you to write me, never absurd for you to come to me, to call me, to lean your face toward me." Yet Albert offered contradictory feelings to her: "Of course I never told you to wait for me. . . . I have no one certain emotion coming from you."

Camus's idea of fidelity was not the usual one. "Right or wrong, I have an assurance that you should have too, that of a singular fidelity, above all the rest and above ourselves, thanks to which we can always meet again. That's what I'm asking you for, if you can't give me the rest. That's what I'm offering you too, because today that's all I have." He was sure that he would find her again: "I know it, even against my own will. That's a fact which is an occasion for neither sadness nor joy."

He went camping for a week with Yvonne, accompanied by Christiane Galindo Davila and two little boys, and these free, happy days were a substitute for the voyages he dreamed about. The Faure family was not pleased, and Camus sent Yvonne a note to break up their relationship: "I will not see you anymore. . . . Excuse me for everything which is absurd in all this. I am unhappy and I love you, but even that is in vain."

In October 1941, Charlot offered him a job in Algiers paying two thousand francs a month, which was not enough for Camus, who saw himself as tied down to Oran: "I feel that in two months I will be a complete Oran dweller." He was in shape, playing center-forward at soccer games: "At the last practice I dislocated my wrist." Pierre Galindo remarked, "That's what you get for trying to act like a young man." But Camus scored the goal anyway.

Apart from the emotional problems he was going through, he may have needed Oran for the book he was thinking of. He asked Lucette to borrow "books about the plague (medical ones) from the university libraries in Algiers," wanting them "as soon as possible." He added other titles to be borrowed along with "the plague books." He also asked the writer Emmanuel Roblès for books about the plague.

Camus encouraged the former members of the Théâtre de L'Equipe to start rehearsing again, but it would be a bad time to stage Charles Péguy's *Jeanne d'Arc*, because the subject might be seen as a bow to the Pétainist cult of patriotism and religious purity: "That would mean following a little too closely the customs of the present day, but everyone knows I am very difficult about these subjects." He decided to move to Algiers at Christmastime, if Charlot could pay a little bit more.

Camus felt drained: "I write as badly as a secretary of state and I haven't much to say." Yet he had embarked on a novel.

Chapter Twenty-two **An Important Thing**

On March 2, 1941, Pascal Pia had written to Camus from Lyons, thanking him for a gift package of dates and nougats and mentioning that a job might be available as an assistant editor at *Paris-Soir*. Pia knew that neither Lyons nor *Paris-Soir* enchanted Camus, but his presence would permit them to resurrect their project of a literary review, *Prométhée*. Pia planned to run it so that even if he could not publish what he called "clinically pure literature," it would have "an orientation that was neither that of Vichy nor of the German Kommandantur." In his typical sardonic style, Pia asked Camus to write for the magazine: "If you weren't an arrant champion of laziness and a well-known good-for-nothing, you'd take an informed stance and say the necessary things. Like what? ... I easily see you writing about Spinoza, or the Palatine Elector, or about Pierre Bayle writing his *Dictionary* in Holland." He knew that Camus was living in poverty and tried to find him a job at a sports weekly. Pia ridiculed the first issue of the "zero" new *Nouvelle Revue Française*, run by the self-declared Nazi Pierre Drieu La Rochelle. In the *NRF*, the novelist Henry de Montherlant, fascinated by power, described an order of chivalry that he wanted to create with other "chosen beings." Camus then distanced himself from Montherlant.

In the first issues of the *NRF* during the Occupation, there were articles by the Fascist Ramon Fernandez and pro-German Frenchmen but also by eminent names such as Paul Valéry, Paul Eluard, and André Gide. Malraux refused to contribute, declaring so publicly in order to contradict Drieu La Rochelle's claim that he would. Malraux's stance influenced Gide, who also decided to avoid appearing in the *NRF*. Jean Paulhan, who had been active in the Resistance from the beginning, continued to work for Gallimard while risking his life. Some saw Paulhan as warped, but others acknowledged that he was a gifted strategist. He held to the principle that the *NRF*, which the Germans had first shut down and then started up again, was a shield for Gallimard. Paulhan agreed in a subtly manipulative way that Drieu should control the *NRF*, and encouraged the collaborationist writer Marcel Jouhandeau to contribute to it, while at the same time discouraging Raymond Queneau and Malraux. Paulhan secretly wrote articles in the clandestine publication *Résistance*, which denounced the same *NRF* for which he worked at Gallimard.

Pia was worried about why Camus hesitated to take the eleven-hour train ride from Oran to Algiers: "Usually, you are more fearless." He impatiently awaited the promised three manuscripts and told Camus not to forget to send them with return receipt requested. He would be delighted to reread *Caligula* and to see *L'Etranger* at last. Pia was confident about the work's quality, for he proposed publishing it in serial form, starting with the first issue of *Prométhée*. François Mauriac and Paul Valéry had agreed to contribute to the new magazine, because as Academicians they could not be muzzled by their fellow Academy member Marshal Pétain. As for possible work at *Paris-Soir*, Pia informed Camus that "pederasts" in the office were favoring their boyfriends in office matters. Sensing Albert's distress, he wrote him nearly every week.

The main difficulty in producing their magazine was to find a stock of paper, not to find a printer. Pia asked Camus's advice about other potential contributors, from Gertrude Stein to Blanche Reverchon, the wife of the poet Pierre Jean Jouve. Pia joked that a man like Camus, "who lunches with Kierkegaard, dines with Heidegger, and sups with Husserl," should have some ideas. Camus suggested that the magazine be called something else, such as *The Red and the Black*, *The Royal Path*, *Dawn*, or *The Gay Science*.

Finally, Pia received the manuscripts of *L'Etranger* and *Caligula* on April 10, 1941, and Camus sent copies to Jean Grenier as well. The latter responded with a professorial letter containing mixed reactions: "I read your manuscripts. *L'Etranger* is very successful, especially the second part, despite the troubling influence of Kafka. The pages about prison are unforgettable. The first [part] is very interesting." Yet Grenier had some complaints about episodic characters, "like the man with the dog, the warehouseman, and especially Marie, who is very touching. By a certain lack of unity and sentences that are too short, the style itself becomes part of the argument. . . . But the impression is often intense." But Grenier did not like Camus's play: "The romantic Caligula in the first act, in the style of Jules Laforgue, does not please me. Love's despair, twilight, women's breasts (which are a Freudian obsession in both your manuscripts)—isn't it all a little bit insipid and false? Perhaps in the theater it will seem different."

A week later, Pia sent a more perspicacious letter: "Very sincerely, it has been a long time since I have read something of this quality. I am convinced that sooner or later *L'Etranger* will find its place, which is among the best. The second part—the pretrial investigations, the trial, the prison—is a demonstration of the absurd put together like a perfect mechanism. Yet nothing betrays the construction, and the last fifteen pages are admirable." Pia felt that *L'Etranger* contained passages on the level of Kafka or Rudolf Kassner; and although he had not yet read *Le Mythe de Sisyphe*, he made connections between Camus's ethics and *L'Etranger* and *Caligula*: "For anyone who knows that you studied the absurd from a philosophical point of view, the path you followed is clear. Unfortunately, it is rare that studying at universities like the Sorbonne results in a great book. Generally, their consequences do not go beyond the *Review of Metaphysics and Moral Sciences*. . . . I frankly admire the mastery which allows you at the same time to describe Meursault's crime and to create Caligula's wild monologue."

Reading *L'Etranger*, Pia was struck by the "constant aptness of tone and . . . the clearness of images, such as when you speak of tears and sweat on old Perez's face: 'they spread out and rejoined and formed a varnish of water on the ruined face.' Incidentally, this is only a detail, but not a negligible one, for generally 'moralists,' with the possible exception of Malraux, have prose styles that are stripped down to bareness (cf. Vauvenargues, Sade, Benjamin Constant) or, on the other hand, are drowned in flowers, like the pre–First World War André Gide." He also liked the new version of *Caligula* very much, with a new act added by Camus: "I have a feeling that Caligula speaks more in it and thus he seems more 'delirious.' It seems to me that in the first version, during the first two acts, the spectator could ask himself whether [Caligula] was a hoax or a possessed man, whereas in the second version there is no more doubt."

Pia resourcefully found money and paper, but *Prométhée* did not receive the necessary authorization to be published. Never easily discouraged in his projects, he decided to publish his magazine in America. His other project was to get Camus published. He gave the two manuscripts to Roland Malraux, who brought them to his half-brother André in Cap-d'Ail in the south of France. Pia spoke to Paulhan about *L'Etranger* and *Caligula*, and Paulhan too wanted to see them. Pia had no doubt that Gaston Gallimard would publish them, and he told the powerful Paulhan that Camus wanted the three absurd works to appear at the same time. Since Gallimard often traveled between Cannes and Paris, he could see Malraux, whose opinion would count. Therefore, if Camus hurried up with the typing of *Le Mythe de Sisyphe*, it was likely that Gallimard would not want to see "an unpublished writer of talent get away from him."

In May, Camus answered Jean Grenier with respect, but resolutely: "I am happy that you found some good things in *L'Etranger*. I get the feeling that you nevertheless do not really like what I sent you." Camus expressed his regrets: "This makes me a little uncertain . . . but I wouldn't hesitate to continue everything I started. . . . I will continue to work. My manuscript on the absurd is not yet typed. It won't be for another month." Before it was typed, he asked to see Grenier's essay on the absolute and sent along a package of dates and figs as a present. Grenier felt that Camus had misunderstood him, and he replied to his former student: "I thought I wrote you that your two manuscripts were very successful. . . . *L'Etranger* is excellent." Camus kept his distance from Grenier's comments: "Your criticisms did not touch me. I just found them useful and usable." He did not really use them much.

In late May 1941, Pia continued indefatigably to look for jobs for Camus. He noted that there were jobs for a few hundred woodcutters near Lyons, and maybe Albert could work as a forestry agent. This job included lodgings, with utilities paid, use of an office and telephone, as well as 2,500 francs a month. Or Camus could be an "independent contributor" to a provincial newspaper, *Le Petit Dauphinois*, based in the Vienne region near Lyons. Pia made great efforts to find "an acceptable job in a healthy climate" for his friend.

Finally, André Malraux, Camus's hero, had read his manuscripts. Pia reported: "It is clear that your manuscripts have shaken him up. It's always like that with the manuscripts he loves. He thinks about them for a long time, then he thinks about them some more, and he suggests some formal corrections." Pia then recopied Malraux's letter to him, sure that Malraux would want Camus to see it.

Malraux, who could be capable of prideful, vague flights of fancy, was simple and clear-sighted here: "I have just finished Camus's manuscripts It's quite annoying that I'm not going to Lyons, because it surely is more serious to speak about things in person than by letters or other abridged means. I read *L'Etranger* first. Its theme is very clear. . . . To sum up, I think *Caligula* should be left in a drawer until *L'Etranger* or something else has familiarized the public with Camus's work. We'll speak some more about this if you like. *L'Etranger* is obviously an important thing. The power and simplicity of the means which finally force the reader to accept his character's point of view are all the more remarkable in that the book's destiny depends on whether this character is convincing or not. And what Camus has to say while convincing us is not negligible."

Malraux lined up his technical criticisms neatly:

1. The sentences are a bit too systematically made up of subject, verb, complement, period. Sometimes it becomes a formula. Very easy to fix, by sometimes changing the punctuation.

2. There would be advantages to working further on the scene with the chaplain, which isn't clear. What is said is clear,

but what Camus wants to say is said only partially. And the scene is important. I know that it's very difficult . . .

3. Same comment for the murder scene. It's good, but not as convincing, to use that word again, as the book as a whole. Perhaps he simply has to try harder, with one paragraph more about the link between the sun and the Arab's knife.

4. For everything that has to do with the sea, tighten all the accents, which are necessary and good there, but there is cotton filler between them.

I am not trying to tell you intelligent things, nor the penetrating kind of thing, I am trying to tell you useful things, which seems a bit like a student supervisor. Too bad. As for the essential questioning which Camus sought, tell him not to worry: it's there.

Pia told Camus that if he so wished, Malraux would pass the manuscript of *L'Etranger* to Roger Martin du Gard, who was also a refugee in the south of France, and full of good advice. They could also give it to Gaston Gallimard. Pia sent Albert his own comments on Malraux's comments:

1. [Malraux's] objection to *Caligula* would fall apart on its own if Gallimard or another publisher accepted your three manuscripts at the same time.

2. The dryness of sentences did not bother me. But I believe that the only valid stylistic objection one can make to an author is when his style is wrong, which is not the case here. The rest is a matter of taste, and thus a personal matter.

3. I noted that you had not exhausted your subject in the chaplain's scene. I don't believe the subject can be exhausted here, and you cannot unbalance the book under the pretext of inserting everything that it implies. *L'Etranger* makes us want to see other works by the same author? Fine. There aren't that many works you can say the same for.

Pia reported that Malraux felt that publishers would "certainly make a comparison with Sartre because of the scenery. The only thing to do about that is not to give a fuck. Camus can be pleased with his book." Pia had answered Malraux, "I agree with you about the advantages he would find in redoing ever so slightly the murder scene. Like you, I had the impression that the murder was carried out too quickly by the author to be convincing to the reader. On reflection, however, we might accept the murderer's tale as it is, since the protagonist is not tormented by worry about being convincing. In fact, why should we demand more of the novelist than we do of the novel? . . . As for the final scene, agreed: Camus said only partially what he had to say. But is it possible to insert what he implied without unbalancing the book? Honestly, I don't think so."

Camus responded to Pia: "Malraux is not a man to speak in order to say nothing. I . . . therefore take his criticisms as proof of his approval of what I've done. . . . His other criticisms are fair: the first chapter was written a year before the others, in Paris. No doubt it has to be rewritten. If the 'formula' in the style is noticeable, then it must be rewritten. Naturally, I sought for dryness in the exposition (I entirely fabricated the long style), but caricature must be avoided in every kind of aesthetic." Camus went back to the murder scene, but had trouble seeing the "mistake."

Pia announced in a May 1941 letter that *L'Etranger* had been accepted in advance by Gaston Gallimard, based on the recommendations by Malraux and Paulhan. The only suspense was whether the three books would be published simultaneously, as all the editors had not yet read them.

In his game of publishing billiards, Pia played with Malraux, Martin du Gard, and Paulhan to push Gallimard to publish all three manuscripts. He also lent a copy of *L'Etranger* to other writers, such as the poet Francis Ponge. Pia received *Le Mythe de Sisyphe*, which Camus inscribed to him, "The little that I could do for you did not merit such a reward."

At Oran, Camus went swimming and bicycle riding, but refused to ride a tandem bicycle with Francine, because he found it ridiculous. In July, Grenier, who had finally received *Le Mythe de Sisyphe*, adjusted his opinions on the trilogy: "I am still holding on to your essay, which I want to reread. It seems to me absolutely remarkable, of the first order, with no comparison to what you have done previously. There are admirable pages of clearness and virile resolution. The novel and play illustrate that well, in addition. Yes, it's really remarkable. Thanks for having entrusted it to me."

Pia also sent *Le Mythe de Sisyphe* to Malraux, who wrote directly to Camus in October, as he finally had his address: "The link between *Sisyphe* and *L'Etranger* has many more consequences than I supposed. The essay gives the other book its full meaning and, above all, changes what in the novel first seemed monotonous and impoverished into a positive austerity, with primitive force." As he believed that Camus's books illuminated one another, Malraux would see Gaston Gallimard and try to arrange for him to publish the books "one on top of the other." Malraux was aware of his own influence: "At other times, I could be sure of making up his mind, and he is far from being impervious to good reasoning. The problem of paper being scarce remains."

Malraux added: "I am leaving out details: the beginning trudges a bit.

Because you are using the light that comes from suicide, there's no point in dwelling on it too much, once it's been pointed out." He firmly envisaged the nearly simultaneous publication of L'Etranger and Le Mythe de Sisyphe: "What matters is that with these two books together, you take your place among the writers who exist, who have a voice, and who will soon have an audience and a presence. There are not that many." Malraux knew he was judging works by a young author: "Afterwards, their own story begins, but that's another matter. . . . You make a sort of morality out of the absurd; it remains to make a psychology from it."

On November 15, Camus wrote to Malraux, heading his letter with a familiar and collegial "My dear Malraux." His letter showed sincere gratitude and just a bit of tension over the fact that Malraux was famous and Camus unknown: "You are among those whose approval I sought, and the way in which you give it adds to my gratitude." After Malraux's comments were relayed to him by Pia, Camus "rewrote two chapters, which have improved from it." Malraux had understood that the books complemented one another: "Certain works can illustrate one another. That's the idea I am working on . . . and that's why I insisted, perhaps naively, on simultaneous publication." But if Gallimard should decide not to publish them together, Camus would understand: "Now these things are separated from me, and they can do as they please. . . . In any case, if my manuscripts bring me nothing but the pleasure and sympathy of some minds I love and admire, it will be quite enough."

Camus explained some of Malraux's writings to Malraux himself, suggesting that Lawrence of Arabia, a "fully absurd character," would have fit into one of Malraux's most famous works: "The psychology of the absurd found some of its finest successes in your characters. That is no vain compliment and you know it is true. Lawrence would have felt at home in La Condition humaine." The false rumor that Malraux would write for the collaborationist NRF had even reached Oran, and Camus let him know that he was doing his best to deny the gossip. Malraux replied that he expected to be able to persuade Gallimard at least to publish Le Mythe de Sisyphe at the same time as L'Etranger.

Pia visited Malraux, who had moved from Cap-d'Ail to Cap-Martin nearby. There they discussed Camus's Mythe, and Malraux later wrote to Pia with his conclusions: "I have finished Camus's essay. It's remarkable, and what he has to say gets through, which is not very easy. The book completely illuminates his novel and greatly reduces my objections about details in the latter." Malraux himself was working on a new novel, which became La Lutte avec l'ange, and was reading Camus from the point of view of a working author: "I read him with all the more interest because in my current novel, the crabs are crawling around in the same basket."

Paulhan had also read Camus's novel, and Pia let his friend know right away what the reaction had been. Paulhan stated, "I finally received the Camus books. I read *L'Etranger* in one sitting. What is there to do about it? [Gaston Gallimard] will of course be ready to publish it." Paulhan wanted to print excerpts in the new *NRF* or in the weekly *Comoedia*, which would pay Camus five thousand or six thousand francs, enough to live on for two or three months. Paulhan continued in his letter to Pia about *L'Etranger*, "It's very fine, frankly very good. Germaine [his wife] and I were very gripped by it. . . . I liked *Le Mythe de Sisyphe* less. It's intelligent, but in fact it's hardly more than an intelligent chronicle of metaphysical events." Paulhan detected a "personal obscurity" in the essay, and had not yet read *Caligula*, but he reaffirmed in a postscript, "Yes, *L'Etranger* is damn good."

Since the novel was recommended by Gaston Gallimard and Jean Paulhan, it passed at the Gallimard reading committee meeting of November 12, 1941, without any problem. Paulhan had given *L'Etranger* the highest grade, a one. Pia told Camus he disagreed with Paulhan's opinion of *Sisyphe*: "Contrary to what he suggests, I don't think that a book like *Sisyphe* can be simply an intellectual curiosity outside of any personal 'problem,' as Paulhan calls it. If there were no problem, there would be no attempt to clear it up. Then at best, it would be a philosophy teacher's old *spiel*, and *Sisyphe* is not exactly that."

Pia advised Camus not to print parts of his book in Drieu La Rochelle's collaborationist *NRF*: "As a place, it stinks worse than ever." He also suggested that Camus not rush to sign with Gallimard, as he knew that Gaston was "too miserly for you to agree to his conditions without first trying to improve them." Finally, on December 8, 1941, Gaston himself wrote to Camus from Cannes, as Malraux had given him the writer's address. The publisher found *L'Etranger* "remarkable" and would be very happy to publish it as soon as possible. Where should he send the contract? A royalty of ten percent on the first ten thousand copies sold was proposed, then twelve percent on the following thousands, with an advance of 5,000 francs. At the time, Pia's monthly salary in Lyons was 4,600 francs.

In Paris, Gaston's secretary, Madeleine Boudot-Lamotte, sent the manuscript to Lieutenant Gerhard Heller of the Nazi Propagandastaffel, a military censor who basked in the French literary milieu during the German Occupation period. Heller later stated that he read *L'Etranger* in one night and had no objection to it, finding it both asocial and apolitical. Heller called Madeleine Boudot-Lamotte to announce his approval and to propose his help "in case of difficulty, at least to obtain all the paper needed."

In Oran, Camus felt isolated and uncomfortable, making pessimistic notes in his *Carnets*: "There is vertigo in losing oneself and denying everything, in breaking forever what once defined us, and which now offers only

solitude and the void, all in order to find the only platform from which des-
tinies may always begin again. The temptation is everlasting, but should one
accept or reject it? Should one bring the obsession with a work to the empti-
ness of a humdrum life, or on the contrary should one make one's life worthy of it by obeying flashes of lightning? Beauty is my direst concern, along
with freedom."

In a time of war, Camus recalled "those who created in troubled times,
like Shakespeare, Milton, Ronsard, Rabelais, Montaigne, and Malherbe."
He was reading the last works of Tolstoy, which he found monotonous,
Hindu literature, the biblical books of the Prophets, the sayings of Buddha,
the Koran, Nietzsche, Pascal, and Leon Chestov. He criticized the "terrible
monotony of Proust and the Marquis de Sade, etc., etc. . . ." He made careful notes on Jean Giono's translation of Melville's *Moby-Dick*, observing,
"Feelings and images multiply philosophy tenfold." He was inspired to find
a new nickname for his mother-in-law, Fernande Faure: Moby-Dick. And he
worked on his new book, which would be a novel and chronicle about the
plague. Camus practiced the aphorism "Willpower is a form of solitude,
too."

On February 2, 1942, Jean Paulhan wrote to Camus: "I should have
written to you long ago to say how much I liked *L'Etranger*. . . . It seemed to
me very great. It made me think of Kafka at times and at others of Eugène
Sue, which is the sign of the book's difference, of all it succeeds in doing,
with the strangest unity. . . ." Sue, an early-nineteenth-century author of
penny serials like *The Wandering Jew*, was hardly a fashionable literary name.

The novelist Raymond Queneau, a Gallimard employee, wrote to say
that *L'Etranger* was in production and would be out by March or April. Queneau added a postscript, "Your essay presents some 'local' difficulties," because in *Le Mythe de Sisyphe* Camus mentioned Kafka, who as a Jew could
not be spoken of in German-occupied territory. Gaston wrote too, to explain
that two proofreaders in Paris would be responsible for the final proofs of
L'Etranger, supervised by Paulhan, since it would be too difficult for Camus
to correct them from Oran. Gaston also mentioned "a delicate question" in
Le Mythe de Sisyphe, which required cutting the chapter "An Absurd Creation," from pages 107 to 121 of the manuscript, because "it deals with Kafka."
Paulhan also wrote to announce that after all, *L'Etranger* would appear at
the same time as *Le Mythe*, and asked if Camus would like to contribute to
a special issue of the *NRF* offering homage to Stendhal.

Despite this invigorating news, Camus was troubled by health woes.
He explained on February 21, 1942, to Jean Grenier, "I've had a serious relapse, exactly like ten years ago. I am getting treatment right now (pneumothorax again, etc.)." On March 4, Gaston wrote to insist that it really was
necessary to replace the passage on Kafka with something else. He knew that
Camus was ill and was very sorry: "I am very annoyed to have to write to you

like this when I would like to publish you without any objections. Be assured that they do not come from me." On March 10, Malraux wrote to say that Gaston seemed "fairly excited" about *L'Etranger* and was also thinking of reprinting earlier work by Camus that had been previously published by Charlot. A week later Pia wrote to say that he was still looking for a place in France where Camus could rest and work, whether at newspapers, prep schools, or on estates that needed running. If Camus refused to let part of *L'Etranger* be printed in the *NRF*, it would not compromise the book's publication, Pia insisted. He explained to Camus: "If Gallimard had to blush or get angry each time an author scorned his magazine, he would have died of shame or rage months ago."

Pia suggested that if *Sisyphe* was not published by Gallimard because of the Kafka question, they might try a publisher in the free zone or in Switzerland. Meanwhile, *Le Mythe de Sisyphe* was being handed around among philosophers: Jean Grenier sent his copy to the noted Catholic thinker Gabriel Marcel, who sent it in turn to the historian of philosophy Jean Wahl. Pia asked Camus to do him a favor and find in Algeria three books by Kafka, *The Trial*, *The Metamorphosis*, and *The Castle*, none of which were available in France, as old copies had been pulped on the orders of the Germans. He added affectionately: "I'd like to hear that you've perked up, and are once again as bold as when you used to run around Kabylia."

Queneau sent a note to say that he had checked the first proofs of *L'Etranger*, and Paulhan would deal with the second proofs: "Allow me to say what sympathy and esteem I have for your work: very great." On March 29, Malraux wrote to say he was sorry Camus was ill; could Camus find him a biography of T. E. Lawrence by Basil Liddell-Hart? And how about a rug of so-called white Tlemcen, measuring around 3.5 meters by 4.5 meters?

As the war advanced, the Germans cracked down on French resistance efforts. The Oran press obeyed the French Vichy collaborationist and anti-Semitic guidelines. In April 1942, Paul Eluard secretly circulated his famous Resistance poem, "J'écris ton nom, liberté," and stopped contributing to the *NRF*. Camus's *Carnets* were still very restrained, since as a known former Communist, he felt he had to be prudent. Yet he did note down some observations about politics, such as an analysis of the current hatred against the British in occupied France: "There are many reasons for the official hostility against England (good and bad, political and not), but one of the worst motives goes unmentioned: rage and a base desire to see crushed someone who dares resist the power which has already crushed you." Camus also examined France's reputation for nonconformity and for individualism as opposed to conservatism: "The Frenchman has kept the habits and traditions of great thinking, he only lacks the guts. . . . He remade the world without moving his ass out of his armchair."

Some Frenchmen, like his friend Pia, were active in the Resistance, but they were in the great minority: "There is always a philosophy or the lack of courage." Camus understood the confusion of most Frenchmen, and their strong or weak adherence to Pétain's preaching, which he rejected: "to return to the Middle Ages, to a primitive mentality, to the soil, to religion, to an arsenal of old solutions." At André Bénichou's home, he heard André's young son Pierre humming the Pétainist hymn, "Maréchal, nous voilà!" which was taught in French schools, and Camus laughingly yelled at the kid.

His *Carnets* were devoted to long passages about his novel-in-progress, comments on books which sometimes read like bizarre clichés, and notes on the pleasures of nature near Oran: "Who can say that he has lived through eight perfect days? Yet my memory tells me this, and I know that it doesn't lie. Yes, this image is perfect, as these long days were perfect. These joys were physical and had all the mind's approval as well. . . . Long mornings on the dunes amid naked bodies, the overwhelming noonday sun, and one must say what has already been said: That is youth, and at thirty all I long for is to pursue that youth. But . . ."

Camus felt himself getting older, and fortunately Pia wrote constantly to break his friend's isolation and get him back in touch with work and with France. Pia was still looking for jobs for Camus, such as forestry agent, in a healthy region. He was also busy trying "to extract an advance" from Gallimard for Camus. Queneau had asked Pia for biographical information on Camus, and Pascal reassured Albert: "I'll send it to him and don't worry, I'll be discreet. Still, if you think I should present you as a Hindu prince or former high-ranking military officer or a defrocked priest, I can send ten kilos of fanciful references to Paris." Pia had met with Jean Grenier, and they spoke of their friend Camus, who with his habit of compartmentalizing people had not told Grenier about his marriage to Francine. Grenier was not offended by this omission, only commenting about Francine, "If I'm not mistaken, his wife is very pretty." Pia told Camus that this comment proved "that there are still some connoisseurs among the philosophers."

Gallimard was still thinking of reprinting some of Camus's earlier works, buying the rights from Charlot, but Camus finally refused. Malraux wrote to say that he approved of Camus's decision: "You are right to prefer that Gallimard sticks for the moment to what he already has." Camus often saw Emmanuel Roblès in the cafés of Oran. A native of that city, Roblès was a demobilized aviator working as a schoolteacher at Turenne. From Morocco he brought smuggled items for Camus like wine, noodles, and rice. He described to Camus the illness of his wife, Pauline: she was stricken with typhus, like hundreds of thousands of Algerians in 1941–42, and most died from it. Typhus was a reality and a symbol, and the plague even more so. A camp for the ill in Turenne was surrounded by a sanitary cordon of Senegalese soldiers. Roblès gave precise descriptions of his experiences to Camus, who noted them down while smoking Bastos cigarettes. To tease Camus,

Roblès claimed to support soccer clubs that Camus did not favor. Camus confided in Roblès that he was a slow worker.

Finally, on April 23, Gallimard sent him a contract, and on April 30, a first payment, but with postal delays, it was a considerable time before Camus received them. Under Pia's pressure, the advance had increased from five thousand francs to twice that amount, which was enough to live on for three months and to pay for a trip to France. Malraux assured Camus that the advance was "large enough to prove that [Gaston] is interested in your books."

In May 1942, Francine hurtled into Christiane Faure's apartment to announce, "Albert is spitting blood again. Dr. Cohen is going to do a pneumothorax on him." The next day, Camus, pale and sweating in his bed, told Christiane, "It's a heavy blow. I thought I was cured." Camus received his treatment and dragged himself between work and illness, counting on his future values.

L'Etranger was printed in France on May 19, 1942, in an edition of 4,400 copies. This was as large as initial printings of works by established authors, like Queneau's *Pierrot mon ami* and Gide's *Théâtre*. Other new Gallimard books by the playwright Jacques Audiberti, the critic Maurice Blanchot, and the essayist Marcel Jouhandeau, had much lower printings. But a new mystery by Georges Simenon had a printing of 11,000 copies, and Saint-Exupéry's aviation memoirs, *Pilote de guerre*, 22,000. Camus could not inscribe copies to journalists in the French publishing tradition, nor could he see copies in bookstores or read the first reviews in newspapers. Gaston had decided to put *L'Etranger* on sale without waiting for the essay, whose proofs Paulhan was correcting, minus the controversial pages on Kafka.

Finally, at the beginning of June 1942, *L'Etranger* appeared in bookstores, priced at 25 francs, in the white NRF cover with red and black printing. Also published at the same time by Gallimard were James Joyce's *Ulysses*, which the Germans considered decadent, and Gide's *Les Nourritures terrestres*, which the Vichy collaborationist newspapers denounced. At the same time, a limited edition came out of a work by the poet Paul Claudel, who admired Marshal Pétain, *Cent Phrases pour éventail*. As usual, Gallimard deftly manipulated both sides of the conflict: ads were bought in the press in both occupied and free zones. Twenty author's copies of *L'Etranger* were sent to Oran, but never arrived at their destination. Albert and Francine asked for travel permits to visit France, but the application process was long and painful. Malraux felt that the publication of *L'Etranger* should facilitate such official matters as travel permits. The word of mouth on Camus's book, then an essential factor in publishing, was excellent, ranking Camus with Stendhal. It was said that even Pierre Drieu La Rochelle supported *Le Mythe de Sisyphe*'s publication.

On June 17, Camus at last received a copy of *L'Etranger*, and he took the occasion to thank Paulhan for correcting proofs for the book and also for inquiring about his health. He replied, "The cure is long, but I intend to be cured." He fought tuberculosis with determination: "They gave my right lung the treatment which they had done some years ago on the left lung (pneumothorax). For the moment this has forced me to undergo every week an inflation of the pleurum. . . . Little by little . . . the inflations will be spaced farther apart. When they are doing them every two weeks, I think I will leave Oran and return twice a month, just for the treatment. . . . Even though I am better and can go outside the house, I cannot think about going 600 kilometers every week [to Algiers] — I'm not in good enough shape."

Later the same month, Camus suffered from what his doctors called an "escalation" in his illness. He told his favorite sister-in-law, Christiane, "I really thought I was done with it," but he needed treatment from Dr. Cohen, a lung specialist. After a few days, Camus stopped spitting blood, when the pneumothorax operation was performed, which consisted of deflating the infected lung. While he was undergoing the follow-up treatment which reinflated his lung, Camus began to look at his in-laws in a different light. They cared for him and clearly loved him. He lived in slow motion, reading a lot, no longer able to go swimming.

He thought about his condition: "Of course, illnesses are solitary adventures, but ten years ago I decided to get out of mine, and I really thought I had done so. It's not always that easy to start again at zero. To have to economize myself, when all that I knew how to say and do was excessive! No doubt the best thing would be to try to turn this to my own advantage, sort of as if I were going back to school." Camus got through his illness and days which were "distended and interminable." He took walks up to the Oran cliffs, "the best place for thinking about the plague and everything I want to do."

In July 1942, Camus hoped to leave for France, but instead stayed for two weeks at La Palestre, a house on the Planteurs slopes, near Oran. He planned to spend all the remaining summer, fall, and winter in the mountains, whether in Algeria or in France. Lucette Meurer filled his reading requests, and he ordered from her Francesco Berni's essay "In Praise of the Plague," adding, "Have I told you that my book is out in Paris? That's all I know."

Camus had not asked himself if he should publish in France at this moment, given that many writers were banned, particularly Jews. But few French writers who had a choice refused to be published during the occupation; apart from the Dadaist Tristan Tzara and the essayist Jean Guéhenno, the list was very short indeed. Both Guéhenno and Tzara had other sources of income than writing. Camus had to earn his living, and he lived with the notion that his days were numbered. Still, he refused to write for the *NRF*: "I would not like to write for the magazine, but if it's a question of the publishing house then that is different." He wanted his pages on Kafka to appear in the free zone, but he went along with Paulhan and Gaston Gallimard's idea that the publishing house was one thing and the collaborationist *NRF*, which it published, was another. Apart from rare saints like Guéhenno, most of the little writers simply survived in Paris, while the great names succumbed to their voracious appetites for fame. Prudent writers published their books, but tried to write as little as possible, or not at all, for magazines and newspapers under German control.

Chapter Twenty-three **Which Absurdity?**

*L*e Mythe de Sisyphe is dense, epigrammatic, and of a deceptive clarity. It looks like a short essay, without technical jargon, cryptic sometimes to a fault. In it, Camus spoke of the world, history, and of his life. The book may be passed through many different filters. Camus sought a lesson in life that went beyond the unadventurous teachings of Jean Grenier and beyond his readings of Pascal, Kierkegaard, Nietzsche, Chestov, Husserl, and Jaspers. He told Christiane Galindo Davila that he was glad to get back to philosophy, but this essay seems more about morality than philosophy. And more about morality than about ethics, if morality aims at establishing rules for living, whereas ethics strives to analyze the concepts of morality, perhaps eventually a morality to be founded outside the one imposed by moral judgments, based for example on God or transcendent reason. Camus asked the question: How should we live?

Le Mythe is also an essay, a formally perfect sketch, and sometimes a philosophical prose poem, falsely cold-seeming and strongly autobiographical. Camus took stock, with an attitude that was neither systematic nor anti-systems. He respected certain creators of doctrine, like Descartes, Hegel, Nietzsche, and those he called the "existentials," led by Martin Heidegger. But although he appreciated these thinkers, he did not really confront them. He was more or less ignorant of those philosophers who did not believe in a philosophical system outside of science, like Bertrand Russell, Rudolf Carnap, and Ludwig Wittgenstein. Until this time, in almost all his writings, Camus had expressed a tragic emotion about life and a massive mistrust of those who built systems. His temperament and his reading of Nietzsche nourished his suspicions of all traditional morality. Faced by the world's incoherence, he believed in modest progressions, by using thought which could be formulated.

Carrying this essay inside him for four years, Camus produced philosophy in spite of himself. As a writer, busy with the relations between aesthetics and ethics, he did not want to propose any universal morality. It was difficult enough to construct one's own individual moral code. Camus saw an "unspeakable universe where contradiction, antinomy, anguish, and impotence reign." From 1938 to 1941 he had a feeling of absurdity about the world, history, and his own life. He began his essay with a bang: "Judging whether life is or is not worth living is to answer philosophy's fundamental question." Although it is unproven that Camus ever felt suicidal, he did have a permanent, deep, although vague, sense of absurdity. This essay was not written quickly, like *L'Etranger*. Camus spoke in the first person as a man: "Conscious of not being able to separate myself from my time, I have decided to become part of it. I focused on the individual so much, because he seems to me insignificant and humiliated today."

In 1940 and 1941, the French and France were certainly humiliated. "Knowing that there is no winning cause, I have a taste for lost causes: they demand a complete soul, which is up to its defeats as well as to its fleeting victories." *One* of the possible interpretations of this multilayered essay is that Camus was referring to defeated France, and fleetingly victorious Germany, in this passage. Camus wrote, "For those who feel solidarity with the world's destiny, the clash of civilizations has something anguishing about it. I have made that anguish my own at the same time that I wished to play my role. . . . One must choose between action and contemplation." Camus addressed his readers: "I am telling you, tomorrow you will be mobilized, and for you and me, this will be a liberation."

Although his illness prevented Camus from wartime action, he wrote: "The individual can do nothing and yet he can do everything. . . . I am on the side of struggle." Camus had defined ideas about conquerors, at a time when the emblematic type of this order was Hitler: "Yes, man is his own end. . . . Nothing remains of the conqueror, not even his doctrines. . . . Those cemeteries which cover Europe and which obsess some of us, are hideous." Camus included an autobiographical insight from the time he worked as a journalist on *Alger Républicain*, when the conquerors Hitler and Mussolini advanced in Europe and Africa: "The absurd creator does not stick to his work. He might renounce it, and sometimes does so. All that is required is an Abyssinia."

Making generalizations about man, Camus often spoke about himself and his own experience: "Man finds himself confronted by the irrational. . . . He feels inside himself the desire for happiness and reason." Absurdity is "born at the confrontation between the human cry and the world's unreasoning silence." Camus generalized further, based on his own experience: "A man defines himself as much by his comedies as by his sincere outbursts."

Powerful pages deal with the actor, whose paradoxes Camus knew well: "Actors in general . . . are not absurd men, but their destiny is absurd." He was referring to the successive lives which actors live, their singularity and diversity. Camus revealed himself considerably: "But to know if one can live with one's passions, to know if one can accept their basic law, which is to burn the same hearts which they exalt—that is the whole question." Here, the subject was not man in general but Camus in particular. Before this, he mentioned the problem of logic: "It is almost impossible to be thoroughly logical. . . . I don't know if the world has a meaning which escapes it, but I know I am ignorant of this meaning, and for the moment it is impossible for me to know it." He referred to Sartre's novel *La Nausée*: "This 'nausea,' as a contemporary author calls it, is also the absurd." However, it is unlikely that Sartre would have agreed.

Camus dedicated the first part of the chapter on "absurd creation" to philosophy and the novel. He did not claim to be writing philosophy himself, or not really. His introduction sets the tone: "The pages that follow deal with a sensitivity to the absurd which can be found here and there in our century, and not an absurd philosophy, which our time, strictly speaking, has not known." For Camus the essayist, the absurd was a point of departure, "the description of mental illness in its pure state. No metaphysics or beliefs are mixed in with it for the moment." The reader must take Camus literally here, as almost everywhere. He found absurdity in the condition of man as Sartre defined him, as well as in the posters displayed during the mobilization for the war. Universalization is a temptation of French culture. He perceived the "absurd little God" in war as in life: "There are absurd marriages, challenges, rancors, silences, wars, and peaces, too." Ever literal, Camus explained that the saying "That's absurd" means "That's impossible" but also "That's contradictory": "If I see a man with a sword attack a group of machine guns, I will judge that his act is absurd."

Camus worked on several different levels here: in the French language the word "absurde" seemed to correspond to two English words, "absurd" and "nonsensical." Camus was the first French writer to give absurdity as many registers. He used it alternatively to mean "contradictory," "false," and "unreasonable." His reasonings seemed rapid, punchy, and fluid. He sought a certain lucidity without quite attaining it, to express this mid-century malady. To affirm as Camus did that suicide is the only serious philosophical problem is not serious from a historical point of view. Yet he was correct in implying that only sociologists like Emile Durkheim had really treated the subject. Rather than absurdity, philosophers have preferred studying a half-dozen problems, from the soul to existence.

To accept or refuse Camus's proposition, we must pose a metaphysical one: Does life have enough meaning so that we should not kill ourselves? Although he mentioned logic, Camus never really examined formal logic. He was referring to the coherence of the behavior chosen by a man, to the morality he set for himself. For the essayist, a vast feeling of absurdity existed between the world and man's rational aspirations. Camus stated that we have a feeling of the absurd at time's passing, or when we see a man making gestures inside a phone booth, or when facing the inevitable mystery of death. There is a contradiction between the irrational character of the world and every thinking man's desire for clarity.

The universe is not absurd in itself, any more than it is yellow or sugary: it simply *is*. Life and the world have a meaning for the believer who has a code of conduct in the Gospels based on the word of Christ. Camus's anguish came from the fact that no morality was imposed by an atheist or agnostic's world. For Camus, truths existed in the sciences, but not a single truth—he knew mainly psychology and sociology. In a summary way, he declared that physics ended up in poetry. Camus's anxiety was psychological, but also metaphysical in one sense: it called for man to be totally in harmony with his universe, the same world in which Camus had dealt with the problem of innocent children's death when he studied theology, and the burden of unacceptable politics when he started working in journalism.

Trying to sketch out a morality, he turned back to Nietzsche: "What matters is not eternal life but eternal liveliness." The artist was the character that Camus understood best. He stated that the creator pushes absurdity aside, which may have been true for him, but not for every artist. He repeated his philosophy conveyed in images, and his rejection of novels of ideas: "The absurd work insists upon . . . an art in which the concrete signifies nothing other than itself." To be appreciated, a "work of art presents itself as such and does not demand explanations. . . . In any case, explanations and descriptions do not exhaust it."

Camus situated his personal morality as a writer and as a man less with conquerors than with artists, such as Don Juan the hedonist, whose work was ephemeral: "There is no destiny which cannot be overcome by despising." Faced with illness and attacks of lassitude, Camus was as heroic as the absurd man described in his book, often scorning and despising his life's contingencies. The absurd was also the inadmissible, the inexcusable, and the incomprehensible. Camus declared that "with respect to intelligence, I can . . . say that the absurd is not in man . . . nor in the world, but in their common presence." Without any clear continuity, he added, "One of the only coherent philosophical positions is . . . revolt." He did not agree with Dostoyevsky that if God did not exist, all was possible. Certain acts, which are crimes, must be rejected. Camus used man to explain man, first and foremost. He took as a goal the human person's fulfillment and happiness. Thus absurdism became a kind of humanism: the world had the meaning one gave it.

For the title of his essay, Camus was influenced by Jean Grenier, whose

Essai sur l'esprit d'orthodoxie spoke of mortals punished by the gods: "We often speak of the myth of Prometheus while forgetting to mention its outcome, which is the principal part of it. Sisyphus is never spoken of." Camus drew three consequences from his meditations on the absurd: revolt, freedom, and passion. And he identified with Sisyphus, ending his essay with a literary cry of hope. Camus advocated a superior kind of faith, "which denies gods and raises up rocks. He [meaning man, Sisyphus, and Camus] also judges that all is well. This now-masterless universe does not seem either futile or sterile to him. Each grain of this stone, each mineral chip of this mountain full of night alone forms a world. The struggle itself towards the summits is enough to fill a man's heart." It was like Camus when he felt happy to finish a manuscript or to begin a new one: Sisyphus' rock rolled down, and he started back up the mountain, an end which had no need of justification in itself. Like writing or any creation.

Camus wrote in *Le Mythe*, "A world that can be explained, even by bad reasoning, is a familiar world. But in a world suddenly deprived of illusions and light, a man feels like a stranger." That was the universe of Meursault, *l'ètranger*, or the stranger, Camus's first protagonist, who was absurd because, among other things, he did not look for meaning in what happened to him. Instead, he abstained from commenting and judging. The protagonist of *L'Etranger* felt no need to justify himself, either: Meursault learned that his mother died in an old-age home in Marengo. He felt no special emotion, went to her funeral, and then walked to the beach, where he picked up a young woman. Later she asked him to marry her, and although he did not love her, he saw no reasonable excuse not to do so. In the same distracted way, he accepted the friendship of a fellow tenant. The latter, something of a pimp, beat up an Arab's sister. Meursault himself killed an Arab man on the beach, in arbitrary and absurd circumstances. He went on trial, where his indifference about his mother absurdly had more effect on the judge and jury than the murder he committed. Meursault was sentenced to death, yet did not want to die, and would have preferred to be pardoned. He refused the help offered by the prison chaplain and felt like knocking him out. Finally, he prepared himself to die, but still wanted to live. The end of this prodigious short novel, a monologue, was a great cry: "I felt ready to live it all over again. As if that great anger had purged me of evil and emptied me of hope, facing the night loaded with signs and stars. For the first time I exposed myself to the tender indifference of the world, feeling that it was so similar to me, like a brother in fact. I felt that I had been happy, and that I still was."

The events in Meursault's life may seem absurd by their novelistic discontinuity, but not because of their randomness in an indifferent world. In imagining this character, Camus also thought of Pascal Pia, the friend of his who, like Meursault, was not simply beyond conventions and traditions, but instead marginal to them. Camus was inspired by several men and women in painting the portrait of the finally inexplicable Meursault, just as the deeper meaning of *L'Etranger* is finally inexplicable. Nor could the current situation between Europeans and Algerians be said to have influenced the apparent desire of a "pied-noir" to kill an Arab.

He thought about a vaster novel than *L'Etranger*, a chronicle in which he would describe men in revolt, faced by the world's absurdity.

Chapter Twenty-four **Short of Breath**

In July 1942, after school vacations freed Francine, Camus was advised by his friend Dr. Cviklinski to spend the coming winter in the mountains in France. Thanks to Gallimard and to Francine's salary, the Camuses had a little money. At the beginning of August, the couple spent two weeks at the Emer farm near Aïn-El-Türck, which belonged to Marguerite Dobrenn's family. Other guests were Jeanne Sicard, Jean-Paul de Dadelsen and his brother, and Francine's cousins Nicole and Manette Chaperon. The young people went swimming and had fun, howling with laughter one afternoon when a small donkey climbed up the steps to the house. Those who slept at the farm were piled one atop another. Camus avoided the sun, and despite the heat he wore a thick tablecloth over his shoulders. He was short of breath and his friends sensed that he was exhausted; but he seemed in remission. Francine and Albert returned to Algiers, but they did not have time to see friends like Claude de Fréminville. They did lunch with Emmanuel Roblès and two other friends. Roblès noticed that Camus was mostly silent and sweated a lot.

The Camuses then took a ship which cruised along the coast of Spain before arriving in Marseilles. The couple slept on the ship's bridge, along with their fellow travelers, such as Louis Joxe, a history lecturer at the University of Algiers and a future participant in the Resistance. Joxe and Camus recognized one another when Camus was reading a new novel by Louis Guilloux and Joxe a volume by Théophile Gautier. After the customs and immigrations formalities at Marseilles, which included an examination for lice, the Camuses boarded the train to Lyons, where Albert was too tired even to see Pia. They took another train to Saint-Etienne, then a winding little train up to Chambon-sur-Lignon. Finally, they rode in a cart for a few kilometers to get to Le Panelier, at one thousand meters altitude, in the Vivarais region.

A distant relation by marriage of Francine's, Sarah Oettly, ran a family hotel in a fortress-farm, Le Panelier, at the center of a hamlet containing four farms. Francine and her sisters had spent summers there during their childhood. Madame Oettly was affectionate and maternal, looking after Camus and even sparing him tiring conversation by serving the Camuses their meals in their room rather than in the communal dining room. The couple relaxed on a second-floor wooden balcony off a room that Mrs. Oettly arranged for them at a special rate. Camus chatted with Madame Oettly's employee Madame Faury, who he felt had plenty of common sense. Like Camus's mother, Madame Faury was completely illiterate. For several days he went out rarely; he lay on the lawn, or at most strolled a short way to the local cemetery. Farther away, along the Lignon River, fishermen angled for trout. On this plateau in the Vivarais region, the Camuses ate better than in Oran. Farmers sold butter, milk, cheese, meat, and potatoes, and Sarah Oettly prepared them special dishes, always at reasonable prices, because in this Protestant region, few of the farmers indulged in the wartime black market for foodstuffs. Camus still complained that the food was not perfect, "not to mention that there is no wine at all." He got in touch with a doctor at Saint-Etienne, and slowly came to appreciate the landscape: "A handsome countryside, a little somber. Fields, forest springs, as far as the eye can see. All along, the smell of grass and the noise of water." It rained, which was agreeable after the stifling heat of Algiers, and the landscape became superb: "I do find it attractive, but it hasn't yet entered into me. It will take many days and many walks."

As a consolation, Camus's second book from Gallimard, *Le Mythe de Sisyphe*, was announced for publication. On September 22, Camus had sent Gaston Gallimard a first draft of an insert for *Le Mythe*: "Modern intelligence suffers from nihilism, and to cure it, we propose that it forget its illness and go backwards. Such are the 'returns' to the Middle Ages, to a primitive mentality, to the so-called 'natural life,' to religion—in short, to the arsenal of old solutions. But to give a shadow of usefulness to these cures, several centuries' contributions must be denied; we must pretend to be ignorant of what we know very well, to pretend we have learnt nothing, and to efface what is ineffaceable. This is impossible. On the contrary, this essay takes into account some clarifications we have learned from our exile. It suggests that the mind should live with its negations and to make them the principle of progress. It uses fidelity and confidence with respect to modern intelligence. In this sense, one can only consider it as a clarification, the preliminary definition of a 'good nihilism,' and to say everything, a preface." Camus also sent his publisher a more concise summary to be printed on the traditional

paper bands wrapped around new books: "Sisyphus, or Happiness in Hell."
He was at Le Panelier to rest and to write the novel he had begun. "I am
waiting for this illness which is suffocating me to go away, and as for everything else, my only wish is to write, and I hope to do so here."

In good weather, Camus would sit on a stone bench in front of the hotel and listen to the toads; he found them pretty animals and enjoyed hearing their flutelike song in the evenings. Sometimes he walked along the rows
of pine trees that led up to the banks of the Lignon River. He became fond
of a cat named Cigarette, who died at the end of the summer. Other guests
came to the hotel, but Camus avoided them, since in France, speaking to
strangers was ill advised, on the theory that what you don't know couldn't
hurt you. Another guest, Raymonde Grumbach, admired the young couple,
but limited herself to saying good morning to them. As a Jew, Grumbach
had been fired from her job as a hospital intern in Paris. The entire region
of Chambon became a refuge for persecuted Jews during wartime.

Camus followed with calm interest the destiny of *L'Etranger*. He was
assured from Paris that even if the book were a failure, it would sell at least
three thousand copies. Pia wrote Malraux urging Gaston to arrange a
monthly retainer for Camus. Pia informed Malraux, "If I know him, he
won't ask anything for himself, even if he lets himself croak out of discretion." Camus was counting on the money he would get for an essay he gave
to Edmond Charlot to publish, "Le Minotaure, ou la halte d'Oran." However, the German censor did not permit its publication because it suppos-
edly attacked regionalism and local patriotism. Pia wrote to Camus: "If you
had added under your name the title 'President of the Society of Oran Folk-
lore,' then they would have no doubt given you all the permissions you
wanted."

The first reactions to *L'Etranger* did not satisfy Camus. He told Claude
de Fréminville, "The reviews have been mediocre in the free zone and excellent in Paris. Finally, everything depends on misunderstandings. The best
is to close one's ears and work." Albert gladly invited Claude to join them,
but wanted to avoid "tears for him. There's no wine or tobacco (four
cigarettes a day), there are milk products but nothing which seduces the
mouth. In short, you'll really have fun here."

Gaston Gallimard cultivated his new author, writing, "True, the reviews have been absurd. However, there was a good article by Arland in *Comoedia* and another, equally favorable, in the *NRF*." The positive articles
had been printed in publications owned by Gallimard. Marcel Arland, a
Gallimard author himself, had written a two-column story in the July 11 issue
of *Comoedia* under the flattering headline "A Coming Writer: Albert Camus." After quoting from *L'Etranger*, Arland offered a favorable, but not brilliant, review of the book: "And whatever reservations one may feel about his

thought . . . the important thing is that M. Camus is sincere and his tone moves us." Arland ended his article with the words "a real writer," which helped sales. In September, a note in the *NRF* seemed as flat as Arland's, if less straitlaced. The reviewer, a certain Fieschi, linked Camus to an insidious *"vachiste"* (literally "bovine," but meaning "vicious") trend, an odd formulation for Camus's apparent nihilism. Nevertheless, the critic praised "a sober and just book, yet on a horribly gaudy tragic subject which smacks a little of Grand Guignol." Fieschi concluded that this was "a great book, one of those which 'lifts the soul' exactly because it does not preach."

Gaston did not mention to Camus an article by André Rousseaux in the free zone's *Le Figaro* which tore apart *L'Etranger*. Rousseaux was considered the pope of book critics, and reading *L'Etranger* made him reflect: "It seems that the crisis of the novel gets a little worse every day. Young novelists' debuts do not just mostly reveal mediocre talents. When a trend presents itself, it is often one that makes us worried and unsure." Rousseaux lamented: "The novel seems to have the sad privilege of reserving for itself spiritual passivity and the moral scrap heap." The critic noted that Camus had an "already formed talent . . . and qualities as a prose writer" but that nevertheless his "reality is excessively poor." Camus made Rousseaux think André Gide's immoralist, and his hero, Meursault, had been "amputated of everything that gives a man value."

Pia sent from Lyons a review from *Le Temps* by another pillar of French criticism, Emile Henriot. Pia observed, "I never doubted that M. Henriot was an ass, and he has insisted on confirming this opinion. Apart from that, what he says is mostly encouraging, because after reading him, one feels it would have been troubling if *L'Etranger* had pleased him. From Rousseaux to Henriot, that's exactly the audience that Meursault was hoping for at his execution. I feel like writing to the Ministry of Justice to put these two characters on the jury lists, if they are not already there."

With supporters like Malraux, Paulhan, and Pia, a young writer might accept the average journalist's hostility. But Camus expressed bitterness in his *Carnets*: "Three years to write a book, five lines to ridicule it with misquotes." He added: "Puny morality is raging. Imbeciles believe that when negation is chosen, that means abandonment. They imagine that virility means prophetic Holy Rollers, while grandeur is found in spiritual affectation." Camus wrote a long response to Rousseaux, more for himself than for the journalist, because he never mailed it. He claimed that the letter he was writing was "not an action taken by an unhappy author," and in the unsent message itself he forbade Rousseaux to publish it. When the critic complained that Meursault never took any initiatives, he "did not notice that Meursault always limits himself to answering questions, those about life and men. Thus he never affirms anything, and I only presented him in a negative image, so that nothing can help you to see his deeply held convictions." Camus feared that his letter would be useless: "It would take too long to tell you some reasons for this, but I may at least regret that a superficial study has led you to pin a shopkeeper's philosophy on me which I am not ready to accept. . . . You have not often seen my name in today's magazines, which are nevertheless quite easy to enter. That's because I have nothing to say in them, and I did not feel like sacrificing myself to self-advertisement. At this time I am publishing books which have taken me some years of work, for the sole reason that they are done and I am preparing those which will follow them." Camus added, in this letter he never sent: "I do not expect any material advantage or any consideration from them, and I only hope that they will obtain for me the attention and patience which is given to every work done in good faith, but it seems that even this hope was exaggerated."

Gallimard, ready to launch *Le Mythe de Sisyphe*, suggested that afterwards he would be ready to publish *Caligula*, but Camus said he preferred to wait with the play. Pia sent him an article by Maurice Blanchot which he called the most intelligent thing written so far about *L'Etranger*. Blanchot noted about Meursault, "The narrator tells the story without seeming to reveal anything about his real inner changes, or by showing feelings so simple that they make him even stranger and more distant than if he said nothing; this leads to an unsurpassable objectivity." Camus's use of the judicial system as "the instrument of horrible fatality" reminded Blanchot of William Faulkner's novel *Sanctuary*. However, Blanchot felt that the details of trial procedure in Camus's novel were "artificial." Pia disagreed, saying that Blanchot was "kidding himself when he calls the trial's staging artificial. It's odd that there are so many reasonable people who have not yet recognized the judicial system's demented aspect, and its funny apparatuses like judges, lawyers, witnesses, etc. . . ."

Pia sent Camus the new book by Jean Paulhan, *Les Fleurs de Tarbes*, and jokingly promised to send him everything he would need "in terms of books, food, or stuffed animals." Pia also assured his friend that *L'Etranger* was well distributed in bookstores, and suggested he contact Swiss newspapers, which might hire Camus to write a regular column after he had done a few articles for them: "These Swiss are a little heavy, but less frivolous and, when all is said and done, less idiotic than the pooh-bahs of the French press."

In October, Camus was relaxed and working. He reported to a friend, "Francine stayed with me all the month of September and has left now, so I must meditate all alone now until the end of November. After that I will return to Algiers and settle down there no doubt, unless something unforeseen happens." He was hoping for an apartment at El Biar or in the Algerian mountains, with the healthful air of higher altitudes.

The landscapes of Chambon finally "entered into him": "In fall the countryside becomes rather pretty. All the trees look like great yellow and red flames. The covered sky makes the lines more harsh—and there isn't anyone on the walkways anymore." The other hotel guests gradually left: "In a week I'll be all alone on this estate with a nice old lady (the proprietor) who looks like something right out of a gynecology textbook, but at least I can continue to work. I've already made lots of progress with *La Peste* but I think I'll have to start it all over again." Camus became an amateur mycologist: "When I have nothing better to do, which is often, I go mushroom hunting. This peaceful occupation helps me to forget everything I see when I go to Saint-Etienne for my medical treatment: the most frightful poverty I have ever seen." To Camus, Saint-Etienne seemed even worse than Kabylia; but to keep him company, he had adopted "three dogs with good mugs."

He loved the smell of a wood-burning fireplace: "I needed silence, and now I don't detest anyone anymore. If only I could be cured and live as I did before (since I've been ill, I haven't gone running once) I think I would once again be capable of happiness, but naturally, it would be better to try to arrange what exists rather than wish for improbable things." The cool season came and life was tiresome at Le Panelier: "It's a long time since the swallows have left for the countries of summer and I am seriously late in doing so, too."

Soon he would be twenty-nine years old. He asked the German occupation military authorities for a travel permit to Paris, where he planned to stay for a week. In Paris there were productions of *La Celestina* by Fernando de Rojas, *Hamlet*, and plays by John Millington Synge, all of which he had first discovered in Algeria: "In sum, Algiers has set the style and Parisians are only little copycats. . . . Sometimes I think of health as a great land full of sun and cicadas which I have lost through no fault of my own. And when I have too much desire for this country and the joy which it brings me, I go back to my work. I will return [to Algiers] with some very advanced work which does not satisfy me, and which must be reworked from the beginning. That's how it always is with me: I must start things over again if I want to do them really well."

There was another conscientious review of *L'Etranger* in the magazine *Fontaine* by Henri Hell, one of Camus's comrades from the Théâtre du Travail. Hell detected in Camus's style the influence of John Dos Passos. This influence risked becoming a "too mechanical procedure," yet Hell believed that "this monotony in fact suited the theme of *L'Etranger* unusually well." Hell concluded that "M. Camus has succeeded, thanks to a technique that is not at all classical, and without writing a psychological, analytical novel, and giving his book the purity and rigor of a classical tale in the best French tradition." Hell knew Camus but seemed to misunderstand Meursault, whom he called "a man without humanity, without human value or truth on a human level, despite the book's only weapon, which is a will towards realism."

Another personal friend, Blanche Balain, accused Camus's book of a certain hardness, and the author replied, "True, *L'Etranger* is an organized, willful book which seems to lack emotion. In this respect what you tell me is true. But the book has a double meaning, and Mersault [sic], whom I tried to make natural and alive, is also a symbol at the same time. On the other hand, there is more meaning which will be illuminated later, because he is at the start of a series of works. He is describing point zero, and what a man at point zero can see of life. But of course there are other things, like sacrifice, fidelity, honor, and explosive life—all these absurd virtues keep their meanings." He added as a postscript: "I could be at Lyons on October 28. If you aren't going there, I'll no doubt put off my departure. But I'm leaving Le Panelier at the end of November (around the 25th) and after a brief stop at Lyons, I'll be on the road to Marseilles. See you soon then, dear Asiatic woman [Blanche's father was a military officer in the French Asian colonies]. Don't forget your friend, he's waiting for your letters."

Jean-Paul Sartre, whose books Camus had reviewed in the *Alger Républicain*, had returned from prison camp more than a year before. A teacher now at the Lycée Condorcet in Paris, Sartre was writing prodigiously: he was finishing his monument of phenomenological ontology, *Being and Nothingness*; he was writing a play, *The Flies*; he was beginning the first volume of a series of novels, *The Age of Reason*; and he was trying to organize a small group of intellectual Resistants in a bulletin, *Socialism and Freedom*, for which both Marxists and non-Marxists wrote articles. In September 1942, Sartre also wrote a twenty-page essay on *L'Etranger*, which would appear in February 1943 in the review *Cahiers du Sud*. Sartre did not make up part of the literary directorship at the Gallimard office, but he saw a lot of Paulhan and Queneau, who recommended the book to him. He also read *Le Mythe de Sisyphe* in proofs.

Sartre's study was the most original analysis of *L'Etranger*, although it was printed under the condescending headline "Explanation of *L'Etranger*," implying that Sartre was explaining not just to the reader but even to Camus himself what he wanted to express, where he succeeded and where he failed. Sartre had rarely devoted as much print to a contemporary writer, having given only a dozen pages to Faulkner and Jean Giraudoux in two essays written before the war. Only François Mauriac had been given twenty pages, in a famous Sartre essay which ended, "God is not an artist: neither is Mr. Mauriac." However, Sartre did think that Camus was an artist, and he finished his review in only three days, looking for the key to *L'Etranger* by applying the model of *Le Mythe de Sisyphe* to it.

Trying to classify *L'Etranger*, Sartre said it was not a tale that "explains and coordinates while it retraces events, substituting causal order for chronological progression." He felt that a real novel "demands a continuous duration, a becoming, the clear presence of the irreversibility of time. . . . I would hesitate to call a novel this series of inert present-times which allow us to see underneath the mechanical workings of a many-tiered cake. Or it might be a moralist's short novel in the style of [Voltaire's] *Zadig* or *Candide* with a discreet touch of satire and ironic portraits; despite influence by German existentialists and American novelists, it stays basically very close to a Voltairean tale." Passing deftly from *Le Mythe de Sisyphe* to *L'Etranger* and back again, Sartre thought about Camus the way he thought about himself. The official Gallimard opinion was that *L'Etranger* was the best book published since France's surrender, a marvelous exotic work which was an ambiguous novel." Unlike bad reviewers who weren't philosophers and who hadn't read *Le Mythe*, Sartre offered an X-ray of Meursault's heart as "neither good nor wicked, neither moral nor immoral." He commented about Camus's version of absurdity: "If one takes them separately, neither man nor the world is absurd, but as man must be 'in the world,' the absurd must finally be part of the human condition." Sartre did not approve of Camus philosophically. He projected the Heidegger-influenced ideas from his own *Being and Nothingness* onto *Le Mythe* and *L'Etranger*. Indeed, Camus had disapproved of Sartre's philosophy in *La Nausée* and *Le Mur* when he had analyzed it four years previously.

In his review, Sartre was like a condescending exam-giver: "The poles of the absurd are made up of Death, the implacable plurality of truths and people, the unintelligibility of reality, as well as chance. To tell the truth, these are not very new themes, and M. Camus does not present them as such. Since the seventeenth century they have been listed with a special kind of dry, brief, and contemplative reasoning which is especially French; they served as commonplaces for classical pessimism." Sartre was quick to attach the label of "classical" to Camus's works, as Henri Hell had done. Sartre continued, "M. Camus used some coquetry in quoting texts by Jaspers, Heidegger, and Kierkegaard, which he seems not always to have understood, incidentally."

Sartre's academic tone did not obscure some real intuitions on his part: "M. Camus reveals a proud humility in the simple choice of delivering his message in novelistic form. This is not because of his resignation, but rather his refusal to recognize the limits of human thought." Trying to explain the mysterious success of this book in 1942, Sartre said that it must be taken as "an abrupt communion between two men, the author and the reader, in an absurdity beyond reason."

Paulhan had told Sartre that Camus was "like Kafka written by Hemingway," but Sartre did not see any Kafka in Camus's work, the way Camus had in *La Nausée*. Sartre wrote, "M. Camus's views are all earthbound. Kafka is the novelist of impossible transcendence: for him the universe is full of signs which we don't understand; there is another side to the stage scenery. But for M. Camus, the human drama is in the absence of all transcendency: 'I don't know if this world has a meaning which escapes me, but I know that I don't know this meaning and that for the moment, it's impossible for me to know it. What can a meaning outside of my condition mean for me? I can only understand it in human terms.' "

Sartre was hypnotized by the novel's tone: "A nineteenth-century naturalist would have written, 'A bridge straddled the river.' Mr. Camus refused to allow himself that anthropomorphism. He would say, 'Over the river there was a bridge.' " Sartre was struck by the originality of *L'Etranger*: "A classical work, a work of order composed about the absurd and against the absurd." But he was not sure that "this was what the author intended." He had not read Camus's reviews of *La Nausée* and *Le Mur*, so this was the first time he was aware of Camus, and the writers met through their best intercessors, their books. Both of them confronted the eternal problem of the basis of morality if one does not believe in God.

In the same February 1943 issue of *Cahiers du Sud*, Jean Grenier published an article which was shorter and far less sparkling than Sartre's. Grenier praised the novel's "dry language that is concise and willfully colorless." He recalled Camus as a theater actor and director: "I remember the play *Le Paquebot Tenacity*, in which he played the role of a man who did not leave. He did not act the innocent victim who touches us, because to be touching one must approach a character, but rather he played a disillusioned dandy who could not withdraw enough from a world he abhorred—it was the death of the wolf!"

Camus did not tell Grenier what he thought of his commentary, but he did say what he thought of Sartre's dissertation: he was happier than not, feeling neither misled nor misunderstood: "Sartre's article is a model of 'taking to pieces.' Of course, every creation has an instinctive element which the writer does not envision, and intelligence does not play such an important role. But in criticism, this is the rule of the game, which is fine because on several points he enlightened me about what I wanted to do. I also see that most of his criticisms are fair, but why that acid tone?"

Making his literary debut in France, Camus was mentioned in all the main newspapers and the highbrow reviews, and even those who disliked *L'Etranger* could not ignore it. Even better, Camus found an audience; and Gallimard printed 4,400 more copies in November and the same number again six months later. Yet at Le Panelier, as he worked on *La Peste*, Camus felt misunderstood, as he stated in his *Carnets*: "Reviews of *L'Etranger* speak of impassivity, but the word is wrong: better to say 'kindness.' " He also noted, "Three characters entered into the composition of *L'Etranger*, two men [Pierre Galindo and] myself, and a woman." The woman was Yvonne Ducailar, whom he frequently called "l'étrangère" in conversations and in letters.

In his last days at Le Panelier, Camus read Plato, Spinoza, and the Bible. A stepped-up German program sent young Frenchmen aged twenty-one to thirty-five to forced-labor camps in Germany, but Camus's illness kept him from being shipped off. From Lyons, Pia still kept an eye out for Camus and promised to visit him. Camus was enjoying autumn in the Vivarais region, with its red forests and beech trees that "made spots of golden yellow or stayed isolated on the fringe of the woods like huge beehives streaming with blond honey." From time to time a pretty girl would go by in the distance, but temptations were fewer than in Algiers or Oran. Camus returned to his obsession with the necessity for asceticism: "Sexuality leads to nothing: it isn't immoral, but it's unproductive. One can abandon oneself to it when one does not want to produce anything. But only chastity is linked to personal progress. There is a time when sexuality is a victory—when one separates it from moral imperatives—but then it quickly becomes a defeat, and in turn, the only victory which is won over it is chastity."

A few days later he wrote: "Uncontrolled sexuality leads to a philosophy of the world's nonsignificance. In contrast, chastity gives back meaning [to the world]." A bit later, Don Juan made an appearance in the role of a cynical, disillusioned man: "Woman, outside of love, is boring, although she doesn't know it. One must live with her and shut up, or sleep with them all and do what one wants. The most important thing is elsewhere."

Camus's difficulty in constructing a sexual morality without God was such that often he felt that artistic creation meant work minus sexuality. He described himself in his *Carnets*: "Idea: he refuses all that is offered to him, all of the joys which present themselves because of a deeper exigency. He spoils his marriage, engages in unsatisfying love affairs, waits, and hopes." To Camus, sexuality often seemed absurd and contingent, not sensual and joyful, with the most important thing remaining his work-in-progress.

This work-in-progress had both social and metaphysical meanings. In *L'Etranger* there was hardly any mention of social matters, apart from the mechanical and imbecilic judicial system. In *La Peste*, social and historical dimensions would be more ambitious and visible. Camus aimed high: "The first thing an artist must learn is the art of transposing what he feels into what he wants to be felt. The first times, he succeeds by accident, but later, talent must replace accidents. There is thus an element of chance in the roots of genius." He used the word "genius" about his own case, although so far the press had only spoken of "talent."

Camus's prolonged stay in the mountains was part of the then widespread, but false, theory that at high altitudes, the tubercular patient could get high doses of oxygen. In fact, at great heights there is less oxygen, and the rate of carbonic acid in the blood does not diminish. To replace blood lost in hemorrhages, patients were encouraged to consume as much red meat and red wine as possible. Camus was a victim of this type of medical mythology. Another remedy with quasimagical aspects was to rest the lungs by collapsing them and thus forcing them into repose. Camus managed to escape sanatoriums, but insofar as he was exiled to the French mountains to be cured, he conformed to the medical conventions of his day.

Camus was given to romantic considerations about his illness: "The renunciation of youth. It's not I who renounce people and things (I couldn't), it's people and things who renounce me. My youth is fleeing from me—that's what it is to be ill." He accepted his illness and decided to be cured quickly, not wanting tuberculosis to take hold of him, but preferring to govern it himself: "Illness is a monastery with its own rules, asceticism, silence, and inspiration."

In North Africa, Allied troops were advancing. On November 8, 1942, American military forces landed in Morocco and Algeria. On the tenth, the Allies occupied Oran, while in France, the Germans crossed into what had been the free zone. Camus was conscious of being trapped, cut off from Algeria and his family, "like rats," he noted in his *Carnets* on November 11. Before the American landings in Algeria, Francine had been terrified, but Albert told her not to worry. However, he missed the last boats out of France and could not get back to Algeria. For a long time afterwards, Camus's *Carnets* would be devoted to his work on the second version of his novel, and on a play, *Le Malentendu* (previously entitled *Bujedovice*).

Every two weeks Camus would go to Saint-Etienne for treatment, without ever centering his existence on his tuberculosis: "Illness is a cross to bear, but perhaps also a protective railing. But the ideal would be to take the strong points while refusing the weak ones. Illness should be a retirement that makes one stronger at a desired moment, and if it were necessary to pay in a currency of suffering and renunciation, then we'd pay up."

In *La Peste*, Camus drew inspiration from a secretive world: "By the Plague, I want to express the suffocation which we have all suffered and the atmosphere of danger and exile which we have all lived in. At the same time, I want to extend this interpretation to the notion of life in general. *La Peste* will show people who have taken the part of reflection, silence, and moral suffering during this war." Albert was also taking notes on the theme of revolt, producing his books slowly, not like a writer under a deadline. During the occupation period, his life was more organized than ever before, and some of the constraints suited him.

Pia thought that a sanatorium at Hauteville in the Ain region would be better for his friend than Le Panelier, as it was at an even higher altitude and in theory would have purer air. He would arrange the money aspect with Malraux; both men were continuing to press Gallimard to pay Camus a monthly retainer. Pia advised Camus to register himself at the Ministry of the Interior, subdivision Algeria, as Frenchmen from North Africa who were retained in France might be given a subsidy.

At Lyons, the writer Jean Prévost had another idea for helping out financially: Camus should take the competitive exam for secondary-school teachers, then by pulling strings he could be admitted to a cure establishment for students at Saint-Hilaire-du-Touvet. Jean Paulhan also took up the battle with Gaston and asked him to send Camus 2,500 francs per month for at least six months. Pia wrote that the stingy Gaston had "the goodwill of a lazy lump," but finally the payment was arranged. Camus asked Paulhan if it was possible to find work in Paris. Pia had been fired by Jean Prouvost and planned to work at a used-book store in Paris as a front for full-time Resistance activities.

Camus thought he might be able to cross the Pyrenees and from there get back to Algeria through Spain. The founder of the newspaper *Alger Républicain*, Jean-Pierre Faure, lived in the southwest of France, and Camus thought of asking him for advice on this subject, until Pia dissuaded him because of Faure's inaccessibility. Pia was truly concerned about Camus's health and wondered if he wouldn't be better off in a milder climate like Saint-Paul-de-Vence in the Alpes-Maritimes region. He gave Camus secret news of Aragon and Malraux by using the first names of their wives: the writers could not be mentioned because they were hiding in the Resistance and a military censor was reading letters.

Paulhan wrote to Camus, asking to meet him in Paris. He tried to think of an employment that Camus would not find too tiring in his present condition. The war in Europe was going against the Germans, and most Frenchmen now believed the Axis powers would be defeated. When the collaborationist author Lucien Rebatet produced a long essay, *The Debris*, in which he sang the praises of the Germans, Gaston Gallimard refused to publish it, under the official pretext that there was a paper shortage.

Chapter Twenty-five **Man's Prejudices**

Winters were rough on the Vivarais-Lignon plateau. Some of the local Protestant families hid Jewish refugees who were hunted by the French collaborationist police, helping the Germans to deport them to concentration camps. Camus was mainly waiting for his travel permit to go to Paris. In December 1942, he wrote to Janine Thomasset, who had married Pierre Gallimard, Gaston's son, at the beginning of the war, asking her to send Maurice Blanchot's two novels and Nietzsche's *Thus Spake Zarathustra*. He complained to Janine, "In this Protestant region, only edifying works can be found, which are instructive but make me feel anemic." Meanwhile, Camus wrote, "we are learning patience, which is a good thing." The hero of *La Peste* also learned patience by waiting.

Camus got to know a new guest at the Oettlys' hotel, a man traveling under the name Fayol. He was really Pierre Lévy, a Marseilles Jew active in the Resistance since 1941. He joined the Resistance movement Combat in 1942 and moved to La Celle, near le Chambon, in the region where Camus was staying. Fayol was in contact with local Resistance leaders. He and his wife, Marianne, made friends with Camus, who presented some of his other friends to the couple, like the poet Francis Ponge and Father Bruckberger, a whimsical, rakish Dominican priest who worked for the Resistance. Fayol, who also traveled under the names Simon, Rivière, Roux, and Vallin, did not offer much information about his activities, but Camus was well aware that he was an active member of the Resistance.

Marianne Fayol gave Camus some German lessons, and he told her that he missed Francine, who was still teaching mathematics back in Oran. Camus complained that during all this time, he could not have any children with Francine because of their separation. Marianne expressed sympathy but privately felt that Camus was an egocentric artist who thought more about

himself than about others. He spoke to Fayol of the slow erosion of love between people separated from one another.

When they met at La Celle or at Le Panelier, Camus showed the Fayols parts of the manuscripts of *Caligula* and *Le Malentendu*. He also told
Marianne that *La Peste* was coming along with difficulty. He would take
walks with a droopy-eared dog named Pauline, saying smilingly, "This bitch
is my cross to bear," and he helped the Fayols' son Serge to write an essay for
homework, for which they got a good grade. The friends laughed together
when the hotel's old window curtains were sewn into pajamas for Camus.

The Fayols showed Camus a way to get letters delivered to Francine
through a postal drop in Portugal. Camus had still not abandoned the idea
of getting back to North Africa. After his travel permit was finally approved
on December 28, 1942, he took the train to Paris on January 4 and arrived at
the Gare de Lyon at 9:55 p.m. He stayed in Paris for two weeks, and at the
Gallimard office this prodigal son was greeted as a prodigy. Everyone wanted
to meet the author of *L'Etranger*, especially since the book was selling well.
Camus was "dazed," but he felt a "real sympathy" for Michel Gallimard,
Gaston's nephew, and he also finally met Jean Paulhan.

He soon returned to the Haute-Loire region and wrote, "To amuse myself, I imagined the story of a victim of the French Revolutionary Terror who
couldn't write more than one sentence of a book about it, because he felt he
couldn't match the reality." Working on *La Peste*, Camus gave the characters
names inspired by people who lived in his region. Le Panelier was transformed into Paneloux, a Jesuit priest in the novel. Montrambert, a sad and
dirty neighborhood in Saint-Etienne, suggested the name of the fictional
journalist Rambert. A local quack doctor named Rioux was remodeled into
Dr. Rieux in *La Peste*. Another local doctor from le Chambon bore some resemblance to the fictional Rieux. Dr. Roger Le Forestier was an active member of the Resistance who, before he was arrested and murdered by the
Germans in 1944, treated Jews and would hide them, as well as other people
working in the Resistance. In 1942, Le Forestier was thirty-five years old, Dr.
Rieux's age in *La Peste*. There the physical resemblance ends, but philosophically there were some parallels: both were independent men who faced
down the authorities, becoming activists fighting against the Plague and
Nazism respectively. Le Forestier had worked with Albert Schweitzer as a
medical missionary fighting leprosy in the Congo, and he noted about his
own Christian engagement, "I have known human misery, the degeneration
and ugliness of man. I refused to see the illnesses that oppress us as a
defeat for man, and I have treated, assuaged, and cured them." Rieux in *La
Peste* might also have subscribed to these words, although he was an atheist,
unlike the devout Le Forestier.

Camus was thinking of another essay, as he told Paulhan: "I . . . have written some pages about a pessimistic revolution, but they are insignificant notes, and besides, they are in Algiers." According to him, the French philosopher Alain had defined the idea of "political relativity," but Camus wanted to introduce "a relativity with passion." There were also lighter parts of his correspondence with Paulhan: Camus jokingly thanked him for ironically claiming to nominate him for the French Academy. Camus was in the company of dogs, but missed his Siamese cat, who was at home with Francine. He wrote to Paulhan, "I am pleased to know that you love animals, something we have in common."

At Le Panelier, Camus gave Fayol a copy of the underground newspaper *Les Etoiles*, telling him, "It's dynamite." The journal contained, among other things, Resistance poems by Louis Aragon. Marianne Fayol made sixty copies of *Les Etoiles* on the mimeograph machine of the public school at nearby Tence. Camus continued his treatments at Saint-Etienne, where he met his friend Blanche Balain. She asked him about the rumors on the fate of French Jews—were they really being deported to extermination camps outside France? Yes, said Camus, the rumors were true, and it was imperative to join the Resistance. A few French Resistance groups had been formed, but they were hampered by lack of munitions and the frequent arrests of their leaders, thanks to the help of French collaborators and informants. When an important Resistance leader, Jean Bonnisol, was arrested the night of December 15, 1943, Fayol confided to Camus that he had been asked to take Bonnisol's place. What did Albert think of the idea? Camus replied that the decision was too serious for him to express an opinion about it.

Thanks to Pia, who also belonged to the group Combat, Camus was aware of what the Resistance was doing, its size and its limits. He still hoped to get back to Algeria through Spain with the help of Father Bruckberger. Marianne Fayol and Sarah Oettly sewed three gold coins into the crotch of a pair of Camus's pants, to be used after he got past the Spanish border. The Fayols tried to dissuade him from going, saying that if he was captured, Franco's troops would lock him up in the Miranda de Ebro prison camp, where he would receive no medical treatment. Camus did not say he was afraid to die, but he felt his mortality more than some others: "From now on the feeling of death is familiar to me, although it is no longer accompanied by pain. Pain makes us hang on to the present, and requires a struggle that keeps one busy. But death, foretold by the mere sight of a blood-covered handkerchief, without any other symptom, means being plunged back into time in a vertiginous way, which is the fear of becoming something else."

Father Bruckberger invited Camus to his little house near the Dominican monastery of Saint-Maximin in the Var region. Bruckberger did not know of any secret route for getting out of France. The priest dreamed of an audacious and poor clergy, conquering with a Nietzschean spirit. Hating any kind of unctuousness, whether from bishops or any other priest, Bruckberger liked to say, "These Christian Democrats bore the shit out of me." Camus told Bruckberger, "When I was young, I thought all priests were happy." To which the father replied, "The fear of losing their faith shrinks their sensitivity, which becomes no more than a negative vocation. They don't look life in the face."

Camus returned to his plateau. At Lyons or Saint-Etienne, he would often see Pia, Francis Ponge, and a new friend, the poet René Leynaud. In June 1943 at Leynaud's home, Camus gave a reading from *Le Malentendu* to a small group, including Ponge and another friend, Michel Pontremoli. Meanwhile, Pia made many mysterious voyages throughout France, going to Switzerland and returning again. Malraux joked with him: "I am told of your upcoming trip to Paris and your sudden interest in the stuffed animal business," a reference to Pia's involvement with the Resistance.

During 1943, Francis Ponge wrote long letters to Camus, developing his ideas on everything from justice to pumpkins, money troubles, and the works of Elsa Triolet, Louis Aragon's wife. Camus was not much interested in modern poetry, but he liked Ponge's "Le parti pris des choses," in which inanimate objects became sources of emotion. Simple and powerful, Ponge's poetry spoke of oranges, butterflies, and oysters, teaching readers to look, touch, and listen afresh. Fourteen years older than Camus, Ponge had also kept his distance from surrealism. He was struck by *Le Mythe de Sisyphe*, which Pia had sent him, even before he had met Camus. He thought that Camus had not included in the book one of the themes of the absurd, "the infidelity of means of expression . . . the impossibility not only for man to express himself, but to express anything at all."

There was a certain coquetry in Ponge's speaking of his incapacity to express or describe anything, and he published prose-poems which he called "failures of description": "In Camus-like terms, when a poem becomes pressing, it is nostalgia I feel, which must be satisfied, and so I let it pour out (or attempt to describe the nostalgia)." Having chosen the absurd as his view of the world, Ponge realized that what he published were recountings of expressive failure.

Ponge met Camus in Lyons and gave him his first notes on *Le Mythe de Sisyphe*. Later he wrote to Camus, "Another thing I did not tell you: Personally, the heaviness of my rock often discourages me and makes me very lazy. Can one imagine a lazy Sisyphus? Wouldn't that be the height of absurdity, or might it only be a contradiction in terms?" Ponge read the issue of the *Cahiers du Sud* with the articles on *L'Etranger* and hastened to write to Camus to tell him what he thought: "I've read Sartre's article, which is very skillful at making the reader find you sympathetic, despite (or because of) that slightly jarring tone which is a bit 'superior' (and quite unjustifiably so). . . . What Sartre says about *L'Etranger's* classicism touches me extremely; classicism that is absurd, or against the absurd—there we are!"

Camus wrote to Ponge that he understood why he was an "activist," a euphemism for "Communist" meant to deceive military censors. Ponge scolded his new friend, "Of course the world is absurd! Of course it does not signify anything! But what is tragic about that? I would gladly remove from absurdity its coefficient of tragedy. . . . Ontological suicide is made for only a few young bourgeois people (incidentally, rather nice ones)."

Sometimes Ponge felt that Camus would like to see him taking philosophy more seriously. But Ponge saw philosophy only as a literary genre, and not his favorite one. Camus suggested he read *Moby-Dick.* Ponge delighted in the prospect of a postwar period and the death of God: "Sisyphus, descending his slope again, will no longer be alone, but arm-in-arm with all his comrades—you, me, Paulhan, Eluard, Pia, and the millions of men who are finally like brothers." Ponge was making many trips to Paris and Grenoble for the Resistance, and he wrote to Camus, "It's not possible to speak of these trips, which were nonetheless instructive. It's a matter of asceticism, of course."

Camus took many notes for his *Carnets* and the third version of *La Peste*, as well as about himself and about man in general. He felt that everyone must be engaged: "The only cowardice is to get down on one's knees. . . . It is our duty to do what we know to be fair and good." Camus felt an admiring tenderness for René Leynaud, the regional head of the Combat movement since the beginning of 1942. A fervent Catholic, Leynaud was also a traditionalist poet. Camus found Leynaud's self-doubts touching, such as when the Resistance leader wrote to him: "I often ask myself if I don't work at poetry in order to demonstrate to myself that I am not a poet, or perhaps to kill my sense of the prestige of words, which is very great in me." Leynaud wrote to Camus that he lacked the philosophical knowledge to appreciate *Le Mythe de Sisyphe*, but he found *Caligula* admirable, "a lightning bolt, the revelation of the impossible in a soul." He sent Camus his poems, often sonnets, and the two writers discussed writers like Agrippa d'Aubigné, Maurice Blanchot, and Martin Buber. They enjoyed boxing matches, swimming in the sea, and camping. They met in Lyons or at Saint-Etienne. Albert felt that if hell exists, it must "resemble these interminable gray streets" of Saint-Etienne, where everyone was dressed in black. He hated Saint-Etienne as the opposite of Algiers; for him, the city symbolized a modern urban horror. "Saint-Etienne and its suburbs: such a spectacle is the condemnation of the civilization that gave birth to it. . . . No people can live outside of beauty. They can only survive for a time, that's all. And this Europe which offers here one of its most constant faces is constantly distancing itself from beauty."

When Camus went to Saint-Etienne for his pneumothorax operations, he therefore suffered doubly. He would take walks with Leynaud in Saint-Etienne, visiting cafés "deserted and full of flies," sipping lemonades sweetened with saccharine in those days of sugar shortages. Leynaud wrote to him at the end of 1943: "May God give us again this year and for some others the joy of serving the same truth. These are my wishes for the year 1944 which I express for you and for myself too, as today I don't want to separate you from a certain idea I have of myself and which I hope is not ignoble."

All through 1943, Camus also corresponded with Elsa Triolet, whom he had met along with her husband, Louis Aragon, in Lyons. Elsa had read *L'Etranger* and *Le Mythe* and saw the novel as a bouquet of despair "even more complete" than the essay. She felt he had evaded the question of old age in his books. Camus compared one of Elsa's books with *Gone with the Wind*, which worried Triolet, who was a simpering Communist. Elsa would sign her letters "Elisabeth Mayzargues" to deceive the military censors. She wrote to Camus to say that Aragon had heard Francine on the radio, asking for news of Albert by name. Aragon stayed in the background, a grand seigneur who was not on the same wavelength as the young, new writer. Elsa's eyes and heart were aflutter as she sensed Albert's reservations about her: "May I ask you a little question? Why are you wary and reserved with us? With me?" She repeated her theme: "As for my husband, you must be very sensitive, and you have preconceived ideas. . . . Anyway, although I hate the people who don't love L., we haven't necessarily the same degree of friendship for every single person." Elsa could not omit a pathetic note: "Yet I . . . have the impression of having made a declaration of love to which you have not responded: I love you like a brother!"

Triolet published a convoluted article in the review *Poésie* in 1943, sixteen pages of allusive criticism of *L'Etranger* and *Le Mythe de Sisyphe*, mixed with an invented story about a fictitious Baroness Mélanie. Her article was subtitled "The Myth of Baroness Mélanie." Camus did not seem displeased about the baroness, telling Elsa: "As for your point of departure, the criticism of my essay, you are absolutely right: there can be absurd myths, but absurd thought is not possible."

In theory and practice, Camus had already gone past the absurd. At Le Panelier and during his trips to Lyons, he felt revolted by the French people's situation; as a writer, his weapons were words. He published a pamphlet, *Des Exilés de la peste*, with Trois Collines Editions in Geneva, which took an approach similar to the eventual novel, *La Peste*, portraying the Plague as Nazism and the rats as Germans. *Des Exilés de la peste* was not widely read, but the text was a form of testimony for Camus. The Plague had no limits, and it could mean the German occupation, terror, suffering, death, exile, and imprisonment. Camus wanted the "great theme of the novel" to be separation. His life in France from 1942 to 1943 provided material for his story without exhausting its meaning, any more than L'Etranger's pages about beaches and courtrooms in Algiers were the only significance of that novel. Camus complained that he lacked imagination, yet he did show some in his two finished plays, although they were based on the real-life struggles and beliefs of people he knew.

When Dr. Rieux and Father Paneloux have a discussion in the novel, Camus found their arguments in his readings and memories of conversations with Pia and Ponge, for the unbeliever's side, and with Bruckberger and Leynaud, for the believer's point of view. On the Vivarais plateau, unbelievers like the Fayols and believers like Dr. Le Forestier worked together to save Jews and to fight in the Resistance. In Camus's novel, Rieux says to Paneloux, "We are working together for something that reunites us beyond blasphemies and prayers. That is the only important thing." Camus's sympathies were clear. The Plague is not absurd in itself, and to face it, man must revolt. As 200 million Europeans were prisoners of the Nazis, so 200,000 imaginary Oran residents were prisoners of the Plague.

In this tale, two women were conspicuous although not often present: Camus's mother and Rieux's mother. As he did in L'Envers et l'endroit, Camus recalled his mother, Catherine Camus, leaning over her balcony on the rue de Lyon: Madame Rieux had a "particular taste . . . for a certain window . . . behind which she would sit in the evenings, a bit rigidly, her hands still and her eyes attentive." Like Camus's mother, Madame Rieux was all "silence and shadow." Camus wrote as a novelist and as a son: "Thus [Rieux] and his mother always loved one another in silence, and she would die in turn—or he would—without being able during their entire lives to go any further in admitting their tenderness." Camus may also have been thinking of Francine and himself when Rieux said to his wife, " 'Everything will be better when you come back. . . . We'll start over again.' 'Yes,' she said, her eyes shining, 'we'll start over again.' "

As the war progressed for Camus as for Pia, Ponge, and Leynaud, any compromise with the German occupants became a dishonest capitulation. Not that all anti-Nazi Frenchmen were militants or members of the Resistance. In La Peste, when it becomes a question of forming teams of sanitary volunteers to fight the Plague, "the results were thin." Active Resistance members in France did not exceed two hundred thousand at the highest estimate. In his final version of La Peste (1946), Camus wrote, "However, the narrator's intention is not to give these sanitary groups more importance than they had. . . . Instead, it is true that many of our fellow citizens give in today to the temptation of exaggerating their role." Camus's view of the Resistance would rapidly change over the years. In La Peste, an allegorical tale, those whom Camus loved, like Rieux, became engaged right away, or with time, like Paneloux and Rambert. Camus implied that reaching an adult age brought a practical morality with it, but his psychology and art also meant understanding others with indulgence. Before committing himself, Camus had also hesitated, like Rambert. The latter wanted to flee Oran, and Camus sought to escape occupied France and return home to the safety of Algeria. He put parts of himself in his characters, with seriousness or humor.

Camus had studied Saint Augustine, Father Paneloux's specialty in *La Peste*. Rieux is the son of a laborer, whose great knowledge derives from "poverty," much like Camus's self-image. The journalist Rambert is a soccer fan, and at Chambon Camus felt deprived of his much-beloved matches. Like Rambert, Camus believed that "the midfielder is the one who distributes the game." He made fun of himself in his self-portrait as the pathetic Grand, who agonizes over writing a book. Grand keeps rewriting the same sentence, and Camus was on his third version of *La Peste*. Camus, who loved to laugh in private, put few smiles into this grave tale, a reflection of the tragic years during which it was written.

His books contained references to each other. In *La Peste*, there is an allusion to *L'Etranger* at a tobacconist's: "In the middle of an animated conversation, the latter spoke of an arrest that was much talked about in Algiers, of a young commercial employee who killed an Arab on the beach." From one book to another, Camus would salute his friends, who might sometimes also be his critics. He was present, barely disguised, in the two characters Rieux and Rambert, the most three-dimensional portraits along with Paneloux and Tarrou. Rieux embodied tranquil courage and an atheism that he felt was inevitable, although he regretted it. He was the embodiment of doubts and worry. In Tarrou there were also elements of Pia, who was convinced of the world's insignificance, which did not keep him from being militantly active in his Resistance unit. To Camus, as to Rieux, the death of children was a "scandal." The novelist writing *La Peste* at le Chambon was like the young reporter who inquired about the death of innocent people in Algiers.

With *La Peste*, the reader can observe the novelist's changing attitude toward the absurd. As soon as he had arrived at Chambon, Camus noted in his *Carnets*: "Although the absurd teaches us nothing, it is an ultimate form of progress." A few months later, he added that the absurd was no more than an "aesthetic justification." He had only one conclusion to this argument: "I see clearly that absurd thought (even in aesthetics) ends in an impasse, and the problem is, Can one live in an impasse?" Camus and his characters in *La Peste* would distance themselves from the absurd in order to find the pathway to revolt.

By the autumn of 1943, Camus seemed to have arrived at a certain wisdom, if not serenity and fundamental satisfaction, in the act of writing. He was not pleased with his long book, *La Peste*, written with less passion than

L'Etranger. But it was possible to see the direction he was headed in: *"La Peste* may be read in three different ways. It is at the same time a tale about an epidemic, a symbol of Nazi occupation (and incidentally the prefiguration of any totalitarian régime, no matter where), and, thirdly, the concrete illustration of a metaphysical problem, that of evil . . . which is what Melville tried to do with *Moby-Dick,* with genius added."

The world no longer seemed absurd, but terrible instead. Revolt was the response that Camus wanted to give in his life and in his chronicle. The absurd man Meursault as well as the abstract heroes of *Le Mythe de Sisyphe* are overwhelmed by events and by the thoughts of man caught up in the torments of European history. Camus had once toyed with the idea that if God did not exist, everything was permitted, with the double temptation of getting rid of conventional morality and creating a new one. Now he stated that "value judgments cannot be suppressed entirely, for that would deny absurdity."

For aesthetics, craftsmanship, and art, Camus kept one of his promises: he had imagined an "author writing each of his novels in a different style." *La Peste's* calm and ample style was radically different from the terse and dry tone of *L'Etranger.* It was similar to a lake after a torrent.

Like his first-person narrator, Rieux, in *La Peste,* Camus felt closer to failures than with saints. Rieux affirmed, as Camus might have: "I don't believe I have any taste for heroism or saintliness; what interests me is being a man."

Chapter Twenty-six **Resistances**

T hirty years old. Man's first faculty is that of forgetfulness, but it is only fair to say that he even forgets the good that he has done," Camus wrote in his *Carnets*. Staying in Paris at the Hôtel Mercure on the rue de la Chaise, near the metro station Sèvres-Babylone in the seventh arrondissement, he continued to take notes for *La Peste*, with his usual uncompromising self-scrutiny: "The greatest economy that one can achieve in thinking is to accept that the world is unintelligible, and that man should be the focal point." On a metaphysical level, the world seemed incomprehensible and meaningless.

At the end of 1943, the planet's political and military history were changing quickly, and among the thousands of Allied soldiers fighting in Italy was Albert's brother, Lucien Camus, a sergeant in the First Anti-Aircraft Brigade. Promoted to company sergeant major, Lucien fought alongside tens of thousands of Algerians of all religions. Lucien would participate in Allied landings on Ajaccio on October 24, 1943; on mainland Italy on June 9, 1944; and in France on September 19, 1944.

Snug in his room on the rue de la Chaise, Albert Camus wrote to his friends Pierre and Marianne Fayol: "I had to find a room, organize my restaurants, gallop around the town halls and police headquarters, get myself yelled at, etc. All that took time." The Hôtel Mercure was a furnished residential hotel, an easy walk to the Gallimard offices, first along the boulevard Raspail, and then a few steps on the rue de Montalembert to arrive at the rue Sébastien-Bottin, where Gallimard was. Hired as a manuscript reader at four thousand francs per month, Camus shared an office with the writer Jacques Lemarchand, known in the literary milieu, but not fully appreciated, which Camus thought was unfair. Lemarchand was rather reticent about his opinion of Camus's plays, but they had lots of fun writing a poetry anthology, which would be accepted by the reading committee, although it was never published. Before he got to Paris, Camus had proposed to Blanche Balain that she become his secretary, but she refused.

With his salary and book royalties, Camus was not rich but was comfortable enough. In November he had "tumbled into the midst of 400 manuscripts for the Pléiade Prize [founded by Gaston Gallimard] which, it appears, was only waiting for me." Camus and Lemarchand were responsible for weeding out the best ones. Camus complained that examining around fifty books and manuscripts left his head spinning. What he had read at first was bad, he told the Fayols, and if the remainder were like that, their little son, Serge, could send in his homework and "he'd have a good chance."

His room at the Mercure was well heated and boasted boiling-hot water. He could cook there, and he received friends from Algiers such as the writer Gabriel Audisio and the painter and set designer Marie Viton, Countess of Estournel. Camus found Paris restaurants good but expensive: "In any case, Paris remains the only city in France where one can forget about food restrictions, or almost." In Paris at the time, there were four categories of restaurants, plus an exceptional class where there was no limit on the prices of luxury dishes, from steak to caviar. Camus went to restaurants in the second and third categories, where meals cost 150 to 250 francs, or around a dollar. Among the restaurants he often ate at were Le Petit Saint-Benoît on the street of the same name, Les Charpentiers near the Mabillon market, Les Casques, Les Assassins, Augustin Cheramy, and Alexandre on the rue des Canettes. In poorer restaurants of the fourth class, where Camus did not eat, diners were served rutabagas, Jerusalem artichokes, and beets, prepared in school-cafeteria style. Destitute authors without Gallimard contracts could eat meals subsidized by the Writers' Union for only four francs at a cafeteria on the avenue de l'Opéra.

Camus kept the Fayols up to date with the latest chatter from Paris. He saw his first play in months, Corneille's rarity *Suréna*, which had been exhumed by the Comédie-Française. He was struck by Corneille's verses and said he had not felt such powerful emotion for a long time. Some evenings, Michel Gallimard and his wife would drop Camus off at a metro station and watch the young writer, who was sensitive to the cold, walking awkwardly away, wearing an overcoat Michel had given him, with the collar turned up. His thin, pale face had the unhappy look of a dying man, a stranger in a city that was hostile, gray, and sinister.

In coded language, Camus told his correspondents that he was working for the Resistance: "You know that I had intended to do a few journalistic pieces. . . . Everything is going well with respect to that, and I am using my small talents as best I can." The Fayols knew that Camus was not doing any journalism, nor did he want to: Camus had made contact with the Combat group, and they put him in touch with the Movement for National Liberation (MLN).

Whatever his involvement was, Camus never touched a gun. He later wrote to René Lalou that in 1940 and 1941 in Algeria he had been "in contact with Resistance groups which prepared a possible invasion landing." In 1943, he told Lalou that he "joined the Combat group. . . . I never touched a gun." Camus said that his "little activity" in the Resistance seemed to him "derisory next to that of some of my comrades who were real combatants."

For the time being, the war continued, and Camus told the Fayols that he was concerned about its duration: "If peace takes too long, it will have no more meaning, or only for a few scoundrels and cowards." He felt that the Parisians were optimistic: "When one is threatened, one prefers to hope."

Only two hundred meters away from the Hôtel Mercure was the luxurious Hôtel Lutétia, headquarters of the German Wehrmacht—one of the many grandiose sites that the Nazis had taken over in occupied Paris, including the Senate, the Lycée Montaigne, the Hôtel Crillon on the place de la Concorde, and the Hôtel Meurice on the rue de Rivoli. On the boulevard Raspail and the boulevard Saint-Germain, Camus could see German military cars and trucks, and at every major crossing there were traffic signs in German. After each terrorist attack from the Resistance, the Germans would put up posters in red and black or in yellow and black, listing French prisoners who had been shot in reprisal. The French *milice*, the all-Gallic militia, which was feared as even more pitiless than the Gestapo, wore black berets and dark blue uniforms; the *milice* occupied the Lycée Saint-Louis on the boulevard Saint-Michel near the Sorbonne, and facing the German Bookstore run by, among others, the French writer and collaborator Robert Brasillach.

Camus found Paris at the time "very lovely in this still-warm autumn that covers all the sidewalks with dead leaves. There are magnificent moonlit nights and at deserted intersections . . . there is a grandeur which this city will never recapture, and pretty things and lovely faces at every street corner."

Parisian women limped around in wooden-soled shoes because of leather shortages, and those without stockings painted their legs to make it appear that they were wearing them. Camus noted: "The city assumes the look of a resigned woman prisoner. It makes you want to get the hell out of here, or to break something, but you shut up and keep walking straight ahead." Albert sent letters to Francine through Armand Guibert, a poet living in Portugal.

On December 20, he finished reading manuscripts for the Pléiade Prize. He saw Paul Claudel's play *Le Soulier de satin* at the Comédie-Française, commenting that "there is a lot to say about it," but not specifying what exactly that might be. He had plenty to eat, and a "diplomaed doctor" was treating him. The Fayols hoped that the doctor was intelligent and understanding, but Camus replied that one shouldn't expect too much, as he thought that doctor-patient rapports were "forcibly false, and on an unequal level, with each party acting out his own comedy. My doctor finally discovered that I write books and he immediately informed me that he was writing one on tuberculosis and that therefore we were colleagues. I congratulated him, he congratulated me, and thus we acted out a brief situation-comedy second act." Seriously, the doctor recommended that Camus use the medication Antigrippine—a kind of aspirin—for his attacks of flu. On December 20, Camus warned the Fayols that he was sending them a friend from Oran who was stuck in France, writing in code, "This woman friend, it turns out, has delicate health from a hereditary infection": i.e., the woman refugee was Jewish.

Camus had to stay in Paris for his job, and found only two hours a day in the evenings after office hours for his own writing, which exhausted him: "I am like everyone, I aspire to peace in every sense of the word." He constantly repeated to the Fayols "I have works to create," and he added, about Francine, "and perhaps a happiness to find once again." At the beginning of 1944, Sarah Oettly came to Paris from Le Panelier, carrying foodstuffs for Camus from the Fayols. He wrote to them gratefully: "All this reinforces my idea that there is no Providence, only friends." He was very occupied by his work at the Gallimard office and by his "journalistic work," the code reference for his errands on behalf of the Resistance. As for his main literary projects, "La Peste is sleeping and wakes up from time to time, only to doze off once again."

And then he was very much taken with Jean-Paul Sartre's one-act play No Exit. He described it as "about Hell, performed in a Louis-Philippe-style living room (which is Hell) with no intermission and no entrances or exits, which makes for rather tough directorial problems." No Exit was to be performed in an experimental theater subsidized by Gaston Gallimard. Camus was seeing a lot of Simone de Beauvoir and Sartre, whom he had met at the dress rehearsal of Sartre's play The Flies in June 1943. Sartre did not often appreciate the company of men, but he liked Camus, a writer who had been an actor and stage director. Sartre proposed to Camus that he play the role of Garcin in No Exit and that he direct the play as well. Camus accepted. Rehearsals were held in various hotel rooms, including Camus's and Simone de Beauvoir's, at the Hôtel Louisiane on the rue de Seine. They were also held at the home of Olga Barbézat, whose husband, Marc, owner of a pharmaceuticals laboratory and editor of the review Arbalète, was producing the play. After a few weeks, Olga was arrested, suspected by the French police of belonging to the Resistance. Sartre decided to replace Camus, who was unknown in the Paris theater world, with a well-known director and to have the play staged at the Vieux-Colombier Theatre with professional actors. So Camus was obliged to give up the project of acting in and directing *No Exit*. The brief letter that Camus sent Sartre to release them from their mutual agreement, Simone found "charming."

Camus and Sartre enjoyed laughing together while Simone—nicknamed "Castor," or "the Beaver"—looked on at their antics with a tender but somewhat haughty expression. Sartre would write at the cafés in the Saint-Germain-des-Près quarter, usually at the Flore and less often at the Deux Magots. At the time, cafés were crowded with writers and artists, some of whom were in the Resistance, some collaborators, and some simply waiting for new developments. The Saint-Germain Aquarium café overflowed with collaborators, including the expert on Marcel Proust, Ramon Fernandez. Camus nicknamed a waiter at the Flore "Descartes" because his real first name was Pascal, and this sort of joke annoyed the Beaver. Simone was attracted by Camus's nonchalant simplicity and good humor, but she was also irritated by his "Rastignac side," referring to Balzac's pushy character in *La Comédie humaine*.

Sartre was short, fat, and wall-eyed, ugly by any standard, while Camus was handsome, slim, and above average height. The two men talked more about women than about philosophy. They seemed to fall for one another, and although Camus did not describe his past in detail, Sartre managed to guess enough about it to appreciate him as a man. Sartre came from an upper-middle-class family, whereas the surly, meditative Camus, who could be heavy-handed though seductive, came from the working class. Sartre was eight years older than his new friend, and although he might have played a paternal role, he preferred to behave like a brother, never pedantic or overprotective.

The Beaver was perplexed, and worried that Sartre was falling too much for Camus's charm—as she herself was doing, by the way. Quickly enough, Beauvoir and Camus became jealous of one another, although decorously so. The Beaver noted that she and Camus were like "two dogs surrounding a bone," the bone in this case being Sartre. Beauvoir planned to write an essay, "For a Morality of Ambiguity," and indeed she had an ambivalent sexuality in general, as well as ambiguous feelings about Camus. Sartre adored Camus's cheeky side and his appetite for joy, as well as the contrast between his refined books and his ribald jokes. While he seemed flattered to be asked to join the Sartre family, Camus nevertheless remained on the edge of their social circle.

Sartre wrote philosophy, novels, novellas, and plays, and his brilliant excess astonished Camus. In the winter of 1943–1944 alone, Sartre had written two screenplays, *Les Jeux sont faits* and *Typhus*, rewrote the first two volumes of his *Les Chemins de la liberté*, wrote articles praising Maurice Blanchot and Kafka and a ferocious study of the collaborator Pierre Drieu La Rochelle. *Being and Nothingness* had been published in August, and though it sold hardly any copies, it was slowly making an impact. Some people avoided giving an opinion about this monstrously ambitious work. Jean Paulhan said that the book was practical for black-market shopping: on one side of the scale you put potatoes, and on the other side *Being and Nothingness*, which weighed exactly one kilogram.

Camus and Sartre would eat lunch and dinner at the Brasserie Lipp on the boulevard Saint-Germain, before going to have a drink at the Rhumerie down the block. Camus never made any public comment about *Being and Nothingness*, nor did he ever really get inside Sartre's ideas. They were not intellectual accomplices, as Sartre was with Maurice Merleau-Ponty or Raymond Aron, writers who recognized one another's merits and were friends as well. By contrast, Sartre once tipsily told Camus, "I'm more intelligent than you, huh? More intelligent!" Camus nodded his head obligingly, convinced that it was true. Once Camus saw Sartre showing off to a pretty young girl and asked him, "Why are you going to so much trouble?" Sartre replied, "Have you taken a look at my mug?"

There were lots of lovely women in the Saint-Germain quarter, which Camus noted "makes a nice change from the toothless horrors of the Haute-Loire region." Sartre and Beauvoir had developed a doctrine for their relationship: Sartre theorized, borrowing philosophical terms from Immanuel Kant, that he would have a "necessary" permanent relationship with the Beaver while also having other "contingent," temporary love affairs. This arrangement suited Sartre. Camus did not moralize about his love life on such philosophic heights, and he still had not quite figured out how to be in love with two women at the same time. He knew about Sartre and Beauvoir's sexual games, but he did not participate in them.

Camus would meet the couple socially in the large apartment of Louise and Michel Leiris on the quai des Grands-Augustins in the sixth arrondissement. Louise Leiris was the daughter of the noted art dealer Daniel-Henry Kahnweiler, who helped make Picasso a star; and Michel Leiris was a writer and ethnologist, an early member of the surrealist group who passionately admired bullfighting and Picasso. While Sartre had his "family," Camus also had his social circle, adopted as he was by the Gallimard family, notably by Pierre and Janine Gallimard and Pierre's cousin Michel. They would go out to nightclubs and take part in "fiestas" where they drank hot wine with cinnamon. Pierre never drank, and Michel indulged only a little, as three glasses of wine would make him drunk. Writers like Georges Bataille, author of the erotic *Story of the Eye*, and Raymond Queneau, also went along. Sartre's family circle included the young writer Jacques-Laurent

Bost, who became an expert at cooking boiled beef with vegetables, known as *boeuf mode*, and veal blanquette, whenever meat was available. After the midnight police curfew, guests would have to stay overnight with their hosts.

The Leirises organized a reading of Picasso's play *Le Désir attrapé par la queue* in their apartment. As stage manager and director, Camus handed out the roles. Picasso's work was surrealist, Dadaist, and realist all at once. The performance, which took place on March 19, 1944, began at 5 p.m. and ended an hour before curfew time. Leiris played the role of "Bigfoot" and Sartre that of "Round Morsel." Simone de Beauvoir was "the Woman Cousin," although she would have preferred to play "the Pie" or "Thin Anguish"; and Queneau played "the Onion." Simone wore a red angora sweater and large blue pearls, which Camus made fun of, and that annoyed her. Some of the play's speeches reminded the actors and the audience about occupation meat shortages, such as when Bigfoot said, "After some consideration, nothing is better than mutton stew, but in fact I much prefer boiled beef in onion sauce, or well-prepared beef stew in red wine sauce."

The photographer Brassaï immortalized the production, whose audience included the actor-director Jean-Louis Barrault, the painter Georges Braque, the dramatist Armand Salacrou, the singer, actor, and writer Marcel Mouloudji, and the poet Henri Michaux. Also present was twenty-two-year-old actress, Maria Casarès, who was lovely, although outside the usual canons of beauty: she had slanted eyes, a stubborn chin, and a hoarse voice. Casarès took note of the stage manager, who used a stick to give the signal to raise the curtain by knocking three times on the floor. Camus also narrated the play, reading the notes about scenery and stage directions. Maria Casarès found this young man enchanting. He spoke with an accent, in a voice that was clear, if hoarse, alternately abstracted and vivid. He had a haughty profile and eyes that seemed lost, which made for a proud but tired appearance. She told herself that he must be an actor. Casarès had just made her theatrical debut at the Mathurins Theatre in John Millington Synge's *Deirdre of the Sorrows*, and the film director Robert Bresson chose her to act in *Les Dames du bois de Boulogne*.

Sartre and Camus did not compromise themselves in the fashionable Parisian literary salons where Nazi collaborators were welcome. They stayed away from invitations from Madame Boudot-Lamotte, the mother of Gaston Gallimard's secretary, and above all from Florence Gould, an American who welcomed guests on Thursdays on the avenue Malakoff in the sixteenth arrondissement. Mrs. Gould hosted a group that included Nazi officers like the military censor Lieutenant Heller and Captain Ernst Jünger, who had a flourishing literary career. Among the odd lot of Frenchmen who also went to Mrs. Gould's home were the writer Marcel Jouhandeau, because he was a Nazi collaborator; Henry de Montherlant and Jean Cocteau, for obscure reasons; Paul Léautaud, because he was a misanthrope; and Marcel Arland and Jean Paulhan, because they were spies for the Resistance.

For an encyclopedia which Gaston Gallimard planned to publish, Sartre, Merleau-Ponty, Simone de Beauvoir, and Camus wrote on ethics, and they planned a group manifesto on the subject. The end of the war was in sight, and the team planned to publish a literary review when Paris and France were liberated. Far away from his wife, Camus enjoyed a double family life with the Gallimards, that was both personal and professional. His official job title at Gallimard was first a vague "secretary," then "reader," and he participated in the reading committee, a strategic position where he worked alongside Janine Thomasset-Gallimard. There was no official hierarchy at the Gallimard office, but power echelons were very well established: The founding father, Gaston, was assisted by his brother Raymond, the company's finance director. Camus was friendly with the second generation of Gallimards, the cousins Pierre, Michel, and Robert.

One evening at the Le Tabarin nightclub Camus started to glance in a hostile way at a group of Gestapo officers. Robert restrained him, saying, "Hey, you're not going to do something stupid, are you?" The charming exile Camus often let his fatigue show through his energetic façade. Michel admired, loved, and adored him, and so did the youngest Gallimard, Robert. Michel had plenty of money, as did Janine and Pierre, so whatever else happened, Camus was always assured of having enough to eat. He was no longer poor, but he would taunt Michel by saying, "You haven't had the experience of poverty."

Gaston Gallimard was Olympian, charming, crafty, generous and cheap at the same time. Gaston had guided the publishing house carefully since the beginning of the occupation. The NRF had been shut down, then started up again. In November 1940, Gaston wrote to Jean Luchaire, a Nazi collaborator, publicist, and director of the newspaper Nouveaux Temps, that Gallimard was concentrating "on collaborating" with the dreaded Dr. Kaiser of the Propagandastaffel, the Nazi propaganda unit based in Paris. This letter would come back to haunt Gaston after the war, although he refused to publish works by Luchaire. On the other hand, the collaborationist press, newspapers like Le Petit Parisien, Le Pilori, and Je Suis Partout, attacked Gaston: Paul Riche wrote in Le Pilori: "Gallimard? Where have we seen that name? . . . at the bottom of books by André Gide, Malraux, Aragon, and Freud, surrealist books, suspicious books afflicted by necrosis. Unhealthy? Yes, unhealthy! . . . books of propaganda for Israel. How many Jewish names there are on Gallimard's list . . . Freud! . . . Benda! . . . Abraham! . . . Wahl! Gallimard is an assassin of the mind."

The resurrected NRF was entrusted to the collaborator Pierre Drieu La Rochelle, and the review published thirty issues during the war with a print run of five thousand copies; before the war, the NRF had a circulation of fifteen thousand. Like all Paris publishers, Gaston had to adhere to the rules of the German ambassador, Otto Abetz. The "Otto list" ordered that publishers destroy all copies of books by Jewish authors as well as non-Jews who had "poisoned French public opinion." More than one thousand titles were destroyed in warehouses—over 2,240 tons' worth of books. To better apply his strategy of long-term survival, Gaston made what he saw as a tactical sacrifice of a number of his authors, like Louis Aragon and Joseph Kessel (Communists), André Malraux (Resistant), and André Maurois (Jewish). But to some authors whose books had been destroyed following Nazi orders, he gave a monthly allowance.

He remained in contact with Malraux, who himself was a friend of Drieu La Rochelle. Gaston knew that Jean Paulhan had been in the Resistance since immediately after the French surrender. He knew how the younger Gallimards and Camus, as well as most of the other employees at the rue Sébastien-Bottin, felt about the Germans. Gaston did not adopt the role of saint, which might have shut down the publishing house. But André Malraux remained a member of the jury for the Pléiade Prize, although he was hated by the violent collaborationist daily *Je Suis Partout*, which spewed out criticism of "Malraux of the Communist Party and the International Brigade."

The Pléiade Prize was given to Marcel Mouloudji for his novel *Enrico*, after Sartre put pressure on the other jurors. The Pléiade Prize, typically enough, was a way for Gallimard authors to give a Gallimard author a Gallimard prize. To celebrate Mouloudji's award, Camus suggested going to one of his favorite North African restaurants, Le Hoggar on the rue Monsieur-le-Prince, with Gabriel Audisio as another guest of honor.

In the beginning of 1944, with the war nearly over, the reading committee, whose members were chosen by Gaston, began to reflect political opinions. Some members of the committee, like Paulhan, Jean Blanzat, and Bernard Groethuysen, also belonged to the National Writers' Committee, a Resistance organization with some Communist members, but which welcomed everyone. Among the latest adherents to the National Writers' Committee were Queneau and Camus, who joined in principle, although he never attended a meeting either in Paris or in Lyons. By the beginning of 1944, Camus was an active member of the Resistance. All of the Gallimard reading committee was on the Allied side, with the single exception of the collaborator Ramon Fernandez.

Camus was on excellent though distant terms with Paulhan, and showed him sections of *La Peste*. He was also on good terms with the charming Queneau, who wrote poems as attractive as his novels and also published Resistance articles in underground journals. André Malraux had refused to join the Resistance as long as it had no guns or money, but by 1944 he too was a member. Camus remained in contact with the Combat group, thanks to his friends Pascal Pia and René Leynaud.

At the end of 1943, Camus had been summoned by the National Resistance Committee director, Claude Bourdet, who, following Pia's advice, wanted to make Camus editor in chief of *La Revue Noire*, an intellectual publication. Camus was given false papers and an identity card in the name "Albert Mathé." According to the card, Mathé was a journalist, the son of Jacques Mathé and Madeleine Pannetier. The card was dated May 20, 1943, and in case of arrest and verification, it would not betray Camus, as the registries for that month had temporarily disappeared from the local archives. Later, Camus would have a birth certificate made to confirm his false identity card, which said that he was born on May 7, 1911, at Choisy-le-Roi in the Seine department near Paris. Almost all active members of the Resistance were given false papers. Sartre never had any; but Pascal Pia, who was back in France after a stay in Switzerland, had been given several fake names since he started in the Resistance in 1942. Pia had been deputy to Marcel Peck, head of Combat for the Lyons region. When Claude Bourdet gave up the idea of *La Revue Noire*, Pia proposed that Camus reorganize the newspaper under a second pseudonym, "Bauchard." Then Bourdet was arrested, and Pia took his place as head of some underground activities, traveling through France, preparing the committees of liberation which the Communists hastened to create.

Pia presented Camus to Jacqueline Bernard, a young woman from a wealthy family who was active in the Resistance under the names "Auger" and "Oger." The same age as Camus, Jacqueline had studied political science until she was asked by Resistance activists if she wouldn't like to type out "little articles to explain that, in fact, Marshal Pétain and Joan of Arc were not really the same thing." Jacqueline's father, a colonel in the French army, gave money to support Combat. Camus remarked to Jacqueline that he was ready to accept any useful task and that he knew how to write for newspapers or do page layouts.

For security reasons, the articles were photo-engraved and sent to as many as fifteen different printers throughout France, as sending newspapers by train or the post was risky. Once, a package of newspapers marked "cleaning products" was delivered by error to an unsuspecting Paris dyer. Frightened, the dyer called the collaborationist police, who suspected him of Resistance activities. Camus told Jacqueline Bernard about this story: "You see, it's as dangerous not to be involved in the Resistance as it is to be involved."

Jacqueline worked in a tiny maid's room and was on the lookout for places where the editorial staff could hold their meetings. A sympathizer offered his apartment, except for Fridays when his mistress came to call, a detail that delighted Camus. Jacqueline also asked her parents' former maid for a room; a Belgian, she was now the concierge of a building on the rue de Lisbonne in the eighth arrondissement, and so the Resistance workers began to meet in a room behind her office. The password was to ask for "Mr. Pineauva," to which the prearranged response was "Third to the right." No one ever wondered why so many people gathered in a room in back of a concierge's office.

Finally Camus revealed to Jacqueline who he was, breaking the general rule of anonymity in the Resistance by telling her that she could reach him at the Gallimard office. She helped him to obtain black-market tires for his bicycle from a boy who worked at the Comédie-Française, which served as a message drop for the Resistance.

Sartre came to one meeting of the newspaper, newly renamed *Combat*, and offered his services "even for stories about dogs run over in the street." The Beaver volunteered to help the newspaper make contacts. *Combat* received funding from Switzerland and the south of France, and some of this money was entrusted to Michel Gallimard, who put it in his personal safe. Camus took on the job of editor in chief of *Combat*, a rather well-printed sheet measuring about seven by ten inches. A cross of Lorraine cut across the "C" in the newspaper's title. *Combat* had "only one leader: de Gaulle. Only one combat: for our freedoms." Its motto was, "In war as in peace, the last word is said by those who never surrender."

The newspaper presented itself as the voice of the United Resistance Movements, which included Combat, Libération, and Franc-Tireur. Issue number 53, dated December 1943, announced that Michel Clémenceau, son of the great French president Georges Clémenceau, had just been arrested and sent to a German concentration camp. *Combat* started by printing ten thousand copies; but by late 1943, 250,000 copies were printed of each issue.

Combat was supposed to appear every two weeks, but often came out only every three or four weeks. The issue of December 1943 contained news about the south of France and German operations against teachers and students at the University of Strasbourg who had taken refuge in Clermont-Ferrand. The newspaper summed up the Resistance's activities: "From November 2 to December 2, the Maquis carried out 310 attacks, sabotages, executions, and resupplying operations, seconded by the Franc groups and the FTP of the Haute-Seine department. In only twenty cases were the police able to identify the authors of these operations. The merchandise taken, including tobacco, wheat, canned food, etc., could fill a whole train. Around sixty traitors have been slaughtered." On the fourth page was a ten-point manifesto for the future, which Pia and Camus approved of: "We no longer want a parliamentary system which is powerless when confronted by capitalist powers. . . . We no longer want to re-experience the Popular Front, to witness reforms applied by a powerless government sabotaged by hostile civil servants and threatened by reigning capitalists who preferred to lose France rather than see it become socialist."

Frenchmen obtained more news about the war by listening to the BBC's French programs or to Radio Brazzaville, broadcast from the Congo, than they did by reading the Resistance press. Still, newspapers like *Libération, Franc-Tireur, Résistance, Défense de la France,* and *Combat* represented the Resistance and were symbolically cohesive, providing centers around which Resistance groups operated. More than anything else, newspapers proved the vitality of the Resistance movement and helped launch slogans, especially those against forced labor, such as "To leave is to betray, to betray is to die" and to recruit for the Maquis: "If you are brave, you will join the Maquis."

Some Resistance workers complained that they were treated as a negligible quantity by General de Gaulle, whose exiled Free French government was in Algeria. But *Combat* identified with de Gaulle, publishing a photocopy of a letter from him: "My comrades, the honor and grandeur of France depend on what you are doing, what you are suffering in the Resistance, which is to say in combat. The end is approaching!"

At work, Camus hid some anti-Nazi documents in Pierre Gallimard's office and dictated to Janine some shorter articles for *Combat.* Camus did not belong to an "action group" and was therefore not responsible for transporting guns, transmitting military information, or participating in sabotage. He chose what news should be covered, counted the lines in each article, and recruited contributors at the Gallimard office, including the writer Dionys Mascolo. His office on the rue Sébastien-Bottin also served as a mailbox. In 1943 and 1944, writing an anti-Nazi tract in France could lead to arrest and deportation to a concentration camp. In *La Peste,* on which Camus was still working, those who fight illness are not presented as heroes. Camus rewrote articles and apparently contributed four original pieces under the pseudonym Bauchard for the *Combat* issues of March, April, and May 1944. One, under the headline "To Total War, Total Resistance," preached engagement against political neutrality. In April he attacked the *milice,* the French militia that aped the evil of the Gestapo, with a reference to the comic servant in Molière's play *Don Juan:* "Sganarelle wants to outdo Don Juan; the domestic goes one better than his master." In May he described the execution of more than eighty Resistance members held hostage by the Germans after a Nazi train was derailed in an attack. Because of his use of pseudonyms, there is still some doubt over which articles Camus actually wrote.

He certainly did write an article for *Les Lettres Françaises* in April 1944, a review of French writers grouped in the National Writers' Committee. He criticized a member of the French Vichy government, Pierre Pucheu, who was responsible for executing prisoners; Pucheu would later travel to northern Africa, where de Gaulle had him shot. Pucheu believed he could make active Pétainism work alongside Gaullism, just as Drieu La Rochelle fantasized about joining the Red Army. The lack of a realistic point of view in "politicians" at the time could be stupefying. Camus ferociously condemned Pucheu: "These laws which he signed in an everyday setting, a comfortable and anonymous office, he lacked the imagination to really see that they would translate into agony for innocent Frenchmen who would be put to death. . . . It must be known all over France (and in the Ministries) that the time for abstraction is over."

A polemic began in *Les Lettres Françaises* between Camus and two Communists, Paul Eluard and Claude Morgan, who felt he had not been hard enough on Pucheu and that his article seemed mostly to fault Pucheu's lack of imagination. In theory, Camus was on the executive committee of *Les Lettres Françaises*, along with Paulhan and Eluard, but in fact Morgan ran the periodical. Camus responded by coming out in favor of the execution of traitors and collaborators.

His most important written contributions to Resistance action were essays grouped under the book title *Lettres à un ami allemand*. The first letter appeared in autumn 1944 in the *Revue Libre*; in it, Camus envisaged the postwar period, influenced by the Resistance writer Vercors's novel *Le Silence de la mer*. Solemnly, he addressed an imaginary German friend to explain why he "had accepted the sword now." He was opposed not to Germans but to Nazism. Camus had shed his pacifist skin: "We have had to overcome our liking for man and the image that we had created of a peaceful destiny. . . . We needed to make a long detour and we are very late." His second letter, written in December 1943, was centered on an anecdote: a chaplain was accompanying prisoners to their execution and saw one of them escaping, so he gave the alarm. The prisoner was caught again by the Nazis. Camus spoke to the French people: "These are our finest sons who are dying; that is my cruelest thought." He said he did not hate the Nazis, "the executioners." When this article was written, few Resistants knew the full details of the German concentration camp atrocities, but it was widely known that Resistance fighters captured by the Gestapo or the French *milice* were tortured to death.

To avoid this fate and possibly betraying fellow Resistants, the printer who produced *Combat*, André Bollier, committed suicide just as he was about to be arrested by the Germans. Claude Bourdet and Jacqueline Bernard had also been arrested and deported to concentration camps. Camus feared that Pia might have been arrested, too, and he thought of assembling a commando group in Lyons to free him. Camus, alias Bauchard, did not participate in military-style actions, but he found himself mixed up in certain operations nonetheless.

He and the actress Maria Casarès asked Dionys Mascolo of the Paris Gallimard office to help move a printing machine. Mascolo lifted the machine into a small van, carrying a revolver in his pocket in case of trouble. He was surprised to find Camus and Casarès waiting for him on the outdoor terrace of a café on the square d'Anvers along the boulevard de Rochechouart in the ninth arrondissement, usually frequented by pimps, collaborators, and Resistants. Camus was at the café more out of solidarity than necessity.

Mascolo had joined the Communist party along with the sociologist Edgar Morin. The writer Robert Antelme and the novelist Marguerite Duras belonged to the National Movement of Prisoners of War, partly directed by François Mitterrand, whose alias was Captain Morland. One day, Antelme was arrested at the home of his sister Marie-Louise on the rue Dupin in the sixth arrondissement, near the rue du Cherche-Midi. A friend warned the other members of the group, and Mascolo alerted Camus. The archives, files, and photographs of the Movement were stored at Antelme's apartment on the rue Saint-Benoît close by. Mascolo went to get them while Camus stood watch.

Camus was ready to offer this sort of fraternal assistance. He helped Malraux find a room in the apartment of the poet Jean Lescure for an officer in his Maquis who was passing through Paris. Compartmentalization, which was one of the principles of secrecy in the Resistance, was not always respected. Some Resistance fighters carried address books written in codes which were easy to break.

Squabbles between different branches of the Resistance reached dangerous levels. In May 1944, the French Communists, led by Jean Marcenac, denounced in a tract certain people pretending to be in the Resistance and in the underground, citing by name Camus, Sartre, and Jean Lescure. This was akin to a poison-pen letter, and the tracts were very quickly in the hands of the Germans. When Lescure showed him the tract, Camus merely shrugged his shoulders.

French intellectuals and writers did not play an immense or decisive role in the Resistance, but Camus had wanted to put out a newspaper, to distribute it, to bear witness, and consequently had risked his life.

Chapter Twenty-seven **180,000 Copies**

The theater director Marcel Herrand gave Maria Casarès a copy of Camus's play *Le Malentendu*, saying, "I think you can play the role of Martha. It's a work by a young author I like. Read it." Herrand was not just a director but also an actor, and he ran the Mathurins Theatre. He was a smart and snobby homosexual and a cynical socialite, and he wanted to stage the five-character play *Le Malentendu*.

Camus's manuscripts were circulating around Paris. The director Jean Vilar was interested in *Caligula*, with its twenty-five characters. Herrand had read both plays and felt that after *L'Etranger* and *Le Mythe de Sisyphe*, Camus would be better off starting with a more intimate theater work. A first work meeting was scheduled in Herrand's apartment above his theater near the boulevard Haussmann.

There Maria Casarès met the young man who had held the stick at the Leirises' apartment during the reading of Picasso's play. She felt herself tremble with an "inevitable instinct of conquest," as she later put it. She found Camus's face "haughty, but not foolish," reflecting "air of indifferent casualness" as well as "extraordinary presence." She also sensed in him a certain boredom, instability, and fragility which were hard to grasp, "a vulnerability matched with the power that exile grants us." She felt in herself a "desire to intimidate and challenge, to take the risk of provoking something, and maybe to be foolish." For his part, Camus was also moved by Casarès's violent, electric beauty. Their love affair began shortly afterwards.

Camus read *Le Malentendu* aloud in a dull voice, easily but also with a bit of stage fright. He stopped to drink a few mouthfuls of water. His listeners were Herrand, Casarès, Hélène Vercors, the writer's wife, as well as the actors Marie Kalf and Paul Oettly. He got through the second and third acts more calmly, although he was soon tired and sweating. Herrand ended the session before Camus had finished reading his play.

Maria Casarès was the daughter of a rich, liberal Spanish Republican who served at different times as Spain's minister of the navy, of communications, of public works, of the interior, and of the War Department, among other government jobs. During the Spanish Civil War, Maria, nicknamed Vitolina, worked in a hospital. Her first lover had been a Marxist labor activist, and Maria felt she had inherited a sense of anarchy as well as the "pride and theatricality of the whole Spanish world." As a refugee in France after Franco's Fascists won, she passed her university entrance exams in 1939 at the Lycée Victor-Duruy in Paris. She impressed her teachers and classmates at Le Conservatoire as she had done at the famous private theater school Le Cours Simon.

Vibrant and warmhearted, Casarès played roles like Racine's Bérénice, the Queen in Victor Hugo's *Ruy Blas*, and Joan of Arc in the verse play by Charles Péguy, *Le Mystère de la charité de Jeanne d'Arc*. Very feminine, and indifferent to what people thought of her, she insisted on being treated equally to men. She had appreciated *L'Etranger* and *Le Mythe de Sisyphe*, and she and Camus shared a Hispanic side, and were mutually attracted to that aspect of each other. Camus had Castilian roots, but Casarès had a much stronger Galician background. Although accepted as a French actress, she performed with a slight Madrid accent. She was nine years younger than Camus, and in private life, just as professionally, she had bewitching charm. The blood of Don Juan flowed in her veins, as it did in Camus's. Like Camus, she was a seething, conquering foreigner in France. They were both independent, prideful, possessive, almost despotic. Like Camus, Casarès took to heart the death of Republican Spain, with more lyricism than political sense. Unlike him, Maria enjoyed perfect health, and her nature was more optimistic than his.

Literally and figuratively, Camus and Casarès were both actors. Camus wrote: "A mime of what is perishable, the actor appears only to practice and to perfect himself. The convention of theater is that the heart can only express itself and make itself understood by gestures and through the body, or the voice, which comes as much from the soul as from the body." Onstage, Casarès had a high-pitched, hoarse voice. As Camus said, "The law of that art is that everything must be enlarged and translated into flesh." Maria loved dancing almost as much as acting, and Camus would take her out to waltz or tango, although he was less skilled at the popular Latin dance the paso doble. They had their favorites among popular songs, mostly by French singer and songwriter Charles Trenet, or Edith Piaf's classic "La Vie en rose." They would soon become Parisian celebrities, and when they arrived at a nightclub, orchestras would strike up in their honor a paso doble called "Pisa morena"—the musicians' way of saluting the pretty brunette.

They would also meet at Maria's apartment on the rue de Vaugirard

near the Necker Hospital in the fifteenth arrondissement, where Albert liked
to sit on the large terraced balcony. Camus would help her to discover writers, or they would both silently do their work. Sometimes she would meet
him in the one-room studio that was added onto the apartment of André
Gide at 1 bis rue Vaneau in the seventh arrondissement. Gide rented the
room to Camus without knowing him beforehand, and received his rent in
cash and in person. That way Camus the Resistance activist could not be
traced by the police, and the parsimonious Gide did not have to pay income
tax on the rent he collected.

On the evening of June 5, 1944, Camus and Casarès participated in a
fiesta at the home of the great actor Charles Dullin, who ran his own theater
company. They returned home by bicycle a bit drunk, with Maria riding on
the handlebars. Operation Overlord had begun that night, and the Allies
landed on the Normandy beaches. Parisian life continued as before, although a championship soccer match was postponed. On June 17, the
Gestapo and the French *milice* raided an underground printing plant that
Combat was using.

Rehearsals for *Le Malentendu* went well, and the director, Herrand,
never yelled at his actors. Camus attended some rehearsals, watching this
professional closely. Herrand was responsible for the play, and Camus kept
his opinions mostly to himself, although he did ask Casarès to transmit one
suggestion: that when two actors embraced onstage, they might perhaps
squeeze each other a bit tighter. The plot of *Le Malentendu*, often evoked by
Camus, was about a young man who returns home without telling his
mother and sister who he is, and his sister, not recognizing him, kills him.
Obvious from the beginning, this plot paralyzed the play's action.

Camus put little of himself into the first play he had completed,
Caligula. The emperor who goes mad from his own lucidity was not Camus,
apart from his sense of humor, perhaps. But a few remarks do seem to reflect
Camus's life in the political world: "It takes one day to make a senator and
ten years to make a worker." Caligula also reflects the author when he says,
"To love someone is to accept to grow old with them. I am not capable of
that kind of love."

By contrast, *Le Malentendu* was a work of solitude in which Camus
looked at himself closely. *Le Malentendu* was almost called *Budejovice*, because it takes place in the Czech town of that name. The hero, Jan, returns
from a sunny country to find that everything in his hometown seems "singular—the language and the people." Like Camus at Chambon, where he
rewrote the text, Jan misses his fatherland and "evenings over there . . . the
promises of joy." Jan's sister, Martha, wants "a lot of money to be able to live
freely beside the sea." Jan proclaims, "One cannot always remain a foreigner.
I want to find my country again and make all those I love happy; I am not

looking farther than that." Martha may seem to be speaking of Camus when she shouts, "Men's love is a heartbreak. They cannot prevent themselves from abandoning whatever they prefer."

Le Malentendu was written in 1942 and 1943 in occupied France, "far from everything I loved," and the play "wears the colors of exile." Camus wrote it while he was working on *La Peste*; at one point he thought of calling the play *L'Exilé* and the novel *Les Exilés*. His second play was not pessimistic. He explained: "When the tragedy is done, it would be incorrect to think that this play argues for submission to fate. On the contrary, it is a play of revolt, perhaps even containing a moral of sincerity." After the fact, the author drew a possible meaning from his work: "If a man wants to be recognized, one need only tell him who he is. If he shuts up or lies, he will die alone, and everything around him is destined for misery. If, on the contrary, he speaks the truth, he will doubtless die, but after having helped himself and others to live."

The dress rehearsal of *Le Malentendu* was on June 24, after a performance for invited guests the evening before. A few days earlier, Sartre's play *No Exit* had opened with great success at the Vieux-Colombier on the Left Bank near Saint-Germain-des-Près. Sartre and Simone de Beauvoir attended the dress rehearsal of *Le Malentendu*, and they had also read *Caligula*, which they felt was a better play than Camus's second effort. The Gallimard family—Gaston, his wife, Jeanne, Robert, Michel, Pierre, and Janine—were faithfully present in orchestra seats. The play did not work, and after the denouement was forecast in the first scene, the action dragged. A friend and acting teacher of Maria Casarès, Béatrix Dussane, left before it was over, wondering if the actors were responsible for the show's frigidity.

But the Gallimards all applauded, and some reviews were favorable, at least for Casarès. In the collaborationist weekly *La Gerbe*, the writer André Castelot, later a popular historian, saluted Maria but classed the play as Grand Guignol. Some of Camus's friends charitably blamed the play's failure on the author's reputation as being involved in the Resistance: presumably, Germans and collaborators had organized the bad reviews.

Nearly a month after the play opened, Albert Beusche wrote in the *Pariser Zeitung*, a German-language newspaper, that the play's "form and idea . . . are bizarrely muddled." Camus was hurt. The play had been meant as the third panel of a triptych on the absurd, and Camus regretted not having staged *Caligula* instead, which he felt was more accessible. One clear error was that the son, a young man in his twenties, was played by Marcel Herrand, who was over forty. But at least Camus saw his work performed in Paris for the first time, and by Maria, whom he called "a marvelous actress." There were some other consolations, such as when Jean Cocteau wrote to him on July 9, 1944, to say that "the solitude onstage was superb."

Another literary colleague, Jean Paulhan, took a while to "speak more frankly" about *Le Malentendu* to Camus: "It seemed to me that the subject was admirable, but the stuffing was of poor quality." However, Paulhan added that he found Camus "more sensitive" than Sartre as a playwright. At the Gallimard office, the philosopher Brice Parain did not much like the play either when he read it, explaining that he had been overtaken "by a sympathetic sadness which didn't have the characters as object. . . . I didn't know who to feel sorry for, you, me, or everybody, and I didn't see what I should rely on. . . . The characters [talked] too much."

Then, suddenly, Camus and Casarès were questioned by the police. Near the Réaumur-Sébastopol metro station, French and German policemen blocked a road at both ends. Camus was carrying a layout page with the heading of *Combat*. First, he put it in his overcoat pocket, and then he slipped it to Maria. The Germans searched the men and asked the women for their identity papers. Maria saw Camus with his hands held up and thought that if the Germans tortured him in front of her, she would talk. Camus often said that one never knew what one might do under torture. The Germans did not find the layout. For the moment, after they were let go, he decided to move from his apartment, to get rid of the documents, and to stay at the home of a friend from his Algerian days, Paul Raffi. Their friend Janine Gallimard ran into the journalist Albert Ollivier, who told her that someone had informed on their Resistance group, and Jacqueline Bernard had already been arrested on July 11. That same night, she was supposed to have met with Camus and Casarès, the latter being used as a courier.

It was better for Albert to disappear, so Pierre and Michel Gallimard took papers and clothes from Camus's room and then left by bicycle for Verdelot, a town sixty kilometers away from Paris, to a house arranged for by Brice Parain. The Gallimards and Camus stayed there for a few days, and Albert cooked his favorite dish, *maizéna*, an Algerian-style corn purée. One day the writer Roger Stéphane, a Resistance activist, showed up at the house to tell them about his plans for launching a review with Jacques Lemarchand, Sartre, and Camus, but Albert nixed the idea.

Pierre Gallimard returned to Paris to his bindery factory, and as soon as he was gone, his cousin Michel confessed his love to Pierre's wife, Janine, who fell into Michel's arms. The scene was like a tragic vaudeville, with Michel and Janine immediately deciding to elope. Janine explained the situation to Albert and wondered if she was really in love with Michel, admitting, "When I think of him, I tremble." Camus replied, "Okay, then you're in love." Pierre returned to Verdelot, and despite Camus's advice to her not to tell Pierre that she was leaving him for Michel, she went ahead and told her husband anyway.

As for Camus, he was trembling with love for Maria Casarès, who did not come to Verdelot, although he expected her to. Their relationship was striking for all those who knew them, as she was a force of nature, fiery and sometimes violently impatient. Albert liked to call her by a Tolstoyan nickname, "War and Peace." With Maria, the writer stopped playing the role of the indifferent man or the foreigner, as she declared her desire to follow him in all his activities.

Finally, the Verdelot refugees returned to Paris. On August 15, Allied troops landed in the south of France, and on the eighteenth, the battle for the liberation of Paris began. General Leclerc's tanks from the Second Armored Division rumbled into Paris. The editorial staff of *Combat*, as well as those from other Resistance publications like *Défense de la France* and *Franc-Tireur*, occupied a building at 100 rue Réaumur, formerly used by the collaborationist press. *Combat* had published fifty-eight underground issues, and now the fifty-ninth issue would be the first free one. Paris rejoiced, but it was bloodstained rejoicing.

A member of the National Theater Committee, Jean-Paul Sartre had been assigned to personally occupy the Comédie-Française because of its status as a cultural symbol, and he did so, although the theater building was empty to begin with. Sartre asked Michel Leiris to accompany him, but Leiris preferred to stay at the Musée de l'Homme with some friends. On his way to the rue Réaumur offices of *Combat*, Camus passed by the Comédie-Française to see Sartre. He found the philosopher sleeping in an orchestra seat, tired out after walking through Paris. Camus woke him up, laughing, "Your armchair is facing in the direction of history!"

After August 21, the Resistance newspapers were hawked freely in the streets, and in some headlines the question was asked if the Germans would recapture Paris. An editorial in *Combat* was titled, "They Shall Not Pass." The article had a Camus-like ring to it: "What is an insurrection? It's the people taking arms. What are the people? They are what in a nation will never go down on its knees." Vaudeville and tragedy were intermingled in some instances. Pierre Gallimard could not accept that Janine would leave him, and he said he wanted to die. Camus decided that Pierre might as well die for a good cause, so he sent him across German lines to write an article for *Combat* about meeting American troops; Pierre returned uninjured.

From a military-strategy point of view, the liberation of Paris was a minor event, less difficult than the taking of Caen or Strasbourg. But on the political and poetic level, it was an essential Gaullist advance. In an editorial for the August 24 issue of *Combat*, Camus conveyed the atmosphere of liberated Paris and the point of view of the Resistants: "Paris fired off all its bullets into the August night. In the immense stage set of stone and water, the barricades of freedom have once again been raised everywhere around that river whose waves are heavy with history. Once more, justice must be bought with men's blood." Camus spoke of a "freedom, conquered amid these convulsions . . . a terrible childbirth [which] is that of revolution." He proposed the slogan "From Resistance to Revolution" as a subheading for *Combat*. The next day he continued: "While freedom's bullets whistled through the city, the cannons of Liberation crossed the gates of Paris amid shouts and flowers." Camus spoke for all Parisians: real Resistants, occasional fighters, the past summer's supernumeraries, and those who a week before had cheered Marshal Pétain and were now on August 26 cheering Charles de Gaulle on the Champs-Elysées. Camus reminded his readers: "Four years ago, men rose amid debris and despair and tranquilly affirmed that nothing was lost." He celebrated the "marvelous joy which fills us like an ocean wave." With the tacit complicity of many French people, and of Camus's journalists, who did not challenge it, de Gaulle started a legend that France and Paris were liberated by the French—civilians and military—with backup help from American, British, Canadian, and Polish soldiers, if one insisted, and the Red Army far in the background.

De Gaulle proclaimed a new law that banned the collaborationist press and that put Resistance titles like *Combat* and *Libération* in the forefront of the French press. Like its colleague *Franc-Tireur*, *Combat* did not depend on any political party or financial power. On August 21, Camus as editor in chief stated that the freedom of the press had been won again: "It would not be enough to win only the appearance of freedom, which France had to settle for in 1939." He continued, "And we should only have accomplished a tiny part of our task if tomorrow's French Republic should find itself like the Third Republic, narrowly dependent on money. We know that one of Pétain's favorite themes has long been the struggle against moneyed powers. But we know too that never has money weighed as heavily on our people as it has since July 1940, when Money, to save and enhance its privileges, deliberately hoisted the traitors to power, linking its interests to those of Hitler."

After the war, French Communists had important positions in the government and press, despite some prudent wariness on the part of de Gaulle's supporters. Men like Camus did not oppose the Communists, and few journalists had any idea of the Soviet prison camp system at a time when the world's attention finally had been drawn to the German concentration camps. Camus was still convinced that the Soviet people supported their rulers. If not, how could have the Red Army have beaten the German army? Men came out of the Resistance with magnificently simplistic and dangerous revolutionary illusions about the organization of national and international society; Camus was among these illusionists.

He was known as a writer, and with his *Combat* articles he became a famous journalist. As a novelist he might touch a few thousand readers, but as an editorial writer he influenced hundreds of thousands of Frenchmen. At

Gallimard, he continued working on the reading committee. Pascal Pia took primary responsibility for *Combat*, acting as editor as well as in his official title of director, although in the first months after the occupation, Camus did not get much other work done, mostly ignoring the still-unfinished *La Peste*. He complained about his lack of progress with the book.

He was working at the newspaper and living out his passion for Maria Casarès, staying out late at nightclubs in Saint-Germain-des-Près, Montparnasse, and Montmartre to relax after the newspaper had been put to bed. Camus threw himself into the world of journalism again in order to develop his ideas, but also because he liked the atmosphere. From 1941 to 1943 he had lived in solitary fashion, above all during the months at Chambon.

At the *Combat* offices on the rue Réaumur, he rediscovered teamwork and the sweet and potent narcotic of journalism. Camus enjoyed dealing with typographers and cultivated their acquaintance in Paris, Clermont-Ferrand, and Lyons. Newspaper printers had their own traditions and slang which Camus savored. If someone made a stupid remark, they would cry "Piot!" which was their slang word for "Hogwash!" There were also the newspaper proofreaders, mostly political anarchists, who defended syntax and grammatical purity by screaming at erring journalists. Camus would be scolded, "We say 'Je vous prie de m'excuser' and not 'Je m'excuse'! And to think that this thing went to college!" Journalists like Pia and Camus had plenty of respect for these acidulous and often erudite proofreaders.

Camus would go to the steel printer's sheets to make final fact-checking and cuts. The steel sheets retained their old-fashioned name from earlier days of printing, "stones." The typographers reigned, telling Camus to cut six lines so that a page design could be perfected. Camus would listen, and felt at ease with such demands. Workers and journalists would gossip together, spending much time at the corner café. Relations between journalists and laborers were all the more cordial since some had participated in the Resistance together. The workday would begin at the café with a dry white wine, followed by a sweet white wine, or perhaps a red. An aperitif was next, followed by a lunchtime Brouilly from the Burgundy region, and a solid Algerian red wine in the afternoon. By then the work shift was over, and some of the newspaper employees would go to "pay a visit to the whores" on the rue Saint-Denis, a few steps away.

This was not Pia's schedule, as he would leave the office and go to sleep shortly before dawn and be back in the office by ten eleven, carrying a thermos of coffee. Pia's wife would bring him another thermos in the afternoon; he hated social responsibilities and ate very little, preferring to work and to smoke endless cigarettes, covering his front with ashes. Camus used to arrive at the office around four p.m. Pia would say, "We're going to try to make a reasonable newspaper, and since the world is absurd, it will fail." For his part, Camus would tell young recruits at the paper, "I'm going to make you do damn annoying things, but never rotten ones."

Pia directed the newspaper as a paternal boss. As editor in chief, Camus was admired by most, but not all, of his employees. *Combat* was a consecration of Camus's moral authority, and he was as happy as on a theater stage or on a soccer field. Although the newspaper was serious and at times solemn, the journalists did have fun. Salesmen would come and hawk products hitherto unavailable, and the French journalists avidly bought American bourbon, Camel cigarettes, and Eversharp pens. Camus discovered Alka-Seltzer, which he found was good for hangovers, and Vicks VapoRub for his attacks of tubercular fever, which he called "flu." Despite his serious attention to work, Pia was capable of kidding around with a young journalist, who taught him how to dance the jitterbug one day in the office. Albert and Pascal openly admired the youngster's wild Zazou dance style, which included neighing like a horse and stomping on the floor as if with a hoof.

Pascal Pia would go from clowning to gravity: he modestly did not want his Resistance achievements made much of, and he rejected careerism with a true disdain for opportunists. The Resistance medal was awarded, unsolicited, to the staff of *Combat*, including Camus, who said, "We used to be old morons and now we're old morons with a medal." In the office, Pia often showed his admiration for Camus by reading aloud the proofs of his editorials.

When Franklin D. Roosevelt died, Camus spoke in his article about the American president's struggle with his physical handicap caused by polio: "He had the face of joy. . . . He knew that there is no pain that cannot be overcome by energy and conscience." Pia remarked that Camus knew he must have been thinking of the tuberculosis that still threatened him when he wrote the Roosevelt article. Even during the most dramatic days of Paris's liberation, Camus had to visit Dr. Georges Brouet's office for lung treatments.

Pia and Camus were horrified by some sections of other newspapers, such as the horoscope, which they felt dishonored a paper. Pia vetoed a letters column, on the grounds that readers were there to read the paper, not to write in it. They were dismayed by the idea of putting crimes on the front page to appeal to bloodthirstiness, rather than treating them as social phenomena.

In their building on the rue Réaumur, on another floor, exactly the sort of newspaper that Pia and Camus loathed was produced: *Défense de la France* was sensational and vulgar, even more so than the popular *Paris-Soir*, whose editor, Pierre Lazareff, had returned from wartime exile and wanted to meet Camus and Pia on a friendly basis, having given them jobs years before on *Paris-Soir*. But the two ex-employees refused to see him. Camus, forgetting some of Lazareff's appealing human qualities, like fidelity and kindness, remembered only his disgust at *Paris-Soir*. Lazareff believed that "a journalist's first duty is to be read," but Camus felt it was to tell the truth as much as possible, with as much style as possible. Camus saw "Lazareffism" as unacceptable journalism, a mixture of political submissiveness, raw crime, and nonsense.

Pia and Camus hated the spineless large-circulation press, which followed orders and catered to its readers' lower instincts. Lazareff was not producing the kind of critical journalism they dreamed of. Having Lazareff working in their very building was a kind of provocation, a reminder of the fact that almost in spite of themselves, Pia and Camus had been obliged to work for *Paris-Soir*. Perhaps they were also settling scores with themselves.

Later, in 1947, Camus wrote to someone who had gone to see Lazareff, saying, "I'm telling you that you have met the real underworld of this unfortunate country. I'll try to get you into contact with more respectable people." A year later, when another journalist asked him to write an article for *Elle* magazine, a weekly run by Lazareff's wife, Camus replied in a letter dated November 5, 1948, "I have no esteem for the publication group that today is attached to *Paris-Soir* and its directors, which represents for me the worst and most contemptible of what I have experienced in journalism. I would not contribute an article even if I were to be paid millions. . . . Regardless of the good opinion I have of you, I cannot contribute to a magazine that is directly or indirectly linked to that miserable enterprise." He added a postscript: "Between you and me, I authorize you to have this letter read by Lazareff and his collaborators, as they say."

At the time, hope, purity, and revolution were very much in the air.

Chapter Twenty-eight   **Combats**

T he love affair between Albert Camus and Maria Casarès was a matter
    of common knowledge, and they still seemed happy together, al-
    though perplexed about the future. While they toyed with the idea of
emigrating to Mexico together, on August 31, 1944, shortly after the liberation
Albert had written to Francine, who was still stuck in Oran:

> My dear,
>   I have a chance to get a letter through to you by rapid post
> and I wanted to reassure you as quickly as possible about my sit-
> uation. I've been without your news for months, and I imagine
> that it's been the the same for you. I am fine, although a little
> tired. I haven't the time to tell you the real story of the past two
> years. After having tried to escape to Spain and deciding against
> it, because it would have meant several months of camp or
> prison, which I couldn't have managed in my state of health, I
> entered the Resistance movement. I thought about it a lot and I
> did it with my eyes wide open because it was my duty. I worked
> in the Combat movement in the Haute-Loire region and then
> right afterwards in Paris with Pia. The rest goes without saying;
> I'll tell you about it later. Six weeks ago I was almost arrested and
> I disappeared from public life. Then there were the marvelous
> days of the insurrection and making the daily *Combat*. At the pres-
> ent moment Pia and I are doing the newspaper—with a certain
> success. I don't know if I can leave Paris, but as soon as it will be
> possible, I will send you money and you'll come here.
>   I have so much to tell you, so much, but I am tongue-tied
> in front of you. Everything will be all right, and I am so glad that

this country is free. I knew that our getting together again also depended on it, so I had two reasons to work for it.

I saw Adrey [a painter friend], who told me about you, that you worked in an orchestra, and I forget the rest. I was sick to hear about it, but I believe it's all over. Now I have some money and you can take it easy and work on your music.

I am going to send this letter right away. I don't have the patience to wait for the normal mail. If you can answer, do so to the newspaper *Combat*, at 100 rue Réaumur, or to the *NRF* at 5 rue Sébastien-Bottin. Tell me that you've waited for me and that I'll find you as you were before.

I embrace you with all my tenderness,
Albert.
Kiss everyone around you, and my mother.

A letter to a friend or a sister rather than to a wife.

The Faures announced that they were coming to Paris. Christiane, Camus's favorite sister-in-law, grasped the situation immediately, as she understood Albert's taste for women. The problem was how to protect her sister and arrange things so that their mother, Fernande Faure, did not notice anything about Albert's affair. In October 1944, Francine arrived in Paris and moved in with her husband at the studio on the rue Vaneau, behind André Gide's apartment. Their separation had been long and the reunion was difficult.

The first issues of the freely produced *Combat* were planned during editorial meetings at the Gide studio. With Pia as director and Camus still editor in chief, journalists were sometimes recruited informally. The screenwriter Alexandre Astruc recalls that while visiting the building on the rue Réaumur as a contributor to *Franc-Tireur*, Camus waylaid him in the stairwell and hired him to write for *Combat*. Roger Grenier was asked to do theater reviews, and later ceded that post to Jacques Lemarchand in order to do major reporting. During Paris's liberation, Jean-Paul Sartre published "Tales of a Pedestrian in Rebelling Paris." Sartre's name was amicably spread across the front page in huge letters. *Combat* also announced that Sartre's *Le Mur* would be read on the radio by the actor Michel Vitold. Then Sartre was invited to the United States by American admirers, and sent back articles for *Combat* headlined "A Frenchman in New York" and "A Frenchman in Los Angeles." He reported that in America, going to a dance hall was an innocent pastime, unlike in France, where not just dancing was the quarry. He noted that food seemed abundant. Sartre also wrote laborious articles about the Tennessee Valley Authority, which exasperated Camus and Pia. Worse, he sent livelier articles to the upper-middle-class daily *Le Figaro*, which shared Sartre's reflections from America with *Combat*. But Camus forgave his chum's misdemeanors.

Pia and Camus had not forgotten Malraux. At first, *Combat* announced worriedly that he might have been killed in the Corèze region. When Malraux subsequently turned up in Paris, they put a photo of their hero on the front page, wearing a colonel's five-gallon hat and smoking a cigarette. Then, in autumn 1944, the newspaper, despite space shortages due to its four-page format, published excerpts from Malraux's book *La Lutte avec l'ange*. It was a way of showing that literature and engagement counted for *Combat*. Pia was as admiring of Malraux as he was suspicious of Sartre, whom he called "that bedroom philosopher." During these first months, *Combat*'s articles and reportages were lively, though classical, more original than those in *Le Figaro* and less stuffy than those in *Le Monde*, which had been appearing again since December 1944. Camus, writing under the pen name Suetonius, was quite vicious about *Le Monde*, the daily founded by Hubert Beuve-Méry. For him, its serious tone, its typography and format recalled the defunct newspaper *Le Temps*. Camus, alias Suetonius, was convinced that *Le Monde* had been created by General de Gaulle—which was true—to serve the general's own interests, which did not turn out to be the case. Camus felt that *Le Monde* had a grudge against the Resistance, and he mentioned the link between *Le Monde* and its prewar predecessor *Le Temps* when he commented: "*Combat* is printed on the rotary presses that used to produce the *Pariser Zeitung*, but the machines of *Le Temps* are so accustomed to their job that they no longer need subsidies from the Ironworks Committee to do serious work in discrediting the Resistance." The accusation was a bit much, and a love-hate relationship was born between Camus and Hubert Beuve-Méry, which was full of contradictions, misunderstandings, and suave nastiness.

Editorials by Camus and his colleagues in *Combat* were carefully written and curt. Camus defined a journalistic approach when he wrote a few days after the liberation: "We have decided to suppress politics and replace it with morality." He posed professional problems, such as what journalism should become after the Vichy collaborators left. Over the next months, Camus tried to answer these questions.

Combat printed as many as 182,000 copies, but sometimes almost one-third of these went unsold. Camus's moralistic obsession with professional ethics exasperated some of the competition. They wondered where this little upstart came from who was trying to deal out lessons to them. Camus's Parisian colleagues knew very little, if anything, about the dailies he worked on in Algeria. Camus liked to use the royal "we" to imply unanimous accord: "What would we like? A clear, virile press that uses respectable language." He wanted to see newspapers freed from money problems, "with a tone and truth that puts the public on the level of what is best in itself." He felt that a good newspaper sought the highest common denominator among its readers, not the lowest.

Ten days after the new liberated newspapers appeared, Camus had already decided that they were "not very satisfying," and he attacked *Défense de la France* for its editorial choices: "We read with definite irritation, the day after Metz was taken at great human cost, an article about Marlene Dietrich's entry into Metz. And we have reason to be indignant." However, Camus added, "this does not mean that for us, newspapers must always be forcibly boring. . . . Simply, we do not think that in wartime, a star's caprices are necessarily more interesting than people's pain, the army's blood, and a nation's persistent effort to find its truth."

Camus did not ask himself if there might be several different types of reading public; instead he concentrated on pointing to the "sensibility of an empty-headed girl" as the targeted readership of some newspapers, just as before the war: "They want to inform quickly instead of informing well, and truth does not win out in the process." At *Combat* as at *Alger Républicain*, Camus wanted his journalists to express their doubts, and not hesitate to use the conditional tense as a way of showing concern and reserve, as was done at *Le Monde*. Sometimes *Combat* made mistakes, such as quoting before the fact a Swiss radio report that Hitler was dead and in the latter months of 1944 announcing that in Spain, Franco's regime was crumbling when it was not.

For Camus, critical journalism "amounted to asking that in-depth articles have depth and that false or dubious news is not presented as real news." For the writer, speaking as a political observer and participant, "news . . . cannot do without critical commentary." But although Camus did not specify it, news had to be separated from commentary; he did so by his editorial choices for the paper's contents. He also called for a "tone" or a style, posing the problem of individual talent and collective honesty. Readers were meant to vote for *Combat*'s objectivity by subscribing. With his "care for objectivity and prudence," Camus and Pia agreed that a journalist must be "a day-to-day historian." A newspaper must not serve any one system, and he invited young reporters and older editorial-writers to challenge themselves.

During these months, Camus never mentioned any moments of lassitude, although, as André Gide complained, "the great misdeed of journalism is to make you write when you have absolutely no desire to do so, when you are uninspired, the weather is heavy, your pen scratches, thoughts do not flow, and the sentence remains shapeless."

Pia and Camus called on literary authors to give some character to *Combat*, like Gide and Georges Bernanos, the novelist who wrote *The Diary of a Country Priest*. Camus did not forget journalism while being a writer. He reserved certain questions for his books, making notes for them on his

Combat stationery: "Man's crisis, or can one believe in Man? . . . Also to believe that he can do something admirable, when it is impossible by being either entirely materialist or entirely spiritual."

Camus had his own formula for his editorials: one idea, two examples, and three typed pages. He took notes, wrote, and then dictated his text to a secretary. Of course, he rewrote his articles less than he did his literary texts. In the first two months of the free *Combat*, he formulated some principles of political morality and moral politics, also approved by Pia: "Here we do not believe in 'definitive' revolutions." Camus was no longer a Communist, or a Marxist, if he had ever been one. He did not believe in the concept of the end of history in Socialist terms. He wrote, "Revolution is not revolt. What carried the Resistance for four years was revolt, which is to say the entire stubborn refusal, practically blind at first, of an order that wanted to make men kneel. Revolt is at first a matter of the heart. But there comes a time when it passes into the mind, where feeling becomes idea, and spontaneous outbursts end up in concerted action. That is the moment of revolution." Because the great models of revolutions were in 1789 in France and 1917 in Russia, Camus, who like many Frenchman, overlooks the American Revolution, insisted: "Revolution is not forcibly the guillotine or the machine gun, or rather, it is the machine gun when necessary." He thus accepted an inevitable dose of violence, while defining the kind of society defended by *Combat*: "For France, we want a collectivist economy and liberal politics."

Condemning capitalism and putting his faith in socialism, he did not explain how a market economy could develop under collectivism, which was the mythical dream for some in his generation. Camus was attracted by the British Labour Party and Scandinavian Social Democrats and declared, "We want to achieve without delay a real popular democracy." But neither Camus nor his friends knew that the "popular democracies" that emerged at this time in Eastern Europe, Asia, Africa, and Central America were anything but popular and democratic.

A different moral problem appeared for Camus with the purging punishment and execution of collaborators. Intellectual purification seemed more popular with the French than economic purification, since the targets of these campaigns were more often writers and journalists than industrialists. Camus felt that it was important to purify in quality rather than in quantity, but this was not everyone's opinion: the weekly *Les Lettres Françaises* and the National Writers' Committee promoted radical vengeance through purification, supported by writers like Aragon, Eluard, Benda, Vercors, Sartre, and Beauvoir. One of the worst was Claude Morgan, who wrote that the novelist Jean Giono's "silence was in itself a crime!" A committee to purify publishing was formed, composed willy-nilly of publishers who had followed the orders of the Nazi Propagandastaffel like Jean Fayard; old Social

Democrats, like Francisque Gay; Communist sympathizers, like Pierre Seghers; and just plain mischevious spirits, like Jean-Paul Sartre. The less they themselves had resisted, the more certain people wanted to punish others for having collaborated.

Jean Paulhan and François Mauriac, both recognized as Resistance activists, argued for moderation, and Paulhan resigned from the editorial committee of *Les Lettres Françaises*, after a list of one hundred expelled writers was printed. He left the National Writers' Committee as well. Camus and Mauriac would disagree in a polemic that appeared in their respective publications, *Combat* and *Le Figaro*. Camus also resigned from the National Writers' Committee, telling Paulhan, "I am too uncomfortable to express myself in an atmosphere where the spirit of objectivity is taken as spiteful criticism and where simple moral independence is so poorly tolerated. . . . You see, it's a first retreat towards the great silence which decidedly tempts me more and more."

Mauriac, a Catholic who meditated on charity, was also a bourgeois who thought of what he saw as a necessary reconciliation among Frenchmen. He might also have been thinking of his brother, Pierre Mauriac, who had been president of the Doctors' Guild under Pétain. Whatever his motivations, Mauriac attacked purification, and Camus agreed insofar as he felt that there were too many personal attacks and too much rhetorical excess in newspapers. He feared that this tendency would result in a situation akin to that of the collaborationist press during the German occupation. Camus was horrified by the death penalty and by that accessory of French justice the guillotine. He would never forget what his mother and grandmother told him about his father coming home from an execution and vomiting. This story, in one sense the fundamental heritage left to him by his father, continued to haunt him, and he referred to it more often as the years went on.

At first, Camus's editorials said slightly less than he really thought about the subject. Mauriac, dubbed "Saint Francis of the Assize Courts" by the satirical weekly *Le Canard Enchaîné*, always mentioned charity when writing about judicial matters, while Camus spoke of justice. Camus wrote, "Each time I spoke of justice with respect to purification, Mr. Mauriac spoke of charity. And the virtue of charity is rather singular in that it seems to make me argue for hatred when what I am really calling for is justice. To listen to Mr. Mauriac, one would really think that it was absolutely necessary to choose in daily life between a love for Christ and hatred for men. Well, no!" The two writers were worthy adversaries, raising the problem of journalists' responsibility, as well as any writer's, during the occupation.

Their moral consciences came from diametrically opposite positions: the old believer (Mauriac was fifty-nine) and the young atheist (Camus was thirty-one). They both came out of the Resistance, Camus famous for having founded *Combat*, and Mauriac for having published books (under a pseudonym) with the clandestine Editions de Minuit. Mauriac and Camus respected, irritated, surprised, and provoked one another. Camus was touched that Mauriac was opposed to Franco's Spain, for example. Neither man argued against the need for purification, and at first Camus did not even exclude the possibility of the death penalty. Both insisted on impartial judges and trials based on solid legal bases. The French Communists were eager to stage rapid popular tribunals, but neither Camus nor Mauriac agreed. At times, the liberation released the finest as well as the lowest instincts. Even Camus's ideas shifted: on September 4, 1944, he had called for "rapid and exact justice," while on September 9, Camus and Mauriac both signed a writers' manifesto calling for "fair punishment for imposters and traitors."

A traitor was more difficult to identify than an imposter. Finally Camus rejected the idea of quick popular justice and declared in *Combat*, "We will maintain freedom, even if it profits those who fought against it." Camus defined traitors as a "foreign body" which must be "destroyed," yet destruction necessarily implied physical liquidation, which he rejected. In the same article, on October 25, 1944, Camus attacked Mauriac, stating that when confronted by traitors, justice should "make mercy shut up." At the time, Mauriac was defending the journalist Henri Béraud, who hated both the British and the Germans and had been sentenced to death. Mauriac felt that bad causes should not be given martyrs and that Béraud's errors were more in the nature of a crime of opinion than of treason. General de Gaulle agreed and pardoned Béraud.

Four months after the liberation of Paris, Camus was scandalized by the actions of some provincial courts as well as those in Paris. He wrote, "A country that spoils its purge is preparing to spoil its renovation. A country wears the face of its judicial system, and ours should have something else to show the world than this messy face." Camus accused Mauriac of being "a writer of moods and not of reasonings." With a straight face, he claimed that a writer should not be influenced by moods, as if his own editorials had been cool and contained in the Raymond Aron style. Camus said he would leave Mauriac with his taste for pardons, and forgive with Mauriac "when Leynaud's wife" would permit him to do so. Camus's friend the poet and Resistance fighter René Leynaud had been arrested and shot just before the liberation. Seven months later, in an article dated January 11, 1945, Camus wrote, "Until our last moment we will refuse a godly charity that cheats men of their justice." When French Nazi collaborators like Georges Suarez and Paul Chack were executed, Camus, then, did not regret it.

One man's case did touch Camus: the writer and journalist Robert Brasillach was sentenced to death on January 19. A number of intellectuals signed a petition asking de Gaulle to pardon Brasillach. Some of the petition's signers felt that a writer should not be judged too strictly by his words, while others felt that the punishments in general should be less harsh. Still others did not want to see a series of hard sentences, or wanted to reconcile Gaullists and Pétain's supporters. Among the fifty-nine signers of the petition were the composer Arthur Honegger, the painter Maurice Vlaminck, and the writers Paul Valéry, Paul Claudel, Jean Anouilh, Jean Cocteau, Colette, Jean Paulhan, and François Mauriac. Of these, only the last two were Resistance activists; others were noted collaborationists.

The novelist Marcel Aymé wrote to Camus for his support on January 25, 1945. Aymé, himself a former collaborator, asked Camus for "a sign of compassion and literary fraternity. . . . I might as well say, of fraternity, period. It seems to me that there is a lot of randomness in political opinions." Aymé seemed sincere and convinced, if clumsy. Frenchmen who had collaborated closely with the Gestapo had been arrested with their boss, Gestapo collaborator Jacques Bonny, and Aymé dared to remark, "I was telling one of my friends the other day that if François Villon had lived during the occupation, he probably would have been part of Bonny's gang." Aymé meant that the medieval poet, known to have been a criminal, in modern-day France would have worked for the Gestapo. Aymé concluded that if Camus agreed with the petition's signers, he should write to Brasillach's lawyer, Jacques Isorni.

On January 27, Camus replied to Aymé with a letter that did not hide his feelings or his anguish. He knew Marcel Aymé by sight, although he had no particular liking for his work. He told Aymé, "You have given me a bad night's sleep. Finally, I have sent the signature you asked for today. . . . I have always been horrified by death sentences and I decided, as an individual at least, that I could not participate in one, even by abstention. . . . That's all, and it's a scruple which I imagine will make Brasillach's friends laugh a lot. And as for Brasillach, if he is pardoned and if an amnesty frees him, as it must, in a year or two, I want this letter to tell him the following, from me: I did not add my signature to yours for his sake, nor for the writer, whom I consider as nothing at all, nor for the person, whom I despise with all the force that is in me."

In his letter to Aymé, Camus referred to Leynaud and to "two or three friends mutilated and slaughtered by Brasillach's friends while his newspaper . . . encouraged [Germans and French collaborators]." As for Aymé's remark about the choice of an ideology or a side, Camus replied, "You say that randomness enters into political opinions, and I have no idea about that. But I know that there is no randomness in choosing what dishonors you." Still thinking about the Resistance fighters who had been shot, he added, "And it's not by randomness that my signature will be found among the others, whereas Brasillach's signature never argued on behalf of [Georges] Politzer or Jacques Decour," two contemporaries of Camus's who had founded *Les Lettres françaises* and had been murdered by the Germans. Camus ended his letter by asking Aymé to communicate all of the above to Brasillach, "and also that [Camus was] not a man of hatred and felt himself more inclined to retirement than to politics. Perhaps [Brasillach] would understand that because of some nuance which no doubt escaped him, he could never shake Brasillach's hand."

Sartre, Beauvoir, and others refused to sign the Brasillach petition. Simone too thought of the martyred Politzer and of the poet Robert Desnos, who died in a German concentration camp. If she raised a finger to help Brasillach, then she would deserve to have her friends "spit in her face." She added that Brasillach's case was not a simple crime of opinion: "By his denunciations and his calls for murder and genocide," Brasillach "directly collaborated with the Gestapo." Despite supporters like Camus and Mauriac, who had signed for varied reasons, Brasillach was not pardoned, and before he was shot at the Fresnes Prison on February 3, he said, "In any event, beyond all the disagreements and the barricades, some French intellectuals have made a gesture on my behalf that honored me the most."

After Brasillach, no well-known writer would be shot, only journalists. Camus also intervened on behalf of Lucien Rebatet, the Fascist author of *The Debris*: "I am asked to add my signature to a request for pardon made in Lucien Rebatet's favor. It is not my intention to dissimulate the latter's offense; on the contrary, I fought until the end the man that he was, but it is a stronger motivation which impels me today to ask that the condemned man be spared. Whatever one may say or think, no country in the world can do without pity, and rather than put a man to death, it is more urgent and more exemplary to give him the occasion to think about his offense. These, briefly stated, are the reasons that impel me to send you this request, which I only beg you to believe is not easy for me." Rebatet was indeed pardoned.

The trials of politicians came after those of writers, and Camus attended Pétain's procedure, calling for "the most pitiless . . . justice" for Pétain. De Gaulle commuted Pétain's death sentence to life imprisonment, and Camus felt that in every guilty man he could detect a "portion of innocence." Camus chose human justice, whereas Mauriac thought of divine justice and therefore of indulgence. Camus felt that unbelievers could choose only human justice, however imperfect it was, and that purification had to be done in the name of that justice. Camus admitted that this often resulted in injustices and aberrations: Justice, with its echoes of absurdity, as depicted in *L'Etranger*, always contains the inherent problems of freedom.

Freedom and justice seemed to be opposed to one another, and Camus noted in his *Carnets* in July 1945: "Revolt. Finally, I have chosen freedom. For even if justice is not done, freedom preserves the power to protest against injustice and to preserve communication. Justice in a silent world, the justice of mute people, destroys complicity, denies revolt and mutual consent, but only on the lowest level. This is where one can see how freedom's importance gradually becomes of primary importance." The purification process raised many moral and metaphysical problems: "But the difficult thing is to never forget that [freedom] must at the same time demand justice." For a year, Camus had been meditating on freedom as much as on justice. He concluded: "Freedom means being able to defend what I don't agree with, even in a government or a world I approve of. It's being able to admit that your opponent is right."

Camus did not express all his doubts in public, but in private he confessed his heartbreak. In his *Carnets* on July 30, 1945, he wrote, "At thirty, a man should get ahold of himself and know the exact extent of his qualities and defects, know his own limits, anticipate his failures, and be what he is. And above all, to accept all of these."

On August 30, 1945, he wrote, "Henceforth it is certain that the purification in France is not only ruined but, even worse, discredited. The word 'purification' has already become rather painful, and the thing itself has become hateful." Certain of the court's decisions seemed incoherent, such as when Georges Albertini was sentenced to five years' hard labor for recruiting people for the Legion of French Volunteers Against Bolshevism while the pacifist René Gérin received an eight-year sentence from the same tribunal for having written book reviews for the collaborationist daily *L'Oeuvre* during the war. Camus felt that such discrepancies were illogical and unfair, and he wrote, "Total pacifism seems to me bad reasoning, and we now know that a time comes when it cannot be upheld . . . [even though] we cannot approve what Gérin wrote, even on literary subjects, in *L'Oeuvre*."

Sartre enjoyed Camus's polemic with Mauriac, and while traveling in Brittany, he wrote to Camus: "I wanted to send along with this letter an editorial from the [local newspaper] to show you the fame of *Combat* in the provinces, but I can't find it. Anyway, note that it declares that you and Mauriac are the two greatest journalists of our time and that anyway, you finally came to an agreement." Camus would later acknowledge that on the "precise point" of pardoning wrongdoers, "M. François Mauriac was right."

Algeria also haunted Camus. As soon as *Combat* appeared freely, he wrote of North Africa in it, saying that the French defeat in 1940 caused "a loss of consideration for the French from a virile people like the Arabs." In April 1945, Camus was at last able to revisit Algeria for three weeks. On May 8, 1945, Camus was back in Paris when the German surrender was announced. He was with André Gide at the time, in his apartment on the rue Vaneau.

This news outweighed any other, but on May 8 there were also widespread violent demonstrations in Algeria for that country's liberation from France. Although most of the Paris press spoke little about the matter, Camus and Pia both had ties with Algeria, and Camus published six articles in *Combat*, starting on May 13. Not fully informed about the events, Camus began his series prudently, putting things into perspective rather than taking sides: "Faced by the events that are agitating North Africa today, extreme attitudes should be avoided. One such would be to present a situation as tragic when it is only serious. Another would be to be unaware of the grave difficulties that Algeria is debating today."

Between May 8 and 13, the Algerian government announced that 103 Europeans had been massacred in attacks on colonial centers, and one hundred more wounded, some severely mutilated, and there were rapes as well. The French press focused on European casualties, although reprisals also took their toll on Arab communities. Camus reminded his readers that Algeria was not France and that a large number of Algerians no longer believed that a policy of assimilation was possible with France: "The North African natives have distanced themselves from a democracy from which they see themselves definitively excluded." They "no longer wish to be French. . . . The Arabs are asking for a constitution and a parliament for Algeria." Camus warned against the notion of an "indigenous mass," unorganized and ignorant.

When another French Algerian, Jules Roy, a career military man with literary ambitions, met Camus, he was surprised by the novelist's fraternal and egalitarian way of speaking about Arabs. Camus looked for causes for the problems, as well as solutions that would give Algeria a future. He blamed "famine in Algeria" and underlined that "the visible crisis . . . is economic in nature." Official government rations were no longer distributed: "In Kabylia, in the Ouarsen, South Oran, and the Aures regions, to cite geographical points distant from one another, only four to five kilograms (of wheat) were distributed per month, which means 130 to 150 grams per day for each person." Even the official ration of 300 grams per day for "natives" was lower than the one for Europeans. Camus asked for "boatloads of foodstuffs, and justice." Faithful to his positions of 1937 and 1938, Camus recalled the project for Algeria proposed by the Popular Front of León Blum and Maurice Viollette, which had not been adopted: "It had nothing revolutionary about it, only according civil rights and voting status to around sixty thousand Moslems. This relatively modest project created immense hope among the Arab populations." Camus was convinced that the entire French policy towards Algeria needed to be revised.

Camus did not offer a real conclusion to his series of articles on Algeria. Instead, he refuted the theory, which some observers held, that the riots were set off by "professional agitators." He felt that the political crisis was a problem of structure, dating back to before the famine. With a certain lack of focus, he asked for a political action that might at the same time be "firm and democratic." The problem was how to export a democratic régime to Algeria. Finally, Camus was concerned and distressed: "Speeches don't need to be exported, but realizations do. If we want to save North Africa, we must show the world our resolution to make France known there by its best laws and its fairest men." Camus did not take sides over the demands which he mentioned for a separate Algerian parliament and constitution. In his views, France and Paris had already lost Algeria and the support of the assimilationist élite as well. He ended his series with the sentence: "The infinite power of justice, and that alone, must help us reconquer Algeria and its inhabitants." Anguished, Camus did not really choose between the prescriptions for a long-term assimilationist policy and the new nationalistic politics advocating total liberation.

Camus's arguments would seem to logically lead to Algerian independence, but behind his rhetorical precautions he sincerely wanted the country to maintain its ties with France. His position was original, but sometimes vague, and it would soon make him into a solitary voice on this issue. *Combat* was sympathetic to the policies of the Socialist governor general of Algeria, Yves Chataigneau, who tried unsuccessfully to force concessions out of European colonists and their pressure groups in Paris.

In May 1945, after the riots and massacres, the Algerian writer Jean Amrouche traveled for six weeks in North Africa and met with Ferhat Abbas. Amrouche offered a ten-page typed article to *Combat*, but was refused on the grounds that it would be redundant, since Camus was already writing his own series of articles on the subject. In them, Camus pointed to dishonorable racism around the globe, and he wanted to keep France from this fate. He felt that in Paris at least, people were not generally racist, although he knew the power of anti-Semitism: "Any day you can always be sure of finding an otherwise intelligent Frenchman who will tell you that the Jews really go too far."

On August 8, 1945, Camus was one of the few French editorial writers to express his horror after America dropped the atom bomb on Hiroshima. Simone de Beauvoir was also horrified by the atom bomb's use, but neither she nor Sartre said so in public at the time. For the overwhelming majority of Frenchmen and commentators, this bomb meant the end of the war, as many Japanese deaths would prevent future American deaths. Camus wrote, "Mechanical civilization has just arrived at its latest degree of savagery. We will need to choose, at a more or less distant future time, between collective suicide and the intelligent use of scientific conquests." Although Camus was nearly alone in reacting immediately in this way, he did not deny the bomb's usefulness: "Let's be clearly understood. If the Japanese surrender after Hiroshima's destruction, as a result of intimidation, we shall rejoice." Camus felt that the bomb's invention meant that all people must plead "even more energetically than before in favor of a true international society where great powers will not have more rights than small ones."

Camus's vocation for moralizing was clearer in his Hiroshima editorial than anywhere else.

Chapter Twenty-nine   **The Ramberts**

As a reader at Gallimard, editor in chief of *Combat*, and a writer, Camus led three different professional lives. He felt tired, as his third occupation in particular required more time. Sometimes he took a leave of absence: in 1945, the newspaper paid him for only seven months' work, and Gallimard for five months. *La Peste* was dragging on, but the character of the journalist in the novel, Rambert, was becoming better rounded.

Camus saw many Ramberts around him at *Combat*, where most of the journalists were under forty, with beginners' enthusiasm and a lofty idea of their trade, and often of themselves. A new recruit to *Combat* was the enigmatic Pierre Galindo, who was perhaps a bit too aware that he had served as one of the models for Meursault in *L'Etranger*. Camus presented Roger Grenier to Pia, who hired him to cover trials, among other things. Albert Palle, a former paratrooper in the Maquis, was presented by Raymond Aron, who himself had been introduced to the *Combat* staff by André Malraux. Palle previously had published only an article in Sartre's review *Les Temps Modernes* and two others in the Resistance newspaper *France-Libre*. Palle found Camus charming but "a bit of a star, pleased with his reporters but also pleased with himself . . . nice and friendly, but a little regal. Not really haughty, but nearly so."

Pierre Kauffmann, whom Pia had known during the war, began writing about national subjects and then was asked to deal with foreign affairs. When Kauffmann asked what a specialist in foreign affairs was supposed to do, Camus replied, "He kicks around the world at the paper's expense." Camus told Kauffmann, a philosopher who had not been able to teach in France because he was Jewish, what *Combat*'s approach was: "We aren't dogmatic and we won't be anti-Communist, but when we disagree with communism, we'll say so." Kauffmann traveled around the world, from Canada to the Middle East, writing articles for *Combat*. He was wary of Camus, whom he saw as a "man who was proud of his prose style," a sort of journalistic version of the nineteenth-century French writer Chateaubriand.

Jean-Paul de Dadelsen, Camus's friend from Oran and secretly a fine and original poet, served as *Combat*'s London correspondent. Jean-Pierre Vivet, who later wrote the first graduate thesis on Camus, wrote humor pieces, then film reviews, and later trial reports. *Combat* lacked staffers, and several journalists wrote about many subjects. The newspaper was enlarged to a four-sheet tabloid format, and friendship and chance continued to play a role in the hiring of journalists. For book reviews, Pia hired the Trotskyite Maurice Nadeau. As a theater critic, Camus's friend Guy Dumur revealed a flair for discovering new talent. Like Camus, Pia appreciated people who wrote well.

The most important editorial writer besides Camus and Albert Ollivier was Raymond Aron. On his first day at work, Aron discreetly retired to an office and everyone forgot about him. Finally, Albert Palle noticed him and introduced him to Pia. Aron, who had spent the war in London, had great expertise in German philosophy and sociology as well as a rare grasp of political economy. According to Aron, the "prize for excellence" for literary talent went to Camus, whose economic and diplomatic analyses notwithstanding lacked rigor. To Aron's taste, Camus was not interested enough in foreign affairs. Camus and Aron had some points in common: they both believed in the need for a revamped national sense of solidarity, and both were wary of Communists. Camus was a partisan of a different kind of socialism than what the Communists offered; his did not sacrifice political freedom and economic justice. At the time, Aron also gave socialism a chance to unite the "governmental direction of economy, under the influence of the popular masses," with "personal and intellectual liberalism which France is not resigned to sacrifice." For Aron, an article had to be devoid of passion, whereas Camus always had evident passions, and therefore also compassion.

Aron expressed his disappointment about France's situation: "The country has not shaken off the weight of the past, it has not eliminated the poisons accumulated during four years of occupation, it has not thrown itself with joyous unanimity into the great task of reconstruction." Camus and Aron agreed only in appearance, for Camus was primarily interested in morality, what existed and what should be desired, whereas Aron was interested in politics as the art of the possible. Camus wrote, "We do not believe in political realism," by which he meant that he disavowed cynical opportunism. Aron was not cynical, but he believed first and foremost in realities. *Combat* had proclaimed a few weeks after it first appeared freely in liberated Paris: "The press has a role to play as advisor to the government and guide to public opinion." Aron thought primarily about advising leaders, while Camus addressed himself to the simple reader. Camus was not attracted to Léon Blum, the intellectual former head of the Socialist Popular Front, and indeed, like Pia, he was wary of all politicians, and had been so since the *Alger Républicain* days. Camus blamed the Socialists for not having imposed upon the French parliament the Blum-Viollette plan to improve the lot of Algerians and also for having abandoned the Spanish Republicans.

One man, Charles de Gaulle, spoke to the French people over the heads of other politicians. Despite Pia's and Camus's allergy to the nationalism that de Gaulle represented, *Combat* wanted France's provisional government to be recognized by the Allies. Pia and Camus were hostile to soldiers in politics, who had to prove that once in power they would not become dictators, as Napoleon and Pétain had done. Camus admitted, as did Ollivier, that de Gaulle was among the first to refuse the legitimacy of the Vichy French government and the German occupants, and they approved when he nationalized French coal and electricity. But that did not mean they supported him in everything, especially as de Gaulle was hard to categorize neatly. Camus had recognized him as the head of the Free French Forces, but did not grant him permanent historical legitimacy. He preferred to judge the general step by step, noting that neither de Gaulle nor France's situation right after the liberation appeared to be revolutionary. *Combat* expressed this slight disappointment by referring to "the general" with a lowercase "g" instead of the almost universally used capital "G."

Camus searched for a political line midway between right-wing Gaullist reformed nationalism and Communist-like internationalism that swept the left wing. He expressed his solidarity with those who resisted the Free French Party's politics, as well as those of prewar politicians such as the unsinkable Radical Socialist Edouard Herriot, mayor of Lyons. Camus wrote, "There are many of us who think that Herriot has nothing more to teach us. If he can still be useful, it's to the extent that considering who he is and what his party was, and observing the prodigious adventure that France needed to have before it could be reborn, we'd say there is no possible comparison with today, and that France's rebirth needs something more than such lukewarm hearts."

Camus often reasoned in terms of generations rather than class struggle. He saw the former politicians of the Third Republic, many of whom had voted Pétain into power, as weak-minded traitors and poor servants of their country. Camus would use the word "bourgeoisie" approximately and pejoratively, like many intellectuals during these years. For him, the French bourgeoisie abandoned its leading role in 1940.

The French Communist Party posed specific problems for the *Combat* journalists. French Communists thrived on the ecumenical unanimity of the Resistance and the glorious reputation of the Red Army, which helped free

Europe of Nazism and fascism. The Communist Party seemed to control more French intellectuals than the Socialists and was given special treatment. Maurice Thorez, the Party's secretary general, was a deserter from the French army in 1940 before the Germans won. *Combat* remained polite and "realistic" with the Communists and never mentioned inconvenient facts like Thorez's desertion or the German-Soviet nonaggression pact of 1939. Camus still felt that the German-Soviet pact could be explained by the Munich peace accords, but abandoning his reserve slightly, he broke with the French Communist Party in January 1945, when the Movement for National Liberation held a meeting in Paris. *Combat* had ties with the latter group, which was under pressure from the Communists to merge with the pseudo-Communist National Front. André Malraux thunderously opposed this merger; and *Combat* backed Malraux in this quarrel, holding that the Resistance must remain pluralist and not slide towards the French Communist Party.

Through their daily, *L'Humanité*, and a weekly, *Action*, the Communists attacked *Combat* and Camus, who took his time before replying. In those days, inhibitions still restrained critics of the left and right wings in French politics. For the larger leftist public, being anti-Communist meant being anti-Soviet. And Camus said, "Anti-Sovietism is as powerful a stupidity as systematic hostility towards England or America would be." Less advanced than André Gide, who stuck to his harsh judgments about communism, Camus did not see the USSR primarily as a totalitarian government. To be fair, Gide had not been immersed in the Resistance's fraternity with wartime Communists. But for many, the tenor of the time was for submission, obsequiousness, and even servility towards national and international communism.

For a while, *Combat* remained fairly prudent, not knowing and perhaps not wanting to know the truth about Soviet totalitarianism. *Combat* started out with an excellent correspondent in London, Jean-Paul de Dadelsen, but none at all in Moscow or Washington. Unable to afford permanent correspondents, the paper would send journalists on spot reportages, such as when Camus sent his friend Amrouche to Algeria. *Le Monde* and *Le Figaro* had much more international coverage than *Combat* because they had more money. Camus himself was more pro-Russian or pro-Soviet than pro-Communist, and, above all, he was not obsessed with details of what was at stake on the international scene.

Combat's world horizons were strictly limited in the East, apart from articles by Colonel Bernard, Jacqueline's father, about Southeast Asia. In 1946 *Combat* published a front-page article headlined, "France Will Make Enemies of Its Colonies If It Refuses Them the Right to Independence." But Camus was not very interested in Vietnam, Cambodia, or Laos. Nor did he take much interest in the pages of *Combat* in the French literary scene: Pia took charge of the literary section. Camus would write about books only occasionally, taking the pen name "Suetonius," which dated back to his Algerian days, to bludgeon Paul Claudel on one occasion.

Camus made enemies and friends among readers. The novelist Georges Bernanos wrote to him, "I do not always agree with you, but I will always contradict you with regret." Camus made a point of declaring without ambiguity that his thought did not end in absolute pessimism any more than Sartre's or Malraux's did: "It is puerile to think that pessimistic thoughts must be despairing ones." *Combat* did not automatically defend Sartre's writings. Jacques Lemarchand praised *No Exit* when it was revived at the Vieux-Colombier, but Maurice Nadeau disliked the series *Chemins de la liberté*, parts of which Sartre said were inspired by John Dos Passos. Camus did not write any substantial article about the books of Sartre or Beauvoir, although the three writers remained friendly.

Camus was still working on *La Peste*. Towards the end of the novel, the journalist Rambert meets his wife again: "When the train stopped, the interminable separations, which often began on the same train platform, would end in a second's time, the moment when arms would close with exultant greed around the body whose living forms had been forgotten. Rambert wouldn't have the time to look at this form running towards him before she would press it against his chest. And holding her in both arms, squeezing her head against him, of which he could only see her familiar hair, he let the tears flow without knowing if they were tears of present joy or of pain too long repressed; at least he was sure that they would prevent him from checking whether this face hidden in the hollow of his shoulder was the one he had dreamed of so long, or that of a stranger instead. He would know later if his suspicions were true, but for the moment, he wanted to be like all those around him who seemed to believe that the Plague could come and go, without men's hearts being changed by it."

In his *Carnets*, Camus was less optimistic about his own marriage: "Eighty percent of divorces among prisoners returned home. Eighty percent of human loves cannot resist five years' separation." Often friends who visited, like Lucien and Mireille Benisti, a couple Camus had known in Algeria, noticed the tension in the Camus marriage. Albert seemed irritated, ironic, and biting, although he always remained courteous to his wife in front of guests; he was not the sort of man to shout and storm about. Francine was presented to Sartre and Beauvoir, but she did not feel comfortable with them, although they found her lovely.

Francine began to participate in certain parties but not all of them. Maria Casarès was no prude, but she was worried by Francine's reappearance, even though Camus assured her, "Francine is like my sister." When

Camus announced that his "sister" was pregnant, Maria, who was understanding only up to a point, broke with him. Camus did not like lies, and neither did she.

Among other problems, Camus spoke of his "respiratory illness," avoiding the word "tuberculosis." He complained about the Paris climate as a contributing factor in his relapses, moments of exhaustion, and shortness of breath: "Imagine . . . that starting in mid-October, you know that you really won't see the sun for six months." He met some Algerian friends with pleasure after *Combat* had been put to bed, and he would drag them to nightclubs and bars, expecially the Méphisto and the Tabou, for late-night revels.

Visiting his friend Charles Poncet, he said that Francine was pregnant and joked about their baby-to-be: "It's a larva!" The Camuses could no longer live in a one-room apartment. They moved to a delightful suburban house, La Vallée-aux-Loups, where Chateaubriand had once stayed, but a bit far from Paris. They remained there only a few weeks, then moved to a furnished house in the eastern Parisian suburb of Vincennes, which was more accessible to the *Combat* offices and Gallimard. They could also put up Francine's mother, who arrived before the baby's birth. In August 1945 Camus wrote to Michel and Janine Gallimard: "My mother-in-law landed at the Bourget airport slightly dazed by the open air and vaguely disgusted because everyone had vomited except her. . . . Her son-in-law has shut himself up in his room and tries to give a form to a story of an epidemic which will finally kill him, but not before I've worked all this month at *Combat*." A publisher friend, Guy Schoeller, offered them a little house that belonged to his mother, along the Seine at Bougival, twenty minutes away from Paris by train or car, so the Camuses moved once again.

On September 5, 1945, Francine Camus gave birth to twins, Catherine and Jean, at the Belvédère clinic near the porte de Saint-Cloud. Coming to pick up his wife, Camus packed her luggage into a car borrowed from *Combat* and called out a joyous "Let's go!"—to which Francine pointed out that he had forgotten about the twins.

At Bougival, he met his former teacher Louis Germain, who was serving in the French army at the age of fifty-eight. Germain stored a trunk with the Camuses, and after his visit he sent a letter in which he expressed mixed feelings. "I think I have a certain part, very modest it's true, in your destiny. . . . I'd like you to assure me that I was not wrong in guiding you towards the lycée." This fine teacher found Paris a noxious place.

Life in France remained hard, even if the French were less rationed that the British, victors in the war. Some Americans got together to help French intellectuals, especially writers, and the Camuses received food packages from a Philadelphia lawyer named Ira Williams. Camus was struck by the kindness of his correspondents and was amazed by how prepared the

Americans were; he was given several different types of food packages, such as "type A," a one-pound can of vegetables, half a pound of sugared cocoa, a pound of powdered milk, a pound of cheese, etc. Camus thanked those who regularly sent packages, and offered to send his books in exchange.

In August 1945, rehearsals began for *Caligula* at the Hébertot Theater, and Camus had to audition actors for the roles. Camus was very satisfied with a handsome, moody, and romantic young actor, Gérard Philipe, who was chosen to play the title role on his way to a great career on stage and screen. Paul Oettly directed, assisted by Camus. Showing fidelity to his Algerian friends, Camus chose Marie Viton to do the costumes and Louis Miquel for the scenery.

The former three-act play *Caligula* now had four acts. More than *Le Malentendu*, *Caligula* fit into the absurd cycle: Camus presented an intelligent tyrant whose motives seemed "both strange and profound. . . . In particular, he was the only one to have turned power itself into derision." Opening on September 15, *Caligula* was very well received, helped by its cast. Gérard Philipe was an unforgettable Caligula, and the distinguished actor Michel Bouquet played the role of Scipion. Jean Oettly, a cousin of Paul, played the role of the First Guard.

The audience appreciated the play's caustic lines: "Everything is on the same level, Rome's grandeur and your arthritis attacks." "Everyone knows that to govern means to steal, but there are ways of doing it." There were also somber speeches: "To lose one's life is a little thing, and I will have the courage when necessary. But to see the meaning of life dissipate, and our reason for living disappear, that's what is unbearable. One cannot live without a reason." Some thought Camus was referring to the attitudes of far-right-wing magazines like *L'Epoque* and *Action*, which attacked him for the line "I cannot disagree with anything without feeling obliged to befoul it or to take away from others the right to believe in it."

His play's success did not keep the author from expressing a touchy bitterness in his *Carnets*: "Thirty articles [about *Caligula*]. The reasons for praise were as bad as the reasons for criticisms. There were scarcely one or two voices that sounded emotionally moved. In the best of cases, fame is a misunderstanding. But I will not put on the superior air of someone who disdains it. Fame is yet another sign of mankind, no more and no less important than their indifference, friendship, or hatred. Finally, what does all that mean to me? This misunderstanding is a liberation to those who know how to take it as such. My ambition, if I have one, is of another order."

He also noted: "At the age of thirty, almost from one day to another, I knew fame, and I don't regret it. I could have imagined worse things, and now I know what it amounts to: very little." Sartre and Beauvoir had the impression that Camus savored his reputation, yet he seemed less happy about it than the jubilant Sartre was tickled by his own renown. Camus wrote in his *Carnets*: "What is a famous man? Someone whose first name does not matter. Everyone else's first name has an individual meaning."

Camus felt constrained by his marriage, and he could not finish his novel. He was solicited for articles, speeches, and panel debates. He did not like his name to be linked with Sartre's, but in American interviews the latter had sung Camus's praises. In the July 1945 issue of American *Vogue*, Sartre placed Camus in the modern Pantheon. "The Resistance," he said, "taught us that literature is not a futile activity, independent of politics." Sartre felt that Camus was the archetype of the committed writer, a hope for a "new classicism." The principal characteristics of future French literature could be guessed in the "pure and somber work of Camus." Sartre maintained that Malraux's generation was opposed to Camus's, which believed that "action is austere, modest, and useful." Sartre's generalizations sometimes seemed as wide as his enthusiasms, but in public he could not have been more flattering to Camus.

Camus had no money worries on the horizon, but he did feel limited by material concerns because he was still looking for a decent permanent home for his family, while refusing to stay in the suburbs. He explained to Jean Grenier that he could not work in a state of exasperation. He had "not had a day of rest for three years." He lived by night and by day, just like Beauvoir and Sartre, who worked ferociously for up to fourteen hours a day. But they had no children and lived at a hotel, without having to take care of one another materially. Francine, by contrast, consulted Albert each time she bought a table, a blanket, or an overcoat. The introverted Francine was more indecisive than she was infantile. Camus wondered how he was supposed to write with women and babies around, and he sometimes envied Sartre's freedom. Camus needed relationships of manly friendship, and although both Sartre and Camus were macho types, Camus was more capable of a serious conversation with a woman. Not so Sartre, who found in the Beaver one of the only women whose brain power was strong enough to make her independent.

Camus and Sartre were acccomplices, although they had few philosophical or literary discussions apart from rapid agreements that François Mauriac was tiresome, Gabriel Marcel kitsch, and Faulkner extraordinary. Camus was reserved and even somewhat wary with Sartre, confiding more in Beauvoir. Sartre had a naturalness and verbal facility, while Camus seemed stuffier. Camus did not describe his metaphysical torments to Sartre, whom he would meet at the cafés and bars of Saint-Germain-des-Prés and Montparnasse and at nightclubs like the Rose Rouge, where they heard the writer Boris Vian play the trumpet and Juliette Gréco sing. Nor did Camus confide these things to Malraux, whom he would see at the Gallimard office. He would speak about them more easily to women, such as when he dined alone with the Beaver at the Brasserie Lipp. Beauvoir claimed that Camus wanted to write the truth about himself one day, as she felt that in him, the gap was wide between the public man, his work, and the private man. Simone, who was part harsh schoolmistress and part liberated young lycée teacher, liked Camus's "bad boy side." She thought that his skepticism was really cynicism but was still seduced by his charm. The Beaver and Sartre were Manichean toward others; Camus was not. Sartre was especially violent, because he was not much involved with the Resistance, and his hardness toward intellectual collaborators was inversely proportional to the risks he had run, while Camus, who had been more engaged, was less inflexible.

Sartre and Beauvoir approved of most of Camus's positions on modern history, although they found his manner of expressing them too preachifying. Sartre, Beauvoir, and Camus all had different ideas about God, although all three were atheists. Sartre and Beauvoir were pleased to be so, but Camus was anxious and perplexed by his own lack of belief. No character created by Sartre ever felt possessed by the Devil or by God. But Camus in *La Peste* was still living with the life and thoughts of the Jesuit priest Paneloux and Dr. Rieux, a non-believer and a man of God whom he met while taking care of human suffering. Camus tried to understand his faith in God, while Sartre felt that this giant superstition wasn't worth the time. But Camus identified with his characters: When Dr. Rieux declares, "I had another idea of love. Until death I will refuse to love a universe where children are tortured," the distressed Paneloux replies, "Ah, doctor! . . . I have just understood what mercy is." Rieux says, "It's what I don't have, I know. But I don't want to discuss that with you."

Camus did not discuss God or mercy with Sartre; nor did he talk about the sacred with Malraux, as he might have done. However, Camus and Sartre did speak about political subjects, like communism. Sartre felt that one must choose to work with the Communists or against them. Camus did not have the same approach, speaking of believers and unbelievers in communism. He noted in his *Carnets*: "The meaning of my works: so many men are deprived of mercy. How to live without mercy? One must try and do what Christianity never did: to take care of the damned."

Sartre and Camus did not think that the world has a meaning, apart from the one man gives it by his actions. More and more, Sartre clung to Marxist historicism with its future revolution, victories, and defeats all programmed in the genes of history. Camus did not accept historical materialism, which he saw as the negation of all freedom. In the name of freedom, Sartre rejected absolute determinism; but stuck between the implications of history and freedom, he did not accord Christianity a privileged place in the twentieth century, as Camus did. Sartre found Camus untalented in metaphysics and theology, whether the subject was Aquinas or Marx.

In his *Carnets*, Camus asked, "By what right can a Communist or a Christian (to choose only respected forms of modern thought) reproach me for being a pessimist?" Writing to a Belgian divinity student, Jacques de Vriendt, in September 1945, Camus rejected the reputation for pessimism he had been given: "I can only tell you this—I have too much taste for life and a feeling for the world to believe that all is nothingness. . . . I do not believe that negation encompasses everything, I only believe that it is at the beginning of everything. Today, when all problems are posed in terms of flesh, it is natural that intellectual doubt has become a vital doubt which challenges all existence."

Like his characters Rieux, Paneloux, and the journalist Rambert, Camus sought a foundation for his values. He felt a certain envy of Christian certainties, writing to de Vriendt, "Values are given to you in advance by the Revelation. Your only concern is to reconcile them with the world. I personally believe that they cannot be reconciled with the world. . . . The only coherent religious state seems to me the monastic state, with all its rigors." Taking note of Europe's atheism, Camus wrote to his religious correspondent, "Tell yourself that three-quarters of the men in the Western world today are deprived of God and that one must try to formulate their thoughts, consciously or not. Now is the time to do something for the damned. . . . God has been and remains, I suppose, one of man's great opportunities. But all those who have turned away from him must find another path, and must do so without too much pride or illusion." Camus concluded by thanking de Vriendt for his kind words about France: "Yes, I love this country. I know its errors and its weaknesses, and I may have judged its people severely, but even at the heart of its worst errors, I swear to you that it has remained great and it merits the respect of all those who know how to judge human quality."

Camus poured out his feelings with this correspondent he did not know, rather than with Sartre's crowd. Michel Leiris, who attended all the theatrical premieres of the group, felt that despite Sartre's poetic touches in *The Flies* and *No Exit*, "Camus's plays, although they do not contain great poetry, are nevertheless better." Simone de Beauvoir talked of Camus and his friends and lovers in a saddened tone. She felt amorous toward him, but he did not return the feeling, and that opened the gates for all misdealings.

The media still spoke of "Sartre and Camus" rather than of "Camus and Sartre," which was understandable, but somewhat irritating for Camus.

Chapter Thirty

The Island with Three Rivers

O n January 31, 1946, in Washington, D.C., Frederick B. Lyon, head of the State Department's Foreign Activity Correlation division, wrote to FBI director J. Edgar Hoover that the State Department had received news that "Albert Camus alias P. F. Corus, New York correspondent of *Combat* (a newspaper in Paris, France), has been filing inaccurate reports which are unfavorable to the public interest of this country." Lyon asked Hoover to "make a preliminary investigation of Mr. Camus and his activities." Two weeks later, an FBI agent in Washington, Guy Hottel, found that "Albert Canus" and P. F. Corus were both unknown to the U.S. State Department, and so the FBI tried to find out more about him. They studied the February 23, 1946 issue of *The Nation*, in which Hannah Arendt wrote about French existentialism, and confirmed that "the subject [of the present report] and Jean-Paul Sartre" were the leading exponents of existentialism. It seemed suspicious that Sartre and Camus had refused the French Legion of Honor when it was proposed to them. Camus had also refused to be a candidate for the French Academy, saying, "The life or death of the French Academy seems to me a futile thing."

Since September 1945, his American publisher, Alfred A. Knopf, had been inviting him to New York. Knopf's wife, Blanche, a frequent visitor to Paris and an ardent Camus fan, served as intermediary for the invitation. So the writer made the request known to the head of cultural affairs at the French Ministry of Foreign Affairs, which would pay his travel expenses, suggesting two topics for speeches: "One Year of Free Journalism" and "A Plea for Europe." He noted that his topics would have no "political impact," and he filled out the usual forms to ask for an American visa, which asked him to promise not to assassinate America's president and to state that he had never belonged to the Communist Party. Camus affirmed without hesitation that he had never been a Communist, not merely on his visa application but also privately to colleagues like Maurice Nadeau, who was astonished when he found out the truth years later.

He boarded the ship *Oregon* at the French port of Le Havre on March 10, 1946, a cargo freighter which contained a few passenger cabins. The ship was slow and comforts were few, among the few luxuries being cocktails in the captain's cabin. Camus shared a stateroom with a psychiatrist named Pierre Rubé and another Frenchman, who refused to wash himself. Camus tried to study a little English in preparation for his visit to America, and although he could read the language fairly well, he spoke it badly. He also kept a travel diary: "Once again I look [at the ocean] as I have done for years, at the drawings which foam and wave create on the water's surface, lace formed and dissolved, liquid marble . . . and once more I look for the exact comparison which will capture for me that marvelous blossoming of sea, water, and light, which has escaped me for so long."

Camus was writing one day in a corner of the passenger's lounge when Dr. Rubé began playing Bach's Italian Concerto on the piano. Camus said, "Well, well, you play that piece—my wife often plays it, too." Rubé asked if Camus's wife was a musician, to which the writer replied, "Yes, she introduced me to Bach."

The *Oregon* arrived in New York by night. "In the distance," Camus noted, "Manhattan's skyscrapers are against a background of fog. My heart is calm and dry and I feel I am watching a spectacle that does not affect me." When the passnegers disembarked at eleven a.m., Camus was the only one to be treated as a suspicious character, because he refused to name friends whom he knew to be Communists. Finally, after diplomatic intervention, the immigration officer begged Mr. Camus's pardon for having delayed him, and a French embassy employee drove him to his hotel on West Seventieth Street in Manhattan.

The French cultural attaché at the time, Claude Lévi-Strauss, worked part-time in a splendid townhouse while writing his anthropological classic, *The Elementary Structures of Kinship*. Before Camus arrived, Lévi-Strauss had already welcomed Sartre and Beauvoir and the essayist Roger Caillois. Lévi-Strauss had some original ideas, such as importing American gray squirrels to French parks and buying collections of American Indian art. His relations with Camus were friendly, if reserved, as he felt that Camus was a "conformist in his left-wing virtues." Camus found Lévi-Strauss quite taciturn, a university professor disguised as a diplomat. The consul dragged Camus, the missionary of cultural relations, through New York's hurly-burly.

The writer explored New York and wrote his friends Michel and Janine Gallimard, "It is beyond human power to give an idea of the curious way in which eight million bison live in this elevated amusement park that geographers call New York, in which 102,000 green, red, and yellow beetles that entomologists call taxis circulate, stop, start, and cross one another . . . using the manners of polite anthills, while 252,000 bison dressed like operetta generals and admirals stand in front of doors of buildings, some to stop the beetles by means of a whistle, and others to open the door for us, and still others to go up and down like multicolored toys in fifty-story cages which commentators call elevators in memory of the Virgin Mary, who didn't make many disciples here as a virgin, which is a blessing in one sense, because that way no one will be crucified."

Camus had trouble adding up his contradictory impressions. He suggested that one could wonder if one was "among madmen or the most reasonable people on earth; if life was as easy as they say here or as foolish as it seems; if it is natural that they hire ten people instead of one, without improving the service; if Americans should be called modest, liberal, or conformist; if it is admirable or immaterial that garbage collectors wear elegant gloves; if it is good that the circus here shows ten simultaneous attractions in four different rings so that although you are interested in them all, you can't see any of them; if it is meaningful that the thousands of youngsters who roller-skated with me the other night to the sound of a giant organ in a sort of indoor bicycle track in a yellowish light seemed as serious and absorbed as if they were solving an eighth-degree equation."

His first guide during his American visit was Dolorès Vanetti Ehrenreich, who spoke the "purest slang I have ever heard," Camus remarked. Ehrenreich, an employee of the American Office of War Information, was a former girlfriend of Sartre's, of whom she would say, "Do you realize, I've slept with Napoleon!" Dolorès explained to Camus that Americans do not like ideas, but he did not take such French clichés as gospel: "That's what they say, but I doubt it."

Camus was interested in the details of American life that he saw: "the large consumption of scotches and soda in the cultural milieu; the luxury and bad taste, especially in neckties; the love for animals, especially the Central Park Zoo's gorillas and the Museum of Natural History's protozoa; the habit of drinking fruit juice in the morning; delicious ice creams, price freezes, rapid changes of temperature, millions of windows lit up at night, hot baths, vitamin doses, and drugstores serving bacon and eggs." Camus saw an exciting and electric megalopolis composed "of fifteen large cities whistling, screaming, working, and amusing themselves with a sort of mechanical despair." He found Americans to be "cordial, hospitable and indifferent, quickly happy and quickly forgetful." Policemen never asked passersby for their identity papers. He learned that "the secret of conversation here [is] to speak in order to say nothing." Camus wrote out in English his own version of a typical American conversation: "Good morning—Nice

weather today, is it not?—It is.—The spring will be wonderful.—I think so.
OK. How do you like America now, Mr. Camus?—OK! I like it very much—
You are right. It's a nice country, is it not?—It is.—Will you come back
again?—Sure.—Etc. etc."

Camus gave a "damned annoying" press conference for a dozen journalists at Lévi-Strauss's office on Fifth Avenue. He talked about his upcoming book but refused to speak of his Resistance activities, and declared that
he had read American novels, by authors from John Dos Passos to William
Faulkner. Yes, American novelistic techniques influenced him, but they also
led to an impoverishment in the means of literary expression: "In any case,
American novelists themselves are freeing themselves from these formulas."

At the end of March 1946, Camus gave a lecture at Columbia University, accompanied by the French Resistance novelist Jean Bruller, known as
Vercors. The University's McMillin Theater was jam-packed with students
who wanted to hear Camus speak on theater, literature, and philosophy. But
the writer suggested it might be more interesting to talk about railway workers, miners, and his generation, who were adolescents during the world economic crisis and who "were twenty years old when Hitler took power." With
all the subsequent world events, Camus said, "I suppose that's what one calls
an interesting generation." He told the young Americans that "the literature
of this period was in revolt against clarity, narration, even against the sentence. Painting rejected the subject, reality, and even harmony. Music rejected melody. As for philosophy, it taught that there was no more truth, only
phenomena, and that Mr. Smith, Monsieur Durand, and Herr Vogel might
exist, but that these three phenomena had nothing in common."

When a student asked if there was a human crisis, Camus replied with
four brutal wartime anecdotes. The first anecdote: Two accused men were
tied down and tortured by the Gestapo in an apartment. Later, the concierge
started to clean up around them, and when one of the prisoners complained
to her, she replied, "I don't get mixed up in the affairs of my tenants." The
second: In Lyons one of Camus's friends had been tortured by the Germans
and was taken out of his cells with his ears torn off for another "questioning."
The German officer who had already interrogated him asked him, full of so-
licitude, "How are your ears doing now?" The third: In German-occupied
Greece, an officer was ready to shoot three brothers who were prisoners.
Their mother pled with the German and he decided to spare one of her
sons, if she would choose the one who would live. She chose the eldest, who
had children of his own, thus condemning the others, which is what the
German officer wanted. Last story: Freed women concentration-camp prisoners were sent back home via Switzerland, and when their train passed a funeral, they started to laugh hysterically. "So that's how dead people are
treated here!"

Camus told his audience that today, intelligent people were affirming that if Hitler had won the war, history would have sanctified him and justified his terror. Camus did not want the students to think that everything was meaningless. The German occupants of Paris thought and acted according to Hegel's hateful principle that "man is made for history and not history for man." Camus said that in action as well as in thought, all forms of realistic and fatalistic philosophy must be rejected: "There is in France and Europe today a generation that considers that whoever puts faith in the human condition is mad, while anyone who despairs because of events is a coward."

Camus respected the American taste for freedom and happiness. A student interrupted to say that something illustrating humanity's crisis had just occurred: the money from admission fees for the lecture, which was meant for French war orphans, had just been stolen from the Columbia cashier's desk. The audience decided to pay a second time and contributed even more than before. Camus found that solution "typical of American generosity. Their hospitality and cordiality is in the same taste, immediate and spontaneous. That's what is best about them."

He gave another speech at Vassar College in Poughkeepsie, New York, to "an army of young starlets who cross their long legs on the lawns." American campuses enchanted him, unlike drab French universities: "What is done for young people here deserves to be remembered." Camus ended his lecture tour on May 1 at Brooklyn College, where he said that he had expected American youth to be more emotionally demonstrative. He pointed out that man's most dangerous temptation was inertia. An ordinary man thought that if he did his job well, he had assumed all his responsibilities; but that was not enough, he must also participate in other struggles. American young people's problems and doubts were the same as those of young Europeans. After a few weeks in America, he had the impression that there were no more national problems, only international ones. He spoke of pessimism and optimism, contradicting himself and simplifying considerably: according to Camus, European pessimism believed that all life was a tragedy, while American optimism believed that all of life is good and even marvelous. A synthesis was needed, which would encourage solidarity between the two countries, a synthesis that would result in a "classic civilization." American students should send packages to French comrades, correspond with them, and thousands of Americans students should go to visit France. A student asked if Camus was an existentialist. "No," he sighed.

Wandering around New York, Camus loved Broadway with its theaters and neon lights, the Bowery and its elevated trains. Like any tourist, Camus adored Chinatown, the Bronx, and Sammy's Bowery Follies, with its grotesquely obese women singers. Camus traveled and appreciated the "gentleness of evenings on Washington, D.C.'s vast lawns, when the sky turns red and the grass starts to blacken, with hordes of joyously crying little black kids knocking a ball between them with a slat of wood; disheveled Americans in shirtsleeves collapse on park benches, coming straight from a saloon out of an old film, using their last bit of energy to suck on ice creams molded in pasteurized cardboard, while squirrels come right up to your feet to unearth some delicacies which only they know the name of, and in the city's one hundred thousand trees, a million birds salute the arrival of the first star above Washington's pyramid in the still-bright sky, while long-legged dames walk along the grassy paths in the perspective of the great monuments, offering to the heavens their splendid faces and loveless glances for a relaxed moment."

Returning to New York, he continued his peregrinations in black Harlem, Jewish Brooklyn, and vulgar Coney Island. The translation of *L'Etranger* appeared on April 11 from Alfred A. Knopf. The novel was translated by James Joyce's friend and exegete Stuart Gilbert, and while the *New York Times* criticized the "Britannic" quality of Gilbert's translation, the book was praised as "brilliantly told." *The New Republic* assigned Camus's friend Nicola Chiaramonte, whom he had helped escape to Morocco in 1941, to review *The Stranger*, and as expected, the article was positive, calling the book "admirable."

American ladies, young and less young, pursued Camus, such as the millionaire Dorothy Norman, who deluged him with invitations, and the writer Eleanor Clark, who sent him a bouquet of flowers. Camus appreciated some American painters whose works he saw—for instance, the turn-of-the-century Romantic Albert Pinkham Ryder. He met a theater producer, Harald Bromley, who offered to back all of Camus's plays for American productions. Bromley took Camus to hear a black American jazz pianist who performed under the name of Rocco: "He plays a piano on casters standing up, while pushing it in front of him. His playing has rhythmic power and precision, and he participates by jumping, dancing, and throwing his head and his hair from left to right."

He also met another new friend, more serious than Bromley, the writer Waldo Frank, a former friend of the poet Hart Crane, who believed that "originality is a form of solitude." Frank told Camus that "to find great art and great poetry in America, you have to go to Spanish America." Camus in turn noted that Waldo Frank "is one of the rare superior men I have met here. He despairs a little about America today, when he compares it to nineteenth-century America. He said, 'The great minds (Melville) have always been solitary here.'"

Camus also ran into André Breton, who had spent the war in America working for the Office of War Information but had refused to learn English so as not to "pollute" his French, according to Breton. The two writers remained on highly reserved and even unfriendly terms. Surrealism had never interested Camus, who began to feel more and more critical about Frenchmen who stayed in America during the war. As for Breton, he recalled Jean-Paul Sartre's nastiness about surrealism and saw Camus as an appendage to Sartre. There was something of a rivalry bubbling up between Camus and Breton, as surrealism was considered out of date compared to Sartre and Camus.

One day a nineteen-year-old student from Wesleyan University, Michel Vinaver, waited for Camus in the vestibule of his New York hotel. He told the writer he had written some short stories, in French and in English, then said, "I want to write, but everything has already been written." "But no!" Camus exclaimed, and suggested that Vinaver contact him back in Paris. Camus himself had been the protégé of Jean Grenier, André Malraux, Jean Paulhan, Pascal Pia, and André Gide, and now could put himself in the affable role of kindly protector. However, he tried to avoid being a chattering missionary of cultural relations. Instead he would spend time with university professors like Germaine Brée, whom he had met years before in Oran, and Justin O'Brien, the translator of André Gide, as well as Nicola Chiaramonte.

On April 16, amid the blaze of publicity for the new translation, he was introduced to a pretty twenty-year-old with blue eyes and brown hair, Patricia Blake. He met Patricia, a copy writer for American *Vogue*, just after he'd had a "damned annoying" meeting with the magazine's managing editor, Jessica Daves, who had published a poor but much-noticed photo portrait of Camus by the famous Cecil Beaton. Patricia had almost finished her history studies at Smith College and spoke good French. She had spent a year at Smith's Maison Française dormitory in Paris, where she perfected her knowledge of French authors from the seventeenth to the twentieth centuries. She also wrote articles for the *New York Times Book Review* to supplement her salary of thirty-five dollars a week from *Vogue*.

Often, Camus treated women the way a bombardier pilot treats a target site: he would strike and, mission accomplished, he would get away quickly. But after seeing Patricia the first time, Camus immediately invited her out the next day, and she accepted. He liked being seen in public with Patricia and told Pierre Rubé that he felt very much in love. Camus was now living in a Central Park West duplex with living room, kitchen, and two bedrooms, put at his disposal by a furrier named Zaharo, who admired his books. Camus asked Rubé, "Don't you find little Patricia astonishing? Does she represent a certain type of American girl?" Rubé found her indeed exceptional, and quite different from the girls he had known, although he was no specialist in young American girls. Patricia seemed to have talent and intellectual maturity, apart from her great candor. Rubé's opinions made Camus smile.

Patricia accompanied him to his speech at Bryn Mawr College, although the couple sometimes shocked people: at thirty-three, Camus was old enough to play the role of Pygmalion, but not quite old enough to act as guru. He guided Patricia along the seas of literature and politics, helping her to avoid certain coral reefs. Patricia had discovered Proust, whom she saw as a great truth, but Camus cautioned her by saying "half-truth." She was more interested in poetry than Camus was, and he scribbled a letter of introduction for her to the poet Saint-John Perse, who was a longtime diplomat working in Washington under his real name, Alexis Léger. Patricia had read Lenin and Marx and felt sympathies for communism, but Camus explained that Communist leaders were not just utopians but also murderers. Later, Patricia would become a specialist in Soviet politics. She was amused by Albert's passion for Chinatown restaurants. Once during a dinner there with French people, he gave her mock-terrified looks because a guest's simpering wife was unexpectedly playing footsie with him under the table.

Camus remained fascinated by nightclubs and Patricia was obliged to follow along, although she preferred the theater to screaming burlesque singers. They saw Laurence Olivier in a double bill of Sophocles' *Oedipus Rex* and Sheridan's *The Critic* during a 1946 New York tour of the Old Vic theater company. Camus took the eminent philosopher Etienne Gilson, an authority on Saint Thomas Aquinas, to the Copacabana nightclub, and when Gilson did not appear to appreciate the atmosphere, Patricia staged a faint in order to cut the evening short. She did not enjoy popular music, but liked the way Albert danced slow dances and fox-trots, keeping his partner at a distance like a well-brought-up working man. He asked her to type some pages of *La Peste*. About the character Tarrou in *La Peste*, Camus wrote in his *Carnets* that he "frequented Spanish dancers, he loves only passion." Patricia and Albert were living a passion, on the "Island with Three Rivers," which was Camus's inexplicable name for New York.

Camus had put on some weight, but he often seemed exhausted, even cadaverous. He thought that he would die, and he indulged in a certain taste for morbidity, collecting the last words of dying men, which he enjoyed reciting to friends; he also became interested in American funeral customs. Camus was sweating a lot and had attacks of high fever; he smoked heavily, as did Patricia, but he drank little alcohol. If he had a coughing fit and had to spit blood, he would leave the company to do so. He repeated in his letters to friends that he was going to die, and he told Patricia that he feared the end was near, perhaps a year or two away. In his *Carnets* he wrote of his need to live intensely: "But why not put a name too to this desire I feel in my heart, and this tumultuous need that seizes me, to find once again the impatient heart I had at age twenty. But I know the remedy—I shall look at the sea for a long time." He had an acute sense of passing time and of time lost.

He noted: "Sadness to feel myself still so vulnerable. In twenty-five years I will be fifty-seven years old. Twenty-five years then to write my works and to find what I'm looking for. Then, old age and death. I know what is the most important thing for me, yet I still find a way of giving in to little temptations, to waste time in futile conversations or in sterile wanderings. I have mastered two or three things inside myself, but I am far from that superiority which I need so badly." He had attacks of suicidal despair, and he kept a copy with him of a suicide note that one of Leon Trotsky's friends had written to the political leader, in which the suicidal Russian complained that his life had "lost its meaning" and that he felt "obliged to leave it, to put an end to it."

While he was in the States, Camus got involved in a publishing squabble, defending the position of Gallimard, who were currently suing the American publisher Reynal & Hitchcock. Gallimard owned the rights to the works of the novelist Antoine de Saint-Exupéry, but during the war the author himself had sold the rights to his books *The Little Prince* and *Flight to Arras* to the American company. Raymond Gallimard, Gaston's brother and Michel's father, arrived in New York for the trial, and the American-based French Resistance weekly, *Pour la Victoire*, attacked him: what was Gallimard doing "against American publishers whose only crime was to help French writers . . . while the *NRF* had as Führer Drieu La Rochelle?" In a letter to Michel, Camus called the weekly "an ass-wipe . . . which only expressed opinions of courageous Frenchmen who stayed in 1941 at Waldorf-Astoria apartments for one thousand dollars per month." He assured Michel that the trial had only relative importance, and that the Gallimard family "doesn't have a worse press here than in France." He said that during the trial, he discovered that he had talents as an orator, and added, "Do you know what the *Vogue* girls call me? 'The young Humphrey Bogart'!!! You know, I can get a film contract whenever I want."

Camus had promised to visit Montreal with Harald Bromley, who bought a used car for the trip, but as soon as they reached the Adirondack Mountains, Camus felt like turning back. However, they pressed on to Montreal. On May 26, 1946, he wrote Patricia a letter from a stopover point, Camp Downey: "Saturday 9 p.m. . . . I arranged to have a moment of peace and solitude which I need to write to you. I think you'd like this place, lost in the Adirondacks, where we have landed after two days of wandering in the mountains of this region. It's an isolated old house which is usually visited by hunters and fishermen, but which is deserted right now. I am in the living room in front of a big fireplace, under a beamed ceiling. There was a storm a moment ago and now the night silence is full of the cries of toads, birds, and crickets. . . . My dear, I was so unhappy to have left you and so displeased with myself. . . . The only desire that is worth anything is the one to keep you near me. . . . Finally, I asked [Bromley] to return earlier." Camus would later mainly recall the "profound boredom that reigned" in Montreal. During the trip he noted mysteriously, perhaps having to do with Patricia, "The only thing I wanted to say, I was incapable of until now, and no doubt I shall never say it."

He was tired of America: "My curiosity for this country has ended all at once, as with certain people I turn away from without any explanation and with no further interest (Francine reproaches me for this). Although I see a thousand reasons one might have to be interested in it, and I could defend them and make an apology for them, I can reconstruct [America's] beauty and its future, but my heart has simply stopped speaking to me here." Writing to Michel and Janine Gallimard, he saw Americans with tired eyes: "So here I am in fact ready to leave America . . . having already left it in spirit, and I am only leaving here a corpse without a soul, well dressed it is true, which continues to circulate amid eight million dead men who also continue to pretend to live in this astonishing great city. . . . This corpse does not resemble that charming, exceptional person whom you had the good fortune to meet."

Camus admitted his incapacity to understand America and Americans as well as New Yorkers, not a common admission among Frenchmen — since Tocqueville, most of them have been convinced that they know Americans better than anyone else. Camus, though, wrote: "I don't have a precise idea about New York myself, even after so many days, but it continues to irritate me and seduce me at the same time. New York is like Oran." This was both a compliment and a criticism in Camus's mind, because while Oran in *La Peste* was unattractive, it was nevertheless part of his beloved country, Algeria: "[The Americans] resemble our colonists in Algeria so much, but I can't live among them anymore." Camus was impatient, he told Michel and Janine, to "rediscover the flaws and defects of Europe, where conversations have wit, even nasty wit, irony, loftiness, passion, and lies, as well as your kind French faces."

Camus took the boat home, and Patricia did not accompany him to the dock. He already had seen mainland France, Czechoslovakia, and Italy, his stay of less than three months in America was the writer's fourth major voyage. He could no longer write, as he had ten years before, "There is no pleasure in travel. I see it rather as a form of asceticism." Camus brought back no generalizations about America, especially not of the Marxist kind which Sartre had made, explaining everything in terms of American economic and military imperialism. When his friend Charles Poncet asked why he did not publish an account of his trip to America, Camus said, "Everywhere I went, I received a warm welcome, and everywhere I expressed myself with total freedom. I'm not going to spit in the plate after having eaten the soup, the way Sartre did." He told Louis Germain that America was "a great country, strong and disciplined in freedom, but ignorant of lots of things, starting with Europe."

Camus had a sort of mythical hierarchy, where the top level of importance was occupied by Algeria's Arabs and Frenchmen. Then came the men of the Mediterranean basin, the French, Spanish, and Italians. Then came the Slavs, literary characters with charm and nihilistic pessimism who also had an appetite for life's joys. But he remained wary about Anglo-Saxons, and for Camus, like many Frenchmen, Americans qualified as Anglo-Saxons.

He noted down what remained of his impressions of New York: "I can only retain powerful, fleeting emotions, and irritated nostalgia, and moments of heartbreak. After so many months, I don't know anything about New York. . . . To tell all, I am out of my depth when I think of New York. . . . Yes, I am out of my depth. I am learning that some cities are like certain women who irritate you, shove you around, and skin you alive, and yet whose burns, which you carry all over your body, are somehow dear to you, who provide at the same time loud violence and delectation." He added: "For days I walked in New York with tears in my eyes, simply because the city's air is full of cinders. . . . That is finally how I carry New York inside me, as you put a foreign object into your eye, unbearable and delicious, with tears of pity and a rage to deny everything. Perhaps that's what we call passion. . . . Yes, I loved New York's mornings and nights, I loved New York with that powerful love which sometimes leaves you full of uncertainties and hatreds: sometimes one needs exile."

Camus returned to Paris with a crate full of eighty kilos of sugar, coffee, powdered eggs, rice, chocolate, farina, baby foods, canned meat, soap, and detergent. He also brought back tender memories for Patricia Blake, to whom he wrote on June 24, 1946: "Dearest Pat, Here I am, arrived in my old Paris after twelve days on the sea and a day on the road, which were filled by you, by my regrets, and by that hopeless and marvelous thing that we shared. It was nice weather on the Atlantic, I spent my days in the sun, and I got off the ship with a face like a Negro's."

Camus rediscovered Paris, which he loved, although not in every way. He told Patricia, "My only consolation is in this Paris which for me is still lovely. I've walked alone through it several times, which was for me the only way to walk here with you." Patricia had given him a keychain with a buffalo nickel attached, and Camus noted sentimentally, "When I take my keys in hand, the bison which you know burns my hand a little. What will happen when I see your handwriting?" By contrast, the reunion with Francine was difficult. Camus sent copies of his books to Patricia and bought her gift subscriptions to magazines like *L'Arche* and *Les Temps Modernes*. At Camus's request she sent him subscriptions for *Casket and Sunnyside* and *The Embalmer's Monthly*, both organs of the American funeral trade: "They made healthy reading," said Camus. At the end of July, he planned to retire to the countryside of the Seine-et-Marne region to finish *La Peste*: "I find this book a failure. . . . I am not disposed at this time to publish it."

He kept recalling New York scenes with Patricia, such as a walk down Eighth Avenue: "the red sky above the ugly houses, the enormous indifferent crowd, and your face turned towards mine to remind me that beauty was stronger than an entire city. Oh, Pat! What would you be if you were in this Paris, which lavishes so much beauty everywhere."

On July 18, 1946, he wrote again to Patricia, "I had a drink with two Americans who didn't speak French. And in my effort to understand them and to find the words in English, I found myself as I had been over there and I thought of New York, that island where we loved each other, and only with difficulty could I suppress a surging-up inside me, the discovery that I had been happy, and that this indeed was happiness." Camus would constantly state his own right to happiness, and realize after the fact that he had once been happy. He added his second constant theme, that creative work can replace happiness: "If I was working, things would be simpler. . . . I don't like anything I am writing, and I have the feeling of an irremediable failure. . . . You tell yourself because you can't have anything you want, it isn't even necessary to have what you can have. In short, I am ready to enter a monastery."

Camus believed he was all right, but his confusion was more than the disappointment of a return from travel, as he told Patricia: "I am not managing to find my equilibrium again. I can't say my life was very happy before I left for America, but I could stand it, and by the way, I ran from woman to woman. . . . Now that no longer interests me, and I can no longer manage to enter into what used to be my life. To that is added the doubt which I feel about my work. But in the end, I'll get out of this, because I must."

He refused invitations from friends, but he did lecture at a sanatorium in the French Alps for tubercular students, seeing himself in their eyes: "The sight of these hundreds of young boys and girls arrested by an illness which is as much mental as it is physical, who are curious about life and yet removed from it, had nothing joyful about it."

On August 3, Camus arrived in the Vendée region in order to finish writing *La Peste*, the novel he had been working on for five years.

Chapter Thirty-one   # The Terror

Camus's young lover Patricia Blake said she wanted to write, and in giving her advice, he also revealed himself: "Don't get alarmed if you dislike what you write. It takes years to find your real voice, your tone and the truth in your heart. People believe that this is given at the beginning, and a writer's work is to translate this given. Not at all! The writer's work consists of writing with as much effort as possible, and at the end of this labor it sometimes happens that he finds what he sought for so long inside himself. Creation is not a joy in the vulgar sense of the term. It is a servitude, a terrible volunteer slavery—and the joy much resembles that of great visionaries: it has an odor of melancholy." He recommended patience and courage, and a rigorous work schedule to Patricia. Camus added some misogynist generalizations for his "treasure from the Americas": "I know . . . that you will never become the dead soul covered with mink . . . that every woman, or nearly every one, aspires to be."

On August 5, 1946, he moved to Moutiers, forty kilometers from Nantes and two kilometers from the sea, which he found cold, to the home of Michel Gallimard's mother, Raymond's first wife. There, Camus regained courage and found time to work. He spent the month of August there in a family setting, in a "very vast and old house filled with lovely old furniture, antique tapestries and portraits of ancestors. There is no electricity, but it's one of the Vendée chateaus that Balzac often mentions. Large grounds with lovely trees and admirable light give this land an air of calm and grandeur."

He told Patricia he had found serenity there, if not joy: "Here I have peace, which is to say that I work from eight to ten hours a day in the most absolute silence and I am busy finishing *La Peste*. . . . I think of nothing but this book and of you (but it's the same thing, because the book often speaks of separation)." He found time for brief horseback rides: "Once I fell off at a

228

full gallop because my horse rolled over, but I got up without a scratch." On August 21 he reported, "I have worked so much that yesterday I finished my book. I should be happy, but I cannot yet judge. I am blind in the face of this bizarre book, whose form is slightly monstrous. I do not yet know whether I will call it *The Terror* or *The Plague*." Invariably, he passed through doubt first and foremost: "I'm not sure if I am expecting that the light will return, that I'll feel once again as if I had talent and strength, that your face be tilted back in front of me."

At the Gallimard home, he looked at Weegee's book of photographs of low life in New York, *Naked City*, sparking further nostalgia, and he read Lewis Mumford's study of Herman Melville. Postponing a planned trip to Algeria, he sent Patricia Count de Gobineau's *Les Pléiades* and Sartre's *Being and Nothingness*.

Back in Paris, he hated the sky, "thick and whitish as if it were going to snow. But it doesn't snow and there remains only the threat and sadness. . . . It is true that nothing has gone well lately: bad health, discouragement, and above all *La Peste*, which I reworked again, rewriting it in part, and which discourages me. Finally I have decided to publish it as it is, and so the failure will be complete and it will teach me modesty."

Never had Camus taken so long to finish a book. In 1943, he had removed a character, Stephan, replaced him with Grand and Rambert, and cut out some grandiloquent passages. Never had he so underlined the moral message of a book. In 1946, the Plague was totalitarianism, Nazism, fascism, and also communism, and Franco's régime in Spain. Camus believed along with Malraux that the principal danger came not from the West and the United States but from the East and the USSR. He made the transition from solitary revolt to collective revolt against the injustices of the Western world and the cruelty of the Communist universe. As he did not believe in realism in art, he felt no need to specify the régime he was aiming at in his novel. Camus wanted his book to be read "with several meanings." The obvious subject was the Resistant's struggle against the Nazis, and the underlying content the inevitable combat against everything that is totalitarian and authoritarian. Camus held himself back a little from expressing his vivid opposition to Stalinism.

La Peste is the most calmly and didactically anti-Christian of Camus's books, but nevertheless it tries to have the Jesuit Paneloux speak about his specialty, Saint Augustine. Rewriting the manuscript, the novelist noted with some simplification in his *Carnets* that "the only great Christian mind who looked the problem of evil in the face was Saint Augustine. He wound up with the terrible 'No man is good,' and since then, Christianity has tried to give only provisory solutions to the problem. Here the result lies, for there is a result. Men have devoted time to it, but they are poisoned by an intoxica-

tion which is two thousand years old. They are exasperated by evil or resigned to it, which amounts to the same thing. At least they could no longer
tolerate lies about the subject."

In December 1946, Camus spoke to Dominican priests in a monastery
on the boulevard de La Tour-Maubourg in Paris's wealthy seventh arrondissement. The Catholic writer Julien Green was present and wrote in
his *Journal*: "There were far too many people, and the two rooms on the second floor were full. They put us in the front row and Camus was seated only
two meters from us. Ill and visibly tired, Camus nevertheless spoke in a way
that I found very moving, about what Catholics are expected to do in France
in 1946. He was moving in spite of himself, without any effort at eloquence;
it's his honesty that does it. He spoke rapidly and simply, with notes. The
look in his slightly pale face was sad, as was his smile. Some listeners asked
questions, but so clumsily that they would have done better to remain silent.
One of them, an ex-revolutionary with an innocent face, said something that
made everyone wince: 'I have found grace, and you, Mr. Camus, I'm telling
you in all modesty that you have not.' Camus's only response was to
smile . . . but he said a little later, 'I am your Augustine before his conver-
sion. I am debating the problem of evil, and I am not getting past it.' "

Camus assigned the character Paneloux the responsibility for "defending God." For himself, Camus rejected Christianity and Catholicism,
whether doctrinaire or tolerant. He never accepted the idea of original sin or
the idea that men deserved their unhappiness. Basically, he admired Pascal
only for his style rather than for his message. In *La Peste*, Paneloux ends his
first sermon with the words "We mustn't be more hurried than God," yet Camus seemed more hurried than that, and he could finally explain neither the
Plague nor God. Evil as an insoluble problem was a mystery for Christians,
and he supported Dr. Rieux, who was a nonbeliever like himself: "Naturally,
a novelist's characters—if I am a novelist, which I'm not sure of—always represent 'temptations.' . . . Rieux is the one who represents me." This mystery
of evil made Christian truth seem illusory. Yet believers were personally attracted by Camus's sincerity, and later Julien Green would write, "His face,
so sensitive and so human, touched me deeply. There is such evident probity
in this man that it inspires respect in me almost immediately. Simply, he is
not like the others." For those who appreciated him, Camus's sensitive honesty was part of his charm.

Father Maydieu of the Dominican monastery on the boulevard de La
Tour-Maubourg wrote to Camus after he had read *La Peste*: "We are all Father Panelouxes. . . . You are helping us to acquire a marvelous knowledge of
man and of Christ." Christians took note of Camus's atheism but expected
him to convert one day, when in fact he never had any faith. France was becoming less Christian, and Christians were pleased each time that an atheist

showed them some respect. Georges Didier, Camus's former classmate at the lycée in Algiers and now a Jesuit priest, also wrote to him after reading *La Peste*: Didier saw a believer's point of view in Camus's "fairness in trying to understand," but unlike Father Maydieu, he did not recognize himself in Paneloux: "nothing in common with him, not even his solitude." The Algerian Jesuit explained, "The entire experience of my sixteen years of religious life has been of deepening and enlarging the heart, which makes friendship a force and a joy that is felt more every day." Didier insisted on the "feeling of being indispensable for one another. . . . Christ's love does not suppress the other affections but flows into them, communicating its own warmth to them and its own tenderness."

Despite these letters, proofs of the existence of a God he found impossible to believe in were less important than the Communist problem, which deified Marxist history. At the end of October, the writer Arthur Koestler, who was occupied with the same political questions, arrived in Paris with his English lover, Mamaine, for the opening of his play *Le Bar du crépuscule*. Koestler spent much time with the Camus-Sartre-Beauvoir group during his visit. Born in Hungary, the energetic Koestler was a militant Zionist and a correspondent in Paris in the 1920s. As a member of the German Communist Party, he had visited the Soviet Union in 1932. Imprisoned by Franco during the Spanish Civil War and in the Vernet camp in France during the Second World War, he escaped to London, where he became a noted writer.

With Camus, Koestler found "instant comradeship." They had things in common: both had gone hungry at times, both had been Communists, and both appreciated the writings of George Orwell. Starting with their first meeting, Camus and Koestler addressed each other with the informal "tu." Although Simone de Beauvoir was attracted to Koestler as a man and a good novelist, she and Sartre felt he was pedantic and "with a poor Marxist education."

Everyone adored Mamaine, a very pretty blonde. Simone appreciated her "acute mind" and "fragile grace," but subsequently she fell in love with Koestler, as she had with Camus. Simone had more romantic success with Koestler than she had had with Camus, who later shuddered to Koestler, "Imagine what [Simone] might say on the pillow afterwards. It's horrible— with such a chatterbox, a total bluestocking, unbearable!"

Koestler, Sartre, and Camus all agreed that intellectuals had to take initiatives against the two superpowers, America and the USSR. The rights of man had to be defended everywhere. In France, the League of Human Rights was in the hands of the French Communist Party, and another organization was needed. A group including Camus, Koestler, and a friend of the latter's, a German Jewish psychologist named Manès Sperber, went to see André Malraux to discuss the problem. At Malraux's grandiose Boulogne home with its staff of servants, Camus observed the statues and paintings and dryly noted that he was seated "between Piero della Francesca and Jean Dubuffet." Refusing to make a final choice between the USSR and America, Camus asked those present at the meeting to imagine a third possible route: "Don't you believe that we are all responsible for the absence of values and if we are descended from Nietzsche and nihilism [as Malraux and Camus would have it] or historical realism [as Sartre and Koestler stated], if we publicly say we were wrong and that moral values exist, and henceforth we shall do what we must to establish and illustrate them, don't you think that would be the start of hope?"

A French intellectual generally does not admit his errors in public. Koestler felt closer to Camus than to Malraux or Sartre, but he found Camus's humanism "just a bit confused." Koestler was mainly concerned about French intellectuals who did not denounce Stalinism. But Camus, Sartre, and Beauvoir had another disagreement: *Combat* had two editorial writers, Albert Ollivier and Raymond Aron, who supported the Socialist party, and Camus agreed with their stance. Jacques-Laurent Bost, who hated Social Democrats as much as Sartre did, protested to Camus about his colleagues' beliefs. Camus told him, "If you don't like it, leave," and Bost did.

During a jazz-inspired party at the apartment of the writer Boris Vian, Camus, in a nasty mood, attacked Maurice Merleau-Ponty, who had written an article parodying a book by Koestler. Camus claimed that Merleau-Ponty's convoluted prose justified the Moscow purge trials. Sartre defended Merleau-Ponty, and Camus left, slamming the door.

Still, Sartre and Camus did not let their different political opinions keep them apart as friends for long. They would meet at the Pont-Royal bar, the Brasserie Lipp, and at Dominique's, a Russian restaurant in Montparnasse. The Koestlers would often stay at the Hôtel Montalembert near the Gallimard offices. Koestler felt that "to really become friends with someone, you have to start when you're twenty years old," and so his relations with Camus "were more connivance than deep friendship."

One night in November 1946, the friends went to an Algerian restaurant, followed by an intimate dance on the rue de Gravilliers. Mamaine noted in her diary: "Also saw the charming spectacle of [Koestler] squeezing the Beaver against him (she who I believe had practically never danced in her life) around the dance floor while Sartre (for whom ditto) squeezed Mrs. Camus against himself." Koestler took the merry group to a nightclub neither Sartre nor Camus knew, the Shéhérazade, where he ordered Russian hors d'oeuvres, vodka, and champagne. Sartre immediately began to get drunk, and Beauvoir, too, who was weeping floods. Francine was tipsy, and Mamaine reported, "Camus told me that from the first time he saw me, he was very attracted to me, but that he couldn't do anything because of [Koestler], and when I told him that it didn't bother K. if I flirted with men so long as it wasn't anything serious, then he said I was the type of girl one could fall in love with."

Simone made declarations of love to Arthur, who was moved, listening to the nightclub's orchestra playing "Ochi chornyje," but replied, "It's impossible to be friends when you don't agree politically." Mamaine was convinced that Camus didn't "care a damn about" Francine, but she sensed how much Francine clung to Camus. Sartre poured large amounts of salt and pepper into paper napkins and drunkenly put them into his pockets. Later that night they made their way to a bistro in Les Halles to eat oysters washed down with white wine. By that time, everyone was using the informal "tu" to address one another. That same morning, Sartre had to make a speech at UNESCO, and Camus said, "Then you will speak without me," to which Sartre replied, "I wish I could speak without myself." Camus asked himself, "Why do we drink? Because with drink, everything becomes important, everything goes along a maximal line. Conclusion: we drink out of impotence and because we are condemned to do so."

Mamaine continued to be charmed by Camus: she wrote to her sister-in-law, "You really cannot imagine how attractive and nice Camus is." An improvised dinner at the Camus apartment brought together Sartre—who rarely agreed to visit his friends' homes—the Beaver, Koestler, Mamaine, and an American journalist, Harold Kaplan, and his wife. Sartre attacked Kaplan as an American and therefore an enemy of freedom. Koestler accused Sartre of defending Stalinist terror and a falling-out ensued, followed by a scene, then mutual apologies. For some time, the Beaver had found Camus unbearable and too anti-Communist, which she saw as a philosophical and political crime. One evening, driving her home in his car, Camus defended de Gaulle over the Communist leader Maurice Thorez. This, to Simone, was inconceivable. Camus was far from General de Gaulle politically, but he was even farther from the French Communist Party.

The round dance of Paris cafés, nightclubs, and restaurants continued. Meanwhile, Albert and Mamaine threw themselves into a passionate love affair. The young Englishwoman kept a diary and also wrote to her sister with details of the relationship. Her journal on November 7: "In the metro . . . Camus told me, 'I can't leave you.' I said I wasn't sure I took things as seriously as he did. Later, Camus said tenderly, 'I only feel good when I'm near you.' I asked, 'What shall we do?' He said, 'Run off.' I said, 'Where?' And he said, 'To the South of France.'"

Mamaine joined Albert at Avignon. After a week there, Camus told her, "You've made me as happy and as unhappy as a man can be." In the train back to Paris, Mamaine noted, she told him, "You know you'll forget me." To which he replied, "Of course we forget everything, but I don't want to live in a world where I have forgotten you."

Back in Paris, the lovers took walks in the Luxembourg Garden and went from café to café. Camus showed Mamaine fragments of *La Peste* and sent her a bouquet of flowers before she had to leave for England, with a letter: "I cannot get used to the idea that you are leaving. If only I could let myself go, there would be such an outburst in me that it would surely carry you away. While I am waiting, I cannot tear you away from that other heart which, nevertheless, you do not find good. Flowers in Spain mean passion and violence, but we are civilized and reasonable. Au revoir, dear foreigner! When you get home, don't leave me alone right away, but turn yourself a little towards me again. It's not easy losing you, I know that now."

For Camus, Yvonne Ducailar was also a "dear foreigner," and he didn't want Patricia Blake to turn away from him, either. All of these women were not mere passing fancies, because they somehow inhabited him, mixing all realities and nostalgias together. One romantic explanation is that he ran from woman to woman to find a single, unique one, as a Don Juan in the style of E. T. A. Hoffmann or Alexander Pushkin. Another hypothetical explanation of Camus's love life is that he seduced out of a passion for novelty every time, like Molière's Don Juan or Mozart's Don Giovanni. Camus went from one woman to the next with the same enthusiasm, as if to fight a certain vertigo made up of fear of illness and death. He told Mamaine, "I am devoured by flu and fever," and she, too, was tubercular. His real fear was to spoil his book, *La Peste*; and as a conquering seducer, Camus grew accustomed to romantic conquest, knowing it was essentially trivial.

He believed that he was not loved enough, and wrote this to Mamaine. His passions, not his transitory affairs, were rarely for Frenchwomen born and bred. He loved women who were foreigners, or just odd: Simone Hié, Yvonne, and Francine had Algerian ties; Patricia was American; Mamaine, British; and Maria, very Spanish. Camus did not choose geographically distant women in all innocence. During the first months of a passion, he would feel reassured, and he found a new balance in rediscovered joy. He would plead with Mamaine and Patricia to turn towards him, not to turn away. As Don Juan, Camus insisted on cures of asceticism, and the idea of a monastery recurs incessantly in his letters and the *Carnets*. As part of the infinite richness of existence, Camus believed in loving several women at the same time. With those he loved passionately, he went from love to affection, maintaining a tenderness for them all. Camus was thus representative of his generation and his profession, which were by definition liberated. Moreover, he was North African. He perforce lied to all of his loves. Mamaine wrote to her sister that Albert had married Francine because she was pregnant—a falsehood that might have been easier for the Englishwoman to understand than his North African code of honor about his word, which he had given Francine. It was just easier to say that Francine was expecting a baby.

At the same time, Camus wrote a thirty-six-page philosophical parody in dialogue, "L'Impromptu des philosophes," but he signed the work with a pen name, Antoine Bailly, and never published it. In the style of Molière he made fun of the pseudo-existentialists of the basement nightclubs of the Saint-Germain quarter in Paris. The satirical target was the heavy-mindedness of some of Sartre's crowd. In a hasty imitation of seventeenth-century style, characters speak dialogue that is alternately spirited and heavy. A typical exchange has one character declaring, "This world is absurd"; another character asks why, and the reply: "For the reason that it cannot be explained." In this sketch, a Monsieur Nothingness visits a provincial mayor and pharmacist, Monsieur Vigne, who is marrying off his daughter Sophie. Nothingness is carrying a book which "denies religion." He states that we are free because we are nothing, there are no causes, and everything happens by chance. Nothingness and Vigne parody certain declarations of both Sartre and Camus. "L'Impromptu des philosophes" seems mainly an effort at self-criticism and letting off steam.

Apart from philosophical satire, the work also contains psychological caricatures. Nothingness defines anguish as "a very general apprehension about accidents one cannot define and which may not happen anyway. . . . Anguish, more anguish, always anguish . . . and we shall be saved." Under the influence of Nothingness, Vigne wants a son-in-law who is a dropout, a criminal guilty of incest and pederasty. Camus had a few homosexual friends, but he was repelled by the pederasty of André Gide and Henry de Montherlant, and was irritated by Sartre's fascination with certain homosexuals, notably Jean Genet. "L'Impromptu" was a way for Camus to get rid of some philosophical exasperation. He also targeted literary critics: the director of the asylum from which Nothingness has escaped declares that the madman is a professional critic and "his method is to never read the books he speaks about, which is common in this fine profession." The rest of the dialogue is equally tense and irritable, such as when Nothingness, on political matters, suggests voting "for those who will suppress freedom. There will be no Republic in France until all Frenchmen have disappeared."

In Europe at the time, the Cold War was in the air. Camus wrote to Patricia, "Europe becomes heavier and heavier. . . . Fear is widespread. I have just taken a stand in a series of articles, 'Neither Victims nor Executioners.' I have understood how one can be solitary as soon as one adopts a certain language. . . . Desertion is impossible, yet the position of victim does not please me." Camus had wanted to clarify his political position in these *Combat* articles, which started appearing on November 11. He refused to give in to leftist pressures to be tolerant of communism: "You must not speak of Russian purges of artists because that will benefit reactionaries. . . . You must stay silent about the Anglo-Saxons maintaining Franco in power because that will finally benefit communism."

In 1946 he felt that men lived in the abstraction of absolutist ideas and messianism without any nuances. A character in "L'Impromptu des philosophes" says, "In the climate we live in, we can't have too many Messiahs." In these articles, for the first time, Camus denounced pseudos of the left and right, tricksters who sought happiness for men in spite of themselves, and blamed more or less equally "Marxist and capitalist ideologies, both persuaded that applying their principles must forcibly lead to the balancing of society." The world was living in a state of terror, and Camus opposed philosophies that "make an absolute out of history (Hegel and Marx who said that the goal was a classless society and everything was good which led to it)."

Camus was still regularly voting for the Socialists in elections: "It is quite obvious that our Socialists, under the influence of Léon Blum, and even more because of the threat of events, have moral problems among their first concerns (the end does not justify every means), which they had not emphasized until now. Their legitimate desire was to refer to certain principles which were better than murder. . . . It is equally evident that these same Socialists want to preserve Marxist doctrine, some because they think you can't be revolutionary without being Marxist, and others by an admirable fidelity to party history that persuades them that they cannot be Socialist without being Marxist, too."

Camus did not seek to condemn the Socialists, but rather to illustrate their problems: either they must "admit that the end justifies the means and that murder can be legitimized, or else they must renounce Marxism as their absolute philosophy, limiting themselves to retaining its critical aspect, which is often worthwhile." For Camus, Marxists accepted in advance the idea of millions killed "for the supposed happiness of those who remain. . . . The price is too high." To avoid wars, which had become too costly in the atomic era, international and national democracies were needed. Camus's ideas of utopia included a world parliament with elections. He believed in the United Nations and in a national order "which will finally bring the lasting structural reforms by which revolution defines itself." Apart from a few generalities, Camus did not say precisely what sort of structural reforms he had in mind. He limited himself to certain formulas and assumptions, such as the nationalization of railways, gas, electricity, coal, and the auto industry. In time, de Gaulle would accept all of these programs, and he was hardly a Marxist.

Camus offered some fine formulas, but he did not give practical ideas in his new social contract: "The plague is not treated with the same formula as a head cold. A crisis that is tearing apart the entire world must be repaired on an international level." Camus refused to hate a single people or country, but he felt there was more of a threat from the East than from the West: "The good way to love the Russian people by recognizing what they have always been, the salt of the earth which Tolstoy and Gorky speak of, is not to wish new adventures of power on them, but to spare them a new and terrible bloodbath after so many past woes. The same is true for the American people and unfortunate Europe." Camus defended the idea of a universal dialogue against servitude, lies, and injustice.

In private, Camus was even clearer about his beliefs. He noted down a meeting with an unnamed old friend from his Resistance days who had become a Marxist. Camus told the friend, "So you will be a murderer." The friend replied, "I've already been one." Camus said, "Me too, but I don't want to be one anymore. . . . Here's the real problem: whatever happens, I would defend you against the firing squad, but you'd be obliged to approve if I was shot. Think about it."

By the end of 1946, Camus had distanced himself from both Marxists and Sartre's existentialists and was trying to better understand the idea of revolution and revolt. He sketched out a chapter of a book, "Relation of the Absurd to Revolt," and privately thought about the subject of suicide: "Our epoch is one that, having pushed nihilism to its extreme conclusions, has accepted suicide. This can be verified in the facility with which it accepts murder, or justifies murder. . . . Men of Terror have promoted suicide's value until the final result, which is legitimized murder, or collective suicide."

Camus used his novels and journalism to attack the most obvious fortress of totalitarianism, communism, as well as bastions of authoritarianism like Franco's régime. He was more or less alone in his struggle, and another handicap was that he accepted and refused at the same time to present himself as a philosopher. Above all, he saw himself as an artist and a moralist: *La Peste* contained a secular form of catechism.

Camus rejected the hypothesis of historical laws leading to inevitable progress; he rejected those who accepted all violence called revolutionary; and he rejected the dialectic that individual misery today will be compensated by universal joy in society tomorrow. As a writer, Camus formulated his credo this way: "I prefer committed men to committed literature. Courage in one's life and talent in one's work is already not so bad. The writer becomes committed when he wants to."

Chapter Thirty-two

Bitterness

A lbert and Francine Camus finally put their names on an apartment lease for a townhouse on 18 rue Séguier which was owned by the Gallimards, a few meters away from the Latin Quarter in the heart of the sixth arrondissement. The high-ceilinged apartment was difficult to heat. The Camuses' new home had an entranceway, a kitchen, a living room, two bedrooms, a dining room, and a bathroom with shower. To walk to the Gallimard office, Camus would get to the boulevard Saint-Germain by way of the rue de Buci, where a colorful street market was located, almost Algerian or Spanish in its intensity.

Camus adored his children, whom he nicknamed "the two comedians," "Sloppy and Mandarin," and "my two heavyweights." But he found them something of a burden, too. He had trouble getting used to married life, although he was attentive to his children's health and well-being: he was concerned that Jean seemed a little fragile. Visitors to the rue Séguier apartment would be aware of the couple's anxieties and Camus's irritations.

Life was difficult and food supplies were chancy. Camus corresponded with Régine Junier, an old French milliner who lived in America, who felt a maternal admiration for Camus and generously sent him packages of powdered milk, coffee beans, sugar, sardines, plum pudding, scarves, sweaters, a teddy bear for Jean and a doll for Catherine. Régine Junier wrote to complain that arthritis, which Camus's mother also suffered from, kept her from tying the packages correctly, and that she was suffering from heart pains. Camus wrote back to her: "Dear Régine, we are upset to know that you are ill. We are sure that with spring finally here, you will feel better. Francine and the twins are in good shape, apart from Catherine's spectacular bronchitis. They are still turbulent and they amuse us a lot. We finally moved into our own place."

Camus stayed at Briançon for Christmas, to take a rest, as he explained to Régine: "Winter dragged on for so long here and I'm so overwhelmed by work. . . . My only desire is to leave Paris and the literary world I live in and get back to the Mediterranean. I long for the sun and solitude." He sent Régine a fashion catalog: "This way you'll know what's being done in Paris at the moment and you can be inspired by it for your demanding clients. . . . For us, life becomes more and more difficult in France. The world grows more and more foolish, and a few of us have had enough." He thought about giving Jean and Catherine to his family for a little while so that Francine could rest. But he was optimistic about his literary output: "As for me, I'm continuing to work. I'm preparing a play and a philosophical essay, which is almost finished."

To all of his correspondents, especially those who did not belong to the Paris milieu, Camus said how much Paris life weighed on him. Short trips to Switzerland, Algeria, and England did not provide much relief. He informed Pierre and Marianne Fayol, who had moved to Morocco: "I am overwhelmed with work. *La Peste* will appear soon and I've taken over the running of *Combat* again for a few months, to avoid a shipwreck which was threatening. There are strikes, financial crises, the cowardice of some, and a general lassitude." Camus asked his friends to excuse his typewritten letters, but to save time he now dictated them to a secretary. Besides, "every day my handwriting becomes more unreadable and I don't want to inflict on you the chore of deciphering it."

In January 1947, Camus was going through the first death throes of *Combat*, although he wanted to remake the newspaper, as he explained to Francine: "For *Combat*, everything is simple. Pia and some others want to give it up, but I said (and maybe I'm wrong) that under current conditions that would be abandonment. Pia replied that to run a newspaper, you have to believe in its success, which he did not believe in and therefore he should leave. Finally he agreed to stay if I became the paper's director, with him continuing to do the physical work and I the reform and supervision. The experiment is limited to six months, and if sales go up, Pia will have his proof that the paper can succeed and he will take up his work again. I said I agreed to try this experiment for a limited time, but no longer (so I can still take a vacation). It will mean being present every evening from six p.m. to nine p.m. I'll arrange it so I don't have to go in on Saturdays, and that will give me nearly three days for myself."

The situation at *Combat* was complex. There was no longer a single editorial line, many readers went elsewhere, and the print run dropped to 100,000, with sometimes as many as a third of the copies remaining unsold. In 1947 *Combat* projected a deficit of 19 million francs. Pia discussed buyouts, including one by Léon Chade, owner of the Lille-based paper *La Voix du Nord*. Camus approved of this possible solution, but was worried about "Chade's Balzacian side." *Combat* continued to sell less and less, was badly distributed, and was further damaged by a newspaper strike from February 11 to 17, 1947. So Pia packed up his coffee thermos and the slippers he enjoyed wearing around the office and left for good. The remaining journalists, including Albert Ollivier, tended to support de Gaulle, until Camus objected on April 22: "If my memory is correct, *Combat* did not choose to be the paper of one political party." Then, using the collective "we" he was so fond of, Camus added: "The Socialist Party is the party which we feel closest to, with all the disappointments that implies."

The *Combat* staff was united when Paris was liberated, but later disunited by the problem of de Gaulle's candidacy. Camus had a strong republican background and was worried about potential Caesars. He would appear often at the paper's office, but contributed only rarely. He wanted to treat de Gaulle's party "on an equal footing with the other parties," but that was not the way his editorial writers thought. Albert Ollivier wanted to publish an update on the problem in April, which Camus initially opposed, afraid that it would finish off the "unfortunate newspaper."

Camus called a meeting at his apartment on the rue Séguier of several journalists from *Combat* to talk about the paper's problems. De Gaulle himself found the *Combat* staff pleasant enough, if loony, and his aide Malraux offered the paper financial help from the Gaullists. The offer was duly refused. In June 1947 one of the founding fathers of the paper, Claude Bourdet with outside help from Henri Smadja, a Tunisian businessman, bought out the paper's shares and became the new owner; but Pia felt that Bourdet was too leftist, and he refused to participate in this new *Combat*.

Pia came to an editorial meeting but declined the check that was due him for the sale of the paper, accusing his colleagues of "conducting yourself in an unacceptable manner, allowing people to say that I had left the paper to join the Gaullists. Goodbye!" Pia could not accept the idea that anyone would think he had made a venal choice, and he privately continued to blame Camus for not refuting such nasty rumors. The assembled staff, including Camus and Ollivier, were stunned. Someone asked Pia why he tended to support de Gaulle, and he laughed: "Because de Gaulle has a sense of humor!" Pia and Camus would never meet again, despite efforts by Jacqueline Bernard to bring them back together.

Disappointed but relieved, Camus finished his second cycle of journalistic activity. He would henceforth devote himself to his own writing, and draw a salary as a reader at Gallimard, holding on to this job for the sake of his independence. Resolutely, he noted in his *Carnets*:

Without a future.
1st series—Absurd: *L'Etranger*—*Le Mythe de Sisyphe*—*Caligula* and *Le Malentendu*.

2nd—Revolt: *La Peste* (and appendices)—*L'Homme révolté*—
Kaliayev.

3rd: *Le Jugement*—*Le Premier Homme*.

4th: Heartbroken Love: *Le Bûcher*—*De l'Amour*—*Le Séduisant*.

5th: *Création corrigée* or *Le Système*: large novel + long meditation + unactable play.

The title *Kaliayev* refers to an early version of *Les Justes*. In ten years, ending
in 1947, Camus had achieved the first two series of his program, and the
other titles were a projection for the next fifteen or twenty years' work.

By June 1947, subscriptions to *Combat* had fallen to only six thousand.
On June 3, Camus bade farewell to the readers of *Combat*, abiding by his
agreement, and noting that the paper would continue without him. He
rather coolly introduced the new owner-editor, Claude Bourdet, to his readers, which irritated Bourdet. To the dozens of people who wrote to regret his
departure, Camus sent a lugubrious form letter: "Thank you for your letter.
It consoles me about many things." He replied more personally to a typeset-
ter named Toumatier, saying that a proper press was impossible to achieve:
"We were disarmed because we were honest. The press, which we wanted to
be worthy and noble, is now the shame of this unfortunate country." Rumors
circulated that Pia was jealous of Camus's fame, which was highly unlikely,
given that Pia, a radical nihilist, always refused to publish anything written
by himself. Camus left *Combat* for a number of reasons, including fatigue,
bad health, and the writing he had planned. As for Pia, he joined a Gaullist
press agency. The political gap between the two men widened.

At the beginning of June, Camus received the first copies of *La Peste*.
Twenty-two thousand copies of the book were printed and put on sale on
June 6. Ten days later there was a second printing of twenty-two thousand.
Between June and September, fifty-two thousand copies were sold—the first
very large publishing success for Camus. Most reviews were positive as well,
but in *Combat* Maurice Nadeau expressed reservations, which angered Camus: Nadeau quoted a passage from *La Peste* where the character Tarrou admitted that what interested him "was to know how to become a Saint. . . .
Can one be a Saint without God? That's the only concrete problem that I
know today." Nadeau perceived a temptation for sainthood in Camus, which
he found neither surprising nor unexpected, but thought it provoked "dis-
comfort" in the reader. Pia had commissioned the critic to review the book
without consulting Camus, and the Trotskyite Nadeau did not appreciate the
secular morality and humanism of *La Peste*. Camus did not admire Nadeau,
either, thinking he had an excessive passion for surrealism. Camus's friends
and acquaintances knew that he was at a vulnerable point and did not always
tell him what they really thought of his solemn, mechanically progressing

narrative. Sartre, who was on a lecture tour in America, publicly praised *La Peste* and its author's talent, but privately he declared that Camus was no genius.

Camus took a vacation at Le Panelier with his wife and children before seeing them off to Oran, which still held a strong attraction for Francine. He was not in a jolly mood, even after he won the distinguished Critics' Prize for *La Peste* on June 25, 1947, when he noted "the sadness of success. . . . If everything was more difficult for me, as before, I would have much more right to say what I'm saying. What remains is that I can help many people—by waiting." He scribbled some fragments of dialogue for a play, and in a letter to Marguerite Dobrenn, he mentioned his gloominess and how pleased he was to be away from Paris: "Here I am, far from everything (and so happy to be so, by the way) . . . and the Critics' Prize does not console me for the end of the *Combat* story, which only left me with disappointments."

He expressed less self-pity when he wrote to Janine and Michel Gallimard. On June 22 he reported, "Today is Sunday. We arrived five years ago and all is calm in the area. Lovely days, gray days, light winds, rain and breezes. . . . We are finding the world's truth again. We have merit in doing so: the night trip with the twins was hellish: . . . In short, we are in a castle keep like Chateaubriand at Combourg, but not alone. On the ground floor are the twins, on the second floor Milord and Milady, and on the third floor, Milord alone. It's at the very top of the keep, in fact, that I devote myself to the disorder of inspiration: 'Early mornings, we are sick in the belly / And by evening, I am quite smelly.' Such is in fact my schedule, with sleep and grazing (I eat and sleep like a Cossack). During lulls I think of you, with that nuance of tenderness and melancholy which is inseparable from great and fruitful loves. . . . By now you've guessed that I'm reading [Chateaubriand's] *Mémoires d'outre-tombe* and I have taken over the style for myself."

Camus received press clips for *La Peste* from Gallimard's publicity department: "I am buried beneath flowers, and that gives me some doubts, or rather that reinforces them." He read his reviews carefully. Camus denounced French journalism in general, but cared about certain journalists, even from rather vulgar weeklies, as he told Janine and Michel: "I was right to have left Paris—although [the weekly] *Samedi Soir* sent a journalist to interview me here, between two trains. The poor fellow, badly informed, came here via Dijon, Lyons, Saint-Etienne, and by bus, plus four kilometers on foot. By the time he arrived, he needed a stretcher. Afterwards, I have been left in peace. . . . Francine is well. She hasn't a damn thing to do, or almost nothing, and that's what she needs. She is reading Plato and says that Socrates is intelligent, which is also my opinion, and she shares it. She adds, 'Although he isn't nice with little Hippias.' Catherine had colic and we gave her rice water; Jean had colibacilli but he gets along with them. As for me, I am slowly resuscitating. . . . Ah, my chicks, it is very difficult to live and even more so to speak of oneself. . . ."

The two Gallimards almost always managed to put Camus into a good mood. When Michel announced rapid reprints of *La Peste*, Camus joked, "Michel may do or say as he likes, but I will never be mixed up with you in your ignominy. Suppose in fact that another fifty thousand copies of *La Peste* are printed, as I've been told. Well then, if I earn a million, the publisher gets five million, and the farther I go, the more the publisher charges ahead, until finally, the more success one has, the more one is exploited. That's why I plan to change my publisher. . . . Here's another joke: they came to propose the Legion of Honor to me. . . . I refused with dignity, saying that I preferred a gift certificate for a new car. Faced by such sordidness and impudence, they could only accept."

After all the kidding (Camus would never have seriously thought of changing publishers), he had some reflections about literary awards, like Gallimard's Pléiade Prize, which he would not participate in that year: he felt it would be better to give such prizes to young writers. And Gaston Gallimard agreed with Camus that it was ridiculous to give the Gallimard Critics' Prize to someone who is already established. "All that is of a rather exasperating thoughtlessness. I know very well that Gaston can't do anything about it. I can't either, in which case, I prefer to deprive myself of the annual lunch [for the Pléiade Prize]."

Fernande Faure arrived at Le Panelier with Francine's young cousin Nicole Chaperon. The presence of the "colonel's wife," as Camus called his mother-in-law, did not improve relations between him and Francine. Yet Fernande was useful and took good care of the hyperactive twins as a devoted, although sometimes overstrict, grandmother. Camus's resignation from *Combat* left a vacant spot to fill, as did *La Peste*, finally delivered to its readers. The author felt he was floating along: "I don't know. I want to change my existence a little, but I can only think of travel." He planned a trip to Brittany to see the novelist Louis Guilloux and went there in Jean Grenier's new Citroën II, covering four hundred kilometers in two days, visiting Combourg, Saint-Malo, and Saint-Brieuc. In the latter city, Camus visited his father's grave. At first, he thought that this stopover had no meaning, as he had never known his father, Lucien Camus. Then an idea struck the writer: "The man buried underneath this stone, and who had been his father, [was] younger than he," Albert Camus, was at the time.

Camus returned to Paris, which he enjoyed in summertime, with the fine weather and the peculiar Saint-Germain crowd frolicking elsewhere. The writer had free time, although the heat in his office overwhelmed him. He wrote to Janine and Michel in his usual comic mode: "I am alone at the *NRF*, courageously bearing the weight of this enormous and enriching business, seeing people who do not speak French and who are asking for foreign rights." He ran from office to office, answering phones for the absent personnel: "Hello, foreign rights. Hello, sales department. Hello, editorial department. Yes, bindery here. *Trojan Horse* [a literary review run by Father Bruckberger] at your service. *Les Temps Modernes* [Sartre's monthly] here. *Geographical Review*, hello. Yes dearie, it's me, Raymond. . . . In short, thanks to a trick known at the Opéra, where the same choristers cross the stage several times during the musketeers' parade, I make the outside world sure that the company has not been abandoned by directors who are heedless of their responsibilities. I hold the *NRF* in the palm of my hand, I perpetuate it, brandish it above the waves, and ensure its survival, which in this heat wave is also causing me to whittle down and die."

On August 17, Camus told the Gallimards that he had taken care of a childhood friend who was going through a depression and whose wife had sent him to see the writer: "He was nice enough, but suffered from amnesia, and the fear that his balls would be cut off. I persuaded him that this did not happen without good reason, and now he is more or less calmed down." Camus was thinking of writing a play, *L'Etat de siège*, with roles for Maria Casarès and Gérard Philipe: "That would be the ideal cast." He worked very little, doodled ideas "in margarine," and went swimming at a pool in the valley of Chevreuse, outside Paris.

Now, after working with temporary office assistants like Renée Thomasset (Janine Gallimard's sister) and Odile de Lalène, Camus was given a full-time secretary at Gallimard, Suzanne Labiche, who was intelligent and ferociously loyal. Camus nicknamed her "the gracious doe"—*la gracieuse biche*. Suzanne, herself tubercular, was a descendant of the French comic playwright Eugène Labiche. She typed the final version of *La Peste*, and as she was impressed by Camus, she saved his rough drafts and started to keep a journal about him. He soon noticed what was going on, scolded the secretary, and burned her journal before her eyes.

Suzanne had the indispensable qualities of a private secretary: devotion, endurance, patience, wisdom in filtering calls and sorting out mail. She also had some incorrigible defects: a devotee's fanaticism and insistent curiosity. She would relate gossip, sometimes improving on reality, and thus creating incidents. Her position was awkward in that she knew almost everything about Camus's life but had to remain silent, respecting the hierarchies. She adored the writer but pouted when he kept a pretty woman visitor too long in his office.

In their youth, Camus and Jean de Maisonseul had resolved to always answer letters, and Camus tried to keep his word. He worked out form letters, leaving it to his secretary to work out the details. At this time he wrote a novella, *Jonas*, about a painter who no longer painted. Jonas, alias Camus, was overwhelmed and spent less time at what was essential, his work, by wasting it on superfluous things like letter writing: "By chance, his reputation grew even more when he worked less. . . . So many obligations prevented him from strolling about lightheartedly, in any case. He always felt as if he were late for something, always guilty, even when he was working, which happened from time to time." Like Jonas, Camus was going through a phase of doubt: "He told himself now that he would never work again, and that he was happy."

This was not Camus's case when he feared he would never write again, yet at that same moment Camus was planning two works: an essay, *L'Homme révolté*, and *Les Justes*. In his *Carnets*, he wrote, "I have reread all these notebooks, starting with the first one, and what was quickly obvious was that little by little, the descriptions of landscape disappeared. The modern cancer is eating away at me too. . . . The most serious problem that challenges contemporary minds is conformity." Later he expressed nostalgia in the form of a joke: "Fortunate Christians, who have kept grace for themselves and left the charity for us."

Very involved in politics at the time, Camus was still opposed to the Soviet and American blocs, seeking a third path. In October 1947 a group of intellectuals including Camus, Sartre, and Maurice Merleau-Ponty launched a call to international opinion in *Esprit* magazine, a French intellectuals' manifesto stating that as a prelude to world peace, it was essential for Europe to be independent of both superpowers. They demanded economic unity for Europe and neutrality in foreign affairs as well in military matters. Almost immediately, Merleau-Ponty decided to withdraw his signature, and he refused to reprint part of the petition in *Les Temps Modernes*, which he co-directed. In November, Camus authorized the journalist Jean Daniel to reprint his articles in the series "Neither Victims nor Executioners" in his magazine *Caliban*. The articles were complemented by an appeal for international opinion: "We all know . . . that the new order . . . cannot only be national or even continental, and above all not Occidental or Oriental, it must be universal."

Caliban was an excellent review that appeared only every two months because of its shaky finances. Jean Bensaüd, who took the pen name Jean Daniel, became its editor in chief in October 1947. Camus was drawn to *Caliban* and to Daniel, who was twenty-seven years old at the time. The son of a miller from Blida, Jean Daniel felt himself to be Algerian, as did Camus. In 1953, Daniel would publish a novel at Gallimard, *L'Erreur*, with a preface by Camus, about a character named Vilmas, who was in good part inspired by the author of *La Peste*: "The charm which ordinarily goes along with versatility was a sign of his rich nature. He possessed comic talent, but he rather used naturalness. Like all of us he played a role, but he really played himself, with accuracy and ease. I only knew a single weakness in Vilmas, his taste for romantic adventure, even though he was married to an adorable woman whom he adored."

Emmanuel d'Astier de la Vigerie, the director of the pseudo-Communist newspaper *Libération* and a deputy in the French National Assembly, offered to print a response to Camus's ideas; it covered six pages of one issue in April 1948. D'Astier felt that the first priority was to rescue victims from the hands of executioners. He saw Camus as an intellectual who fled politics to take refuge in morality. Although d'Astier did not know of Camus's health problems, he hit upon the metaphor of tuberculosis to explain the writer's point of view: "I am a pacifist and so are you, but your social movement for peace resembles a social movement against tuberculosis that aims to eradicate the illness while refusing the means to prevent it." D'Astier felt that Camus was being unrealistic in his plans for a third path between the two great superpowers and his ideas for a social contract and an international parliament: "We are astonished to see you codifying worldwide anarchy under the pretext that you can't avoid it."

Camus wrote to Jean Daniel to express his "impatience, irritation, and intolerance" toward d'Astier, whom he saw as a fellow traveler and a Stalinist adventurer: "Daniel, you don't understand the seriousness of all this. . . . Mr. d'Astier de la Vigerie is pretending to believe that the real danger comes from me and that I'm going to forget all the victims, whom he never cared about in the least!" Camus replied to d'Astier in a nine-page article under the headline "Where Is the Mystification?" He emphasized that he was not a resigned intellectual: "Real resignation leads to blind orthodoxy and despair leads to philosophies of violence." He spoke about Marxist theory with prudence but firmness. He was reproached by some for not knowing enough of Marx and for never having learned about freedom in Marx's writings: "That's true, I learned it in poverty. But most of you do not know what that word means. . . . You say that to get rid of war, we must get rid of capitalism, and I agree. But to suppress capitalism, you must wage a war against it. That would be absurd, and I continue to think that you cannot combat what is bad with what is worse, but with what is least bad."

The polemic continued in various periodicals, with Camus thundering, "We will never be in favor of concentration camps!" a dig at Soviet practices. Sartre entered the polemic, supporting d'Astier, but without directly opposing Camus, either. In *Caliban*, Camus argued for a Churchillian style of politics, defining democracy as "the exercise of democracy itself . . . the least bad régime." He flatly opposed Marxism as unacceptable in its pretensions to solve every problem, and he criticized utopianism and totalitarianism, which he felt blended with one another. He agreed with those "who refuse to worsen poverty in the name of a blind theory or messianism." As he advanced in his essay *L'Homme révolté* he attempted to separate Marx's critical analysis from his activity as prophet.

He also published in *Caliban* a letter in which he defined the rapport between a possible journalism and a wide readership: "(1) A novel cannot be condensed, if it can sometimes be summed up. (2) Popularization is not the same as vulgarity. (3) One can be interested in a large public without ceasing to observe the laws of language and even giving a role to style and originality. (4) The public is not despicable to the point where it must endlessly be told like a dying man that everything is fine. (5) Only one thing is stupider than absolute pessimism and that is absolute optimism."

Although Camus saw journalism as "the finest profession" he knew he could also be harshly critical. "With one or two exceptions"—like *Combat*, *Franc-Tireur*, and sometimes *Le Monde*, according to Camus—"sniggering, cheek, and scandal form the basis of our press." Camus firmly believed in journalism's didactic role: "The public must be directed; that's the press's role." Camus's tone seemed overemphatic, but he had lived through too many failures with three dailies and felt a lasting bitterness. He saw journalists as members of an elite, but he reflected, "When the élite betrays society, society dies. . . . In this case, our society's consolation will be to be the first to die openly of foolishness and vulgarity."

It sounded like a requiem for a kind of journalism partly achieved but in practice often impossible to sustain.

Chapter Thirty-three **Dear Comrade**

W hen a reader had written to ask him if he was worried about being trapped in an ivory tower of literature, and hadn't he better organize a new political party, Camus had replied on January 2, 1945, "Far be it from me to say that given the choice between creation and political engagement, I choose creation. For some years now I have done the contrary." Camus had spent more than half his work time at *Combat*, even if certain staffers thought he took too much time off: "And for the past six months it is also true that I have not written a line for myself—I suppose that's what being engaged means. But you asked me if I thought that a new party must be created, because I do not feel like registering in any existing one. To create a party takes all of a man's time and energy, and I don't believe I am that man. I'm already serving politics, history, and man in my own way, which is a double way. First, I fight as a basic militant; second, I use language to define what I think is right. When this political party which we were discussing is created, I will adhere to it and serve it in the double way I've told you about. But I won't be its leader, because I know my limits. Yet I don't think this engagement will keep me from creating the work I am busy with, because my writing is meant to serve that engagement."

The author of *La Peste* was also a columnist. "I will reply categorically: Yes, it is essential to be committed. But neither you nor I should conclude that one must embrace the first forum which comes our way. Serving man requires sustained political far-sightedness and difficult fidelity." Unlike Sartre, Camus did not think of himself as omniscient in politics. Camus strove to be faithful to a reasonable left wing that rejected the notion that the ends justify any means.

By now, the Communist and pseudo-Communist left wing saw Camus as a key target. In turn, he saw as cynics writers and journalists like Louis

Aragon, the czar of French literary Communists, and Pierre Courtade, a journalist at the magazine *Action*. Aragon and Courtade knew the reality of Socialist society in the USSR and knew about communism's economic inefficiency, privileged nomenklatura, and concentration-camp police apparatus. Camus felt there was no excuse for the elite of the French Communist Party, who were accomplices of Soviet leaders, and that whatever literary aesthetics French Communists pretended to, everything was subordinate to Marxist doctrine.

In 1947 and 1948, the Soviet Union opposed what they saw as "bourgeois" science with the falsified genetic research of a "proletarian" scientist, Trofim Lysenko, who placed environment over heredity, and was defended by such as Louis Aragon. Camus had no grasp of the physical sciences, but he saw Lysenko's faked experiments as comparable to phony Soviet purge trials. Camus could not be as friendly with Communist leaders as he was with Resistance members, although he was willing to meet some notables. At one such meeting, an old friend, Charles Poncet, invited Camus to lunch with a French Communist Party apparatchik, Raymond Sigaudès, who said the French ambassador in Warsaw told him it was necessary to fake the Polish elections, otherwise those wily Poles would vote as a group against the USSR out of sheer hatred for the Russians. When Camus tensely observed that this was a curious idea of democracy, Poncet quickly changed the subject.

At a December 13, 1948 meeting of an abortive leftist organization, the Revolutionary Democratic Union, Camus spoke to the public, on the condition that Maurice Merleau-Ponty not be invited to speak, as their previous disagreement still rankled him. Camus had a somber message: "It is better to be wrong by killing no one rather than to be right with mass graves. . . . The world is in misery and already inquisitors are seated in ministerial armchairs." Camus was more comfortable in defending an American former war pilot, Garry Davis, who tore up his U.S. passport and took refuge in the Palais de Chaillot in Paris, temporary headquarters of the United Nations, where he claimed to be a "world citizen." In September 1948, Davis launched a movement, Citizens of the World, which the French press made much of. A support group of French intellectuals was formed, led by Camus, André Breton, Vercors, Raymond Queneau, Jean Paulhan, the philosopher Emmanuel Mounier, the advocate for the homeless Abbé Pierre, as well as the African-American expatriate writer Richard Wright. By contrast, Jean-Paul Sartre refused to participate, as he was wary of utopian world views and evangelism, and François Mauriac was skeptical as well. When Davis tried to give a speech at the United Nations, he was arrested, and Camus and Breton went to the UN secretary general's office to ask that he be released. Camus was recognized by the officials, although Breton was not, and both were told: "You see, if anybody at all could come here and make speeches . . ."

Camus took all the journalists present to a brasserie at the place de Tro-cadéro to improvise yet another press conference, and then organized yet another meeting to support Davis at an indoor bicycle track in Paris, the Vélodrome d'Hiver, attended by Breton, Jean Paulhan, Vercors, and the Abbé Pierre. When Davis came onstage, he spread his arms out like the cru-cified Christ for as long as the applause lasted. Camus stated that the United Nations was floundering and that world government was desirable. The Davis affair seemed surrealist, which may have been why André Breton ap-preciated it.

As for Camus, he soon lost interest in Davis when the American began selling grotesque "World Citizen passports" as a source of income. Camus was less naive than some people thought, and he did not actually encourage anyone to tear up his passport, as he privately explained: "I don't think that belonging to Garry Davis's movement is the only way to prevent the return of the plague, but I think that those who refuse both dictatorship and the plague find themselves rather in the situation of plague doctors, who do not have a vaccine that cures everything. They struggle from day to day with the means available. But nothing prevents us from thinking that new and more efficient means will finally appear, and as a matter of fact, I believe so."

After the Davis affair, Camus withdrew from high-profile politics, but he did not abandon all political activity, seeking instead other means with more immediate results. Hoping for peace, Camus helped to found the Group for International Liaisons in the Revolutionary Union Movement. He denounced two ideologies found in both the USSR and the USA: "The first, Stalin's idolatry of technology, seems more spectacular because it is newer and fresher, and also because it does not hesitate to sacrifice the masses, today in Europe and tomorrow in Asia. It is the most violent move-ment . . . impatient to counteract the more advanced American idolatry of technology, [which] in fact presents signs of a permanent idolatry of tech-nology. Less brutal and less complete than totalitarianism, it is more pene-trating and destructive because it has been able to call for the least effort, in films, radio, and the press, to make itself psychologically indispensable and even to make itself loved."

Camus suggested two forms of action: "(1) Concrete international friendship expressed by mutual aid . . . especially reserved for victims of to-talitarian tyranny. Each group's rule will be to try to help itself. . . . We will not imitate European governments which cynically beg for American sup-port without believing themselves obliged to gratitude. (2) The creation of a news agency where our differences will be confronted, and where we will try to gather accurate news to make the actions of American dissidents known in Europe, and to influence American opinion so that it can tell the difference between Soviet leaders and the Russian people themselves. . . . This attempt, limited to these measures, is the only one that can justify us today, on the condition that we accept the necessarily nonconformist lifestyle that it will bring. It is not a question of further adding to the world's hatreds by choosing between two technolatries, even though we know that one of them represents the lesser evil."

To help victims of Stalin's and Franco's terror, Camus preferred libertarians to Socialists, Social Democrats, or Liberals. He wrote a manifesto published in the bulletin of the Group for International Liaisons that, while not abandoning his old ideas, did drop hitherto available ideologies, such as love of communism, capitalism, or neutrality: "The [Liaisons Group] propose[s] to create communities of men beyond borders which are united by things other than the abstract ties of ideology." Camus compromised neutrality by believing that the principal danger came from the East at a time when Communists received one-quarter of the vote in France and Italy: "When one-quarter of the electors in France and Italy vote for the enemy, whether or not there is rearmament, we are not in a position to resist effectively." He ended by expressing envy of the British, who had no Communist Party.

Camus preferred the fraternal climate of libertarian meetings to discussions bogged down by rhetoric. With new friends, he began using a word, "comrade," which he had not used since before the war, as in a letter to Alfred Rosmer: "My dear comrade . . . Chiaramonte and I think that our American friends' formula must be slightly changed in order to make the group really international, and develop the positive part (mutual aid) rather than the negative part (politics)." Camus knew that in a Western country, even the best will in the world could not create a party without a platform or representation in parliament, without social and socio-professional bases, and without money. He also reflected on nonviolence, admiring Gandhi's results: "I have studied . . . the theory of nonviolence, and I am not far from concluding that it represents a truth worthy of being preached as an example. But for that, grandeur is needed, which I lack."

In France, Camus saw the working masses as duped by the Communist Party. It was natural that workers should be drawn to its basic militancy, which seemed to speak to them; but they had to be ignorant of Soviet history in order to believe that tyranny did not exist there. Camus stated: "I don't believe in the real usefulness of large crowd actions." His lassitude seemed as subjective as it was objective: "The objectives which seem to me preferable to all others are education, clearer definitions for the vocabulary we use, and retirement when that is necessary."

Solidarity, he felt, must nevertheless be more important than solitude. Camus maintained an old affection for the workers of the Book Union and had some contacts with the militants of the labor union Force Ouvrière and the teachers' union, despite the lack of places where intellectuals and workers could possibly meet in France. Camus did not consider himself as a writer for the workers, who did not read him, he felt. He clung to a form of Socialist hope in his heart and hated the "society of money." For him, capitalism continued to exist because the alternative of a revolutionary society retained so many vices, and he was seduced by the labor parties in England and Sweden, feeling that they represented another form of socialism, with union autonomy. While he accepted the supposed virtues of collectivism as a means of production and distribution, he looked for another society beyond capitalism and free enterprise in the market economy. He did not give a clear opinion about the class struggle, as he saw politics not just in terms of the organization of a city, a country, or the world but also as a human being's relation to himself. He felt that a man must have his honor, a mixture of frankness, sincerity, and coherence in his behavior, noting on a stray piece of paper: "Nobility obliges one to honor, but being a man obliges one to nobility. Honor is a style of life. . . . There are parts of honor. [The writer Alfred de] Vigny saw very well that honor was the only possible morality for man without God, as man's reasons cannot stand by themselves; it is man who stands by himself in their place. . . . Man is nothing without men. That's why a revolution which is separated from honor betrays its origins. . . . Look at the Spanish libertarian movements."

Camus made friends with a group of revolutionaries, whom he found honorable and noble, with exemplary lifestyles. These marginal rebels who never gave up their faith in socialism impressed him more than the intellectuals from related movements. He would call them "dear comrade" and even gave them his personal phone number, which he did only with intimate friends, saying, "It's BAbylone 1293. . . . Every morning, I am available at home, for you." Although these revolutionary friends did not have exactly the same concerns as Camus, they worked together to create an acceptable society, and Camus felt their influence on his play and the essay on revolt he was writing at the time.

One such friend, Nicolas Ivanovitch Lazarévitch, a pure and just man, became a brother to Camus as well as a new political father. Lazarévitch put together some documentation on nineteenth-century Russian terrorists for the writer. A huge, mustachioed man with a crew cut, fond of wearing black leather, Lazarévitch would beat on his chest during conversations like a character out of Dostoyevsky, and for Camus he incarnated the workers' movement and its history. Camus was eager to meet such militants, who had experiences he had not lived through himself. Lazarévitch denounced not only the Communist Party but also the Trotskyites, the Social Democrats, and the right wing, among others.

Camus had even more affinity for Alfred Rosmer, a small and distinguished-looking man known for being uncompromising. Rosmer was an executor of Leon Trotsky's will and a former contributor to the French Communist newspaper, *L'Humanité*. When Rosmer opposed Bolshevik tendencies among Communists, he was obliged to leave the newspaper, but his beliefs as a Communist union worker were unshaken, and Camus's children enjoyed visiting the Rosmers outside Paris: Francine also got along better with the Rosmers than she did with Sartre, for example. When the Camuses would have arguments, Rosmer's wife would stand up for Francine.

Camus did not simply admire such revolutionaries, who had struggled for thirty years, he actively sought publishers for their books and wrote prefaces for them. Since Gallimard could not be persuaded, Camus tried Rosmer's memoirs on a smaller publisher, Sullivan Editions, writing, "In tortuous times, Rosmer has kept to a straight path, navigating between despair that aimed at his own servitude and discouragement that tolerated others' servitude. . . . He has repudiated nothing of what he has always believed." Back in 1914, Rosmer had refused to agree with the nationalist feelings of the day, unlike French and German Socialists, who were nationalist and prowar, and thus Camus partly blamed them for his father's death in the First World War.

Like those of most French leftists circa 1948, Camus's views of the Russian Revolution reflected the simplistic thinking that before Lenin's death everything was wonderful, that the world seemed to begin over again, as history finally commenced on the ruins of an empire. Camus had a romanticized and homogenized image of the Soviets. By listening to men like Rosmer, Camus changed his mind about Lenin in part, just as he had stopped supporting Stalin in 1946. His revolutionary friends informed him about Soviet society's economical and political positions, and Rosmer condemned Stalinist dictatorship in a way that was "measured, but definitive." Camus appreciated Rosmer's sense of balance and the fact that although he had supported the Russian Revolution, he "also knew how to recognize its perversion." For Camus, the essential fact was that the Russian Revolution's failure did not condemn every revolutionary enterprise.

Camus felt that the right wing had no authority to criticize the outcome of the revolution: "To think well about this subject, one must not be among those who insulted the revolution itself and who hasten to see in every birth an abortion." For the writer, European leftists should oppose Stalin's regime, not "because it inherited a revolution that destroyed bourgeois property, but because by its insanities, it strengthens bourgeois society." Camus still adhered to one of the founding myths of Marxism, that the ideal society can be realized only after the bourgeois class has disappeared. He sometimes disagreed with his revolutionary comrades, something not possible for the members of the doctrinaire French Communist Party. His freedom of tone was complete and opposed to any hegemonic thought.

Armed with his friends' insights, Camus noted down some conclusions about recent political history: "The war and resistance have not only taught us about themselves and perhaps about ourselves as well, they made us understand that the worst evil is totalitarian hatred," which he vowed to fight. He added with candor: "As for the rest, we are walking in darkness." Camus believed in the chances of the rebirth of socialism, led by the minority revolutionary left wing, which he saw as the salt of the earth: "Yes, our comrades in struggle, our elders are those who are laughed at because they have no power and are apparently alone. But they are not alone. . . . The enslaved individual is solitary, even when his solitude is drowned out by a cheering throng that celebrates the slaveowner's power."

For Camus, Rosmer clung to Socialist and revolutionary truth without sacrificing freedom. Camus focused on the integrity of those militants who did not give in to the ways of Paris's bourgeois literary society, but he did not accept misstatements from his libertarian and anarchist friends. When one activist, Paul Rassinier, indulged in anti-Semitic remarks, Camus rebuked him: "The libertarian spirit cannot permit itself the slightest indulgence in anti-Semitism without renouncing its integrity." Camus was always available to support isolated figures of the non-Communist left wing, such as when he intervened on behalf of Louis Lecoin, who had defended conscientious objectors during the war. Camus understood Lecoin's somewhat chaotic path to pacifism, which had led to the older man's publishing a pamphlet in September 1939, *Peace Immediately*. Although Lecoin had also been defended by collaborationist newspapers like *Je Suis Partout*, Camus felt that the old man had already been punished enough in jails and prison camps. Camus also appreciated Maurice Laisant, a libertarian who was propaganda secretary of the Free Forces of Peace group and had been accused of sticking up seditious posters against the war in Southeast Asia.

Camus did not commit himself on the Viktor Kravtchenko trial, which took place in Paris in January 1949. Kravtchenko, a defector who formerly had worked at the Soviet embassy in Washington D.C., sued the pseudo-Communist weekly *Les Lettres Françaises*, run by Louis Aragon, and won. In his autobiography, *I Chose Freedom*, Kravtchenko had denounced Stalin's dictatorship, and *Les Lettres Françaises* naturally accused him of lies and anticommunism. The non-Communist left wing remained reserved about the affair, since Kravtchenko did not seem a pleasant person and, despite ample proof, they did not wish to believe in the horrors of the Communist world. Even Camus felt that Kravtchenko was a "profiteer of the Stalinist regime" and thus had no right to criticize Stalin's dictatorship, unlike Rosmer and his other revolutionary friends.

However, Camus's favorite subject for political intervention remained Spain, to which he was attached as to no other country except Algeria. He tried to do some genealogical research about his Spanish roots, despite poor reading knowledge of the language, and in 1948 he discovered that his maternal grandmother, Catherine Maria Cardona, had been born in 1857 in a village near Mahón in Spain called San Luis. In 1948, he was working on a play, *L'Etat de siège*, set in Spain, which he saw as a country incarnating grandeur and excess. He attended numerous meetings in Paris to protest the nonliberation of Spain by the Allies after the war, and he was opposed to Spain's admission to the United Nations and UNESCO, through what he saw as the American State Department's short-sighted view that Franco's regime would be the lesser of two evils. "Maintaining a totalitarian regime [in Spain]," he wrote, "means a short- or long-term reinforcement of communism" there to oppose it. Camus stated endlessly that the Republican government in exile was the only legal Spanish government, and signed dozens of petitions to this effect. In February 1949, he personally went to the Spanish embassy in Paris to present a petition to protest a death sentence against a Republican opponent of Franco's government, Enrique Marcos Nadal, and wrote many articles to back up his beliefs.

After he was awarded the Resistance Medal, Camus had refused most other decorations, but he accepted being named Commander in the Order of the Liberation of Spain, for its symbolic value. In a grandiose ceremony at the Paris official residence of the Republican government at 35 avenue Foch in the sixteenth arrondissement, Camus expressed his thanks to the assembled VIPs. In 1949, Franco's régime seemed so solid as to be eternal, and although no one thought Franco would fall, Camus believed it was important to speak as if he would indeed be toppled. In a draft for one speech, Camus said, "Spain? I don't think I know how to speak about it anymore. In 1938, men of my blood and my age shared in the revolt and despair of Republican Spain." Camus was angered that Spain was not liberated, as France was, after the war: "Because we had shared the same defeat, my thought was that we should share the same victory, but apparently my idea was not considered reasonable. . . . And we spoke in vain, and there is victory for no one today because there is no justice for Spain. . . . Justice is like democracy, it is total or it doesn't exist. Who will dare tell me that I am free when the bravest of my friends are still imprisoned in Spain?"

Among Camus's closest friends were French and Spanish libertarians, and this was clear when he spoke of his "Spanish comrades," saying "We now know that the world is cowardly. . . . You believed that you were an example, when you were only one element at stake. The story goes back a long while and it's a ridicule that we share. Blood, struggle, exile, madness—for the moment, all of this is vain." When Western powers were passive about Spain Camus's penchant for poetry and morality led him proudly to idealistic, unrealistic ideas: "When one's only weapons are justice, nobility, and moral rights, in the eyes of realists one has nothing at all." Camus defined realism as the USSR's and America's idea of practical politics: "Realists govern the world today and they are tearing each other apart. You Spaniards believed that your world was the world of Cervantes, Calderón, Machado, and Goya, but realists prove to us every day that it is only a land of mercury deposits and some ports that interest the military experts. . . . But perhaps a day will come when the greatness will no longer be measured by the number of cannons and in capacity for destruction, and our already dying civilization may decide to return to its spiritual sources and rediscover an art of living. That hour, which will be an hour of truth, will belong above all to Spain, the last country of true civilization." Camus concluded by returning to the first person singular: "On that day, for the first time in eight years, an enormous weight of bitterness and shame will be lifted, and I will be able to breathe once again, and that day our freedom will be yours, just as we share your hard silence today."

Beyond politics, morality, and literature, Maria Casarès was an unmentioned reason for Camus to be moved by the fate of Spain and the Spanish Republicans.

Chapter Thirty-four **The Unique One**

F riends who spent time with the Camuses, such as Janine, Michel, and
Robert Gallimard, saw clearly that Albert had only a fraternal affection for Francine. Sometimes tender and at other times impatient, he
would make her suffer, although Francine's charm, good nature, timidity,
and controlled little voice finally would make him melt. She sometimes still
seemed to live in a state of permanent indecision, whether it was about buying a record or choosing a vacation place. When they had a luncheon appointment, Camus would come to fetch her, worried that she would get
stuck over which shoes to wear, and he said, "If we're going to see Evelyn
Waugh, I have to remind her that Evelyn is in fact a man."

Francine practiced music with teachers, and tried to work for six
months at Gallimard in the foreign-rights department, an experiment that
was not attempted again. When her mother, Fernande Faure, came to Paris
to visit, the couple's tensions grew. Camus would say with exasperation, "I
didn't know I married four women."

Francine's mother and sisters sought to protect her, but they ended by
separating her from Albert, who was surprised to always find them underfoot.
Francine let herself be manipulated by Fernande, and by her sister Christiane, who was less stubborn and had a better sense of humor. By contrast,
Madame Faure was a strict, moralistic widow, whose devotion was over-
possessive.

Camus kept his distance from Fernande and from Francine's other
sister, Suzy. Christiane would amuse him when she would swipe his under-
pants and wear them herself. Francine's family felt that she was a jewel in the
hands of a successful man who was involved with other women. Francine
went through periods of depression, which made Camus even more uncomfortable in the role of husband, since he felt his in-laws were sometimes

frankly hostile. His wife never complained, and never played the victim, but remained painfully in love with her husband.

Camus took care of practical home matters, such as writing checks for household bills. When he was in America briefly, Francine could not manage to pay their taxes without his advice. While insisting on his freedom, Camus enjoyed his role as father and kept an eye on the children, even if he did not feel he was made for family life. He never said he wanted to live with a wife, children, and a tribe of relatives, and sometimes he was clearly exasperated. When he was ill, he could not help take care of the twins, who were three years old in 1948, and Fernande stepped in ably.

He did feel free in the Gallimard family, with Michel and Janine, who became his closest friends, along with Robert Gallimard, Michel's cousin, who would marry Janine's sister Renée in 1952. With Robert Camus talked mainly about their passion for sports, Robert's for rugby and Albert's for soccer. Camus became an adoptive uncle for Anne Gallimard, Janine and Pierre's daughter. Michel adored gadgets and loved buying mechanical toys for Camus's kids. Their father would protest, but let it go.

Albert talked with Michel and Janine about all his problems, and Janine particularly was a strong support for him. Lovely, with an exquisite lilting voice, and seemingly lighthearted and uninvolved, she in fact idolized Camus, and flattered him in all sincerity, learning lines from his plays and reciting them by heart to him. He would exclaim "Janine, really!" but secretly he was pleased. Camus wanted all the people he liked to love his books as much as they cared for him; always sensitive and self-doubting, he needed reassurance.

Michel had long been the favorite of Gaston Gallimard, which may be why he never got along with Gaston's son Claude. Michel was a redhead, with pale skin and slightly slanted eyes, naturally elegant and courteous, but also bad-tempered, and a passionate friend, sometimes excessively so. Yet Camus never complained about Michel's flamboyance, such as the expensive Saturday-night dinners he hosted at the restaurant Le Relais Saint-Germain near the Gallimard office. Michel had the jealous temperament of a hospital patient needing care, and he wanted everyone, especially Janine, to be at his beck and call. Albert would tease Michel for spending so much money on fine cars and rented yachts for cruises. He realized that although Michel was very much a part of Paris, he was not really defined by the Paris establishment. And Michel never criticized him. Michel, Janine, and Robert would never betray him, Camus felt. They knew everything about him and accepted it all, or almost all. With them, he could adopt a cheeky tone. One boring evening, for example, when time seemed to pass slowly, Albert joked, "Well, when do we all undress?"

Back in Paris after going with Janine to visit Michel, who had tuberculosis, at a sanatorium in Leysin, Switzerland, Camus wrote them about professional matters: "I've just seen a distinguished chap who offered me a pile of gold for the film rights to *La Peste*, but earning money doesn't interest me, because it means more profit for my publisher and for the taxman. . . . I found a sobriety on my return here which is more natural to me, and therefore I've regained my inner balance. It seems that I enjoyed [Leysin], but real paradises are the ones that are lost."

In April 1948, Camus went with Francine to Algeria, and they stopped at Algiers first for one of his three or four annual visits to his mother. He again wrote to Michel and Janine, still at the Leysin sanatorium: "Dear Cavaliera [sic] and Rusticana . . . I fainted slightly in the airplane from claustrophobia, but by the time we landed, I was fresh as a daisy." He enjoyed the trip with Francine, going sunbathing on the deserted beaches between Algiers and Oran: "We found once again a kind of life which we like, and this has influenced our happiness. . . . While we were tanning under the sun, someone pinched my electric-blue suit while Francine surrendered to the enemy her African lizard handbag, a Mexican bracelet, an American rain coat, and a Vichy skirt. We went to the police, not because we had any illusions about getting the things back, but because we'd lost our identity papers as well. The policemen looked at us with suspicion and we almost wound up in jail."

Michel responded with a complaining letter, and Camus tried to cheer him up in his reply: "Mighty Saint Michel . . . I wasn't in the right mood to receive your last letter stuffed with prodigiously asinine things. Let me recapitulate the numerous illnesses you claim to have: tuberculosis, sterility, probable impotence, sciatica, hemorrhoids, smallpox, and prostatitis. And this list which provokes a distinguished melancholy in you causes me to break out into wild laughter, for which I genuinely apologize. But you must admit it was irresistibly funny."

Camus spoke to Michel as one tubercular patient to another: "As for knowing the solution to your medical and metaphysical problems, I'm not the one to ask, since your only serious illness as far as I can see is the current one. What's more, it's in a modest form, and well treated, so not dangerous. . . . I can't even feel pity over a certain number of things it deprives you of, since I know perfectly well that you never liked those things. As for the other hardships, even though they are temporary ones, I know that they are difficult, and so my heart is truly with you. . . . Goethe said that only a narrow-minded person is capable of hope, which in simple language means that you only have to be an ass and everything works out fine. That, however, is not your case, and it is quite clear that pains which a president could put up with are painful to anyone with sensitivity. Confidentially, few people have considered their case with as much horror as I did, when it happened to me. That horror explains a lot about the man I've become, but finally, these are not the noblest things, and now I'm working towards a more worthy attitude. Dostoyevsky, announcing the new man, said he wouldn't care about dying. I'm not speaking about myself, but I think that all the heartbreaks of modern sensibility are heading towards that new man."

Camus associated illness with religion: "Even if you don't believe in religion, even if God is dead (killed from behind, as one of my friends said), something true remains in religious experience, just as in any experience, which is that personal life has only a distant relationship to happiness. The Greeks understood that well, and they are the ones who answered the question you asked and I asked: they did not deny the mystery, but simply gave it an idea of balance, which is a profound truth that Christians can't understand. Each evil is compensated by a pleasure—or a grandeur attached to it—and only love for life can justify a man (Epicurus said, 'Death is not our business'). Of course, love for life is the opposite of wife swapping and boogie-woogie, or driving at 150 kilometers an hour. When one has quality, and although I'm not extravagant in praising you, one must admit that you do, one ends up benefiting from every experience. . . . I have expressed poorly what I sometimes think clearly for a few instants, and I later miss and feel nostalgia about these moments. Let's say that it's a secret, and secrets can't be divulged skillfully."

Fifteen days later, Camus wrote to the Gallimards about their imminent return to Paris: "The news of Janine and Michel's return has provoked a real outburst of jubilation at the NRF. People ran up and down stairs, kissing on the landings, champagne corks popped in every corner, and these rejoicings will finish as they usually do at the NRF, and you know so well what that means! We've started to prepare the welcome ceremony: a band will play in the courtyard, and Auguste [the building's janitor] will be dressed as a drum major . . . and Gaston, dressed as Admiral of the Fleet (since he's gone on a diet), will bestow the welcome kiss upon you. . . . As for us, the true friends, the little ones, without rank, modestly hidden away in the ping-pong room, we shall take our part in the common joy by discreetly hiding real tears of tenderness behind our fingernails. While waiting for this blessed day, we work actively, each in his corner, to add to this company's fortunes and thus ensure the constant vacations you've indulged in for nearly two years now."

Francine left the twins in Oran. He said that in a philosophy of marriage which he would write someday, "the chapter on woman must be called 'The Obstacle,' and the one on children, 'The Really Big Obstacles.' " The rue Séguier apartment seemed too small for the whole family, and Francine wanted a few weeks of freedom from the children to reorganize their lives and find a new apartment. Camus reported, "The result is that by consecrating all her time to our life's definitive organization, its current temporary state has been endangered. . . . I'm speaking of provisions: we don't have any butter, sugar, soap, or other simple necessities; my shirts are deprived of their most elementary buttons; the apartment, itself temporary, has become the victim of a blind fury for straightening up, which seizes our little Breton maid daily, during which she is happy to mix my immortal creations with the mediocre manuscripts that the NRF forces me to read, for derisory pay." He added with a sigh, "I won't dwell on the subject, but I must say that I'm beginning to despair over getting anything out of these projects, given Francine's nature, although she is generous."

In May 1948, Camus went to England with Francine, invited by the French Institute, and visited Edinburgh with their friends Annie and Jean Guéhenno. Camus still admired Guéhenno very much as a man and as a writer. A shoemaker's son, Guéhenno felt at ease with people from humble backgrounds, like Camus.

When he and Francine returned to Paris, their friends noticed a certain relaxation in the couple, despite Albert's continued boredom. On June 18, 1948, Camus ran into Maria Casarès on the boulevard Saint-Germain. By now, Maria was a famous actress of stage and cinema. Camus asked where she was going, and she replied, "To the theater—and you?" Camus said, "I was going to Gide's." From then on, they were never separated.

The lovers felt distressed, because since their separation a few years before, they had only noticed one another from afar, but had had no contact. Maria had taken lovers, and she left her latest, the actor Jean Servais, to go back to her relationship with Camus. Albert would still not think of leaving Francine, mainly because of the children.

Soon Maria became all-important to Albert, and he would write her twice a day, without any sense of the ridiculous. He said that if she died, he would never want to laugh again, and that he was jealous of her profession: "You must work, but think of me while you do it." He told her that no other man was to lay a hand on her, and when they were separated, he expected a letter from her every day.

He was anguished, and claimed to be insane, although Maria urged him to calm himself and take it easy, as she nursed him through his episodes of flu and relapses into tubercular fever. Maria regretted that they could not run away together, but told him: "Be happy with your children." Albert spoke kindly of Francine, of how he esteemed her with a deep, affectionate friendship, unlike the passion he felt for Maria.

Francine was aware of her husband's double life and had the courage to accept it, or nearly so. For New Year's, 1949, Albert sent his greetings to Maria: "Happy New Year, my love, a year together, and may I not die far away from you." The Faures knew that Camus had taken up his affair with

Maria again, although attempts were made to hide the news from Fernande. Christiane tried to console her little sister, saying, "Francine, it's not as serious as all that; you can't expect Albert to fight against tuberculosis *and* his passions as well, that's too much to ask." Their other sister, Suzy, could not understand how a husband and wife could deceive one another. Francine simply gritted her teeth. She could not personally imagine being unfaithful to Albert. Sometimes he returned at three a.m., but she rationalized that journalism could allow for all sorts of strange hours, and even if Camus spent so much time away from home, Francine was always with him.

He wrote down one dream where she appeared: "He is led to the guillotine, with a woman called Véra. Francine appears and hands him a revolver. He tells her, 'I knew you'd be there to help me.' "

But Francine's interior tensions were terrible. Such situations are not easy to live with, and her nerves were not solid to begin with. She was less simple-minded than some of Camus's friends thought; not wishing to blame him for infidelity, they took her to be the kind of conventional lower-middle-class woman who prevented an exceptional man from living fully.

"I'm a warped person," Francine told Albert. "I can only know my capacity for loving by my capacity for suffering. Before I suffer, I never know." Emulating the composer Richard Wagner, who called his wife Cosima "the Unique One," Camus gave this nickname to Maria, and their liaison was public, even if Camus made some attempts to spare Francine's feelings. He once described his ties with Maria this way: "We lived some magnificent times together in 1944, but they were long marred, even after we got back together again, by mutual pride, and although prideful love has a certain grandeur, it does not have the astonishing certainty of self-abnegating love."

Camus's friends realized that Maria was then the most important woman in his life, and he was perfectly at ease, relaxed, and laughing when he was with her. "Why are you laughing?" she would ask. "From sheer pleasure," he would reply. She accepted him as he was, faithful in spite of his sexual infidelities. He often used a prepared formula: "I deceived you, but I never betrayed you." However, the sexual freedom did not work both ways, and if anyone spoke about one of Maria's passing love affairs to him, he would glower. He was particularly jealous of handsome young Gérard Philipe, with whom Maria acted in Henri Pichette's play *Les Epiphanies*.

Maria felt no guilt, saying, "I didn't take anything from anyone, because in this domain, one can only take what is already available or made available." Maria never thought about possibly marrying Camus herself, as she later explained in a memoir: "In the outsized and overwhelming love that we lived, I never had the idea of formalizing ties that would attach [Camus] to someone new. . . . And on his part, he never fought with anyone else who I had ties with."

An ardent, raging star, she asked herself fewer questions about love in general than did Camus in *Le Mythe de Sisyphe*. When Camus picked up other women for fleeting affairs, Maria remained calm: "We felt so sure of one another that nothing could make us doubt, and once we were certain to have been mutually chosen, everything was possible. Nevertheless, to get to this state of mind, we both had to conquer every inclination to excessive possessiveness, in both of us, during a risky and tormented period."

They shared a life without living together. Camus would pick her up at the theater after a performance, and he was not afraid of admitting to her that he felt ill or short of breath. She could sense when he felt claustrophobic, and knew how to deal with his moods, whether happy and talkative or not. Casarès was an independent actress before Camus knew her, and thus he did not create her but created with her instead. And so the theater came back into his life. He began rewriting his plays, and Maria would act in the next two. *L'Etat de siège* opened at the Marigny Theater on October 27, 1948, and *Les Justes* at the Hébertot Theater on December 15, 1949.

The main character of *L'Etat de siège* represented the Plague, meaning the totalitarian system, or dictatorship. But the only thing the play had in common with the novel *La Peste* is that both dealt with an absurd and terrifying world. Camus wanted to "imagine a myth that might be intelligible for every spectator in 1948. (1) It must be clear, no matter what anyone says, that *L'Etat de siège* is in no sense an adaptation of *La Peste*. (2) It isn't a traditionally structured play, but a spectacle whose ambition is to mix all forms of dramatic expression, from the lyric monologue to collective theater, and including pantomime, simple dialogue, farce, and choral declamations." The playwright was inspired by Pedro Calderón's ritual dramas, and collaborated on the project with the famous actor, director, and mime Jean-Louis Barrault. In *L'Etat de siège*, Camus returned to a kind of total theater he had aimed for in his earlier play *Révolte dans les Asturies*.

His play was almost called *The Inquisition at Cadix*, and its message was revolt. Its implicit moral was that to conquer the plague—meaning all types of totalitarianism, above all the Soviet kind, or authoritarianism such as Franco's—one must let go of fear. Diego, the hero of the play, who fights the plague, states, "As far as I can recall, a man had only to conquer his fear and rebel in order for the machines of tyranny to begin to squeak, although they don't always stop right away, but they sometimes finally do get jammed." Played by Barrault himself, Diego was opposed by Nada, the villain, portrayed with brilliant flamboyance by the formidable actor Pierre Brasseur. In his sermon to the citizens of Cadix, Diego cries: "Fear no more. . . . Stand up, all those of you who can! . . . Throw away the gags from around your mouths and shout with me that you are no longer afraid."

Nada, who represents the plague, proclaims, "Over centuries across five continents, I have killed without respite, never getting tired. . . . If you want to know my opinion, a dead person is refreshing, but you can't get anything out of him, and so in that sense he isn't worth as much as a slave. The ideal would be to acquire a maximum of slaves, by trading them in for a minimum of well-chosen deaths. Today, the technique is finely honed. That's why, having killed or besmirched as many men as necessary, we can bring entire populations to their knees." There were other clear references to Franco's Spain and the Soviet bloc in such passages as this, when a messenger says, "It is strictly forbidden to help any person struck by the plague, except for denouncing him to the relevant authorities. Denunciations between members of the same family are particularly recommended, and will be rewarded by a double food ration, called a civic ration."

Jean-Paul Sartre and Simone de Beauvoir did not appreciate the play's allegorical content, and neither did the audience, despite the scenery and costumes by the noted painter Balthus and incidental music composed by Arthur Honegger. Faced by a total failure, Camus said with bittersweet sarcasm, "*L'Etat de siège*, as it opened in Paris, received with no effort unanimous reviews. Indeed, few plays have benefited from such a unanimous panning, which is all the more regrettable because I still believe that *L'Etat de siège* for all its faults may be the work I have written that resembles me most."

The character Diego was like Camus in his lyric or novelistic flights, while Victoria was a blueprint for Maria Casarès; and in their love dialogues, friends in the audience could not help thinking of Camus and Maria. However, some spectators were puzzled: for instance, the Catholic philosopher and drama critic Gabriel Marcel, who wondered why Camus had set the action in Spain instead of an Eastern-bloc country, and why the Catholic Church was portrayed so harshly. Camus responded to Marcel that elsewhere in his writings he had already denounced the Russian concentration camps and the Western democracies that tolerated Franco's Spain, and as for the Church, its holy-water sprinklers had blessed Franco's firing squads.

Meanwhile, he was busy rewriting *Les Justes* to try to avoid a similar fiasco. He announced to Francine, "The new version . . . is typed, and I recast it into four acts, as influenced by Jacques Hébertot. I've lost all confidence in myself, and almost anything makes me change almost anything. Then I went back to my original idea of five acts, and I sent Hébertot to hell. So the latest version is the one you know, with some changes (Voinov returns in the fifth act). Hébertot is unhappy with me, as I am with him. Each time I suggest an actor to him, it seems 'that one has behaved badly with the Hébertot Theater.' Soon I'll be seeing my terrorists played by boy scouts or passive sodomites, and this may all end badly. . . . When one is in agony, one must read Epictetus, who is useful now, and for the rest of the time one simply admires things and does everything differently. I saw [the revival of] *Le Malentendu* and was moved, since it's the play that resembles me the most."

In *Les Justes*, directed by Paul Oettly, Maria Casarès played the lead role of Dora Doulebov. In this moving play, which was well received and touched the audience, Camus dealt with the prerevolutionary era of the Russian Nihilists. It was a subject he had discussed at length with his friend Lazarévitch, and Camus drew on the stories of terrorists of the 1905 Russian Socialist Revolutionary party. Retaining the real name of one man, Kaliayev, he stuck to historical facts while inventing other characters in the play. Dora, a young woman, makes a bomb which her lover throws under the carriage of Grand Duke Serge, Moscow's governor. The terrorist does not dare throw the bomb, because he sees the Grand Duchess and her children in the carriage, so the police arrest Kaliayev. This much of the play was historically accurate. The Grand Duchess visits the Nihilist in prison to urge him to repent and to find God. There is also a villain, Stepan (who was played by one of Camus's favorite actors, Michel Bouquet), a revolutionary who feels that any means is justified to reach a goal, like the Communists who held power in the USSR: "When we've decided to forget about children, that day we will be masters of the world and the revolution shall triumph."

The moral behind Camus's play was clear: before the Bolsheviks arrived, Socialist Revolutionaries like Stepan wanted justice, but because they did not value human life, they created another police state instead. At one point Dora screams to another character: "Yes, you're my brother, all of you are my beloved brothers . . . but what awful taste fraternity sometimes has!"

In his private life, Camus followed parallel paths with Maria, who represented passion, and Francine—up to a point—the mainspring of his existence. To many acquaintances who weren't his friends, he seemed too sure of himself, even arrogant. But that wasn't how he judged himself: "I never saw into myself very clearly, but I've always instinctively followed an invisible star. . . . There is in me an anarchy and frightful disorder. Creating makes me die a thousand deaths, because it means making order, and my entire being rebels against order. But without it I would die, scattered to the winds."

In his *Carnets*, he summed up the essential problem of his personal life: "People persist in confusing love and marriage on the one hand, and love and happiness on the other, whereas all these things have nothing in common. That's why happy marriages are most often the ones where love is absent."

He did not exactly despise women, although he would say of a cute pickup who wanted to prolong a brief liaison, "I made her understand that she really wasn't up to the class of the establishment." In his draft for a screen adaptation of the novel *La Princesse de Clèves*, one character claims that "loving every woman" can only mean that one feels "a bit contemptuous about those one is said to be in love with."

Camus was uncomfortable in his family life, and so he would relax at Maria Casarès's apartment, where he was pleased to be with the Unique One, her maid and dog. But he needed Francine in her role as wife and mother, while Maria filled the more glittering role of official mistress. Michel and Janine Gallimard were in the know and discreet, and would go out with either Albert and Francine or Albert and Maria, depending on the evening. He felt free to complain to the Gallimards about his domestic troubles. For instance, when he came back to Francine after a voyage in the provinces, he said: "Returning here, I found domestic pains-in-the-ass—an apartment that is too small, nowhere to put the children, nowhere to put the mother-in-law, no coal cellar, no coal either but wood instead, which takes up even more space, no maid. It's enough to drive you mad. I am so fed up that I feel ready to do something terrible. . . . I've become pessimistic. I no longer feel that one can confide in everyone, because there are few people one really wants to call friends, and men in general seem to me cowards and very cruel. . . . I'm becoming an old crab . . . and the best thing would be to retire from the world and stop writing."

A bit manic-depressive and subject to the attacks of tuberculosis which he still called flu, he relied on work. Before taking off on further travels in 1948, he explained to Michel and Janine: "Before leaving for South America, I have set myself the project of giving my contractual exploiter of a publisher five new books: a five-act play, La Corde; a 250-page-long essay, L'Homme révolté, a volume of critical essays; another of political essays; and one of literary essays on the Mediterranean. Therefore I must get rid of projects that I have been planning for years, stop writing for a few months, and then begin a second cycle which will bring me universal glory. While waiting for that, the five books should pay enough for me to live modestly, if Gallimard's take is not too excessive. But to finish what I want to do between now and June, I must work furiously, not be bothered by any asshole, and put considerable pressure on my natural nonchalance. I'm being encouraged, and it will only take a little luck."

Camus still worked at the Gallimard office, only a few minutes' walk from Janine and Michel's apartment at the rue de l'Université, where the friends would play card games. In 1951 the Gallimards bought a country home at Sorel in the Eure region, eighty kilometers from Paris, where Camus would visit to play charades and ping-pong and make carefully scripted sixteen-millimeter home movies. Michel and Albert would take a lot of photographs and do a lot of reading, aware that as tubercular patients, their days might be numbered. Raymond Gallimard also had a country home, on the banks of the Eure, which Camus would visit with the twins. While others swam, Camus would sit fishing in the river in the shade of a lime tree, and would sometimes land a pikefish.

The group of friends would often dine outside Paris, at Carrières-sur-Seine, where Camus expressed his affection for the Gallimards' daughter by inscribing books to her, "Your old uncle . . ." He gave Anne advice as he did to his own children: "When you walk in the street, smile at people, and if someone says good morning, answer back, because you'll always benefit from it." When Anne was in high school, she failed her take-home graduation exam, even though her essays had been written by Camus and by her father's mentor, René Etiemble, another Gallimard author.

Camus liked to socialize with writers who had ties to Algeria, such as Emmanuel Roblès, Jules Roy, and Jean Sénac, and he was particularly fond of the working-class novelist Louis Guilloux. In 1953, he wrote in a preface to a reprint of Guilloux's novel *La Maison du peuple*, "I have always preferred that writers give their testimony after having had their throats cut. Poverty makes those who have experienced it intolerant of hearing others speak about it, unless they have lived it, too. In 'progressive' magazines and books, the working class is often treated as a tribe with strange customs, in a way that would make the working class nauseous, if they only had time to read the specialists on how progress keeps marching on." Guilloux knew how to speak about people without despising them, as had French Socialist novelists such as Jules Vallès, and Camus appreciated Guilloux's "modesty and the refusal to take someone else's poverty as a stepping stone for oneself, which is a rare thing in the world we live in." Camus particularly admired *La Maison du peuple*, in which Guilloux "used everyday poverty to better reveal the world's suffering. . . . I've never been able to read it without a pain in my heart, because reading it brings back memories for me. . . . Too much poverty shortens the memory and undoes the ties of friendship and love. If he earned fifteen thousand francs a month in a factory workshop, Tristan would have nothing more to say to Isolde. Love too can be a luxury, which means it can be eliminated." Guilloux was a modest man who lived mostly in Brittany and was known to bathe very rarely. Francine got along with him well, because he had none of the snobbery towards her that many of her husband's other literary colleagues showed.

Another close friend among many, was his former teacher from Algeria Jean Grenier, who settled in the Paris suburb of Fontenay-aux-Roses in 1950. Camus wrote a preface for a reprint of Grenier's novel *Les Iles*, and Grenier was often obsessed by Camus's ever-growing fame compared with his own relative obscurity. Grenier often asked Camus to use his official connections to get him out of having to pay parking-ticket fines, and when he bought a house in the town of Bourg-la-Reine, he borrowed money from Camus to do it. For Camus, Grenier was an important confidant, and Albert explained to him that marriage wasn't his and Maria Casarès's style, and he wouldn't think of divorcing Francine.

Despite all his attentive friends, Camus felt stifled and threatened in Paris. And the two men who would soon become his most important friends were not residents of the city.

Chapter Thirty-five   **Three Friends**

I n 1948, Albert Camus was thirty-five years old and the poet René Char forty-one, and although Camus was not a great reader of contemporary poetry, he convinced Gaston Gallimard to publish Char's book of poetry, *Feuillets d'Hypnos*, which he considered "brilliant." He reassured Gallimard, who was perplexed by Char's work: "It's hard to judge our contemporaries, but if anyone has genius, Char does." Camus saw him as a poet-philosopher: "Char rightfully continues the tragic optimism of pre-Socratic Greece. A secret was transmitted from Empedocles to Nietzsche, from one summit to another; now Char displays the hard, precious tradition, after a long hiatus. . . . His poetry is both old and new, combining refinement with simplicity."

Char's life and work were a moral lesson for Camus, who appreciated that the poet had abandoned surrealism: "Char only kept what was best of surrealism, which is what that movement will be remembered for, having dared to speak of love in a necessary way." Char was saying, "Beware of surrealism, because that once excellent school is now fossilized."

Camus called Char a classic, but the admiration was not mutual. Char had read *L'Etranger* and *La Peste*, and didn't like novels in general, as he later recalled: "I am on bad terms with the contemporary novel; I don't know how to be drawn to its subject, or get close to its plot, its basics, and what it revolves around." When a friend, Urbain Polge, asked what he thought of Camus's work, Char replied in his southern French accent, "He's a *bong, très bong* journalist."

But ever since the autumn of 1946, when Camus went house-hunting near Avignon and found Char to be "an adorable, brilliant, and consoling handsome boy," the friends saw each other regularly. Char introduced Camus to some of his Resistance comrades, and he appreciated Albert's "cheerfulness that could be airborne or thoughtful." As Char showed him around the region, Camus was delighted to discover similarities to the Algerian landscapes of his childhood. So he decided to rent a country house for three years near L'Isle-sur-la-Sorgue, where Char lived, in the south of France.

Camus wanted to introduce Char to one of the women of the Gallimard family, but none was available at the moment, and the poet, who had many girlfriends, was not the marrying kind. Camus had already found substitute fathers such as his teachers Louis Germain and Jean Grenier, and new brothers such as Robert Jaussaud, Claude de Fréminville, and Pascal Pia. René Char became a sort of older brother whom he admired. When Camus's mother and his niece Lucienne arrived at the Marignane airport, he presented Char to them, saying, "Here's my brother—you'll like him."

Over six feet tall and with the hands of a blacksmith, Char was like a tree or a standing stone, living modestly in a small house, where he offered visitors pastis to drink and an unending stream of apocryphal anecdotes. Camus was fascinated by Char's Resistance activities, which had started in September 1943. As a member of Combat, Char had plenty of stories to tell, and he admitted that he sometimes went overboard with them. But Camus always listened admiringly, and he repeated that he himself did not do much for the Resistance. Camus noted down some of Char's anecdotes about the occupation, and also one about "Char's love affair with a female lion in the Jardin des Plantes zoo—he took her head in his hands through the bars, and she rolled over and spread out her little paws." The novelist appreciated that his poet friend refused jobs and honors in Paris. Both were sports fans. Char had broken a finger during a rugby game, which he bragged about more than his Resistance injuries. And both were ladies' men, although Char had some anxieties and fears, which he covered up by his brutal manner.

On November 7, 1949, Camus wrote to his friend, "The truth is that one must know love before one can know morality, or otherwise both will perish. The world is cruel. . . . One loves more if one has lived more, and life itself can separate us from love." He praised the poet's latest book, *Matinaux*: "You are advancing with certainty, and at least on that road you'll never hesitate; everything is fruitful for you, and you are one of today's rare creators." When he was with Char, Camus was often in a grave or even grandiloquent mood: "I have passed the age of dreams, and my constant effort has been to avoid solitude and difference; I wanted to be with someone. . . . The only thing I believe is that destiny exists, and my destiny is that struggle where nothing is easy." He ended his letter by saying, "I'm writing to you like a friend and brother, but don't think that I'm too sad, because as you know, I've got my own philosophy." He inscribed a copy of *Noces*, "To René Char, to bring back those years when I didn't know him yet, but which already contained the reasons for our friendship. Fraternally . . ." He also signed a copy of "L'Eté," a collection of lyrical essays, to "that brother in suffering and joy, whose affection" helped him to survive.

Camus gave Char records, notably of Mozart's *Don Giovanni*, and they took auto trips in Camus's trusty and rusty Citroën from Paris to Provence. At one country inn during a July 1948 excursion, at Tain-l'Hermitage, they were taken for gangsters at "a hostelry for patricians of the black market," as Camus gleefully wrote to Michel and Janine Gallimard, whom he addressed as "Dear Port and Starboard." Camus explained that the hotel owner, "whom I had seen a hundred copies of in Montmartre, living on the generosity of ladies, stationed amid refined clients and two dozen pink lampshades, saw a car pull up and two unwashed bruisers get out, one shaped like a door-frame." The doorframe-shaped client was Char, and he and Camus were told by the hotel owner, "You understand, we're being watched, but you can sign the register with any names you want, I won't ask for your identity cards." Char put his profession as "businessman" and Camus as "journalist," which was all right with the owner, who just did not want them to sign with the name "Pierrot le Fou," a notorious gangster of the time. How lovely to be taken for gangsters, for a poet and novelist who also knew how to write about sage and thyme, Epicurus and Heraclitus.

In *Jonas* Camus based the character Rateau on Char; it is he who consoles the painter who represents Camus. The two friends created a literary magazine, *Empédocle*, in April 1949, which lasted for eleven issues, until June 1950. "Don Quixote, that's my guiding light," declared Char, who advised on poetry at Gallimard but didn't socialize there. When they were together, the friends made fun of the Paris literary crowd and their pretensions.

Camus felt that Char "was quite alone, without having a taste for solitude, and cannot conceive of life without friendship, and he cannot love most of the men around today. Therefore he is very demanding, sometimes violently so, of the few men he esteems. . . . He deserves to be encouraged and accepted wholly because he himself is whole, and of a quality so rare that without him, it would take the world too long to be reborn."

Char introduced Camus to a friend, Urbain Polge, a pharmacist at nearby Saint-Rémy-de-Provence, whose wife and children soon became close to Francine and the twins. Polge was a devoted reader of Proust and Tolstoy and the philosopher Emmanuel Berl, and he had a calmness that appealed to Camus, apart from his total separation from the Paris literary world.

The Polges and the Camuses would spend vacations together regularly in the Vaucluse or the Alpes-Maritimes department, staying at Cabris with a friend of André Gide's, Pierre Herbart. Whereas the bachelor Char could offer little experienced advice to Camus about his marriage and children, Polge was a reassuring confidant on these subjects. In Paris, Albert was sometimes accused of cultivating his friendship with the Gallimards in order to advance his literary career; but with Urbain and Jeanne Polge, he could relax, abandoning the grand manner that offended many people in Paris. His children got along with the Polge sons, Gérard and Jacques, the latter nicknamed "the Genius" by Camus. Camus would try out literary opinions on Urbain without fear of censure, saying, for instance, that the French essayist Paul Bourget wasn't as bad a writer as was commonly thought, and that everyone should read the complete works of Balzac. Younger than Polge by two years, Camus would demand, "You've got to tell me how it feels to be forty years old." He invested some money in Polge's project to open a medical analysis laboratory in Grasse. Francine, too, felt entirely at ease with the Polges. Perhaps even more than Albert, she accepted the Paris milieu, but felt that she was always being watched there. In the Polges' rural retreat, their friendship developed its secret codes. It was a ritual for Camus to say to Polge's mother-in-law, Marcelle Mathieu, "Whenever you make your squash-and-bean soup, just let me know."

Camus appreciated the Vaucluse countryside, where a farmer once watched him writing in the shade of a plane tree and remarked, "Hey, you write down the first stupid thing that comes into your head, right?" Camus's comment to Polge was that the same thing could be said about lots of writers. At Grasse, a city famous for its perfume, Camus was invited to socialize with perfume factory owners, who asked him solicitously, "Do you think we treat our workers well?" To which Camus replied, "Try living for a month on what they earn and you'll see for yourself."

Camus took up fishing, having bought and studied *The Perfect Fisherman's Book*, and would stand in streams, laughing and once almost falling into the water after catching a big fish. He would laugh at stories from visitors like Paul Oettly, who would tell the male company how "the train ride from Lyons and Valence takes forty minutes, and I fucked a girl in the train and had just enough time! . . . If you're poor, you might as well have sex!" With such friends, Camus forgot his somber public façade, as he did with the Faure family, who kept in close touch with Francine, sending telegrams if she forgot to write for one week: WORRIED ABOUT NO NEWS STOP.

Fernande Faure did not just love her youngest daughter, Francine; she adored her and—without realizing it—stifled her. Francine hoped at times that one day her husband would behave himself and be sexually faithful, but Fernande and Christiane seriously doubted that would ever happen. In front of Fernande, no one dared mentioned Maria Casarès's name. Fernande bustled with energy, showing how she adored *her* twins, "our" children. She washed, ironed, knitted, baked cookies, and ruled Catherine and Jean with an iron hand, in order that Francine might get some rest. She was imperial and servile, imperious and considerate, seeming as enegetic as Francine was hesitant. Fernande also dictated the day's schedule. Breakfast became a ceremony where Madame Faure weighed the chocolate for making chocolate milk and measured the grain for the babies' gruel, which had to stay on the fire for a long while, otherwise, as was well known, it might cause constipation. Often Fernande behaved according to absolute laws; once when Jeanne Polge was preparing a vinaigrette, she criticized, "You haven't whipped it—a good vinaigrette must e-mul-si-fy."

Jeanne and Urbain Polge sensed how Camus was constantly irritated by his bossy mother-in-law, but he held back his resentment. Christiane would joke with Albert to lessen the tension in the house, but not the refined other sister, Suzy. She would scold him with remarks such as "Oh, Albert, you mustn't drink *that* sort of wine with couscous!" Of course, the Faures had known Camus as a bohemian with no future and no income. Now it was somehow worse: apart from his infidelities, he lived in an odd and disreputable world of letters. It was strange how Francine seemed to enjoy the Paris literary life.

Francine was always sweet and gentle with the children, and concentrated on playing Bach and Scarlatti on the piano; but she seemed more and more disoriented when she needed to make the slightest decision: she could not even pack suitcases on time. She easily panicked. One day Jean limped into the house because of a thorn in his foot, and before the thorn was discovered, Francine became seriously worried, half convinced that her son might have polio.

Yet despite tensions, Camus told Urbain Polge, "You know that Francine and I will end up our lives together." Privately, Urbain felt that Albert was developing a bad conscience about his marriage and that interfered with his happiness. To Urbain, Camus seemed like a kid who could never refuse a piece of candy. He seemed genetically programmed for love. Camus loved to love the way other people loved to eat, hike, or swim. Some people are passionate about chocolate, strawberries, smoked salmon, blood sausage (as Camus was), English soaps, German beer—or women (Camus again). Others are not.

In the south of France, Camus and Polge would go to the bullfights at the famous arena at Nîmes and to rugby matches at Perpignan. As this family-oriented friendship, involving both wife and children, developed, Camus's association with Jean-Paul Sartre languished somewhat. On November 8, 1949, Camus wrote to the critic René Lalou about Sartre, saying that his meetings with the philosopher "are widely spaced, but warmhearted. I think Sartre has a great and persuasive talent, but his books have never influenced me, because our surroundings are incompatible. In terms of art, the sky at Le Havre [where Sartre was born] is not the same as Algiers. In terms of ideas, Sartre was inspired by German philosophers, whom he knows admirably, while I've always preferred Plato to Hegel." Camus felt that his "real master" was Jean Grenier. Essentially, Camus saw himself as an artist, whereas Sartre was a philosopher who wrote literary works to illustrate his theses. Camus owned two copies of Sartre's *Being and Nothingness*, but in the one he read and annotated, he does not seem to have gone past page 183 of the vast tome. Whereas Sartre was sure of his genius, Camus was always prey to self-doubt, and neither Jean Grenier nor René Char could reassure him. Sartre could sit nailed to his chair for a dozen hours to write, but Camus's limit was four or five hours, spent pacing nervously around a room while he was preparing a new work. The two gave up their weekly lunch, because Camus could not go along with Sartre's philosophy and especially not with his political stances. Sartre, whom Camus once called "our Diderot," did not suffer psychological anguishes the way Camus did about solitude, for example. Sartre never thought about retiring to a monastery, as Camus had, and he might have laughed at Camus's noting in his *Carnets*: "I have retired from the world not because I had enemies there, but because I had friends, and not because they usually abused me but because they thought I was better than I am, which I could not stand."

Sartre accepted himself good-humoredly, but Camus, even when he was in the presence of his friends René Char and Urbain Polge, wanted to be someone else. He wrote in his *Carnets*: "The greatest luck of my life is that I've only met, loved, and disappointed exceptional people. I've known virtue, ease, and nobility, through other people, an admirable and painful experience. . . . As Dostoyevsky said, 'Can a conscious man ever respect himself, even a little?' "

Chapter Thirty-six

Forty Grams of Streptomycin

C amus no longer overindulged in whiskey, as he did after the liberation (in the fiesta days), and unlike Sartre, he did not use Corydane
or other stimulants. Tired, weak, and irritable, he made no progress
in the beginning of 1949, particularly on his essay on revolt. What was the
point in his planning an early retirement from journalism if it did not help
him to further his work as a writer? He still had trouble adjusting to his double role as husband and lover, knowing that Francine did not live well with
this situation either, although she kept quiet about it.

The political scene worsened on the national and international levels.
Some of Camus's friends and acquaintances distanced themselves from him,
and vice versa, as partisans and adversaries of the USSR organized themselves amid widespread fear of a coming world war. Camus refused to align
himself unilaterally with one or another of the groups. Moscow had recently
created a Movement for Peace to organize sympathizers and mobilize pacifist intellectuals, and it was hoped that the masses would follow behind
them. Some of Camus's acquaintances, such as the actor-director Jean-Louis
Barrault, were among the official directors of the Movement for Peace in
France. Camus was glad to condemn the arms race, but not as unambiguously as did Louis Aragon, Paul Eluard, Vercors, and Picasso, who denounced "American colonialism and imperialism."

Camus was also depressed by the journalistic scene in France. A new
radio show, *Derrière les Coulisses* (Behind the Scenes), featuring nasty gossip, falsely announced that Camus had sold the screen rights for *La Peste* to
an American company for a high sum, and Camus wrote to the director of
the radio station, sending a copy of his letter to the Ministry of Information,
to complain that the journalist in question had not even bothered to phone
him to check.

About this time, Claude Mauriac, the son of François Mauriac, launched a new monthly, *Liberté de l'Esprit*, intended to dissuade young people from being seduced by communism. In the first issue, a right-wing polemicist, Roger Nimier, mocked Camus for staying silent while French-intellectual Nazi collaborators were executed under pressure from former Resistance fighters. Nimier wrote, "Mr. Camus's silence, amid the universal silence, would not be at all remarkable if the same writer had not raised his voice (eloquently) in favor of niggers, Palestinians, and yellow men." Nimier also feared the war, but he stated, "We won't be fighting it with the shoulders of M. Sartre or the lungs of M. Camus." Did Nimier know that Camus was tubercular? Interviewed recently, Robert Gallimard believes that he could not have been ignorant of this fact, whereas Nimier's biographer, Marc Dambre, is ambiguous about the matter. In a later issue of *Liberté de l'Esprit*, one of the staff writers, Jean Lescure, a poet who knew Camus during the Resistance, protested against Nimier's harsh joke. Later, Nimier would apologize to Camus, but one wonders whether he meant the apology sincerely.

Camus longed to get away from Paris, but instead of moving once and for all, he decided to take a holiday. The director general of cultural relations at the French Foreign Ministry, Roger Seydoux, proposed that Camus go on a lecture tour of South America. It was suggested that Camus give five speeches, which the writer reduced to only two, one on "the contemporary world's spiritual crisis" and another about literature, "Novel and Revolt." Usually Camus refused to speak in public, making an exception for speeches to patients in tuberculosis sanatoriums. But the South American tour allowed him to get to know that continent as well as to flee Paris.

Yet he could not admire South America's democracy. In Argentina, Juan Perón made his political party an instrument of his personal power. In Brazil, the Communist Party was dissolved by the government and its leader lived in hiding. In Chile, a law banned Communists from union leadership and prevented them from voting or running for office. Camus hoped to address opposition groups in Argentina under the auspices of the intellectual group Sur, led by Victoria Ocampo. At fifty-nine, Ocampo was an ardent jet-setter and friend of writers such as Jorge Luis Borges, Jules Supervielle, José Ortega y Gasset, Roger Caillois, and Waldo Frank. Ocampo had broken quite early with the Communists, and her literary review *Sur*, had a total circulation of four thousand copies in America, Madrid, and Paris and Argentina. Among its notable articles was André Gide's "Return from the USSR," which was critical of Stalinism, and it also featured excerpts from André Malraux's novel *La Condition humaine*.

Roger Seydoux advised Camus to avoid being invited only by Ocampo's group and to speak to at least one other group with a less notorious political stance. Camus preferred private meetings to speeches at banquets, and he began to find negotiations for the trip rather annoying. He almost considered dropping the idea, and began to talk about going to South America as an "onerous duty," as it was not clear how to bring the Good News to totalitarian countries. On hearing that an Argentine censor had banned a production of his play *Le Malentendu*, Camus canceled his planned trip to that country.

Although not usually impressed by premonitions, horoscopes, and the irrational, Camus felt some odd fears before he left, telling Maria Casarès that perhaps he shouldn't go because he sensed that evil was floating in the air. Nevertheless, he boarded the ship *La Campana* in Marseilles on June 30, traveling first class. Camus noted in his diary that he felt ashamed of the relative luxury of his accommodations after seeing fourth-class passengers lodged in vertical bunk beds "in concentration-camp style." To pass the time, Camus read the *Journal* of Alfred de Vigny, which pleased him, apart from Vigny's "constipated-swan side." He seemed to be going through long depressive crises: "Twice I've had thoughts about suicide."

Yet public interviews show him relaxed, amused, and flattered by the welcome that greeted him in South America after his landing in Rio de Janeiro, Brazil, on July 21. Two years earlier in the United States, he had been well known, but now he was a celebrity, even if he was still annoyingly presented as "existentialism's number-two man," after Jean-Paul Sartre. It was bad enough being called an existentialist, but to be ranked as number two was infuriating.

In Brazil, he accepted the necessary invitations while eyeing pretty girls and chatting in a somewhat dazed manner. He made slightly self-satisfied statements to the press, such as "I wonder why society ladies are always attracted to me." Camus seemed less restrained than in America, as he understood very little Spanish and no Portuguese at all. His Brazilian hosts were smitten when he asked to see a soccer match, which was not what most visiting lecturers requested. In Rio de Janeiro, Camus did not want to live in a hotel, so he stayed at the French embassy. He suffered over the separation from Maria, writing, "Whoever has not dreamed of a perpetual prison for the woman he loves, has never really loved." He ate lunch with VIPs and toured the city and its famed nightclubs, going to bed late (the writer Albert Cossery had given him a list of interesting cabarets and nightclubs to visit, such as the Tabaris in Bahia), and generally fulfilled a cultural missionary's duties.

South America's underdevelopment surprised him, particularly the contrast between rich and poor neighborhoods, modern buildings and *favelas*. It reminded him of Algeria, and he compared poor Brazilian women carrying water jugs on their heads to Kabyle women, who carried water that way, too. Camus gathered a mass of impressions he had no time to organize, and he knew that he lacked the needed sociological and cultural background to make something of them. His trip to America had been calm though disorganized. But Camus's diaries and letters from Brazil reveal a man somewhere between fatigue and madness, although he put on a good face in public. About Brazil he wrote, "Here nature suffocates man," and he too had the impression of suffocating.

He saw no Arabs in Brazil, but there were plenty of blacks, who were well assimilated in spite of frightful poverty. Camus said, "I like black people a priori and am tempted to find all sorts of qualities in them which they don't have." He had a friendly time with a young black theatrical troupe that wanted to stage his play *Caligula*. Escaping from solemn official ceremonies, Camus went incognito for fun to a black dance with one of the actors, who kept repeating, "Segreto, segreto. . . ."

Camus objected to yet another proposed version of *Caligula* when the Brazilian director wanted to "throw in some goddamn ballet, which is the new fashion on the international stage." A theater troupe in London had come up with the same idea. Amid speeches to academics and press conferences, Camus was taken on a tour of the Bahia jail, known as the "handsomest in Brazil." He was impressed by the jail, "like a prison in an American film, except for the smell, the frightful smell of men which is found in every prison." In the Bahia jail, inspirational posters could be seen, multiplied to the vanishing point, that read "Be Good" and "Optimism." He felt ashamed to see some privileged prisoners who were employed as servants by the director. He was also disconcerted by one of the jail officials who kept insisting that Camus "make [himself] at home" there.

Camus was aware that his speeches went well and that his listeners found him charming, but he felt a sense of failure. When he arrived in Brazil, he wrote to Michel and Janine Gallimard, joyously addressing them as "Dear Samba and Rumba," but in his *Carnets* he wrote that he was stricken by fever and flu once again, "and this time it seems to be serious." Although he did not mention the word "tuberculosis," two weeks later he wrote that he clearly realized that he "wanted to die." A week later he described himself as in "the middle of a psychological debacle. The strong balance which has stood up to everything has now collapsed in spite of all my efforts." He called his depression "a kind of hell. If the people who welcomed me here could feel the effort I am making to appear normal . . ."

Camus traveled through landscapes that seemed surrealistic to him. After dozens of hours in cars, arriving by night in cities he did not know, he would return to other cities to speak with professors, novelists, and philosophers. He also found time to keep company for a few days with a pretty young woman with "the green eyes of a wicked mother." He also attended snake fights and boxing matches and performed his public duties, although his public face hid a terrified man.

Camus had been an actor long enough to be able to conceal his true feelings. He answered the public's questions about Sartre, Faulkner, and Char, Hitler's Nazism and Zola's naturalism, France, Spain, and Italy, and the excesses of Soviet and American imperialism. Always attentive, Camus prepared his speeches with care, the way his uncle Etienne had repaired wine barrels. For Camus, an artist was a conscientious artisan.

In Rio he spoke at the Itamaraty Palace, where the Ministry of Foreign Affairs was housed. A young woman was seated in the front row, devouring his words, and after his talk, Camus made a gesture for her to approach. He was surprised that the young woman, Gilda Gabaglia, had read several of his books, and even quoted one of Camus's lines, "I hasten to arrive at a country where the sun burns away all questions." Camus also recognized in the audience a Spanish Republican he had known in Paris, who was working at a distant ranch in Brazil but had made the trip in order to offer Camus a pack of cigarettes which were the closest available to the "gusto francese." Camus was moved to tears by this gift.

The notes for his speeches give a good idea of how the lectures were organized: a neatly written introduction and conclusion with well-ordered ideas in between, ready to be developed according to the audience. After each speech, indifferent and exhausted, he would perform the social duties that irritated him more and more. He felt the voyage was turning into a corrida, as he was sometimes obliged to give two speeches in a single day. South America's cities astonished Camus, and he wrote to René Char about São Paulo, "The termites are going to devour the skyscrapers."

He managed to get to Chile as well by traveling through Uruguay, despite visa mixups. In Chile he met the poet Rafael Alberti; as he noted, "I know that he's a Communist, and finally I explained my point of view, and he approved of it. But calumny will do the rest and will one day separate me from this man who is and who should remain my comrade." On August 14 he arrived at Santiago's Hotel Crillon, saying, "During this stupid voyage, only the sights and people of Chile have brought me comfort. . . . Chile has taught me that volcanoes can be tender."

Camus did not remain relaxed for long. He gave his ritual lecture on "this time of murderers," the foul world where torture had become a governmental necessity. Camus also spoke about the aphorist Nicolas de Chamfort: "Chamfort was right: when one wants to please high society, one must agree to be taught lots of things by total ignoramuses." He also tried out his work in progress L'Homme révolté on the public. Although at first Chile seemed more restful than Brazil, on August 17 there were riots about a public transportation issue. After attending a Spanish-language production of Le Malentendu, Camus left for Rio de Janeiro on August 20 and flew back to Paris shortly thereafter. Camus had been impressed by the Spanish writer

José Bergamín, who refused to choose between communism and Catholicism so long as the Spanish Civil War was not over. Camus noted down a quote from Bergamín: "My deepest temptation is suicide, and a spectacular suicide at that."

Meanwhile, he gathered material for an enigmatic novella, *La Pierre qui pousse* (The Growing Stone). In this tale, an engineer named Arrast travels to the jungle between gigantic rivers. The author gave great importance to the Brazilian magic religion, macumba. The story's hero was on a sort of redemptory voyage, perhaps akin to Camus's wandering from lecture to lecture. Finally Arrast "is filled with tumultuous happiness by the sound of water. Eyes closed, he joyously celebrates his own strength, as once again he celebrated life's beginning over again." Never again would a Camus story be so close to the unconscious, lining up a series of sentences that exploded the barriers of logic.

Camus had escaped from two months of everyday life, but he returned to Paris with insomnia, eczema, and depression. At home he went to several doctors, who found Koch's bacillus in his sputum and diagnosed tuberculosis at the lesional stage. They ordered him to rest for some months, so he was unable to take up his duties at Gallimard right away. Camus believed that he was about to die without having achieved his great work, and he thought of Tolstoy, who wrote *War and Peace* between the ages of thirty-five and forty-one. At that moment, Camus was thirty-six. He also thought of Herman Melville, who wrote at age thirty-five, "I have consented to annihilation."

During difficult times, Camus always referred to his novelistic leading lights, Melville and Tolstoy. He felt that from then on, "my life's only effort will be to live the life of a normal man; all the rest has been generously given me, except money, which I am indifferent to. I didn't want to be a man of the lower depths, and this outsized effort has been useless. Little by little, instead of succeeding better and better in my efforts, I can see the abyss approaching."

At the end of October he noted that his tubercular relapse was devastating, especially as he had been certain for so long that he was cured. However, this realization, coming after "an uninterrupted series of devastations, finally makes me laugh. Here I am, liberated: madness is also a liberation." He read novels by Hawthorne, Melville, Tolstoy, and Stendhal, poems by Rimbaud, Shelley, and Keats (another tubercular writer), the painter Eugène Delacroix's *Journal*, and essays by philosophers Jacques Maritain and Johann Gottlieb Fichte. He became interested in the characters of the British novelist Graham Greene, jotting down from *The Heart of the Matter* a declaration from the unhappy Scobie: "Human love knows nothing that might be called victory, barely a few strategic successes before the final disaster of death or indifference."

Camus was divided between a powerful desire to live and the temptation of death, and for the first time in his life, suicide seemed the only serious problem. Meanwhile, lung specialists found a treatment for him, and although he was usually discreet about medical treatments he received, this time Camus did tell friends about his prescriptions: "40 grams of streptomycin from November 6 to December 5, 1949. 360 grams of P.A.S. from November 6 to December 5, 1949, plus 20 grams of strepto from November 13 to January 2."

He was not satisfied with this strong new treatment, so he also consulted another specialist, Dr. Jacques Ménétrier, whom he would recommend to Michel Gallimard. He told the doctor that he was at an impasse about everything, from finances and family to career matters and the fact that he was not able to finish his book. Ménétrier used so-called total medicine to treat the exhausted and desperate patient, hoping to restore Camus's natural defenses. He prescribed small doses of minerals like copper, iron, cobalt, and magnesium—a fashionable therapy that came from America, based on oligo-elements. However, this treatment was unable to cure Camus's tuberculosis.

But the antibiotics, plus Camus's willpower, did achieve results, and his health improved slowly, rebounding once again. Although he was still fatigued, work was a therapy and a relaxation for him, and now that he was not wasting any more time traveling, or at the Gallimard offices, his book on revolution and revolt could take shape unhindered. He consulted a psychiatrist, as much about Francine as about himself, since he had real reservations about psychoanalysis. In theoretical terms, Camus was unsure what exactly was meant by the unconscious, whereas practically speaking, he feared that a writer might be dried up by too many sessions with an analyst. Nevertheless, Camus toyed with the idea of going through analysis, although not as seriously as Jean-Paul Sartre did.

With a sense of friendship, Camus compared his health with Michel Gallimard's, and openly doubted the value of alternative treatments with oligo-elements. Yet the treatments did permit him to get away for working holidays at Cabris, near Grasse, in the southern Alpes-Maritimes region of France, where he often went between 1949 and 1951. There in the almost Florentine countryside, he stayed in the Chèvre d'Or Hotel, huddling close to a wood-burning fireplace. Camus felt alone with his thoughts, although he recalled philosophical conversations he had once had with Sartre, Jean Grenier, and Nicola Chiaramonte. He wrote to Francine, "The heart of the matter is, I don't believe in thoughts expressed during discussions or in the clash of ideas. I'm not a philosopher, and for me thought is an interior adventure that matures, that hurts or transports one. . . . It's a meditation that takes days and years to formulate, to move forward, and to find expression." Camus had been reflecting on his essay about revolt for five years and doubted that even one hundred hours of discussion with friends would advance his work by a second's time. "And then," he concluded, "one is always a zero through one's own fault."

To Maria Casarès he wrote that he was thinking of *Les Justes*, and that "the only possible justice is a new repartition of justice. We make revolutions so that others may travel by wagon-lit." Fortunately, Camus was able to rely on these two women, the crystalline lover Maria and the mother of his children, Francine. He complained humorously to friends that Francine always wrote him using express mail, which cost more than the regular post, although it arrived no faster: "Unfortunately, I told her that there was money in my author's royalty account." Camus felt that although Francine was still dear to him, he needed to "pick her up and hold her at arm's length, but to do so, I'd need to gather all the energy I'm using in writing, in wanting to change the world, and in asking myself about destiny."

Considering that he was convalescing, he had a full work schedule. Getting up at nine a.m., he read and took notes on Hegel until eleven. He wrote from four p.m. to eight p.m., and after a brief pause for dinner he worked again until ten-thirty. He would read Montaigne's *Essays* in bed until he fell asleep. Francine arrived for a few weeks to give him Spanish lessons, then left again.

Friends came to visit, as well as his brother, Lucien. Camus also visited the novelist Roger Martin du Gard, whose life and works he found exemplary. He showed a different face to different people at this time: his friend Blanche Balain, who lived in Nice, found him "lugubrious," although he did gain weight and get some sleep at last. Camus felt that all of his work was ironic, but that his current project was not. He thought cynicism was a constant danger in what he wrote, but although *L'Homme révolté* is quite skeptical, it is not cynical. The first two "cycles" of his work, Camus said, dealt with the absurd and revolt, depicting people who never told lies, and who were therefore unreal. He stated that for this reason, he was not a novelist in the usual meaning of the term, but rather an "artist who creates myths to the measure of his passion and anguish." Camus added that this might be why in his personal life, the people who had "transported" him also possessed "the power and the exclusivity of these myths."

He could hardly wait to finish his essay in order to begin a new imaginative work. He planned after *L'Homme révolté* to devote himself to "creation in freedom," dreaming of a big novel to be inspired by friends he had met in Algeria and in France, from Marguerite Dobrenn to Mamaine Koestler. Of one character he wrote, "Love became possible for him, and he only had the right to lies and adultery." After the myths of Sisyphus (the absurd) and Prometheus (revolt), this novel would deal with the myth of Nemesis.

Camus traveled between Paris and Cabris to Chambon, continuing to write *L'Homme révolté*. He refused to allow *L'Etranger* to be published in a cheap paperback edition, not wanting the book to leave the more expensive "Collection Blanche" of Gallimard. He felt that *L'Etranger* was "not a book for everyone, as *La Peste* is. Later, maybe." At this point he also explained to Michel Gallimard that he no longer wanted to perform his administrative duties at the publishing house, as reader and editor. He had continued to receive his pay while he was on sick leave, but just as *Combat* had gotten rid of him, he would get rid of Gallimard.

He was looking for another apartment for his family and relied on Michel to read the real estate pages of *Le Figaro*. At Le Panelier, despite the heat, his children, and flies, Camus managed to get work done. In August, he met Maria Casarès at a hotel in Grand-Valtin, a village in the Vosges near Gérardmer, at 850 meters altitude, in a valley framed by prairies and forests. Telling Michel Gallimard about his tryst with Maria, Camus insisted that Michel remain discreet about the holiday, not wanting to hurt Francine's feelings unnecessarily. He enjoyed looking at the villagers, who resembled "amiable bulldogs. . . . The beautiful faces can be counted on a goose's foot." The rather primitive hotel cut off guests' electricity at ten p.m., which Camus felt was perfect for a healthy regime. He and Maria sometimes went to a nearby town for hydrotherapy treatments. Albert worked hard and wrote faithfully to Francine, lying by omission about Maria's presence. "Here is external nothingness and the foul ugliness of people in general."

Camus was rediscovering the pleasures of life. Back in Paris, he finally found a five-room apartment that suited him, and which was practical for his family, at 29 rue Madame near the place Saint-Sulpice in the sixth arrondissement.

He constantly relied on Maria, writing to her: "You belong to me absolutely and forever, like a mother belongs to the one she has created." After two months of treatment with streptomycin and three months at Cabris, his health was restored, he no longer thought about suicide, and his essay on revolt was finally done.

On July 1, American troops had landed in Korea as part of an ominous new war, but Camus wrote to a friend, "I can forget the world and the Koreans, and the prodigious pain in the ass of living in an interesting epoch."

Chapter Thirty-seven # 5 rue Sébastien-Bottin, Facing the Garden

A fter *La Peste*, Camus could have lived on his author's royalties, but he did not want his daily life to depend on his books' sales. His second job, working for Gallimard, had given him a certain freedom, but also obligations. Gallimard remained the most prestigious publishing house, not only because of its financial success but because of its list. Gaston Callimard, the head of the house since 1911, outdid his French publishing rivals, like Bernard Grasset and René Julliard, by virtue of his distinguished authors. Camus had been discovered during the war and remained faithful to Gallimard, even when the publisher had problems because he had allowed the NFR to be run by the notorious Nazi collaborator Pierre Drieu La Rochelle.

Drieu was a member of the Gallimard editorial committee, but he attended meetings only five times. Gaston Gallimard did not frequently go to collaborationist parties, but he did hobnob with Lieutenant Heller of the Nazi Propagandastaffel, part of the German occupation forces. When Paris was liberated, Gaston was suspected by the French army government of having been "an agent of the German espionage and propaganda services."

Camus helped to defend Gaston and testified for him in court to explain that the NRF directed by Drieu was "completely separate" from the rest of the publishing house, which was "public knowledge." Furthermore, Camus said, Gaston "sheltered and protected" him even though he had a vague idea that Camus was using his office at the publisher's to meet activists from the Resistance group Combat. Indeed, many Resistance, or otherwise politically laudable, writers continued to be published through the war by Gaston, and condemning him would mean also condemning not only Camus himself but Valéry, Gide, and Sartre. Thanks in part to Camus's testimony, Gaston Gallimard was acquitted of all charges against him.

The truth lay somewhere between the charges against Gaston and Camus's generous defense. Gaston was no hero during the war, but he was not an infamous villain, either. Gaston appreciated and respected Camus, but he did not see him as an immortal author, much preferring writers like León-Paul Fargue, Valéry Larbaud, Marcel Proust, and Saint-John Perse. Gaston, the founder of the firm, had hired his only son, Claude Gallimard, who was more legal-minded than literary, and when Claude became a prisoner of war, Gaston replaced him with his favorite nephew, Michel Gallimard, who everyone thought would really run the house after Gaston. Camus was enthralled by this rich family with their passions, sympathies, and conflicts, and he treated them with a certain familiarity. He also enjoyed listening to the stories of Gaston's brother Jacques, who was an artillery soldier in the First World War and now worked in the accounting department. Jacques Gallimard would gush forth with neurasthenic recollections, often repeating himself, but Camus was moved by the war tales. They made him think of his father, Lucien Camus.

Camus was not at the heart of Gallimard's publishing activity. He participated in the reader's committee and directed one series, called "Espoir." The weekly meeting of the reader's committee at Gallimard was a bit like mass in the Catholic Church, a communion with books. It was held in Gaston's office, where three windows of the large oval room looked out on a garden where snooty cocktail parties were held, which Camus rarely attended. In front of the right-hand window was Gaston's desk, where he would sit with his back to the wall, his hand posed on a telephone or a bottle of mineral water. He presided like a wheedling lay clergyman, governing visitors with charming or stormy glances. Some felt that with his habitual bow tie, he looked like a tipsy maître d', dressed in town clothes. Claude would sit facing him, silent but busy. In the same symmetrical distribution around the left-hand window were Raymond Gallimard and *his* son, Michel. In the 1950s, leading lights of literature, whether famous or little-known, would be placed in a semicircle around the family members during weekly meetings, everyone within eyesight of Gaston and Raymond. At the two ends of the room were literary secretary Robert Gallimard, Michel and Claude's cousin, and Dionys Mascolo, a reader-secretary before he became head of the foreign department. Between them were the places, as unchanging as copper-plated prie-dieus in parish churches, of Brice Parain, Albert Camus, Jacques Lemarchand, Jean Blanzat, Raymond Queneau, Roger Caillois, Marcel Arland, Jean Paulhan, and the only woman, Dominique Aury.

Of the fifteen participants having the right to express themselves, the five Gallimards made up a strong minority, capable of filibuster, and although they might disagree, they usually maintained a tacit accord, the family motto being "I Shall Maintain." The atmosphere in Camus's time is hard to define—there wasn't an ounce of vulgarity or populism, nor any excessive tendency towards the avant-garde. The best-selling writer was definitely Camus; the most original, Queneau; the most refined, Caillois; the most mysterious, Paulhan; the most respectable without being conformist, Blanzat, Lemarchand, and Arland; the most philosophical, Parain; and the most confused, Mascolo (he had been torn ever since the Resistance about the "impossibility of not being a Communist and the impossibility of remaining a member of the Communist Party"). Paulhan, for his part, remained the most powerful reader as well as the most active and closest to Gaston.

GG—Gaston—presided over the meetings without applying obvious pressure. It was tacitly agreed that the reading committee's debates and their grading of books from one to three would remain confidential; but as with cabinet meetings, leaks could not be avoided. Paulhan opened each meeting by talking about what he had read that week, and he read a lot; he adored digressions, for the pleasure of joking or telling gossipy bitchy tales. Then each member's reading notes were collated and everyone gave his report. When present, Camus read aloud seriously the long descriptions he'd written when he felt that a book deserved attention, and he'd sometimes say to Gaston, "I'd gladly take that for my series." If the book was of little interest, four lines sufficed. (His handwriting grew more and more difficult to read, like flyspecks, and that caused problems for the secretarial staff.) Robert Gallimard would sum up the conclusions in writing, and Gaston would turn to him and say whether a book was accepted or not. If a book was graded only one and a half on a scale of one to three, then a committee member might ask for a second reading from whoever agreed to do so. Reading assignments went according to the genre of book in question. Camus took charge of essays as well as novels. But Gaston did not even ask his distinguished committee to read popular authors like Joseph Kessel and Jacques Perret, because "they would only find them trash," and he intended to publish them anyway, to make money.

Camus's personal secretary, Suzanne Agnely, née Labiche, was massive and hatchet-faced, but she was fanatically devoted to her boss. She would protest wearily, "He's impossible with his phone calls and his women whom I have to keep apart. He puts me in untenable situations!" But she remained devoted, and he appreciated her. Like numerous women at Gallimard—the personnel was seventy percent female—she seemed to be in love with Camus, and even began by referring to him as "maître" until he quickly asked her to desist.

Certain men at the publisher's were jealous of him, and because he had climbed the ladder, some thought of him as a climber. When *La Peste* was so successful, Camus received a constant deluge of mail, and Suzanne

Agnely helped him to deal with it. After the liberation, the French were looking for intellectual leaders, and packets of letters would arrive every day for Camus, sometimes a hundred per week. Requests for interviews became demands from the mad, the half-mad, the obsessed, boy scouts, and photographers. At least some of the photographers were distinguished, such as Yousef Karsh and Henri Cartier-Bresson. The Sorbonne professors, the handicapped, and the climbers who wanted help with literary juries and ministries all hassled Camus, not to mention lycée students, actors and actresses, biographers, and authors requesting articles, reviews, and prefaces. When Jean Galtier-Boissière, editor of the magazine *Le Crapouillot*, politely asked for a response to a questionnaire about his height, weight, favorite sports, domestic animals, etc., Camus replied that while he was willing to briefly state his age and whether he was married, "the rest, all the rest from pets to the second woman in my life is my business alone. Such miserliness about my private life can only be justified by my unreasonable taste for personal freedom."

Well-known and lesser-known magazines asked him to join their editorial committees, and he refused, but often would send a subscription check to them. Out of courtesy, strategy, or even masochism, he always answered flattering requests, even to say no, and if he was asked for books, he sent them. He was particularly attentive to letters from "unfortunate" countries, from Spain to Greece. If certain correspondents scolded him too much, Camus would reply that he was a laborer's son, that he had known poverty, and that he worked not as a quest for some abstract intellectual glory, but to support his loved ones.

He admitted that his much-vaunted reputation was at times a heavy burden: "Let me tell you that my great rule is never to despise anyone." Asked to sign a petition circulated by the publisher Maurice Nadeau to defend the American writer Henry Miller against charges of pornography, Camus signed. Some propositions merited lengthy reflection, such as when the filmmaker Jean Renoir wanted to make a movie of *L'Etranger*. Gallimard's financial wizards demanded an exorbitant ten million francs for the screen rights, and the project died.

Sometimes Camus's responses were summary: when one correspondent wrote to ask his opinion of homosexuality, Camus replied, "Dear Sir, I have no time, and no taste, for this investigation."

Camus's position was enviable, but also difficult, in that when his friends' manuscripts were refused by Gallimard, he was considered the guilty party, and he was not necessarily thanked when they were accepted. When Claude de Fréminville's request for an advance on a book for Gallimard was turned down, Camus had to explain that this was because Fréminville's previous book, *Bien sous tous les rapports*, had sold a total of four hundred copies. When his doctor friend Stanislas Cviklinski sent him a manuscript, Camus replied, "I'm speaking with the frankness of comradeship: you have written this in an impossible and often incomprehensible language."

Camus was generally thought to be all-powerful at Gallimard, but he was aware that his decisions were debatable, saying that "a literary judgment is the most relative thing in the world, and it must be expressed as simply as possible." He had no illusions about his ability to judge poetry, and always disclaimed having any skill in the matter, even for prose poems. Still, with the poetry of Algerian militant Kateb Yacine, he kept an open mind, and he wrote to Kateb, "I was interested by your poems, which I felt were sometimes too calculated, but the cry breaks through and that's what touched me." Although Camus could not publish Kateb's poems, he did propose them to magazines like *Présence Africaine*, and wrote to the poet: "You and I were born on the same soil, and that makes for a resemblance, above all the quarrels of the moment."

Camus also dealt with scientific essays at Gallimard, although he lacked technical knowledge, and he negotiated the publication of Carl Gustav Jung's works as well. He would often claim to have liked a rejected book, but he was outvoted by others on the readers committee, and tried to encourage disappointed authors with his own experiences: "I might confide in you that I wrote two very bad novels before being able to publish a third." He was alluding to *La Mort heureuse*, which remained in his drawer, and was probably referring to a second abortive project only for effect, unless an unknown, potential novel has disappeared without a trace.

In 1949 and 1950, Camus worked rigorously with Gaston, although less with Paulhan and Queneau. He complained that being a publisher's reader exhausted his faculty for discovery and admiration, and he could not remain permanently fresh if he was always bent over manuscripts. Unless he stumbled on something really extraordinary, he felt that he was mostly walking along an uncertain line. Camus explained to Gaston and the other Gallimard bosses that employees should be granted sabbaticals in order for them to clear their heads. Taking his own advice so that he could finish one of his own books, he retired to the countryside.

Although Camus was not a real discoverer of talent, he did encourage some young writers of value, like Romain Gary, Roger Ikor, and the young Michel Vinaver, whom he had met in New York and whose novel *Lataume* was accepted with Camus's support. And Camus warmly received the young author Jean-François Revel, who later became an important essayist and political philosopher. When he liked an author, he would even cable his American publisher: TO MADAME KNOPF . . . AMONG FRENCH WRITERS PIERRE MOINOT IS ONE OF OUR BEST HOPES STOP HE IS IN CONTRAST WITH CURRENT FRENCH LITERATURE.

Camus would, of course, be happy to see writers whose work was accepted, but he preferred to simply write consoling letters to those who were rejected. When Gallimard refused to publish Marguerite Yourcenar's volume *Dramatis personae*, Camus explained that he admired the text's beauty, but that Gallimard "is not disposed to publishing plays." This was not quite true; but then, Yourcenar may not have had a Gallimard catalog in front of her in order to verify this excuse.

Camus asked friends like François Bondy, editor of the magazine *Preuves*, to be on the lookout for manuscripts and books, and he even took an interest in the original publication of foreign-language works, trying to sign up books before they appeared abroad, such as Rex Warner's *The Aerodrome*. Camus was never highly erudite, but he did have a publisher's instinct. For instance, he asked the director of the Geneva library if the complete manuscript of the eighteenth-century writer Benjamin Constant's journals might finally be available. He also gave André Belamich the task of translating into French the works of the Spanish Republican poet and martyr Federico García Lorca, and Belamich went on to translate four-fifths of that writer's voluminous works. Camus was so fond of the charming and modest Belamich, who was always so kind, that with his taste for irony Camus would call him "the viper."

Why did so many writers, foreign as well as French, cling to Camus? The Polish poet Czeslaw Milosz gave a clue when he wrote to Camus: "I am not looking for a master in you, but rather someone who makes my life a bit legitimate." Still, the vast swamp of correspondence exhausted Camus. He sent a note to his close friend Louis Guilloux, which was typed by Suzanne: "Dear Louis, I am dictating this letter because it's much simpler. In fact I'm in bed, and probably for a long while. What I was sick with, when you saw me, was the return of my old illness."

Despite the advances of medicine and treatments, Camus lived every day under a mortal threat.

Chapter Thirty-eight　　**On the Courtyard Side**

The house of Gallimard was an enterprise like any other: Gaston was boss, and employees got moving when a general strike started in France. Some of the top-level staff, like Dionys Mascolo, supported the workers' claims, devising a discreet and tactful petition with Renée, the sister of Michel Gallimard's wife. Camus had no union card, nor would he have wanted to enroll in the Communist-sympathizing French trade union the CGT, or the Christian Social Democrat Union either. But he had prestige in the office, and so he was asked to sign the petition, and he was the first to do so. The lower-level Gallimard employees liked Camus, even if his success as a Don Juan and a writer irritated male employees higher up the ladder. Although he seemed exquisitely polite in the corridors of the house, some colleagues felt this was forced.

The petition was presented to the five Gallimards—Gaston, Claude, Raymond, Michel, and Robert—in their offices. After seeing it, an enraged Claude threatened to fire a whole group of employees, and the workers' delegates retreated unhappily. Michel was irked by Claude's reaction, but Raymond, who hated conflicts, remained silent. Gaston was annoyed, and Robert did not want to find himself caught between his uncles and cousins, so he tried to discreetly leave, but Gaston ordered him to remain. Michel explained that after all, Gallimard was not a reactionary office, but Claude acidly remarked that it was bizarre that Michel's friends Mascolo and Camus as well as Renée, Michel's sister-in-law, were the strike's ringleaders. At this point the conversation turned into a Gallimard brawl.

More literary than the businessman Claude, Michel was also more left-wing politically, and he felt that the petition was not offensive; he spoke about it with Camus, who was offended by some of the clan's reactions, since France was supposed to be a democracy, after all. Salary raises were granted and the strike ended, but not before a chasm was created between Michel and Claude, and Albert was Michel's friend. Whether a likely prospect or a mere fantasy, at one point Michel thought he would leave Gallimard and set up his own publishing house, in which case Camus was ready to go along with him.

Camus had his own difficulties at the office: He had hired translators for an edition of the works of Federico García Lorca, while Robert Gallimard handled the contractual details. One of the translators complained that the payment offered him was insufficient, but the budget had already been fixed, and Gallimard refused to raise the pay, which the translator took very badly. Since Camus had recommended this translator, Robert went to his office to ask advice about what to do, and Camus adopted a snooty air, as if to say, "After all, old boy, the nickel-and-dime stuff is your responsibility." Robert was offended, but Camus later apologized. Camus was hardly a typical Gallimard employee, and the books he wrote were no longer submitted to the readers' committee, any more than were Raymond Queneau's or Jean Paulhan's, or those of eminent nonemployees like Jean-Paul Sartre and André Malraux.

Camus's series, "Espoir," was launched in 1946 and would grow to a list of twenty-four works. A number of Sartre's friends were published with respectable sales: Colette Audry's *On joue perdant* (2,750 copies sold); Jacques-Laurent Bost's *Le Dernier des métiers* (3,300 copies); and among the poets, René Char's *Feuillets d'Hypnos*, which dazzled Camus (3,850 copies sold rapidly, a lot for poetry), and *Lettera amorosa*. Jean Sénac contributed a volume of poems, with a preface by Char. Camus's only really original discovery was Jean-Paul de Dadelsen's poetry, which, influenced by T. S. Eliot, invented a sort of French blank verse. After the publication in 1955 of "Bach en automne" in the *NRF*, Dadelsen would be recognized by other literary reviews.

Camus also published novels, and judicial chronicles like Roger Grenier's *Le Rôle d'accusé*. Camus was friendly with Grenier, who was six months younger than he, and when the younger writer said he was planning a church wedding to please his future parents-in-law, Camus laughed: "Good idea. Whenever we do something really asinine, we might as well do it to music."

Camus also published *Tu peux tuer cet homme*, a collection of scenes from the Russian Revolution chosen, translated, and presented by Lucien Feuillade and Ida Lazarévitch, his wife, with a preface by Brice Parain, whose *L'Embarras du choix* Camus published in 1947. Two years later, he discovered and helped to make known a work by the late philosopher Simone Weil, to which Parain had drawn his attention. Camus would publish eight works by Weil, the mystic scholar who wanted to live like a laborer and participated in the Spanish Civil War by serving as a cook, which made Simone de Beauvoir laugh. As a radical, visionary Catholic convert, Weil denounced the proletariat's inhuman living conditions, and that fascinated Camus. But he was less drawn to her penchant for unhappiness, and her premature death from anorexia was disturbing. Through Weil, Camus felt he understood how to get away from nihilism, the work of a laborer having the same kind of meaning as art.

As an author, Camus had hoped that his "modest" series, "Espoir," would help to "denounce tragedy and to show it is not a solution, nor is despair a reason. Necessary trials depend upon us to turn them into promises."

As an author, Camus was not maniacal about weekly or monthly sales reports. He wasn't like Montherlant, who was convinced that Gallimard cheated him, or Sartre, who didn't care about his royalty statements. Camus had neither undue respect nor hatred for money. He feared money's influence in journalism and in the cinema. He didn't like the fact that Sartre enjoyed carrying bills of large denominations in his pockets, as if to show his lack of concern for money, handing out royal tips. Camus never spent extravagantly himself. He drove a used front-wheel-drive car, while feeling nostalgic for an even simpler B14 car he'd driven at age twenty. He never locked his car doors when he parked, because he did not like "being distrustful, and besides, if someone steals it, that means he really needs it." At a time when French trains had three classes, Camus always traveled in second; and he was never clothed by famous tailors, preferring simple flannel pants, tweed jackets, and an occasional loud tie about which the younger Gallimards would tease him. His only extravagance was getting haircuts at Ortega's fashionable barber shop on the rue Pasquier.

He wanted his children to learn the value of money and vowed that they would never see cash thrown out the window. Evoking his own childhood, Camus made them understand that poverty was noble, but utter destitution was not, and successful people must never own too many cameras, cars, thick rugs, or sumptuous furniture. Camus was not against property, so long as it remained modest. According to him, luxury softened people.

He still had difficulties getting accustomed to Paris's literary institutions. When he was almost awarded the Renaudot and Goncourt prizes for *La Peste*, afterwards, he decided to stick to his original position not to accept literary prizes, feeling that their juries were breeding grounds for what he hated in Paris intellectuals and pseudointellectuals: perfidy, nastiness, coldness, meanness, influence peddling, vengeance, and snobbery. When his friends Jeanne and Urbain Polge asked him what he would do if he were awarded the Nobel Prize, his only response was a smile. In general, he disliked honors. Walking along the quai Conti with his friend Jules Roy, he pointed to the impressive French Academy building and said, "Swear to me that you'll never belong to that."

When Camus had arrived at Gallimard during wartime, everyone welcomed him with joy. Relations later became more nuanced, warmer with some and colder with others. As the years went by, the most influential men on the readers' committee, Paulhan and Queneau, were on good terms with him, and Camus never forgot that they were his first correspondents about *L'Etranger*. No friendship existed between him and Queneau, but there was an evident esteem. Queneau was his elder by ten years, a timid man with a loud laugh, who did not have the same interests as Camus, but in his own way he felt as close to downtrodden poor people as did the author of *La Peste*. Camus once wrote a brief appreciation of a Queneau novel, *Pierrot mon ami*: "Raymond Queneau's books are ambiguous enchantments wherein the spectacles of daily life are mixed with ageless melancholy."

The tall Jean Paulhan, whose bullish head contrasted with his precious way of speaking, left no one indifferent. At Gallimard, he took no interest in financial matters, but for literature he was like a second boss, advising Gaston to publish the Romanian-French aphorist E. M. Cioran for literati, and the novelist Joseph Kessel for the readers of the popular daily *France-Soir*. Camus felt that in the highly neurotic literary world, Paulhan would never stab him in the back. He might be unctuous, falsely friendly, and even truly nasty, but he was also courageous in peacetime as well as during the war. In Camus's eyes, Paulhan remained the man with a mimeograph machine at home during the occupation, printing out Resistance tracts in his own highly recognizable handwriting. The publishing house still existed thanks to Gaston and Paulhan, even if the latter's jokes, insinuations, and little notes in violet ink irritated Gaston. Without ever writing anything about Paulhan's works, Camus believed that they deserved respect and attention, and he acknowledged that Paulhan had doubts before he did about the violence of the postwar purging of Nazi collaborators.

Jean-Paul Sartre disagreed with Camus's praise; he had tried to woo Paulhan before the war, but later told Camus that Paulhan was "an ass, a mediocrity, and a thin-pisser." As for Paulhan, he trusted Camus's work but did not think it would last, preferring the author André Dhôtel, whose work has not lasted. Paulhan never wrote anything about Camus, either: each knew that the other was faithful to literature, but not to the same kind. Yet in politics, they could be allergic to the same things: well-meaning critics like Jules Roy and Jean Amrouche spoke of a North African literary school, but Camus told Paulhan, "Between you and me, I'll admit that North African literature is starting to bore me about as much as the absurd does."

Camus felt closer to Brice Parain than to Paulhan. Parain was reassuring-looking, with his little sunken eyes, salt-and-pepper hair, and farm laborer's body. Parain analyzed Plato in simple terms, and he also knew the Russian language and the USSR, breaking with communism for theoretical reasons, while Camus did so out of disappointment.

So long as Camus stayed at the level of Michel, Janine, and Robert Gallimard, the office atmosphere delighted him, but otherwise, he was irritated to find himself mixed up in intrigues. Camus called the postwar *NRF* a "curious milieu whose function is supposed to be to stimulate writers, but where in fact one loses the joy for writing and for creation." He noted there "the hatred of writers, such as one can contract in a publishing house." Even the greatest writers surveyed one another jealously and felt that their publisher did not do enough for them. A few rare ones escaped professional pettiness, such as Malraux and Sartre, and although Malraux's support of Charles de Gaulle irritated Camus, he strongly admired the writer and especially adored his books' titles: "Can you find better titles than *Le Temps du mépris, La Condition humaine, L'Espoir?*"

In 1948, a conflict broke out between Sartre and Malraux. In an article in *Les Temps Modernes*, Merleau-Ponty wrote that Malraux belonged to the "league of lost hopes." In response, Malraux wanted Gallimard to stop publishing the magazine, and murmured threats that files kept about the publisher's activities during the German occupation might be brought to light. Gaston was furious, refusing to take this kind of blackmail. The Gallimard family held private meetings, discussing the matter. Raymond, Claude, and Michel thought that it was better to lose Sartre than Malraux. Camus agreed, valuing Malraux's literary work over Sartre's. Gaston gave in. In 1948, *Les Temps Modernes* switched publishers, being produced henceforth by Julliard Editions; but Sartre's books continued to be published by Gallimard.

By his literary stature, his temperament, and his lifestyle, Roger Martin du Gard elicited Camus's complete respect. Thirty-two years older than Camus, he shared with the younger writer a nearly boundless admiration for Leo Tolstoy. Neither old-fashioned nor avant-garde, Martin du Gard's style was pared-down. He worked, and spent no time in tittle-tattle, although like Camus, he was a writer with self-doubt. Camus understood Martin du Gard's need to protect his private life: "Roger Martin du Gard believes that a writer owes his work, and not his person, to the public. Therefore he practices and recommends to his friends the most extreme discretion about his private life."

Camus hated the spirit of literary cabals and longed to be rid of Paris, and not just for a few months at a time. He complained to Jean Grenier that he was allowed to spend only four or five hours a day on his personal writing, and he was angry at himself for not working more. As it was, he saw the bare minimum of people at the office, only those who pleased him. He claimed to use his illness with "cynicism" to filter out those people he had no desire to talk with. He declared, "The Parisians have had me for two years in their literary fun fair. I don't like their cheek." He would have preferred to live in Provence, Antibes, Cannes, or especially Menton—places that at the time were not yet overcrowded by tourists. Tormented by illness and the desire to write, Camus wanted to leave, and Gaston willingly gave him vacation time. Like Sartre, Camus did not care for society life. When Francine accepted an invitation for him to lunch with the French president, Vincent Auriol, Camus furiously cancelled the engagement, as he later explained to his mother, who exclaimed, "That's right, son—these people aren't for us!" Camus also refused to see the Count and Countess of Paris, the couple who claimed to represent the monarchy in France. Apart from some weekends with Maria, Camus preferred above all to retreat to Cabris and its olive trees, or Chambon with its pines, or, for family holidays, Le Panelier.

Camus seemed happier and more relaxed at friends' houses or in hotels than at home. It seemed impossible for him to adhere to the material forms of marriage. He said, "The place where I prefer to live and work (and even rarer, where I wouldn't mind dying) is a hotel room. . . . The happiness we call bourgeois bores and terrifies me." From his younger years, Camus maintained a respect not for money per se, but for the work it represented. Simple in his tastes rather than stingy, he would always joke about the withdrawals made by Gallimard from his accounts, but never complained about the royalties he received as author or as director of his series. Neither a miser nor a spendthrift, he regularly sent checks to buy books for patients at tuberculosis sanatoriums and to the Federation of Spanish Deportees, among others. He would meet Blanche Knopf in Paris at the Ritz Hotel restaurant, but on his own he would never choose fancy hotels or famous eateries. In Paris or Algeria, in the homes of rich friends, Camus was scandalized by excessive luxuries.

He argued with some organizations that he felt sucked the blood of writers, like the French copyright guild, the SACEM. His suspicions of associations and clubs of writers, even inoffensive ones like the Société des Gens de Lettres, dated from the wartime days of the National Writers' Committee. He remained distant from such groups, asking a friend, Mireille Dorion, to act as agent for his literary and dramatic rights.

By the beginning of the 1950s, Camus lacked a most important commodity—time. It was easier and less demanding to correct other people's manuscripts than to get working on his own. Camus called himself lazy, but he always thought of work, and felt he was really alive only if he had a book in progress. At home or in a hotel, he would write by hand, and few people apart from Francine, Maria, some friends, and his Gallimard secretary were able to read his handwriting. He rewrote a lot, jotting down ideas in notebooks and on bits of paper, and kept an immense working plan in his head, knowing where he wanted to arrive, but feeling unworthy of ultimate success. Before La Peste, he noted, "What makes my books a success is the same thing that makes them a lie for me."

He also feared creative impotence, telling a number of friends that he lacked imagination. Camus needed the ascetic setting of Cabris, Paris's Right Bank hotels, or studios lent by writer friends. Based at the rue Sébastien-Bottin office, what he called "my perpetual address," he longed to flee once and for all, yet sometimes he also feared the solitude which forced him to write. He did not like being obliged to reprint certain texts of his youth, like *Noces*, and *L'Envers et l'endroit*, but he finally agreed, going over his "bad errors." He treated himself with a special mixture of hardness and indulgence. Already famous, he still had self-doubts, and strove to find a continuity in his works.

Brice Parain said enthusiastically that the texts of *L'Envers et l'endroit* were the best things he had written, but Camus disagreed, because "at twenty-two, one hardly knows how to write, except for geniuses. But I understand what Parain, knowing that enemy of complaisant art and philosophy, means to say. . . . There is more real love in these clumsy pages than in all those that have followed." Camus felt that in French society in particular, the writer's profession "is to a large extent one of vanity." He strove to find a balance between what he was and what he said, and felt that the day he achieved this, "and I can scarcely dare to write it, I might be able to build the works I am dreaming of." He often repeated that after twenty years' effort, his work had barely begun, but few people believed that he was sincere when he said that.

He would feel obliged to take other people's manuscripts with him on vacations, but this work would invade his own. At Cabris he once again labored over *L'Homme révolté*, and he asked Francine to send him books, especially Lenin's analysis of Hegel's dialectics, Bertrand Russell's essays on nineteenth-century thought, and the art historian Elie Faure's *L'Esprit des formes*. He was working ten hours a day on his own book, and he declared to his wife, "Only work and creating keeps the soul standing tall. I . . . I am not happy, and in fact I've never been in such a black mood, but at least those dishonorable days are over when I dragged myself around, ashamed of doing nothing and incapable of accepting my shame or of doing what was needed to stop it."

On February 27, 1951, he wrote to René Char, saying that he was working ten hours a day and hoped to be finished by March 15, "but the childbirth is long and difficult, and it seems to me that the baby is quite ugly and this effort is exhausting." By March 8, he announced to Francine that he had finished the book, although curiously he felt no joy in the accomplishment. "I would have liked the book to force me to make a decisive step forward, for myself and for many others as well. . . . But I doubt very much that I have succeeded." He felt he lacked the necessary genius for this kind of transforming book: "I always choose tasks that are beyond my powers, and that's what makes me live in continual effort, and what exhausts me."

He wrote to Maria with the same message, that he had finished the book yet was not happy, "whether because of doubt or fatigue, I don't know." He explained that having finished, he could rework his text in Paris without any problem, because in his solitary retreat he was almost "hallucinating, without rest or distractions." He was also sleeping badly. To René Char he expressed his "anguish at putting aside" the book: "I would have liked to have been true and useful at the same time, but that would have meant possessing a kind of generosity at every moment." He went on to say that he felt in a state of "airborne depression" at having finished the lengthy task.

For the month of July 1951, he rented a villa at Chambon to go fishing with his children. To Jean Grenier, who was passing through, he said that he felt closer to Hellenism than to the Judeo-Christian tradition, although within the latter he felt "closer to Catholicism than to Protestantism, and rather removed from Judaism because of its antinaturalism, which causes their minds to close up." Grenier objected, pointing out that Camus was close to the Jews in his feeling of revolt against injustice and his sense of humanity, to which Camus insisted, "I feel one must revolt in order to arrive at happiness, to love nature, and possess wisdom about life in an immediate way, not from a great distance."

Strolling through the village of Chambon, Camus and Grenier passed a Salvation Army poster that said, "God Is Looking for You," and Camus wisecracked, "He wouldn't be looking for me if he hadn't already found me."

Chapter Thirty-nine **Rebellions**

*I*n 1950 Camus had bought the apartment that he occupied at 29 rue
Madame, forming a real estate company with Michel Gallimard to do
so. Eventually Camus bought back from Gallimard all the shares in the
company, becoming the sole owner. This was the first time Camus did not
live in borrowed or rented accommodations.

The rue Madame was a calm, upper-class street only fifteen minutes'
walk from the Gallimard offices. It was also near a bistro, the Café de la
Mairie, on the place Saint-Sulpice, where Camus liked to pause to read the
newspaper. Slightly to the north were the boulevard Saint-Germain's cafés
and brasseries, and to the south, the Luxembourg Garden, where Camus
would walk with the twins, who loved the merry-go-rounds, puppets, and
donkey rides.

In this domestic setting, Camus was quickly irritated by Francine's
mother, and would complain, "I don't have a mother-in-law, I've got three."
When exasperated, he would call Madame Faure "Tartuffe." Fernande
Faure always took good care of the children, giving them a slap when necessary. Camus had the impression that she was stifling his wife, but he kept
quiet about it, and in any case he was not usually present, what with all his
trips to the country, the mountains, and abroad.

At the rue Madame apartment, Camus installed a divan in the office,
where he worked mornings before going to Gallimard. During his absences,
Francine would practice the piano, and when a friend suggested how nice it
must be to have a musical wife, Camus grumbled, "If you had to swallow six
hours of Bach a day, you wouldn't say that."

Although he was only a part-time father, he tried to fill the paternal
role by telling his children stories, such as how he was born "in the mover's
wagon" that transported his mother to Mondovi in 1913. He spoke to the

twins about his mother, whom they saw very little, although at Christmastime Madame Camus sent bags of candy for the children and blood sausage for Albert from Algiers.

Tender but strict, Camus loved his children, who were symbols of hope and innocence for him. He playfully called the twins "Plague and Cholera" as they all sang rounds together. Jean resembled his father physically and his mother psychologically. He played the piano well, and Camus and Francine were proud of his musical abilities. Catherine was more even-tempered than her brother, good at gymnastics (Camus worried about her being too much of a tomboy) and she was gifted in French composition. Her little bespectacled face was funny and serious at the same time. Camus decided that his daughter was open-minded and decisive and would have no problems in later life but he worried about Jean's introversion. Camus could not conceive of his son being different than he was, so he forced the boy to play soccer when Jean would have much preferred to spend his time playing chess. In a very Algerian way, Camus wanted to "make a man of" the boy. He was worried about Jean's health, and the fact that he was "raised by women," although the boy's amusing comments would sometimes reassure his parents. Once when his mother asked him if he hadn't anything to do, the boy replied, "It isn't amusing to do nothing when there's nothing to do." And once when the word "God" was mentioned, Jean asked, "What exactly do you mean by that?"

Catherine was enamored of her father, whom she would call "the Reassuring One." Jean was close to his grandmother Faure and his aunt Christiane, who spoiled the children with toys, which did not please Camus. Nor was he happy when Michel Gallimard smothered them with playthings. Camus complained as usual, "Michel, you'll never understand, because you have no experience of poverty." When the children were too old for teddy bears, Camus preferred to give them "useful" gifts, even for Christmas, like overcoats, books, records, and other "honorable objects," as he called them.

While playing with the children, Camus would give them lectures about not spending money thoughtlessly and how they should respect the servants and polish their own shoes. At mealtimes they had to serve themselves, not be served by the maid, and had to finish everything on their plates, especially greens, leaving nothing behind. Camus could not understand why it took Jean a full two minutes to reply to a dinnertime question like "Would you care for a second helping of potatoes?" There were no elbows on the table, no cursing or fighting. During meals he would remind them of a rule of silence. The children would chant the rule in chorus, followed by a mock "minute of silence," interrupted by their laughter.

Camus preferred a secular education for the children and refused to enroll Catherine and Jean in the prestigious neighborhood private schools, the Collège Stanislas, for the Catholic upper classes, or the Ecole Alsacienne. He wanted them to go to public schools, even though they were overcrowded, particularly because the children would eat lunch at school and escape the feminine atmosphere at home for a little.

Camus used authority with the twins, and he knew how to be severe, but he also listened to them and did not pretend to be infallible. He allowed himself to be criticized, which gave them the impression that children's opinions were as valuable as adults'. He taught them to be civil and respectful of others and wanted them to work hard at school. If Jean got bad grades, Camus told him, "I'm going to make you an apprentice in a garage." He did not scold Catherine when she declared that she wanted to celebrate her first communion, but only asked, "Why? Because you want a pretty dress and presents, or because you believe in God?" She admitted that it was because she wanted the presents, and her father replied, "Isn't that marvelous!" and the subject was dropped.

To his children, Camus never showed his often rigid public face, but he did teach them moral lessons, such as that lies can kill. He often told his friends that he was not made for marriage, but he never said that he was not made to be a father. Never letting on to his children that he had been or still was ill, Camus often joked about the subject with Michel: they would indulge in macabre humor over the idea that they both should get life insurance, but because of the state of their lungs, no company would be foolish enough to insure them. And they would tell Janine, "Of course we'll die before you do, so you can have us embalmed and put us both in the living room and come to talk to us every night."

Francine was an excellent mother, and she never complained, even during her bouts with depression. Whenever Camus was staying away from the rue Madame, he would try to visit his children every Thursday at noon, so that they could show him their grades after lunch. Although he would speak quietly, he could be severe if they were not up to his expectations.

In 1950 and 1951, Camus rebelled against the marital tensions at the apartment on the rue Madame. He felt guilty, but he also believed that every person should be free in his life; he did not want to hurt anyone, but he was doing so in spite of himself. To his children, Camus seemed serene and joyful, but he confessed to Maria that he "always had the feeling of being at high sea, my heart threatened by a regal happiness." He admitted that although he sought harmony and balance in his life, he needed to get there "by the steepest paths, disorders, and struggles." Often he could not bear himself: "For entire days I have the most frightful opinion of myself."

His life was still his work: The first six months of 1951 were devoted to finishing *L'Homme révolté*. It was complicated to write, to be a part-time father, and to be faithful, even to "the Unique One," Maria Casarès. The center of his private life remained Maria, whom he called "the genius of my life," although he continued to have fleeting relationships, often with actresses.

Tragic events Camus tended to keep to himself in the form of dry entries to his *Carnets*, where he noted down on June 11, 1951: "Letter from Régine Junier announcing her suicide." Régine, the elderly milliner who had sent so many generous packages to Camus and his family from America, had ended her life. Generalizing ironically about the somber events of the past year, Camus wrote, "1950 Man—he fornicated and read the newspapers."

To flee the rue Madame apartment, Camus used the pretext of research for his essay. Three years before, he had announced to his publisher that it was "almost finished," adding, "No novel in sight, not for a long while." The idea of revolt had obsessed Camus since at least 1943. In 1945, he had published a fifteen-page article, "Remarks on Revolt," in the magazine *L'Existence*, in which he asked, "What is a man who revolts? First of all, it's a man who says no. But if he refuses, he does not only renounce something, he is also saying yes. Let us examine the moment of revolt in detail." These words were repeated almost identically in the first chapter of the book, *L'Homme révolté*.

He dedicated the work to Jean Grenier, who had greatly influenced his political thought by pushing Camus to join the Communist Party before the war, while Grenier wrote an essay against mental orthodoxy. In his book, Camus sought to examine the revolutionary orthodoxy of the pseudo-Communist left wing, who took Karl Marx as their messiah. When Camus and Grenier met at the Paris suburb of Fontenay-aux-Roses, Grenier had read the manuscript of *L'Homme révolté* and he told him that the book was in "the reactionary line of [Charles] Maurras," the Fascist leader of the Action Française movement in the 1930s. Camus replied, "Too bad, but one has to say what one thinks." Then Grenier observed that he would make a lot of enemies with the book, and Camus said, "Yes, no doubt my friendships are not very solid."

For Camus, this work of artistic and political theory was in the nature of a confidence. As he wrote once in a letter, "Our generation has had no other faith than in revolution, but the tragedy is that even when it succeeds, revolution shows us a horrible face." Camus compared the French, who had lived through four bloody revolutions in 150 years, to the British, who Camus erroneously believed had never experienced a popular rebellion over the same period of time. For Camus, France lagged behind England, "an indubitable social democracy, the most advanced in the world along with the Scandinavians. Revolution is thus not an end in itself and cannot be an object of faith, but rather a means for serving justice and truth."

Camus believed that when a revolution was not serving its aims, its failure must be pointed out; but at the end of the 1940s, progressive French intellectuals, such as those who wrote for Sartre's *Les Temps Modernes*, chose to ignore Communist police-state abuses and gulags in order not to imperil the revolution in general. Realizing that these people were lying to themselves, Camus would say, "I hate my epoch." He did not hate realities, but rather the "lies in which they wallow." Camus saw that the USSR was a land of slaves, and yet its "concentration-camp rule is adored as an instrument of liberation and a school for future happiness." He vowed to combat this lie until the end of his life, and summed up his feelings in the sentence "We don't need hope, we only need truth."

By 1951, Camus was very isolated from the left-wing intelligentsia, although some French intellectuals were gradually leaving the Communist Party. He did his best to speed up this trend by telling with irony how in the Soviet embassy in Paris, he had heard an official bragging about how the USSR had made a "great effort," because instead of the ten thousand political prisoners the country used to have, there were now "far fewer."

In *L'Homme révolté*, Camus tried to incorporate his experiences, knowledge, and readings in sociology, literature, and philosophy, as well as politics. He had already stated some years before that he did not mind being caught contradicting himself: "I don't want to be a philosophical genius." He felt that past revolutionaries had justified murder in the name of future happiness, but now he felt it was essential to find a new humanism. He asked the question: How did certain men accept collective murder in the name of revolt, which became a revolution? Militants who had rightfully revolted became professional revolutionaries who created our century's totalitarian governments.

Camus's book analyzed his epoch and its evils. He felt that nowadays, philosophy could be used for everything, "even changing murderers into judges." Through revolt, man can free himself from his condition and recreate the unity of the human race: "I revolt, therefore we are," to paraphrase Descartes. Once man gets rid of God, he can enter history by himself, and revolt becomes revolution.

Some readers found his arguments obtuse, but Camus carefully divided his study into five main subjects: man in revolt, metaphysical revolt, historic revolt, artistic revolt, and, finally, what the author called "thought from the South." This latter part was less analytical and more lyrical, in a personal spirit. He contrasted a Mediterranean sense of measure with a totalitarian imbalance, which he saw as Nordic, and he sang the praises of measure, as he had for listeners at Algiers's Maison de la Culture in 1937.

Camus blamed German thinkers, who saw history as determined by irresistible forces, for our century's intolerance, and for the intellectual and political absolutism that encouraged inquisitions. An early German villain in this respect was the philosopher G. W. F. Hegel, an ardent defender of nationalism who made success in history the moral principle of all group conduct, according to Camus. This legacy was continued by Karl Marx, the Marxists, and the Communists, and Hegel's precedent made possible propaganda's lies, the idealizing of wars and the spilling of blood. Camus's study of Hegel was hardly academic, based mostly on a selective reading of excerpts and of studies by experts like Jean Hippolyte and Alexandre Kojève; and his reading of Marx was also fragmentary, mainly from a standard anthology.

Some of his theories Camus based on his experiences, but mostly he relied on what he read in books, as his own revolutionary experience was limited. As a member of the Algerian Communist Party, he saw Communists use ruses and double-talk when confronted by Algerian nationalists. Camus's revolutionary friends like Nicolas Lazarévitch and Boris Souvarine explained to him how in the USSR the Bolsheviks betrayed the pure revolutionary ideal, and they urged him to read books of testimony about Soviet gulags. Camus had the unusual merit of actually listening to the critical witnesses of the Russian Revolution, who were plentiful but almost entirely ignored by the French intellectual world.

Camus tried in vain to get works by Boris Souvarine, "the first man disillusioned with communism," published. In June 1950, he signed a "Manifesto of Free Men" drawn up during a Congress of Cultural Freedom in Berlin, declaring that "intellectual freedom implies first of all freedom of thought and word, above all if these are in opposition to ruling powers." The petition declared that the theory and action of totalitarian states were "the greatest threat to confront humanity in the course of civilized history." Adding a Camus touch, it said, "Deprived of the right to say no, man becomes a slave." At the beginning of *L'Homme révolté*, Camus wrote, "A slave who had received orders all his life often finds a new ruling power unacceptable."

Camus's book mentions Marx often, Lenin a few times, and Stalin not at all. He felt that in its recent form, the bloody spirit of revolution was only a forum where "absurdity outdid itself." He sought a new purity in revolt, which would give a new coherence to action. *L'Homme révolté* may be seen as a theoretical illustration of *La Peste*, as part of the same cycle as *L'Etat de siège* and *Les Justes*. The heart of the work is what was then a radically original questioning of revolution in general and the French and Russian revolutions in particular.

This was a brave project, especially for a highly visible left-wing writer, who had always been taught at school that revolution equaled democracy, and that any criticism of revolution must be reactionary. To criticize the French Revolution was to conspire against freedom, just as in the 1950s

Marxist historiography dominated university studies in France, which turned the Russian Bolsheviks into the heirs of the French Jacobins. By intuition rather than by reasoning or research, Camus linked the French period of postrevolutionary Terror to contemporary Soviet terror. Thus he took on a whole mythology of the French educational system and the left-wing intelligentsia.

In his critique of the French Revolution, Camus attacked sacrosanct historical figures like Robespierre and Saint-Just, who were admired by nearly every French lycée student. He demolished Saint-Just's "absolute tone, that cascade of peremptory affirmations, that sententious, axiomatic style.... His sentences purr like the very wisdom of a nation.... It's the guillotine style." He also rejected Saint-Just's fanaticism and the Jacobin revolution's cynical attempt to create a religion of virtue.

Camus even opposed the necessity of King Louis XVI's execution, universally accepted by historians as necessary: "It is a repugnant scandal to present as a great moment in our history the public murder of a weak and good man. That scaffold does not mark a summit, it must be said." Camus also denounced fashionable literary heroes like the Marquis de Sade, admired by the surrealists, whom he saw as exalting totalitarian societies: "Sade's success in our era can be explained by a dream which he shares with contemporary sensibility: the calling for total freedom, and cold-hearted dehumanization operated by intelligence." Camus found Sade's novels frightfully monotonous, but he did admit that the marquis opposed the death penalty as much as Camus did.

Camus was less justified in attacking the poets Arthur Rimbaud and the Comte de Lautréamont, who wrote *Les Chants de Maldoror*. He criticized Rimbaud for being a man of revolt in his poems but not in his life as a trader in Abyssinia in later years: "The magus, seer, untouchable convict continually locked up as a galley slave, the semideity on a godless earth, always carried eight kilograms of gold in a belt squeezing his belly, which he complained gave him dysentery," and he suggested that Rimbaud's young revolutionary admirers should "die of shame at the mere notion of that belt." He scorned Rimbaud for being an adolescent in revolt who became a colonialist adult attached to his gold; but one critic replied to this argument by asking, "Where did Camus want Rimbaud to carry his gold?"

Camus never claimed to be a specialist in poetry, and he didn't hesitate to call Lautréamont's *Chants de Maldoror* "the book of an almost-brilliant junior-high-school student." Lautréamont was an icon of the surrealist movement, and Camus also criticized the surrealists, although more politely than he treated the Communists. He admitted that André Breton, "the pope of surrealism," was a fine love poet, but he took Breton's statement literally that the simplest surrealist act was to go down to the street with a revolver in hand

and shoot at random into a crowd. Camus was horrified by the stupidity of that remark and felt that Breton must regret it by now.

Since *Le Mythe de Sisyphe*, Camus and the surrealists were also in open disagreement over the question of suicide, and Camus disagreed with the views of a surrealist poet, René Crevel, who was gay and tubercular and killed himself in despair about his health problems. Possibly ignorant of the reason for Crevel's suicide, Camus showed no empathy. He blamed the surrealists for speaking "of suicide as a solution, and Crevel felt that this solution was the 'most realistically fair and definitive.' . . . To celebrate self-destruction to the point of rushing to do it in the company of others does honor to no one."

He even accused the surrealists of being the accomplices of Bolshevism and Jacobinism, but in fact, the 1950s surrealists were a diffuse and fragmented bunch, unlike the 1920s group, and they were not guilty of complicity with the Communist Party. No sooner had Breton returned from his wartime exile in America than he denounced the Soviet regime. Camus used surrealism, aspects of which displeased him, to try to destroy communism, but his excessively negative attack was motivated almost as much as by personal hatred as by rigorous arguments.

At the end of *L'Homme révolté*, Camus praised the lyrical "Mediterranean thought" of Plato and Saint Augustine, as opposed to Northern European thought, personified by Hegel and Marx. Solemnly and pompously, Camus declared, "Cast into ignoble Europe where the most proud races die, starved of beauty and friendship, we other Mediterraneans still live in the same light. In the heart of the European night, solar thought, double-faced civilization (with northern and southern faces) awaits its dawn. But it already illuminates the roads to true mastery."

The essay ended not with reasoning but with grandiloquent rhetoric that sought to defeat nihilism: "At this time when each of us must work to start his efforts over again, to earn what he already owns in spite of history: his field's lean harvest and brief earthly love . . . we must break with the present epoch and its adolescent furors. The bow will bend backwards and the wood will squeal, and at the summit of the highest tension there will spring forth the energy of a forthright arrow, in the straightest and freest fashion."

As a pioneering attack on Stalinist communism, *L'Homme révolté* was published before other notable books, such as Raymond Aron's *L'Opium des intellectuels*, and twenty-five years before Jean-François Revel's *La Tentation totalitaire*. At the beginning of the 1950s, Camus was the only widely known French writer coming from the left wing to take such decisive positions. At the beginning of the summer of 1951 he corrected proofs of *L'Homme révolté*. It remained to be seen whether readers would give more weight to the arguments of a novelist than to those of an economist or sociologist.

Before *L'Homme révolté* was published in October 1951, the magazine *Les Cahiers du Sud* published Camus's chapter on Lautréamont. He was not surprised to read an outraged response from André Breton in the October 13 issue of the weekly *Arts*. The pope of surrealism saw Camus as a conformist who had committed the fundamental crime of attacking Lautréamont's poetry, "the most brilliant work of modern times." A week later, *Arts* published Camus's reply, explaining that he was neither conformist nor resigned, but felt that nihilism "generates conformity and servitude, and is against the still-valuable teachings of true revolt." A bitter controversy began, with Breton asking an interviewer in the November 16 issue of *Arts*, "What is this phantom of revolt that Camus is striving to promote and hide behind? A revolt in which 'measure' has been introduced?" Camus's book did advocate a certain sense of "measure" in revolt, which Breton saw as a contradiction in terms. Camus offered yet another response a week later, saying, "Breton limits his insufficient philosophical critique to Marxism. . . . [He] would prefer that in today's world decline, Marxists were the only guilty party. That's why he gives my book the privilege of being important, because it contains a critique of Marxism, but that would be too easy. There is no good or bad nihilism, only a long and fierce adventure in which we are all allies."

Along with Louis Aragon, Breton was one of the few living writers attacked by Camus in *L'Homme révolté*. He did not mention Malraux in his essay, which Camus privately explained was because Malraux was still alive, while Breton was "practically dead": "I didn't speak of Malraux in *L'Homme révolté* because I relied on works that were already finished as examples and illustrations. The only living man whose attitudes I studied turned out to be André Breton, but one may consider that surrealism already belongs to history. . . . As for Malraux, he is still in operation."

A few days before *L'Homme révolté* appeared, Camus lunched with a friend at the brasserie of the Lutétia Hotel in Paris, and before parting he said, "Let's shake hands, because in a few days, not many people will want to shake my hand." The book was launched successfully, with a first printing of 16,800 copies on November 2, 1951, and 11,000 more copies printed two weeks later. Two further printings made a total of 60,800 books sold in the first four months. Interest declined thereafter, and the fifth printing had to wait until February 1954.

Camus was not surprised by attacks from the Communist-influenced press. The writer Albert Béguin said, "Too bad, but your book is a success with the right wing!" Camus felt that Béguin's comment was grotesque: if a right-winger happened to say the earth is round, was it necessary to deny that fact? He left the scene of the polemics when his mother broke her leg; he rushed to Algeria to be at her bedside, writing home to Francine: "I arrived in a pouring rain, typically Algerian, which is still continuing. Mother had already gone into the clinic, and I only left her for a few hours to get some sleep. They operated on her this morning, and everything went well. . . . She's sleeping right now, and her general condition is excellent. She was very brave and sensible and I love her. . . . As for myself, I feel tired, but I suppose everything's better now. I must say that since this book came out, I've been in terrible shape, and have been getting worse right up to these last few days. I don't know if I can continue to put up with this business and its solitary struggles."

On November 22, he described his state of mind to Maria: "It's my hesitation over what to do and say now, and there are days when I prefer to have precisely nothing to do or say. Maybe it's a kind of fear when faced by my vocation, but I never felt this fear before, which may come from fatigue, and maybe also because I can see more clearly now that the demands that have got me this far have no limits except exhaustion and the final plunge. Yet without these demands, I wouldn't be anything at all, and neither would my work. I sometimes feel an exhausted dizziness when I think about the future."

Mamaine Koestler wrote to say that her favorite chapter in the book was "Revolt and Art," and Camus agreed, stating that he had abolished literary realism in the Socialist style: "To be truly realistic, a description is forced to be endless. . . . Realism is endless enumeration."

In the right-wing *Figaro Littéraire* of November 24, Camus's friend Jean Guéhenno praised the book, putting it on a level with with Malraux's *Condition humaine*. Guéhenno felt that Camus was a humanist; and although the writer's ideas on Sade and Lautréamont worried him, he nevertheless realized that Camus was "on the high road." Malraux himself was less measured, telling Gallimard colleagues that Camus "was right to demolish Breton and even Rimbaud."

Although the book was a commercial success, Camus complained to his friend Ilo de Franceschi in February 1952, "*L'Homme révolté* is a book that sells but isn't read, or almost not. Whether it has stirred anything up is unclear, although it has given rise to bubbles which have burst quickly." On February 10, Jean Amrouche sent him a letter which was partly critical, and Camus replied evasively, "I'd like to discuss it with you one of these days." Offering as an excuse for his lack of time the fact that unlike other French intellectuals, who were obsessed by France's problems in Southeast Asia, in his case "events in North Africa have created an anguish that weighs on me almost nonstop."

On February 22, Camus saw Sartre at the Salle Wagram in Paris at a rally to plead for Spanish labor union members who had been sentenced to death by Franco's tribunals. Despite their disagreements, Camus had suggested that André Breton be invited to sit on the honorary panel. Camus met Sartre in the street afterwards, and they want to have a drink. Sartre told friends that he was embarrassed because it was "a pain in the ass" to have to tell Camus that there would be a bad review of his book in *Les Temps Modernes*. According to Simone de Beauvoir, Sartre had wanted a review that was firm but courteous, and had assigned the critic Francis Jeanson to the job.

Meanwhile, the book was winning approval abroad from the political philosopher Hannah Arendt, who wrote to say, "I've read *L'Homme révolté*, which I like very much," and the Polish novelist Witold Gombrowicz, then living in Argentina, who had read Camus's book and asked his friend the poet Czeslaw Milosz to send Camus copies of his own books in French translation as an act of homage. Gombrowicz wrote to Camus, "I believe we are fighting the same battle."

During his Easter vacation of 1952, he wrote to Janine and Michel Gallimard ("Dear Recto and Verso") to say that he was pleased to be far from Paris, at Le Panelier: "Everything is going well, except for my work and my mood. I swim as the cuttlefish does, in the dark, and I play at being one of the Dead Souls." Finally, in May 1952, Francis Jeanson's article appeared in *Les Temps Modernes*, twenty violent pages which began by reproaching Camus for the good reviews his book had received in *Le Monde* and *L'Observateur*, saying that he "should be worried" by praise from these quarters. Jeanson, a specialist in Sartre's philosophy, complained that Camus's thought was "infinitely flexible and malleable, apt to acquire many different forms . . . vague humanism with just a touch of anarchism." He praised the book from a literary point of view, but admitted that he had no use for the "thirst for moderation" in Camus's self-assured art. Jeanson was shocked by Camus's view of historical revolt, such as comparing Louis XVI's execution to the Passion of Christ, and felt that the writer's dismissal of Hegel and Marx was so extreme that it "denied any role at all to historical and economic elements in the birth of revolutions." Dismissing Camus's approach as "the divinization" of individual man, and rejecting his idea that Marxist thought led to Stalinism, Jeanson wrote: "Stalin was the one who created Stalinism." Camus was described as a pseudophilosopher who had written a pseudohistory of revolutions: "*L'Homme révolté* is above all a missed opportunity to write a great book."

Sartre's secretary, Jean Cau, let the stunned Camus know that *Les Temps Modernes* would of course print his reply to the review, and Camus polished a sixteen-page essay which appeared in the August issue of the magazine. In his first draft, Camus mentioned Jeanson by name, but then he decided it was better to demolish his opponent by not actually naming him. As was his habit when writing letters to the editor, Camus began his reply with "Monsieur le Directeur," which exasperated Sartre, who expected a less grandiose formula, like "Dear friend" or "Dear Sartre." Camus declared, "One doesn't decide the truth of an idea according to whether it is left- or right-wing, and even less by what the left or right wing decides to make of it. . . . In fact, if the truth seemed to me to be with the right wing, I would go along with it." Camus had already received hurtful reviews from the far-right and right-center press, and he "found offensive" Jeanson's comments on his literary style, which suggested that "a beautiful style is forcibly right-wing, and left-wing writers must write in slang and gobbledegook. . . . If it is true that my ideas are inconsistent, then it's better to write them well in order to limit the damage. Imagine if confused thoughts had to be read in a dismaying style—better to call it a day!"

He told "Monsieur le Directeur" that he was weary of receiving lessons from critics who "never placed anything but his armchair in the direction of history." This was a coded reference to the quip Camus had made when he discovered Sartre sleeping in one of the orchestra seats of the Comédie-Française during the liberation of Paris, when the philosopher was officially responsible for "liberating" the theater.

Sartre felt obliged to respond to this provocation, and the result was nineteen vitriolic pages mixing personal remarks with criticism, and practicing excommunication with even more verve than the pope of surrealism, André Breton, Sartre began his excommunication tenderly, by stating, "My dear Camus, our friendship was not easy, but I shall miss it. . . ." Sartre said he had hoped their disagreement might be about basic issues and not "wounded vanity. . . . You have so deliberately blamed me, and in such an unpleasant tone, that I cannot remain silent without losing face." Sartre announced that he would now treat Camus with total frankness, for the first time since they had met. He first attacked Camus's personality, his "somber self-importance . . . vulnerability and . . . mournful immoderation." He claimed that Camus had lost touch with his literary characters Meursault and Sisyphus, and that now "a violent and ceremonious dictatorship has installed itself in you, based on an abstract bureaucracy and claiming to impose moral law." Sartre hated Camus's preachy, self-assured stance: "Tell me, Camus, by what mystery may we not discuss your works without taking away humanity's reasons for existing?"

In his reply, Camus had called Sartre bourgeois, and the philosopher retorted, "I don't think you are the brother of the unemployed Communist worker in Bologna, Italy, or the poor daily laborer in Southeast Asia fighting against Bao Dai's colonialists. . . . You may indeed have once been poor, but you are poor no longer. You are a bourgeois, like Jeanson and myself." The "may indeed have once been" was a nasty crack, since Sartre knew very well about Camus's humble origins, but Sartre felt that Camus had no more right than anyone else to speak in the name of the working class: "From this distance, you resemble Saint Vincent de Paul or a nun who has taken a vow of poverty. . . . You see, I have heard too many paternalist speeches not to be wary of your kind of fraternalism. Poverty has not charged you with any kind of mission."

Sartre sensed a form of blackmail in the methods of Camus's letter: "I don't reproach you for its pomp, since that comes naturally to you, but for the smoothness with which you handle your indignation." Camus's reply had seemed too well written to him, and the references to "Monsieur le Directeur" were absurd "when everyone knows we have been linked for ten years." Sartre blamed Camus for not even naming Jeanson in his reply, thus dehumanizing his critic, as if Camus were according himself some kind of superiority: "What if your book simply shows your philosophical incompetence? What if it is made up of secondhand knowledge, hastily collected? . . . And if your reasoning is inaccurate? And if your thoughts are vague and banal? . . . At least I have this in common with Hegel, that you haven't read either one of us. What a mania you have for not going back to the original sources. . . . I don't dare advise you to go back to *Being and Nothingness*, since reading it would be needlessly difficult for you. You hate difficulties of thought and you hastily decree that there is nothing to understand, in order to avoid reproaches of not having understood things, before they develop."

Since Camus felt that Soviet prison camps were a fundamental problem, Sartre pointed out that, "yes, Camus, I find these camps just as unacceptable as you do. But I find equally unacceptable the use that the so-called bourgeois press makes of them every day." Sartre felt he was taking the long-term view by believing that every anti-Communist was "a dog." He pointed out that Camus's approach could not be applied to the situation in Southeast Asia: "If we apply your principles, the Vietminh are colonized and therefore slaves, but because they are Communists they are also tyrants at the same time."

Despite his harsh rhetoric, Sartre left open a door for friendship with Camus: "You have represented for us the admirable conjunction of a person, his action, and his creative work, and tomorrow you may be this person again. . . . How we liked you then." He offered the final death-blow: "You are only half-alive among us. . . . If you find me cruel, have no fear, soon I shall speak of myself, and in the same tone." Sartre was plugging his next book, the semiautobiographical *Les Mots*. Sartre left the pages of *Les Temps Modernes* open to Camus if he wished to reply again, but Sartre promised to say no more on the subject: "I have stated what you were for me and what you are now. But whatever you may say or do in return, I refuse to fight with you. . . . I hope that our silence will soon make this polemic forgotten." However, Jeanson wanted to have the real last word in the magazine, and added twenty-nine pages of further insults, such as that Camus was more concerned with God than with his fellow man.

The hard core of disagreement between Camus and Sartre was communism, or "socialist realism." Although Sartre was not a member of the Communist Party, he still believed in socialism with a human face. Sartre continued the myth of the bourgeois as liar, swine, exploiter, social climber, and philistine who might in theory approve of the rights of man but was in fact a colonialist. By denouncing Camus as bourgeois, he made him into an accomplice of the exploiting class. Sartre admitted that he too was bourgeois, but he tried to distance himself from this world.

Sartre accused Camus of secondhand knowledge of Marx, but it is not clear that Sartre's own scholarship was any less shoddy: Raymond Aron, who had read Marx thoroughly, maintained in his *L'Opium des intellectuels* that on the subject, Camus and Sartre were "equally incompetent." Aron, the former editorial writer for *Combat*, now working for *Le Figaro*, was generally considered the most informed right-wing thinker, and thought *L'Homme révolté* was simply a bad book: "The main lines of argument are lost in a series of disconnected studies. The writing style and moralistic tone hardly permit any philosophical rigor." Aron felt that Camus's actual ideas expressed in the book were banal and reasonable, and the polemic with Sartre was ridiculous because neither man was a Communist: "They both recognize evil on both sides. Camus wants to denounce both sides, whereas Sartre . . . only wants to denounce the West, but does not deny the reality of evil on the other side. To be sure, this is a nuance, but one that casts doubt on Sartre's entire philosophy." Aron had once been a friend of Sartre's, but never of Camus's, of whom he came to approve more in later years, admitting that "Camus not only objected to certain aspects of Soviet reality, but he also saw the Communist regime as total tyranny, which had been inspired and justified by a philosophy. . . . [Camus reproached revolutionaries] for sacrificing living people to a supposed historical good, a historical good whose exact image was contradictory and in any case incompatible with existentialism."

Camus and Sartre both wanted a new, more humane social order, but Sartre remained a violent revolutionary in theory, while Camus was a man in revolt who rejected revolutionary excess, whether Jacobin or Communist in origin. Sartre enjoyed far more prestige among the French leftist press than did Camus, and the two friends parted much as they had met: As a critic on the *Alger Républicain*, Camus had admired *La Nausée* and *Le Mur* but felt wary about the philosopher who wrote them; and in his essay "Explication de *L'Etranger*," Sartre admired Camus as a writer but gave him poor marks as a thinker. He really despised Camus intellectually, telling Jean Cau that Camus was "a kind of schoolteacher, worthless in philosophy, but radiating a moralizing hubris."

Sartre saw Camus as a "vedette" of French thought, using the two meanings of that word in French, a media "star" and also a "little patrol boat," whereas Sartre saw himself as "an unsinkable battleship," according to Cau.

Chapter Forty   **In a Glass Bowl**

On September 5, 1952, Camus wrote to Francine: "I am anguished by Paris, as always when I get back here. *Les Temps Modernes* came out with twenty pages of response from Sartre and thirty from Jeanson. Even before the magazine appeared in bookstores, excerpts were printed in *L'Observateur*. The affair is well, if not elegantly, launched. As for the replies, one is nasty and the other foolish. Neither answers my questions, except for Sartre at one point, but the fifty pages are deliberately insulting. Thus I have the pleasure of being called a cop and a ham actor, among other things. All told, it's a long disquisition on my pride, which nevertheless has been decimated by all this, as you can see, and that will delight a lot of people. Decidedly, this book has cost me dearly, and today I only have doubts about it, and about myself, who resembles it too much."

On the seventeenth, he wrote again to his wife: "I've lived almost alone all this time, with somber thoughts, a bit somnolent. I'm trying to arrange all this as best as I can, as one tries to find a good position on an uncomfortable bed, and it isn't always easy. I understand that they are just discussing my work, and I was the first one to find it debatable, even on the deepest levels. But I have nothing to say if they are accusing me personally, because then every defense becomes a self-apology. This explosion of long-suppressed hatred is striking, and it proves that these people were never my friends and that I always offended them by what I believe, hence this nasty spewing and incapacity to be generous. There is no other explanation for the extreme vulgarity of these attacks, which I won't reply to, because it's impossible to do so. I just have to try to tell true from false in the midst of all this sludge, and not be vexed or humiliated by other people's logic. I must resist the temptation of despising too much, as well as of not despising enough. I must know how to break with others (yes indeed), but without resentment. Such acrobatics are not easy, but they are my destiny, while unfortunately I have many things to arrange and less life energy than before."

Camus showed his irritation to friends such as Jeanne Terracini, whom he spoke to after returning to the rue Madame apartment, confiding his exasperation with Sartre: "What do you want me to do about it, punch him in the kisser? He's too little!"

Les Temps modernes's circulation increased during the battle, which was covered by the popular press with headlines like "Spat Among the Existentialists" and "Sartre vs. Camus," to the point where Camus told Urbain Polge, "Enough is enough. I'm not going to keep on answering and give them more publicity." To Polge, Camus privately wondered if he had really been right in the affair. Unlike the lighthearted and self-confident Sartre, Camus was plagued by painful regrets, constantly casting into doubt his own talent and reasoning power. Robert Gallimard, one of the few people to know and appreciate both Sartre and Camus, called the breakup of their friendship the end of a love story.

Francine and Maria loyally tried to help Camus forget the controversy. Although he did not speak about it directly to the Unique One, he once arrived at her apartment on the rue de Vaugirard stifling from an attack of claustrophobia and almost in tears. Maria advised him to try to look at it from a distance, but he was unable to do so.

At Gallimard, many colleagues laughed sarcastically about the affair, giving out grades, with Sartre getting an eighteen out of twenty for his response but Camus earning a barely passing ten out of twenty. The day after Sartre's reply was published, Camus made the rounds of the Gallimard offices looking for support, but he found few people willing to agree with him. Gaston, accustomed to putting up stolidly with squabbles among the great, seemed bored by the whole affair. Claude was amused because the affair seemed to distress Michel, Camus's friend. Robert was noncommittal, saying, "I happen to be Sartre's editor at Gallimard and I know that in this debate you'd like people to take sides, but I feel it is strictly your own business." Camus replied, "So let's remain on good terms and not speak about it anymore." Jean Paulhan sent Camus supportive little notes, for which Camus thanked him: "Since I have become, in part thanks to you, what we call a writer, I've always been astonished by my colleagues, sometimes positively so, but today in another way. As ever, I also feel my own inadequacies."

Sartre told Robert Gallimard blithely, "Camus chews me out all the time," but what was a mere anecdote for him had become a drama for Camus. Outside the Gallimard office, Camus kept stumbling on real or imagined Sartre supporters, so he took to avoiding public spots on Saint-Germain-des-Prés. In Montparnasse, he stopped going to restaurants like Le Dome, La Coupole, and La Palette because Sartre often lunched there. Ca-

mus felt himself a pariah in the non-Communist left wing, with every acquaintance a potential enemy, and he tortured himself over it. He noted in
his *Carnets*: "Paris is a jungle, where the beasts are fleabitten. . . . Sartre, as a
man and as a mind, is disloyal."

He considered a second response to Jeanson and Sartre, or an article in
another magazine, but no left-wing magazine sympathized with his point of
view, and although some of the right-wing journals would print him, he did
not want to take that political direction. He considered publishing a pamphlet, and wrote twenty pages, which were destined to remain in a drawer,
written more for himself than for any public: "I wrote *L'Homme révolté* because in the 1940s, I saw men whose system I couldn't explain and whose actions I couldn't understand. In brief, I could not understand how men could
torture others while continuing to look at them. . . ." He felt capitalism "no
longer maintains itself by its virtues, now extinct, but by the spectacular vices
of revolutionary society. That's why I felt it was good and useful to try to
make a reasoned criticism of the only instrument that might free workers, so
that this freedom might be something other than a long and hopeless hoax."
In his private notes, Camus complained, "The time for sedentary artists is
over"—perhaps another reference to Sartre snoozing at the Comédie-
Française. He continued to question the motivations of his enemies, some of
whom used to be his friends: "Each adversary, however repugnant he may
be, is one of our interior voices which we would like to shut up, and as such
we must listen to him in order to correct, adapt, and reaffirm new truths
which we may glimpse this way." In a lugubrious mood, but determined
to bounce back, Camus ended his essay with the observation "Nothing is
useless."

The literary critic Pierre de Boisdeffre asked Camus to participate in a
debate at the Catholic Center for French Intellectuals with Raymond Aron,
among others, but Camus refused, saying, "At this point, the least sentence I
might say will be used in a way that disgusts me in advance. . . . It would be
impossible for me in that case to continue expressing myself with academic
politeness. I am mistaken for a deliberately polite man whom one may insult
in all safety."

Friends and family begged him to drop the subject, but he wrote to
Francine, "I suppose you are all right, but in that case I should let everything
go hang. After all, why should I defend what is my property and my life,
when it would be simplest to abandon it for others to do what they like with
it, to eat, deface, or throw it up. Ganged up all together, they are too much
for me, and in a word, I cannot go on any longer. The best thing for me to
do is to shut up, put earplugs in, and try to work."

In December, he visited Algeria to see his mother and to go on a tour
of regions he had not yet seen in that country's south. He returned to Paris

the following month "bucked up and calmed down. . . . This country and these men always help me to become myself again." But after this pause, he resumed his familiar obsession in letters to friends: "I don't believe in Sartre's honesty anymore. Now I speak about it without anger, but henceforth I know that he and his friends are capable of falsifications and lies."

There were some consolations: René Char wrote to say he thought *L'Homme revolté* was in his opinion Camus's best book so far. Another correspondent was the Polish painter and writer Josef Czapski, who worked to reveal the secret Soviet atrocities at the wartime prison camp of Katyn, and whose book on Soviet prisons, *Terre inhumaine*, had been published in Paris in 1948. Czapski told Camus, "Immediately after the attack that was concentrated on you, I wanted to write to tell you why I love you, and why you have more friends than you might think." In response, Camus went to see a gallery show of Czapski's figurative paintings. He wrote to Czapski to tell him not to worry that his paintings were not avant-garde in style: "It doesn't much matter that you are not in what is called 'the movement,' since these days the movement is not moving much. . . . If the words 'left wing' no longer have much meaning, it's because leftist intellectuals in particular have chosen to be the gravediggers of freedom, which may be seen from the example of *Les Temps Modernes*. That's what must be fought head-on and neutralized."

For a week in mid-December 1952, shortly after the execution for alleged treason of several Czech Communist leaders, Sartre traveled to a Vienna meeting of the Movement for Peace. Camus commented, "Ordinarily, going to Vienna means participating in a cold war act, but going there with a backdrop of eleven hanged men whose names were followed by the word 'Jew' in Czech newspapers is beyond description. . . . Just as our rightwingers were fascinated with Hitler's power, so our leftists are entranced by Communist power, tarted up with the name 'efficiency.' " Three months before Stalin's death, Soviet authorities discovered a so-called plot of Jewish doctors against Stalin and launched a violent anti-Semitic purge in Russia. Camus remarked that French leftist intellectuals' "only disgusting work is to carefully distinguish between good and bad concentration-camp jailers and good and bad anti-Semites. It makes you vomit." And in his *Carnets* he still dwelt on the Sartre polemic: "A noble trade, where one must let oneself be insulted without flinching by a lackey of literature and of the Communist Party! In other, so-called primitive times, at least one had the right to challenge somebody to a duel without ridicule, and to kill him. It was idiotic, of course, but it made insulting less comfortable."

Meanwhile, Camus had become so well known that biographers began to materialize. When one, Roger Quilliot, submitted a study of Camus's "La Mer et les prisons" for the author's approval, he praised the work, adding, "I have removed . . . your references to Sartre for the excellent reason that his books never influenced me, unlike those of Malraux, which you mention." Camus still felt that *L'Homme révolté* was his strongest work: "It's a book that has provoked lots of noise, and which has earned me more enemies than friends (at least the former have screamed louder than the latter). I'm like everyone else, I don't like to have enemies, but if I had to do it all over again, I would rewrite my book just as it is. It's the book of mine which I value the most."

Despite tension with Francine at home, the year 1953 did not begin too badly. Mamaine Koestler sent him a Burberry raincoat from London, which he claimed made him look like Humphrey Bogart. Camus became friendly with Robert Ceresol, the associate director of the Mathurins Theater in Paris, who asked the writer to organize a small theater festival to be held in the courtyard of the castle of Angers by the banks of the Maine River. Feeling abandoned by French literati, Camus found warmth, friendship, and complicity among theater people, but as he had no inspiration to write any new plays, Maria helped Camus to translate and adapt the seventeenth-century Spanish baroque playwright Pedro Calderón's *Devotion to the Cross*.

At the same time he mechanically compiled an uneven collection of press articles he had written from 1948 to 1953, called *Actuelles II*; it was Gallimard policy to allow their most distinguished authors to publish collections of their occasional essays, such as Paul Valéry's *Variétés*, and Sartre's *Situations*. Camus's earlier such volume, *Actuelles I*, dedicated to René Char, had assembled his articles from *Combat* and had more unity than the hodge-podge that followed in 1953, which was largely devoted to the Sartre polemic.

He also reprinted a preface to his friend Alfred Rosmer's book, *Moscow Under Lenin*, to show that he remained anchored to the left wing. To those who claimed that he had become reactionary or had lost hope, Camus stated, "Some men, like [Rosmer], have known how to survive the collapse of their hopes by surviving twice: first by refusing to abandon themselves to the comforts of so-called temporary servitude, as many revolutionaries do, and secondly by refusing to despair about the power of revolt and freedom which is at work in every one of us." In the same essay, Camus predicted, "True liberation is certainly not for tomorrow, but nihilism already belongs to the past, even if its last screams still echo in our newspapers and magazines." He also added, on a more personal note: "Creation, which is still possible, becomes more necessary than ever. The contradictions of history and art are not resolved in a purely logical synthesis but in a living creation."

During these painful months, Camus rewrote literary essays which would be published in the collection *L'Eté*, and after the combat over rational ideas, he found a lyric breath once again by returning to the subject of Algeria. The Angers festival went well, but his friend the actor and director

Marcel Herrand died two days before it opened, and Camus returned to Paris sad and weary, not knowing what he would do for the rest of the summer of 1953. Francine and the twins were vacationing with the Polges in the south of France. Camus wrote to Mamaine Koestler about his troubled marriage, "I must make a decision that I don't have the heart to make, but that's childish, and we are all adults."

In the fall, Francine's mother, Fernande, suffered a bad sprain, and Francine herself was weary, so Camus wrote to Mamaine, "I am living in the middle of a hospital, but happily, I have enough vitality for ten people." He wrote to the Polges on October 10, "Francine stays in her room and sleeps most of the time. My mother-in-law with her leg stretched out looks like the Viceroy of Peru in [Piero della Francesca's painting] *The Coach of the Holy Sacrament*. By some miracle, Catherine has become a silent adult, and I wander around, conscious of my uselessness. I must tell you, however, to make up for Francine's letter, that I am not worried about her. She is suffering from a moderate depression as I see it, which doesn't mean that it's a pleasant one for us. Continued remedies and rest will be enough to cure her definitively." Francine was dejected, speaking very little and repeating herself when she did. On October 21, Camus wrote, "She is my greatest worry. . . . Her depression has developed and she is receiving treatment now." A bit later, he felt that she had improved: "She hasn't blossomed totally, but there is a little springtime, tentative but undeniable. She is already talking about going to Oran, which is a good sign."

Meanwhile in Paris, Simone Hié, who on occasion still introduced herself as "Madame Camus," had married a certain Dr. Cottenceau and was living at 57 boulevard Saint-Michel. Since 1947 the police had caught her several times buying heroin and morphine. She had persuaded doctors to write her prescriptions for morphine pellets, as she had done in Algeria before the war. Despite an attempt at detoxification at the Bellevue clinic, she still regularly injected herself with doses of two grams of heroin. In October she was arrested once again, this time at the Café de Flore, by the antidrug brigade of the Paris police, who found almost six grams of heroin in her possession. On October 28 she was taken to the infirmary at Fresnes prison; she was sentenced to a fifty-thousand-franc fine, and freed on November 3.

For some months Simone's mother, Dr. Sogler, had been calling Camus for help, but he was unsure what to do: "I have thought about it, and I really don't know what to tell you. Seventeen years ago, with an intuition that was ahead of my young age, I realized that there was no way out of this situation. That's why I ended it abruptly, even though that cost me more than I have ever admitted to anyone. Today I only feel for Simone and above all for you, with all the understanding I am capable of. As for her husband, although I don't know him, it goes without saying that I understand what he must be feeling. Damage must be limited . . . first by avoiding that the worst happens . . . and to spare her the judicial consequences of her madness." Camus advised Dr. Sogler that Simone should look for a reasonably priced clinic in Algiers: "Unfortunately I fear that I am as powerless in the matter as I was seventeen years ago." His former mother-in-law, for whom he still felt affection, asked him to find Simone a job in France. He wrote back to her in Algiers: "Dear friend . . . As difficult for your health as this may prove to be, I believe that Simone will find the best shelter near you. . . . It is better to see things clearly, and without ever giving up hope of a possible cure, we must realize that relapses are probable. Thus I find it difficult to recommend Simone to a publisher without telling him frankly what he would be up against."

Simone was arrested yet another time in Paris, but not convicted. Wandering around the city, she ran into Professor René Poirier, Camus's former teacher from Algiers, on a metro platform and told him some incoherent things about Camus, such as that he had turned her "into a guinea pig."

Francine had returned to Oran to rest, and Camus joined her there On December 26, 1953, he wrote to Jean Grenier after postponing a planned trip to Egypt: "Francine's state, which had remained steady for several days and which I hoped would improve, suddenly got worse when Catherine became ill with scarlet fever. I can't give you the details here, but from now on we have to watch her constantly. She must have treatment, and the only question is whether it will be possible to do so here or if we must return to Paris." On December 28 he added to friends, "I found Francine in a worse state than when I left Paris, which I found particularly astonishing the first day, but since then she seems to be getting better."

For a short time he thought he still might be able to go to Egypt, leaving Francine at home. He wrote to Grenier again: "I'm sorry to ask you to send the money to cancel Francine's ticket, but I think it would be the most practical thing. I do have serious problems here, as I found Francine in an alarming condition. I hoped that returning to her childhood home would help her to regain her balance, but on the contrary, I found that her depressed mood had deepened into clinical depression, complicated by signs of anguish and obsession. I am very worried and I blame myself for not having taken the first symptoms more seriously. In truth, had the thing been possible, I would have preferred to delay again this trip to Egypt, as it would have been too painful to leave Francine alone at a time when apart from my sister-in-law [Christiane], there is no one in her family who can really help or understand her, but it's too late now. All I can do is to speed up my return and to reduce my stay in Egypt to the bare minimum."

He planned to return to France first, leaving his son with the Polges. But after the Christmas holidays, Francine's state of health became even worse; and one day she headed out onto the terrace that joined the Faures' two apartments on the rue d'Arzew, where Albert and Christiane had to restrain her from what may have been a suicide attempt. His travel plans were now out of the question. On January 4, 1954, Camus wrote to the Polges, "F. is under observation in a clinic here and I had to give up my trips to Algiers and Egypt." Francine spent twenty-four hours at a hospital, followed by four days at the Gasser clinic, during which time Camus did not leave, even to visit his mother in Algiers. He reported about Francine, "The doctors feel that it isn't a very serious case, but surveillance and treatment are necessary."

Camus and Francine returned to Paris by plane, accompanied by André Bénichou, while Christiane took Jean to stay with the Polges, to whom Albert confided his distress: "I am so disoriented that I turn first towards you." Francine was placed in a clinic on the rue Jeanne-d'Arc in the Paris suburb of Saint-Mandé. Camus felt by turns guilty, overwhelmed, and irritated. Friends recalled his exasperation as he explained that at the clinic, Francine would sit on her bed, looking directly in front of her, while Albert waited by her side. Christiane, who was inspector of public education at Oran, came to visit every three weeks, while her sister Suzy, who lived with her husband in Paris, came more often.

At the Saint-Mandé clinic, the doctors seemed to disagree about Francine's treatment. All she did was cry, sleep, and talk obsessively about Maria Casarès, her husband's lover. Christiane was sure that her sister would get well with time, and when a treatment using iodine injections was proposed, Camus and Christiane refused to authorize it. Francine's illness brought Camus closer to the Faure family, as Camus feared for Francine's life, noting on January 30, 1954, that "F. is not better or worse, and my impression is that her medical diagnosis is uncertain, and although I am convinced that she will recover, it will take more time than I had previously thought. I see her now in the afternoons and try to help her to get out of it, but I sometimes feel cruelly how powerless I am. At other times, I notice lots of positive signs, and that is what I must believe in."

As winter ended, Camus fell ill with a bad flu, and Francine did not get better. Her room at the clinic was on the second floor, and one day clinic employees found her window wide open: Francine had jumped. Christiane believed that her sister had just wanted to escape from the clinic, but Albert knew that she had wanted to kill herself. Francine had fractured her pelvis in the fall and would be immobilized in a plaster cast for over a month, which would give her bedsores.

Good friends like the Polges, the Jaussauds, and the Bénichous visited the Camuses to offer their support. Camus would tell his children about the Polges: "You must love them twice as much as before, because they are good and intelligent, and good and intelligent people are rare." About his wife's condition he noted: "The pelvis fracture and immobilization in plaster, plus a fever, which they are trying to reduce with penicillin, do not encourage psychological improvement. We now find ourselves with the prospect of a long treatment with insulin, which offers no hope of improvement until June." The doctors tried insulin shock therapy on Francine, but the treatment caused memory loss and finally a hypoglycemic coma. Camus was upset, saying, "Events have grown to proportions that are a little out of our control, and I am greatly worried."

Urbain and Jeanne Polge offered to take care of Catherine as well as Jean, so that the twins, now eight years old, could remain together; but Camus decided to send Catherine to be with her grandmother Faure at Oran, a place the girl loved. Camus counted more on Christiane's teaching skills to help Catherine than on Fernande's grandmothering. His in-laws came more and more to blame Francine's depression on Albert's infidelities, and above all on his affair with Maria Casarès. Camus told Francine, "They think I'm the guilty one," but Francine was blaming herself for not being a good wife and mother. Usually, Camus's escape and his shield was work, but he told a number of friends at this time, "I cannot write." Instead, he thought about compiling his novellas into a new book.

On March 28, 1954, Camus wrote to Mamaine Koestler, "No, Francine isn't any better. She had a woman psychiatrist, apart from an assigned doctor who works at the clinic, and she likes her a lot and talks with her, but in general she speaks less and less, and I have the terrible impression that she's going farther and farther away. But maybe that's wrong, although I fear the worst in this case, and if it happens, I will be desperate." Camus tried to remain a lucid observer at this moment of great trouble in their marriage: "I have no gift for love, nor for suffering, and I wander around without knowing what I am here for."

Whenever he had visited the apartment of late, he found that his separation from Catherine and Jean was too painful; "I miss my children a lot," he wrote to Michel and Janine Gallimard. It had been a comfort knowing that even if he did not see them often, Jean and Catherine were ensconced on the rue Madame, where he could visit them in between travels, working vacations, and other escapades. He was accustomed to speaking with them on the telephone, despite his dislike for that instrument, but now Jean was far away in Provence and Catherine in Algeria. René Char finally found a two-room apartment for Camus on the third floor at 4 rue de Chanaleilles in the seventh arrondissement, a building where Char kept a pied-à-terre. Until he found this place, Camus stayed with friends, in hotels, and in borrowed studio apartments.

Camus felt that one cause of the misunderstandings between himself and his wife might have been their immaturity, but he also went through moments of guilt: "I am the first one responsible, because a part of me has never stopped thinking instinctively that human affairs are not serious. It's also that I have hurt so many people around me. . . . And really I don't know how to get out of it, when I think that Francine may continue to be what she is right now."

Mamaine wrote from England to say that she had spoken to a British doctor about Francine, and the doctor was optimistic. Camus was encouraged, although not convinced by this long-distance diagnosis: "Finally, your doctor's prognosis consoles me a little. I'm also told that however long it may take, there will be a cure. I am making my heart patient and stubborn in order to wait, and above all, to help her. . . . I've always had enough strength to get myself out of anything, and here, too, I feel that everything will work out for Francine. What will remain for us is the memory of a nasty nightmare and the obligation to arrange our lives on a decent basis which will finally be a good one."

For Camus, decency meant a clear and public separation from Francine, who was being stuffed with medications and had shrunk to only 45 kilograms, although Camus remained resolutely optimistic in letters to friends, as well as confessing his lack of inspiration: "Being unable to work at anything, but needing money, I agreed to write the screenplay for a film on *La Princesse de Clèves*, which will take me a lot of time, but I will learn a craft I didn't know before. Otherwise, I go to soccer matches and walk in summery Paris, which is hot and stormy."

But the film project to adapt the novel for the director Robert Bresson came to nothing: "I am not doing anything. . . . For a month I worked on *La Princesse de Clèves* and then Bresson was such a pain in the ass—he's a maniacal madman—that I had to quit." Since the film's producer never sent any contract, Camus had worked for nothing. Francine's clinic cost a lot of money, and to earn some income, Camus made some recordings of his works: "My financial situation has become disastrous. . . . F. is better, but I daren't say anything about myself."

It was hoped that at the end of six months of treatment, Francine could leave the clinic and stay in the south of France, without her husband or children, but at the beginning of June she had a slight setback, which postponed these plans. Finally, Christiane left for a thermal station, Divonne-les-Bains, with her sister Christiane looking after her for six weeks. But Camus was feeling exhausted, and a doctor whom he consulted at Lausanne warned him that his respiratory capacity was much diminished.

The news from Divonne was fairly good, despite Francine suffering another little setback. Camus rented a house outside Paris to live in with Jean and Catherine, whom he was proud of.

Suddenly he received word from England that Mamaine Koestler had died of tuberculosis. Camus was deeply upset. Mamaine represented for him a successful human being with intelligence and courage, a woman who accepted him as he was.

By August, Francine seemed to be past the worst; and whether out of sincere belief, self-protectiveness, or sheer egoism, Camus believed that he could do no more for his wife: "Francine is much better and I hope that by autumn it will be over, and it had better be, as I am tired and can't help her anymore." On the train back to Paris, Christiane followed Francine around whenever she walked in the corridors, until the poor woman cried, "Stop it, I'm not going to kill myself!" In September, after a further stay at Grasse, Francine returned to the apartment on the rue Madame, and since Camus could not for the moment think of leaving her, he tried to re-establish a life with her there. He refused invitations from friends, saying, "I try to eat all my meals at home."

Then Francine's mother moved to Paris, and the Faures asked Camus to leave the rue Madame apartment. Francine had not been consulted. Usually, Camus made such important decisions for himself, but this quasi-official departure was imposed on him, even though he secretly wanted to leave anyway. He got used to the idea that Francine's illness would last a long time, and doctors agreed. Her suffering was awful, and at that time there were few medications for mental illnesses. Pills calmed the patient down but could not cure her. Camus considered psychoanalysis for Francine, but finally decided against it.

In November, he noted that it was more and more difficult for him to write, as he told Jeanne Polge: "I feel all dried up . . . like ink by a blotting paper. F. is in about the state you saw her in, with the added good news that she is doing some little chores for the children and she has some fairly good moments. Nevertheless we had to choose a treatment a month ago, and in the last few days, we decided on a new series of three treatments. If after this, Francine does not emerge from her cocoon of depression, we'll just have to trust in time, which as you know never seems to be in a hurry."

Francine underwent twenty-three treatments of electroshock therapy, which used curare as an anesthetic, to reduce the epilepsy set off by the shocks. Arranging electroshock treatments for his wife was a task that was "beyond him," according to Camus. Yet although he seemed out of commission as an artist, he continued to function as a husband, drawing on his emotional resources as "the old maniac of happiness that I am," as he put it.

He consulted many specialists about medication for Francine, including one who told him that "feeling the need to spare Francine's health was making [him] live in a fishbowl, and the doctor prescribed freedom and self-fulfillment" for him. Camus replied, "That's a superb prescription, far and away the easiest one to live with." He admitted to Christiane what another doctor had told him about his own health: "What I thought were colds have in fact been attacks of tuberculosis, and I'm going to have to start taking antibiotics again."

Chapter Forty-one **November 1, 1954**

On May 7, 1954, French forces surrendered at Dien Bien Phu in Southeast Asia, in a political disaster. Camus noted in his *Carnets*: "The fall of Dien Bien Phu. As in 1940, mixed feelings of shame and rage. The evening of the massacre, it was clear that right-wing politicians had put the unfortunate men in an indefensible position while the leftists shot them in the back." Camus had no profound knowledge of Asian problems, but he had some intuitions. In leftist mythology, French soldiers in Southeast Asia were brutes or Nazis, but Camus understood why Prime Minister Pierre Mendès-France, one of the few politicians he felt any sympathy for, signed a treaty to keep Vietnam free beneath the seventeenth parallel, with French assistance.

Camus always paid more attention to what was happening in North Africa than to Indochina, and on March 22, 1954, he wrote to French President René Coty asking him to pardon seven militant nationalist Tunisians sentenced to death for killing three policemen. Camus introduced himself to Coty as "an independent writer who knows about North African questions because of his origins, and who tries to judge without prejudice whenever possible."

On the night of October 31, dozens of terrorist attacks broke out all over Algeria. Mendès-France declared reassuringly, "Our departments in Algeria make up an integral part of the French Republic." The French minister of the interior, François Mitterrand, declared, "Algeria is France." Camus was upset, because while he did not deny the offenses of colonialism, "there are not just moneybags who live over there." Apart from a few thousand major colonialists and captains of industry, many Europeans living in Algeria were from the working class, manual laborers and small tradesmen — people like his own family. The standard of living of the European residents of Algeria (the so-called pieds noirs) was 20 percent below that of mainland France. In 1954 there were 984,000 Frenchmen in Algeria and nearly ten times as many "natives," whose birth rate greatly exceeded the French families. The organization for independence from France, the Front pour la libération nationale (Front for National Liberation) or FLN, militated against colonialism, with an egalitarian, socialist discourse.

Camus knew that elections in Algeria had been falsified and that the crushing majority of Europeans were against the assimilation of Moslem people. He was worried about the problem, and each time he had an opportunity, he denounced the daily racism against North Africans, whether in France or in Algeria.

On December 11, on a trip to Italy, Camus was stricken by fever and flu. He wrote in his *Carnets*, "To get back my health at all costs, as I need all my energy, not because I want an easy life but I want to be up to life's challenges, when they are difficult." On December 12 in Rome, Camus noticed in a newspaper that Simone de Beauvoir's novel *Les Mandarins* had won the prestigious Goncourt Prize in Paris: "I saw by chance in a newspaper the Parisian comedy I had forgotten about and the Goncourt farce. *Les Mandarins* won this time, and it seems that her novel's hero is really me. In fact the author took some things out of context, such as the director of a newspaper that began in the Resistance, but all the rest is false, whether dealing with thoughts, feelings, or acts. Even better, the dubious acts of Sartre's life are generously dumped on my shoulders. Otherwise, it's garbage, but not intentionally so, just naturally, the way one breathes."

Camus explained to Charles Poncet that Beauvoir was profiting from the Camus-Sartre quarrel in order to get her revenge. Camus said, "You can't imagine how far she goes in her cynicism. She imputes to Henri [modeled after Camus] some fairly dubious actions of Sartre's, for example Henri has a play produced in a theater run by a woman who was implicated in the Nazi collaboration, but I didn't give a play to Simone Berriau during the occupation, Sartre did." Camus told Poncet about de Beauvoir, "She couldn't stand the friendship between Sartre and me. You know, we three had lunch on a given day each week, for years. . . . One day she came into my office to tell me that she had a woman friend who wanted to sleep with me, but I replied that in these matters, I was accustomed to choosing for myself. That was a humiliation that such a woman never forgets."

In the wake of rumors and scandal after *Les Mandarins* was published, Camus remarked, "They've thrown all their goddamn slime on my back." He took consolation in work, making extensive notes for a book he planned to call *Le Premier Homme* and another, more hypothetical work, which would be his version of *Faust*.

Simone de Beauvoir claimed that her Goncourt Prize–winning novel did *not* have characters based on real-life people, because that was not her style; but it is clear that one of its protagonists, Henri Perron, was closely modeled on Camus, and another, Robert Dubreuilh, on Sartre. *Les Mandarins*, written just after the Camus-Sartre polemic, was a major way of getting even. In the novel, Henri runs a newspaper called *L'Espoir*, which recalled *Combat* as well as the name of the series of books that Camus directed at Gallimard. Beauvoir saw Camus as a deeply divided person, and her hero Henri reflected this, saying, "I'd very much like readers to know who I am, but I'm not very sure myself." The main female character, a psychoanalyst named Anne, a clone of Simone de Beauvoir, studies Henri, calling his novels "mortally classical." This was an echo of Sartre's criticism of Camus's writing in *Les Temps Modernes*, which stated that his style was overwritten and "too constructed."

Dubreuilh judges the fictional newspaper *L'Espoir* in the same terms Sartre had used to demolish Camus's *Combat*: "If your newspaper pleases everyone, that's because it doesn't bother anyone. It attacks nothing and defends nothing, and escapes from all the real problems." Just as Camus had confided his torments to Beauvoir, so Henri confides in Anne, Robert's wife: "I will confess everything to you—I have nothing more to say, or rather, what I have to say seems like nothing to me." Henri Perron was condemned to write only articles, a kind of literary sterility that also seemed to threaten Camus.

Beauvoir did change a few minor details. A few years earlier, a journalist named Antoinette Nordmann had infiltrated Camus's home by posing as a chambermaid, and a visiting journalist, Alexandre Astruc, unmasked her. Nordmann confessed that she planned to write an article about the writer's home life, and she was thrown out. Beauvoir's novel placed a journalist in exactly the same situation at Anne and Robert Dubreuilh's home.

Sartre's circle was well aware of the tensions between Albert and Francine and of the latter's depression. In the novel, Henri's wife, Paule, is ill; and although she has a profound admiration for her husband, he no longer loves her: "I didn't want to behave like a swine, but I have no vocation for martyrdom. Sometimes the situation seems simple to me: when you aren't in love anymore, you aren't in love. Other times, it seems unfair to have stopped loving. She's the same Paule as before, after all."

In *Les Temps Modernes*, Francis Jeanson had reproached Camus's *L'Homme révolté* for being praised by the right-wing press, and in Beauvoir's novel, Henri Perron is praised by the conservative newspapers: "The entire right wing covers you with flowers, it's disturbing. You say that you can't do anything about it, but it's disturbing all the same." Even more cuttingly, in the novel Henri has an affair with an actress, Josette; and all of Paris's cultural world knew about the affair between Camus and Maria Casarès. The descriptions of Camus in *Les Mandarins* were even crueler than what had been published in *Les Temps Modernes*. According to Simone, the Camus character "wanted to enjoy himself, which led him inexorably to the right wing, because on the left, pretty faces found few admirers."

Les Mandarins was a fierce exercise in the denigration of Camus, and as such it provoked many smiles and cackles at the Gallimard office. Gaston kept away from the controversy, although Camus's loyal friends Brice Parain and Janine, Michel, and Robert Gallimard were all irked. The Polish poet and essayist Czeslaw Milosz, who was living in France at the time, asked Camus why he didn't respond, and Camus said, "Because you don't discuss things with a sewer."

The controversy over *Les Mandarins* passed by, but the Algerian crisis remained. Outside in the street around the rue Sébastien-Bottin, demonstrations of sympathy for the Algerian rebels were held. Some French progressives, led by Sartre, offered immediate support for the Algerian revolutionaries, the FLN. Others founded committees against continuing what they called "the Algerian war," a name it merited by now. The government in Paris and the Algerian administration were still referring to "operations to maintain order," or "police operations." Some writers not at all considered leftists, like Roger Martin du Gard and Francois Mauriac, supported the war's opponents. René Char, who was still a close friend of Camus's, refused to support the FLN, as he saw that group as part of a nationalist movement rather than a movement of liberation. Camus was isolated on the issue. FLN supporters like Dionys Mascolo, Marguerite Duras, and Robert Antelme tried to persuade him, and some found him pompous and stuffy on the subject.

Robert Gallimard was a founding member and treasurer of the Committee of Intellectuals Against the Continuation of the Algerian War, and Michel Gallimard signed the committee's petition. Camus felt betrayed by Michel's adherence, saying, "I don't say you were wrong to sign, or that these people's intention is bad, but I'm saying that it's dangerous and that you might have blood on your hands." A few weeks after the first Algerian terrorist attacks, Camus expressed his opinions in a letter: "Obviously it's easier to be anticolonialist in the bistros of Marseilles and Paris." Camus knew he was accused of colonialism, but he said, "I know where such accusations usually come from, and the Arabs know who their real friends are." He pointed out that the Communists "betrayed [the Algerian Arabs] in 1936 . . . at the time when I was by their side."

A friend from Algeria, Jeanne Terracini, felt that the revolutionaries would be eliminated by the French. Camus admitted that the French were giving the Arabs a hard time, "making burnooses sweat," but that "a modus vivendi can be found." André Malraux disagreed with Camus on the issue, feeling that France could no longer hold on to its North African colonies, and he found Camus too stubborn on the subject, rejecting all discussion.

Premier Pierre Mendès-France was voted out of office in February 1955, and a newspaper was founded in October of that year with the object of returning him to power. L'Express was run by Jean-Jacques Servan-Schreiber, an ambitious journalist who defined himself as left-center or liberal in his politics, but not Marxist or Communist. Servan-Schreiber was assisted by the professional journalist Françoise Giroud. Camus's memories of journalism in Algeria were largely negative, and after he left Combat he had always refused to work for newspapers, agreeing with Tolstoy that journalism was "a whorehouse for the intellect." But Servan-Schreiber and Giroud were after literary heavyweights to write for them, such as François Mauriac, Jean-Paul Sartre, and Camus. Servan-Schreiber knew that Camus felt sympathy for Mendès-France, and so he asked the journalist Jean Daniel, who already was working for L'Express and who knew Camus, to act as intermediary, promising Camus total freedom of speech if he would contribute regularly. Despite his reservations, Camus agreed.

Trying to escape from the isolation L'Homme révolté had imposed on him, Camus told Daniel, "Solitary in my epoch, but as you know, I am also in solidarity with my epoch, very much so. . . . Journalism has always seemed to me as a most agreeable form of engagement. . . . I want to help to bring Pierre Mendès-France back to power. . . . From the very first time I met him, he seemed to me to be a true statesman."

Having agreed to write for L'Express, Camus left for three weeks' vacation in Greece to see places he had long dreamed of, including Argos, Delphi, Delos, Olympia, and Mykonos. During his trip he took notes for two stories, "L'Hôte" and "Le Rénégat," and a novel, Le Premier Homme. He also worked on a preface to a new edition of Jean Grenier's Iles, and he sent his first article to L'Express, a plea on behalf of the Greek city of Volos, which had been destroyed by an earthquake. Camus compared the Greek architects and archeologists favorably to Frenchmen and their "puny resentments," but the article left Servan-Schreiber aghast and wondering who could possibly be interested in reading it, even if it was drastically cut. Jean Daniel warned Servan-Schreiber that Camus had been promised freedom of expression and that if the article was not printed, Camus would certainly quit L'Express. So Servan-Schreiber cabled to Camus, ARTICLE SUBLIME STOP.

After he returned to Paris on May 16, and ten days before his first article appeared in L'Express, a short article in the weekly France-Observateur made fun of Camus for working with Françoise Giroud although "he must have other ideas than she does about the press." Camus sent a long reply to this brief jab, saying, "As for Madame Françoise Giroud, whom you wish to pit me against. . . . I have no difficulty in approving of her conception of the press and I feel I have every right to contribute to this newspaper with the total freedom that they granted me. . . . However, I would not be able to contribute to *France-Observateur*, as I do not share the same ideas as its directors on the role and objectivity of a political weekly." Camus saw *France-Observateur* as pharisees with "demagogic facility," and he told Giroud, "Don't let yourself be intimidated, they are dogs."

France-Observateur replied in a two-page article, explaining that Giroud came from the women's magazine *Elle*, for which she continued to write editorials, and *France-Observateur*'s directors did not like the way magazines like *Elle* were run. In truth, Camus did not like *Elle* either, but he felt that certain of its journalists could still be valid. *France-Observateur* added that Camus, as part of the newfangled *L'Express*, which reeked of Servan-Schreiber's fascination with flashy modern American journalism, was betraying the old French Resistance press like *Combat*. Moreover, *France-Observateur* reminded Camus that it had been one of the few periodicals to devote much space to praising *L'Homme révolté*.

Camus replied to these arguments in the next issue of *L'Express*, saying that they sounded like "the concierge who finds that the artist living on the fourth floor is decidedly snobby about his little world which won't bring him happiness." This quarrel involved personalities more than anything else, with Giroud more of a high-flying, stylish Parisian journalist while the *France-Observateur* editors, Claude Bourdet and Gilles Martinet, were Marxist theoreticians more than journalists. Given the choice, Camus sided with Servan-Schreiber, who opposed any ties with the French Communist Party.

Otherwise, Camus was hardly on the same wavelength as Servan-Schreiber, apart from some comparable personality traits. Both men took themselves very seriously, Camus as a political moralist and Servan-Schreiber as a technological prophet. Both were well known among colleagues and friends for being Don Juans, and Servan-Schreiber was particularly noted as a charmer, despite his hauteur. Even old François Mauriac, who contributed essays to *L'Express*, was said to have a crush on Servan-Schreiber (and to be still more enamored of the editor's younger brother, Jean-Louis).

Camus was not at ease in the dynamic, snobby, and fashionable world of *L'Express*. He felt real affection for one staffer, the rebellious daughter of André Malraux, Florence. But Camus was bewildered by Servan-Schreiber's stunts borrowed from America for his staff, such as TV-dinner-style meals in the cafeteria and gym classes, plus the odd habit of calling secretaries by their first names instead of "Mademoiselle" and, worst of all, when deadlines approached, of forcing editors to swallow vitamin pills so as "not to give up."

Servan-Schreiber's magazine had been founded to oppose the war in

Southeast Asia, and now it was opposed to the war in Algeria. The editor's secret ambition was to be elected president of France—no less—and the magazine was merely a means to an end for him, so he left journalistic matters in the hands of Françoise Giroud. Camus had professional esteem for Giroud, but he was also wary of her, one of her serious faults being that she did not succumb to the charm of his smile. Giroud found the legendary seducer's smile too automatic, and she found his taste for self-torment a little too much for her taste.

Camus approved more readily of *L'Express*'s foreign politics expert, Jean Daniel, and would go along with him on evening prowls to bars and bordellos. Daniel recalled they used to have "chaste" discussions with whores who called Camus "Albert la Peste."

From May 14, 1955, to February 2, 1956, Camus wrote thirty-five articles for *L'Express*, under the headline "Current Events." His passionate resolve was to prove that there were paths open for Algeria other than the solutions proposed by the far left or the far right. So he wrote in *L'Express* on behalf of Algeria and, he thought, every Algerian.

Laughingly, in his familiar accent—sounding somewhere between Algiers and Paris—Camus would describe his looks: "I'm a mixture of Fernandel, Humphrey Bogart, and a samurai." Camus had fun lunching and dining with friends, listening to music with his women. His tastes were simple. He adored *Don Giovanni* and the string quintets by Mozart, the Beethoven quartets, and Mahler's *Song of the Earth*, particularly as sung by Kathleen Ferrier. At the movies, he was an eclectic fan of modern film, without being a connoisseur, and he liked the directors Federico Fellini, Max Ophuls, Orson Welles, and Ingmar Bergman. He was wild about the blond Swedish actress Ingrid Thulin in Bergman's *Wild Strawberries* and also had a weakness for Bogart in Howard Hawks's *The Big Sleep*. It was hard to persuade him to go to the opera, however; and even after an evening spent at the theater or the movies, if he heard the news on the radio, suddenly politics would be back at the forefront of his mind. When there was talk of events in Algeria, his green eyes would often seem to darken.

In May 1954, a few months before a rebellion broke out in Algeria, Camus sent a message to the Committee for the Amnesty of Overseas Convicts, pointing out the weaknesses and contradictions of French colonialism, which "has the Declaration of the Rights of Man in one hand and a stick for repression in the other." Algeria was Camus's obsession, even though he also wrote in *L'Express* about nuclear armament, Franco's Spain, ossified communism, and the plight of manual laborers.

He spoke endlessly to his friends of popular misunderstandings about Algeria. He told Jean Grenier in July 1955: "We needed serious events to happen before we paid attention to Algeria, and the colonists don't have a bad conscience because they see things simply." Camus did not ignore the racism of Algerian poor whites, even if it was softened by a paternalistic attitude. He would say about Frenchmen from Algeria, "We are the Jews of France," and he may have been only half joking. He meant to say that Algeria's European pieds noirs were victims of discrimination in Paris.

In *L'Express* on July 9 and 23, 1955, he wrote two articles about his thoughts on terrorism, repression, and the future of Algeria. These followed along the lines of his articles in *Alger Républicain* seventeen years before. Now he told *L'Express's* readers that elections were still falsified in Algeria and that the Arab people lived "with no future and in humiliation." He was not an apologist for violence, but tried to understand its causes: "In Algeria, as elsewhere, terrorism can be explained by a lack of hope."

The nationalist movements were "poor in doctrine but rich in audacity," according to Camus. He condemned terrorism, by which he meant that of the Front for National Liberation. Describing colonists under siege on isolated farms, he insisted to the liberal readers of *L'Express* that Parisians had no right to treat this tragedy lightly. Some observers compared the FLN terrorists to the fighters of the Vietminh and the French Resistance. For Camus, these parallels did not hold, but he did believe that the crisis could be abated.

He suggested holding an immediate conference in Paris to unite representatives of the French government, colonials, and some of the Arab movements. Sadly, Camus's information was out of date, based as it was on his knowledge of Algeria in 1937 and 1938. His informants were not the people who were leading the struggle in the countryside, in the casbahs, at the United Nations, or even in Paris. He stated optimistically: "If colonialization can ever find an excuse, it would be to the degree in which it favors the personality of the colonized people."

On August 21 and 22, 1955, seventy-one Europeans and fifty-two Moslems were massacred at North Constantine, near Philippeville, Algeria. In reprisal, 1,273 "rebels" were executed. In the midst of these events, the Algerian essayist and poet Jean Amrouche wrote to a friend that Camus's solutions in *L'Express* were not credible: "The evil is much too profound. . . . No agreement is possible between the natives and French of Algeria. . . . In short, I no longer believe in a French Algeria."

Camus spent part of that summer in Italy, putting together a collection of novellas, *L'Exil et le royaume*. One, which would be called *La Chute*, kept getting longer, and soon turned into a separate novel.

Back in Paris, he wrote to Edmond Brua: "Let me take the occasion to express my anguish about the events in Algeria and the tone of the press there. No matter what justified resentments may be felt after the events at Philippeville, it is up to the rest of us to keep our cool, we French adults who are politically more aware of historical realities than these ignorant and so easily cruel masses." Camus advised the journalist, "To the degree, very slight of course, that you may have an influence on your newspaper's orientation, use it . . . to help calm the crisis."

Everywhere, Algerians and observers expected a strong statement from Camus about his point of view, as he was the most famous Algerian writer. He reassured a worried young Frenchman who had been drafted to serve in the French army in Algeria that draftees protected European people morally and physically, notably working-class people. Camus was opposed to the creation by French colonists of militias called "self-defense groups." He wrote to Charles Poncet, "I am very anguished by events in Algeria, a country that is stuck in my craw to the point where I can think of nothing else. My days are poisoned by the idea that I . . . am going to write more articles . . . unfortunately so, because both the left- and right-wing people irritate me on the subject." He asked Poncet for information: "Perhaps you will prevent me from saying stupid things."

Jean Grenier complained to Camus about an article by another contributor to *L'Express*, François Mauriac. The seventy-one-year-old novelist described the Sultan of Morocco as a venerated monarch who ought to be put back on the throne, which in fact happened. Camus was surprised, given that the sultan did not criticize a massacre of Europeans at Oued-Zem in Morocco on August 20, the same day as the Philippeville killings in Algeria. Commenting on his work for *L'Express*, he distanced himself from Mauriac: "After some hesitation, I agreed to write for *L'Express* because Mendès-France was involved, and he knows what one can say and do reasonably. But Mauriac . . . is surrounded by young Arabs, and he has decided that now is the time . . . to write his own *Amyntas*." Camus found Mauriac's article embarrassing, but concluded, "Arabs and Frenchmen must find a way to live together."

Grenier wanted to know if daily life in Algeria was still calm, and Camus replied, "No, you have to go out armed in the evening. My mother is terrified because the other night in her quarter, Belcourt, an Arab shopkeeper was stabbed while he was lowering the iron gate of his store." When Grenier commented that French Algerians would not let themselves be cheated, Camus replied, "They are very determined and unsubtle. The thing that's the most amusing, when you know how completely anti-Semitic the European Algerians are, is their present admiration for Israel. 'Those people know the way to deal with the Arabs,' they say."

French President of the Council Edgar Faure declared on the radio: "All of France's honor and its humane mission obliges us absolutely, unequivocally, and outspokenly to keep Algeria for France and in France." Camus responded to this view in an article, "L'Absente," in *L'Express*, once again calling for elections: "Algeria is not France, it isn't even Algeria, it is that unknown land which a cloud of blood hides from its incomprehensible natives, bothersome soldiers, and exotic Frenchmen. Algeria is the absent one, whose memory and abandonment pain the hearts of a few people. . . ."

In his didactic writings, Camus was endlessly opposed to the caricatures of left-wing newspapers, whether Communist or not, as well as the pious images of the right wing: "To read a certain press, it would really seem as if Algeria were populated by millions of settlers holding riding crops and smoking cigars, riding around in Cadillacs." Camus denied that the modest white settlers of Algeria enjoyed privileges, but he did not deny their racism.

In letters to Urbain Polge, he often seemed pessimistic, but to his readers in *L'Express*, he declared that the future was uncompromised: "I therefore propose that the present two parties simultaneously promise in public not to touch the civilian population under any circumstances. This agreement would not modify any situation for the moment, but it would simply try to remove from the conflict its actions that are impossible to atone for, and would preserve innocent lives in the future."

Camus was critical of the sort of French press that devoted little space to the deaths of two roofing workers after a fall but many columns to England's Princess Margaret's tiffs with her fiancé, Peter Townsend. Camus noted, "Princess Margaret's crucifixion, terrifying as it has been, has had its good results, because the interminable tale of her sufferings, which have personally so exhausted me that I'm not sure I will ever get over it, has at least allowed the public, finally overwhelmed, to distract itself with the trivialities of existence."

L'Express had a circulation of about 135,000 copies at the time, and half a million readers, so Camus's pronouncements had a certain echo. He received letters from readers, such as one from a teacher in Bordeaux who told him to let the Arabs and Frenchmen of Algeria work out their problems by themselves—another example of ignorance and resignation, according to Camus. His friend Jean Grenier had long imagined a political career for Camus, and when elections for deputies approached, he asked Camus why he didn't run for office. Camus replied, "My uncle Acault used to say when somebody had the ambition to be a deputy or minister, 'I see, he's a modest chap!' "

He also said that his mother and Uncle Etienne could not imagine moving to France, even to the south, which had some similarities to Algeria. When Hélène Camus did come to France, she would station herself at a window on the quiet rue Madame and look at the passersby, much less colorful than in Algiers. She missed the rattling of trams and the hurly-burly of the crowds. She told her son, "What do you expect? There are no Arabs!" and he understood why she did not want to live in France.

Camus's editorial writing took time away from his creative work, and he told Charles Poncet, "I lead an exhausted life. . . . I'm constantly late for everything. . . . I'd need three lives to take care of everything." He expressed his "horror, which has become pathological, of appearing in public . . . but anyway, one cannot abandon one's responsibilities." Although he privately supported Pierre Mendès-France in the upcoming presidential elections, in *L'Express* he remained impartial: "Until now I have not participated in the electoral campaign, as you may have noticed, and my reasons are simple: first, I don't feel comfortable with it, and I can't master the necessary language."

Camus hoped for shared mutual respect between the two peoples, French and Algerian, and saw two solutions, either a form of association between the two or else "to continue . . . the policy of previous governments, to give the illusion of progress by a few unimportant reforms, which is like giving aspirin to a cancer patient."

Camus would go twice a week to the editorial offices of *L'Express* to dictate his articles. There he would often discuss politics with Jean Daniel, whom he told, "You cannot live in disagreement with yourself. That is, it is impossible to accept the FLN's methods, or the sacrifice of one's own community. Our community consists of non-Moslems in Algeria, so let's stop hearing about the French, Italians, Spanish, and Jews in Algeria, because there are really just the Moslems, and then there are the rest." Camus felt that certain Parisians' ignorance about North Africa was ridiculous, and regardless of their gender, he referred to them in macho style as members of the "female left wing." He said, "In fact there is a murderous frivolity in this vision of an occupied Algerian nation seeking to free itself from an occupant, with the right to use any means to obtain freedom by taking revenge on non-Moslems."

He told Jean Daniel, "Today they speak to us about an Algerian nation, and that exasperates me, although the FLN has the right, and perhaps the duty, to fight to create a nation, which is at least conceivable. But then they try to put across the idea of a pre-existing nation. . . . You know very well that all this has nothing to do with the idea of a nation. Today Algeria is a territory inhabited by two peoples, and I mean two peoples, one Moslem and the other not, and Algeria's two peoples have an equal right to justice and to equal rights in holding on to their fatherland." French supporters of the Moslem separatist group, the FLN, were forgetting, he felt, that any solution had to take into consideration the French in Algeria: "There is no reason to resign oneself or to believe that history will be fair if left to work out for itself. The fight for justice is what is important, and in terms of this, French repression cannot be justified, and neither can the violent methods of the Liberation Front."

In the January 10, 1956 issue of *L'Express*, Camus proposed a civilian truce. Two days later, Camus lunched with Jean Grenier and seemed pessimistic about the idea of a truce, but felt that the main point of his proposal was "to make people come out of the shadows" and declare their positions. About the French settlers, who felt more or less abandoned by the French mainland, Camus joked, "If need be, they'll become like Americans [in cowboy films], and they've already developed a four-shooter technique when they go from one village to another by car: they always carry a revolver, which they call a French-Arab dictionary, and when they met a native with an even slightly suspicious attitude, they shoot him twice, the second shot being in case the first one misses, and then with another gun they shoot the chassis of the Arab's car twice as well."

Grenier felt it was a shame that people like Camus, who was neither a settler nor a native, had not remained in Algeria to help build a livable country. Camus replied that he would have stayed in Algeria "if they hadn't thrown me out in 1940."

But Camus did decide to go to Algeria to promote his idea of a truce. He called it not the same thing as a movement for peace, since for him, remembering the Movement for Peace launched by Moscow, the word "peace" had Communist connotations. The day before he arrived in Algiers, he published in *L'Express* an article that opposed the doctrine of total war. Charles Poncet and Pierre Miquel met him at the Maison-Blanche airport, and Camus smilingly introduced them to his *L'Express* colleague Patrick Kessel, saying, "We've both come here to make our own jihad."

Although violent death was on the rise in Algeria, Camus said that once inside the country, "that anguish I felt in Paris about Algeria has left me, because at least here one is in the midst of the struggle, as difficult as it is for those of us who go against popular opinion. Finally, I have always found peace in struggles, and the professional intellectual who gets involved in public matters only by writing about them lives like a coward and tries to make up for his impotence by verbal exaggeration. In fact, only by taking risks can we justify thought, and besides, anything is better than France, a place of resignation and wickedness, a swamp where I was stifling. Yes, I woke up happily for the first time in months."

Camus was convinced that the FLN would launch a campaign of urban terrorism, to provoke civilian and military reactions. He wanted to have a public meeting to encourage dialogue, and the mayor of Algiers had promised an auditorium in the town hall; but local officials changed their minds, and when a second auditorium also suddenly became unavailable, Camus thought of renting out a movie theater for his meetings. Several took place in an atmosphere of excited confusion, and although Camus was unaware of it, most participants knew that the FLN would be there. At one meeting, an Algerian Moslem schoolteacher screamed at Camus, "We don't give a damn about your civilian truce! What we need is independence — immediate, absolute, and without any conditions!" Later Camus said to Pierre Miquel, "I asked myself what I was doing there. It's a hell of a mess, but they don't really expect us to take down our pants, do they?"

Camus defined his plan during a series of discussions with a wide range of Algerian groups, explaining that during the truce he hoped for, combatants would promise to respect civilians, prisoners, and all other unarmed people. Despite Poncet's protests, Camus continued to speak and write about "the French" and "the Arabs" instead of referring to the latter as simply "the Algerians." He explained that it was not a question of condemning the current struggle or approving it, but of humanizing the war. Some listeners approved, but others raised the problem of traitors, as the FLN felt obliged to execute them. Camus replied that he had strong hopes for an agreement with the FLN.

After one lunch at an Algiers restaurant, Camus realized with some distress that his Moslem interlocutors were only interested in the FLN; but like Charles Poncet, he did not wish to play favorites with this group. At another meeting, on January 19, a Moslem man told Camus in so many words, "You ask us to stop terrorism, but we can only do it if you realize that independence must come first." Camus had no reply and simply left the hall.

Before a final meeting on January 22, a thousand invitations were sent out, and Camus prepared a thirty-five-minute speech which he dictated to a secretary. A few days before his arrival, some friends had advised him not to stay at the Saint-Georges Hotel, as there had recently been some disturbances there during a speech by the progressive politician Charles Hernu. However, Camus did register there, and he was now receiving death threats by phone and in the mail; but despite the risk of kidnappers, he refused to move somewhere else. Reactionaries who opposed the French liberals had phony invitations printed up to get them admitted to the January 22 meeting, and when local police discovered this ruse at the last minute, the real invitations had to be changed and sent out again.

A separate Moslem security force was organized for the event, and in an impromptu meeting with Moslem shopkeepers in a friend's home, Camus tried to press for his plan to force the French government and the FLN to spare civilian victims. One of the shopkeepers, Mohamed Lebjaoui, said he doubted whether the French government would agree to this proposal, since the repression of civilian populations was at the heart of their peacekeeping policy. Camus said, "If the FLN accepts the plan and not the French government, I will take up my pilgrim's staff and journey through France to denounce the government, and that will create a scandal! But first, the FLN must agree." Lebjaoui claimed that his group had contacts with the FLN, and suggested that Camus organize a meeting with a French government representative in order to discuss the idea. Camus was ready to speak with Moslem supporters of the FLN, but he had no patience with the group's European sympathizers. While he felt he understood Algerians, he remained very much a European from Algeria himself. Thus he refused to meet with André Madouze, a French professor of religious history who had become an energetic supporter of the FLN.

The day of the big meeting arrived, and Camus entered the Cercle du Progrès flanked by two friends of his brother, Lucien, whom he laughingly introduced as "my two gorillas." By 4:30 p.m. the auditorium was full, mostly with Europeans, with lots of women, intellectuals, and upper-middle-class people, but only a few modest folk and Moslems. Outside in the street, a thousand protesters yelled "Death to Camus!" although a few voices could be heard crying "Camus is on our side!"

Camus read his prepared text gravely, hammering home that he was there not to divide but to reunite the opposing parties, as a writer who had devoted part of his life to serving Algeria. He claimed that his request "was beyond political matters," which was unrealistic, since by that time in Algiers, everything was a political matter. He said that he had "more doubt than certainty to express," but that for twenty years he had sought the agreement of Algeria's two peoples. Outside the hall, a few protesters still hoped that Camus would support an independent Algeria, or "Algeria for the Algerians," as their slogan went.

Camus made an appeal to moderate Arabs, urging them to speak alongside liberal Frenchmen, because otherwise they might soon "have their mouths shut for them. . . . We are too easily resigned to fate. We believe too readily that after all, only bloodshed makes history advance, and then the strongest make progress at the expense of the weakness of others." Just as Camus spoke these words, pebbles struck the windows of the hall. Growing pale, Camus hurried on with his speech: "Men of culture and faith have the duty . . . not to abandon historical studies nor to serve what is cruel and inhuman in them. They must maintain themselves and help men against what oppresses them, to support them against the fates that surround us."

He concluded, "We are in a duel with knives, and the world is moving ahead at the speed of a supersonic jet. The same day that newspapers print the horrible story of our provincial quarrels, they announce European atomic stockpiles. If only Europe could come to terms with itself, waves of richness would cover the continent and overflow as far as our home, making our problems and hatreds obsolete."

Applauded by a moved public, Camus dwelled in lyric fashion on the idea of free men "who refuse both to employ and to submit to terror." Once again he addressed the theme of "neither executioners nor victims." After him, a number of other speakers talked briefly, asking the public for signatures on a petition for a civilian truce; among them was Emmanuel Roblès.

Camus saluted Sheik El Okbi, whom he had defended seventeen years before in the *Alger Républicain.* Roblès had visited the old man at his home in Saint-Eugène to ask him to attend the meeting; the sheik arrived on a stretcher.

The hall emptied slowly, in order to avoid confronting the opponents massed outside. Some participants regrouped in a back room. Louis Bénisti chatted with Amar Ouzegane, reflecting on a common French-Algerian platform, that would unite France and Algeria.

Camus sensed that his speech had disappointed Jean de Maisonseul, who felt that the idea of a truce was a lovely one, but that even if it was agreed upon, it could not last more than eight days. However, Maisonseul loyally traveled to Paris to meet with the secretary of the Jewish Agency to push Algerian Jews to cooperate with Camus. Jews had been significantly absent at the writer's speech, which had attracted Moslem religious leaders but no rabbis.

The day after the speech, Camus visited with the governor general, Jacques Soustelle, who said he was interested by the proposed truce but was unsure of how to enforce it. Camus's friend Edmond Brua wrote of the speech in *Le Journal d'Alger:* "Yesterday Albert Camus launched an emotional appeal for protecting innocent civilians. . . . One would like to believe that if the hostile protesters who crowded the place du Gouvernement to scream while Camus spoke to an overflowing audience at the Circle of Progress had heard his words, they might have been ashamed of their yells. One hopes that they would have sincerely applauded the great writer, as the audience did."

After a long visit with his mother, Camus returned to Paris, where he published a last editorial about Algeria in *L'Express,* headlined "One Step Forward." There had been much gossip in Paris about his trip to Algeria, and Camus wrote, "I am well aware that this type of action inspires more ridicule than support, and people like to see it as an admission of ignorance or powerlessness. If they feel that way, let them, but I firmly believe in the possibility of an unconstrained association between the French and Arabs in Algeria. I also believe that this association of free and equal people represents the most equitable solution, but as for the means to achieve it, after much thought and a long comparison of the different ways to arrive at this goal, I must honestly confess to lingering hesitation."

French President René Coty named a new president of the council, Guy Mollet, who announced that a free election would determine Algeria's fate. Camus told Jean Grenier that the Arabs "are making insane demands for an independent Algerian government, where the French will be considered as foreigners unless they want to convert [to Islam], and war is inevitable." Grenier wondered what would happen if France abandoned everything, which looked likely, and Camus replied, "She cannot, because she could never agree to throw one million, two hundred thousand Frenchmen into the sea."

Camus called the atmosphere a "Munich of the left-wing," evoking the notorious 1938 Munich agreement betwen Hitler and British Prime Minister Neville Chamberlain, who falsely believed he had negotiated a lasting peace treaty. He praised a French radio personality, Claude Terrien (really Claude de Fréminville), who often criticized the searches and the use of torture by the French army in Algeria. The writer told Terrien, "I can imagine the sort of courage it takes for you to treat the same problems every morning and to try to clarify things, and turn the egoism of the Frenchmen in France into feelings. I can imagine the kind of courage it takes for you to speak out loud about your suffering and ours. . . . You see, Claude, at least you have the advantage over me that you are listened to."

On February 2, Camus published an article that had nothing to do with the news, and which turned out to be his last for *L'Express*, headlined "Thanks to Mozart." He discussed Don Giovanni, who "died amid divine fire. . . . Mozart knew that every artist learns from his own experience that to grow as a creator and as a man, one must recognize one's own limits and respect them, because in trying to go past them, one can get smashed up. . . . [Mozart] lived and created very close to us in time and space, and our lives and struggles therefore are instantly justified."

He explained to Jean Grenier that he had quit *L'Express* on February 8 because he disagreed with Servan-Schreiber's position on Algeria. Camus had put his letter of resignation into the rapid-post "pneumatique" at the post office on the rue des Saints-Pères, and before dropping it into the slot, he held on to the letter for a moment, wondering whether or not to send it, then decided, "Yes, that's what I must do, I must make up my mind, and now I am free. Yet *L'Express* paid me thirty thousand francs per article." To another friend, André Rosfelder, Camus explained, "I left *L'Express* . . . for two apparently contradictory reasons, which define my position: Mauriac's joining the 'France-USSR' movement, and Guy Mollet's sideshow in Algiers." "France-USSR" was not simply a cultural organization, because according to Camus, "nothing Communist is cultural." He saw in the revolution of the Algerian nationalists, the FLN, the long arms of the governments of Moscow and Cairo, which supported the group's terrorism.

At *L'Express*, Camus had not found the fraternal spirit that he had felt at *Alger Républicain* and *Combat*. He felt alone and powerless, and asked Robert Namia, a staffer at *Alger Républicain*, what could be done for Algeria. Namia was an admirer of Camus's and would have liked to see him become editor in chief of *L'Express*, but he replied, "There is nothing to do except shut up, because whatever we say, we will be thought traitors." Camus replied, "You're right."

Deciding that silence could also be a form of action, Camus resolved to remain silent about Algeria, "in order not to add to its unhappiness or to the foolishness which is being written on the subject." He was guided by two principles: he violently condemned the murder of civilians, and he understood that some Algerian freedom fighters who were not full-fledged terrorists might nevertheless one day kill his mother. Secondly, unlike many contributors to *L'Express*, such as François Mauriac and Jean Daniel, he never emotionally or intellectually accepted the idea of Algerian independence. For Camus, independence would make the country's humble white folk, such as his own family, into foreigners and second-rate citizens in a land that was nevertheless theirs. Namia was right, in that Camus was seen as a traitor not only by the pieds noirs and the right wing, because he did not sing the praises of French Algeria, but also by the Paris left wing, because he did not support the violence of the FLN.

Independence was at the heart of the matter; but curiously, he never had a frank discussion on the matter with either Servan-Schreiber or Françoise Giroud before leaving *L'Express*. Servan-Schreiber considered it a personal failure not to have managed to convince Camus to stay on as a contributor, because although he was considered hypersensitive, he was an excellent journalist, as Giroud felt too. Still, he confidently declared, "We'll see Camus back here again!"

Servan-Schreiber was wrong. Camus confessed to a colleague that he had even stopped reading the magazine, and when after his departure, Jean-Paul Sartre published some articles in *L'Express* about the Hungarian uprisings in 1956, that did not further endear Camus to the magazine. He simply could not understand how anyone could see the Algerian problem differently than he did.

André Rosfelder wrote to him from Algiers to say that some of their mutual right-wing friends regretted having demonstrated against Camus when he spoke at the Circle of Progress in Algiers, and Camus answered, "I understand why your friends are upset, and you can tell them that I was not upset with them even for one minute because of their demonstrations against me. But it ought to make them think, that the current situation of ignoble massacres of civilians and children by terrorists gives valid arguments to the most hard-headed faction of Frenchmen in Algeria. . . . Inside me there is someone right now who is dying of shame, and if I thought that some action was possible, even the most insane one, I would try it . . . but we are hurtling toward the abyss and we have already arrived at its edge. Bit by bit, French public opinion accepts the idea of war, a development that I have tried to make clear to Arabs of goodwill, or at least of less bad will. But the only result, I suppose, is that I have won their mistrust."

Camus was concerned about Rosfelder's "continuing trust" in the French governor Jacques Soustelle, who started out as a liberal but was so horrified by terrorism that he rejected any so-called abandonment of Algeria by the French. Camus said, "After considerable thought, I must say that I have no confidence [in Soustelle], and you can explain to your friends what I am saying. They should only try to understand that a man like myself, who has never known discouragement, and who is horrified by all easy ways out, does not write this to you without a reason. I am torn apart, and that's the truth."

In Paris, Camus made some attempts to convince the French government that his plan for a truce was not merely utopian; but his efforts were lost in administrative quicksand. Camus's friends in Algeria, like Camus himself, never were clearly approved of by the FLN, which more than ever, through terrorist attacks and reprisals, took control of events in the writer's homeland. Algeria entered into the era of plastic bombings and the cycle of revolution-repression-violence.

In 1955, a state of emergency was declared in Algeria, and censorship was re-established.

Chapter Forty-three

The Prisoner's Shout

*I*n mid-March 1956, Camus sent a typed manuscript of what would be called *La Chute* to Vivienne Perret, the wife of his friend Jean Bloch-Michel, the associate foreign affairs editor of *L'Express*: "Do you have the time to read these 120 pages? Looking at them, I hesitate a little and you will see why. If Jean could read them too, you might advise me. . . . The book might hurt Francine. . . . In any case, I'm glad I did it. For one year I really thought I wouldn't be able to write anymore." He added in a postscript, "No title so far, except for *A Hero of Our Time*, which has already been used, or *The Last Judgment*, or maybe *The Good Apostle*."

On March 31 he wrote to Vivienne again, saying, "The book will appear under the title of *The Shout: A Tale*. But now I feel completely detached from it, and I still have the same appetite, or I should say fever, for work, like a prisoner who wants to catch up on lost time."

For more than a year, Camus had repeated to his friends at Gallimard and to Francine and Maria that he was "empty." But in addition to his journalistic activities, he had been busy with theater for the past eighteen months, and he finished seven stories: "La Femme adultère," "Le Rénégat," "Les Muets," "L'Hôte," "Jonas," "La Pierre qui pousse," and *La Chute*, the story that emerged like a pearl into a long tale, as if by independent growth. Twenty years before, Camus had noted, "Sometimes I need to write things which partially escape from me, but which prove that what is inside is stronger than I am." Camus decided to publish *La Chute* before his novellas, and toyed with the idea of other titles, like *The Shout, The Pillory, A Puritan of Our Time, The Mirror*, and *The Day's Business*. It was Roger Martin du Gard who suggested *La Chute*—The Fall—and Camus adopted it, despite André Belamich's warning that "people will talk about 'Camus's *Fall*' with all that it implies."

La Chute was described by Camus as follows: "The narrator in *La Chute* makes a calculated confession. . . . A refugee in Amsterdam, a city of canals and cold light, where he pretends to be a hermit and a prophet, this former lawyer is waiting for sympathetic listeners in a sleazy bar. He has a modern heart, which is to say that he cannot bear being judged, and therefore he hastens to prosecute himself, but only in order to better judge other people. He looks at himself in a mirror, but finally pushes it towards others. Where does he stop confessing and start accusing others? Is the narrator putting himself on trial, or his era? Does he represent a specific case, or is he the man of the hour? There is only one truth in this game of mirrors: pain, and all that it promises."

Reading this tale, Robert Gallimard exclaimed, "You took us all for damn fools! So this is the literary impotence you were complaining about?" In interviews, Camus stressed that he was not meant to be the work's narrator, Jean-Baptiste Clamence, but in fact, Camus was never as profoundly and subtly autobiographical as beneath the mask of Clamence, and friends recognized him behind the fictional guise.

On May 16, 1956, Gallimard published *La Chute* in a first edition of 16,500 copies. On June 1, 11,000 more copies were printed, and on June 8, another 11,000. By November, 126,500 copies had been sold. Francine joked, "You owe me this one," because she understood that her husband wanted to depict a part of himself, as well as the Parisian milieu where he felt ill at ease. She and several other readers knew that the episode in *La Chute* when a young woman throws herself into the Seine from the Pont des Arts referred to Francine's suicide attempts in Oran and Paris in 1954. In October 1954, Camus had spent four days in Holland, including two in Amsterdam, which provided the basis for the story. When Camus showed Francine parts of the book prior to publication, she told him, "You're always pleading the causes of all sorts of people, but do you ever hear the screams of people who are trying to reach you?" The cry of the young woman who isn't saved by Clamence was also the stifled cry of Francine, which Albert did not hear or understand, as well as that of other women. His friend Roger Quilliot would recall the day when Camus, working in the large room of the rue Madame apartment, told him he couldn't go out to lunch, and would explain at another time. He did so, stating, "My wife tried to commit suicide." Of course, *La Chute* was not purely autobiographical in content.

Eight years before, in 1948, Camus wrote in his notebooks that ever since his first books, such as *Noces*, he had tried "to depersonalize myself (each time in a different tone). Only then can I speak for myself." He stated, "Only great spirits interest me, but I am not a great spirit." Camus revealed himself in the character of Jean-Baptiste Clamence, haunted by guilt and lies, duplicity and cynicism. Simone de Beauvoir read *La Chute* and felt that in projecting his resentments into his confessions Camus's narrative lacked acuity and bite. Jean-Paul Sartre, who also received a copy of the book, without any personal inscription, felt it was a masterpiece and perhaps Camus's best book, because his estranged friend both revealed himself and hid himself completely in it. But Sartre's crowd could not embrace it, nor could the journalists who reviewed the book.

In his final speech, the character Clamence speculates on what would happen if he were beheaded and his "still-fresh head" were lifted above the assembled crowd for them to recognize it: "I would end, unseen and unknown, my career as false prophet crying in the wilderness and refusing to leave it." Just as in *L'Etranger*, where Meursault asks for a crowd to witness his guillotining, Camus dealt with a recurring nightmare, his own execution. The final cries in *L'Etranger* and *La Chute* are of guilt recognized by others, which leads to punishment of the hero, according to whether he accepts or rejects his guilt. Meursault is in fact guillotined, whereas Clamence, like Camus, only dreams of his own execution.

Jean-Baptiste Clamence in *La Chute* is a forty-year-old man, and Camus was forty-three when he finished the book. Clamence has left Paris, "a superb stage set inhabited by four million silhouettes," and Camus always longed to get away from the city and its fickle literary crowd. *La Chute* contains some hints of the joking and cheekiness that friends appreciated in Camus the man. Clamence dryly describes himself: "Nature served me well in terms of physique, a noble pose comes easily to me." Jean Grenier and others enjoyed joking about Camus's "noble" Castilian side. In another coincidence, the intellectual sports fan Clamence says, "I'd rather have looked like a rugby player," and Camus too would have preferred to have an athlete's stocky build. Clamence is a "tireless dancer" at bars and nightclubs, as was Camus. Clamence does not sleep with prostitutes, but he respects them; and on at least one occasion, Camus introduced a Paris whore to his wife, Francine.

Clamence displays a "well-known courtesy," and Camus, whether in stores, restaurants, banks, or at the Gallimard office, was always polite, although he could snub pushy people with a brusqueness that Michel and Robert Gallimard reproached him for. Clamence is described as generous, and although Camus did not broadcast the fact, he regularly responded to requests for donations from charitable organizations, especially for victims of disease and for destitute singers and writers. Otherwise, he could only be convinced with difficulty to spend his money, and refused to throw it around.

Clamence says, "I have only been sincere and enthusiastic when I played sports and in the regiment, when I acted in plays we put on for our own pleasure," and Camus himself stated, "The only places on earth where

I feel innocent are at Sunday soccer matches in a jam-packed stadium and at the theater, which I have loved with an unsurpassed passion." Even their attitude toward honors was the same: both Clamence and Camus refused the Legion of Honor repeatedly.

Quite a bit of *La Chute* is devoted to women, with whom Clamence is successful "without much effort," and the same was true of Camus, to put it mildly. Clamence states, "Sensuality alone ruled my love life. . . . I have judged almost all the women I have known as better than myself. . . . For a ten-minute love affair, I would have renounced both my parents. . . . It is painful for me to admit that I would have exchanged ten conversations with Einstein for a date with a pretty walk-on extra. But after ten dates with her, I would usually be longing for Einstein, or serious books."

Friends like Roger Quilliot had often seen Camus abandon serious conversations about Marx or the Russian anarchist Mikhail Bakunin in order to concentrate on a charming young woman; and friends, less gifted seducers, in both Algiers and Paris, could never forgive him for his conquests.

Clamence and Camus also shared negative qualities. The writer could be tender and charming, or odious and arrogant, with a smile that could seem natural or forced, according to the moment. And Clamence exclaims, "I am considered charming, just imagine that! . . . You know, charm is a way of answering 'yes' when no clear question has been asked." Clamence never seduced his friends' wives, preferring to stop being friends with a man before sleeping with his wife; but in real life Camus did not always have this scruple. When Camus slept with their wives, some of his Paris friends acted resigned, complaisant, or even flattered.

Clamence spends much time picking up women: "Standing on the sidewalk in the middle of a fascinating discussion with friends, how many times have I lost my train of thought because at that very moment, a ravishing woman crossed the street?" Large numbers of friends recall Camus looking at lovely women of the sixth arrondissement as if he were undressing them in his mind. Speaking with Robert Gallimard about a pretty girl he had not yet met, Camus made a gesture with both hands to trace her breasts and asked, "Is she . . . intelligent?"

Clamence is afflicted by sexual jealousy, saying, "Sometimes I would go so far as to make [a woman] swear never to belong to another man." After leaving Simone Hié, Camus swore to himself never to be jealous again, but he could never keep that promise. Clamence couldn't either. French and Mediterranean to the core, Camus reproached Maria Casarès for love affairs she had had even before they met. When Casarès acted with Gérard Philipe in the play *Les Epiphanies*, the two actors had to roll over on top of one another onstage, and then the director added another detail: Philipe's hand poised on Casarès's groin. An upset Camus told Robert Gallimard, "You know, all of Paris is saying that Maria slept with that moron Gérard Philipe."

When he slept with a woman, and she insisted on further involvement, Camus would explain that his real attachments were elsewhere; and although brief sexual adventures posed no problem for him, he did have difficulty in leaving women whom he truly loved. This contributed to his cluttered emotional life; as Clamence declares, "I thought about my difficulty in definitively separating from a woman, which has led me to have several affairs simultaneously."

In public and in the media, Camus denied that Clamence was meant to be himself, saying in *Le Monde* three months after the book was published that his only point in common with Clamence was that they "shared a lack of imagination." Camus's denials were meant to protect his family and his private life. Separated now from Camus, Francine understood the book perfectly. Camus would say to friends at Gallimard and elsewhere that a man cannot sacrifice his own interests for the real or supposed interests of his children, and by his own standards, Camus remained loyal towards Francine. But like Clamence, who could never forget the "scream" of a young woman throwing herself into the Seine, the writer felt intermittent guilt about his domestic relationship.

Clamence speaks of being harshly judged, much as Camus had been by the Sartre crowd: "I felt vulnerable and publicly accused, and I felt that my peers stopped listening respectfully, as I was accustomed to. I had been the center of a circle, which broke apart and the people lined up in a single row, like a tribunal. . . . I received every wound at once, and immediately lost all my strength." Camus did not mention Sartre directly, although Clamence caricatured the philosopher's literary activity by writing an "Ode to the Police" and an "Apotheosis of the Meat Cleaver." Although Camus did not name the specific Montparnasse watering holes where Sartre hung out, he referred to "the little cafés where our professional humanists meet . . . our atheists of the bistros."

In the past three years, Camus had discovered he had many enemies, although he pretended to understand them. Camus found a new reason for disliking Jean-Paul Sartre when the philosopher stated that he supported total independence for Algeria. Camus felt that Sartre and his disciples accepted sanctified violence and so-called historical necessity in Algeria as well as in communism's bloody history. Clamence speaks with irony about temptations toward totalitarianism, and Camus may have had his literary enemies in mind: "I realize that one cannot avoid either dominating or being enslaved. Each man needs slaves the way he needs pure air, and to command is as natural as breathing, don't you agree?"

Even after he got *La Chute* out of his system, Camus still was aggressive about existentialism, whether Marxist or not. In a 1956 letter to a Harvard student, Nicolas Daniloff, he wrote, "I am not an existentialist in the current sense of the term. Sartre's existentialism seems to me a contradictory

philosophy in which confusions and bad faith abound. . . . Far from leading
to a decent solution of the problem of freedom versus authority, [existential-
ism can only lead] to servitude." As a lawyer, Clamence was steeped in his
specialty, "noble causes," as was Camus, who joked, "You'd think I slept with
Justice every night."

As for religion, *La Chute* accepts the existence of God, which Camus
did not, but seriously questions the "terrible law" of divine fate. Clamence
feels that he will be damned, or at least go to Purgatory, and the Amsterdam
canals which he walks by remind him of the concentric circles of Dante's
Hell. Camus, who had studied Saint Augustine and Pascal, spoke with ease
about sin and grace.

Readers and critics wondered if Jean-Baptiste Clamence's name was
chosen as a reference to Saint John the Baptist and to the Latin root of the
name Clamence, *clamans*, "he who shouts." Camus replied to a letter from
a Belgian student, Malvina Eeckhout, about these matters: "(1) Yes, there is
a play on words in Clamence's name, as you have suggested. (2) This character is sincere when he realizes his own duplicity, and I approve of him at
that moment. He is not sincere when he beats his own breast in order to better attack others, and I disapprove of this very modern attitude, which is why
he ends his long monologue with a sarcastic comment."

In some ways, the character Clamence gave Camus the chance to
rewrite his own trajectory. He knew that some Parisians complained that his
participation in the Resistance had been belated, but Clamence becomes involved even more slowly when he learns about the Resistance after arriving
in the French free zone: "Once I was informed, I hesitated, as the enterprise
seemed to me a bit mad and romantic, to tell the truth."

As *La Chute* was written with feverish spontaneity, it was not fit into a
cycle, as Camus tried to do with his other works. In *La Chute*, he summed
up his life and gave it unity almost in spite of himself. Never before had he
been as inspired, as transported by a style, very different from the first-person
tone of *L'Etranger* and the third-person of *La Peste*. Alternating paroxysms of
joy with lofty serenity, Camus added maxims, dry little phrases, and metaphysical questions in the tradition of his beloved Nietzsche and Chamfort:
"When you have no character, it's better to have a method." Modern man
would be remembered only for having "fornicated and read the newspaper."
He also described modern man in 1956 as having "a modern heart, which is
to say that he cannot stand being judged."

Pascal Pia had been out of touch with Camus and read his new book
critically, telling a friend: "I asked myself if I didn't have a 'modern heart'
and maybe I used to have one, but I lost it, because I don't care if I'm
judged, although that doesn't mean that I'm happier with myself today than
I was yesterday. No doubt the reason is that I'm older now, and my wisdom

must be plain old lassitude. In fact, I don't believe in the 'modern heart' which Camus denounces, nor in its opposite, which I suppose would be the 'antique heart.' . . . Clamence can say that we are all judges, but I don't believe him."

The philosopher and gadfly Emmanuel Berl, who got along very well with Camus, had just published a book, *Présence des morts*, in which he said that the French collaborator Drieu La Rochelle's suicide left him feeling guilty. Pia was as much irritated by Berl's book as he was with *La Chute*, and noted, "Mr. Berl speaks about Drieu in a way similar to Clamence in *La Chute*. Could an epidemic of penitent justice be afflicting the authors of Gaston Gallimard, to whom *Présence des morts* is dedicated?"

No critic could hurt Camus as much as Pia, now a supporter of Charles de Gaulle. His former comrade and big brother, once so present in his life, indirectly associated Camus with the villainous Drieu La Rochelle.

Other readers, whether close to Camus or not, sympathized with the story, even if they understood it imperfectly. Georges Didier, the former lycée classmate, now a Jesuit wrote to Camus, "I like the book's art in which the monologue, interminable to the vanishing point, expresses, almost as much as the content of the sentences, the painful impossibility of getting away from oneself. I liked the soul in it, too." The priest saw a Platonic quest for ecstasy in the book and suggested some theological parallels, pushing Camus towards a belief which he knew that the writer could not accept.

Another reader, François Mauriac, sensed the absence of God in *La Chute*: "Camus has omitted to put his life in the crucible of God's judgment, to which Christians are submitted. . . . Camus shows me that we Christians are not always the ones with the greatest passion to examine and delouse ourselves." Camus's friend Charles Poncet said that while he thought that the lucid, cruel book was one of the writer's best, it was a little jarring, all the same. Camus replied, "That must be because you see the world as a place of smiles."

Jean-Claude Brisville, who was preparing a book about Camus, said that Clamence seemed discouraged and wondered if the hero expressed Camus's current feelings. To which Camus replied, "True, my hero is discouraged, and that's why as a good modern nihilist, he exalts servitude, but when have I ever chosen to exalt servitude?"

Those who knew Camus as a man and a writer recognized him more easily in the calculated confessions of *La Chute* than in the cryptic declarations of *L'Etranger*. For such readers, Camus did not really cover up the autobiographical roots of *La Chute*. With his infinite game of mirrors, Clamence drew readers in and disconcerted them. Such readers included Fernande Faure, who said about Albert and Francine, "He hasn't been much happier than she has."

Meanwhile, although Camus had left Algeria, the country did not leave him. Amid terrorist attacks and army operations, his mother still refused to move to France, despite her son's insistence. Camus's longtime friend Jean de Maisonseul was arrested by French authorities under mysterious circumstances. Maisonseul awaited trial in jail and amused himself by discussing Camus's works with another prisoner who was also a fan of the writer's books. When Camus heard about the arrest, he wrote to the daily *Le Monde* on May 30, 1956, to express his "indignant stupefaction": "Until now I have forced myself to remain silent about the Algerian matters so as not to add to French misfortune there, and because in fact I did not approve of what was being said either by the right wing or the left wing." He explained that Maisonseul, whom he had known for twenty years, was a talented architect and painter and was in no way political, apart from supporting Camus's project for a civilian truce. One news report had implied that Maisonseul belonged to a subversive organization, but Camus insisted that the imprisoned man could not be accused of either trying to negotiate a cease-fire or "the establishment of an independent Algerian republic."

In his letter, Camus asked whether one still had the right to be liberal: "As for me, I am firmly opposed to any sort of capitulation and also opposed to the French far right wing in Algeria, who represent another sort of resignation, and an infinitely blameworthy one." He suggested that if Maisonseul had to be arrested, then it was also necessary to arrest Camus, Red Cross workers, and all those who were aware of the civilian truce project. He pointed out that only a month before, French Prime Minister Guy Mollet had sent him an enthusiastic note about the truce committee's actions, and Camus added sarcastically, "These congratulations will of course help keep my friend cool in his prison cell."

Camus also put private pressure on the government through his friend Roger Quilliot, a Socialist who had access to Mollet's staff. Since Maisonseul was not freed immediately, Camus published another article in the June 3–4 issue of *Le Monde* with a hostile command to Guy Mollet under the headline "Govern!" Camus attacked government policy and ended with a threat to "appeal directly to public opinion about it . . . to obtain protest about this by every means." He also insisted that reparations should be paid to Maisonseul for his prolonged and arbitrary detention.

In this open letter, Camus broke definitively with Guy Mollet: "Jean Maisonseul's friends cannot be satisfied by regrets expressed in a restrained manner. The reputation and freedom of a man are not bought with condolences and nostalgia. On the contrary, they are carnal realities by which we live or die, and I would even say that between eloquent speeches in the French National Assembly and a man's honor, that honor is the more urgent." Camus stated that relations between Algiers and Paris had degenerated to "bureaucratized anarchy, and France has become like a worm wriggling around, trying to find its head." He condemned French policy outright, saying, "Weakness can become a delirium which excuses all aberrations."

L'Express followed the controversy with attention, naming Camus its Man of the Week in an article signed by a certain Thomas Lenoir, a pen name for Françoise Giroud. The paper praised Camus for seeing and criticizing "Stalinist deviation," and charted the writer's relationship with Sartre, the "deadly destruction of a difficult friendship, tumultuous and intense, in which two men complemented and enriched one another." Camus was called "too famous at thirty-four years old," and his personal charms were enumerated: "He has eyes which are the color of twilight and all of the art of an actor, which he was between the ages of twenty-two and twenty-five." It went on to say that Camus was a "prisoner of his own glory, which quickly changed him into a statue, and it's possible that he may never get out of the desert where his voice is echoing, that of *L'Homme révolté* and an entire generation." Finally he was described as "a man flayed alive, who always seems to have an arrow sticking into his side, and who has as much trouble putting up with you as leaving you, acting as not acting, and believing instead of despairing."

Camus asked that the Algerian judiciary system hand over the Maisonseul case to be prosecuted in Paris, and wrote to Charles Poncet on May 30, "Recent events have made me beside myself, and I am now trying to move heaven and earth for Jean." If Maisonseul was not freed, Camus planned to organize demonstrations and labor strikes, but without the help of the massive French trade union, the Communist CGT, which would not have intervened on behalf of the anti-Communist Maisonseul. Poncet explained to Camus that Maisonseul had been found in possession of a letter containing a list of Moroccans who sympathized with the Algerian revolution, and that had aroused the suspicions of the local government.

Maisonseul was let out of prison on "conditional freedom," and Camus joked, "All of us are always under conditional freedom." As Maisonseul's case bogged down, the accused man spent his time at home painting, until charges were finally dropped on July 10, 1957.

By now, Francine had more or less resumed her normal life, teaching ten hours of mathematics classes each week at the Marcel Proust private school. The real litmus test was music, as Camus always encouraged her to play more, hoping she might become a professional musician. When Francine started playing the piano and organ again, everyone agreed that the worst of her tragic mental illness must now be over.

Chapter Forty-four **A Black-Hearted Anemone**

rancine spent her 1956 summer vacation in Palerme, near L'Isle sur-la-Sorgue, with the twins and her husband, who was finishing his new collection of stories. On August 6, Jean Grenier visited them, and Camus showed him the new manuscript, dedicated to Francine, which would be published in 1957 as *L'Exil et le royaume*. Camus, who always complained of not being able to write, was in fact experimenting with new styles, and he told Grenier, "I wanted to change the writing style with each novella, and work out something original."

In the title *L'Exil et le royaume*, the Exile was historic, geographical and moral, while the Kingdom was a Paradise Lost, beyond suffering and self-denial. Grenier particularly admired the story "Les Muets," in which Camus described a workers' strike, from memories of his childhood and of his uncle, a laborer. Camus joked with Grenier, "Oh, you liked 'Les Muets,' a story where I wanted to offer social realism for the people down the block." In the quite realistic "Les Muets" the author returned to the working-class neighborhood of his childhood in Belcourt, far from the Paris offices of the *NRF* and the abstract ideas of Jean-Baptiste Clamence in *La Chute*. "Les Muets" is redolent of sardines, blood sausage, wood fires, and the sweat of workmen. Camus criticized those who "made discourses about manual labor" without knowing what they were talking about. In Paris, Camus was often accused of being a privileged reactionary, and "Les Muets" was his way of pointing to lower-class characters and replying, "This is my family!"

Camus asked Grenier what he thought of the story "L'Esprit confus," and Grenier admitted that he hadn't understood anything about it, and if Camus had not told him that the subject was left-wing intellectualism, he never would have guessed it. It was hard to see the principal character, an African missionary awaiting his replacement, as a symbol of leftist intellectuals. Camus promised to rewrite "L'Esprit confus" to make it clearer, and Grenier said that he also liked the novellas "La Femme adultère" and "L'Hôte," although he did not see Arabs as Camus did. In these stories, Arabs are silent and impassive, sitting in buses as "mute escorts," in the way that Moslems almost always appear in Camus's books. As a journalist, Camus often spoke about Arabs, but as a novelist he had little to do with them, compared to his deep knowledge of and care for the Frenchmen of Algeria. He often portrayed Arabs conventionally as "free but impoverished lords of a strange kingdom." In "L'Hôte," he described a schoolteacher named Daru, who lives alone and feels exiled, and to whom a policeman entrusts an Arab prisoner. The Arab's hands are bound because he has murdered someone, but Daru refuses to guard the prisoner, telling the policeman: "All this disgusts me, and your boy there most of all, but I wouldn't turn him in, and I'd fight to avoid doing so, if necessary." Daru gives dates, bread, and sugar to the Arab and lets him free, but the prisoner decides of his own volition to go to jail.

Daru is another of the author's many masks. In the novella's symbolic ending, someone writes anonymously on Daru's classroom blackboard, "You turned in our brother, and you will pay." The teacher's no-win situation had some parallels with Camus's situation with Algeria. Daru, "in that vast country which he had loved so well . . . was alone," and Camus had stressed nonviolence only to find himself caught between two warring communities.

Before the new collection of short stories appeared, Françoise Giroud sent Camus a friendly note, asking for authorization to print one of the stories in *L'Express*, adding, "It's sad not seeing you here anymore." Camus replied with a curt letter of refusal, dryly conveying his "faithful and respectful memories" to Françoise.

By now, Camus had returned to work at the Gallimard offices. One day Robert Gallimard noticed him in the courtyard of the NRF gazing tenderly at a young actress, Catherine Sellers, and he realized that Camus was once again in love. Before Camus presented Sellers to Janine and Michel Gallimard, awaiting her arrival at a restaurant, he said, "You'll see, she's a marvelous actress and an exquisite woman, and it's extraordinary how she eats nothing. She'll order a slice of ham, cut off every last bit of fat, nibble three tiny pieces, and push her plate away, you'll see."

Camus wrote in his *Carnets*, "I love this anxious, hurt little face, which is sometimes tragic, and always handsome. This little being gets too involved, and her face is lit up by a dark, sweet flame of purity and spirit. It's the first time in a long while that I am touched in my heart by a woman, without any desire, any design, or game playing, and I love her for herself, with a certain sadness." It was untrue that Camus felt "no desire" for Sellers, as both would soon find out.

He was working on his theatrical adaptations. However, he did not just want to translate some plays, but to establish a theater troupe with an ambitious program, to direct his own theater. Camus had definitely bounced back, as he was planning his latest cycle of a novel, a play, and an essay. He even thought he might try to be an actor again as well.

He had been an amateur theater director in Algeria, and now he could become a professional. In 1955, while he worked on *La Chute* and his novellas, he adapted the Italian writer Dino Buzzati's play *Caso clinico* under the title *Un Cas intéressant*. Camus told the actor Michel Bouquet that he would reread Shakespeare's *Romeo and Juliet* as another candidate for possible adaptation. Camus still ranked Shakespeare very high; as he wrote to Bouquet in 1956, about *Romeo and Juliet*, "A project like that ought to have from the beginning . . . a sensitive and lucid mind to translate its beauties."

With an admirable sense of organization, Camus sketched out plans for a repertory theater that would give eight performances per week: five of a modern French play, two of a foreign classic, and a matinee of a French classic. He imagined taking over the Hébertot Theater for his plans. Camus always had ongoing projects, and he used calculated stamina rather than madness in his methods. Like a real craftsman, if he started writing a book, he would finish it. Although Sartre was more prolific than Camus, he did not complete a good number of the projects that he began.

Among the foreign plays that Camus hoped to produce were Ben Jonson's *The Silent Woman*, which he had already staged in Algiers; Eugene O'Neill's *Strange Interlude*, which he thought he might act in; and the Russian writer Griboyedov's verse play *Gore ot uma* (Woe from Wit). Other projects were Tolstoy's *The Power of Darkness* and Camus's own adaptations of Shakespeare's *Othello*, *The Tempest*, and *Timon of Athens*. Camus was able to acquire a real taste for Shakespeare thanks in good part to Sellers, who spoke fluent English and knew Elizabethan literature well. He also seriously considered staging Pirandello's *Tonight We Improvise*, Tirso de Molina's *El burlador de Sevilla*, Calderón's *The Wonder-Working Magician*, Strindberg's *Ghost Sonata*, and Kleist's *Katharina von Heilbronn*. The second part of his repertory theater would consist of classic French plays like Corneille's *Sophonisbe*, Racine's *Bérénice*, and Molière's *Le Misanthrope*, in which Camus would have liked to act the role of Alceste. The third part was modern French plays, which would include the reworked version of *Le Malentendu* and theatrical adaptations of his friend Louis Guilloux's novel *Le Sang noir* and Dostoyevsky's *The Possessed*. Camus was rereading Dostoyevsky at this time; since childhood this Russian mystic novelist had haunted him, the way Melville and Nietzsche did.

Camus was willing to devote ten years of his life to the theater, and he wanted to commission new plays from other great writers. Among his own playwriting projects was a version of Don Juan that would also include the

Faust myth, an idea he had been mulling over since his student days in Algiers.

Stage directors also solicited Camus, such as Jean-Louis Barrault, who wanted him to adapt Kafka's *The Castle*, despite their mutually disappointing experience with *L'Etat de siège*. Jean Vilar, who had lost Camus's manuscript copy of an adaptation of John Webster's *The Duchess of Malfi*, wanted Camus to adapt Calderón's play *The Mayor of Zalamea*.

Camus, who could be good at persuading himself that he was used up as a writer, was ready to plunge into the theater works of Prosper Mérimée, Alexander Pushkin, Christopher Marlowe, Miguel Cervantes, and Paul Claudel, according to various lists he made, which were preserved by Catherine Sellers. He also considered writing a play entitled *Lespinasse, ou le double amour*, which would illustrate his practical thesis that one can love two people at the same time. By the summer of 1956, Camus had already written ten plays, including six adaptations or creative collaborations. For nearly twenty years, he had been making adaptations, but as a director he was a relative neophyte.

Camus felt somewhat misunderstood as an adaptor of plays, saying, "People ask me with acute concern, 'Why do you adapt texts when you could write your own?' Of course . . . in fact these are my own too, the adaptations I have written, and I'll write other original ones which will no doubt create a yearning for my adaptations one day." He explained the difference between the two forms of writing: "When I wrote my plays, then the writer is foremost, in a work that answers to a vast, calculated plan. . . . But when I adapt them, then the stage director is foremost in my mind." Camus felt as though he was going back to his youth, when he co-wrote *Révolte dans les Asturies*: "I believe in the total spectacle that is conceived, inspired, and directed by the same mind, and written and directed by the same man, which allows a unity of tone, style, and rhythms that are the essential resources of a spectacle."

Camus repeated to his actors that he insisted on "the right to evolve," and his strongest theatrical law was that "everything must be enlarged and translated into flesh." Silences must be audible, and even immobility must be spectacular. He encouraged his actors to scream so much in rehearsal that Catherine Sellers's doctor, his friend Stacha Cviklinski, worried that he would destroy his actresses' voices. Before, he had urged Maria Casarès toward new crescendos with her own hoarse voice. He felt especially at ease with a group of actors that included Michel Bouquet, Jean-Pierre Joris, and Serge Reggiani and actresses like Maria Casarès, Catherine Sellers, and Tatiana Moukhine. Among his actors, Camus ruled without any question. During one walk with Jean Daniel, Camus praised actors for working all year, unlike academics, whom he called "titled heirs of the bourgeoisie"—Jean-

Paul Sartre and Simone de Beauvoir, for example, who even though they had stopped teaching years ago still took vacations in accordance with academic schedule. Camus told Daniel, "I prefer the company of theater folk, virtuous or not, to the company of my brothers the intellectuals, not only because intellectuals are rarely pleasant and can never get along with each other, but because in intellectual society I always have the impression of having done something that I must be forgiven for."

Camus did not like a certain media mythology that "wants you to believe that theater people are animals who go to bed late and divorce early, and I will doubtless disappoint you by saying that the theater has even less divorce than the textile, beet growing, and journalistic industries. When it happens to actors, we talk about it more, because Sarah Bernhardt's heart interests the public more than that of [the rich industrialist] M. Boussac." Camus needed the physical activity of rehearsals and performances, finding this fatigue exalting: "Only in my youth, playing team sports, have I known this powerful feeling of hope and solidarity that go with long days of training up to the game, whether you win or lose. . . . The little morality I know, I learned on the soccer field and the stage, which remain my real universities." Camus had learned the morality of fraternity and loyalty, without which any troupe dissolves.

He knew his trade well: "Theater also helps me to escape abstraction, which threatens any writer." For the festival at Angers in 1953, he had worked with model sets designed by the painter Leonor Fini and was lyrical about the pleasure he felt: "I love this trade which forces me to think not just about the psychology of various characters, but also about where to put a lamp or a pot of geraniums, the texture of a fabric or the weight and relief design of an architectural coffer that must be displayed on an arch." As a director, he would ask himself questions aloud, scribble notes, and run a sort of "disorganized race through the theater . . . a singular art that has its own laws, accidents, and voice." Camus told Catherine Sellers that all arts need an audience, and "if I could have chosen a talent at birth, I would have been a sculptor, and not a writer, a soccer player, or an actor. For me, sculpture is the first among the arts." Yet for him, theater's total dependence on an audience gave it a unique power and attraction. Camus had his own ideas about the relative importance of text, actors, and direction in a play: "The greatest actor is . . . the one who is most submissive to an author's will." When a play displeased him, Camus was not afraid to show it, and he walked out of Marcel Achard's comedy *Patate* at intermission, although the play was a crowd pleaser.

Camus wrote to Francine, who was in the south of France with the Polges: "Rehearsals [for *Requiem pour une nonne*] have begun in the afternoon and evening, and therefore I have only mornings free, when I still have to go to the *NRF* sometimes. I have revised all of my novellas based on your criticisms and Grenier's observations. . . . At least the whole thing has gained in truth. As for quality, heaven shall judge, since there are no critics there. Thank you, in any case. The rehearsals right now are about blocking, and they are rather dull because it's very detailed work, but of course it's amusing to begin this business over again, and I've got stage fright because it's a difficult game."

Three years before, Camus's literary agent, Nicole Lambert, the sister of Michel Gallimard, had asked William Faulkner for permission to adapt his novel *Requiem for a Nun*. In general, Camus did not approve of theatrical adaptations, telling Arthur Koestler, "I know from experience that the theater magnifies things and makes them banal, and when you have chosen the novelistic form to tell a story, that's because it permits nuances and shadow-play that only a novel can." But Faulkner's novel had a natural theatrical structure, and the American writer had himself helped a student, Joan Williams, adapt the work for the theater. First published in 1951, Faulkner's story was divided into three sections or "acts." Camus transformed this into two acts and seven scenes.

At the same time, the French translator of American literature Maurice Edgar Coindreau was preparing a French version of Faulkner's novel for Gallimard. He and Camus discussed how best to translate the title, containing the troublesome word "nun," which in an antiecclesiastical country like France had grotesque and comic overtones. Coindreau thought that *Requiem pour une réligieuse*, would be frightful, since "réligieuse" means not just a nun but also a kind of pastry. *Requiem pour une bonne sœur* was considered even worse, since "bonne sœur" had a pawky, homespun aura that might evoke a dowdy provincial religious school. *Requiem pour une sainte* sounded better, but the only problem was that there was no saint in this tragic play. Coindreau feared that the word "nonne" would give French audiences the giggles. But the versions of the play and the novel absolutely had to have the same title, and Camus finally decided that it would be *Requiem pour une nonne.*

Camus found the story of Nancy compelling, a servant who murders the child of her employers and is sentenced to hang for the crime. He did not follow Faulkner word for word in his adaptation, but wanted to remain faithful "to certain particularities of his style," which reminded him of longwinded tirades in classical French tragedies. He wrote to Coindreau that he had changed Faulkner's lengthy, involuted style only once, "in the final scene [in the prison] where it really became like preaching, which might have been badly received in 1956 Paris. But through all this, Faulkner was first priority and despite the difficulty of the project and my own flaws, I believe that I have served him faithfully." Camus saw Faulkner as a profoundly tragic dramatist, and his novel contained the theme of a hero torn between his responsibilities and fate. Some theatergoers were surprised by the religious tone of the text, and Camus said, "It's true that I don't believe in God, but that doesn't mean I'm an atheist, and I would agree with Benjamin Constant, who thought a lack of religion was vulgar and even hackneyed." He was no more a believer in 1956 than he had been in 1936, but he was still interested in the dialogue between believers and agnostics, and he would discuss religion in his apartment on the rue de Chanaleilles with the Abbé Altermann, a well-known personality in French religious circles.

In order to spare Francine's feelings, Camus did not invite Maria Casarès to work on this project with him. When he spotted Catherine Sellers acting in a production of Chekhov's *The Sea Gull* in April 1956, he made a date with her at the Brasserie Lipp, and gave her the manuscript of *Requiem pour une nonne*, saying, "Read the play, and if you like the role [of Temple Stevens, Nancy's employer], it's yours."

Catherine Sellers's father was a French doctor who died during the German occupation after being deported to a concentration camp, and her mother was an amateur violinist. Catherine had written a college thesis on Elizabethan theater, focusing on John Webster's *The Duchess of Malfi*. By coincidence, as an actress, Sellers had already once replaced Maria Casarès for a touring production of Luigi Pirandello's *Six Characters in Search of an Author*. Catherine had been briefly married to an Englishman, and kept his name, Sellers, after their divorce. Both serious and funny by temperament, Sellers was the most erudite actress whom Camus had met. She had lived in Algeria during the war and so could discuss the place with him. With her elfin body and dark eyes, she would meditate for hours about the slightest detail of her performances.

Camus had offered her a compelling part that went to the brink of insanity. He was reliving the experience he had had with Maria, the Unique One, of seeing a beloved woman speak his words and play a character he had imagined. Maria and Catherine, both highly sensuous actresses at the height of their powers—the one as a Spanish Pasionaria, and the other an intense Elizabethan woman—were for Camus the embodiment of a dream.

Camus explained to Sellers that the theater was the highest and most universal of literary activities, and to write plays was the summit of a writer's art, although he did not imply that his own plays were his most important works. His version of Faulkner was an odd combination of classical French and a romantic American English. The adaptor felt that Faulkner was "the greatest American writer.... I mean to say that he has created his own world, always recognizable and irreplaceable, as did Herman Melville, Fyodor Dostoyevsky, and Marcel Proust. *Sanctuary* and *Pylon* are masterpieces." Camus asked Sellers to visualize an "endlessly unwinding spiral of words and sentences which lead the person speaking them to an abyss of suffering." Although the character Nancy was African-American, Camus was not primarily interested in racial questions in the story, but rather the problems of suffering and redemption.

In rehearsals he insisted that the actors express the range and weight of that unhappiness. In some scenes, Camus as director saw parallels to his own past life. Temple Stevens's husband showed sexual jealousy after discovering erotic letters written to his wife in a scene that Michel Auclair played badly. Camus had discovered such a letter in Salzburg when he was married to Simone Hié, and he knew that the scene needed more passion. Simone still reappeared from time to time in his life, via letters from her mother. To obtain drugs, an addict learns to lie, and Simone lied a great deal. Temple Stevens, too, had this problem, saying in the play, "Why can't I stop lying? It should be easy to stop lying the way one stops running or drinking or eating sweets, because one has had enough. But it's as if one never gets tired of lying." For Camus, lies were often inevitable, and could take on metaphysical proportions. He made *Requiem* into a story of abjectness and redemption.

Catherine Sellers also did research for Camus, and he nicknamed her Sherlock Holmes when she tracked down Faulkner's works for past appearances of some of the characters in *Requiem pour une nonne*. After a first reading seated around a table, Camus would climb onstage with his actors and show them how to make gestures and read certain lines, reminding them that "theater is a story of grandeur told by two bodies." Never bossy or self-critical, he would tell the actors, "Above all, don't imitate my intonations," and he quoted Nietzsche that one must be wary of any thought that did not come from the "celebration of muscles." As a director, Camus favored flamboyant gestures, telling his actors to open their arms very, very wide.

With his hint of a Mediterranean or Algerian accent, Camus was low-key, and he enjoyed changing little details, like moving a chair or a piece of rope, or a lighting cue. Often he was not enough of a stickler, and he learned not to be disappointed by the inadequacies of some actors; he wanted at all cost that rehearsals be full of joy. While working on this Catholic play, he would make surprising Jewish references, such as saying that the theater was his phylactery and his kibbutz. He called *Requiem pour une nonne* his bachelor's degree, his first diploma as a professional stage director, and he planned to go for later graduate degrees by directing Shakespeare and Dostoyevsky.

Catherine Sellers admired Albert as much as the passionate Maria had, but she did not see herself as his equal, as the older actress did. Catherine was twenty-five years old when Camus was forty-three. He could easily be didactic with her, without playing the role of Pygmalion in a heavy way. She would constantly keep notebooks, until they would be so overburdened that her notes were unreadable; then Camus would send her cartons full of fresh notebooks to replace them. If he advised her to read a novel by the Victorian novelist and poet George Meredith, she would read his complete works. Together they discovered the novels of Robert Musil and listened to music. Camus had such a passion for Mozart, especially his Requiem, he wanted to hear it when he was dying. He would read aloud to Catherine the poems of René Char and Saint-John Perse. While Maria Casarès's well-established career continued just as before, Sellers's had just begun when she met Camus. Working with him, she became very well known. Maria and Catherine both accepted their complementarity and rivalry in their relations with Albert, also taking into account his obligations to Francine, though Maria accepted Camus's further indiscretions and adventures with more tolerance than Catherine did.

Camus had twenty-four rehearsals for *Requiem pour une nonne*; they ran from one p.m. to one a.m., with only a one-hour break. He would swallow a meal in a restaurant behind the Mathurins Theater, while for her meal, Catherine would buy chopped meat from a butcher's shop and eat it on the street. Camus nursed a sense of revenge at the Mathurins, as *Le Malentendu* had failed there some years ago. He would direct Catherine in a much more demanding way than the other actors, whom he allowed to freely discover their characters' inner motivations. But the play rested on Catherine Sellers. She didn't like her hands, and Camus had asked her to make a gesture when Temple emerged from a bordello: "You don't separate your fingers, and besides, it isn't the hands themselves which are beautiful, but the way they move."

As usual, Catherine took notes, some limited to simple stage movements, others more psychological, such as that Temple was "a tragic person, but not morose or exhausted or sad: she is a black-hearted anemone, with energy and elation in her unhappiness, showing all of life's colors. . . . Act the role with generosity and despair, with talent and exaltation, with detachment and tenderness, with distance and fever. . . ." Catherine scribbled another comment by Camus in her copy of the published adaptation, that "Temple is like an unwinding bobbin that in the end remains full." By coincidence, René Char made a similar comment to Sellers when he saw the play after its fiftieth performance: "It's like a ball of wool that unravels down to its last strand, and you realize that it's still full."

In order to help Camus, Catherine even learned to type. At Gallimard, Camus's official secretary, Suzanne Agnely, still served at the hub of his professional, and in part his personal, life, and she would tell women friends that Camus was working on a project with a typist. Whether his lady friends chose to believe the story was another matter. Agnely implied that she was being used as a front; who could say what Camus was working at and with whom?

Although she did not live with Camus, Catherine was among the few people allowed to visit him at his apartment on the rue de Chanaleilles, where he had lived permanently since June 1956. Camus had bought the needed furniture for his quiet apartment at the nearby Bon Marché department store, and he paid a rent of 50,000 old francs per month to his landlord, Jean de Tocqueville, a director of the Treasury, for the flat, which consisted of a bedroom and an office. The building was Anglo-Norman in design, located near the townhouse of the Greek arms dealer Stavros Niarchos. Maria always found reasons not to go to the apartment on the rue de Chanaleilles, but those who did go noticed on a lectern in Camus's office—he liked to write standing up—photos of Tolstoy, Nietzsche, and Albert's mother. Catherine Sellers also visited the Camus family apartment on the rue Madame, for the ostensible reason that she was acting in his current play, and Francine pretended not to be aware of their love affair, which had started in September 1956.

As he had done with Maria, Camus took Catherine to his favorite couscous restaurants and cafés. He was careful about his own health and advised Catherine about hers. He drank very little, and if he was lunching alone, ate only scrambled eggs and oat flakes. He and Catherine continually made grave resolutions to quit smoking, and Camus would stick to his plan for two weeks and then go back to his Disques Bleus, which he knew were particularly bad for his lungs. The choking, the panic, the claustrophobia—the old symptoms would return, and he thought himself about to go mad. He tried to calm down by practicing yoga. Catherine had introduced him to her yoga instructor, Jean Klein.

He told Catherine that actors should never socialize with critics or write them letters, no matter what their reviews said, although this was the exact opposite of what Camus did as a writer. He was still on excellent terms with Guy Dumur, who was one of France's most acidulous critics.

Just before the dress rehearsal for *Requiem pour une nonne*, Camus began to write an essay about the death penalty, "Réflexions sur la guillotine." The guillotine had been one of Camus's obsessions ever since childhood, as described in both *L'Etranger* and *La Peste*. Camus wanted the death penalty abolished, and not only for humane reasons. As he wrote: "For thirty years, government crimes have far exceeded individual crimes," and he felt that human lives must be worth more than the state. His essay appeared in a book along with rather better-reasoned writings by Arthur Koestler and Jean Bloch-Michel on the same subject. Catherine helped Camus in his research by going to the Santé prison in Paris to interview the chaplain, and she returned with the news that this priest actually favored the death penalty, as indeed most Frenchmen did, according to polls.

Yet Camus helped create a climate in which the French government some decades later abolished capital punishment, by discussing an important event from his early life: "Shortly before the First World War began in 1914, a man was sentenced to death in Algiers for having committed particularly revolting murders, massacring a farmer's family, including the children. The killer was a farm worker who had done the deed in a sort of blood delirium, and he further aggravated his case by robbing his victims. The affair was much discussed, and it was generally felt that decapitation was too good for such a monster. I am told that this is how my father felt, for he was particularly indignant about the murder of children. One of the few things I know about him is that he wanted to attend the execution, for the first time in his life. He got up when it was still dark to get to the place of execution, on the other side of town, where a giant crowd gathered. He never told anyone what he saw that morning, and my mother only said that he returned home quickly, his face looked distressed and he refused to speak, and he lay down on his bed for a minute, then suddenly began to vomit. He had just discovered the reality hidden behind the impressive slogans, and instead of thinking about the massacred children, he could only think of that trembling body which had just been thrown on a board to be beheaded."

Requiem pour une nonne opened and was a considerable success, running for over six hundred performances. When the actor playing the governor, Michel Maurette, became ill, Camus himself enjoyed playing the role four times, and apparently did not overact.

The French actor Louis Jourdan, who had been based in America for some years, met Camus in Paris to ask if he would direct him in an English-language production of *Caligula*. Camus was generally wary of movie actors who dreamed of being stage stars, and he turned Jourdan down in a letter: "I was very much tempted by your proposal. . . . For me, directing is not just controlling actors' movement, appearance, and all-important speaking rhythm, but also the problem of giving them instructions, and my weak knowledge of English would be a major obstacle. . . . Of course, I could speak directly to you and have my comments translated to the other actors, but I would be completely unable to say if an English intonation was true or false, and at best you would have only half a stage director where what you need is a total unity of direction. But I feel that I could help you even from afar by giving advice, which you could ignore or not according to the question you might ask me."

Deeply immersed in the theater, Camus had neglected journalism and politics, although he approved of a French-English military expedition that was sent to Egypt after the nationalization of the Suez Canal, and in this he differed from his liberal and leftist friends. Like his fellow French intellectuals, Camus closely followed events in Hungary, a general strike that was suppressed by Soviet invasion.

Camus still disapproved of Algeria's FLN, considering them puppets of

Moscow and Cairo; but when the French government tried to cover up the hijacking of a Moroccan government flight that carried FLN leaders, he considered this act of air piracy to be against the interests of French-Algerian relations.

There was still no sign of a truce, civil or otherwise, in Algeria, and left-wingers reproached Camus for complaining about Communist repression in Hungary but not protesting against the use of torture by French troops in Algeria. Camus refused to sign certain petitions that he felt placed the blame in only one direction in Algeria. Instead of signing petitions, he preferred action.

Chapter Forty-five

The Ways of Silence

*T*he worsening Algerian crisis made the year 1957 a terrible one for Camus. Isolated from his family, he said he suffered from Algeria the way one suffers from a pain in the lungs. The French military operation to maintain order there, which had changed in nature, was now openly referred to as "the war in Algeria." Arab nationalists lost ground in military matters, but advanced on diplomatic and political fields.

Camus thought continually about his family, who were threatened by the situation. Lucien wrote to Albert, "Mama is fine, except for her feet, of course, which are getting more deformed, and she has a lot of trouble putting on her shoes." Lucien informed his brother that he had been drafted into the French army in Algeria: "As if I didn't have enough professional problems, now the army has called me up again to guard railways and trolleys. I assure you that it would be a nuisance if Algiers didn't have such pretty girls. . . . Your new book came out, could you send me a signed copy? I give you a big hug, Lucien."

Camus's mother, Lucien, and the Faures were constantly in danger of being killed by FLN bombs in trolley cars, which was part of the nationalists' campaign of urban terror. Yet some Paris intellectuals continued energetically to support the FLN, and even Raymond Aron was in favor of Algerian independence, although he could not say so in the right-wing *Le Figaro*, where he was a columnist. Aron published a book, *La Tragédie algerienne*, in which he foresaw the pieds noirs' destiny as exiles. He demonstrated that integration was impossible in Algeria, that the colony cost France dearly, and that independence was inevitable. Aron never justified Algerian terrorism, and Camus accepted many of his ideas, but only if France could remain in Algeria. Camus rejected the hegemony of the FLN, while Aron said that the Algerian nationalist movement had no choice but to concentrate on the goal of independence.

Camus told Jean Grenier, "The French government should not negotiate with the FLN. . . . The government should refuse unambiguously." the President of the French Council Guy Mollet invited Camus to participate in a commission to safeguard freedom by studying the problem of torture in Algeria. Camus refused the offer, because he felt that the commission's powers were not clearly defined, and the government offered it no guarantees of independence and effectiveness, nor was it granted discretionary powers for its investigations.

Camus had in effect shut up about Algeria in public, but not privately, where he fought on several fronts. The Algerian poet Jean Sénac published a small magazine, *Exigence,* and attacked the writer in an article: "Camus once declared, 'He who writes will never attain the level of those who die.' But at that time he had not yet repudiated the justice of *Les Justes.*" Camus was sent the article anonymously, and he replied to the magazine that he saw no contradiction between his attitude about Algeria and what he expressed in his play *Les Justes:* "The subject of *Les Justes* is precisely the one that is occupying us today, and I still think now what I thought then. The hero of *Les Justes* refuses to throw a bomb when he sees that he might kill children, in addition to the Grand Duke he planned to kill. In the play and in *L'Homme révolté* I gave examples of such refusals, the passionate certainty that there is a limit in murder and injustice that must not be transgressed. I cited these examples because for me they are the only ones that maintain truth and grandeur in revolt, and my position on this point has not changed. Though I can understand and admire a fight for liberation, I have only disgust for a killer of women and children. The cause of the Arab people of Algeria has never been worse served than by terrorism against civilians, now practiced systematically by Arab movements. Terrorism delays, perhaps irremediably, the solution of justice that will eventually come. The objection that the French are doing things as bad would be worth discussing if Arab leaders and intellectuals had protested against the murder of innocents as we did against the collective repression of Arabs, but this did not happen. Do not describe me as approving acts that even in the past repelled me. On the contrary, I continue not to repudiate my past but to absolutely condemn the murder of innocent civilians, today as yesterday."

Camus stated that he did not want to lecture Sénac, but added, "Many people . . . are dying today in Algeria, on both sides. You writers should think about that seriously before you criticize me and the so-called 'injustice' of *Les Justes.* That expression, easily said here, bears its full bloody weight in Algeria." Sénac responded by breaking with Camus, as many other Algerian writers did, but not before sending him a poetic postcard from Fiesole, Italy, hoping for a future day when the two might reunite.

Almost twenty years after it was first published, Camus reprinted *L'Envers et l'endroit,* in a one-hundred-copy luxury edition published by

Jean-Jacques Pauvert, who bought the rights from Charlot Editions. In his preface, Camus said that the texts still seemed "clumsy" to him in terms of form, but that he did "not disown anything that is expressed here." The preface was taut, subtle, and melancholic: "To correct a natural indifference, I was placed midway between poverty and the sun. Poverty kept me from believing that everything was good under the sun, and the sun taught me that history is not everything." Camus spoke of his "Castilian side," of his lack of taste for comfort and riches: "I am a miser when it comes to the freedom that disappears when excessive wealth appears. . . . [In the past] I have known fear and discouragement, but never bitterness."

As a response to killings and guillotinings in Algeria, Camus published parts of his "Réflexions sur la guillotine" in the NRF's June–July 1957 issue. Soon afterwards, Calmann-Lévy Editions published a book containing Camus's essay. At a lunch with Jean Grenier, Camus bemoaned the fact that Algerian nationalists had turned down Mollet's offer of free elections, which probably would have been in favor of the nationalists. Camus felt that the Communist Party was trying to weaken French resolve about Algeria in order to benefit the USSR, and he said, "The natives are getting weary of the continuing war." He cited an example that his brother had told him about of a farm worker who came to Algiers looking for work and explained to Lucien that he had left his village because nationalist fighters had stolen his chickens and as a reprisal, the French authorities had seized his barley fields. For Camus, the men of the FLN were not politicians and did not understand what was in their own interest. At another lunch with Grenier, in April, Camus told him that he had met bitter Algerians in Paris: "I told the Algerians who accompanied [André] Bénichou that it was a mistake to believe that French public opinion was indifferent about, or favorable to, their country's independence. There was a strong movement against it, and one day they would have to reach a compromise to share power, as three radical French deputies had proposed, with an exchange of populations. If the Arabs complained that Algiers, Oran, and the industrialized areas would be taken from them, the answer is easy: these areas were made valuable by the French."

At the same time, Camus was preparing a new staging of Caligula at Angers, and afterwards he planned perhaps to go to the south of France. He avoided the crowds of vacationers on the Côte d'Azur. But politics in Paris still worried him, and he told Grenier that Pierre Mendès-France was "isolated and he is suffering from it: he is going through a bad depression. Edgar Faure is ready to sell everything, to give everything up, because he has no conscience. De Gaulle will return. . . ."

Camus sometimes still clung to the idea of dividing up Algeria: "Even if division is not desirable for France, it's better to fight with a project in mind than none at all." Camus remained hypersensitive to every criticism, no matter where it came from. For instance, the British monthly *Encounter* attacked him for remaining silent about Algeria. Camus replied with a letter to the poet Stephen Spender, the magazine's editor: "As a Frenchman, I cannot join the Arab Maquis, and as a Frenchman from Algeria . . . I cannot approve of terrorism against civilians, which incidentally strikes far more Arab civilians than French." The same day, replying to a letter from a union leader about a meeting where Camus spoke, he mentioned his continued abstention from journalism: "I have renounced regular journalism for myself, because I disagree with all the editorial staffs. That does not mean I have no opinions or that I have retired to a theatrical convent. . . . I will continue my activism on the day I choose."

Camus disdainfully attacked a "certain kind of political intoxication. . . . I have publicly denounced using torture, whether in Budapest or Algiers."

On March 15, 1957, he participated in a meeting at the Salle Wagram to defend Hungary against the Russian Communists as he informed his correspondents: "I denounced collective repression even before it took its present form. No doubt I chose my moment badly, because my articles did not enumerate enough dead bodies to attract sufficient attention."

The Algerian tragedy did not make him forget Hungary: "Admit that a man who has pled the same cause for twenty years may now remain silent, until the day when he will speak again, when Paris frivolity has forgotten the Algerian tragedy, just as it has already forgotten Hungary, and ask yourself if this same man, who lived the Algerian tragedy in his flesh because all his family is in danger there, deserves to be spoken to in the way you have just done."

He begged his mother endlessly to move to France, but she disliked the climate and lifestyle of Paris, and only wanted to live in Algiers. Camus told friends that she no longer dared go out of her house, and each time the radio reported a terrorist attack or a bomb that went off, he thought of her.

When the secretary of the French teachers' union, Denis Forestier, asked him to explain his silence, Camus replied, "Most public declarations in Paris result in deaths of both Arabs and French people, and today all of my family is in Algeria, exposed to terrorism against civilians. Personally, I cannot agree to do anything even from afar that might indirectly justify someone who would attack my family." The writer Jean Amrouche, who was as solitary as Camus although he had different opinions, told someone at this time, "No, there is nothing to be done with Camus, he does not want to compromise himself with a dialogue. He has just written to me that he will bear witness all by himself."

Camus agreed with Germaine Tillion, an ethnologist who wrote a book on Algeria in 1957 saying that independence would throw Algeria into poverty. But Amrouche disagreed adamantly with this view, in a violent article in the magazine *Témoignage Chrétien*, claiming, "The dramatic and desperate situation of Algeria in 1957 was caused by the colonialism's 127-year reign." Amrouche felt that Tillion was sketchy on the subject of colonial bullying, a racist regime that took Algerians to be a subhuman species.

In June, Camus's friend from Oran and *Combat*, the gifted poet Jean-Paul de Dadelsen, died of a brain tumor. The summer began horribly for Camus, who felt powerless in his work and in terms of the world around him. He wrote to Catherine Sellers, "I feel well, but I am in a strange state of mind. . . . I am incapable of any work other than the mechanical kind, which I do meekly while waiting for inspiration's wing to rustle by me and shake me up. I am also pessimistic, amnesiac, ignorant, etc. . . . and I'm discouraged. I'm waiting, although I don't know for what, a new energy or joyful power? I don't know how to write, and in short, I'm a barbarian!"

In August, he told Catherine, "I'm still insane, and it's a sterile insanity, to be sure! . . . The sum total is negative, and in fact for two days now, for the first time in my life I wanted to give up writing since I reread *Crime and Punishment*. I could work in the theater and do adaptations now and then, and I could be free inside, without that striving when you are empty, that dries you up so much. Yes, perhaps I had better give up writing, right now."

In September, he wrote to her again: "I've never known such a state as I find myself in now, with no memories or even feelings, and deeply humiliated to no longer feel the heart inside me which I always found indispensable. How can anyone write, make things, and create under such circumstances? If this were to last until I die, it would certainly be hell."

Regarding Algeria, Camus did not see only one side of the question, and he was aware of colonial injustices, although his reaction to them was not that of "frivolous repairs" suggested by intellectuals like Jean-Paul Sartre. He told Jean Daniel, "I'd be very glad to fight injustice, because I was not born to resign myself to history, first because I don't believe in doing so, and secondly because my duty is not to believe in it. . . . Yet all the arguments invoked by intellectuals to justify Moslem violence against innocent civilians implies a belief in history, and in history being fair." He had not changed the opinion expressed in *L'Homme révolté* that any solution of the Algerian problem must involve Frenchmen remaining in Algeria.

In October, Camus met Germaine Tillion and agreed to write the preface for the English translation of her book. He was fascinated by her tales of having met FLN leaders in Algeria and calling them murderers to their faces. Camus wrote in his *Carnets* that Tillion also "showed me the compositions of thirty Arab students aged eleven and twelve whose Arab teacher gave them the subject to write about 'What would you do if you were invisible?' Everyone wanted to get a gun and kill Frenchmen or French paratroopers, or government leaders, so I despair for the future."

He refused to sign leftist manifestos for "peace in Algeria," but he always intervened on behalf of prisoners or those sentenced to death. For him, even before the Algerian troubles started, a writer was obliged to support all those who were persecuted by governments in any country, regardless of fashion and who was in power at the time. He protested to save Greeks and Iranians and remained vigilant about Algeria. When on July 14, 1953, French police fired on Algerian demonstrators at the place de la Nation in Paris, killing seven, Camus was among the writers who expressed their indignation.

Although he had taken a vow of public silence, he intervened endlessly, motivated first by his hatred of the death penalty. He tried to be useful, asking for prisoners to be freed or transferred to France, and acted in secret not from shame but to be more effective. He understood that most Moslems rejected France's extortionate politics and use of torture, and he wrote, "You Arab democrats must do all you can on your side to lessen mass francophobia." Sometimes a mere threat could prompt Camus to action, such as when he learned that the liberal writer Mouloud Mameri would be arrested for publishing an unsigned article in the monthly *Espoir* Camus protested, and the journalist was not prosecuted after all.

Camus would write to ministers, to the prime minister, to the president of France, to leaders of political parties and of other nations. When he learned that an Algerian suspected of being a Communist, Pierre Léonardon, was detained in a camp, he wrote to the prisoner's lawyer, Irène Dayan, "These arrests are of course idiotic and do not help anything, but what can we do in this specific case?" Prisoners would write to Camus to complain that the civil code was dissolving in Algeria, insofar as it had ever existed for Arabs, while the new laws were defended by policemen and paratroopers.

One imprisoned letter writer, Pierre Liddi, had known Camus when he belonged to the Algerian Communist Party before the war. Louis Miquel had previously warned the prisoner's daughter that despite the injustice of his imprisonment, Camus would never intervene on behalf of a Communist. Yet Camus did intervene, responding directly to Liddi in January 1957: "As for me, I despair a little about Algeria, not only because of the errors that we have made over the years, but because the present attitude of the FLN systematically ruins the situation, putting independence as a primary goal and at the same time practicing blind terrorism that kills women and children. The FLN is pushing the French population to despair and making any solution except stupid and hateful war impossible." Camus was aware that French policies deserved to be criticized, but what did the nationalists propose? He stated that he had "not found a single Arab militant who will say today that the murder of children and innocents has never served any cause or any action, no matter how justified it may be in principle." Camus explained to his old comrade Liddi, "I tell you all this to inform you about my state of mind, which is shared by many liberal Frenchmen, for a long time in favor of deep reforms in Algeria. . . . I wish you courage, and do not doubt the affectionate memories of your Albert Camus."

A feverish Christian leftist writer, Maurice Clavel, asked Camus to intervene on behalf of an Algerian, Moktar Debache, sentenced to death for attempted homicide, although the man he attacked was almost unharmed. Camus studied numerous dossiers and intervened in over a dozen cases by writing letters to President René Coty on behalf of men condemned to death although they had not actually killed anyone, or who were young and the only support of a large family. Camus told the president that if he used mercy and indulgence, he might "preserve a little of Algeria's future which we are all hoping for." Coty's aides replied with form letters acknowledging his notes, but the condemned men were usually executed by the time the responses arrived. Despite the suspicion he felt for Prime Minister Guy Mollet, Camus also sought his support in October 1957, admitting his powerlessness in such matters: "I have intervened several times with the president to ask him to pardon [men with death sentences], but the men in question have almost all been executed. . . . At a time when terrorism is slowing down, I fear that more executions will set it off again." The same day, Camus also wrote to Coty's office, receiving the usual form letter from a presidential aide; but Camus decided that no matter what the outcome was, he would continue his activism.

He agreed to write letters to help a leftist lawyer, Pierre Stibbe, defend a nationalist Algerian accused of killing an Algerian pacifist, but only if Stibbe did not announce publicly that Camus had done so: "In no way do I wish to give a good conscience to a stupid fanatic in Algiers who may shoot into a crowd where my mother and all my family may be, although I would not personally be in danger. . . . For me this reason, which may seem naive in Paris, has taken the force of a passion that is affirmed by reasoning." If the judge in the case did not agree to keep Camus's letter a secret, then Stibbe would be limited to quoting from Camus's book on capital punishment, because it was "written exactly in the hope that lawyers of all causes would use it." Camus had no illusions: "Furthermore, I am at your disposal after the death sentence, if it happens, for all direct intervention that may prevent execution." In his draft of a letter to the judge, Camus stated that he was pleading for the life of the accused man "even though I entirely disapprove of his act." News was leaked to *France-Observateur* magazine that Camus's letter would be used by the defense lawyer, and Camus withdrew it, because it could no longer be used secretly. Stibbe made further efforts to convince Camus to become involved to save the prisoner from the death penalty, but Camus would not budge.

He did, however, intervene in other cases, such as that of Taleb Adberrahmane, a student, who Camus felt was "not a killer without scruples, but rather a weak and tormented mind who participated in an action because of extreme poverty and unfortunate circumstances, without really understanding all its consequences." According to Jean Daniel and Germaine Tillion, Camus intervened in more than 150 affairs. Despite his disagreements with Daniel, he stayed in contact with him about requests for pardons. The men did not see each other, but felt that their activism was more important than their disagreements.

Whatever the reason for prisoners' detention, arrest, and sentencing, Camus almost always reacted by becoming involved. One of the writer's last such letters was to an Algerian army judge on behalf of Amar Ouzegane, his Communist Party comrade before the war, who had "skillfully duped" Camus about his ties to the FLN during his projects for a civilian truce. Although he was often bitter during polemical exchanges, Camus did not often hold grudges in political matters. He wrote to the judge that Ouzegane "tried to organize a truce meant to spare French and Algerian Moslem civilians. . . . He did all that was in his power for the enterprise to succeed, for a purely humanitarian purpose." In fact, Ouzegane was an important FLN leader who did not disavow terrorist violence, which he saw as inevitable, as did many "progressive" Frenchmen. Some of the prisoners Camus defended were pardoned; and after Charles de Gaulle was elected president in 1958, the executions of prisoners declined substantially.

In his solitude, Camus also fought for the rights of Hungarians. After the Russian suppression of Hungarian independence in 1956, the novelist Robert Merle wrote to Camus to reproach him for having spoken of "genocide," and wanted to know why Camus had not also condemned the French-English intervention in the Suez Crisis of the same year in the same terms. Camus replied that Merle would possibly agree with him one day, "as others have done who in the past have criticized and insulted me in order to justify the Russian government's totalitarian policies." Camus signed petitions on behalf of the Hungarian insurgents along with two French Nobel Prize–winning writers, Roger Martin du Gard and François Mauriac, and T. S. Eliot. On behalf of the Hungarian writer Tibor Déry, who had been sentenced to nine years in prison, Camus wrote to authorities in Budapest, along with Eliot, Ignazio Silone, and Karl Jaspers, struck by Déry's fearlessness in claiming responsibility for his acts and his role in the Hungarian insurrection.

Camus used a double method for more efficiency, intervening both in public and in private, through diplomatic channels in certain cases. A Hungarian literary weekly, Magyar Orsa, attacked Camus and another protester, the British philosopher Bertrand Russell, claiming that writers had no right to incite people to revolt, and that it was normal to put these "madmen" away to remove them from contact with "healthy people."

In *France-Observateur*, Roger Stéphane accused Camus of remaining silent about the horrors of repression in Algeria, pointing out that his sense of morality was "abstract." Stéphane himself was in prison for his activism about Algerian matters, but Camus refused to defend him because *France-Observateur* had got hold of the letter that the lawyer Pierre Stibbe had solicited to defend a client, and printed it. Camus complained to the editor of *France-Observateur*, Claude Bourdet, "You really ought to stop attributing all the difficulties in your field to my nasty pride, which cannot be blamed for everything. Your argument is a bit vulgar and really too easy. . . . you published my doubts, which just might damage Stéphane, and you omitted to publish the two sentences that show that I am on your side. This is precisely the sort of thing I dislike about you: to use a letter that was solicited by you in the first place in so scandalously manipulative a way can be called disloyalty or blindness, but in this case you were blinded by something other than friendship or even plain sympathy."

Other interventions had better results, and Camus's liberal Algerian friends approved of his activism when they were aware of it, although others felt he was too anti-Communist. Some old friends in Algeria whose opinions counted for Camus reproached him again for not advocating independence. Raymond Sigaudès, who had worked with Camus at the Théâtre du Travail and had gone to football games with him, called one day at the Gallimard office to ask why Camus could not join the Algerian nationalists, and suggested angrily, "It's because if you take sides, you're afraid you won't get the Nobel Prize!"

Sigaudès broke with Camus, another sign to the writer that he was losing old friends over the Algerian question, including those from the leftist working class.

Chapter Forty-six

The Prize to Pay

O n October 16, 1957, Camus was lunching with Patricia Blake on the second floor of the restaurant Chez Marius when a young man sent from the Gallimard office approached him and, after dismissing the waiter, announced that the writer had won the Nobel Prize for literature. Camus seemed to "suffocate," and he kept telling Patricia, "Malraux should have got it, you know . . . Malraux." When Jean-Paul Sartre was told the news, he quipped ironically, "He deserves it!" Shortly afterwards, Camus sent a telegram to his mother in Algiers: MAMA, I MISS YOU MORE THAN EVER.

Even a decade before, Camus had been mentioned as a Nobel Prize candidate by the Swedish Academy, and in the 1950s, a Swede who worked in the French office of the Stockholm publisher Bonniers confided to Camus that the Academy had asked him to make a study of the writer's work. The night before the award was announced, rumors from Stockholm were already circulating in Paris.

Camus informed Francine by telephone, and at the family apartment on the rue Madame, his daughter, Catherine, and a friend who had worked briefly as the writer's secretary, Odile de Lalène, ran downstairs to buy champagne. Camus arrived at the apartment and said, "Life is a novel." "Is there a Nobel Prize for acrobats?" asked twelve-year-old Catherine, a budding gymnast. Odile joked, "Poor Albert—you would have made such a handsome marginal character!" But Camus was not in a joking mood, and he even considered refusing the prize. Then he thought he might accept it, but send a speech rather than attend the ceremonies, but Gaston Gallimard vetoed that idea.

At Robert and Renée Gallimard's home on the rue de l'Université, Camus paced up and down the living room, watching his mother on television news broadcasts. Renée Gallimard had the feeling that he did not want to sit still because he was afraid he might cry.

Journalists and photographers hunted him down, and during a Gallimard office cocktail party to celebrate the news, with Francine and the twins present, Camus was in a tolerant mood with the press. Catherine said, "I really want to go to Stockholm to use Swedish ice skates—wow!" Jean asked, "Does this mean Papa's literary work is going to last?" Not long before, Jean had yelled at his father in a moment of anger, "You second-rate writer!" There were flashbulb explosions and hugs from friends like Jules Roy, Jean Bloch-Michel, and Jacques Lemarchand, and the theater was represented by the great actress Madeleine Renaud, although Francine had banned Maria Casarès and Catherine Sellers from the party. The Swedish ambassador in Paris congratulated Camus in an otiose speech, and the writer thanked the Swedish Academy "for having honored my country first, and secondly a Frenchman from Algeria." Before Camus's prize, the recent Nobel Prize–winning writers from France included Roger Martin du Gard (1937), André Gide (1947), and François Mauriac (1952). Camus was a month away from his forty-fourth birthday when his prize was announced; only the British novelist Rudyard Kipling had been a younger winner, at age forty-two. More Frenchmen than any other nationality had won the literature prize since it was established, including Sully Prudhomme, Frédéric Mistral, Romain Rolland, Anatole France, and Henri Bergson. French President René Coty sent Camus a ritual telegram of congratulations, and a deluge of official lunches and dinners followed.

To Roger Quilliot, who saw him at this time, Camus seemed "anguished, like someone buried alive." Camus told everyone that Malraux deserved the prize more than he did. Some people felt Malraux did not receive it because he ardently supported Charles de Gaulle and others believed that the present anti-Gaullist French government had intervened to force the Swedish government to put pressure on the Academy. However unlikely this seemed, Camus continued to repeat everywhere, "I wish Malraux had got the prize," which may have meant, "Malraux deserved it more than I did," or, "He would have won it if it wasn't for his politics." Malraux finally sent him a note, "Dear Camus, I have just read your public statements, which do honor to us both, and I thank you. Friendly wishes." Malraux commented to Jean Grenier that by his declarations, Camus had "chosen the most dignified way" of reacting, but Florence Malraux found that it was best not to mention the Nobel Prize in the vicinity of her father.

Camus genuinely admired Malraux, saying, "It was one of the luckiest things of my life to have read Malraux as one of my masters when I was a young writer and afterwards to have met him as a friend. . . ." But although Malraux had a certain esteem for Camus, he considered him more of a protégé than a friend; indeed, it may be doubted whether Malraux had any friends at all, if that meant people he saw as his equals.

The Nobel Prize ceremony demanded preparation, and Francine told Renée Gallimard at the hairdresser's, "Albert asked me to come to the Nobel Prize with him, and I know he did that to please me, but should I go? I'm afraid I'd bother him." Renée exclaimed, "Not at all!" Camus explained to a new young Danish girlfriend, Mi, who was also not invited to the Gallimard party, "Francine was there for the suffering, so it is normal that she should be there for the honors." Albert's feelings for his wife remained complex, and he mentioned in a letter to her cousin Nicole Chaperon how he was moved by the generosity of Francine, "whom I have never stopped loving in my bad way." In the same letter he said that Francine had "forgiven" him. He also pointed out to Nicole that the Nobel Prize gave him "more doubts than certainties. Success is a balm, but a temporary one, and an artist's discontent remains incurable. . . . He dies without attaining knowledge."

When Jacqueline Bernard organized a round of drinks with former *Combat* staffers, including Roger Grenier, Camus joked with them, parodying Genesis, "Here is the speech I will make at Stockholm: "Remember that shit thou art and into shit thou shalt return." Meanwhile the press made Camus a star, with personal interviews and plenty of flattery. In *Le Monde* on October 18, Émile Henriot of the French Academy praised the "high literary qualities" of Camus, a "pure artist" and "director of public conscience." But Henriot was completely off the mark when he referred to Camus's work as "existentialist."

In the *Figaro Littéraire*, Mauriac expressed himself suavely in only eleven lines, writing, "The Nobel Prize is most often the recompense for a life's work and for a life. . . . This young voice, which represents an entire generation, I imagine has appealed to the Nobel Prize jury." In the same issue of *Figaro Littéraire*, Jean Grenier wrote that Camus's "greatness derives from his distance, and his distance is only the natural manifestation of his greatness." At lunch that day, Camus told Grenier privately, "Don't say that I filled a gap that challenged my generation, just say that I tried to fill it. . . I'm going to have more enemies than ever."

There were a few attacks, in Paris rather than the provinces, and Camus commented that the Communist daily, *L'Humanité*, "criticized me, but fairly." He felt, however, that the far right wing had no such compunctions: "If you want to know how far ignominy can go, read [fascist writer Lucien] Rebatet in *Dimanche Matin*, who says that I would have liked to command a firing squad, whereas I was in fact one of the three Resistance writers who got him pardoned." Rebatet, who had been threatened with execution after wartime Nazi collaboration, wrote about Camus, "This prize which falls most often to septuagenarians is not at all premature in this case, because since his allegorical *La Peste*, Camus has been diagnosed with an arteriosclerosis of style."

Another critic, the influential Kléber Haedens, was equally scornful about Camus, writing, "Is it possible to write more dreary and dead language . . . to pile on the platitudes with more pompous expression?" In the same newspaper, *Paris-Presse*, there was a bittersweet article by Pascal Pia, who recalled that Camus, who had accepted the 42,000-dollar Nobel award, had criticized the poet Arthur Rimbaud in *L'Homme révolté* for walking around carrying gold in a belt around his waist: "Where did [Camus] want [Rimbaud] to put it? Unlike Monsieur Camus, Rimbaud did not have a bank account." Pia went on to say that he had admired the young Camus for his writing style, "which is rarely seen in a writer under thirty years old," but he confessed that today he did not appreciate Camus the man, who was less like "a man in revolt than a secular saint." Pia blamed Camus and Sweden itself, which had been easily invaded by Germany during the Second World War: "A citizen of the world, pacifist, signer of lengthy petitions, declared enemy of the death penalty, Albert Camus in his recent works and public statements could only please Stockholm, where, as we saw when their neighbors Finland and Norway were invaded, the stubborn love of peace triumphs over every other emotion."

The most ferocious attack was from the literary critic Bernard Frank, an artisan of book talk: "Each time the critics as a group think he is going to speak, they get excited, bustle around, shudder, undulate, and anything else you can imagine. But nothing happens; Camus stubbornly does not cease to shut up. In this domain, he remains an artist and hides his effects, because a few years ago you couldn't hear him when he was silent and now he jabbers about it. . . ."

At the Mathurins Theater, where *Requiem pour une nonne* was still playing, a new poster was printed to proclaim that the play was the product of *two* Nobel Prize winners, as Faulkner had received the same honor in 1949. On hearing of Camus's award, Faulkner sent a telegram in slightly unidiomatic French, saying, "We salute the spirit that is constantly searching for himself and asking for himself" (Faulkner's message used the verb "se demander" instead of the correct "s'interroger," which means to question oneself).

Among the congratulatory calls was one from a stranger, a Citroën salesman, who proposed that Camus buy an expensive new car. After the prize, Camus received a plea from the daughter-in-law of the novelist Sigrid Undset, who wanted him to help pay for buying the former home of the late poet Sully Prudhomme, another Nobel laureate. So many money-grubbers appeared that when Madeleine Jaussaud phoned him at his Gallimard office to see how he was, the exhausted Camus asked, "You're telephoning me to ask for money?" He quickly apologized, but the post-Nobel period had emotional highs and lows for Camus, forcing him to weed out enemies from friends.

He wrote to his former teacher Louis Germain, "Without that affectionate hand you held out to the poor boy I was, without your teaching and example, none of this would have occurred. I don't make too much of this kind of honor, but at least this is an occasion for telling you what you were and still are for me, and to assure you that your efforts, your work, and the generous heart you put into them are still alive in one of your little schoolchildren who, despite his age, has never stopped being your grateful pupil."

He turned down an interview with *L'Express*, telling the journalist Madeleine Chapsal, "Above all, I'd like the noise made by this Nobel to die away quickly and I want to disappear for a while. However, I am very grateful for what you say about certain articles, which haven't hurt me because I was vaccinated years ago. Besides, one must live among one's contemporaries, smiling when it is possible. You see, our intellectual society, whether leftist or rightist, is almost always frightfully mean and nasty, and would be a sure sign of decadence, were there not some warm-hearted exceptions."

There were some faithful friends, like the worldly French Dominican priest Father Bruckberger, who wrote to him, quoting the medieval chronicler Joinville telling a friend, " 'Seneschal, let the dogsbodies howl, and we shall laugh all the better in bedrooms of noble ladies.' Joinville was no Christian Democrat." What with his mixed emotions about the prize and the reactions it evoked, Camus told Bruckberger, "France is not limited to this pathetic poultry yard whose squawking I don't even listen to." Still, he felt that the Nobel award was "too great." He contributed a little of the prize money to charity, including enough to buy a record player for a tuberculosis sanitorium in the Basses-Pyrénées region.

During the ceremonies in Stockholm, Jeanne Polge looked after the twins. Camus rented a tuxedo from a shop on the rue de Buci, and Francine borrowed Mado Bénichou's only piece of jewelry, an old pearl necklace, as well as a white mink stole from another friend.

The day he left for Sweden, Camus ate lunch with the philosopher Emmanuel Berl, to whom he said, "Above all, I don't want to offend Malraux." Berl, a quizzical character who despite his Judaism had written some of Marshal Pétain's most famous speeches, said that he had the paradoxical experience of "always feeling like I agree with Camus, without ever understanding" the writer's ideas.

His doctors forbade air travel, so Camus took the Nord-Express train at the Gare du Nord, with Francine and friends like Michel, Janine, and Claude Gallimard, as well as his American publisher, Blanche Knopf, whose green fingernail polish caused general astonishment among those traveling in the French train. Only a few weeks before, Mrs. Knopf had sent Camus one of the Burberry raincoats he liked, and some records that were still unavailable in France, including performances of Schoenberg's *A Sur-*

vivor from Warsaw and *Ode to Napoleon Bonaparte.* On October 18, Camus had replied to Mrs. Knopf, in somewhat stilted English, about his plans for a new novel, *Le Premier homme*: "I hope the First Man goes on." Also on the train was Camus's translator Carl-Gustav Bjurström, who was finishing a book about the writer's work. Camus noticed that Claude Gallimard was reading a book that he'd disguised with a false jacket. What was it? When Claude put the book down and went into the corridor, Camus sneaked a look. It was *L'Etranger.* Was Claude rereading it, or reading it for the first time? the author asked himself.

The corrida began when they arrived in Stockholm on December 9. A Swedish career diplomat, Hans Calliander, was in charge of Camus's group. He led them through a series of press conferences and cocktail parties with Swedish arts personalities, many of whom spoke no French. Camus minded his manners and did not get drunk, unlike the prizewinner three years before, Ernest Hemingway, whose alcohol capacity astonished even the Swedes.

Some local journalists expected Camus to be more of a political guru than a writer, and the largest Stockholm newspaper, the liberal *Dagens Nyheter,* felt that the choice of Camus was inexplicable. The paper stated that his ideas were neither numerous nor interesting, that he lacked both depth and imagination as a writer, and that with the possible exception of *L'Etranger,* he had produced only second-rate work. The conservative *Svenska Dagbladet* was rather more respectful, comparing Camus's successes despite his life's difficulties to the hard times France had lived through since 1940 and that country's literary triumphs.

The prize was conferred on December 10, after a minor episode in which Camus mislaid his speech, which he found again, in time for it to be put into Swedish by his faithful translator Bjurström. As Camus climbed the rostrum to accept the award from King Gustav VI, the slim writer looked like the young man who had danced at the Padovani Bathhouse in Algiers and in Paris nightclubs. Simone Gallimard, Claude's wife, thought that she could see a childlike worry in his eyes, like a schoolboy who had won an academic award he wasn't sure he deserved, but who had decided to enjoy all the pomp. Simone had had little previous contact with Camus, because of Gallimard family feuds, but in Stockholm she finally understood his famous charm.

As the ceremony went on, the secretary of the Swedish Academy, Anders Osterling, made a gaffe by calling Camus an existentialist. Finally the gathering moved on to a gilt salon, where diplomas, medals, prize checks, and a banquet were lavished on the Nobel winners in various fields. Then there was a ball, everyone in formal dress, with a Swedish student choir singing.

Following tradition, Camus gave his speech at the Stockholm City Hall after the final banquet of the ceremonies on December 10. Solemnly addressing the crowd, "Sire, Madame, Your Royal Highnesses, ladies and gentlemen," Camus gave what sounded like a eulogy for himself, using the words "art" and "artist" thirteen times, and referring to himself countless times, in a dense and prosaic text. With a mixture of coquetry and sincerity perhaps, he said that his only riches were his doubts and a new work in progress. He called himself a writer who "cannot put himself in the service of those who are making history today." He spoke of art that relieves a prisoner's silence, and how a writer must criticize princes and never serve or submit to them. A writer can become engaged by refusing to lie about what he knows and by resisting oppression. Camus placed himself in a generation who were "twenty years old when Hitler came to power and the first Soviet trials began, and to perfect their education, witnessed the Spanish Civil War, the Second World War, the concentration camps, and a Europe of torture and prisons." When he spoke of the Frenchmen of Algeria, his full, deep voice vibrated with barely contained emotion, as can be heard on the official recording. King Gustav VI was delighted by the speech.

Later, the beautiful Francine smiled at everyone during the receptions, as she and Albert played at being husband and wife. The Swedish popular press dubbed Madame Camus the "Number One Nobel Pinup." But Camus was considered by some to be a "cold war troublemaker," and the Communists of Eastern Europe and Asia complained that the Swedish Academicians had shown the "political nature" of their prize by not giving it to a French Communist writer like Paul Eluard or Louis Aragon.

On December 12 at 5:30 p.m., Camus met students at Stockholm University, and after yet more choral singing, a debate began, which Camus always liked better than a simple speech. Asked what he thought of cinema, Camus replied that films "serve propaganda on one hand and money on the other. . . . I pay a lot of attention to the cinema, but the cinema doesn't pay any attention to me." A student asked what he thought of conscientious objectors, and Camus replied, "I was a pacifist until 1940, and I respect conscientious objectors and have asked that they be given legal protection, but I don't think it will be easy. . . . I think that peace is the greatest possession, but not worth entering servitude to protect." His listeners wanted to know if French writers were afraid to express their opinions, and if government reprisals were possible, to which Camus replied, "Certainly there are pressures, but those of conformity are usually greater than those from the authorities. In France we reproach the government for being weak rather than for being strong."

Another youngster, the son of a correspondent at *Dagens Nyheter*, which was critical of the writer, asked if there was racial discrimination at Algiers University. Camus said, "No, but there is a restricted admission of [Arab] students, because the fact is, most [Arab students] are poor. . . . Doubtless more Arabs come from very poor backgrounds and don't have the money to study." Camus changed the mood in the room by suddenly declaring, "I haven't yet given my opinion about Algeria, but I will if you ask me." An Algerian man about thirty years old, who was with a group of friends, climbed on the dais and said accusingly, "You signed lots of petitions for Eastern European countries, but in the past three years you haven't done anything for Algeria!" This protester's long speech, not always comprehensible, ended with the shout "Algeria will be free!"

A correspondent from Le Monde, Dominique Birmann, reported that the confused dialogue degenerated into a fanatic monologue "by the representatives of the FLN." Camus kept his cool while the young Swedes tried to hush up the intrusive questioner. After asking them whether they believed in democracy, Camus finally was granted the silence necessary for answering the question.

"I have kept quiet for a year and eight months," he said, "which does not mean that I have stopped acting. I have always been and still am a partisan of a fair Algeria, where the two populations must live together in peace and equality. I have said and repeated that we must give justice to the Algerian people and grant them a fully democratic regime, until the hatred on both sides became such that it was no longer appropriate for an intellectual to intervene, because that might have made the terrorism worse. It seemed better for me to wait for the appropriate moment to help in uniting rather than dividing. I can assure you that you have comrades who are alive today thanks to actions that you are not aware of. I feel a certain repugnance about explaining myself in public, but I have always condemned terrorism, and I must condemn a terrorism that works blindly in the streets of Algiers and one day might strike at my mother and my family. I believe in justice, but I will defend my mother before justice."

In his article, Birmann, who was the only French journalist present, noted that "this speech was interrupted with applause." What Camus said about his mother and justice would become famous in France and around the world. But it was not quoted in any source other than the December 14, 1957 issue of Le Monde, as neither British nor Swedish journalists who were there printed it.

Camus's translator Bjurström was present and felt uneasy about the discussion between the Algerian and Camus. According to Bjurström, Camus meant that if what you mean by justice is that my mother could be on an Algiers trolley where a bomb explodes, then I prefer my mother to that terrorist's kind of justice. It was poor logic in any case to compare an abstract idea like justice to the destiny of an individual, Camus's mother. But Camus wanted this statement to convey his rejection of all terrorism, as he had stated in his *Lettres à un ami allemand*, the article in the series *Ni Victimes ni bourreaux*, and the essay "Sauver les corps" as reprinted in the book *Actuelles I*. Interviewed years later, Bjurström recalled that what Camus said differed slightly from the only printed transcript, in *Le Monde*. According to Bjurström, Camus really said, "At this moment, bombs are being thrown in the trolleys of Algiers, and my mother might find herself in one of these trolleys, and if that's your justice, I prefer my mother to justice."

At the office of *Le Monde*, the newspaper's director, Hubert Beuve-Méry, asked his reporter Birmann to confirm that Camus had actually said, word for word, what he was quoted as saying, before the article was printed. Birmann listened to a tape recording he had made of the meeting and confirmed the quote, but he has since lost the recording, which would have been the only objective proof. Once the quote was confirmed, Beuve-Méry said, "I was totally sure that Camus would say some fucking fool thing."

Camus had wanted to express tenderness when faced by a lack of reason, but lots of Algerians and "progressives" interpreted his words in another manner, as if he were saying that the justice due to millions of Algerians was not worth as much as Camus's mother. In fact, Camus was only criticizing the so-called justice of terrorism, and his mother was not being compared to real justice, any more than she herself was meant to symbolize justice.

In Stockholm, there were other questions to answer, such as when the university students showed they were better informed than the secretary of the Swedish Academy by asking Camus if he was for or against existentialism. He replied, "I am not an existentialist, although of course critics are obliged to make categories. I got my first philosophical impressions from the Greeks, not from nineteenth-century Germany, whose philosophy is the basis for today's French existentialism." When a member of the club for liberal students asked Camus why he was liberal, the writer mentioned Walt Whitman, for whom nothing could exist without freedom. He was asked about the influence of Dostoyevsky on his work, and just said, "*Considérable!*" Asked if he felt close to any Swedish writers, he named another Nobel Prize winner, the novelist Pär Lagerkvist, author of *Barabbas*. Then he was asked what he thought of the French writer Françoise Sagan, whose novel *Bonjour Tristesse* had recently made her a worldwide success. Camus said that Sagan was "one of the most charming and pleasant young Frenchwomen" he had ever met, but that "apart from failure, there is nothing more dangerous than success, and if one is very young, success is a difficult trial." Sagan was in that position and had to put up with it. She had talent, even if she was "not Colette." For listeners interested in other young French writers, Camus mentioned some friends, including Jean-Claude Brisville, Jean Bloch-Michel, and Michel Butor. The debate finished with a salvo of applause as Camus put on a Swedish student's cap and a ribbon from the Humanist Association.

At the hall's exit, Francine was in tears, and the four Gallimards,

Claude, Simone, Michel, and Janine, were indignant. It was pointed out to Camus that in between his verbal attacks, the Algerian had consulted his Swedish friends, who briefed him. Later, Camus told Bjurström that the most painful thing was to see "a face of hatred in a brother."

The Swedish press was not sympathetic to the Algerian's attack, and one newspaper headlined the story, "Charming Camus Disarms Aggressive Algerian Student." But the controversy did not end there: after Birmann's article appeared in *Le Monde*, the French embassy asked him for the tape recording he had made, but Birmann suspected that they wanted to destroy it, so he refused to give it up.

The festivities continued, and on Friday, the feast of Saint Lucia, the Camuses were astonished to be served breakfast in bed by young girls wearing nightgowns and crowns decorated with lit candles. No one had warned them in advance of this local custom, and the couple stared as the girls sang folksongs before leaving.

For Swedes who asked literary questions, Camus repeated the same answers: that Jean Grenier was his best friend, and that René Char was the most revolutionary poet since Apollinaire. Camus explained his work plan, that first he had wished to express the idea of negation in three different forms: the novel, with *L'Etranger*; drama, with *Caligula* and *Le Malentendu*; and essay, with *Le Mythe de Sisyphe*. He said that he could never have spoken of negation had he not lived through it: "I have no imagination." He had learned from Descartes's metaphysical doubt that he could not live by negation, and he planned a third cycle on the theme of love.

To small groups, he described his two-volume novel in progress, *Le Premier Homme*, as being in a traditional form. He was also planning a play, in the form of Paul Claudel's *Le Soulier de satin*, which might be called *Le Docteur Juan* or *Juan Faust*, a mixture of the Don Juan and Faust themes. And then he wanted to do an essay on the theme of Nemesis to express his appetite for life.

At Stockholm, audiences often spoke to him about God and Christ, and Camus would reply, "I have Christian concerns, but my nature is pagan." He explained that he felt at ease with the Greeks, especially pre-Socratic writers like Heraclitus, Empedocles, and Parmenides. And he believed in certain ancient Greek values, although he knew that this was frowned on ever since the time of Hegel.

On December 14, Camus gave another speech for students, at Uppsala University, seventy kilometers north of Stockholm. This time Hans Calliander phoned ahead to the Uppsala student union to prevent another incident like the one with the Algerian student at Stockholm. Camus spoke of "the artist and his time," noting that if writers appear in public, "they are immediately criticized and attacked. . . . Every artist who wants to be famous in

our society must know that it isn't he who will be famous, but someone using his name who will get out of his control and perhaps one day kill the real
artist inside him." Speaking to these students, Camus rejected literary realism as well as socialist realism: "How . . . can socialist realism be possible
when reality is not entirely socialist?" He called his own art "neither a total
refusal nor a total consent to what exists, it's both at the same time. . . ." He
quoted a writer he had always respected: "Gide said something that I have always approved of, even though it may sometimes be misunderstood: 'Art
lives from constraints and dies from freedom.' " He said he also rejected all
notions of art for art's sake, because the important thing was to accomplish a
literary work that was a form of testimony: "Personally, I cannot live without
my art, but I have never placed this art above everything else." In the somewhat controlled meeting at Uppsala there were no questions about Françoise
Sagan or Algeria, and several of the students had even read Camus's books.

Overall, the trip had been a success, and the French ambassador explained to the French Ministry of Foreign Affairs that in Sweden, Camus
had "faced points of view that were mostly open to influence, rather than
hostile ones." Only twice did Camus get a chance to wander the streets of
Stockholm alone. On one expedition, he deposited his prize check at a local
bank, made a donation of seven hundred Swedish kroner to the Reform
Church, visited a school, promised to send books to a local French Institute,
and did not appreciate the local food specialties of Swedish meatballs and
fried herring. The Camuses returned to Paris with the obligatory gifts of ice
skates for the children and a handbag for Jeanne Polge.

Apart from the fun, Camus sometimes felt that the prize was a crushing burden. He told the journalist Robert Mallet, "The Nobel gave me the
sudden feeling of being old." He felt as if he had become a statue—and in
fact he was in danger of becoming a medal, because the curator of the
medals department at the French National Library asked him to pose for "a
few sessions" so that a portrait medal of the writer could be sculpted. Camus
responded with embarrassment: "Although I am not very young, I am not
old yet, and I feel my work is still quite insufficient. . . . Perhaps we might
wait."

The Association of Algerians in Sweden wrote to him to say that the
questioner at the Stockholm lecture did not belong to their group, or any
other nationalist group, and his questions represented only himself.

On December 17, Camus wrote to the editor in chief of *Le Monde*, André Chênebenoît, about the articles the paper had run: "I have been quoted
with perfect exactitude, except once, and I ask your permission to permit me
to explain. I never said that the government committed only minor faults in
its way of treating the Algerian problem. In fact, I believe that the opposite is
true. Answering questions about French writers' freedom of expression, I said

it was total. When someone cast doubt on the freedom of the press, I said that until now, restrictions had been minor in dealing with the Algerian tragedy, which does not mean that I approve of these restrictions, even partial ones." He added a personal note: "I wanted to say again, about the young Algerian who challenged me, that I feel much closer to him than to lots of Frenchmen who speak about Algeria without knowing it. He knew what he was talking about, and his face was not one of hatred but rather of unhappiness and despair. I share this unhappiness, and its face is that of my country. That's why I wanted to give this young Algerian, and him alone, a personal explanation in public, which I had withheld until then, and which your correspondent reproduced faithfully."

When he wrote this letter, Camus had just returned to Paris, having left Stockholm on Sunday, December 15. He had not yet realized the public impact of his sentence about justice and his mother. The polemic went on until Chênebenoît asked Camus if he wanted to explain his position on Algeria in the pages of *Le Monde*, in either an article or an interview. But Camus refused the offer with thanks, saying that he planned to explain himself in a book that would be a collection of his articles on Algeria over twenty years, with an additional update. In this letter to Chênebenoît, Camus was haughty and tightly controlled: "In the intellectual society of bad faith and denigration that we have the misfortune to live in, a scrupulous writer can only reveal himself in books about serious matters, which protects him in part from the inevitable deformation of polemic campaigns."

Now Camus had to live with the inconveniences of glory, such as being bothered by autograph hunters in restaurants. He refused to have the words "Nobel Prize winner" added to his signature on articles. But people remembered that he had been honored—that is, except for one old pal, a plumber who ran into Camus walking along the rue de Lyon in Algiers and greeted him, unaware of world events, saying, "Hey, Albert, how's it going? What's happening with you?"

One of the rare critics to hold a moderate position about Camus was the Tunisian Jewish writer Albert Memmi, who expressed both sympathy and disagreement. Books by Memmi had been prefaced first by Jean-Paul Sartre and then by Camus—a rare combination. Memmi understood Camus's sufferings as a native of Algeria, but he wrote in a small monthly, *La Nef*, in December 1957 that Camus was a Frenchman from Algeria first and foremost: "Far from being able to speak of North Africa because he comes from there, Camus has been forced to become silent because everything about North Africa paralyzes him." Memmi saw Camus as well-meaning, but a colonizer all the same: "It must be understood that his situation is by no means easy; it is not intellectually or emotionally easy to have all of one's family on a side that is morally condemned." He went on to explain that Camus "was sure of attracting suspicions from the colonized, indignation from leftist Parisians, and anger from his family at the same time."

Some of the anger had grown violent, like that of the poet Jean Sénac, who wrote to Camus on September 18, 1957, to say that "the only reason I'm not in the Maquis is that on three occasions they refused to accept me." Eleven years before, in his first letter to Camus, Sénac had declared himself a "Christian anarchist," but now he wrote in a text for publication, "Day after day Camus takes positions that not only distance him from moral probity, but they put him at the service of dubious politics." He added ironically: "Apparently the enemies of Madame Camus [the writer's mother] are terrorists, and the political, military, and police suppression ensure Madame Camus's security."

Camus replied to Sénac, "If you want to continue speaking of love and fraternity, don't write any more poems about the glory of bombs that kill children, without any distinction between them and awful 'blind' adults. . . . Good luck to you."

Chapter Forty-seven **Algerian Griefs**

For Camus, 1958 began as badly as the previous year had. Late in December 1957, he was not on time for an appointment with Emmanuel Roblès, and Camus was usually so punctual that Roblès became worried and called the writer's secretary at Gallimard. When Camus finally appeared, he explained that in the taxi he had felt himself suffocating and had stopped at a doctor's to inhale some oxygen.

Later, a specialist would diagnose that he was living in a state of partial asphyxiation. So once again Camus started respiratory exercises with a physical therapist. Almost all of his intimates had witnessed his respiratory attacks, but now he was anguished enough to consult a psychiatrist, and he shut himself up in the apartment on the rue de Chanaleilles, where he thought about suicide and went through crises of suffocation and claustrophobic panic. Noting that he felt "given up now to a sort of madness," he kept a dry, precise account of his experiences:

> December 29 [1957], 3 p.m., another panic attack. Exactly four years ago today, [Francine] became unbalanced, no, it's the 29th today, so it's a day after that date. For some minutes, a feeling of total madness, then exhaustion and trembling. I'm writing this one hour later, after sedatives.
> Night of the 29th to the 30th: endless anguish.
> December 30th, sustained improvement.
> January 1st, doubled anxiety.

On January 1 he wrote to René Char, "Don't worry, I am feeling better. Helped by the doctors I saw, I am going to take the steps needed to find relaxation and gay science again." Three months after this reference to Nietzsche's book *The Gay Science,* Camus noted again, "January–March. The heavy attacks have vanished, and there is only dull and constant anxiety."

Mi, his new young girlfriend, helped his mood. They had met at the Café de Flore on the boulevard Saint-Germain ten months before, in February 1957. Camus was having a drink with Pierre Bénichou, André's son, and Albert Cossery. Mi was seated facing the café's entrance, writing something. Camus stared at the lovely young woman, and she recognized him. The friends invited Mi to their table and asked what she did for a living. She explained that she was an artist, and she and Camus began speaking of Piero della Francesca, whom they both adored, and then everyone decided to go dancing. Afterwards, Camus, always the good strategist, drove his friends home first in order to be left alone with Mi.

Born in Denmark, Mi had studied at Copenhagen's Fine Arts School and in Paris, where she continued to study drawing and painting at the renowned Grande Chaumière School just off the boulevard Montparnasse. She also worked there, choosing models and deciding on poses for them, in exchange for free courses. To further pay for her studies, she became a model at Jacques Fath's boutique, and soon switched to touring as a model for Boussac fabrics throughout France, since they paid better than Fath did. Camus would join her on these tours to provincial towns like Saint-Omer, Perpignan, Beziers, and Narbonne. Robert, Michel, and Janine Gallimard noticed that the new relationship made Camus suddenly seem younger. The couple could be seen together in public at Paris restaurants like the Brasserie Lipp and the Petit Pavé, or in nightclubs like the Nuage.

Mi would visit Camus at his apartment on the rue de Chanaleilles. She did not feel much sympathy for his great friend René Char, who could sometimes be gruff in manner. Mi was one of the rare women who ever attended a soccer match with Camus. She would take him to the Vilennes swimming pool. They would speak of the books of Melville, Dostoyevsky, and Nietzsche. Camus told Mi that he admired Nietzsche's "continual struggle against physical pain. . . . He spoke of himself as if he were God himself, yet he never stops being pitiable, because he wasn't God himself."

Mi accepted Camus's moods and adapted to them. She recalls that they felt as if they were protected in "a limitless time bubble." He loved the young people and the passion of Mi, who treated him as if he were her age, twenty-one, and helped him to relax.

Elsewhere in France, Camus was still being summoned to take part in political events, although some people who knew him in Algeria had already given up his case in despair. On January 11, 1958, Jean Amrouche published a full-page article in *Le Monde* condemning colonial France as "racist, greedy, oppressive, inhuman, and destructive" and seeing Algerian independence as the only solution. Jacques Heurgon replied in the January 16 issue, criticizing Amrouche for being excessive. Camus was on Heurgon's side, writing to him on March 18, "I agreed one hundred percent with what you wrote about Amrouche." He told Heurgon that few people loved Algeria as they did, "with the same obstinate hope." Jules Roy told Camus that he regretted that Amrouche was no longer their friend, and Camus said that Amrouche had become a dangerous sophist.

Retired from public affairs, Camus dedicated himself to the theater and his novel. He told Jean Grenier, "I don't read L'Express or France-Observateur anymore." He felt ostracized and told Grenier, "My enemies are numerous."

His former mother-in-law, Dr. Sogler, often wrote to him to say that Simone was still falling apart, and Camus felt that he could not do anything more for her. He saw Simone once, and she was thinner, with a swollen face, having made little progress with psychoanalysis and her time in a substance-abuse clinic in Switzerland.

To Grenier, Camus generalized about marriage: "It goes better when the bodies are kept separate. I realized that my first wife, Simone Hié, was someone who wanted to destroy herself. She was lovely, strong, and intelligent, but she was never able to shake her drug habit. She would go out sometimes at night to the Hydra Park, leaving me a note, 'I'm going to kill myself.' Although I didn't believe her, you should never take chances with these things, so I would go out into the night and find her in some gully. I didn't suspect that she was a morphine addict before we were married, and I took her on a trip . . . to Linz, and opened a valise and discovered a whole suitcase full of vials. She came back to the hotel and saw me tying my shoes with my foot on a stool and asked me, 'What are you doing?'—she was the only woman ever to use the formal 'vous' with me—and I told her, 'I'm leaving.' "

But politics took precedent over personal revelations: Paris-Match magazine announced that Camus was regularly consulted by President René Coty about pardons, but the novelist denied the report, saying that he only intervened on a case-by-case basis to ask for pardons for prisoners. He was bored by the readers' committee meetings at Gallimard. He went to Belgium to see a performance of Requiem pour une nonne and planned to follow the touring production to Nice.

He told Grenier that he had recently met Charles de Gaulle, who had been in a political desert for more than ten years. The meeting probably took place in Paris: "An intermediary brought us to him, and de Gaulle told us that Africa was lost and that the French are in a period of discouragement, that they lack self-confidence, and there was nothing to do about it, and he must stand aside, so that his example may serve the French people in two and three generations' time." In his Carnets, Camus noted, "March 5th. Conversation with de Gaulle. As I spoke of the risk of trouble from the fury of Frenchmen of Algeria if the country was lost [de Gaulle said], 'French fury? I'm sixty-seven years old and I've never seen a Frenchman try to kill another Frenchman, except myself.' "

Camus told Francine that he had asked de Gaulle about the future of the poor whites of Algeria, and the general replied, "They will demand huge indemnities," terrifying Camus with his cynicism. When Camus suggested giving French citizenship to all Algerians, de Gaulle replied, "Right, and we'll have fifty niggers in the Chamber of Deputies."

On March 26, Camus left for Algeria, where he planned to spend three weeks. He stayed at the Saint-Georges Hotel and went to visit his mother each day. He also saw Emmanuel Roblès as well as another writer he admired, Moloud Ferraoun. He told Ferraoun, "When two of our brothers are caught up in a merciless fight, it is criminal madness to root for one or the other. I prefer the virtues of silence, if I must choose between wisdom reduced to silence and yelling off my head madly. When words can dispose of someone's life without remorse, being silent is not a negative attitude."

Camus also reported on his meeting with de Gaulle to Charles Poncet. Camus had found the general pessimistic and a partisan of a federal solution for Algeria. De Gaulle would only agree to return to power by legal means, but what he called "this fucking party system" would never elect him. Camus told Poncet, "You see, there's no hope from that side." For the first time, there was tension between the two men, because Poncet believed that it was necessary to negotiate with the FLN. Camus had been impressed when some visitors told him about a project for a new law that would turn Algeria into a federated dependency of France, but Poncet warned him, "I think you're wrong to give so much credit to your visitors, as they represent only an infinitesimal part of Algerian public opinion. This project has only the appearance of federalism, and you know that even if the system were truly federal, we cannot be sure it will be accepted by the FLN. If by some extraordinary means this law could bring peace, which I don't believe, then it would be sabotaged, as the 1947 statute was."

Camus insisted, "But you are forgetting the decisive importance that economic development could have for Algeria." He was struck by the economic boom, the fever for building, and the importance of oil. Poncet admitted that a boom was underway, linked to the discovery of oil in Algeria, but this boom would only last a few years. He said it was necessary to address the FLN, and Camus's face darkened: "No, to negotiate with the FLN under present circumstances would be to recognize its legitimacy, whereas the FLN backed by Egypt is the rebirth of the dream of an Arab empire, and an Arab empire means world war."

Poncet asked what was to be done, and Camus replied, "Fight the FLN."

Camus's position was rigid, but Poncet felt that the idea of "personal federalism as advanced by a deputy and approved by Camus, was a "weird idea" that showed a surprising unreality. Friends like Maisonseul, Charlot, Miquel, and Bénisti were saddened to see that Camus seemed to have lost a real sense of Algeria. Albert told his brother that General de Gaulle perhaps represented some hope. Camus described the federal solution in his collection *Actuelles III—Chroniques algériennes 1939–1958*, which was published by Gallimard in June 1958. Camus had not spoken about Algeria publicly in France for almost two years. These texts would serve as his political acts, and perhaps the Nobel Prize would help him to be heard. He collected twenty years' worth of articles that had appeared in *Alger Républicain*, *Combat*, and *L'Express* and the full text of his "Call for a Civilian Truce." For Camus, Algeria's two communities were condemned to live together.

On May 9, Camus attended the opening of an exhibit of Jean de Maisonseul's paintings at the Au Pont des Arts Gallery. Maisonseul was struck by the fact that Camus behaved disagreeably to journalists at the show. The writer had prepared a text to introduce his friend's painting: "If one can speak of pure painting, then one must do so about these works, where the play of values, the study of transitions, backgrounds and unity of material play such a great role. Yet this technique does not vainly delight in itself. It is indebted to African nature for its rocks, clay, dry soil, and stone surfaces . . . with pure light revolving around square white stones."

Events in France changed the Algerian situation dramatically when de Gaulle took power after a sort of legal coup d'état by the political majority. On May 17, the French National Assembly voted a three-month state of emergency in Algeria, and although Camus was glued to the radio, he noted in his *Carnets* on May 29, "My business is to write books and to fight when the freedom of my family and my people is threatened, that's all."

He added a brief introduction to the texts of *Actuelles III*: "Vast changes of mind are occurring in Algeria, and these changes authorize great hopes as well as fears. But the facts have not changed, and tomorrow we must still take them into account to arrive at the only acceptable future, in which France knows how to bestow justice based unconditionally on freedom to all of Algeria's communities without discriminating against anyone." In this preface, written before de Gaulle took power, Camus distanced himself from the "public game" and confessed with some pride the weakness that justified his withdrawal: "First of all, I lack the assurance that lets you decide everything. . . . It is good to know how to recognize your enemy's reasons, to be able to defend yourself against him."

Camus handed out blame, saying, "Reprisals against civilian populations and the practice of torture are crimes against which we are all in solidarity." He also condemned terrorism: "To be useful as well as fair, we must condemn with the same force and without sparing our language the FLN's terrorism, whether operated against French civilians or, more often, Arab populations." And he targeted French progressives: "Alas, the truth is that part of French public opinion believes confusedly that Arabs have in some way acquired the right to slit throats and mutilate people, while another group approves legitimizing every excess."

Camus called for the French left wing to return to a position of decency, and he remembered his father, killed in the First World War: "When a French partisan of the FLN dares write that the Frenchmen of Algeria always considered France as a prostitute to exploit, that irresponsible writer must be told that he is speaking of men some of whose [Alsatian] grandparents chose France in 1871 and left their Alsatian soil for Algeria, Alsatians whose fathers died in droves in the east of France in 1914, and who themselves were drafted twice in the last war, and who have not ceased, with hundreds of thousands of Moslems, to fight on every front for this 'prostitute.' "

Actuelles III appeared on June 16 and was not a success. Six weeks after it was published, *Le Monde* printed an article by Jean Lacouture which said respectfully but critically that Camus brought to Algeria today "a look that is apparently less intrepid than on prewar Algeria." Lacouture was irritated by Camus's will to play referee in "this demented dialogue between paralytics and epileptics" in Algeria, and he made further objections: "It is disappointing that certain reasons are given to reject the idea of an Algerian nation by the same man who wrote in 1955, 'The Arab people have kept their personality, which cannot be defined by ours.' There is certainly a lot to say about the Algerian 'nation,' its historical foundations, and the economic and human consequences of that country's possible independence, but we expected other arguments from the author of *Les Justes* than this one: 'As far as Algeria is concerned, national independence is a purely passionate phrase, as there has never yet been an Algerian nation, and the Jews, Turks, Greeks, Italians, and Berbers would have as much right to demand the leadership of this potential nation.' " Lacouture ended by saying that *Actuelles III* deserved "attention and esteem," but it received little of either. In ten years only 32,621 copies of *Actuelles III* would be sold, which was not much for a Camus title.

Camus wrote to Francine about his reviews, saying, "They squeezed me, but not for Algeria's benefit, just to make me look bad. Isn't that great, because that's what motivated me to clarify what I think, which is a good use for one's enemies, may they be beloved, Amen."

At the end of 1957, he had met with a small committee of members of a study group from the Proofreaders' Union, who asked him to comment on the contacts needed between writers and book artisans. All sorts of technical workers in book production and journalism were present, and Camus told them, "Defending workers' rights is the same as defending the rights of intellectuals. The union could be their natural meeting place, except the workers' union is politicized and a writers' union does not exist. How can we develop one? By calling on intellectuals as you have done today, to participate in debates with study groups and by recreating 'popular universities.' " Before the war, Camus had led study circles in Algiers with Marguerite Dobrenn, Jeanne Sicard, and Charles Poncet. He told the proofreaders, "It is evident that intellectuals would remain silent and have no contact with what could be called a workers' movement . . . if it existed, but there is no workers' movement worthy of that name, and how can we insert ourselves into a nonexistent movement?" Camus mentioned his story "Les Muets," from the collection *L'Exil et le royaume*, which dealt with a strike in an Algiers barrel factory, admitting, "I felt very nervous and couldn't forget that to describe a strike in communicable language, or more precisely its effect, was a delicate task. . . . I didn't receive a single letter from a worker, and no workers' magazine asked for permission to reprint this text. We realized that the book itself did not sell in the working-class milieu, no doubt because books cost too much."

A member of the audience pointed out that the circus and music hall cost a lot of money, yet workers brought their families to this sort of show. To which Camus replied soberly, "I would be unhappy with myself if I made the least reproach to a worker, who surely has the right to seek some kind of entertainment after being tired by his work week." To these people, who were sympathetic with revolutionary socialism and left-wing opponents of communism, Camus spoke of journalistic enemies he did not enjoy making: "There is constant suffering for me, since it is clear that we are in a metropolis of wickedness, of denigration and systematic lying. We live constantly in a pathetic conspiracy which makes this country's atmosphere unbreathable."

Camus remained loyal to Spanish Republicans, those forgotten people of history, and he also defended the state of Israel, which was threatened by the Arab anticolonialism movement. When a young man asked if he should accept to serve in Algeria, Camus gave the reasons that he felt justified the presence of draftees as well as career army officers in Algeria. But he also supported Louis Lecoin, who defended conscientious objectors in France, where they were not given any legal protection.

Camus also sent dossiers to de Gaulle to support Algerians sentenced to death, and after de Gaulle took power, the condemned prisoners were no longer executed, The writer also addressed the new president to defend the friends of Louis Lecoin. The General responded in a rather distant tone, without saying yes clearly, in a letter that began, "Mon cher Maître . . ."

André Malraux, who had been named minister of cultural affairs, against the advice of Pascal Pia, wanted the three living French Nobel Prize winners in literature, François Mauriac, Roger Martin du Gard, and Camus, to speak out about the morality of France's presence in Algeria. Malraux suggested that Camus could be "a sort of permanent Ambassador of French Conscience in de Gaulle's name." But Mauriac was very skeptical about the idea, Martin du Gard died, and Camus wrote from Athens on July 1, 1958, to refuse for the moment, saying that he would think about it later.

Camus had left with Maria for Greece on June 9, and after traveling through the Cyclades islands, they stayed with Janine and Michel Gallimard at Rhodes for two weeks. Michel rented a yacht, and the friends sailed with another Gallimard employee, the artist and graphic designer Mario Prassinos, who drew an illustrated sea log to which Camus contributed humorous and obscene entries. On the island of Mykonos, Camus ran into Father Bruckberger wearing a checked cowboy shirt, in the company of a girlfriend.

The Gallimard boat, *La Fantasia*, was a restored old warship, with a crew of a two Greek sailors and a British captain, who sat swilling gin as his wife cooked meals. Maria Casarès left the group early to go back to work in Paris, and she and Albert joked that fifteen days' cohabitation was the limit for them.

Camus was happy, as the little group smeared themselves with olive oil and sunbathed on the boat's roof. They did not really discuss politics, but Camus told Janine that de Gaulle fascinated him by his sheer height and his way of thinking. A number of Paris intellectuals would reproach Camus for taking a holiday in Greece when history was being made in Algeria and Paris, but of course these intellectuals did not miss their own habitual vacations to the south of France, the Balearic Islands, or Tuscany.

During this, his fifth trip to Greece, Camus once again found the country he had dreamed of, but he felt limited by his body: "Alas, I don't know how to swim anymore, or rather, I can't breathe as I used to, but no matter, I regret leaving the beach, where I have been happy."

Returning from Greece, he once again plunged into the Algerian situation, and on August 4, he wrote to Jean Grenier, "I believe as you do that it is no doubt too late for Algeria, although I didn't say so in my book . . . because some chance must be left to historical randomness and besides, one does not write simply to say that everything is screwed up. In that case, it would be better to remain silent, and I'm preparing myself for that."

Camus told Charles Poncet that he was counting on fraternization between Arabs and pieds noirs, but Poncet said that he thought the cheering crowds that welcomed General de Gaulle on a recent visit to Algeria had been arranged. Camus's face grew grim and he said, "Then it's all fucked up." Poncet replied, "Not necessarily, because it's possible that de Gaulle will be firm and skillful enough to impose negotiations on the FLN that won't sacrifice the French community."

Pierre Mendès-France could not forgive de Gaulle for seizing power, disguised with a parliamentary ritual; but Camus disagreed, as he was truly intrigued by de Gaulle, not seeing him as a budding dictator, although he was wary of the General's power barons, like Michel Debré. Camus discerned in Debré traces of fascism, even if they were not overt. Both Camus and Jean Daniel thought it possible that de Gaulle, as an individualist rightwinger, might be able to get France out of the Algerian impasse. Camus was not among the protesters who marched in Paris from the Bastille to the place de la Nation, chanting, "Down with de Gaulle—fascism will not win!" Camus told Charles Poncet, "For the moment, none of our fundamental freedoms is threatened, and if they are one day, believe me, I wouldn't limit myself to signing manifestos, I would be in the streets fighting alongside the workers to defend them."

Poncet once again regretted Camus's silence about Algeria, and the writer replied, "But I *have* spoken! You read my *Chroniques algériennes*, and you saw how the leftist press strangled that book." Poncet was glad that Camus had published something, but he still could not understand how Camus could have supported as ephemeral a concept as "personal federalism" for Algeria. Poncet saw Camus that summer as being on "the edge of misanthropy," constantly feeling that he was being persecuted. He was a whipping boy for the non-Communist left, who saw him as an anti-Communist and a colonialist because he rejected Algerian independence as well as the FLN. For the left- and right-wingers who both wished to claim him, Camus was at best an idealistic dreamer. In Raymond Aron's 1958 book, *L'Algérie et la République*, detailed economic arguments showed that although cooperation was still necessary, integration between the French and the Algerians was impossible. Aron placed the Algerian problem in a European context and concluded that Algeria cost France more than it brought in as income.

When Charles Poncet criticized his silence, Camus became tense, but he did want to participate in the "masquerade of signing manifestos." His actions were more useful, in that he had obtained pardons for several Algerians who were sentenced to death, and he thought that a life saved was worth more "than so many signatures given lightly and uselessly." Camus was obsessed with the opinions of the progressive press and felt that for a long time *Le Monde* had not been impartial, and its director, Hubert Beuve-Méry, "favored abandonment" of Algeria. Poncet wondered how Camus, who once had publicly defended Moslem rights in the *Alger Républicain* and *Combat*, could now stick to a position that contradicted his past. Camus felt that for twenty years, leftists had grown accustomed to injustices committed against "natives," and now the same leftists were forgetting the modest pied-noir folk and supporting abandonment. Poncet, in turn, was convinced that Camus was "immunized against the guilt complex" that motivated the left wing; but above all he opposed evicting the French, "sacrificing a community," an idea that Aron and de Gaulle accepted. To Camus, the idea of independence often seemed likely but remained unacceptable. On other subjects Camus could be lucid, Poncet thought, but about Algeria he was "myopic."

At his Gallimard office, Camus met several young Algerians from a student friendship league, including a medical student, Ahmed Ibrahim Taleb, who worked with Jean Sénac, who was also present, in the underground liberation group Moujahid. There were enough chairs for only two guests, so Camus told the students, "Let's do as we do at home and sit on the floor." The students felt that he was treating them like little boys. Sénac thought Camus was behaving odiously and called him a coward. After the visit, Suzanne Agnely saw Camus in tears, holding his head in his hands. He told her, "And what if these little fellows should be right?" He no longer relied on de Gaulle as he had a few months before, as the General would clearly never create the great dreamt-of community, a sort of French Commonwealth, in Algeria. The vast majority of pieds noirs despised de Gaulle and felt betrayed by him, and Camus told Roger Quilliot, "If we go on like this, we'll be headed towards independence and I will leave, I'll move away from France, I'll go to Canada."

Once again Camus found a certain peace in Provence at L'Isle-sur-la-Sorgue, where "the landscape which I recognize nourishes me again and I arrive happy." Staying with Jeanne and Urbain Polge, he relaxed at Camphoux. He took walks with René Char on the road to the crests of Lubéron, a famous natural wonder, and in the cedar forests. As in Greece, the sense of light and space overjoyed Camus, and he wanted to buy a house nearby.

Camus was not in fact as entirely rejected as he felt, as shown by the September issue of the magazine *Preuves*, which published a letter from an Algerian Moslem reader directed at Camus: "I am perhaps less surprised than you are by the silence which surrounds your latest book, *Actuelles III,* and which will end up by stifling it. . . . Your book's reception had nothing surprising about it. Not only do you say what you think about what has been commonly called the Algerian problem, but you think correctly and you express your thoughts well. . . . Sir, that is why from suffering Algeria that you love well, at least that is sure, I send you a friendly greeting with all the admiration due to a lucid mind and a courageous man." On October 30, 1958, even *France-Observateur* printed readers' protests against the ostracizing of Camus, for example: "I wish to express my astonishment over your silence about the last three books by Albert Camus, *L'Exil et la royaume, L'Envers et l'endroit,* and *Actuelles III.* This silence is even less understandable about the last-mentioned book, which deals with Algeria, a subject that your journal's readers are told about every week. Reading [Camus's] book irritated me at many points, but it did deserve to be read."

Roger Quilliot also praised Camus in a little-noticed article that recognized the importance of *Actuelles III*. Quilliot felt that Camus described "a country close to his heart with a rare good faith and force of conviction. . . . He speaks of it with controlled fervor, measure, and objectivity and deals with many people's reasonings, trying to be fair to all." Camus told Quilliot, "If I had to become a foreigner in Algeria, my own country, I would leave France. . . . I always fought so that Moslems would stop living like foreigners in their countries, but who listened to us? All the regimes, all the politicians share the responsibility, Parisians as well as the Frenchmen of Algeria. I'm sure that the catastrophe could have been avoided."

He refused to be fatalistic—"Yet I don't want to despair"—and although he avoided cocktail parties and ceremonies, he agreed to be guest of honor at a dinner for Frenchmen of Algeria. He had a warm feeling for the pieds noirs even if some, like Maurice Papon, the Paris police prefect, or the artist Pierre Blanchard, were too far-right-wing and Manichean. As Camus grew closer to his compatriots, his friends from before the war, both leftists and rightists, distanced themselves from him. Some thought Algeria should remain French and others were for immediate independence, and Camus satisfied neither group. At Gallimard, where Camus had resumed his work routine, he was surrounded by supporters of the FLN.

To the less ardent ones, he could speak confidentially. Robert Mallet noted in his diary that a disillusioned Camus told him he felt he could no longer be useful: "I am suspected by nationalists from both sides. One side thinks I am not . . . patriotic enough and the other thinks I'm too patriotic. I don't love Algeria in the same way a soldier or colonist does, but can I love it other than as a Frenchman? What most Arabs don't understand is that I love it as a Frenchman who loves Arabs and wants them to be at home in Algeria, but I don't want to feel like a foreigner there myself."

In the autumn and early winter of 1958, Camus felt as foreign in Algiers as in Paris. On December 21, Charles de Gaulle was elected president of France by seventy-eight percent of the electoral college, and most Frenchmen saw him as a providential hero. But not Camus, who nevertheless once more clung to the distant hope that de Gaulle might do something to save the forgotten people of Algeria, the poor whites.

Chapter Forty-eight

I Don't Know How to Repeat Myself

C amus adored the theater. He even loved the Grand-Guignol, and would stop by often to sample its bill of three or four short plays peppered with burlesque, provocation, horror, blood, and farce. Camus used to say, "Now *that's* what I call theater! We have just seen Aeschylus or Plautus, and I wouldn't be surprised if [the Grand-Guignol] performed a fellow named Shakespeare one day—without any intermission, of course." Instead of situation-comedy plays, Camus much preferred going to music halls such as the Bobino, where Edith Piaf sang.

Since October 1953, he had been working on his most ambitious adaptation, of Dostoyevsky's novel *The Possessed*. He would jot down ideas in a notebook about his first version, which would have taken five hours to perform—shorter than Paul Claudel's play *Le Soulier de satin* but still very long. Camus felt drawn to Dostoyevsky almost as much as to Tolstoy: "I put *The Possessed* among the four or five supreme works, and in several ways it has nourished me and educated me. I've been imagining its characters onstage for nearly twenty years." In his adaptation and staging he wanted to shift "from satirical comedy to drama to tragedy." For Camus, Dostoyevsky's characters were "neither strange nor absurd. They resemble us, in that we have the same hearts. *The Possessed* is a prophetic book, not just because it predicts our nihilism, but also because it puts heartbroken characters onstage, with dead souls." Camus attributed the play's atmosphere partly to Russia's weather, telling Catherine Sellers that "an extreme climate, whether hot or cold, is nature's way of encouraging people to excess."

To create his text, Camus used the 900-page-long French translation by Boris de Schloezer, including the Russian author's notes for his novel. Apart from the novel itself, Camus also drew on Dostoyevsky's notebooks and consulted a few critics, like Leon Chestov, author of *Revelations of Death* and

395

The Philosophy of Tragedy. Years before, Camus had dedicated a chapter in *Le Mythe de Sisyphe* to a theory of logical suicide described by a Dostoyevsky character, Kirilov, and even before then, as a young man, he had read with interest André Gide's study of Dostoyevsky. In April 1958 he got down to the actual work of adaptation for what became the play *Les Possédés*. He was still considering buying a house in the south of France and financing a theater, and he had so many plans at this time that he wrote to his theatrical agent, Micheline Rozan, "I tell myself that at least one of my projects has to fail."

He arrived at a version of the play that had twenty-three characters in seven scenes, reduced from an earlier version with twenty-eight characters, both having fewer than the forty-four characters in Dostoyevsky's novel. By cutting out scenes, Camus freely eliminated characters, and since it was difficult to show riots onstage, he left them out.

Suzanne Agnely told a friend in June 1959, "Camus is invisible or else he complains that literature is boring. . . . Since everything that has to do with literature bores him, I let things go on my side as well, with a boredom at least equal to his." His secretary worried that "this will all end up badly . . . and an experimental theater will be given to Camus, which will make him give up literature for good, and if that happens, we will go our separate ways, and I honestly think it will happen soon."

Camus gave a lot of thought to Russia in the nineteenth and twentieth centuries, and decided that for Dostoyevsky, "it was evident that the solution was not Christ plus Marx, it was rather Christ plus the Russian people." Camus treated his subject gravely, with certain glints of references to his own troubles. One of the play's characters, Professor Verkhovensky, is described in the play as holding "the job of exiled and persecuted thinker, with much dignity, but three or four times a year he had attacks of civic sadness." Camus was still coming to terms with his own role as exiled thinker. Another character in the play states, "One cannot at the same time love one's wife and justice," a clear reference to Camus's famous comment about justice and his mother, made less than a year before, in Sweden during the Nobel Prize visit. And in the third scene, the character Kirilov speaks very much in the vein of the author of *Le Mythe de Sisyphe*: "I am interested in the reasons why men do not dare kill themselves."

Unlike Dostoyevsky's characters, who were married for life, Camus at times was thinking of getting a divorce, and spoke about it to Francine's sister Christiane. Apart from her lack of enthusiasm about this news, Christiane was also displeased by Camus's theatrical projects and disappointed that he would write no more novels.

At the heart of Camus's theater team was the agent Micheline Rozan. She had been presented to Albert by Maria Casarès and was one of the first people to read *Les Possédés*. When he asked her opinion, Rozan replied, "I was fascinated by your play." She also admitted, "I'm ashamed to say I've never read the novel. . . . Therefore I took the play as it is, dense and airy, intelligent and touching. It seems to me prodigiously difficult from a technical point of view, and you're going to have a whale of a time. . . . I wonder if it doesn't just lack bite and sharpness."

Camus and Rozan looked around for financing, a theater, and actors. Apart from a few companies, the theater in France seldom got government grants. The money needed for *Les Possédés* was given by a group of investors led by Michel Gallimard. Another potential investor found by Rozan, the Swedish-American financial entrepreneur Lars Schmidt, was rejected by Camus, who told her: "I don't like this type of person, nor the publicity he would use about me, nor having the French theater infiltrated by dollars and Swedish kroner."

A dozen theaters refused the production, and some of the actors Camus hoped to cast were not available. A large publicity campaign was started on the strength of Dostoyevsky's and Camus's names, but Rozan was worried about the length of the play. She felt it might work, but she could not be wholly optimistic. Jean-Louis Barrault was interested in the project, and a contract was drawn up with Barrault and Camus's groups dividing the profits or losses fifty-fifty, but then Barrault withdrew. Finally, Camus signed an agreement with Simone Berriau, director of the Antoine Theater, and he started casting the play. To avoid sending Francine into another grave depression, Maria Casarès was banned from acting in Camus's plays, but he could choose other favorite actors, like Pierre Blanchard, Michel Bouquet, and Pierre Vaneck. Then there was Catherine Sellers.

The final play was in three acts and twenty-two scenes. Rozan pressured Camus to involve Peter Brook in the Paris production: "As we hope that Brook will agree to direct the play on Broadway, would you consider involving him with the scenery design in Paris? Do you see any problem with the play being performed with the same scenery in Paris and New York? For Peter, the work done here would mean less work to do over there."

Rehearsals began at the end of November 1958 and ran smoothly, and Camus enjoyed the way the show was taking shape. Later he grew tired of it, although he did not show his feelings: "These rehearsals bore me, in fact I don't know how to repeat myself." However, he pressed on, making more corrections and telling the actors, "Move just as you like and sit down when you feel the need to. Do what the text inspires you to do." Afterwards, he observed and listened but did not intervene. Actors like Pierre Blanchard were glad to see that Camus understood it was better for an actor to discover his own gestures and tones rather than having them mechanically imposed by a director. Camus felt that a text did not limit a character, and let his actors go through their own exercises. Although Camus did not demand changes of intonation in Blanchard's line readings, he did intervene more with Catherine Sellers, who asked for his advice.

Despite violent attacks of fatigue, Camus gave of himself as director in *Les Possédés* more than for any play since *Le Temps du mépris*. To create a mood before work sessions and during breaks, he would play records of Russian folk songs for the actors. He told the stage designer, Mayo, that he wanted both sets and costumes to be stylized, as they had been at the Théâtre du Travail. As a director, Camus was not simply a writer inside a theater, but a creator using a different kind of language. He surveyed the movements of bodies in action, and did not skimp on grand gestures, unlike most French directors of the time who were mostly interested in diction.

Les Possédés opened on January 30, 1959. André Malraux, the government's minister of cultural affairs, attended with Georges Pompidou, former director of General de Gaulle's office. Malraux expressed only polite interest in what he saw. All of Paris society came, including Louis Aragon and his wife, Elsa Triolet, who had prominent orchestra seats.

Stationed in the wings, Camus was encouraging to all the cast, and offered Blanchard the last-minute gift of a Russian handkerchief as a final touch for his costume. The curtain rose at 8:10 p.m., but there were many latecomers, including the prefect of police, Maurice Papon. The audience laughed when an imprisoned character in the play said the line "I need a passport." The play lasted almost three and a half hours, including two long intermissions, with a buffet dinner where lots of vodka and whiskey were consumed, until the play finally finished around midnight.

The Paris critics had mixed emotions, like *Le Figaro's* Jean-Jacques Gautier, who felt the evening was admirable and painful, disappointing and satisfying all at once. Gautier praised the stunning set changes and the risks taken by the production, but concluded that it was mostly a "curious literary and theatrical experience." After praising Pierre Blanchard, Gautier added a harsh comment: "I am a bit surprised that Mlle Catherine Sellers gave up the role of Prouhèze in *Le Soulier de satin* for the pleasure of playing Maria, which as a role is more of a long grimace than a pretext for drama. It's as if a tragedian had relinquished the role of Oedipus Rex to play Quasimodo." Camus was so infuriated by this review that he seriously considered challenging Gautier to a duel.

Le Monde was enthusiastic: "What a magnificently upsetting show *Les Possédés* is. . . . M. Albert Camus has triumphed over all fears in his weighty enterprise." The daily *Paris-Presse* praised the production but concluded, "All the same, these Russians really do exhaust you." The Communist *L'Humanité* examined the show from the perspective of socialist realism and attacked Dostoyevsky as much as Camus. The newspaper *Libération*, also backed by the Communist Party, took the occasion to protest a movement in

Western literature that opposed Dostoyevsky to Karl Marx. *Libération* felt that "Albert Camus, in that stuffy and vague style that has won him the highest international literary consecration," confirmed the Dostoyevsky-versus-Marx trend in his play. The newspaper further noted that they did not appreciate Camus's program note for the show, which made a "reference to a certain loss of heat in the mental powers of the left wing, particularly in France." Orthodox Communists ruminated over the brand-new attribution of the 1958 Nobel Prize in literature to Boris Pasternak. He thanked the Nobel committee, but under pressure from the Soviet authorities, refused the award. *Doctor Zhivago* was not really an apology for Communism.

Camus would often attend performances, and after the show he would meet Catherine Sellers. As an actorish prank on the hundredth performance of the play, he replaced the water in vodka glasses which the actors drank onstage with real vodka. Michel Bouquet conscientiously drank up, and his long tirades as Stepanovich showed the effects. As director, Camus knew how actors needed reassurance, and if he planned to be away for ten days, he would prepare ten little notes and ask that each day a new one be posted for the cast to read, messages like "Couragio [sic]! Hang in there."

Les Possédés was losing money, and even before the dress rehearsal, the theater owner, Simone Berriau, had worried, "What we have here is a success that may be compromised by the length of the play." Berriau was making slightly less than her usual box-office receipts at the beginning of the run, and receipts dipped even lower when the weather improved. She suggested cutting part of the beginning of the third act, but Camus refused. In order to lessen the deficit, he preferred to ask the Culture Ministry to intervene with the Finance Ministry in order to lower taxes on the theater, but the Finance people would not hear of it.

It was decided that to make money, *Les Possédés* would go on tour, and the impresario Marcel Karsenty, who had created galas that were much despised by the Théâtre du Travail, was interested in the production. He lunched with Camus and told him that André Malraux was planning a reform of French theater and wanted to open new cinemas and experimental theaters. Camus thought that the term "experimental theater" was standoffish and elitist, feeling that it was better "to experiment without saying so." He preferred the term "new theater," "which compromises nothing but authorizes everything." Rozan and Camus exhausted themselves trying to get a theater funded by the government. Malraux's assistants Pierre Moinot and Georges Elgozy asked Rozan to submit proposals to them. Camus became impatient, as he did not like being told which theater to choose. He wrote to Rozan, "As for El Ghozi [sic] I mostly have the impression that he doesn't give a crap about me. He starts off by recommending [anti-Fascist Spanish writer José] Bergamín, whose French texts are literally impossible to perform, even before we know what the theater itself will be. I suppose that could be chalked up to his sheer enthusiasm, right? I'm convinced he hasn't arranged anything with Hébertot."

Pierre Moinot was more interested than Malraux was in how exactly Camus's project would fit into the Culture Ministry's budget. Camus hoped to be given the Récamier Theater, but Malraux, who was reorganizing subsidized theaters, gave that to director Jean Vilar, head of the Théâtre National Populaire. Camus's friends could not understand why Malraux gave Vilar a theater for experimental plays when Vilar already had one, while Camus, who had been promised a theater, still had nothing.

Camus felt it was understood that he would receive a solid subsidy, and negotiations began with Jacqueline Grammont, who owned the lease on the Athénée Theater. He prepared five pages of "theoretical propositions for a new theater," which was long enough to show that his project was serious but not too long for bureaucratic minds. Ministry officials proposed the Sarah Bernhardt Theater, but Camus and Rozan felt that that would be too big for their purposes.

He wanted to create a repertory theater that would inspire new works. The new theater would also present masterpieces from the great epochs— the classical Greek era, Spanish Golden Age, the Elizabethan period, and the French classical and preclassical eras. As director, he wanted to use foreign literature from the past few years and to commission new plays from writers who were "alive, but far from the theater because of their scruples or their demands." He would guarantee "that they will be read with attention and ... performed under honorable conditions." The young directors who would work with Camus, like the actors, would have to put themselves in the service of the text alone: "Quality of language will be the first criterion in the choice of plays." Camus wanted to react against what he saw as an "abandonment of rules" in the French theater.

The new theater would have a repertory of three new productions a year, alternating for a total of 210 performances, including one world première. Camus wrote, "If by extraordinary luck it were possible to find three good, modern works in a single year, then they would make up the three new productions." Among the writers Camus contacted was Emmanuel Roblès, who was just finishing a play, *Plaidoyer pour un rebelle*, about a Communist named Yveton who was guillotined in Algiers.

Camus said it would be "prudent to ask that the chosen theater be empty, so that the director can install and educate his own team for administration and finances." The alternating shows suggested a group of permanently employed actors in the troupe, with additional actors recruited from outside when needed. Camus had in mind a medium-sized theater in order to be able to present *Othello* as well as *Le Paqueboat Tenacity*, a play in memory of his Théâtre du Travail days. The ideal size of the theater would be seven hundred seats. Camus thought of theaters like the Hébertot, the Renaissance, the Ambigu, the Bouffes-Parisiens, and the Palais-Royal.

Les Possédés finally did not do badly, with over six hundred performances at the Antoine Theater and on tour. An experimental theater would have a chance at even greater successes, especially if it were located on the Left Bank of the Seine.

Rumor had it that Malraux was thinking of giving the Comédie-Française to Camus, but this proved to be false. Malraux had a grasp of reality, and Camus had proved his talents as a playwright and a stage director, but not as an administrator.

Chapter Forty-nine   **Grand'rue de l'Eglise**

For the new life he was planning, Camus wanted a new setting, and he decided to leave the rue de Chanaleilles. Friends and acquaintances were asked to look for a new apartment for him, three large rooms, or four medium-sized rooms, with a kitchen and a bath. His theatrical agent, Micheline Rozan, asked him to fill out a questionnaire to indicate his preferences. First choice of neighborhood was Faubourg-Saint-Germain, near the Chamber of Deputies and not far from the rue de Chanaleilles; next came the place Vendôme, Saint-Germain-des-Prés, the Ile-Saint-Louis, Montparnasse, the Opéra, the Jardin du Luxembourg, and the Jardin des Plantes, in that order. If he bought something, he would be ready to spend from three to six million francs, "but closer to the lesser figure, of course."

Camus wrote in his *Carnets* on September 30, 1958: "A month spent revisiting the Vaucluse and to look for a house. Found one in Lourmarin. Then left for Saint-Jean to meet Mi, traveling exalted through hundreds of kilometers through the scent of grape harvest. Then the great, foamy sea. The pleasure like those long waves which flow and sheer away."

Albert and Francine Camus had visited twenty houses and country farms, accompanied by the Polges, acquaintances like Henry Bonnier, and realty agents. Francine had seen a house on the Grand'rue de l'Eglise in Lourmarin, a village of a few hundred inhabitants. The town was in the Vaucluse, at the heart of the triangle made by the three cities Aix, Avignon, and Apt. After seeing the house, Camus said, "It's this one or nothing." He bought it from a surgeon, Dr. Olivier Monod, for 9,300,000 old francs, and set his family up there. René Char remarked, "A Nobel Prize check is useful for that, at least."

The lovely, damp location, a former silk farm, had a subtle odor of wax. On the ground floor, above the wine cellar, were the entranceway, the kitchen, the living room, and the two children's rooms, which opened onto a small courtyard. The garden spread out beyond a low wall to a small road shared by the Camuses and their neighbors. Camus assured the Monod family that he would tend the olive trees they had planted. On the second floor were a large room and a bathroom, and to the left was Albert's monastic room with an uncomfortable wooden bed, a table, and a writing lectern. To the right was Francine's room, nicknamed the Pink Room. The couple lived like brother and sister, and Francine seemed resigned to it. On the third floor, the attic was redesigned into an office. Camus made a few other changes, such as having an alcove wall knocked down by a stonemason, whose wife, Suzanne Ginoux, became Francine's maid. Madame Ginoux had worked for the Monods before Camus bought the house, and she helped Francine get used to the place. Francine would say, "I don't have a chambermaid, I have a sister." The Ginouxes lived on the same street near the church, and they kept the keys to the house when the Camuses weren't there. Camus shopped in the region's antique stores, ordered kitchenware, and a piano from Paris for Francine. He hung Algerian lithographs on the wall and chose dark furniture, preferring black wood from Spain. The writer wanted to present the house to his wife as an entirely prepared "gift package."

The grape vines of the nearby Lubéron region reminded him of his homeland, and he told Suzanne Ginoux, "I feel when I reach out my hand as if I were touching Algeria." In Lourmarin in the Vaucluse, just as in Mondovi, Algeria, grape growers made local specialties. Both white and red grapes were plentiful. Camus wanted his mother to visit this house, and he felt that in this region she would not be homesick. Camus had originally learned about Lourmarin from Jean Grenier, and had written about the region in "L'Enigme": "Fallen from the heights of heaven, waves of sunshine radiate violently on the countryside around us. Covered by this roar, everything becomes still, and the Lubéron over there is just an enormous block of silence that I listen to endlessly." Camus had traveled through the region in his different cars, his successive Eleven-CV Citroëns which he nicknamed Desdemona and Penelope. Driving with René Char or Mi, he visited villages and hamlets by the Vaucluse mountains—Bonnieux, Lacoste, Menerbes, Gordes. Char would tell him about the underground Resistance fighters of the Ventoux.

Far from Paris, which he detested, Camus gathered his family and worked on *Le Premier Homme*. He wrote in his *Carnets*: "April 28 [1959]. Arrival at Lourmarin, under a gray sky, and in the garden, marvelous roses are weighed down by rain, juicy like fruits. The rosemary is blooming, we take a walk, and in the evening, the iris's shade of violet becomes even darker, and I'm exhausted." Later he noted: "For years I've tried to live according to everyone else's morality and I forced myself to live like everyone else and to re-semble everyone else. I said what was needed to unite people, even when I myself felt estranged from them, and in the end, the catastrophe came. Now I wander amid the debris as an outlaw, drawn and quartered, alone and ac-cepting to be so, resigned to my singularities and weaknesses. And I must re-construct a truth after having lived a sort of lie all my life."

Crossing the plains and plateaus, Camus found other villages perched high among the gorges and limestone cliffs, with masses of fallen rocks, and thorny bushes. Mi would stay in a big traditional farmhouse nearby, and when the Faure family was visiting, Camus would go out "to take a walk" and would return with a ferocious appetite. Christiane Faure was not de-ceived by the ruse.

The writer thought a lot about the theater. He also had acting plans, to play the lead role in an adaptation of a book by Michel de Saint-Pierre, *Les Ecrivains*. But he still refused public honors, including an invitation to kick off the first soccer ball at that year's French Cup game.

He was no longer a full-time husband or a full-time father, and his ex-tended family included Michel and Janine Gallimard. He more or less adopted their daughter, Anne Gallimard, whom he called "Anouchka," en-couraging her, "You've got to have confidence in yourself, defeat your demons and march straight ahead. If you enjoy the theater, take advantage of the fact that I'm going to be giving time to it in the next years. After that, I'm not sure that I'll spend much time on rehearsal stages, since I have an old project to go to a monastery."

For the moment, Camus worked on his novel, and he wrote in a note-book for *Le Premier Homme*, "J. has four women at once and therefore leads an empty life." J., or Jacques, the protagonist of *Le Premier Homme*, resem-bled Camus, who also had four important women in his life: Francine, Maria, Catherine, and Mi. Camus noted, "I spoke to Mi in a half-serious and half-joking way about extreme old age when delight and the pleasures of the senses etc. would be over and she burst into tears and said, 'I love love so much!' . . . Mi fills the day with beauty and sweetness, and far from keeping me from my work, this continuous joy motivates me."

Camus was planning a new book and a second theatrical career, and his new young girlfriend had to be accepted by his other women, as they had accepted his brief love affairs. Francine was better, still teaching math at the Marcel Proust School in Paris. Camus's life was beginning over again at age forty-six. To all his women, he confided his horror of old age, especially his own.

On August 13, Camus was calm and balanced between his work and his loves, writing, "Absence and painful frustration, but my heart is alive, fi-nally alive, so indifference did not win out over everything, and I owe gratitude and passionate acknowledgment to Mi." Despite some melancholic moods, Camus felt appeased during these months, with Lourmarin as a port of call as satisfying as the hotel rooms where he used to love to write. The novel worked through him, Camus said, like an underground stream. A year earlier he had written to Catherine Sellers, "I'm still not working, but I must say that I feel something working inside me . . . but I must wait."

Throughout a creative summer, Camus developed his last hero, Jacques Cormery. He had carried this book inside him for six years. Before the start of the Algerian war, he told Charles Poncet that he had the ambitious idea to write a fresco of the contemporary world, like *War and Peace*, but with the humor that was lacking in Tolstoy's book. In *Le Premier Homme* as it was begun, there was no humor, as if the writer could not yet get beyond pity and tenderness for his characters.

Le Premier Homme was ambitious and autobiographical. Camus told Georges Blin, a professor of French literature and a friend of Char's, that he was seized by the idea of writing "a pure novel about 'education.' " He told Jean-Claude Brisville that for the first time he would speak about women in a novel, and they would have a major role because they were vitally important to him. Camus felt that in his previous books, women were only "mythical." He assured Brisville that his work in progress would be his first real novel; until now, he had only been practicing scales—he mentioned *War and Peace* as a reference, as he had with others. Francine asked him, "How can you write about love when you are incapable of it?"

He planned for *Le Premier Homme* the way painters make cartoons for a fresco. For documentation, Camus went in the spring of 1959 to Ouled Fayet to look for traces of his father, but did not find anything. During this trip, the novelist did research at the new National Library in Algiers and attracted admiring glances, especially from lycée students and staff who recognized him. He showed Urbain Polge elaborate parchment documents relating to his maternal grandparents, dating back to 1845 and 1872. He said, "I'm writing a book about my family, and I'm happy about it, I've done good work." In his first rapid draft, the writer sometimes forgot to change the names: although the Saint-Paul farm from his boyhood was called "Saint-Apôtre," the character of the old teacher is often "Germain," the real-life name of Camus's beloved instructor. By August 1959, Camus had already started a second draft of his novel; he told Robert Mallet that he had destroyed many pages of an earlier draft.

In September, General de Gaulle proposed self-determination for Algeria, but the Algerian Republic's government insisted on independence as the first step for any negotiation. In *Le Premier Homme*, Jacques Cormery chats with a farmer near Solférino, asking him about the Arabs. The farmer replies, "We're born for each other, since they're as stupid and brutal as we are, but we do share the same blood as human beings. We'll kill each other a little while longer, cut off each other's balls and torture a bit more, and then we'll start to live together as men, which is what the country wants. Would you care for an anisette?" Camus had lost all hope for a solution in Algeria that could please him, but the novel expressed his former optimism, radiating a joy in writing that recalls *Noces, L'Eté,* and *L'Exil et le royaume.* Through his protagonist, Cormery, Camus connected with his father, "that man who seemed closer now than any other living person." Although Camus had filial feelings towards Louis Germain and Jean Grenier, he realized, "I cannot find a second father for myself." In *Le Premier Homme,* the character Victor Mallan, based on Grenier, told Cormery, "You don't need a father anymore, you raised yourself all alone and now you can love him in the way you know how to love." In Cormery, Camus drew a self-portrait up to the age of twenty-nine: "fragile, suffering, tense, willful, sensual, daydreaming, cynical, and courageous."

Camus reported to Jean Grenier from Lourmarin, "I retreated here to work on November 15, and in fact I have worked. For me, work conditions have always been those of the monastic life—solitude and frugality. Except for frugality, they are contrary to my nature, so much so that work is a violence that I do to myself, but a necessary one. I will return to Paris at the beginning of January and then leave again, and I really hope that this alternation is the most efficient way to reconcile my virtues and vices, which finally is the definition of knowing how to live."

For Camus, knowing how to live also meant fleeing some inconveniences of celebrity. Four new books had just appeared about him, including two from Gallimard, by Roger Quilliot and Jean-Claude Brisville. An American who had known the Camus family at Oran, Germaine Brée, had also published one. The latest was Philip Thody's study from England. There was talk of Germaine Brée's book being translated into French, but the Gallimards felt that three books in French about their Nobel Prize winner might be premature, at least for the moment. Camus wrote to the prospective translator of Brée's book, his friend Marguerite Dobrenn, on November 17, 1959, "It's hard for me to argue with [the Gallimards] that they are wrong." However, he encouraged Dobrenn to find a French publisher other than Gallimard who might want the book, suggesting Calmann-Lévy, Denoël, and Grasset, and promised to help her update it: "It goes without saying that in this case, I would send you all the unpublished works you want." He informed Dobrenn merrily, "I've changed my haircut, going back to the one from my happy years in Algiers, which has rejuvenated me, or at least my heart!"

Having found inspiration once again, Camus was joyful, although it was hard to be separated from his friends, to be without a fixed work schedule, as he wrote to Micheline Rozan: "I don't know when I'll be back, as I must finish the first draft of my enormous story, and I am far from completing it. But it is only here that I can write, and this solitude is really unbearable, so I am croaking from it, but only when you croak from it do you really get work done. I have eight months to finish this before getting back to the theater, only eight months, so the bottom line is, I will hang on as long as possible."

The region was at its loveliest in November. The oak groves had taken on red, brown, and golden colors while the pine and cedar forests remained green. On November 20 at 9:30 p.m., Camus wrote to Mi, "I've worked almost all day, and it's true that solitude is hard, because I love life, laughing, and pleasures, and you, who are like that plus a little more, and what with my nature and the force I have in my blood, it's terrible to chain myself up here and cloister myself. I hope I'll learn some patience, as I am working, and prove to myself that this is the only way to deal with my filthy disorganization, but I kick and stamp and gnash my teeth until I take myself by the scruff of the neck and go back to a blank sheet of writing paper. Having lounged about idly for a good half-hour yesterday, I insulted myself aloud for five minutes. Then I behaved well, by going back to work with my tail between my legs. It isn't that I'm pleased by what I'm doing; I lose heart sometimes before the enormity of what I've started. I tell myself that it's impossible, I am only writing foolish things, and I call for a tiny bit of genius that will allow me to work in joy instead of this endless illness, and finally I carry on."

Two days later, he wrote again to Mi, "I have never worked with such dense material, and this afternoon I had the fleeting impression that my characters had taken on that density and for the first time in the twenty years that I've been searching and working, I've finally arrived at the truth of art. It was a delicious lightning bolt to the heart, but a fleeting one, followed by blind work again and constant doubt."

He was already planning future work, as he had told Jean de Maisonseul at the end of the summer: "I've written only a third of my complete works and I'm really starting them with this book." On December 6, Camus informed Patricia Blake that he would not be able to go to New York to see *Caligula* performed in English, as he had planned, because he was busy "with a book that requires months and months of work, so *Caligula* and Broadway are very far away, as you can imagine. The only thing that I will miss is you, because for thirteen years, New York has meant you, but I will return there later, when the translation of the book I am writing appears."

On December 7, he toyed with the idea of paying a visit to Catherine Sellers; and Francine asked him if he was planning to prolong his stay at Lourmarin, and if so, should she come with the children for the Christmas holidays? He replied, "Yes, I'm staying on at Lourmarin, because I have no desire to be back in Paris, and because I am obstinately accumulating pages and continuing on the blind march which I began. . . . My visitors did not disturb me, but I'm glad they're gone." The visitors were Mi and Robert Ceresol, who had spent a few days at the house. Camus told Francine that he was "happy to find once again the days entirely empty of words, so that I can really work profoundly. . . . That said, don't worry, I'm glad you're coming and I know you won't keep me from working."

He agreed to speak about the writer's job to foreign students at the French Institute at Aix-en-Provence on December 14. He explained to them that writing was "a man's trade" and not "God-given inspiration." Asked whether he was a leftist intellectual, Camus replied, "I'm not sure I'm an intellectual, and as for the rest, I support the left wing in spite of myself and in spite of itself." Camus had once told Jean-Marie Domenach, "I was born into the leftist family, and I'll stay there until I die, but it's hard not to see some decay." He did not feel like a typical French intellectual, and he had said years before, "I am not a philosopher, because I don't believe in reason enough to believe in a system. What interests me is knowing how we must behave, and more precisely, how to behave when one does not believe in God or reason."

Driving near Lourmarin, Camus was stopped by a highway policeman who, seeing the profession "writer" on his identification card, asked what he wrote. Camus explained that he wrote novels, and when the officer asked, "Romance or detective stories?" the writer replied, "A bit of both."

At the Gallimard office, Suzanne Agnely filtered his correspondence, answering the serious propositions, such as the one on December 16, 1959, asking him to add his name to a petition to U.S. President Dwight D. Eisenhower on behalf of Morton Sobell, a young scientist who had been convicted as a Soviet atomic bomb spy along with Julius and Ethel Rosenberg in 1951. The petition had already been signed by François Mauriac, Jean-Paul Sartre, and Bertrand Russell, but Camus remained prudent: "I do not know the Sobell affair well, and I can't say that I'm convinced of his innocence any more than I'm convinced of his guilt."

An American television station wanted the director Sidney Lumet to make a film based on La Chute, starring Laurence Olivier, but unfortunately the project was stillborn. On December 18, Camus wrote to Micheline Rozan to turn down the starring role of a writer in a Peter Brook film, Moderato Cantabile, where his co-star would have been Jeanne Moreau: "Cinematically, I would have been very interested in Brook's film, and part of me still regrets having said no, but I was obliged to, as I have only eight months left to finish the first draft of my book, which will be barely enough. I told Brook that if the film isn't made this year, I'd do it next year, but he seemed determined to do it in February [1960]. I'm delighted for him and Jeanne Moreau, and please explain my reasons to her and make special excuses." Camus had a weakness for actresses, and repeated to Micheline Rozan later, "I keep working to prevent me from missing Brook and his film too much." The film's writer, the novelist Marguerite Duras, had also wanted Camus to play the role, but she and Brook ended up with Jean-Paul Belmondo in the part.

Camus also kept alive his plan for a theater company, although it was hampered by Malraux's bureaucrats: "I have the constant impression that these people have something else in mind, and I am wasting my time with them. I'll have to haunt their hallways and offices for years, and I'm not suited for that, so we'll probably be given the Mathurins Theater, and I'll have to accept or not when I get back on January 4th or 5th." Rozan informed Camus that the Athénée Theater was another possibility.

Far from the rest of the world, Camus filled out a questionnaire sent to him by the Argentinian libertarian magazine *Reconstruire*, which would be Camus's last interview, written or spoken; he responded to it because his correspondents were foreigners and libertarians. Asked if summit meetings between America and the USSR gave him hope that the cold war might end, he replied, "No, power makes anyone who holds it insane." Did he think that capitalism and communism could coexist peacefully? Camus replied, "There is no purely capitalist regime anymore, nor any purely communist one, and powers coexist because they frighten each other." *Reconstruire* wanted to know whether countries were forced to choose between America and the USSR, or was there another choice? Camus said, "When the nationalist virus becomes less virulent, I believe in a unified Europe, based on Latin America and later on Asia and Africa." Asked if he approved of the space program, or was it better to spend the money on earth, Camus remarked, "Science progresses, for better or worse, and there's nothing we can do about it, but there is nothing to be proud or happy about in magnificent achievements that are politically abject to say the least!" Finally, he was asked about the future, and how to make a freer world where there would be less poverty. He replied, "By giving, when one can, and not hating, if one can."

The questions answered, he went back to *Le Premier Homme*, getting up at five a.m. to start work, three hours before his housekeeper, Suzanne Ginoux, arrived. He would always tell her, "I've taken a walk around the plain," a stroll that included the road to Cavaillon, passing in front of a wayside cross and the Lourmarin castle, a one-kilometer walk that stretched his legs in the morning. Camus worked standing in his office or seated on the terrace, smoking Gauloises or a pipe. He would help Suzanne Ginoux make the bed, saying, "It's so much easier for two," and would tell her about his mother, saying, "She worked hard." In Francine's absence, the house seemed very quiet. When he was alone, Camus almost never listened to music.

In letters from November and December 1959, he wrote to Catherine Sellers about a writer's highs and lows: "The solitude here is devastating, because in wintertime the empty village is closed, and the countryside bare, and except for lunch, I don't see anyone all day. These are good conditions for work, and in fact I am working, but dull and continuous anguish is still there. . . . I look at the fine landscape or the blank page, and I am discouraged about the road that must still be traveled. Then I get over it and I forget, and get desperate about writing rubbish, and then start over again, only to throw it all away, and go around in circles, and ask myself what I want to do, not knowing the answer, but trying anyway, and screaming for a little genius that will cure nothing but at least stop this endless suffering. In spite of everything, I'm making progress, but without any satisfaction. I move ahead for the sake of moving ahead, to tell myself that I've done it, that it's very good, and that's why I'm here, and not to have genius, which I don't believe in, because what I believe in is a work schedule. . . . To work, one must deprive oneself, and die brutally, so let's die, because I don't want to live without working. . . . I continue to work, but with less output, and it's true that I couldn't have maintained the former rhythm. This long solitary tension is exhausting, but I must continue it for as long as possible. The weather is spoiled now, but for five days it was like being present at the earth's creation. . . . I don't know what I am going to produce, but I'm sticking to it. How hard, unhappy, and unique an artist's life is! . . . I still have almost ten days alone before the tribe arrives, and I want to profit from them. . . . You might say that my writing faculty has been exhausted from too much use, and the result is a stylistic fiasco, with my work out of order for the past three days, and I hope it will get a little better before I get back to Paris."

At first he lunched at the Ollier Hotel restaurant, but other diners would interrupt his meal, and so the restaurant owner asked the waiter not to speak the writer's name aloud, but to call him any name instead. The waiter immediately yelled, "Is Monsieur Anyname's table ready? Monsieur Camus is here waiting for it." Visitors and tourists often recognized the writer, but locals seemed to confuse him with the French filmmaker Marcel Camus, who directed *Black Orpheus*. Albert would be congratulated, "Oh, Monsieur Camus, you didn't say you were famous, but now I know it, because I saw your film." Finally Camus decided he'd had enough, and asked Suzanne Ginoux to prepare his meals at home, where he could eat in peace. He was neither a gourmet nor a big eater, and she would bring his favorite dishes, like boiled beef with vegetables, stuffed tomatoes, pepper pie, and fruit for dessert. He would always cut a pineapple in two and offer half to the Ginouxes' son, André.

The weather was good until Christmas, and Camus ate his meals on the terrace facing south. Mornings, wearing flannel or velour pants and a shirt lined with lamb's wool, Camus would walk to buy the newspapers and pick up his mail at the post office. Once, he asked Madame Ginoux for a detail to help him in his portrait of Jacques Cormery in *Le Premier Homme*: "At what time of the year do first communions take place?" To avoid disturbances to his work, if the phone rang, Camus would answer it, saying, "No sir, Monsieur Camus isn't in, this is the gardener."

Relaxing, he would caress the cat, Lolita, and pat his female donkey, Pamina, who came from Algeria. He socialized with locals like the garage owner Henri Baumas and a gardener he had hired to plant rosebushes, Alfred Landi, as well as the members of the regional soccer club. He was establishing roots, and told Urbain Polge that it would be amusing to be mayor of Lourmarin, to speak to the inhabitants of the town as well as the surrounding countryside in meetings, as he had in Algiers over twenty years before. He added, "Finally I've found the cemetery where I will be buried, and I'll be fine there." On December 21, he wrote to his mother, who was seventy-seven years old, "Dear Mama, I hope that you will always stay as young and beautiful and that your heart will remain the best in the world, although it could never change. . . . You're going to receive my little end-of-the-year gift, so buy something for yourself with it. . . . I hug you very tightly and kiss you with all my heart. . . . P.S. Best wishes to [Uncle] Etienne, Lucien, and all the family." On the first page of his manuscript of *Le Premier Homme*, he wrote this dedication to his mother: "To you, who can never read this book."

Francine and the twins arrived for the holidays, and Camus was rather pleased with the children's academic results, although he wrote to Louis Germain, "They do not have a M. Germain to teach them spelling, and they disappoint their father on this point."

On December 29, he wrote to Mi, who was in Denmark but would return to Paris shortly: "This frightful separation will at least have made us feel more than ever the constant need we have for each other. I knew it before, and I know it even better now. I bless my need and I await you, full of force and passion, yes, I await you, my beloved and ardent one, my little girl, dear lover! By the time you read this letter, we will only be separated by two or three days."

On the thirtieth he wrote to Catherine Sellers, "The weather is good, the wind is blowing and I hope it will also blow away my cold. I have closed my file folders, because it isn't possible to work seriously with the family here and perpetual visitors. . . . I will therefore live painfully until Monday and I'll try to start over in Paris, and if not, then I'll sadly be obliged to leave again."

The same day he wrote yet another letter to Maria Casarès: "All right, this is a last letter just to say that I'm arriving Tuesday by car, leaving with the

Gallimards on Monday. They are passing this way on Friday, and I'll phone you when I arrive, but maybe we can already set a dinner date for Tuesday. Let's say Tuesday in principle, taking into account surprises on the road, and I'll confirm our dinner by phone. I send you a cargo of tender wishes, and may life splash up inside you all year long, giving you that dear expression that I've loved for so many years, but I love your face when it's worried or any other way. I am enclosing a check for your raincoat in this envelope and with it I'm sending all my heart's sun power. See you soon, my superb one, I'm so happy at the idea of seeing you again that I'm laughing as I write it. I have closed my file folders and I'm not working anymore, because there is too much family and friends of family here. Therefore I have no more reason to deprive myself of your laugh and our evenings together, nor of my homeland. I kiss you and hug you tightly until Tuesday, when I can start all over again."

On December 31, he wrote again to Catherine Sellers: "This is my last letter, my tender one, to wish you a heart-fulfilling year plus a crown of tenderness and glory. . . . But now I am returning and glad about it, so see you Tuesday, my dear, I'm kissing you already and bless you from the bottom of my heart. . . . As long as this monstrous book is not done, I'll have no peace."

The family celebrated the New Year in traditional Provençal style, with thirteen desserts, including a *fougasse*—oranges, tangerines, figs, and almonds. During this holiday with Francine and the twins, Camus told his wife, "You are my sister, you resemble me, but one shouldn't marry his sister."

The Gallimard family, Janine, Michel, and Anne, arrived from Grasse in their car, a Facel-Vega. Before the Gallimards had left Paris for Grasse, their friend the publisher Robert Laffont advised Michel to take the train, but Michel replied that it was impossible, because they wanted to visit Camus in out-of-the-way Lourmarin.

The reunited friends celebrated Anne Gallimard's eighteenth birthday, and Camus gave her a one-volume encyclopedia of contemporary theater as a gift. On January 2, they had lunch at the Ollier Hotel; then Camus dropped Francine and the twins off at the Avignon station to take the train for Paris. Michel had insisted that Camus join the Gallimards for the car ride back, and although Albert had already bought his train ticket, he agreed.

Michel invited René Char, who needed to get to Paris, to accompany them as well, but Char had already bought a train ticket and didn't want to overload the car. When Char went to see his friend at his home on the Grand'rue de l'Eglise, Camus vanished for a few moments, then reappeared with a leaf of his personal stationery with a scribbled, crossed-out message on it. Camus said, "Since you're staying, here's a little note."

The note read, "Char stands alone, without being in the background.

Nothing resembles him, yet he resembles his time, which he never ceases to confront. He abides in his time like a rock." Camus added a final sentence of advice to Char, which he underlined, "Respond to your powers, which are real."

On January 3, as always before leaving, Camus gave the front-door key to Suzanne Ginoux, who had the flu, telling her, "Take care of yourself—I'll only be gone for a week, and we still have lots of things to do."

The travelers—Janine, Michel, and Anne Gallimard, their dog, and Albert Camus—climbed into the car. In his briefcase, among other things, was the manuscript of *Le Premier Homme*, 144 pages of closely written text, of which the first 68 were on his personalized stationery, with writing in the margins and between the lines.

The group went to nearby Camphoux to greet their friends the Mathieu family, and Camus once again said that he would be back in a week's time. Jacques Polge, the son of Urbain and Jeanne, was impressed by Michel Gallimard's powerful Facel-Vega. The friends took the Nationale 7 highway, stopping at Orange for lunch, and then went to the Chapon Fin Hotel, near Mâcon, where they dined and stayed the night.

They left the next morning, drove for three hundred kilometers, and had a light meal at Sens. The Gallimards were teasing Albert about all his women friends, and he replied that he managed to make them all happy. Michel was at the wheel, and Albert was beside him. Janine had given up her place in the car, saying, "You're taller than I am."

Twenty-four kilometers outside Sens on the Nationale 5 road, between Champigny-sur-Yonne and Villeneuve-la-Guyard, the Facel-Vega swerved, went straight off the road, slammed into a plane tree, bounced off another tree, and broke into pieces. Michel was seriously injured, Janine and Anne were unharmed, the dog had disappeared, and Albert Camus was killed instantly.

The dashboard clock, which had been thrown into a nearby field, was stuck at 1:55 p.m. Camus had often told friends that nothing was more scandalous than the death of a child, and nothing more absurd than to die in a car accident.

The same day, January 4, Malraux's aide Pierre Moinot wrote from the Ministry of Culture: "Dear Camus, what a joy to be able to tell you . . ." Finally, the writer would be given his theater. The project had taken eight months to arrange, so it could not be said to have bogged down, according to bureaucratic standards. That afternoon, Roger Grenier arrived late at the offices of *France-Soir* on the rue de Reáumur, and a secretary stopped him on the stairway, asking, "Where were you? We were looking everywhere for you—to get Pia's address!" Grenier asked why they wanted Pia's address, and the secretary exclaimed, "You mean you don't know?"

Five days later, Michel Gallimard died in a Paris hospital. In Algiers on the fourth, a journalist had telephoned the Camus family physician, Dr. Séror, who informed Lucien. Lucien could not bear to tell his mother, so he asked his daughters, Paule and Lucienne, to do so. The girls went to the Camus family apartment on the rue de Lyon and informed Catherine Hélène Camus, who was not even able to weep. "Too young," she said.

Conclusion

According to his physician, Dr. René Lehmann, Camus's lungs were too seriously damaged for him to have lived into old age.

The most discussed obituary of Camus was a full page written by Jean-Paul Sartre in *France-Observateur*. Sartre wrote perversely, "We were on bad terms, he and I, but bad terms mean nothing, even if we'd have never met again, it's just another way of living together."

Sartre's article blamed Camus for having been "too prudent" in his silence about Algeria, but he felt that Camus "represented in this century the current heir of the long line of moralists whose works make up perhaps the most original part of French literature." Sartre continued his posthumous analysis: "His stubborn humanism, narrow and pure, austere and sensual, was a dubious weapon against the massive, deformed events of our time. But on the other hand, by his unrelenting refusals he reaffirmed the existence of moral facts against our era's Machiavellians, and the golden calf of realism."

Emotion could be sensed in the article, and Sartre confided to a critic, Michel Conta, that he had let himself go a little because he saw Camus's obituary as an opportunity to write "some fine prose." Ten days after Camus's death, Sartre told a seventeen-year-old admirer, Patrice Cournot, "Camus never did anything 'nasty' to me, as far as I know, and I never did anything like that to him." It is unsure whether Sartre said this out of forgetfulness, insensitivity, or thoughtlessness.

Sartre did at least generously propose to Robert Gallimard to help Francine and the twins financially. Years later, in the summer of 1972, Sartre told his friend John Gerassi, who was working on his biography, "There is a little falsehood in the obituary I wrote about Camus, when I say that even when he disagreed with us, we wanted to know what he thought. . . . Generally in life, writers are inferior to their books. . . . Camus was probably the last who was a good friend. . . . So we'd be there with his wife and the Beaver, who pretended to be scandalized when we'd tell a lot of smutty jokes. I had two or three years of very good relations with Camus, very good. He wasn't a boy who was made for all that he tried to do, he should have been a little crook from Algiers, a very funny one, who might have managed to write a few books, but mostly remain a crook. Instead of which, you had the impression that civilization had been stuck on top of him and he did what he could with it, which is to say nothing."

Sartre and Camus's story of fraternal love ended badly, and on the intellectual level, they ended where they had begun. Camus, like the literary critic of the *Alger Républicain* he had been, was wary of Sartre the thinker, while Sartre appreciated Camus as a novelist (he thought *La Chute* was "superb," just as he had liked *L'Etranger*) but thought him a poor philosopher.

Shortly after his death, without naming Camus, Sartre wrote a series of articles in which he criticized the late writer's slogan "Neither victims nor executioners." For Sartre, an oppressed colonized man proves his humanity by killing his colonizer: "They look real fine, the nonviolent ones, neither victims nor executioners!"

In Japan in 1965, Sartre commented, "Lots of phony intellectuals in France have said about our war in Southeast Asia or during the Algerian War . . . 'I am against all violence, no matter where it comes from, I don't want to be an executioner or victim . . . and that's why I'm opposed to the revolt of natives against their colonizers,' " which for Sartre was the same as saying, "I am for the chronic violence that colonizers use against the colonized."

Another point of view was expressed by the screenwriter Jean-Loup Dabadie, when he explained what Camus meant to some twenty-year-old students in 1960: "We were in philosophy class and they put Camus's books into our excited hands. Some of us swallowed them whole and, intoxicated by the limpid prose, went off confusing the absurd with absurdities. These students led rag-day processions of revolt, while others walled themselves up inside the books, trying to despair intelligently, daring to imagine a happy Sisyphus, and grew weary from the exercise. . . . Others abandoned Camus almost immediately, and when he called for solidarity, they left him alone with his challenge."

But today, Albert Camus no longer crosses the desert alone, as he did in 1940, 1952, and 1957, because he has millions of faithful readers. Toward the end of his life, Camus wrote, "I have escaped from everyone . . . and in a certain way I wanted everyone to escape from me."

His friend Charles Poncet believed that although Camus had experienced real love, "he apparently did not attach any more importance to the sexual act than having a drink with different women." Camus loved several women right up to his death. Although unfaithful himself, he did not like being deceived. He wrote to Catherine Sellers in September 1959 about a love affair of hers: "I suffered over what you told me, that's a fact, but you mustn't be sad about my sadness. . . . I know I've done everything to detach you from me, and all my life, when someone has become attached to me, I've done everything to make them back off."

Charming and moody, sincere and theatrical, humble and arrogant, Camus wanted to be loved, which he often was, and to be understood, which he did not achieve. He spoke too much about happiness to have really been happy, and his unhappiness was like that of Sisyphus. He was marked by sufferings and heartbreaks, as well as separations, but without these, he might not have been able to write *La Chute*.

Camus was not a poet in the usual sense of the term, although he enjoyed scribbling verses on occasion, but the author of *Noces* and *L'Eté* wrote pages of a magnificent poetic density. *La Chute* and *L'Etranger* should survive for generations to come, and *L'Envers et l'endroit*, *Noces*, and *L'Eté* should be with us a long time in whatever political context they may be read. Gallimard Editions all-time bestseller is *L'Etranger*. Camus has a varied public, which is always renewing itself. In a recent readers' survey in France, Camus is well placed among classic favorites like Balzac, Corneille, and Molière. Among twentieth-century writers, Camus leads the pack of those who interest readers most, followed by Marcel Pagnol and with Jean-Paul Sartre lagging far behind.

This does not mean there are no more dissenting voices: In 1979, a French writer, Jean-Jacques Brochier, reprinted his pamphlet *Camus, Philosopher for High-School Students*. Brochier attacked Camus for "always silently or openly supporting the established order," and for being a writer who "never disturbed anything in our capitalist, Christian civilization." Brochier concluded that Camus's "calls for pity are perhaps the most repugnant thing about him." Asked today if he still holds these opinions, Brochier declares that while *L'Etranger* and, to a lesser extent, *La Chute* were great books, there was still a troublesome side of "Algeria for the French" in Camus, and he thought that the newly published *Le Premier Homme* read like a story called "A Little Lad in the House of the Pieds Noirs." Even when *Le Premier Homme* sold fifty thousand copies in the first week after its belated publication in 1994, *Le Monde*, the prestigious French daily, gave it at first only minimal attention.

Camus wanted Algeria to remain somehow in the French Republic, but he did *not* have what is seen today as typical colonialist mentality, condoning the OAS counterterrorist groups' torturing Algerian nationalists. Those who claim that he did falsify his life and works: The erroneous image of Camus as colonialist and imperialist is widespread in the English-speaking world, nourished by critics like Conor Cruise O'Brien and Edward Said. The latter asserted in his 1993 book *Culture and Imperialism* that Camus's work "is informed by an incapacitated colonial sensibility."

Camus's achievement in the theater was more mixed: he wanted to be a playwright, and while *Caligula* is still stageworthy, his other plays are weaker. Camus's acting talent was also debatable; although he may have been acceptable as Molière's Don Juan and as the Governor in *Les Possédés* during brief acting stints. On television he was embarrassingly poimpus playing the role of Albert Camus.

Above all, he felt himself to be an artist, a "creator of myths, who might be unlikely to succeed," but who at least felt "assured of being nothing else" than a creator. Unlike other great novelists in literary history, Camus did not invent his own universe, but his two best eforts, *L'Etranger* and *La Chute*, have the original and powerful tone of masterpieces. In terms of philosophy, Camus cannot be placed in the Plato, Jean-Paul Sartre, or Wittgenstein league. Camus kept repeating that he was no philosopher, and above all, no existentialist, but evidently he did not insist enough. He contributed to advances in political philosophy by being opposed to systematic thinking. Some of Camus's maxims are more like the crash of a cymbal than a philosophical idea, such as "I call truth that which continues." Not being a philosopher did not prevent him from being a stimulating thinker.

Some of his ideas in political philosophy are more palatable today than the ideologies that died when the Communist world collapsed. In 1957 Camus declared, before many other fashionable pundits, "We know that the era of ideologies is over."

Until the end of his life, he advised others not to confuse creation with propaganda: "It seems to me that a writer must know everything about the dramas of his time and must take sides every time he can, but he must also keep a certain distance from history, at least from time to time." He wrote in *L'Homme révolté* nearly a half-century ago, "The proletariat fought and died to give power to intellectuals, who as soldiers of the future, enslaved them in turn."

Camus sought a rule for living, and in the public sphere he refused lies and despotism. He diagnosed certain evils of his time, which reflected his era's anguishes and his own penchant for nihilism. As a thinker and moralist, he was isolated from the French mainstream, where a crude Marxism flourished.

Typical of his generation, Camus at first adhered to communism and then was tempted by pacifism. Camus was atypical as a libertarian and a Social Democrat reformer, worried by nationalism. In *L'Homme révolté*, he stated that the "struggle of nationalities has turned out to be at least as important for explaining history as the class struggle."

In 1957 he spoke about Europe with some reservations, "I don't believe in a Europe unified by the weight of an ideology or a religion that will make all its differences forgotten. . . . If Europe is not destroyed by fire, it will create itself, and Russia will join in turn, with its own individuality."

L'Homme révolté was partly a failed work, but not because of the political reasons given by *Les Temps Modernes* but because, apart from fifty pages on revolutions and their makers, there was too much literature, philosophy, and politics jumbled together.

As the most famous French left-winger, Camus saved the honor of intellectuals who were caught up in a drift towards totalitarianism. So he was treated like a traitor by the Communists, because, given the political climate in France, he was correct too early.

For two and a half years, Camus was considered the most gifted editorial writer of the French press, and his articles in *Combat* made their mark. His best writing in journalism, I feel, may have been done for the *Alger Républicain*.

He told Jean Daniel that Paris intellectuals were wicked and the best vengeance to have on them was to be madly happy. In the last ten years of his life, he was a whipping boy for the French left wing. It is impossible today to claim, as critics did decades ago, that because Camus was anti-Communist, he was forcibly reactionary or conservative.

With Algeria, the problem is more complex, because Camus is still reproached, especially in Algeria, for not featuring Arabs or Kabyles in his work. Like many of his compatriots of European origin, Camus did not really know Algerian Moslems, and one cannot easily write about what one does not know. Some years ago, in a critical study of the Frenchmen of Algeria, the historian Pierre Nora stated that Camus, "unconsciously obsessed with historical immobility," could not deal with the problem of relations between Europeans and Arabs. Nora saw *L'Etranger* as "a troubling admission of historical guilt [which] begins to seem like tragic foresight." When asked about his opinion today, Nora states, "Camus was a liberal who had nothing to do with 'Algeria for the French' in the political and terrorist sense of the slogan, but his heart and guts could only be revolted by the idea of a final 'abandonment.' I perfectly understand his heartbreak, and why at the height of passion he could only rely on, and proclaim, his beliefs, and there was courage in his position."

But after Nora's book, some commentators even accused Camus of being racist. Young Algerian readers today seem more open about Camus than their elders. In 1960, the city council of Mondovi changed the name of the former rue de la Pépinière to the rue Albert-Camus. In 1962, after the French left, the village was renamed Dréan, and the rue Albert-Camus was renamed in honor of "Feddaoui Messaoud, Fighting Martyr." In future years, perhaps there will be a boulevard Albert-Camus in Algiers.

A new generation of Algerian university critics are rather more subtle than certain Paris intellectuals. Lamria Chetouni, formerly of the University of Annaba and now residing in Paris, published a thesis on *L'Etranger*, in which he said, "In the novel, the Arab is anonymous, depersonalized, belittled, and seen according to racist clichés. Albert Camus showed by his journalism that in real life, the Arab's fate was the same. The author struggled all his life to fight injustices done to Arabs in his country. He sounded the alarm against insensitivity and repression, and tried to put an end to exclusion and social inequalities, by condemning 'mad European pride.'" Chetouni concluded, "A foreigner and a solitary man, Albert Camus was personally the victim of the social contradictions into which he was born. And perhaps that is why Algerian Arabs today pay him homage, for they too have experienced the heartbreak that comes from living upside down." Mohammed Dib, one of Algeria's greatest contemporary writers, declared in 1995, "Camus is an Algerian writer."

But some members of the French intelligentsia still have a quarrel with Camus. Today, the critic Francis Jeanson still thinks that *Les Temps Modernes* was fair more than forty years ago, because the magazine was fighting anticommunism, which as he puts it, "acted ruthlessly" in France at the beginning of the 1950s.

Camus refused politics without morality, which made French leftists smile as much as rightists. One cannot ignore, simplify, or caricature his exemplary positions, when compared with those of so many other writers. Nothing permits us to despise Camus, and there are many reasons to admire him.

His endearing human warmth and goodness embarrass some thinkers. The present book is neither an exposé nor a hagiography, nor is it a list of Camus's good deeds. Camus could seem brusque or unpleasant, but he was more often understanding and kind. Vulnerable, he was faithful in friendship and love, despite his numerous affairs. He gave an encapsulated view of his emotional beliefs: "No great work . . . has ever been based on hatred or contempt. The true creator always reconciles people through some part of his heart and life. . . . An artist cannot refuse reality, because he must give it a higher meaning. How can one justify reality by ignoring it, and how to transfigure it if one accepts to be subservient to it?"

Every successful page he wrote was a bitter victory. On hearing of Camus's death, William Faulkner seemed to echo the late writer's mother's comment, "Too young": "You might say that [Camus] died too young, that he didn't have time to fulfill himself. . . . But the question isn't how much time or which qualities he had, but simply what he did."

And that "what" looks likely to remain important for many generations of readers to come.